Musical Instrument Auction Price Guide

1999 edition

STRING LETTER PUBLISHING

String Letter Publishing, Inc.
255 West End Avenue
San Rafael, California 94960
(415) 485-6946

Editor: Jessamyn Reeves-Brown

Consulting Editor: Mary VanClay

Assistant Editor: Maria Riley

Design Director: Ann Leonardi

Production Coordinator: Christi Payne

Production Assistant: Donna Yuen

Cover Photograph: Rory Earnshaw

The Publishers wish to thank Sarah Allen and Peter Horner of Bonhams, Todd Phillips of Butterfield & Butterfield, Emma Sully and Jonathan Stone of Christie's, Rebecca Herbert and Philip Scott of Phillips, Cindy Tashjian and Kerry Keane of Skinner, and Tim Ingles of Sotheby's for their kind assistance in providing photographs for this guide. Photos on pages 122, 125, 257 and 265, courtesy of Bonhams; photo on page 128, courtesy of Butterfields; photos on pages 124, 126, 259, and 262, courtesy of Christie's; photo on page 121, courtesy of Phillips; photos on pages 127, 258, and 263, courtesy of Skinner; and photos on pages 123, 260, 261, and 263, courtesy of Sotheby's.

ISBN 1-890490-20-2

TABLE OF CONTENTS

STRINGS

REFERENCE LIBRARY

These publications offered by the publishers of *Strings* Magazine give you the information you need to save time and money. Now you can confidently negotiate the price of a rare instrument, shop for the best place to buy strings or get your bow rehaired, or, with our instrument "owner's manual," you can avoid costly accidents and repairs. Your instrument means a great deal to you; let us guide you through ownership with these comprehensive books.

Strings Magazine

Nothing comes close to the pleasure of making music on the instrument you love. And if yours is a stringed instrument, we'd like to send you something that will greatly enhance the pleasure you find in music—and help you play with even greater knowledge and confidence. That something is STRINGS, the magazine for all string players—and for those who are passionately interested in the sounds of the violin, viola, cello, bass, or fiddle . . . in the personalities of those who play and make them . . . and in the lore, the literature, and the future of stringed instruments.

As part of your paid subscription you'll also receive the STRINGS Magazine 2000 *Resource Guide* issue. This comprehensive guide contains listings of the services you need most and tells you how to get in touch with dealers, makers, repairers, and specialists all over the world.

You can make up your own mind about the value of STRINGS: just call us at (800) 827-6837, fax us at (415) 485-0831, or send e-mail to subs.st@stringletter.com. We'll rush you the latest issue of STRINGS and reserve your year's subscription for seven issues, plus the 2000 *Resource Guide* issue, all for just $32.95, a savings of 44% off the single-copy rate.

Musical Instrument Auction Price Guide, 1998 Edition

(1997, 1996, 1995, 1994, 1993, 1992 Editions also available.) This is the definitive reference work on the values of antique and hand-made musical instruments offered at the world's most prominent auction houses. Prices are provided in dollars, pounds, marks, and yen of all instruments by an identifiable maker offered in 1997. The 1998 Edition of the *Musical Instrument Auction Price Guide* furnishes you with an exclusive five-year price summary of more than 5,000 instruments and bows offered at all major auction sales from 1993 through 1997, arranged by instrument and maker. You'll see at a glance the recent market for the work of hundreds of historical makers and workshops, from Amati to Zanotti. $47.95 each, including postage. (1997 and 1996 Editions are $39.45 each, including postage; 1995, 1994, 1993, and 1992 Editions are $22.45 each, including postage.)

Resource Guide, 1999 Edition

No matter what your string-playing needs and interests, you'll find what you're looking for in this incredibly handy 196-page reference tool. The *Resource Guide* contains listings of instrument makers, dealers, and specialists from all over the world who will help you find answers to your questions regarding your instruments, accessories, and printed music. This new 1999 Edition is the most complete ever. (Note: The 2000 Edition will automatically be included as the October 1999 issue with all subscription orders.) $11.95 each, including postage.

Commonsense Instrument Care

The second edition of *Commonsense Instrument Care*, a player's guide by James N. McKean, takes you step by step through the basics of instrument care, from the selection of a case and strings to whether or not to insure. Why risk a costly repair or restoration due to neglect or misconceptions about proper instrument maintenance, when you can easily and routinely be taking good care of your violin, viola, or cello, and bow? It's the perfect companion for both conscientious beginners and younger students. $11.95 each, including postage.

INTRODUCTION

This guide offers descriptions and prices of musical instruments and bows offered at auction by identifiable makers at 23 sales held in the United States, Great Britain, and Italy during 1998. (For a complete list of sales, see page 8.)

It is emphatically not a guide to the playing qualities of these instruments, nor to their physical condition. Nor does the guide generally reflect "retail prices," since many items bought at auction are subsequently resold.

The guide is divided into three sections. The first section presents a report on the 1998 stringed-instrument sales, reprinted from *Strings* Magazine. The second section contains auction results in an Item-by-Item Listing. It provides the details on each item: where it was offered, lot number, where and when made, low and high estimated prices, the specifics of the most recent certificate—if any—with which the item was offered, and the actual selling price shown in four currencies. The first currency is U.S. dollars, followed by pounds sterling, Deutsche marks, and yen. The order of currencies is fixed, regardless of the currency in which the sale was conducted.

The third section contains the Summary by Item and Maker, which briefly encapsulates the offerings of the last five years in four currencies. The summary is subdivided alphabetically by item, from Accordion to Zither-Banjo. Within each subdivision, you will find an alphabetical list of makers whose work appeared at auction, along with the barest of facts: how many items by that maker were offered, how many sold, and what were the lowest, highest, and average selling prices. If no items were sold, you will find no price information. If no items were offered by a particular maker, you will simply not find that maker's name.

Please note that all the basic information in this guide was supplied by the auction houses themselves, and it mirrors whatever inconsistencies or ambiguities you will find in the catalogues and the salesrooms. To cite one such example, you may find bows stamped "A. Vigneron," with no attempt to lump them with bows by Joseph Arthur Vigneron or his son, André. Although authorities may tell us that it was the father who used this stamp, while his son used a stamp reading "André Vigneron," we are not prepared to second-guess the auction houses who offered these bows under the sobriquet "A. Vigneron."

At the same time, we have attempted to clear up merely stylistic inconsistencies. For example, Italian forms of proper names are used rather than Latin forms; thus Hieronymus Amati II is listed as Amati, Girolamo (II).

Let the reader then be wary. When in doubt, first refer, if possible, to the catalogue of the auction house itself. If the catalogue is unavailable to you, contact the auction house directly, using the directory of names and addresses on page 9 of this guide, and request further clarification.

SUMMING UP THE STATE OF INSTRUMENT SALES

by Jessamyn Reeves-Brown

"The market is a lot fussier now than it was five years ago," declares Tim Ingles of Sotheby's. As the millennium comes to a close, the world is in a period of financial turmoil and luxury markets feel the heat. The instrument market is no exception—but as collectors hold more tightly to their cash, new buyers are rising to the fore.

Violin maker and dealer Michael Weisshaar of Costa Mesa, California, says that particularly toward the end of the year, his sales were concentrated on student outfits, items selling for $400 to $3,500. "It's more subdued than it was up to a year ago," he says. "Before the Asian [financial] crisis, people spent money in our field more freely; people are just a bit more careful now."

Philip Scott of Phillips agrees that world economics have a big impact on the violin market, perhaps even more so in Britain. "All buyers are price-sensitive and you have to react to those realities. I think the pound-dollar rate remains equitable, but not enough to tempt American buyers to come to London. And people are constantly being told how uncertain everything is, which doesn't encourage buying."

Jonathan Stone of Christie's is more moderate. "I've been encouraged by the results of the sale in November in particular—people from the Far East were buying. And in both the fall and spring sales, there was sort of a good feeling in the room. I don't think one should be at all complacent, but nor do I think one should be totally depressed. We've been able to sell a good range of instruments and bows right across the board."

Unsurprisingly, fine examples in excellent condition continue to sell well, regardless. "People like to know what they're buying, and they want absolutely no condition problems," says Ingles. He points to two "magnificent cellos" Sotheby's sold in 1998, a Giovanni Francesco Pressenda (lot 135 in the March sale, which sold for £205,000 [$343,170]) and a Michele Deconet, ca. 1750 (lot 102 in the June sale, which didn't sell in the auction but went afterward to a British cellist). "They're pretty rare," he says of the Pressenda. "We think there are about eight of them. And to get one in perfect condition was a really fabulous thing. They come onto the market so rarely, and just handling things of that quality is a privilege."

In fact, 1998 seems to have been the Year of the Cello. "Some of the more exciting pieces that came through, both in terms of violin making and record prices, were cellos," says Kerry Keane of Skinner. "Lot 39 in the May sale, a Celeste Farotti cello from 1912, which is a terrific example, sold for $68,500. We don't see many cellos from Farotti surviving, and this was a magnificent piece; the majority of the original varnish survived. Another cello from that same sale was the Hippolyte Chrétien Silvestre from Lyon in 1881 [lot 49]. It had been in private hands since 1948 and was fresh to the market. It has spectacular workmanship and the condition was just immaculate—this instrument hadn't been polished, I don't think, since 1948." It sold for $36,800.

Why are cellos doing so well? "There just don't seem to be enough really great cellos out there, and when they come up for auction, people really fight for them," Keane theorizes. "Cellos are much more labor-intensive to make than violins, the materials are more expensive, and you only have to look at a symphony to see why fewer cellos were made. But I think there is this postwar baby-boom demographic—more cellists have graduated university and are out there plying their trade. I've been told that in the 1960s and '70s, kids were pushed toward the cello and thus we've produced a community of proficient, dynamic cellists, so great cellos are in demand."

Cellos also featured strongly at Butterfield & Butterfield. Says Todd French, a cellist himself, "In the February sale there was the wonderful Bernardo Calcagni, lot 4110—there was a paper from J. & A. Beare saying that this was only one of two Calcagni cellos he knew about, and I'm sure that created a bit of mystique. That, combined with the condition it was in—which was excellent—meant that it sold well, and deservedly well [at $156,500]. The September sale had a magic little cello too, the Vincenzo Sannino [lot 4581]. It had some very heavy bidding. That was a fun one to see go, because the bidding was active and then it stopped quite low, under the low estimate, and then it picked up again and stopped, and then picked up again and just went up and up" to $61,900.

"It ended up going to a player," French continues, "which I'm very happy with, because I'm really encouraging players to buy at auction." He claims to see a rise in the number of players making bids at auction—and winning. "Of course, it's scary to buy at auction; you have to know what you're doing and there are things a dealer has to offer such as setup and repair. But if you do your homework, you can get a great deal. Just have someone you trust, a maker or restorer, [check the instrument out]. I think when you have a lot of players bidding, they will tend to buy more because they don't have to turn a profit on an instrument, and it's still a lower price than they would pay a dealer."

"There is a strengthening market from players, who after all are our end clients anyway," confirms Ingles. "We sold a number of instruments to players, particularly in November, when two of three major instruments went to players." These were a Nicolas Lupot violin, lot 41, which went for £80,700 ($134,769), and a Francesco Ruggieri violin, lot 57, which took £90,600 ($151,302). And the third instrument, a Giuseppe Guarneri (filius Andreae), "was actually bought by a collector in the end but was pushed up by players" to £166,500 ($278,055).

At Bonhams, players and dealers alike vied for a number of very fine instruments from the collection of the late Robert Lewin, a man who bought only the best. "We sold probably one of the great [Giovanni] Grancino cellos, which made a record [£184,000 ($307,280), lot 54]; and we made another world-record price for a Camillo Camilli violin, which was accompanied by a letter and photo from Hill saying it was the finest one they'd seen," says Bonhams expert Peter Horner. Sold as lot 91, the Camilli took £80,500 ($134,435). "We also made a world-record price [£43,700 ($72,979)] on a very fine Annibale Fagnola violin, lot 138; and we got £34,500 [$57,615] for lot 125, a Giuseppe

Pedrazzini violin, which was quite astonishing, although again it was probably the finest example in the world."

Such record prices for Italian instruments may force players to think hard about what else they can get for their money, believes French, who, ironically, touts French instruments. "They seem to be doing surprisingly well; I think there's a lot of neglected quality there. We had a Georges Chanot violin in excellent condition, lot 4174 in the February sale, that did very well [$32,200]—everybody wanted it. And in the September sale, everybody wanted the Claude Pirot violin [lot 4600], which was also in excellent condition." It went for $17,250. "Back in the 1920s, '30s, and '40s, the French instruments were preferred by players because they enjoyed their sound so much. It seemed the same in our auctions: the players were the ones pursuing the French instruments."

Players are also turning to contemporary makers. "We see players choosing new instruments, particularly as a second instrument," says dealer Philip Kass of William Moennig & Son in Philadelphia. "There are a lot of good reasons for doing that. There's no substitute for dealing with the maker of your instrument. It's new, it's healthy, it doesn't have any structural problems. If you're paying a low enough price for it, you can afford to take a loss on it if you resell. And the provenance of a new violin is usually pretty ironclad!"

New bows, adds Kass, are clearly improving in quality. "There are so many wonderful modern bow makers out there, you can get something very fine and new for $3,000–$4,000 tops that will do as well as the older bows. The quality of wood isn't what was available 100 years ago, but I've spoken with a number of bow makers who feel that the quality of wood available today is better than what it was five years ago. To me, it's a classic case of supply and demand—there's a lot of good makers now and they're getting a lot of orders and they need good wood. Of course," he cautions, "the big question on this is at what point we drive pernambuco stocks to the point where they can't be replenished."

Contemporary violin and bow makers were a focus for Butterfield & Butterfield in 1998. The auction house held an exhibition of American making in conjunction with its February sale (see "A New Golden Age," Market Report, July/August 1998). "I think the combination of the exhibition and the auction was unique," says French. "The local players seemed appreciative just to have a chance to meet some of the makers, and the makers enjoyed it too. They've asked us to do it again, so I hope to this year, maybe in September. It was interesting to have the new makers there with their current masterpieces along with the masterpieces of makers past. And not just for the buyers to see, but for the makers themselves to go from room to room."

Ralph Rabin, a dealer in Madison, Wisconsin, sees more student-level players turning to contemporary Asian instruments. "If there's an improvement area, it's in what's available in the student market, which for a long time was dominated by the German and Eastern European manufacturers. Asian commercial manufacturers are listening to suggestions and incorporating them quickly. There's still a filtering process that needs to take place, but there are better options opening up that way for students. It's evolving rapidly."

Keane sees the effects of that improvement in the auction rooms. "The flood of fairly high-quality student instruments coming in from Asia has sort of watered down that market. I think 1998 was a great shakeout year in terms of what the lower end of the market has done. All across the board, the demand for the very inexpensive "trade" instruments—the lower tier of trade work—has gone a bit soft. I think what we saw this year was a larger majority going without selling and the ones that did sell hitting well within their estimate; there's not the feeding frenzy there was. In the past you could sell a Thibouville-Lamy with a few damage problems and someone would buy it. Now, if they're looking in the $1,000 price range, people say, 'Let's pay a few hundred less and get a new Asian instrument instead.' They would rather buy something that's clean and healthy and in good condition."

This was also the year that the instrument and bow making competition held biannually by Violin Society of America (VSA) included a category for basses. "Bass making will be the next frontier," declares Rabin. The quality of instruments in this inaugural competition was mixed, he says, but he saw much to like. "There weren't a lot of them, and a lot of them were incorporating a lot of innovations, but it was a start. Regarding craftsmanship, they have a lot of ground still to cover. But the violin is defined—we know what we like; the bass is still evolving. You still have a sense of exploration, creativity. You have these virtuoso bass players now who can do anything and everything, and the instruments need to catch up with the skills that are there."

New technology is starting to affect the market of older instruments, too. "There's a lot of talk right now about scientific analysis coming into the field," says Ingles. "Eventually perhaps we'll all have dendrochronology machines on our desks, and when a Strad comes in we'll just flash it in front of the camera!" (Dendrochronology is the technique of dating an instrument by examining the tree rings in the wood from which it's made.) However, Ingles isn't worried that human appraisers will become obsolete any time soon. "It only gives you a negative confirmation, as in 'not before 1740,' so there's obviously a long time before that sort of thing replaces the expert eye, which is good news for all of us. But," he adds, "It's basically healthy for the market that people are exploring new techniques."

One area players don't seem to be affecting is the Baroque-instrument market. Despite early music's rise in popularity, Ingles doesn't see much effect on sales of early instruments (although Sotheby's early-instrument sale in November did quite well). "The profile of early music has risen, but the market isn't influenced so much by what's played on classical FM. There is a hard core of early-music players who may be working more, but I think they've always been there. Really, we're looking at a collector's market, not a player's market. Many early instruments are not really playable; [they're bought by people with] extensive collections looking for something by a maker they don't have or a design they don't have." Still, the stringed instrument that took the top price in that auction (£21,850 [$36,271]) was lot 153, an Austrian bass viola da gamba by "a chap who's practically unknown," Johann Seelos—bought by an early-music enthusiast whom Ingles believes will actually play it. "We're very used in the violin world to sending instruments to homes where they'll be played, and it's nice to know that this one will be," he remarks.

"That's a sort of difficult question, isn't it—would you rather sell to a player or a collector?" he continues. "There are some things you'd like to see preserved, such as the

4

'Messiah' Strad or the 'Lady Blunt.' But if you travel around the world and go to museums, you'll see more Strads than anything else. It's nice to see them side by side, but wouldn't it be nicer to see them being played?"

Christie's was lucky enough to be able to offer not one but two Strads for sale in 1998—and neither will be gathering dust. "The first was the 'Kreutzer' Stradivari of 1727, and it was really a great-sounding instrument," says Stone. "It quite rightly made a new auction record for a musical instrument and was bought by a very distinguished young player." Lot 173 in the April sale, it took £947,500 ($1,582,325). "The second was the 'Kortschak' long-pattern Strad, which was sold in November and which again made a record auction price for a long-pattern and a pre-1700 Strad. It was bought by someone who does play but also loans to players." Lot 189, it took £529,500 ($884,265).

Scott points out that the amazing thing about such acmes of violin making is that "the best instruments in the world were constructed before the great repertoire, before Viotti's treatises on technique, before the great orchestras. The builders of those instruments had no idea of what was to come." It's important to keep that kind of long view through the rough spots in the market, he adds philosophically; people will never stop buying violins. "These 'blips' don't need to be taken seriously. There is still a hunger for melody. People neglect playing violins at their peril, because it is such mental and spiritual nourishment."

Auction Activity

1998
instrument
sales

SALES INCLUDED IN THIS GUIDE

The bracketed code is shorthand that consists of a letter (or letters) denoting the auction house, followed by a number for the month in which the sale took place. If a particular house held two sales in the same month, the code consists of the letter for that house and a four-digit code for both the month and the day. You will find these codes used throughout the detailed item-by-item listings later in the guide.

House	Place	Code	Date	Rate of Exchange
Butterfields'	Los Angeles	[Bf2]	2/9/98	$1.00
Bonhams	London	[B2]	2/18/98	$1.64
Bonhams	London	[B3]	3/31/98	$1.67
Sotheby's	London	[S3]	3/31/98	$1.67
Christie's	South Kensington	[C4]	4/1/98	$1.67
Phillips	London	[P4]	4/2/98	$1.67
Skinner	Boston	[Sk5]	5/3/98	$1.00
Bonhams	London	[B5]	5/13/98	$1.63
Sotheby's	London	[S6]	6/16/98	$1.65
Bonhams	London	[B6]	6/18/98	$1.67
Bonhams	Knightsbridge	[B7]	7/20/98	$1.65
Butterfields'	Los Angeles	[Bf7]	7/20/98	$1.00
Butterfields'	Los Angeles	[Bf9]	9/15/98	$1.00
Bonhams	Knightsbridge	[B10]	10/7/98	$1.70
Phillips	London	[P10]	10/15/98	$1.70
Sotheby's	Milan	[S10]	10/22/98	$.00062
Sotheby's	London	[S1104]	11/4/98	$1.66
Skinner	Boston	[Sk11]	11/8/98	$1.00
Phillips	London	[P11]	11/16/98	$1.68
Sotheby's	London	[S1117]	11/17/98	$1.67
Bonhams	London	[B11]	11/18/98	$1.67
Christie's	South Kensington	[C11]	11/18/98	$1.67
Phillips	London	[P12]	12/10/98	$1.67

DIRECTORY OF AUCTION HOUSES

These are the firms in the United States and Great Britain that regularly conduct sales of musical instruments, particularly stringed instruments and bows.

Bonhams
Montpelier St.
Knightsbridge
London SW7 1HH, England
Telephone: (44) 171 393 3900
Fax: (44) 171 393 3905
Web site: www.bonhams.com
Enquiries: Peter Horner

Butterfield & Butterfield
7601 Sunset Blvd.
Los Angeles, CA 90046 USA
Telephone: (213) 850-7500
Fax: (213) 850-5843
Web site: www.butterfields.com
Specialist: Todd French

Christie's
8 King St., St. James's
London SW1Y 6QT, England
Telephone: (44) 171 839 9060
Fax: (44) 171 839 1611
Web site: www.christies.com
Specialist: Jonathan Stone

20 Rockefeller Plaza
New York, NY 10020 USA
Telephone: (212) 636-2259
Fax: (212) 636-4927
Consultants: Frederick Oster,
Genevieve Wheeler

Phillips
101 New Bond St.
London W1Y 0AS, England
Telephone: (44) 171 629 6602
Fax: (44) 171 629 8876
Web site: www.auctions-on-line.com/
phillips/uk/index.html
Specialist: Philip Scott

406 E. 79th St.
New York, NY 10021 USA
Telephone: (212) 570-4830
Fax: (212) 570-2207

Skinner
357 Main St.
Bolton, MA 01740 USA
Telephone: (508) 779-6241
Fax: (508) 779-5144
Web site: www.skinnerinc.com
Expert: Kerry K. Keane

Sotheby's
34-35 New Bond St.
London W1A 2AA, England
Telephone: (44) 171 408 5342
Fax: (44) 171 408 5942
Web site: www.sothebys.com
Experts: Tim Ingles, Adam Watson

1334 York Ave.
New York, NY 10021 USA
Telephone: (212) 606-7938
Fax: (212) 774-5310
Consultant: Charles Rudig

A KEY TO THE ITEM-BY-ITEM LISTINGS

1. Name of Maker   2. Sale/Lot   3. Item   4. Where/When Made

GUADAGNINI, LORENZO [P11/154] Fine and Handsome Violin w/case: Piacenza, 1742 (W. E. Hill & Sons, London, June 1933) 122,960/184,440
$304,326   £198,000   DM480,942   ¥57,370,500

    5. Certificate   6. Estimated Prices ($)   7. Selling Prices

1. Name. An "attributed" work signals an attribution made, or agreed to, by the auction house; when "ascribed," a traditional ascription is acknowledged but not necessarily agreed with.

2. The lot number assigned by the auctioneer is preceded by an initial to identify the house (B Bonhams; Bf Butterfields'; C Christie's; P Phillips; S Sotheby's; Sk Skinner) followed by a number for the sale. If there were two sales at one house during the same month, the numbers for the month and day are both used to identify the sale.

3. A description of the item as it appears in the sale catalogue. When the item is sold with accessories or when additional items are part of the same lot, a brief itemization appears here. This is also the place where defects or repairs, as reported in the sale catalogue, are noted.

4. Place and date of manufacture, if known.

5. If sold with a certificate attesting to its provenance or identity, the most recent issuer is indicated in parentheses, along with the place and date of issuance.

6. Low and high estimated prices (in dollars) are separated by a slash (/). This is the price range within which the item was expected to sell, in the opinion of the auctioneers. On occasion, no estimate is made—most often involving an important instrument by a famous maker. In these cases, only the selling price appears in the tables.

7. The actual selling price includes the buyer's premium, at Bonhams, Christie's, Phillips, and Sotheby's: 15% on the first £30,000 of the hammer price and 10% on the amount above; and at Butterfields' and Skinner, 15% on the first $50,000 plus 10% on the amount above. Prices are given in four currencies, converted from local currency at their value on the day sold. You may determine the country in which the sale took place from the "Sale" information in "2" above. An unsold item is recorded as "NS." These listings do not provide details on size, weight, color, etc., which often help to identify or distinguish particular items. You are advised to consult the catalogues published prior to the sales, which may be obtained directly from the auctioneers.

ACCORDION

CASALI [P11/10] Piano Accordion in good condition: Verona, Italy 420/588 NS

SCANDALLI [P12/14] Good Piano Accordion w/case 668/1,002 NS

SOPRANI, PAOLO [P11/11] Piano Accordion w/box 252/420 NS

ARPANETTA

KARP, JOHANN [S1104/174] Arpanetta w/case: Copenhagen, 1709 4,980/8,300
$11,836 £7,130 DM19,679 ¥1,378,514

BANDURRIA

ANDRADE, JOAO MIGUEL [S1104/281] Bandurria: Lisbon, c. 1920 166/332
$324 £195 DM538 ¥37,701

BANJEAURINE

HAYNES CO., JOHN C. [Sk11/47] American Five-String Banjeaurine: Boston, c. 1890 200/300 NS

BANJO

BACON & DAY [Sk11/53] American Tenor Banjo w/case: Groton, c. 1937 500/600
$978 £587 DM1,652 ¥119,255

BACON & DAY [Sk11/55] American Tenor "B & D Special" Banjo w/case: Groton 500/600
$144 £86 DM243 ¥17,538

DOBSON, E.D.W.G. [Sk11/37] American Five-String Banjo: New York, c. 1880 600/800
$345 £207 DM583 ¥42,090

DOBSON, GEORGE [Sk11/38] American Five-String Banjo: Boston, c. 1875 200/300
$230 £138 DM389 ¥28,060

DORE BROS. [Bf9/4527] Rare Banjo: New York 700/1,200 NS

EPIPHONE [Sk11/44] American Tenor Banjo w/case: New York, c. 1927 400/600
$690 £414 DM1,166 ¥84,180

ESSEX, CLIFFORD [B2/43] Five-String "Boudoir Grand" Banjo w/case 246/410
$415 £253 DM755 ¥52,406

FAIRBANKS & COLE [Sk11/42] American Five-String Banjo w/case: Boston, c. 1880 250/350
$374 £224 DM632 ¥45,598

FAIRBANKS CO., A.C. [Bf9/4528] Rare American Banjo 1,400/2,400
$3,163 £1,898 DM5,345 ¥420,834

GREY & SONS, JOHN [B2/45] Four-String Gravure-Model Banjo 492/656
$604 £368 DM1,098 ¥76,228

HAYNES CO., JOHN C. [Sk11/46] American Five-String Banjo: Boston 200/300
$150 £90 DM253 ¥18,239

HAYNES CO., JOHN C. [Sk11/48] American Five-String Banjo: Boston, c. 1885 300/400 NS

JEDSON [B7/43] Five-String "Conservatoire" A-Model Banjo w/case 413/578
$380 £230 DM674 ¥52,645

LOCKE, G.S. [Sk11/45] American Five-String Banjo w/soft case: c. 1880 250/350
$316 £190 DM534 ¥38,583

LYON & HEALY [B2/41] Seven-String Banjo w/case: c. 1870 131/197
$132 £81 DM240 ¥16,675

MANSFIELD, E.B. [Sk11/41] American Early Fretless Five-String Banjo w/case: Boston, c. 1872 250/350
$518 £311 DM875 ¥63,135

MORRISON, JAMES A. [Sk11/39] American Five-String Banjo w/case: New York, c. 1882 400/600
$460 £276 DM777 ¥56,120

STEWART, S.S. [Sk11/54] American Tenor Banjo w/case: Philadelphia, c. 1920 100/200 NS

THOMPSON & ODELL [Sk11/40] American Five-String Banjo: Boston, c. 1885 250/350
$201 £121 DM340 ¥24,553

TURNER, JOHN ALVEY [B7/42] Five-String Banjo w/case 165/248
$209 £127 DM371 ¥28,955

VEGA COMPANY [Sk11/43] American Tenor Banjo w/case: Boston, c. 1926 1,800/2,200 NS

VEGA COMPANY [Sk11/49] American Tenor Banjo w/case: Boston, 1933 250/350
$374 £224 DM632 ¥45,598

WEAVER [B10/25] Four-String Banjo 102/136
$196 £115 DM315 ¥24,175

WELTTON [B2/42] Four-String Plectrum Banjo w/case 164/246
$132 £81 DM240 ¥16,675

BANJOLELE

DALLAS, J.E. [B2/40] Model B "George Formby" Banjolele w/case: c. 1940–50 131/197
$151 £92 DM275 ¥19,057

BARITONE

BUNDY [Bf7/10430] Baritone in good condition, w/case 275/350
$184 £112 DM328 ¥25,561

BASSOON

BESSON & CO. [P12/9] Bassoon w/box, accessories: London, c. 1930 334/501
$288 £173 DM476 ¥33,689

BUCHNER, F. [P4/21] Good Contemporary German Bassoon in good playing condition, w/case: Nauheim
1,000/1,334
$3,259   £1,955   DM6,037   ¥435,242

BUFFET CRAMPON & CO. [B5/42] Metal-Keyed Wooden Bassoon w/case
130/196
$262   £161   DM467   ¥35,248

DE LUIGI, GIACOMO [S1104/389] Eight-Keyed Maple Bassoon: Milan, c. 1830   1,660/2,490
$1,527   £920   DM2,539   ¥177,873

FELCHLIN, JOSEF KARL [S1104/269] Ten-Keyed Stained-Maple Bassoon with later simulated ivory bell mount, bocal absent: Bern, c. 1850   830/1,162
$993   £598   DM1,650   ¥115,617

HECKEL [B2/26] Very Fine German Contrabassoon w/case, 2 crooks: Biebrich am Rhein, c. 1900
4,920/8,200 NS

HECKEL [B5/43] Fine German Bassoon w/case: Biebrich am Rhein   4,890/8,150
$6,561   £4,025   DM11,673   ¥881,193

HECKEL [P4/20] Bassoon in playing condition, w/case, crook: Biebrich, 1896   6,668/8,335 NS

HIRSBRUNNER FAMILY (MEMBER OF) [S1104/370] Eight-Keyed Maple Bassoon: Sumiswald, c. 1840   1,660/2,490
$1,622   £977   DM2,697   ¥188,893

HIRSBRUNNER FAMILY (MEMBER OF) [S1104/377] Eight-Keyed Maple Bassoon: Sumiswald, c. 1840   3,320/4,980
$3,054   £1,840   DM5,078
¥355,74oxwood Flute in F: London, early 19th C.
299/415 $400   £241   DM665
¥46,595

MONZANI [P11/7] Eight-Keyed Patent Rosewood Conical-Bore ConcUDWIG, FRANZ [S1104/268] Eleven-Keyed Maple Bassoon: Prague, c. 1850
1,660/2,490 $1,527   £920   DM2,539
¥177,873

MILHOUSE, WILLIAM [C4/421] Six-Keyed Bassoon lacking crook and one keypad   1,002/1,336 NS

MILHOUSE, WILLIAM [S1104/373A] Nine-Keyed Stained-Pearwood Bassoon without crook: London, c. 1820   1,660/2,490
$1,718   £1,035   DM2,857   ¥200,107

PARKER, JOHN [S1104/383] Six-Keyed Stained-Pearwood Bassoon: London, c. 1810   830/1,162
$725   £437   DM1,206   ¥84,490

RUDALL, CARTE & CO. [P12/10] Stained-Maplewood Bassoon w/2 cases, bassoon, accessories: London   334/501 NS

TRIEBERT & SONS, GUILLAUME [S1104/345] Nine-Keyed Stained-Pearwood Bassoon w/bassoon: Paris, c. 1840   498/830
$458   £276   DM762   ¥53,362

BUGLE

CLEMENTI & CO. [Bf9/4569] B-Flat Seven-Keyed Bugle w/mouthpiece: London, c. 1830   2,700/3,200
$4,025   £2,415   DM6,802   ¥535,607

FIRTH HALL & POND [Bf9/4565] Six-Keyed B-Flat Bugle: New York, c. 1840   2,500/3,000
$3,163   £1,898   DM5,345   ¥420,834

LOGIER, JOHN BERNHARD [Bf9/4568] Rare and Important Bugle, mouthpiece probably original: London, c. 1809–11   2,000/2,500
$3,163   £1,898   DM5,345   ¥420,834

SAURLE, MICHAEL [S1104/55] Six-Keyed Bugle: Munich, c. 1835   2,490/4,150 NS

WHITE & CO., H.N. [Bf9/4570] I-Valve Marching Bugle: Cleveland, 1930s   300/500 NS

CITTERN

BRODERIP & WILKINSON [C11/544] Keyed Cittern w/case   501/835
$730   £437   DM1,219   ¥88,707

CLARINET

ALBERT, EUGENE A. [S1104/373] Thirteen-Keyed Blackwood E-Flat Clarinet w/original case: Brussels, c. 1865   498/664
$764   £460   DM1,270   ¥88,936

AMMANN, ULRICH [S1104/23] Five-Keyed Boxwood Walking-Stick Clarinet in D: Alt St. Johann, early 19th C.   4,150/5,810
$6,491   £3,910   DM10,792   ¥755,959

BAUMANN [S1104/205] Six-Keyed Boxwood B-Flat Clarinet: Paris, early 19th C.   996/1,328
$1,680   £1,012   DM2,793   ¥195,660

BILTON [Bf9/4540] Thirteen-Keyed Boxwood Clarinet: London, c. 1830   1,800/2,200
$1,725   £1,035   DM2,915   ¥229,546

BRAUN [B10/13] Twelve-Keyed Boxwood Clarinet: early 19th C.   510/680
$587   £345   DM945   ¥72,526

BUESCHER [Bf7/10429] E-Flat Clarinet w/case, mouthpiece   300/400
$230   £140   DM409   ¥31,952

BUESCHER [C11/525] Clarinet w/case, flute
$77   £46   DM128   ¥9,338

BUFFET CRAMPON & CO. [B10/15] Blackwood Clarinet w/case, clarinet: c. 1950   1,360/2,040 NS

BUFFET CRAMPON & CO. [C11/526] Clarinet w/case, clarinet   501/835
$1,055   £632   DM1,763   ¥128,290

CHRISTIANI [C4/423] Boxwood Clarinet lacking mouthpiece   668/835
$576   £345   DM1,070   ¥77,087

DISTIN, HENRY [S1104/4] Twelve-Keyed Metal
Clarinet: London, c. 1860   3,320/4,980
$133   £80   DM221   ¥15,467

ELKHART [B2/25] Rosewood Boehm-System
Clarinet w/case, wooden flute   98/131
$132   £81   DM240   ¥16,675

FINGERHUTH, CHRISTIAN [S1104/248] Twelve-
Keyed Boxwood Clarinet in A: Cassel, c. 1840
                                                  664/996
$1,240   £747   DM2,062   ¥144,425

GILMER & CO. [B5/38] Simple-System Rosewood
Clarinet w/case   65/98
$131   £81   DM233   ¥17,624

GOODLAD & CO. [B2/24] Six-Keyed Boxwood
Clarinet: c. 1830   131/197
$283   £173   DM515   ¥35,732

GOULDING & CO. [C11/524] Boxwood Clarinet
                                                  334/501
$730   £437   DM1,219   ¥88,707

GOULDING & CO. [P4/19] Attractive Boxwood and
Ivory Clarinet: London, c. 1810   333/500
$383   £230   DM710   ¥51,205

HALL & SON, WILLIAM [Bf7/10432] Rosewood
Clarinet w/case, mouthpiece: New York   400/600
$230   £140   DM409   ¥31,952

HASENEIER, H.F. [S1104/213] Twelve-Keyed
Boxwood Clarinet: Coblenz, c. 1875   996/1,328
$1,431   £862   DM2,379   ¥166,659

HAWKES & SON [P10/8] Excelsior Sonorous-Class
Clarinet w/2 boxes, E-flat clarinet: London   340/510
$391   £230   DM637   ¥46,018

KLEMM & BRO. [Bf9/4541] Six-Key Boxwood
Clarinet: Markneukirchen, c. 1830   900/1,200
$920   £552   DM1,555   ¥122,424

KOHLER & SON [S1104/371] Double-Walled Metal
Clarinet in C, w/case: London, late 19th C.   498/664
$1,336   £805   DM2,222   ¥155,639

KOHLERT, VINCENZ FERARIUS [S1104/347]
Nine-Keyed Boxwood Clarinet in high E-flat,
w/clarinet: Graslitz, c. 1850   714/996 NS

KRUSPE, C. [S1104/212] Ten-Keyed Boxwood
Clarinet in high E-flat: Erfurt, mid 19th C.
                                                  498/830 NS

LEBLANC, GEORGES [S1104/3] Boehm-System
Contrabass Metal Clarinet: Paris, early 20th C.
                                                  3,320/4,980 NS

LEDUC [Bf7/10433] B-Flat Clarinet w/case   70/120
$58   £35   DM102   ¥7,988

MARTIN BROS. [Bf9/4546] Ten-Keyed Boxwood
Clarinet: Paris, c. 1860   600/800
$575   £345   DM972   ¥76,515

MEINEL, CLEMENS [S1104/244] B-Flat German-
System Clarinet w/clarinet in A, case, cover:
Wernitzgrün, mid 20th C.   664/996
$764   £460   DM1,270   ¥88,936

METZLER & CO. [B7/22] Eight-Keyed Boxwood
Clarinet: c. 1830   165/248
$247   £150   DM438   ¥34,219

METZLER & CO. [S1104/17] Ten-Keyed Boxwood
B-Flat Clarinet: London, c. 1840   415/581
$420   £253   DM698   ¥48,915

METZLER & CO. [S1104/388] Six-Keyed Boxwood
B-Flat Clarinet: London, c. 1840   415/581
$496   £299   DM825   ¥57,809

MEYER, KARL [B10/14] Boehm-System Ebony
Clarinet   170/255
$176   £104   DM284   ¥21,758

MILLER, GEORGE [S1104/208] Five-Keyed
Boxwood Clarinet: London, c. 1780   996/1,328
$2,673   £1,610   DM4,444   ¥311,277

MOLLENHAUER, JOHANN ANDREAS
[S1104/352] Five-Keyed Boxwood Clarinet: Fulda,
mid 19th C.   498/830
$438   £264   DM729   ¥51,042

MONNIG GEBRUDER [S1104/245] Metal Bass
Clarinet w/metal alto clarinet: Markneukirchen, early
20th C.   664/1,328
$1,718   £1,035   DM2,857   ¥200,107

NICHOLSON, CHARLES [B2/23] Six-Keyed
Boxwood Clarinet without mouthpiece   98/131
$151   £92   DM275   ¥19,057

PAN-AMERICAN [Bf7/10445] B-Flat "Propeller"
Clarinet w/case   400/600 NS

PASK, JOHN [S1104/362] Twelve-Keyed Metal
Clarinet in C, w/case: London, c. 1865   664/996
$611   £368   DM1,016   ¥71,149

POTTER, SAMUEL [P12/11] Six-Keyed Clarinet
w/single-key flute: London, c. 1840   501/668
$461   £276   DM762   ¥53,903

RAMPONE, AGOSTINO [S1104/14] Fifteen-Keyed
Double-Walled Metal B-Flat Clarinet w/original case:
Milan, late 19th C.   498/830
$1,336   £805   DM2,222   ¥155,639

ROUSTAGNEQ [S1104/393] Five-Keyed Boxwood
B-Flat Clarinet: Toulon, early 19th C.   996/1,328
$1,718   £1,035   DM2,857   ¥200,107

SCHUSTER & CO., G. [S1104/233] Seven-Keyed
Boxwood B-Flat Clarinet without mouthpiece:
Neukirchen, c. 1825   830/1,162
$1,107   £667   DM1,841   ¥128,958

SELMER [B5/41] Rosewood Boehm-System Clarinet
w/case, clarinet   326/489
$525   £322   DM934   ¥70,495

SELMER, HENRI [S1104/247] Boehm-System
Blackwood B-Flat Clarinet w/clarinet in A: Paris, mid
20th C.   664/996
$611   £368   DM1,016   ¥71,149

SELMER BUNDY [Bf7/10431] B-Flat Clarinet needing cork, w/case   200/250 NS

SELMER BUNDY [Bf7/10443] Clarinet w/case,
mouthpiece   200/250
$115   £70   DM205   ¥15,976

THIBOUVILLE [Bf7/10441] E-Flat Clarinet w/case, mouthpiece   300/400
$230   £140   DM409   ¥31,952

THIBOUVILLE-LAMY, J. [Bf7/10444] D Clarinet
                                              300/450
$316   £193   DM563   ¥43,933

UHLMANN, JOHANN TOBIAS [S1104/204] Five-Keyed Boxwood Clarinet in high F: Vienna, c. 1830
                                              996/1,328
$1,431   £862   DM2,379   ¥166,659

WHITELY [Bf9/4544] Five-Keyed Boxwood Clarinet: Utica, New York, c. 1820   800/1,000
$805   £483   DM1,360   ¥107,121

WOOD, JAMES & SON [P12/12] Boxwood and Ivory Six-Keyed Patent Clarinet   134/200
$125   £75   DM206   ¥14,599

WOOD & IVY [Bf9/4539] Eight-Keyed Boxwood Clarinet: London, c. 1840   1,400/1,800
$1,380   £828   DM2,332   ¥183,637

WOOD & IVY [S1104/382] Twelve-Keyed Boxwood Clarinet in C: London, c. 1845   415/581
$649   £391   DM1,079   ¥75,596

WREDE, H. [B5/39] Five-Keyed Boxwood Clarinet: London   163/244
$319   £196   DM567   ¥42,801

CONCERTINA

CHIDLEY, ROCK [B7/34] Forty-Eight-Button English-System Concertina   413/578
$380   £230   DM674   ¥52,645

CHIDLEY, ROCK [B10/20] Forty-Eight-Button English-System Concertina w/case   425/595 NS

CRABB, HENRY [B5/49] Thirty-Button Anglo-System Concertina with price list, w/case 1,630/2,445
$2,905   £1,783   DM5,169   ¥390,243

CRABB, HENRY [C4/435] Forty-Eight-Button English-System Concertina w/case   501/835
$807   £483   DM1,497   ¥107,922

JEFFRIES [C4/433] Thirty-Nine-Button Anglo-System Concertina w/case   2,004/3,006
$4,225   £2,530   DM7,843   ¥565,303

JEFFRIES [C4/434] Sixty-Two-Button Duet-System Concertina w/case   668/1,002
$1,055   £632   DM1,959   ¥141,214

JEFFRIES, CHARLES [B5/48] Thirty-Button Anglo-System Concertina w/case   1,304/1,956
$4,124   £2,530   DM7,337   ¥553,893

JEFFRIES, CHARLES [B7/40] Thirty-Button Anglo-System Concertina w/case   1,320/1,980
$3,605   £2,185   DM6,402   ¥500,125

JEFFRIES, CHARLES [S1104/184] Thirty-Seven-Button Anglo-German-System Concertina w/case: London, c. 1900   1,162/1,660
$4,200   £2,530   DM6,983   ¥489,150

JEFFRIES, CHARLES [S1104/190] Thirty-Seven-Button Anglo-German-System Concertina w/case: London, c. 1900   1,162/1,660
$4,009   £2,415   DM6,665   ¥466,916

JEFFRIES, CHARLES [S1104/191] Forty-Four-Button Anglo-German-System Concertina w/case: London, early 20th C.   2,490/3,320
$4,009   £2,415   DM6,665   ¥466,916

JONES, GEORGE [S1104/187] Forty-Eight-Button English Concertina w/case: London, late 19th C.
                                              498/830 NS

LACHENAL [B2/31] Forty-Eight-Button English-System Concertina w/original case   164/246
$189   £115   DM343   ¥23,821

LACHENAL [B5/45] Forty-Eight-Button English-System Concertina w/case   244/326 NS

LACHENAL [B7/28] Twenty-Button Anglo-System Concertina w/case   165/248 NS

LACHENAL [B7/30] Forty-Eight-Button English-System Concertina w/case   132/198
$161   £98   DM286   ¥22,374

LACHENAL [B7/32] Forty-Eight-Button English-System Concertina   248/330
$247   £150   DM438   ¥34,219

LACHENAL [B7/33] Forty-Eight-Button English-System Concertina   165/248
$209   £127   DM371   ¥28,955

LACHENAL [B7/36] Fifty-Six-Button English-System Concertina w/case   330/495
$398   £242   DM708   ¥55,277

LACHENAL [B7/38] Thirty-Button Anglo-System Concertina w/case   330/495
$569   £345   DM1,011   ¥78,967

LACHENAL [B10/19] Twenty-Button Anglo-System Concertina w/case   68/102
$59   £35   DM95   ¥7,253

LACHENAL [Bf9/4537] Concertina w/accordion: London, c. 1920   1,000/1,200 NS

LACHENAL & CO. [S1104/183] Forty-Eight-Button English Concertina w/case: London, early 20th C.
                                              498/830
$764   £460   DM1,270   ¥88,936

LACHENAL & CO. [S1104/185] Forty-Eight-Button English Concertina w/case: London, late 19th C.
                                              332/664
$878   £529   DM1,460   ¥102,277

LACHENAL & CO. [S1104/186] English Concertina w/case: London, mid 19th C.   498/830
$573   £345   DM952   ¥66,702

VICKERS [B10/22] Forty-Eight-Button English-System Concertina w/case, lesson book 425/595
$508   £299   DM819   ¥62,856

WHEATSTONE, C. [B2/32] Forty-Eight-Button English-System Concertina w/original case 328/492
$641   £391   DM1,167   ¥80,992

WHEATSTONE, C. [B2/33] Forty-Eight-Button
English-System Concertina w/original case   246/410
$151   £92   DM275   ¥19,057

WHEATSTONE, C. [B2/35] Single-Action 48-Button
Concertina w/original case   492/820
$1,282   £782   DM2,333   ¥161,983

WHEATSTONE, C. [B7/31] Forty-Eight-Button
English-System Concertina w/case   248/330
$304   £184   DM539   ¥42,116

WHEATSTONE, C. [B7/35] Forty-Eight-Button
English-System Concertina w/case   330/495
$342   £207   DM607   ¥47,380

WHEATSTONE, C. [B7/39] Thirty-Two-Button
Anglo-System Concertina w/case   990/1,320
$2,846   £1,725   DM5,054   ¥394,835

WHEATSTONE, C. [B10/21] Forty-Eight-Button
English-System Concertina w/case   510/680 NS

WHEATSTONE, C. [P12/15] Treble Concertina
w/case: London   668/752 NS

WHEATSTONE & CO., C. [B2/34] Single-Action
48-Button Concertina w/original case   492/820
$1,169   £713   DM2,128   ¥147,691

WHEATSTONE & CO., C. [S1104/192] Sixty-Seven-
Button McCann Duet-System Concertina w/case:
London, 1922   830/1,162
$1,145   £690   DM1,904   ¥133,405

WHEATSTONE & CO., C. [S1104/193] Thirty-
Button Anglo-German-System Concertina w/case:
London, 1917   1,328/1,992

CORNET

BESSON [S1104/261] Cornet w/case: Paris, c. 1840
                                          996/1,328
$1,049   £632   DM1,744   ¥122,191

BESSON & CO. [Sk5/8] Silver-Plated Cornet w/case,
mouthpiece: London   150/250
$173   £104   DM307   ¥22,939

BOOSEY & CO. [Bf9/4560] Cornet w/case: London,
c. 1898   800/1,000
$805   £483   DM1,360   ¥107,121

CONN, C.G. [Sk5/1] American Cornet w/case,
3 mouthpieces, crook, 2 mutes, music holder: Elkhart,
Indiana, c. 1900   150/250
$748   £449   DM1,331   ¥99,403

CONN USA [Bf9/4551] Cornet: Elkhart, Indiana,
c. 1904   800/1,200
$690   £414   DM1,166   ¥91,818

DUPONT, M. [Bf7/10435] Cornet needing valve keys,
w/soft case, mouthpiece: Paris   70/150
$92   £56   DM164   ¥12,781

GLASSL, EGIDIUS [S1104/71] Circular Cornet:
Komotau, early 20th C.   498/830
$802   £483   DM1,333   ¥93,383

GRAVES, J.G. [B2/27] Cornet w/case   33/49
$113   £69   DM206   ¥14,293

HULLER, EMMANUEL [S1104/75] Cornet: Graslitz,
mid 19th C.   66/100
$1,145   £690   DM1,904   ¥133,405

LYON & HEALY [S1104/272] Cornet: Chicago,
c. 1900   498/830
$916   £552   DM1,524   ¥106,724

MORITZ, C.W. [Bf9/4550] Cornet: Berlin, c. 1890
                                          1,200/1,500 NS

OLDS & SON [Bf9/4552] Cornet: Los Angeles,
c. 1940   700/900
$690   £414   DM1,166   ¥91,818

SCHUSTER & CO., G. [Bf9/4558] Cornet:
Markneukirchen, c. 1890   700/1,000
$690   £414   DM1,166   ¥91,818

WURLITZER CO., RUDOLPH [Sk5/11] American
Cornet w/case, 2 mouthpieces, tuning crook, mute
                                             75/150
$144   £86   DM256   ¥19,116

CYMBALUM

SCHUNDA, JOSEF V. [S1104/307] Cymbalum:
Budapest, c. 1900   1,328/1,992 NS

DOUBLE BASS

VILLA, LUIGI [S1117/195] Double Bass: Cesano
Maderno, 1981   5,845/7,515
$9,218   £5,520   DM15,401   ¥1,120,505

VILLA, LUIGI [S1117/205] Double Bass: Cesano
Maderno, 1992   5,010/6,680
$5,762   £3,450   DM9,626   ¥700,316

VILLA, LUIGI [S1117/213] Double Bass: Cesano
Maderno, 1985   5,010/6,680
$5,377   £3,220   DM8,984   ¥653,628

DOUBLE BASS BOW

MORIZOT, LOUIS (II) [S3/94] Silver Double Bass
Bow: Mirecourt, c. 1950   1,172/1,674
$1,828   £1,092   DM3,382   ¥243,614

RAU, AUGUST [S1117/432] Silver Double Bass Bow
                                           668/1,002
$1,344   £805   DM2,246   ¥163,407

VICKERS, J.E. [C11/218] Nickel Double Bass Bow
                                          334/501 NS

VICKERS, J.E. [P4/237] Contemporary Nickel
Double Bass Bow   250/417
$345   £207   DM639   ¥46,084

WERNER, ERICH [B2/64] Nickel Double Bass Bow
                                            492/820
$528   £322   DM961   ¥66,699

EDEOPHONE

LACHENAL & CO. [S1104/189] Forty-Eight-Button
Edeophone w/case: London, early 20th C.   166/332
$782   £471   DM1,300   ¥91,063

ENGLISH HORN

FORNARI, ANDREAS [B7/18] Fine Italian English
Horn w/case: Venice, 1798   6,600/9,900 NS

LOREE, F. [S1104/341] Conservatoire-System English
Horn w/case: Paris, early 20th C.   996/1,328
$993   £598   DM1,650   ¥115,617

TRIEBERT & SONS, GUILLAUME [S1104/231]
Eleven-Keyed Curved English Horn w/crook: Paris,
1840   3,320/4,980
$3,054   £1,840   DM5,078   ¥355,746

ZIEGLER, I. [S1104/232] Twelve-Keyed Stained-
Fruitwood Angled English Horn: Vienna, c. 1850
                                            4,150/5,810
$3,818   £2,300   DM6,348   ¥444,682

EPINETTE DES VOSGES

LAMBERT, A. [S1104/305] Epinette des Vosges:
Vosges, late 18th C.   498/830
$476   £287   DM792   ¥55,489

FIFE

MILHOUSE, WILLIAM [S1104/47] Boxwood Fife:
London, early 19th C.   166/249
$191   £115   DM317   ¥22,234

SIMPSON [B7/11] Eight-Keyed Rosewood Marching
Fife w/case   132/198
$142   £86   DM253   ¥19,742

FLAGEOLET

BAINBRIDGE, WILLIAM [S1104/1] Boxwood
Double Flageolet: London, c. 1815   664/996
$764   £460   DM1,270   ¥88,936

BAINBRIDGE, WILLIAM [S1104/52] Boxwood
Double Flageolet without mouthpiece, w/box:
London, 1827   830/1,162
$916   £552   DM1,524   ¥106,724

BAINBRIDGE & WOOD [S1104/220] Single
Boxwood Flageolet w/double flageolet   1,660/2,490
$3,627   £2,185   DM6,031   ¥422,448

BAINBRIDGE & WOOD [S1104/376] Boxwood
Double Flageolet w/case: London, c. 1820   498/830
$878   £529   DM1,460   ¥102,277

BUHNER & KELLER [S1104/353] Two-Keyed
French Flageolet: Strasbourg, mid 19th C.   415/581
$955   £575   DM1,587   ¥111,171

LAMBERT, JEAN NICOLAS [S1104/360]
Blackwood Boehm-System Single French Flageolet
w/case, flageolet: Paris, late 19th C.   498/830
$955   £575   DM1,587   ¥111,171

MARGUERITAT [S1104/35] Five-Keyed Blackwood
French Flageolet w/flageolet: Paris, late 19th C.
                                            299/481
$1,240   £747   DM2,062   ¥144,425

PROWSE & CO., KEITH [B5/35] Twelve-Keyed
English Double Flageolet w/case   652/978
$712   £437   DM1,267   ¥95,672

SATZGER [S1104/5] Ebony French Flageolet:
Karlsruhe, late 19th C.   498/830 NS

SIMPSON, JOHN [S1104/320] Boxwood Double
Flageolet: London, c. 1840   664/996
$955   £575   DM1,587   ¥111,171

FLUGELHORN

BESSON & CO. [Bf9/4561] Flugelhorn: London,
c. 1903   600/800
$575   £345   DM972   ¥76,515

LOW, JACOB [S1104/73] Flugelhorn: Münster,
c. 1900   830/1,162
$1,909   £1,150   DM3,174   ¥222,341

OTTO, FRANZ [S1104/67] Flugelhorn:
Markneukirchen, mid 19th C.   664/996
$916   £552   DM1,524   ¥106,724

SCHUSTER & CO. [Bf9/4547] Flugelhorn:
Markneukirchen, c. 1900   600/900
$633   £380   DM1,069   ¥84,167

FLUTE

ALEXANDER GEBRUDER [S1104/342] One-Keyed
Ebony Flute w/case: Mainz, early 19th C.   498/830
$458   £276   DM762   ¥53,362

ARMSTRONG, W.T. [P12/7] Silvered Flute in good
condition, w/case: Elkhart, Indiana   134/200 NS

ASTOR & CO. [S1104/53] Four-Keyed Boxwood
Flute: London, c. 1810   249/415
$764   £460   DM1,270   ¥88,936

BILTON, RICHARD [B5/24] Four-Keyed Boxwood
Flute: London   130/196 NS

BOOSEY & HAWKES [B2/21] Boehm-System Metal
Flute w/case: London   246/328 NS

BOOSEY & HAWKES [B10/8] Metal Boehm-System
Flute w/original case   136/204
$137   £81   DM221   ¥16,923

BOOSEY & HAWKES [B10/11] Silver-Plated Flute
w/case   102/170
$98   £58   DM158   ¥12,088

BOOSEY & HAWKES [P12/4] Silvered Flute in good
condition, w/box: London   251/334 NS

BUFFET CRAMPON & CO. [C11/517] Silver-Plated
Boehm-System Flute w/case   167/334 NS

CAHUSAC [B10/7] One-Keyed Stained-Boxwood
Flute missing a key   680/850 NS

COLAS, PROSPER [S1104/381] Five-Keyed
Rosewood Flute w/5-keyed piccolo: Paris, c. 1890
                                            249/332 NS

COLONIEU, MARIUS HENRY [B2/19] Good
Rosewood 1867-System Flute w/case, extra mouthpiece: c. 1890   328/492
$264   £161   DM480   ¥33,350

COUESNON [B5/27] Rosewood Flute w/case
                                            98/130 NS

CUVILLIER [S1104/328] Eight-Keyed Blackwood
Flute: St. Omer, c. 1830   830/1,162
$1,145   £690   DM1,904   ¥133,405

D'ALMAINE & CO. [B2/16] One-Keyed Boxwood
Flute: London   131/197
$179   £109   DM326   ¥22,630

DOLLING FAMILY (MEMBER OF) [S1104/202]
Six-Keyed Boxwood Flute: Potsdam, c. 1825
                                                           531/747
$840   £506   DM1,397   ¥97,830

DROUET [C11/521] Eight-Keyed Ivory Flute w/case
                                                        1,670/2,505
$2,113   £1,265   DM3,529   ¥256,782

DUBOIS & COUTURIER [S1104/372] Five-Keyed
Blackwood Flute: Lyon, c. 1840   664/996
$573   £345   DM952   ¥66,702

ELKHART [B5/31] Boehm-System Flute w/case
                                                         326/489 NS

FIRTH HALL & POND [Sk5/9] Eight-Keyed Cocuswood and Nickel-Silver Mounted Flute w/case: New
York, c. 1855   300/400
$230   £138   DM409   ¥30,585

FISCHER, CARL [Bf7/10436] Silver Flute w/case
                                                          200/300
$115   £70   DM205   ¥15,976

GARRETT [C11/522] Four-Keyed Boxwood Flute
w/box   167/334
$230   £138   DM385   ¥28,013

GAUTROT (AINE) [S1104/2] Five-Keyed Blackwood
Flute: Paris, c. 1845   498/830 NS

GEROCK, CHRISTOPHER [S1104/386] Six-Keyed
Boxwood Flute: London, c. 1815   199/299
$324   £195   DM538   ¥37,701

GLIER, JOHANN WILHELM [S1104/207] Eight-
Keyed Boxwood Flute that converts to six keys:
Klingenthal, mid 19th C.   996/1,328
$1,909   £1,150   DM3,174   ¥222,341

GODEFROY, CLAIR (AINE) [S1104/331] Five-
Keyed Blackwood Flute w/case: Paris, 1830
                                                        830/1,162
$2,291   £1,380   DM3,809   ¥266,809

GODEFROY, CLAIR (AINE) [S1104/332] Five-
Keyed Cocuswood Flute: Paris, c. 1835   1,328/1,992
$1,336   £805   DM2,222   ¥155,639

GODEFROY, CLAIR (AINE) [S1104/334] Four-
Keyed Boxwood Flute w/case: Paris, c. 1825
                                                      996/1,328 NS

GOODLAD & CO. [S1104/46] Five-Keyed Boxwood
Flute: London, 1828   498/830
$840   £506   DM1,397   ¥97,830

GOULDING D'ALMAINE [P4/18] Elegant Silver-
Plated Six-Keyed Flute in good condition, w/period
box: London   417/583
$498   £299   DM923   ¥66,566

GOULDING D'ALMAINE POTTER [S1104/243]
Four-Keyed Boxwood Flute w/case: London, c. 1820
                                                          664/996
$955   £575   DM1,587   ¥111,171

GOULDING D'ALMAINE POTTER [S1104/385]
Six-Keyed Boxwood Flute w/case: London, c. 1820
                                                          498/830
$535   £322   DM889   ¥62,255

GRENSER, CARL AUGUSTIN (I) [S10/115] One-
Keyed Boxwood Flute: Dresden, late 18th C.
                                                    4,960/7,440 NS

GRENSER, JOHANN HEINRICH [S1104/329]
Eight-Keyed Ebony Flute: Dresden, c. 1800
                                                   9,960/13,280 NS

GRENSER, JOHANN HEINRICH [S1104/330]
Four-Keyed Ebony Flute: Dresden, c. 1800
                                                    6,640/9,960 NS

HALL, WILLIAM [Sk5/3] One-Keyed Boxwood and
Ivory Flute: New York, c. 1850   200/300
$288   £173   DM512   ¥38,232

HAYNES CO., WILLIAM S. [Sk5/2] American
Boehm-System Silver Flute w/case: Boston, 1956
                                                        800/1,200
$2,070   £1,242   DM3,685   ¥275,269

JACOBS, HENDRIK [C4/201] Fine Flemish Flute
w/case (Lyon & Healy)   25,050/33,400
$30,728   £18,400   DM57,040   ¥4,111,296

JULLIOT, DJALMA [Bf9/4573] Silver Boehm-System
Flute   1,600/2,000 NS

KOCH, S. [S1104/196] Nine-Keyed Rosewood Flute
w/case: Vienna, c. 1839   1,992/2,490
$4,009   £2,415   DM6,665   ¥466,916

LAWSON [S1104/50] One-Keyed Boxwood Flute
w/flute: London, c. 1800   581/830
$878   £529   DM1,460   ¥102,277

LEBRET, LOUIS LEON JOSEPH [S1104/337] Silver-
Plated Boehm-System Flute w/flute: Paris, c. 1900
                                                          415/664
$382   £230   DM635   ¥44,468

LEROUX (AINE) [S1104/333] Five-Keyed Rosewood
Flute: Mirecourt, mid 19th C.   498/830 NS

LOT, LOUIS [B10/11A] Very Fine Silver-Keyed
Rosewood Flute w/case: c. 1870   1,700/2,550
$1,662   £978   DM2,678   ¥205,490

MAHILLON, C. [S1104/234] Nickel Boehm-System
Flute w/2 flutes: Brussels, late 19th C.   581/913
$535   £322   DM889   ¥62,255

MARTIN BROS. [Bf9/4545] Six-Keyed Cocuswood
Flute: Paris, c. 1870   700/900 NS

MATEKI [B2/22] Fine Handmade White-Metal Flute
w/case: Japan   1,312/1,968
$2,452   £1,495   DM4,461   ¥309,674

METZLER, VALENTIN [B5/25] Four-Keyed
Boxwood Flute w/case: London   130/196 NS

METZLER & CO. [B5/29] Rosewood Boehm-System
Flute w/case   130/196
$112   £69   DM200   ¥15,106

MILHOUSE, WILLIAM [S1104/214] Six-Keyed
Figured-Boxwood Flute w/leather wallet: London,
c. 1815   498/830
$1,565   £943   DM2,603   ¥182,320

MILLIGAN [S1104/364] Four-Keyed Stained-
B6

KOHLERT'S SOHNE, V. [S1104/321] Heckel-System
Maple Bassoon w/bassoon: Graslitz, early 20th C.
                                                 415/830
$382   £230   DM635   ¥44,468

LÍS SOHNE, V. [S1104/321] Heckel-System Maple
Bassoon w/bassoon: Graslitz, early 20th C.
415/830$38EBALDO [S1104/239] Five-Keyed
Rosewood Flute w/case: London, 1807   830/1,162
$858   £517   DM1,427   ¥99,957

MONZANI & CO. [C11/523] Eight-Keyed Ivory
Flute w/case, ivory pull cleaner   2,004/2,672
$3,841   £2,300   DM6,417   ¥466,877

MONZANI & CO. [S1104/318] Five-Keyed Box-
wood Flute in F: London, 1815   498/830
$591   £356   DM983   ¥68,829

NEDDERMANN, JOHANN ADOPH [S1104/241]
Eight-Keyed Boxwood Flute: Hanover, c. 1830
                                               830/1,162
$764   £460   DM1,270   ¥88,936

OPPENHEIM, H. [S1104/391] Eight-Keyed Boxwood Flute: London, c. 1835   498/664
$802   £483   DM1,333   ¥93,383

PAN-AMERICAN [Bf7/10440] Silver Flute w/case:
Elkhart, Indiana   200/300 NS

PAXMAN BROS. [P12/5] Nickel and Rosewood
Three-Section Boehm-System Flute in good condition,
w/box, cover: London   334/501 NS

POTTER, WILLIAM HENRY [Bf9/4542] Eight-
Keyed Rosewood Flute: London, c. 1830   900/1,300
$690   £414   DM1,166   ¥91,818

POTTER, WILLIAM HENRY [C4/424] Rosewood
Flute missing some keys, w/case   NS

POTTER, WILLIAM HENRY [C11/516] Eight-
Keyed Boxwood Flute   501/668 NS

POTTER, WILLIAM HENRY [S1104/380] Six-
Keyed Boxwood Flute: London, c. 1810   498/830
$764   £460   DM1,270   ¥88,936

PROSER [S1104/349] One-Keyed Stained-Boxwood
Flute w/case: London, late 18th C.   664/996
$1,107   £667   DM1,841   ¥128,958

PROWSE, THOMAS [Bf9/4538] Eight-Keyed
Rosewood Flute: London, c. 1840   800/1,200
$1,093   £656   DM1,846   ¥145,379

RUDALL, CARTE & CO. [B2/18] Good Bakelite
Silver-Keyed Flute w/case, matching piccolo, spare
mouthpiece: London   164/328
$321   £196   DM583   ¥40,496

RUDALL, CARTE & CO. [B2/20] Good Silver-Plated
Flute w/case   164/328
$132   £81   DM240   ¥16,675

RUDALL, CARTE & CO. [B5/26] Good Ebonite
1867-System Flute w/case   244/408 NS

RUDALL, CARTE & CO. [B5/32] Silver-Plated
Boehm-System Flute w/case   98/130
$94   £58   DM167   ¥12,588

RUDALL, CARTE & CO. [B5/34] Handmade Silver
1867-System Flute w/case   652/978 NS

RUDALL, CARTE & CO. [B7/12] Cocuswood
Boehm-System Flute w/case: 1899   165/248
$285   £173   DM505   ¥39,484

RUDALL, CARTE & CO. [B7/17] Handmade Silver
1867-System Flute w/case   413/578
$607   £368   DM1,078   ¥84,232

RUDALL, CARTE & CO. [B10/10] Handmade Silver
1867-System Flute w/case: 1874   340/510 NS

RUDALL, CARTE & CO. [P12/8] Silvered Flute
w/case: London   167/334
$192   £115   DM317   ¥22,460

RUDALL, CARTE & CO. [S1104/338] Eight-Keyed
Rosewood Flute w/case: London, c. 1875   498/830
$4,963   £2,990   DM8,252   ¥578,087

RUDALL & ROSE [P4/23] Interesting Silver-
Mounted Rosewood Conical-Bore English Flute with
some cracks, missing one key: c. 1830   667/1,000
$652   £391   DM1,207   ¥87,048

RUDALL, ROSE, CARTE & CO. [B5/33] Handmade
Silver 1851-System Flute w/case: c. 1860–70 326/489
$469   £288   DM834   ¥62,942

SCHAEFFER, EVETTE [S1104/314] Blackwood
1832-Patent Boehm-System Conical Flute w/flute:
Paris, mid 19th C.   415/664
$840   £506   DM1,397   ¥97,830

SCHOTT, B. (FILS) [S1104/15] One-Keyed Flute
w/case: Mainz, c. 1820   332/498
$573   £345   DM952   ¥66,702

SICCAMA, ABEL [S1104/197] Ten-Keyed Blackwood Siccama-System Flute w/case: London, c. 1850
                                                 166/249
$305   £184   DM508   ¥35,575

SICCAMA, ABEL [S1104/238] Rosewood Siccama-
System "Diatonic" Flute w/case, rosewood grease pot:
London, c. 1850   1,162/1,660
$1,145   £690   DM1,904   ¥133,405

SICCAMA, ABEL [S1104/242] Rosewood Siccama-
System "Diatonic" Flute: London, c. 1850
                                           830/1,162 NS

SZEPESSY, BELA [P4/52] Fine and Handsome Flute
in immediate playing condition, w/case: London,
1885   6,668/10,002
$8,818   £5,290   DM16,336   ¥1,177,713

THIBOUVILLE, MARTIN (L'AINE) [S1104/235]
Eight-Keyed Blackwood Flute w/2 flutes: Paris, mid
19th C.   498/747
$764   £460   DM1,270   ¥88,936

THORSEN, NIELS CHRISTENSEN [C11/514] Silver
Koch-System Flute   1,002/1,336
$960   £575   DM1,604   ¥116,719

WHITAKER & CO. [B7/13] Eight-Keyed Boxwood
Flute w/case: London, 1819   330/495 NS

WOOD, JAMES & SON [S1104/48] Eight-Keyed
Ebony Flute w/case: London, c. 1825   332/498
$1,049   £632   DM1,744   ¥122,191

YAMAHA [B7/16] White-Metal Boehm-System Flute
w/case   165/248
$247   £150   DM438   ¥34,219

YAMAHA [B10/9] White-Metal Flute w/case
                                                     1,020/1,360
$1,075   £633   DM1,733   ¥132,964

YAMAHA [C11/519] Silver Boehm-System Flute
w/case   668/1,002
$863   £517   DM1,442   ¥104,946

FRENCH HORN

DALLAS [P4/25] Silver-Plated French Horn w/case:
Italy   417/583 NS

MAHILLON, C. [S1104/266] French Horn w/French
horn, bugle: Brussels, mid 19th C.   349/498
$496   £299   DM825   ¥57,809

GALOUBET

LONG [S1104/354] Fruitwood Galoubet w/ivory
galoubet: La Ciotat, mid 19th C.   664/996
$1,069   £644   DM1,777   ¥124,511

GIRAFFENFLUGEL

SCHEHL, KARL [S1104/100] Giraffenflugel: Graz,
c. 1830   8,300/11,620 NS

GUITAR

BARRY [S1104/140] Harp-Lute Guitar: London,
c. 1820   299/415
$1,336   £805   DM2,222   ¥155,639

BERTET, JOSEPH R. (attributed to) [S1104/166]
Five-Course Guitar w/case: Paris, 1762
                                                     2,490/4,150 NS

BERWIND, J. [Sk11/9] Good American Guitar
w/original case: Philadelphia, c. 1880   1,800/2,200
$1,380   £828   DM2,332   ¥168,360

DOBRO [Bf7/10367] Resonator Guitar w/case:
c. 1938   900/1,200
$546   £333   DM972   ¥75,885

EPIPHONE [Sk11/20] American Archtop Guitar
w/case: New York, 1938   300/500
$546   £328   DM923   ¥66,643

FABRICATORE, GENNARO [P11/9] Italian Guitar:
Napoli, 1847   1,680/2,520 NS

FABRICATORE, GIOVANNI BATTISTA [S10/112]
Guitar: Naples, c. 1815   1,240/1,860
$1,783   £1,035   DM2,875   ¥209,875

FENDER [Bf7/10399] Telecaster Guitar w/case: 1993
                                                      900/1,400
$518   £316   DM921   ¥71,891

FENDER [C4/427] Stratocaster Guitar   501/835
$479   £287   DM890   ¥64,127

FENDER [C11/507] Telecaster Custom Guitar w/case
                                                     668/835 NS

FERNANDEZ, ARCANGEL [C11/511] Flamenco
Guitar w/case   2,505/3,340
$5,377   £3,220   DM8,984   ¥653,628

FERNANDEZ, ARCANGEL [S1104/285] Concert
Guitar w/case: Madrid, 1968   13,280/16,600 NS

FISCHER, CARL [S1104/126] Guitar w/case:
Regensburg, 1832   498/830
$535   £322   DM889   ¥62,255

FLETA & SONS, IGNACIO [S1104/300] Concert
Guitar w/case: Barcelona, 1980   16,600/24,900
$19,090   £11,500   DM31,740   ¥2,223,410

GIBSON, WILLIAM [S1104/301] English Guitar:
Dublin, c. 1770   830/1,162
$1,049   £632   DM1,744   ¥122,191

GIBSON CO. [Bf7/10377] Tenor Guitar   250/450
$184   £112   DM328   ¥25,561

GIBSON CO. [Bf7/10394] ES-150 Guitar w/case:
1946   900/1,200
$690   £421   DM1,228   ¥95,855

GIBSON CO. [Bf7/10457] L-50 Guitar w/case: 1952
                                                      300/500
$288   £175   DM512   ¥39,940

GIBSON CO. [Bf7/10459] Les Paul Studio Guitar in
near-perfect condition, w/case: 1983   600/1,000
$575   £351   DM1,024   ¥79,879

GIBSON CO. [Bf7/10473] Archtop Model L Guitar
w/case   700/1,200
$690   £421   DM1,228   ¥95,855

GIBSON CO. [C4/425] ES-345 Guitar w/case
                                                     1,169/1,503
$1,247   £747   DM2,316   ¥166,910

GIBSON CO. [C4/426] L-50 Guitar w/case
                                                     835/1,169 NS

GIBSON CO. [Sk11/3] American J-200 Guitar
w/case: Kalamazoo, 1960   3,000/5,000
$3,738   £2,243   DM6,316   ¥455,975

GIBSON CO. [Sk11/17] American Style L-4 Archtop
Guitar: Kalamazoo, 1935   1,000/1,500 NS

GIBSON CO. [Sk11/18] American "Hummingbird"
Guitar: Kalamazoo, 1974   300/400
$546   £328   DM923   ¥66,643

GIBSON CO. [Sk11/19] Electric Model ES-125
Guitar w/case: Kalamazoo, 1953   450/550
$546   £328   DM923   ¥66,643

GIBSON CO. [Sk11/22] Tenor Guitar w/case: c. 1940
                                                      200/300
$460   £276   DM777   ¥56,120

GIBSON CO. [Sk11/23] Archtop "Recording King"
Tenor Guitar: c. 1935   200/300
$259   £155   DM437   ¥31,568

GIBSON CO. [Sk11/24] Archtop Guitar w/soft case:
Kalamazoo, 1920   250/350
$460   £276   DM777   ¥56,120

GIBSON CO. [Sk11/26] American Archtop Guitar
w/case: Kalamazoo, 1918   200/300
$345   £207   DM583   ¥42,090

GUILD [Bf7/10368] X-350 Electric Guitar in very
good condition, w/case   1,200/2,250 NS

HAYNES CO., JOHN C. [Sk11/14] American Guitar
w/case: Boston, c. 1865   800/1,200 NS

LACOTE [C4/428] French Guitar   668/1,002 NS

LACOTE, RENE (attributed to) [Bf9/4530] Fine
French Guitar in a remarkable state of preservation,
w/case: Paris, c. 1830   3,500/5,500 NS

LARSON (workshop of) [Bf9/4534] Good Parlor
Guitar   1,600/2,400 NS

LARSON BROS. [Sk11/10] American Guitar:
Chicago, c. 1900   500/600 NS

LIESSEM, R. [S1104/125] English Guitar: London,
mid 18th C.   498/830 NS

LION, ARTHUR [Bf7/10373] Viennese Parlor Guitar
                                600/900
$374   £228   DM665   ¥51,921

LONGMAN & BRODERIP [S1104/134] Keyed
English Guitar w/case: London, 1798   5,810/8,300
$5,727   £3,450   DM9,522   ¥667,023

LONGMAN & BRODERIP [S1104/144] English
Guitar: London, c. 1795   664/996
$1,145   £690   DM1,904   ¥133,405

LONGMAN & BRODERIP [S1104/278] English
Guitar: London, c. 1790   664/996 NS

MARTIN, CHRISTIAN FREDERICK [Bf9/4533]
Very Fine and Rare Guitar w/case: New York,
c. 1850–1855   20,000/30,000 NS

MARTIN & CO., C.F. [Sk11/1] American Guitar
w/original case: Nazareth, c. 1865   800/1,200
$1,610   £966   DM2,721   ¥196,420

MARTIN & CO., C.F. [Sk11/6] American Style OO-
42 Guitar w/case: Nazareth, 1904   3,000/5,000
$5,750   £3,450   DM9,718   ¥701,500

MARTIN & CO., C.F. [Sk11/8] Fine and Rare
American Style O-44 Guitar w/case: Nazareth, 1923
                                10,000/15,000 NS

MARTIN & CO., C.F. [Sk11/9A] American Style
D-18 Guitar w/case: Nazareth, 1944   1,000/1,500
$2,300   £1,380   DM3,887   ¥280,600

MARTIN & CO., C.F. [Sk11/12] American Guitar
w/soft case: Nazareth, 1910   1,400/1,600
$1,495   £897   DM2,527   ¥182,390

MARTIN & CO., C.F. [Sk11/15] Fine American Style
OOO-18 Guitar w/case: Nazareth, 1936 5,500/7,500
$6,210   £3,726   DM10,495   ¥757,620

MARTIN & CO., C.F. [Sk11/16] Fine and Rare
American Style O-45 Guitar w/case: Nazareth, 1927
                                8,000/12,000
$16,100   £9,660   DM27,209   ¥1,964,200

MAST, BLAISE [S1104/133] Guitar: Mirecourt,
c. 1820   3,320/4,980 NS

MOITESSIER, LOUIS [S1104/131] Guitar:
Mirecourt, 1808   2,988/4,150 NS

MONTRON (attributed to) [S1104/284] Guitar:
Paris, 1806   1,992/2,988 NS

MONZINO, ANTONIO [Sk11/11] Italian Classical
Guitar w/case: Milan, 1960   700/900
$690   £414   DM1,166   ¥84,180

MOSELEY, SEMI [Bf7/10389] "Black Widow"
Acoustic-Electric Guitar   500/700
$288   £175   DM512   ¥39,940

NADERMAN, JEAN-HENRI [S1104/132] Five-
Course Guitar: Paris, 1772   6,640/9,960 NS

NATIONAL [Sk11/4] American Resonator Style 2
Guitar w/case: 1928   2,000/3,000
$2,300   £1,380   DM3,887   ¥280,600

NATIONAL [Sk11/7] American Style 3 Resonator
Guitar w/original case: 1928   4,000/6,000
$3,450   £2,070   DM5,831   ¥420,900

PANORMO, LOUIS [S1104/171] Guitar w/case:
London, 1833   2,988/4,150
$4,582   £2,760   DM7,618   ¥533,618

PANORMO, LOUIS [S1104/296] Guitar w/case:
London, 1834   830/1,328
$2,673   £1,610   DM4,444   ¥311,277

PETITJEAN (L'AINE) [S1104/146] Guitar:
Mirecourt, c. 1810   1,660/2,490 NS

PRESTON, JOHN [S1104/143] English Guitar:
London, c. 1775   498/830 NS

RAMIREZ, JOSE (III) [S1104/293] Concert Guitar:
Madrid, 1971   1,328/1,992 NS

RAUCHE, MICHAEL [S1104/139] English Guitar:
London, 1767   1,328/1,992 NS

REGAL CO. [Bf7/10379] "Le Domino" Parlor
Guitar w/case   400/600
$259   £158   DM461   ¥35,946

RHOUDLOFF, H. [S1104/142] Lyre Guitar: Paris,
c. 1820   1,660/2,490
$1,527   £920   DM2,539   ¥177,873

RUBIO, DAVID [S1104/286] Concert Guitar w/case:
Oxford, 1968   6,640/9,960 NS

SALOMON (attributed to) [S1104/135] Triple-
Necked Guitar: France, c. 1830 3,320/4,980 NS

SILVERTONE [Bf7/10398] Guitar w/case   170/300
$104   £63   DM184   ¥14,378

SILVERTONE [Bf7/10464] Archtop Guitar w/case, amplifier: 1948   300/500
$345   £210   DM614   ¥47,927

STAUFFER (attributed to) [Bf9/4531] Good Parlor Guitar   1,800/2,600 NS

STROMBERG, ELMER [Sk11/5] Rare American Archtop Cutaway Guitar w/case: Boston, c. 1953
                                                      18,000/22,000
$18,400   £11,040   DM31,096   ¥2,244,800

VEGA COMPANY [Sk11/2] Archtop Guitar w/original case: Boston, c. 1935   600/800
$2,990   £1,794   DM5,053   ¥364,780

VEGA COMPANY [Sk11/21] Early Hollow-Body Electric Guitar: Boston, c. 1947   150/250
$345   £207   DM583   ¥42,090

VEGA COMPANY [Sk11/28] Electric Lap-Steel Guitar w/2 cases, archtop guitar: c. 1937   250/350
$489   £293   DM826   ¥59,628

VELASQUEZ, JOSE LUIS [Bf7/10400] Guitar w/case, guitar   150/250
$115   £70   DM205   ¥15,976

VENTAPANE, PASQUALE [S10/110] Guitar with four double courses: Naples, 1873   1,240/1,860 NS

VILLA, LUIGI [S1104/287] Concert Guitar: Cesano Maderno, 1977   415/581 NS

VILLA, LUIGI [S1104/288] Concert Guitar: Cesano Maderno, 1981   1,162/1,660 NS

VILLA, LUIGI [S1104/289] Concert Guitar: Cesano Maderno, 1979   1,162/1,660 NS

VILLA, LUIGI [S1104/290] Concert Guitar: Cesano Maderno, 1995   415/581 NS

VILLA, LUIGI [S1104/291] Concert Guitar: Cesano Maderno, 1979   415/581 NS

VILLA, LUIGI [S1104/292] Concert Guitar: Cesano Maderno, 1979   498/830 NS

VINACCIA, GENNARO & ACHILLE [S1104/137] Guitar w/case: Naples, 1890   1,660/2,324 NS

WASHBURN [C11/508] A-20 Electric Guitar w/case
                                                      334/501 NS

GUITAR-LUTE

HAUSER, HERMANN [Sk11/66] German Guitar-Lute w/soft case: 1914   1,400/1,600
$1,093   £656   DM1,846   ¥133,285

GUITARRA

ANDRADE, JOAO MIGUEL [P4/28] Portugese Guitarra in good condition, w/case: Lisbon, c. 1920
                                                      167/333
$182   £109   DM337   ¥24,322

HARP

BANKS, BENJAMIN [S1104/170] Aeolian Harp w/case: Salisbury, 1787   498/830
$1,431   £862   DM2,379   ¥166,659

DELVEAU [P11/14A] Attractive Grecian Patent Concert Harp in good condition   4,200/5,040
$3,864   £2,300   DM6,440   ¥461,817

ERARD, SEBASTIAN & PIERRE [C11/545] Double-Action Pedal Harp   1,670/2,505
$1,728   £1,035   DM2,888   ¥210,095

ERARD, SEBASTIAN & PIERRE [P11/14C] Fine Gothic Patent Concert Harp in good condition: London   8,400/10,080
$12,751   £7,590   DM21,252   ¥1,523,996

ERARD, SEBASTIAN & PIERRE [S1104/109] Double-Action Gothic Pedal Harp: Paris, c. 1850
                                                      1,992/2,656
$1,909   £1,150   DM3,174   ¥222,341

ERARD, SEBASTIAN & PIERRE [S1104/112] Double-Action Gothic Pedal Harp: London, 1837
                                                      4,980/6,640
$6,109   £3,680   DM10,157   ¥711,491

ERARD, SEBASTIAN [P11/14] Grecian Concert Harp in playing condition: London   1,680/2,520
$3,091   £1,840   DM5,152   ¥369,454

ERARD, SEBASTIAN [S1104/110] Double-Action Grecian Harp: London, 1823   332/664
$2,100   £1,265   DM3,491   ¥244,575

ERARD, SEBASTIAN [S1104/111] Double-Action Grecian Pedal Harp: London, 1831   2,490/3,320
$2,291   £1,380   DM3,809   ¥266,809

ERARD & CIE. [P11/12] Magnificent Concert Harp with minor old worm: c. 1840   13,440/2,016 NS

ERARD & CIE. [S1104/113] Double-Action Gothic Pedal Harp: Paris, late 19th C.   3,320/4,980
$4,200   £2,530   DM6,983   ¥489,150

ERAT, I. & I. [P11/13] Attractive Grecian Concert Harp requiring cosmetic restoration: London
                                                      3,360/5,040 NS

ERAT, J. [P11/14B] Regency Harp in immediate play-ing condition: London   2,520/3,360 NS

HOLDERNESSE, CHARLES [S1104/114] Portable Harp: mid-19th C.   1,328/1,992
$1,336   £805   DM2,222   ¥155,639

MOFFAT, J.W. [S1104/279] Dital Harp w/case: London, mid 19th C.   2,490/4,150 NS

NADERMANN, HENRY [C11/546] Crochet-Action Pedal Harp   8,350/13,360
$9,603   £5,750   DM16,043   ¥1,167,193

NADERMAN FAMILY (MEMBER OF) [P11/14D] French Harp in well-restored condition: Paris, c. 1800
                                                      16,800/20,160 NS

VENTURA, A.B. (attributed to) [S1104/282] Harp Ventura w/case: London, early 19th C.   2,490/3,320
$2,291   £1,380   DM3,809   ¥266,809

HARP-LUTE

BARRY [S1104/129] Harp-Lute: London, c. 1810
498/830 NS

CLEMENTI & CO. [S1104/124] Harp-Lute:
London, c. 1815   415/664 NS

LIGHT, EDWARD [S1104/127] Harp-Lute w/case:
London, early 19th C.   830/1,162
$840   £506   DM1,397   ¥97,830

HARPSICHORD

PLEYEL [S1104/118] Two-Manual Harpsichord:
Paris, 1912   1,328/1,992
$5,345   £3,220   DM8,887   ¥622,555

SHUDI, BURKAT & JOHN BROADWOOD
[S1104/97] Single Manual Harpsichord: London,
1779   99,600/132,800
$104,746   £63,100   DM174,156   ¥12,199,754

HELICON

DE CART FRERES, FERDINAND & LOUIS
[S1104/83] Helicon: Lierre, early 20th C. 498/830 NS

DE CART FRERES, FERDINAND & LOUIS
[S1104/263] Helicon w/tenor horn: Lierre, early
20th C.   548/830 NS

HORN

BESSON [Bf9/4553] Alto Horn w/case: London,
c. 1883   1,000/1,400 NS

BOOSEY & CO. [P10/13] Brass Three-Valve Horn
with some dents, w/three-valve horn   136/204
$156   £92   DM255   ¥18,407

CERVENY & SOHNE, V.F. [S1104/95] Baritone
Horn: Königgrätz, c. 1900   830/1,162
$764   £460   DM1,270   ¥88,936

GROSS & BRAMBACH [S1104/91] Brass Bass
Horn: Innsbruck, mid 19th C.   830/1,328
$1,813   £1,092   DM3,014   ¥211,127

KOHLERT'S SOHNE, V. [S1104/57] Baritone Horn:
Graslitz, mid 19th C.   498/830
$458   £276   DM762   ¥53,362

LAPINI [Bf9/4559] Tenor Horn: Florence, c. 1930
400/600
$403   £242   DM680   ¥53,561

MULLER, C.A. [S1104/268] Tenor Horn w/circular
horn: Mainz, late 19th C.   581/913
$535   £322   DM889   ¥62,255

SCHOPPER, ROBERT [S1104/80] Alto Horn:
Leipzig, c. 1910   498/830 NS

WEBER, CARL AUGUST [S1104/56] Tenor Horn:
Löbau, mid 19th C.   664/996
$1,049   £632   DM1,744   ¥122,191

ZEDLITZ, EDUARD [S1104/255] Natural Horn
w/case, crook: Mariaschein, early 19th C. 830/1,328
$764   £460   DM1,270   ¥88,936

LUTE

CHALLEN, CHRISTOPHER [B7/48] Modern Eight-
Course Lute w/case: 1975   2,475/3,300
$3,036   £1,840   DM5,391   ¥421,158

HARWOOD, IAN [B10/24] Modern Seven-Course
Lute   510/850 NS

MANDOLIN

BOHMANN, JOSEPH [Bf7/10370] Bowl-Back
Mandolin   200/400 NS

BOHMANN, JOSEPH [Bf7/10375] Bowl-Back
Mandolin w/case   200/400
$115   £70   DM205   ¥15,976

BOHMANN, JOSEPH [Bf7/10378] Fancy Mandolin
in excellent condition   350/550 NS

CALACE, RAFFAELE [P4/29] Fine and Handsome
Mandolin in good condition, w/case, various accessories: Naples, 1938   667/1,000
$1,534   £920   DM2,841   ¥204,820

CECCHERINI, UMBERTO [P12/6] Neapolitan
Mandolin w/mandolin   134/200
$154   £92   DM254   ¥17,968

DE MEGLIO & FIGLIO [P4/30] Neapolitan
Mandolin w/case   250/417
$230   £138   DM426   ¥30,723

DEL PERUGIA, FERNANDO [S10/109] Milanese
Mandolin: Campi-Bisenzio, 1898   930/1,240
$1,212   £704   DM1,955   ¥142,715

EMBERGHER, LUIGI [S1104/159] Roman
Mandolin w/case: Rome, 1926   6,640/9,960
$8,018   £4,830   DM13,331   ¥933,832

GIBSON CO. [Sk11/29] American Mandolin w/origi-
nal case: Kalamazoo, 1924   600/800
$3,335   £2,001   DM5,636   ¥406,870

GIBSON CO. [Sk11/30] American Mandolin w/case:
Kalamazoo, 1917   300/500
$633   £380   DM1,069   ¥77,165

GIBSON CO. [Sk11/31] American Mandolin w/case:
Kalamazoo, 1913   400/600
$690   £414   DM1,166   ¥84,180

GIBSON CO. [Sk11/32] American Mandolin:
Kalamazoo, 1914   450/650
$863   £518   DM1,458   ¥105,225

GIBSON CO. [Sk11/34] American Mandolin:
Kalamazoo, 1912   400/600
$748   £449   DM1,263   ¥91,195

GIBSON CO. [Sk11/36] American Early Style A-4
Mandolin: 1905   600/800
$978   £587   DM1,652   ¥119,255

GIBSON CO. [Sk11/51] American Mandolin w/case:
c. 1950   250/350
$633   £380   DM1,069   ¥77,165

HOWE, ELIAS [Sk11/35] American Mandolin
w/case: c. 1900   150/250
$518   £311   DM875   ¥63,135

KAY [Bf7/10451] Flat-Back Mandolin 150/250
$92 £56 DM164 ¥12,781

LYON & HEALY [Bf7/10462] Interesting Baritone
Mandolin 250/400
$150 £91 DM266 ¥20,769

MARTIN & CO., C.F. [Sk11/59] American Bowl-
Back Mandolin w/soft case: Nazareth, 1919 150/250
$345 £207 DM583 ¥42,090

MARTIN & CO., C.F. [Sk11/62] American Bowl-
Back Style 2 Mandolin w/case: Nazareth, 1920
150/250
$288 £173 DM486 ¥35,075

PECORARO, P. [B5/62] Mandolin w/mandolin,
2 cases: 1968 652/978
$675 £414 DM1,201 ¥90,637

STEWART, S.S. [Sk11/33] American Mandolin w/case
250/350
$431 £259 DM729 ¥52,613

VEGA COMPANY [Sk11/60] American Bowl-Back
Mandolin w/case 100/200 NS

VINACCIA, ANTONIO [S1104/162] Mandolin
w/case: Naples, 1777 1,660/2,324
$2,864 £1,725 DM4,761 ¥333,512

VINACCIA, ANTONIO [S1104/169] Mandolin
w/case: Naples, c. 1775 3,320/6,640
$9,927 £5,980 DM16,505 ¥1,156,173

WASHBURN [Bf7/10369] Bowl-Back Mandolin
w/case 250/400
$150 £91 DM266 ¥20,769

WASHBURN [Bf7/10383] Bowl-Back Mandolin
w/case 200/400
$316 £193 DM563 ¥43,933

MANDOLIN-LYRE

CALACE FRATELLI [Sk11/63] Neapolitan
Mandolin-Lyre: 1900 800/1,200
$1,035 £621 DM1,749 ¥126,270

MANDOLINO

FONTANELLI, GIOVANNI GIUSEPPE [S10/113]
Mandolino: Bolgna, 1750 1,550/2,170
$2,496 £1,449 DM4,025 ¥293,825

NONEMACHER, CRISTIANO [S1104/156]
Mandolino: Genoa, 1739 4,980/8,300
$6,872 £4,140 DM11,426 ¥800,428

MARTINSHORN

MARTIN, MAX BERNHARDT [S1104/65] Soprano
Martinshorn w/bass Martinshorn: Markneukirchen,
c. 1920 664/996 NS

MELLOPHONE

HOLTON & CO. [Bf7/10426] Mellophone in complete condition, w/case 150/250 NS

PEPPER [Bf9/4564] Mellophone: Chicago, c. 1895
400/600 NS

YORK [Bf7/10448] "Master" Mellophone
100/200 NS

NORMAPHON

WUNDERLICH [Bf9/4555] Soprano Normaphon:
Siebenbrunn, c. 1935 3,000/3,500
$5,463 £3,278 DM9,232 ¥726,895

OBOE

ADLER, FREDERIC GUILLAUME [S1104/9] Ten-
Keyed Boxwood Oboe w/original case, reed case:
Paris, c. 1840 4,150/5,810 NS

ANCIUTI, JOHANNES MARIA [S10/116] Three-
Keyed Ivory Oboe in an excellent state of preservation: Milan, 1722 NS

ASTOR & CO., GEORGE [S1104/11] Two-Keyed
Boxwood Straight-Topped Oboe: London, c. 1800
1,992/2,656
$3,436 £2,070 DM5,713 ¥400,214

GOLDE, CARL [S1104/246] Thirteen-Keyed Stained-
Boxwood Oboe w/case: Dresden, mid 19th C.
3,320/4,980 NS

HORAK & SOHN, W. [S1104/19] Twelve-Keyed
Boxwood Oboe: Prague, c. 1845 1,162/1,660
$1,909 £1,150 DM3,174 ¥222,341

HULLER, G.H. [S1104/30] Conservatoire-System
Oboe w/oboe: Schöneck, early 20th C. 415/614
$382 £230 DM635 ¥44,468

KATTOFEN, AMMON [S1104/43] Conservatoire-
System Oboe w/case, oboe: Wernitzgrün, mid 20th C.
415/780
$382 £230 DM635 ¥44,468

KOHLERT & SONS [B5/36] Military E-Flat
Rosewood Oboe 98/163
$150 £92 DM267 ¥20,142

LAFLEUR, J.R. & SON [B5/37] Rosewood Oboe
98/163
$150 £92 DM267 ¥20,142

LOREE, F. [P4/24] Ebony Oboe in good condition,
w/2 cases, oboe: Paris 667/1,000
$1,189 £713 DM2,202 ¥158,735

LUDWIG, FRANZ [S1104/8] Eight-Keyed Boxwood
Oboe: Prague, c. 1835 1,660/2,490
$4,582 £2,760 DM7,618 ¥533,618

LUDWIG, FRANZ [S1104/10] Eleven-Keyed
Boxwood Oboe w/original case: Prague, c. 1840
2,490/4,150
$3,436 £2,070 DM5,713 ¥400,214

LUDWIG & MARTINKA [S1104/7] Twelve-Keyed
Boxwood Oboe: Prague, mid 19th C. 1,162/1,660
$4,963 £2,990 DM8,252 ¥578,087

MILHOUSE, RICHARD [S1104/12] Two-Keyed
Straight-Topped Stained-Boxwood Oboe w/box:
Newark, late 18th C.   3,320/4,150
$3,627   £2,185   DM6,031   ¥422,448

MONNIG, OTTO [S1104/51] Simple-System
Stained-Boxwood Oboe: Leipzig, c. 1890   664/996
$764   £460   DM1,270   ¥88,936

MONNIG, OTTO [S1104/216] Eleven-Keyed Rosewood Oboe w/12-keyed oboe: Leipzig, late 19th C.
                                                282/498
$802   £483   DM1,333   ¥93,383

PINDER, HEINRICH FRANZ EDUARD [S1104/37]
Eleven-Keyed Rosewood Oboe: Dresden, c. 1890
                                                498/830
$916   £552   DM1,524   ¥106,724

SCHLEGEL, JEREMIAS [S1104/42] Two-Keyed
Boxwood Oboe: Basel, mid 18th C.   996/1,328
$1,240   £747   DM2,062   ¥144,425

SHARPE, JOHN [S1104/31] Combined Boehm-and-
Barret-System Blackwood Oboe w/case: Pudsey,
England, c. 1900   664/996
$1,527   £920   DM2,539   ¥177,873

SIMPSON, JOHN [S1104/237] Eight-Keyed Boxwood Oboe: London, c. 1835   996/1,328 NS

STARK [P10/9] Oboe w/oboe, flute: London 170/255
$196   £115   DM319   ¥23,009

STEHLE [S1104/32] Thirteen-Keyed Boxwood Oboe:
Vienna, mid 19th C.   1,162/1,660
$1,049   £632   DM1,744   ¥122,191

TRIEBERT & SONS, GUILLAUME [S1104/325]
Boehm-System Oboe: Paris, late 19th C.   996/1,328
$1,622   £977   DM2,697   ¥188,893

UHLMANN, JOHANN TOBIAS [S1104/34] Twelve-
Keyed Boxwood Oboe w/oboe: c. 1840   498/830
$2,291   £1,380   DM3,809   ¥266,809

WEYGANDT, T.J. [S1104/13] Eight-Keyed Ebony
Oboe: Philadelphia, c. 1850   3,320/4,980
$6,109   £3,680   DM10,157   ¥711,491

OPHICLEIDE

HENRI [S1104/66] Nine-Keyed Bass Ophicleide:
Dijon, mid 19th C.   1,660/2,490 NS

PHONO-FIDDLE

EVANS & CO., GEORGE [S1104/151] Phono-Fiddle
w/case, bow: London, early 20th C.   498/830
$840   £506   DM1,397   ¥97,830

STROH, CHARLES [S1104/150] One-Stringed
Phono-Fiddle w/2 experimental violins: London, early
20th C.   315/564
$687   £414   DM1,143   ¥80,043

PIANO

CHALLEN & HOLLIS [S1104/101] Upright Piano:
London, c. 1840   1,162/1,660 NS

CLEMENTI, MUZIO [S1104/108] Square Piano:
London, c. 1805   4,980/8,300 NS

COLLARD & COLLARD [S1104/99] Upright Piano:
London, mid 19th C.   2,490/4,150
$2,291   £1,380   DM3,809   ¥266,809

HAXBY, THOMAS [S1104/120] Square Piano: York,
1793   1,162/1,660
$1,240   £747   DM2,062   ¥144,425

KIRCKMAN, JACOB & ABRAHAM [Bf9/4536]
Fine Square Piano: London, 1779   4,500/6,000 NS

KLEIN, F.A. [S1104/116] Lyre Piano: Berlin, c. 1835
                              11,620/16,600 NS

LONGMAN & CO. [S1104/107] Square Piano:
London, c. 1805   1,162/1,660
$1,240   £747   DM2,062   ¥144,425

LONGMAN & BRODERIP [C11/538] Square Piano
                                          1,002/1,670
$960   £575   DM1,604   ¥116,719

PRESTON, THOMAS [S1104/105] Square Piano:
London, c. 1800   1,162/1,660
$1,145   £690   DM1,904   ¥133,405

WEBLEN, ALEXANDER [S1104/122] Square Piano:
London, c. 1810   996/1,328 NS

PIANOFORTE

BROADWOOD, JOHN & SONS [S1104/102]
Grand Pianoforte: London, 1799   16,600/24,900 NS

BROADWOOD, JOHN & SONS [S1104/104]
Grand Pianoforte: London, c. 1850   4,980/6,640 NS

BROADWOOD, JOHN & SONS [S1104/117]
Grand Pianoforte: London, mid 19th C.   4,150/5,810
$1,909   £1,150   DM3,174   ¥222,341

COLLARD & COLLARD [S1104/106] Grand
Pianoforte: London, mid 19th C.   1,328/1,992
$3,245   £1,955   DM5,396   ¥377,980

FIRTH & HALL [Sk5/13] American Square Pianoforte w/stool: New York, c. 1835   1,400/1,600
$920   £552   DM1,638   ¥122,342

HAWKINS, JOHN ISAAC [S1104/115] "Portable
Grand" Pianoforte: London, c. 1805   33,200/49,800
$34,362   £20,700   DM57,132   ¥4,002,138

LONGMAN, CLEMENTI & CO. [S1104/98] Grand
Pianoforte: London, c. 1800   4,980/8,300 NS

STODART, M. & W. [S1104/121] Grand Pianoforte:
London, c. 1800   13,280/16,600 NS

PICCOLO

HAYNES CO., WILLIAM S. [S1104/375] Silver
Boehm-System Piccolo w/piccolo: Boston, early
20th C.   415/664
$382   £230   DM635   ¥44,468

KRUSPE, C. [Bf7/10449] Good Six-Keyed C Piccolo
w/case   300/400 NS

LOT, LOUIS [P12/6] Attractive Rosewood Boehm-System Piccolo in immediate playing condition, w/case: Paris, c. 1890   1,336/2,004 NS

RUDALL, CARTE & CO. [B5/19] Cocuswood 1867-System Piccolo w/case   163/244 NS

RUDALL, CARTE & CO. [B5/20] Six-Keyed Rosewood Piccolo w/case   130/196 NS

RUDALL, CARTE & CO. [C11/518] Rosewood Piccolo w/case   167/251
$210   £126   DM352   ¥25,577

SELMER [B5/21] Silver-Plated Piccolo w/case
                                                              244/326 NS

WALLIS, JOSEPH [S1104/36] One-Keyed Blackwood Walking-Stick Piccolo in D, w/incomplete walking-stick recorder: London, mid 19th C.   664/996
$725   £437   DM1,206   ¥84,490

RECORDER

RIPPERT, JEAN JACQUES [S1104/221] Ivory Treble Recorder in G, w/case: Paris, early 18th C.
                                                    13,280/19,920
$17,181   £10,350   DM28,566   ¥2,001,069

STANESBY, THOMAS JR. [S1104/217] Stained-Boxwood Treble or Alto Recorder: London, mid 18th C.   13,280/19,920
$20,999   £12,650   DM34,914   ¥2,445,751

VON HUENE, FRIEDRICH [Sk5/7] American Rosewood and Ivory Tenor Recorder w/case: Boston, 1960
                                                              500/700
$1,610   £966   DM2,866   ¥214,098

ROTHPHONE

BOTTALI, A.M. [S1104/277] Alto Rothphone w/case: Milan, early 20th C.   2,490/3,320
$2,291   £1,380   DM3,809   ¥266,809

BOTTALI FRATELLI, A.M. [S1104/39] E-Flat Baritone Rothphone w/case: Milan, early 20th C.
                                                          3,320/4,980
$6,109   £3,680   DM10,157   ¥711,491

BOTTALI FRATELLI, A.M. [S1104/40] E-Flat Alto Rothphone w/case: Milan, early 20th C.   3,320/4,980
$3,054   £1,840   DM5,078   ¥355,746

SARRUSOPHONE

ORSI, ROMEO [S1104/38] Soprano Sarrusophone: Milan, c. 1925   2,490/4,150 NS

RAMPONE [S1104/41] Bass Sarrusophone: Milan, 20th C.   3,320/4,980
$5,345   £3,220   DM8,887   ¥622,555

SAW

FELDMANN, C. [S1104/182] Musical Saw w/bag: Remscheid, late 20th C.   50/83
$56   £34   DM94   ¥6,574

SANDVICKENS, JERNVERKS A.B. [S1104/177] Musical Saw w/bag: Sweden, 20th C.   166/249
$133   £80   DM221   ¥15,467

SAXHORN

KLEMM AND BRO. [Bf9/4548] Over-the-Shoulder Baritone Saxhorn w/mouthpiece: Philadelphia, c. 1860   2,700/3,200
$3,163   £1,898   DM5,345   ¥420,834

ZOEBISCH & SONS, C.A. [S1104/273] Alto Saxhorn: New York, mid 19th C.   498/830
$802   £483   DM1,333   ¥93,383

SAXOPHONE

BUESCHER [B7/26] Alto Saxophone w/case 330/495
$493   £299   DM876   ¥68,438

BUESCHER [C11/530] Brass Tenor Saxophone w/case   334/668
$384   £230   DM642   ¥46,688

CONN, C.G. [B2/29] Alto Saxophone w/case
                                                              328/492
$981   £598   DM1,784   ¥123,870

CONN, C.G. [B5/51] Tenor Saxophone w/case
                                                              326/489
$394   £242   DM700   ¥52,872

CONN, C.G. [B5/53] Soprano Saxophone w/case: c. 1926–27   489/815
$656   £403   DM1,167   ¥88,119

CONN, C.G. [Bf7/10447] Model 6M Alto Saxophone   250/400
$345   £210   DM614   ¥47,927

CONN, C.G. [Bf7/10502] Alto Saxophone   250/400
$431   £263   DM768   ¥59,909

HAWKES & SON [B5/52] Alto Saxophone w/case
                                                              244/408 NS

HAWKES & SON [B7/25] Alto Saxophone w/case
                                                              132/198
$171   £104   DM303   ¥23,690

HULLER, G.H. [S1104/6] Baritone Saxophone w/case: Schöneck, early 20th C.   996/1,328
$916   £552   DM1,524   ¥106,724

SELMER BUNDY [Bf7/10439] Alto Saxophone w/mouthpiece   150/250
$150   £91   DM266   ¥20,769

STRASSER MARIGAUX [Bf7/10437] Alto Saxophone w/case, neck, mouthpiece   275/375
$161   £98   DM287   ¥22,366

SERPENT

CRAMER, JOHN [S1104/267] Three-Keyed Serpent without mouthpiece: London, c. 1820
                                                          3,320/4,980 NS

PRETTY, ROBERT [B7/19] Three-Keyed English Serpent: London, c. 1840–44   3,300/4,950
$2,277   £1,380   DM4,043   ¥315,868

WOLF & CO., ROBERT [S1104/269] Four-Keyed
Serpent: London, c. 1840   1,660/3,320
$4,200   £2,530   DM6,983   ¥489,150

SOUSAPHONE

BESSON [Bf7/10438] B-Flat Sousaphone 1,500/2,200
$805   £491   DM1,433   ¥111,831

DE PRINS GEBRUDER [S1104/275] Sousaphone:
Antwerp, early 20th C.   664/1,162 NS

SPINET

BARTON (ascribed to) [P11/15] Attractive English
Spinet: c. 1730   13,440/16,800 NS

SHEAN, CHRISTIAN [S1104/103] Spinet: London,
c. 1750   24,900/33,200 NS

TAROGATO

MOGYOROSSY, G.Y. [S1104/199] Rosewood
Tarogato: Budapest, early 20th C.   830/1,162 NS

TIPLE

MARTIN & CO., C.F. [Sk11/57] Tiple w/case:
Nazareth   150/250
$259   £155   DM437   ¥31,568

TROMBONE

BOOSEY & CO. [Bf9/4563] Trombone w/mouth-
piece: London, c. 1900   400/600
$403   £242   DM680   ¥53,561

BOOSEY & HAWKES [B2/28] Trombone w/case
          98/131
$160   £98   DM292   ¥20,248

BURGER, JULIUS MAX [S1104/84] Tenor Valve
Trombone w/bass valve trombone: Strasbourg, late
19th C.   664/996
$428   £258   DM712   ¥49,882

DE CART FRERES, FERDINAND & LOUIS
[S1104/87] Tenor Valve Trombone w/valve trombone:
Lierre, mid 19th C.   498/830
$840   £506   DM1,397   ¥97,830

FICKHERT, WILHELM [S1104/85] Tenor Trombone
w/tenor trombone: Plauen, mid 19th C.
          830/1,162 NS

RIVIERE & HAWKES [S1104/62] Tenor Valve
Trombone w/tenor slide trombone: London, c. 1880
          581/830 NS

ROUSSEAU, A.F. [S1104/79] Valved Trombone:
Brussels, early 20th C.   664/996
$611   £368   DM1,016   ¥71,149

SENECAUT, PIERRE [S1104/63] Tenor Valve
Trombone: Brussels, late 19th C.   498/830
$878   £529   DM1,460   ¥102,277

VAN ENGELEN, H. [S1104/94] Six-Valved
"Adolphe Par" Model Trombone: Lierre, early
20th C.   1,328/1,992 NS

WHITE & CO., H.N. [Bf7/10427] "American
Standard" Trombone w/case   100/150 NS

ZELENKA, ANTONIN [S1104/90] Bass Valve
Trombone: Prague, c. 1900   498/830
$420   £253   DM698   ¥48,915

TROMPE DE CHASSE

GAUTROT (AINE) [S1104/254] Trompe de Chasse:
Paris, mid 19th C.   996/1,328
$916   £552   DM1,524   ¥106,724

TRUMPET

COUTURIER, ERNST ALBERT [Bf9/4572] Alto
Trumpet: c. 1896   700/900
$748   £449   DM1,263   ¥99,470

DE CLERCQ, L. [S1104/78] Fanfare Trumpet w/two
fanfare trumpets: Bruges, early 20th C.   581/913
$535   £322   DM889   ¥62,255

MAINZ, ALEXANDER [P10/10] Interesting Early
and Rare Three-Rotary-Valve Trumpet w/trumpet:
c. 1860   1,020/1,360
$1,173   £690   DM1,911   ¥138,055

OTTO, FRANZ [S1104/74] Trumpet: Markneukirchen, mid 19th C.   498/664
$878   £529   DM1,460   ¥102,277

TUBA

BESSON & CO. [P12/13] Silvered Three-Valve Class-
A Tuba with some depressions: London   251/418 NS

HALARI [S1104/276] Tuba: Paris, mid 19th C.
          498/830 NS

SUDRE, FRANCOIS [S1104/59] Tuba w/trompe de
chasse: Paris, early 20th C.   531/747 NS

UKULELE

ALOHA [Bf7/10461] Koa-Wood Ukulele w/case
          200/400
$288   £175   DM512   ¥39,940

KUMALAE [Bf7/10454] Koa-Wood Ukulele w/case
          200/400
$150   £91   DM266   ¥20,769

MARTIN & CO., C.F. [Sk11/58] Ukulele w/soft case:
Nazareth, c. 1925   150/250
$374   £224   DM632   ¥45,598

UNION PIPE

ROBERTSON, HUGH [S1104/316] Scottish Union
Pipe w/case, another union pipe: Edinburgh, c. 1780
          6,640/9,960
$7,636   £4,600   DM12,696   ¥889,364

VIOL

GUGGENBERGER, ANTON [P10/18] Fine and
Handsome Viola d'Amore w/case: Vienna, 1961
          4,250/5,100 NS

JORDAN, HANS [S1104/152] Tenor Viola da
Gamba w/case, bow: Markneukirchen, 1960
                                    830/1,162
$955   £575   DM1,587   ¥111,171

ROY, KARL [C11/102] Seven-Stringed Bass Viola da
Gamba w/case, bow   3,340/4,175 NS

SEELOS, JOHANN [S1104/153] Bass Viola da
Gamba: Linz, 1691   24,900/33,200
$36,271   £21,850   DM60,306   ¥4,224,479

STEBER, ERNST [Sk11/205] German Viola da
Gamba w/soft case   1,800/2,200 NS

VIOLA

ALBANELLI, FRANCO [S3/118] Viola w/case:
Bologna, 1983   4,185/5,859 NS

ARTMANN, GEORG VALENTIN [S3/124] Viola
w/case, bow: Wechmar, 1797   3,348/5,022 NS

ASHFORD, LAWRENCE [S3/128] Viola w/double
case: Cremona, 1989   2,511/3,348 NS

AVERNA, GESUALDO [S10/96] Viola: Caltanissetta,
c. 1920   4,960/6,200 NS

AYERS, PAUL [P11/72] Good Viola in immediate
playing condition, w/case: London, 1981
                               1,680/2,520 NS

BAILLY, PAUL [S3/129] Viola w/case: 1890 (Etienne
Vatelot, Paris, March 28, 1996)   10,044/13,392 NS

BARBIERI, BRUNO [S6/89] Viola w/case: Mantua,
1967   2,475/4,125
$2,846   £1,725   DM5,123   ¥410,464

BARBIERI, ENZO [Sk5/17] Italian Viola w/case:
Mantua, 1979   1,800/2,200 NS

BARGELLI, G. [S3/133] Viola w/case: Florence, 1957
                               5,022/6,696 NS

BEYER, GEORGE W. [Sk5/32] American Viola
w/case: Bloomington, Indiana, 1923   1,200/1,400 NS

BEYER, GEORGE W. [Sk11/300] American Viola
w/case: Bloomington, Indiana, 1923   800/1,200
$690   £414   DM1,166   ¥84,180

BIGNAMI, OTELLO [B11/66A] Italian Viola
                               13,360/20,040 NS

BIRD, RICHMOND HENRY (attributed to) [P11/34]
Good English Viola in good condition, w/case:
Liverpool, 1934   2,016/2,520 NS

BISSOLOTTI, VINCENZO [Bf9/4577] Modern
Italian Viola w/case: Cremona, 1976   2,000/3,000
$2,070   £1,242   DM3,498   ¥275,455

BLANCHI, ALBERTO [C11/122] Viola w/case
                               8,350/10,020 NS

CANDI, CESARE [P10/31] Fine and Handsome
Italian Viola in immediate playing condition, w/case:
Genoa, 1923 (Claude Lebet, La Chaux-de-Fonds,
Switzerland, April 14, 1997)   23,800/27,200 NS

CAPELA, ANTONIO [Bf2/4157] Fine Viola:
Portugal, 1973 (maker's, January 23, 1974)
                               6,500/7,500 NS

CAPELA, ANTONIO [Bf9/4576] Fine Viola:
Portugal, 1973 (maker's, January 23, 1974)
                               6,500/7,500
$7,475   £4,485   DM12,633   ¥994,698

CAPELA, D. [B6/73] Fine Viola: 1972
                               20,040/25,050 NS

CAPELA, DOMINGOS [B11/64] Fine Viola: 1972
                               16,700/20,040 NS

CARESSA & FRANCAIS [S6/94] Viola: Paris, 1904
                               11,550/16,500 NS

CASTELLI, CESARE [S6/92] Viola w/case: Ascoli
Piceno, 1966   2,970/4,125 NS

CAVALINI, DINO [S10/91] Viola: Pontedera, 1976
                               1,860/3,100 NS

CAVANI, VINCENZO [Sk11/162] Contemporary
Italian Viola w/case: 1965   6,000/8,000 NS

CONIA, STEFANO [C11/114] Italian Viola
                               5,010/6,680
$5,762   £3,450   DM9,626   ¥700,316

CONIA, STEFANO [S3/130] Viola: Cremona, 1982
(maker's, May 28, 1982)   10,044/13,392 NS

CONIA, STEFANO [S3/134] Viola: Cremona, 1988
(maker's, November 15, 1988)   10,044/13,392 NS

CONIA, STEFANO [S1117/323] Viola: Cremona,
1988 (maker's, November 15, 1988)   7,515/9,185 NS

CONIA, STEFANO [S1117/325] Viola: Cremona,
1982 (maker's, May 28, 1982)   7,515/9,185 NS

CONIA, STEFANO [S1117/326] Viola: Cremona,
1974   6,346/7,515 NS

CONTAVALLI, PRIMO [Sk11/177] Modern Italian
Viola: Imola, 1970   2,200/2,400
$3,680   £2,208   DM6,219   ¥448,960

COPLERE, JEAN [Sk11/171] Contemporary French
Viola: Paris, 1969   1,800/2,200
$1,495   £897   DM2,527   ¥182,390

CRASKE, GEORGE [P4/69] Fine and Handsome
Viola in immediate playing condition, w/case, bow:
c. 1860   5,001/6,668 NS

CURLETTO, ANSELMO [S10/97] Viola w/bow:
Turin, 1966   11,160/14,880 NS

CURLETTO, ANSELMO [S10/99] Viola: Turin,
1959 (maker's, November 1963)   18,600/24,800 NS

CURTIN, JOSEPH [Sk11/160] Good Contemporary
Viola w/case: Toronto, 1983   8,000/12,000 NS

DIEUDONNE, AMEDEE [C4/101] French Viola
w/case   2,505/3,340 NS

DUKE, RICHARD [C11/116] English Viola w/case,
bow   3,006/4,175
$3,649   £2,185   DM6,096   ¥443,533

EBERLE, EUGENE [C11/117] Dutch Viola w/case,
bow   6,680/10,020
$7,682   £4,600   DM12,834   ¥933,754

EDLER, ERNEST [Sk11/170] American Viola w/case,
bow: Boston, 1940   2,500/3,500 NS

ERICIAN, MARTIN [Sk11/174] Contemporary
Viola: 1960   6,000/8,000 NS

FAROTTI, CELESTE [C4/97] Italian Viola
                                   2,505/3,340
$4,225   £2,530   DM7,843   ¥565,303

FAROTTO, CELESTE [Sk5/14] Good Modern Italian
Viola w/case: Milan, 1971   5,000/7,000
$5,750   £3,450   DM10,235   ¥764,635

FENDT, BERNARD SIMON JR. [Sk11/164] English
Viola w/case: London, 1830   12,000/14,000
$13,800   £8,280   DM23,322   ¥1,683,600

FERRONI, FERDINANDO [Sk11/175] Italian Viola:
Florence, 1934   3,000/4,000
$2,645   £1,587   DM4,470   ¥322,690

FICHTL, JOHANN ULRICH [S10/89] Viola:
Mittenwald, 1764   1,240/1,860
$1,910   £1,109   DM3,080   ¥224,840

FLETA, IGNACIO [S6/96] Viola w/case, 2 bows:
Barcelona, 1936   6,600/9,900
$5,693   £3,450   DM10,247   ¥820,928

FORSTER [C4/88] English Viola   3,006/3,674
$4,225   £2,530   DM7,843   ¥565,303

FORSTER, WILLIAM (II) [Sk11/165] Fine English
Viola w/case: London, 1777   10,000/15,000
$12,650   £7,590   DM21,379   ¥1,543,300

FOSCHI, GIORGIO [S1117/334] Viola: Carate
Brianza, 1982 (maker's, Milan)   6,680/8,350 NS

GAGLIANO FAMILY (MEMBER OF) [P11/106]
Fine, Handsome, and Rare Italian Viola with skillful
restoration: Naples, c. 1800   100,800/117,600 NS

GAND & BERNARDEL [S3/131] Viola: Paris, 1885
                                  13,392/20,088
$18,288   £10,925   DM33,835   ¥2,437,258

GIULIANI, R.G. [S10/94] Viola: Verona, 1932
                                   1,860/2,480 NS

GOULDING [C4/95] Good English Viola
                                   5,010/6,680 NS

GUADAGNINI, GIUSEPPE (ascribed to) [P11/105]
Fine, Handsome, and Rare Italian Viola in good
condition, w/case: Como, c. 1780
                                  201,600/252,000 NS

HARRIS, CHARLES [B11/67A] Viola: 1824
                                   3,340/6,680 NS

HARRIS, CHARLES [C11/99] English Viola w/case
                                   3,006/3,674
$4,225   £2,530   DM7,059   ¥513,565

HARRIS, RICHARD [B11/73] Viola
                                   6,680/10,020 NS

HEBERLEIN, HEINRICH TH. (JR.) [C11/113]
German Viola   3,006/4,175
$2,881   £1,725   DM4,813   ¥350,158

HILL, JOSEPH [B3/116] Very Fine English Viola:
London, 1770 (J. & A. Beare)   20,088/25,110
$23,101   £13,800   DM42,739   ¥3,078,642

HILL, JOSEPH [B6/77] Fine English Viola in an
almost perfect state of preservation: London, c. 1770
                                  13,360/20,040 NS

HILL, JOSEPH [B11/62] English Viola: London,
1779   5,010/8,350 NS

HILL, JOSEPH [B11/69] Fine English Viola in an
almost perfect state of preservation: London, c. 1770
                                  13,360/20,040
$13,444   £8,050   DM22,460   ¥1,634,070

HILL, JOSEPH [P4/130] Good Viola in immediate
playing condition, w/case, bow   8,335/10,002
$10,352   £6,210   DM19,176   ¥1,382,532

HILL, JOSEPH [S1117/330] Viola w/case, cover:
London, c. 1770   5,010/6,680
$5,762   £3,450   DM9,626   ¥700,316

HILL, LOCKEY [B3/117] Very Fine English Viola:
London, c. 1800   4,185/5,859
$3,850   £2,300   DM7,123   ¥513,107

HOING, CLIFFORD A. [B11/72] Viola: 1951
                                   6,680/10,020 NS

HOWE, ROBERT [S3/117] Viola w/case: Windsor,
1884   1,004/1,339
$963   £575   DM1,781   ¥128,277

HUSSON [B3/118] French Viola (Jean-Jacques
Rampal, Paris)   5,022/8,370 NS

HUSSON FAMILY (MEMBER OF) [S1117/327]
Viola w/case: Mirecourt, late 19th C. (Jean-Jacques
Rampal, Paris, December 2, 1997)   5,010/8,350
$8,642   £5,175   DM14,438   ¥1,050,473

JAIS, ANTON [Bf2/4160] Viola converted from a
viola d'amore: Tolz, 1745   1,500/2,000
$1,610   £985   DM2,924   ¥199,930

KAUL, PAUL [C4/112] French Viola   5,845/6,680
$6,914   £4,140   DM12,834   ¥925,042

KLOTZ, AEGIDIUS (II) [S1117/328] Viola w/case,
viola bow, violin bow: Mittenwald, 1799 5,010/6,680
$4,801   £2,875   DM8,021   ¥583,596

KLOTZ, JOSEPH (attributed to) [C4/110]
Mittenwald Viola w/case   6,680/8,350 NS

KLOTZ, JOSEPH (attributed to) [C11/120]
Mittenwald Viola w/case   5,010/6,680
$4,609   £2,760   DM7,700   ¥560,252

LABERTE, MARC [Bf7/10417] Viola w/case
                                   700/1,000
$489   £298   DM870   ¥67,897

LABERTE, MARC [Sk5/90] Viola w/case: Mirecourt,
late 20th C.   800/1,200
$690   £414   DM1,228   ¥91,756

LANARO, UMBERTO [S3/119] Viola w/case: Padua, 1993 (maker's, March 14, 1993)　　　3,348/5,022
$3,850　　£2,300　　　DM7,123　　　¥513,107

LANARO, UMBERTO [S3/132] Viola w/case: Padua, 1987 (maker's, July 5, 1991)　　　4,185/5,859
$3,850　　£2,300　　　DM7,123　　　¥513,107

LANARO, UMBERTO [S1117/324] Viola: Padua, 1981 (maker's, November 30, 1981) 5,010/8,350 NS

LANARO, UMBERTO [S1117/332] Viola: Padua, mid 20th C.　　　　　　　5,010/8,350 NS

LANGONET, ALFRED CHARLES [C11/118] English Viola w/case　　　　6,346/7,515 NS

LEONI, GUIDO [S6/95] Viola w/case: San Benedetto del Tronto, 1966　　　　2,475/4,125 NS

LODGE, JOHN [C11/283] English Viola w/case
　　　　　　　　　　　　668/1,002
$576　　£345　　　DM963　　　¥70,032

MAAG, HENRY [Bf2/4156] Viola: Glendale, California　　　　　　　300/400 NS

MAAG, HENRY [Bf7/10406] American Viola: Glendale, California, 1965　　　200/300
$219　　£133　　　DM389　　　¥30,354

MANGIACASALE, SALVATORE [S10/93] Viola: Turin, 1982　　　　　1,550/2,170 NS

MANTEGAZZA, PIETRO GIOVANNI [C4/115] Fine Italian Viola w/case (Rembert Wurlitzer, New York, October 11, 1950)　　　63,460/75,150
$85,170　£51,000　DM158,100　¥11,395,440

MELLONI, SETTIMO [Sk11/172] Modern Italian Viola w/case: Ferrara, 1925　　6,000/8,000 NS

MOUGENOT, LEON (workshop of) [Sk5/27] French Viola: 1929　　　　　2,800/3,200
$1,725　　£1,035　　DM3,071　　¥229,390

NEUNER & HORNSTEINER (workshop of) [Sk5/23] Mittenwald Viola w/case, bow: c. 1870
　　　　　　　　　　　1,500/2,000
$1,610　　£966　　　DM2,866　　¥214,098

NIGGEL, SYMPERT [S3/126] Viola w/case: Füssen, 1783　　　　　　　3,013/4,185
$4,428　　£2,645　　DM8,192　　¥590,073

NUPIERI, GIUSEPPE [S3/115] Viola: Rome, 1979 (maker's, March 12, 1992)　　　2,511/3,348
$1,040　　£621　　　DM1,923　　¥138,539

NUPIERI, GIUSEPPE [S1117/333] Viola: Rome, 1982 (maker's, March 12, 1992)　3,006/3,340 NS

ODOARDI, GIUSEPPE (attributed to) [C4/114] Fine Italian Viola w/case　　33,400/50,100 NS

ODOARDI, GIUSEPPE (ascribed to) [C11/110] Fine Viola w/case　　　　16,700/25,050
$17,285　£10,350　　DM28,877　¥2,100,947

PARESCHI, GAETANO [S10/100] Viola: Ferrara, 1945　　　　　　　12,400/18,600 NS

PAUL, ADAM D. [C11/303] English Viola
　　　　　　　　　　　1,670/2,505 NS

PERRY, L.A. [P10/45] Good Viola in good condition: N. Wales, 1989　　　　　　765/935
$880　　£518　　　DM1,433　　¥103,541

PETERNELLA, JAGO [Sk11/173] Modern Italian Viola: Venice, 1930　　　2,500/3,500 NS

PICKERING, NORMAN [Sk11/169] Contemporary American Viola w/case, bow: North Bellmore, New York, 1953　　　　　　800/1,200
$805　　£483　　　DM1,360　　¥98,210

PUSKAS, JOSEPH [Bf2/4159] Fine American Viola w/case: Los Angeles, 1970　4,000/5,000 NS

RADIGHIERI, OTELLO [B3/120] Italian Viola
　　　　　　　　　　　3,348/5,022 NS

RINALDI, GIOFREDO BENEDETTO (ascribed to) [P11/80] Interesting Viola in immediate playing condition, w/case (Hans Schmidt, Mittenwald, February 10, 1971)　　　　12,600/14,280 NS

RITTER, HERMANN [Sk5/22] German Viola w/case: 1884　　　　　　800/1,200
$460　　£276　　　DM819　　　¥61,171

ROBINSON, WILLIAM [C11/97] English Viola w/case　　　　　　　2,505/3,340
$4,225　　£2,530　　DM7,059　　¥513,565

ROBINSON, WILLIAM [C11/121] Good English Viola w/case　　　　4,175/5,010 NS

ROTH, ERNST HEINRICH [C11/297] German Viola w/case　　　　1,336/1,670 NS

SALF [C4/90] French Viola　　1,002/1,336 NS

SCHMITT, LUCIEN [S3/121] Viola w/case: Grenoble, 1960 (maker's, April 15, 1961)　5,022/6,696
$5,775　　£3,450　　DM10,685　　¥769,661

SCOLARI, GIORGIO [S1117/329] Viola: Cremona, 1976　　　　　　　4,676/5,845
$6,530　　£3,910　　DM10,909　　¥793,691

SEGAMIGLIA, GIUSTINO [S10/90] Viola: Montopoli Val d'Arno, 1976　　1,860/3,100 NS

SERDET, PAUL [C4/119] Fine French Viola
　　　　　　　　　　18,370/23,380
$19,205　£11,500　　DM35,650　¥2,569,560

SICCARDI, SERGIO [B6/76] Viola　2,505/4,175 NS

STADLMANN, MICHAEL IGNAZ [C4/94] Viola
　　　　　　　　　　　6,346/7,515 NS

STADLMANN, MICHAEL IGNAZ [C11/100] Viola
　　　　　　　　　　　4,175/5,010 NS

STYLES, HAROLD LEICESTER [P11/198] Good Viola in immediate playing condition, w/case: Bath, 1970　　　　　　　840/1,176 NS

THIBOUVILLE-LAMY, J. [C11/285] French Viola w/case　　　　　　　501/668
$1,440　　£862　　　DM2,405　　¥174,977

THIBOUVILLE-LAMY, J. [P4/168] Good Viola in good condition: Mirecourt, c. 1900　1,167/1,500
$1,572　　£943　　　DM2,912　　¥209,940

VETTORI, PAULO [S10/101] Viola: Florence, 1988
6,200/8,680 NS

VILLA, LUIGI [S1117/197] Viola: Cesano Maderno, 1992
1,670/2,338 NS

VILLA, LUIGI [S1117/199] Viola: Cesano Maderno, 1994
2,505/3,340 NS

VILLA, LUIGI [S1117/200] Viola: Cesano Maderno, 1978
2,004/2,672 NS

VILLA, LUIGI [S1117/203] Viola: Cesano Maderno, 1988
2,004/2,505
$1,824   £1,092   DM3,047   ¥221,665

VILLA, LUIGI [S1117/206] Viola: Cesano Maderno, 1984
2,338/3,006 NS

VILLA, LUIGI [S1117/218] Viola: Cesano Maderno, 1988
2,338/3,006 NS

VILLA, LUIGI [S1117/222] Viola: Cesano Maderno, 1986
2,338/3,006 NS

VILLA, LUIGI [S1117/232] Viola: Cesano Maderno, 1978
3,340/5,010 NS

VOIGT (attributed to) [B3/114] Viola
1,674/2,511 NS

WARD, ROD [B10/66] English Viola   850/1,190
$743   £437   DM1,197   ¥91,866

WILLER, JOANNES MICHAEL [S1117/331] Viola w/case: Prague, 1802   3,340/5,010 NS

VIOLA BOW

BAUSCH [B3/79A] Nickel Viola Bow   837/1,172 NS

BAUSCH [B6/11] Silver Viola Bow   835/1,169 NS

BAUSCH [B10/29] Silver Viola Bow   170/340
$293   £173   DM473   ¥36,263

BAUSCH, LUDWIG [Sk5/142] Nickel Viola Bow
800/1,200
$863   £518   DM1,535   ¥114,695

BAZIN [B3/76] Fine Silver Viola Bow   3,348/5,022
$3,850   £2,300   DM7,123   ¥513,107

BAZIN, CHARLES [Bf9/4503] Good Silver Viola Bow
1,400/1,800
$2,588   £1,553   DM4,373   ¥344,319

BECHINI, RENZO [S10/29] Silver Viola Bow: c. 1960
1,550/2,170 NS

BECHINI, RENZO [S10/78] Silver Viola Bow: Bresso, c. 1960   1,550/1,860 NS

BERNARDEL, LEON [Bf2/4077] Silver Viola Bow
1,800/2,250
$1,093   £669   DM1,984   ¥135,667

BULTITUDE, ARTHUR RICHARD [Sk11/141] Gold and Tortoiseshell Viola Bow   2,000/3,000 NS

CHALUPETZKY, F. [C11/51] Gold Viola Bow
1,670/2,004 NS

COLAS, PROSPER [Sk5/76] Silver Viola Bow
1,600/1,800
$2,300   £1,380   DM4,094   ¥305,854

DODD [B6/4] Ebony Viola Bow   1,670/2,505 NS

DOLLING, KURT [C4/372] Silver Viola Bow
501/668
$730   £437   DM1,355   ¥97,643

DUGAD, ANDRE [S1117/434] Silver Viola Bow: Paris, mid 20th C.   1,336/2,004
$1,536   £920   DM2,567   ¥186,751

DURRSCHMIDT, OTTO [S6/79] Gold Viola Bow: Markneukirchen, c. 1900   1,155/1,650
$1,422   £862   DM2,560   ¥205,113

DURRSCHMIDT, WILLI CARL [S10/80] Gold and Tortoiseshell Viola Bow: Markneukirchen, c. 1935
1,860/2,480
$1,426   £828   DM2,300   ¥167,900

FETIQUE, JULES [C4/23] Silver Viola Bow
1,169/1,503
$1,344   £805   DM2,496   ¥179,869

FETIQUE, VICTOR [B3/79] Fine Silver Viola Bow
6,696/10,044 NS

FETIQUE, VICTOR [B6/50] Fine Silver Viola Bow
5,010/6,680
$4,801   £2,875   DM8,596   ¥660,618

FETIQUE, VICTOR [P11/127] Silver Viola Bow with minor, restorable blemishes: Paris   3,360/4,200 NS

FINKEL, JOHANNES S. [S3/237] Chased-Gold and Tortoiseshell Viola Bow: Brienz, c. 1975
3,013/4,185 NS

GRANIER, DENIS [S10/81] Nickel Viola Bow: Marseilles, c. 1950   620/930 NS

HERRMANN, LOTHAR [S3/204] Silver Viola Bow: Schönlind, c. 1950   1,172/1,674
$1,348   £805   DM2,493   ¥179,587

HERRMANN, LOTHAR [S10/107] Silver Viola Bow: East Germany, c. 1960   496/744
$713   £414   DM1,150   ¥83,950

HILL, W.E. & SONS [B6/48] Silver Viola Bow
1,670/2,505
$2,305   £1,380   DM4,126   ¥317,096

HILL, W.E. & SONS [B11/38] Silver Viola Bow
3,340/5,010
$3,649   £2,185   DM6,096   ¥443,533

HILL, W.E. & SONS [C4/41] Silver Viola Bow
2,004/3,006
$2,305   £1,380   DM4,278   ¥308,347

HILL, W.E. & SONS [P11/111] Silver Viola Bow: London   1,680/2,520
$1,932   £1,150   DM3,220   ¥230,909

HILL, W.E. & SONS [P11/123] Silver Viola Bow requiring rehairing: London   1,680/2,520
$3,478   £2,070   DM5,796   ¥415,635

HILL, W.E. & SONS [P11/130] Gold Viola Bow:
London   1,344/2,016
$3,864   £2,300   DM6,440   ¥461,817

HILL, W.E. & SONS [S6/60] Silver Viola Bow:
London, 1931   1,980/2,970
$3,036   £1,840   DM5,465   ¥437,828

HILL, W.E. & SONS [Sk11/128] Silver Viola Bow
                                    3,000/3,500 NS

HILL, W.E. & SONS [Sk11/235] Silver Viola Bow
                                    3,000/3,500
$3,220   £1,932   DM5,442   ¥392,840

KUN, JOSEPH [Sk11/129] Silver Viola Bow
                                    1,200/1,400 NS

LABERTE, MARC [C4/68] Silver Viola Bow (Jean-
François Raffin, Paris, August 30, 1997) 1,169/1,503
$1,632   £977   DM3,029   ¥218,301

MALINE, NICOLAS (attributed to) [B11/29] Silver
Viola Bow (Bernard Millant)   5,010/8,350
$6,146   £3,680   DM10,267   ¥747,003

MILLANT, JEAN-JACQUES [S3/55] Gold Viola
Bow: Paris (maker's, March 23, 1995)   2,511/3,348
$5,775   £3,450   DM10,685   ¥769,661

MOINEL, DANIEL [C11/14] Silver Viola Bow
                                    1,336/1,670 NS

MOLLER, MAX [C4/3] Silver Viola Bow
                                    1,169/1,670
$1,921   £1,150   DM3,565   ¥256,956

MORIZOT, C. [B3/78] Nickel Viola Bow
                                    1,004/1,339 NS

MORIZOT, LOUIS (II) [S3/76] Gold and Ivory Viola
Bow: Mirecourt, mid 20th C.   1,674/2,511
$2,888   £1,725   DM5,342   ¥384,830

PIERNOT, MARIE LOUIS [S10/106] Nickel Viola
Bow: Paris, c. 1920   930/1,240 NS

RICHAUME, ANDRE [P11/119] Silver Viola Bow:
Paris   3,360/4,200
$12,558   £7,475   DM20,930   ¥1,500,905

SARTORY, EUGENE [B3/71] Extremely Fine Silver
Viola Bow   20,088/25,110
$23,101   £13,800   DM42,739   ¥3,078,642

SCHICKER, HORST [C4/385] Silver Viola Bow
                                    334/668
$461   £276   DM856   ¥61,669

SCHUSTER, ADOLPH CURT [Sk11/249] Silver
Viola Bow   1,200/1,400
$1,495   £897   DM2,527   ¥182,390

SCHUSTER, ALBERT [Sk5/140] Silver Viola Bow
without hair   400/600
$1,035   £621   DM1,842   ¥137,634

SEIFERT, LOTHAR [C4/386] Silver Viola Bow
                                    501/835
$576   £345   DM1,070   ¥77,087

SEIFERT, LOTHAR [S3/233] Chased-Gold and
Tortoiseshell Viola Bow: Bubenreuth   2,511/3,348
$2,888   £1,725   DM5,342   ¥384,830

SIMON (workshop of) [B6/49] Silver Viola Bow
                                    5,010/8,350 NS

THIBOUVILLE-LAMY, J. [B3/77A] Silver Viola Bow
(Jean-François Raffin)   2,009/2,511 NS

THIBOUVILLE-LAMY, J. [B6/47] Silver Viola Bow
(Jean-François Raffin)   1,336/2,004 NS

THIBOUVILLE-LAMY, J. [C11/36] Silver Viola Bow
(Jean-François Raffin, Paris, March 26, 1996)
                                    1,002/1,336 NS

THOMASSIN, CLAUDE [S1117/74] Silver Viola
Bow: Mirecourt, c. 1900   1,169/1,670 NS

TUBBS, JAMES [C4/22] Silver Viola Bow with
repairs   835/1,169
$922   £552   DM1,711   ¥123,339

TUBBS, JAMES [Sk11/152] Silver Viola Bow
                                    3,000/4,000
$6,038   £3,623   DM10,203   ¥736,575

VIGNERON, ANDRE [S1117/429] Silver Viola Bow:
Paris, c. 1910 (Bernard Millant, Paris, April 18, 1988)
                                    5,845/7,515
$6,722   £4,025   DM11,230   ¥817,035

VIGNERON, JOSEPH ARTHUR [C4/77] Silver
Viola Bow   5,845/6,680
$6,722   £4,025   DM12,478   ¥899,346

WATSON, D. [B11/37] Gold and Tortoiseshell Viola
Bow: London, 1968   2,505/3,340
$4,801   £2,875   DM8,021   ¥583,596

WILSON, GARNER [C11/62] Silver Viola Bow
                                    1,169/1,503 NS

WILSON, GARNER [P11/152] Rose-Gold Viola Bow
                                    1,344/1,512
$1,893   £1,127   DM3,156   ¥226,290

VIOLIN

ACOULON, ALFRED (attributed to) [P11/194]
Good French Violin in good condition, w/case:
Mirecourt, c. 1920   840/1,008 NS

ALBANELLI, FRANCO [S3/244] Violin w/case:
Bologna, 1989   4,185/5,859 NS

ALBANELLI, FRANCO [Sk11/83] Contemporary
Italian Violin w/case: Bologna, 1990   3,000/5,000
$2,990   £1,794   DM5,053   ¥364,780

ALBERTI, FERDINANDO (attributed to) [B3/176]
Milanese Violin: 1737 (A. Eisenstein)
                                    8,370/11,718 NS

ALLEN, JOSEPH S. [Sk5/68] Good American Violin
w/case, bow: Boston, 1896   1,800/2,200
$3,335   £2,001   DM5,936   ¥443,488

ALLISON, JOHN L. [Sk5/291] American Violin
w/case, bow: 1942   800/1,200
$518   £311   DM921   ¥68,817

ALTAVILLA, ARMANDO [S3/282] Violin w/case:
Naples, 1930   3,348/5,022 NS

ALTAVILLA, ARMANDO [S6/132] Violin w/case,
cover: Naples, c. 1930   9,900/13,200 NS

ALTAVILLA, ARMANDO [S1117/25] Violin w/case: Naples, 1930   3,006/3,674
$4,609   £2,760   DM7,700   ¥560,252

AMATI, ANTONIO & GIROLAMO [S3/252] Violin w/case: Cremona, c. 1620   92,070/108,810
$94,581   £56,500   DM174,981   ¥12,604,585

AMATI, DOM NICOLO [B6/128] Fine Italian Violin: Bologna, c. 1730   33,400/50,100
$42,251   £25,300   DM75,647   ¥5,813,434

AMATI, NICOLO [Bf9/4618] Very Fine and Impor-tant Violin: Cremona, c. 1620 (William Moennig & Son, July 24, 1974)   150,000/200,000 NS

AMATI, NICOLO [S6/148] Violin: Cremona, c. 1680
132,000/198,000 NS

ANDERSON, A. [P12/226] Violin w/case, bow: Edinburgh, 1932   334/501 NS

ANTONIAZZI, RICCARDO [S3/17] Violin w/case: Milan, 1910   16,740/23,436
$21,176   £12,650   DM39,177   ¥2,822,089

ANTONIAZZI, RICCARDO [S3/339] Violin w/case: Milan, c. 1890   8,370/11,718 NS

ANTONIAZZI, RICCARDO [S1117/362] Violin w/case: Milan, c. 1890   5,010/8,350
$6,914   £4,140   DM11,551   ¥840,379

ANTONIAZZI, ROMEO [P11/63] Good Italian Violin in good condition, w/case, bow: Cremona, 1909   20,160/23,520
$28,014   £16,675   DM46,690   ¥3,348,173

ANTONIAZZI, ROMEO [S3/243] Violin: Milan, 1913   16,740/23,436
$25,026   £14,950   DM46,300   ¥3,335,196

ANTONIAZZI, ROMEO [S1117/128] Violin w/case, bow: Milan, c. 1910   13,360/20,040
$21,126   £12,650   DM35,294   ¥2,567,824

ANTONIAZZI, ROMEO (ascribed to) [S1117/380] Violin w/case, cover: Milan, 1925 (Giuseppe Lucci, Rome, October 21, 1975)   20,040/25,050 NS

ANTONIAZZI, ROMEO (workshop of) [Sk11/114] Modern Italian Violin: Milan, 1920   14,000/16,000
$10,925   £6,555   DM18,463   ¥1,332,850

APPARUT, G. [B6/87] French Violin: 1944
1,670/2,505 NS

APPARUT, GEORGES [B2/85] French Violin: 1936
1,640/2,460
$1,697   £1,035   DM3,088   ¥214,390

APPARUT, GEORGES [B3/134] French Violin: 1944
2,511/3,348 NS

APPARUT, GEORGES [S3/348] Violin w/case: 1943
3,348/5,022
$3,080   £1,840   DM5,698   ¥410,486

APPARUT, GEORGES [Sk5/123] French Violin: Mirecourt, 1936   2,400/2,600
$2,070   £1,242   DM3,685   ¥275,269

ARASSI, ENZO [B3/138] Italian Violin: 1930
2,009/2,511 NS

ARASSI, ENZO (workshop of) [Sk11/459] Modern Italian Violin w/case: Milan, 1930   2,000/3,000
$3,738   £2,243   DM6,316   ¥455,975

ARBUCKLE, WILLIAM [P4/125] Good Scottish Violin in immediate playing condition: Glasgow, 1900
1,667/2,501
$1,917   £1,150   DM3,551   ¥256,025

ARCANGELI, ULDERICO [S3/283] Violin w/case: Morciano di Romagna, 1932   5,022/6,696 NS

ARCANGELI, ULDERICO (attributed to) [B11/140] Violin   4,676/5,845
$6,146   £3,680   DM10,267   ¥747,003

ATKINSON, WILLIAM [B3/142] English Violin: Tottenham, 1891   2,511/3,348 NS

ATKINSON, WILLIAM [Bf2/131] English Violin: Tottenham, 1891   1,000/1,500 NS

ATKINSON, WILLIAM [P11/41] Good English Violin in immediate playing condition, w/case: Tottenham, 1909   3,360/5,040
$4,250   £2,530   DM7,084   ¥507,999

ATKINSON, WILLIAM [S3/14] Violin: Tottenham, 1902   2,511/3,348
$2,888   £1,725   DM5,342   ¥384,830

ATKINSON, WILLIAM [S3/259] Violin: Tottenham, 1891   2,511/3,348 NS

ATKINSON, WILLIAM [S1117/364] Violin: Tottenham, 1891   1,670/2,505 NS

AUDINOT, NESTOR [B3/168] French Violin: 1898
3,348/5,022 NS

AUDINOT, NESTOR [C11/197] French Violin
5,010/6,680
$9,603   £5,750   DM16,043   ¥1,167,193

BAADER, J. (workshop of) [Sk5/228] Mittenwald Violin w/case   350/450
$546   £328   DM972   ¥72,640

BAILLY, CHARLES [P4/127] Good French Violin in good condition   1,667/2,501
$2,492   £1,495   DM4,617   ¥332,832

BAILLY, CHARLES (attributed to) [P11/30] Fine French Violin in good condition, w/case: 1925
2,016/2,520
$2,512   £1,495   DM4,186   ¥300,181

BAILLY, CHARLES (workshop of) [Sk5/377] French Violin w/case: 1919   1,600/1,800
$2,185   £1,311   DM3,889   ¥290,561

BAILLY, PAUL [B3/175] French Violin
6,696/10,044 NS

BAILLY, PAUL [B6/112] French Violin
5,010/8,350 NS

BAILLY, PAUL [B11/98] Fine Violin   5,845/9,185
$10,755   £6,440   DM17,968   ¥1,307,256

BAILLY, PAUL [B11/101] French Violin   3,340/5,010
$2,689   £1,610   DM4,492   ¥326,814

BAILLY, PAUL [P4/113] Good Violin in immediate playing condition   6,668/10,002 NS

BAILLY, PAUL [P11/38] Good Violin in immediate playing condition   5,040/6,720 NS

BAILLY, PAUL (attributed to) [P4/154] Good French Violin in immediate playing condition, w/case, bow: c. 1900   2,000/2,501
$2,109   £1,265   DM3,906   ¥281,627

BAILLY, RENE [Sk5/221] French Violin w/case: 1951   1,400/1,600
$1,380   £828   DM2,456   ¥183,512

BALAZS, ISTVAN [Sk5/388] Hungarian Violin w/case: 1965   1,500/1,700
$1,610   £966   DM2,866   ¥214,098

BALESTRIERI, TOMMASO [B3/200] Fine and Rare Child's Violin: Mantua, 1760 (J. & A. Beare, 1993)   46,872/58,590 NS

BALESTRIERI, TOMMASO [Sk11/126] Fine and Important Italian Violin w/case: Mantua, 1761 (Geigenbau Machold, Bremen, January 8, 1988)   175,000/200,000 NS

BALL, HARVEY [Sk11/349] American Violin w/case, 2 bows: Nashua, 1875   1,200/1,400
$1,150   £690   DM1,944   ¥140,300

BALLERINI, PIETRO [S10/3] Violin: Florence, c. 1920   1,240/1,860 NS

BANKS, BENJAMIN [B3/169] Fine English Violin   13,392/16,740 NS

BANKS, BENJAMIN [B6/113] English Violin   8,350/11,690 NS

BANKS, BENJAMIN [C4/165] English Violin   5,010/6,680 NS

BANKS, BENJAMIN [S3/27] Violin w/case, 2 bows: Salisbury, 1775   6,696/10,044 NS

BANKS, BENJAMIN [S1117/376] Violin w/case, cover, 2 bows: Salisbury, 1775   4,676/5,845 NS

BANKS, JAMES & HENRY [C4/160] Fine English Violin w/case, bow   8,350/13,360
$12,483   £7,475   DM23,173   ¥1,670,214

BARBE FAMILY (MEMBER OF) [P10/42] French Violin or small viola, w/case: c. 1840 1,360/2,040 NS

BARBE, TELESPHORE AMABLE [B11/141] French Violin   4,175/5,845
$4,801   £2,875   DM8,021   ¥583,596

BARBIERI, ENZO [C11/143] Italian Violin (maker's, Mantua, 1996)   4,175/5,010 NS

BARBIERI, ENZO [S3/256] Violin w/case: Mantua, 1990 (maker's, May 12, 1990)   3,348/5,022 NS

BARTON, GEORGE [C4/255] English Violin
$192   £115   DM357   ¥25,696

BATCHELDER, A.M. [Sk11/311] American Violin w/case: Frankfort, Maine, 1928   300/400
$431   £259   DM729   ¥52,613

BAZIN, GUSTAVE (attributed to) [P4/43] Good Violin in good condition: Mirecourt, c. 1930   1,000/1,334 NS

BEDOCCHI, MARIO [B11/82] Italian Violin (Giuseppe Lucci)   10,020/13,360 NS

BEDOCCHI, MARIO [S3/33] Violin: Reggio Emilia, 1936   13,392/20,088 NS

BELLAFONTANA, LORENZO [B3/152] Italian Violin: Genoa, 1948   10,044/16,740 NS

BELLAFONTANA, LORENZO [B6/97] Italian Violin: Genoa, 1948   10,020/16,700 NS

BELLAFONTANA, LORENZO [S3/43] Violin: Genoa, 1976 (Carlo Carfagna, Rome, November 18, 1997)   5,022/8,370
$8,085   £4,830   DM14,959   ¥1,077,525

BELLAROSA, VITTORIO [Sk11/75] Modern Neapolitan Violin   10,000/15,000
$9,775   £5,865   DM16,520   ¥1,192,550

BELTRAMI, GIUSEPPE [C11/183] Italian Violin   11,690/15,030
$12,483   £7,475   DM20,855   ¥1,517,350

BELTRAMI, GIUSEPPE [S3/273] Violin: Vescovato, 1888   2,009/2,678
$2,310   £1,380   DM4,274   ¥307,864

BELTRAMI, GIUSEPPE (attributed to) [B11/107] Violin   4,175/5,845 NS

BENOZZATI, GIROLAMO [S3/287] Violin w/case: Rome, 1938   5,022/8,370 NS

BENOZZATI, GIROLAMO [S1117/15] Violin w/case: Rome, 1938   4,175/5,010 NS

BERGONZI, RICCARDO [S10/46] Violin: Cremona, 1983 (maker's, January 16, 1996)   4,960/6,200
$4,991   £2,898   DM8,050   ¥587,650

BERNARDEL (workshop of) [Sk11/115] French Violin w/case, bow   4,000/6,000
$3,565   £2,139   DM6,025   ¥434,930

BERNARDEL, AUGUST SEBASTIEN PHILIPPE [Bf2/4152] Good Violin: Paris, 1843 (Etienne Vatelot)   20,000/25,000 NS

BERNARDEL, AUGUST SEBASTIEN PHILIPPE [S3/26] Violin w/double case, 6 bows: Paris, 1827   10,044/13,392 NS

BERNARDEL, AUGUST SEBASTIEN PHILIPPE [Sk5/58] Fine French Violin w/case: Paris   18,000/22,000
$19,550   £11,730   DM34,799   ¥2,599,759

BERNARDEL, AUGUST SEBASTIEN PHILIPPE (attributed to) [C11/179] French Violin   7,515/8,350 NS

BERNARDEL, AUGUST SEBASTIEN & ERNEST AUGUST [Bf9/4593] Good French Violin w/case, blanket: Paris, c. 1860   17,000/22,000 NS

BERNARDEL, GUSTAVE ADOLPHE [S6/120] Violin w/case: Paris, c. 1880   9,900/13,200 NS

BERNARDEL, LEON [B2/121] Violin: Paris, 1920   1,640/2,460
$1,320   £805   DM2,402   ¥166,748

BERNARDEL, LEON [B3/179] French Violin: Paris, 1900   5,022/8,370 NS

BERNARDEL, LEON [C11/165] French Violin
                                                1,336/2,004
$1,344   £805   DM2,246   ¥163,407

BERNARDEL, LEON [C11/176] French Violin
                                                1,169/1,670
$1,344   £805   DM2,246   ¥163,407

BERNARDEL, LEON [S1117/59] Violin w/case:
Paris, 1900   4,008/4,676
$5,762   £3,450   DM9,626   ¥700,316

BERNARDEL, LEON (attributed to) [P4/61]
Superior Violin in good condition: Mirecourt, 1922
                                                3,001/3,667 NS

BERNARDEL, LEON (workshop of) [Sk11/304]
French Violin: Paris   400/500
$1,150   £690   DM1,944   ¥140,300

BETTS [B2/84] English Violin   984/1,312 NS

BETTS [B3/195] English Violin: London
                                                3,348/5,022 NS

BETTS [B5/217] English Violin   652/978 NS

BETTS [B6/91] English Violin: London, c. 1820
                                                2,505/3,340 NS

BETTS [B7/162] English Violin   413/578 NS

BETTS [B10/91] English Violin   850/1,190 NS

BETTS [B10/94] English Violin   255/425
$332   £196   DM536   ¥41,098

BETTS, JOHN [B2/110] English Violin missing table,
w/a quantity of violin parts   246/328
$321   £196   DM583   ¥40,496

BETTS, JOHN [P11/48] Good English Violin with
minor table corner-fragment restoration, w/case:
London, c. 1810   10,080/11,760 NS

BEUSCHER, PAUL (workshop of) [Sk5/121] French
Violin w/case: Paris, 1927   1,400/1,600
$1,725   £1,035   DM3,071   ¥229,390

BIANCHI, CHRISTOPHER [Bf7/10515] American
Violin w/case: Schenectady, New York, 1986
                                                900/1,200 NS

BIANCHI, PASQUALE [Bf7/10514] American Violin
w/case: Schenectady, New York, 1984   1,000/1,400
$863   £526   DM1,535   ¥119,818

BIMBI, BARTOLOMEO [S3/36] Violin w/case:
Tuscany, c. 1760 (Max Möller, Amsterdam, October
2, 1962)   46,872/58,590 NS

BIMBI, BARTOLOMEO [S1117/394] Violin w/case:
Tuscany, c. 1760 (Max Möller, Amsterdam, October
2, 1962)   33,400/50,100 NS

BIRD, RICHMOND HENRY [P11/88] Good English
Violin in immediate playing condition, w/case: 1925
                                                2,520/3,360 NS

BISCH, PAUL (workshop of) [Sk5/74] French Violin
                                                1,800/2,200
$1,725   £1,035   DM3,071   ¥229,390

BISIACH, LEANDRO [B11/112] Very Fine Violin:
Milan, 1895   30,060/41,750
$36,490   £21,850   DM60,962   ¥4,435,332

BISIACH, LEANDRO [C4/172] Italian Violin
(Kenneth Warren & Son, Ltd., Chicago, May 6,
1997)   33,400/41,750 NS

BISIACH, LEANDRO [P4/97] Good Italian Violin in
immediate playing condition, w/double case: Milan,
1896   25,005/33,340 NS

BISIACH, LEANDRO [P11/55] Good Italian Violin
in immediate playing condition, w/double case:
Milan, 1896   23,520/30,240
$27,048   £16,100   DM45,080   ¥3,232,719

BISIACH, LEANDRO [S10/53] Violin w/case, bow:
Milan, 1906   43,400/49,600 NS

BISIACH, LEANDRO & GIACOMO [Sk5/70] Good
Modern Italian Violin: Milan, 1972 (maker's, Milan,
May 14, 1972)   16,000/18,000 NS

BISIACH, LEANDRO (II) & GIACOMO [S6/22]
Violin w/case: Milan, 1964   24,750/29,700
$26,565   £16,100   DM47,817   ¥3,830,995

BISIACH, LEANDRO (II) & GIACOMO [S1117/37]
Violin: Milan, c. 1960   20,040/25,050 NS

BISIACH, LEANDRO (II) & GIACOMO [S10/119]
Violin: Milan, 1973   12,400/15,500 NS

BISIACH FAMILY (MEMBER OF) (attributed to)
[P4/81] Fine and Handsome Italian Violin in immediate playing condition, w/case   16,670/25,005 NS

BISIACH FAMILY (MEMBER OF) (attributed to)
[P11/47] Fine and Handsome Italian Violin in immediate playing condition, w/case   11,760/15,120
$13,138   £7,820   DM21,896   ¥1,570,178

BLANCHARD, PAUL [P4/67] Good French Violin
with some rib and upper-back restoration: Lyons,
1897   5,001/8,335 NS

BLANCHI, ALBERTO [S3/13] Violin w/case, bow:
Nice, 1932   13,392/20,088 NS

BLONDELET, EMILE [B5/284] Violin   2,445/1,956
$2,062   £1,265   DM3,669   ¥276,946

BLONDELET, H. EMILE [C11/159] French Violin
                                                1,670/2,004
$1,632   £977   DM2,726   ¥198,321

BLONDELET, H. EMILE [P4/84] Good French
Violin in immediate playing condition: Paris, 1928
                                                3,334/5,001 NS

BLONDELET, H. EMILE [P10/29] Good French
Violin in immediate playing condition, w/case: Paris,
1924   3,400/5,100 NS

BLONDELET, H. EMILE [P12/26] Good French
Violin in immediate playing condition, w/case: Paris,
1924   2,505/3,340 NS

BOCQUAY, JACQUES [C4/191] French Violin
w/case (Fernand Billottet, Paris, November 29, 1936)
                                                5,010/6,680
$17,285   £10,350   DM32,085   ¥2,312,604

BODOR, JOHN JR. [Sk5/127] American Violin w/case: Churchville, Pennsylvania (maker's, Churchville, Pennsylvania, February 14, 1990)
3,000/4,000
$2,875   £1,725   DM5,118   ¥382,317

BOERNER, LAWRENCE E. [Bf2/4119] Violin: El Cajon, California, 1978   2,000/2,500 NS

BOERNER, LAWRENCE E. [Bf7/10475] Violin w/case   1,800/2,250 NS

BOLLER, MICHAEL (ascribed to) [C11/342] German Violin   1,670/2,505 NS

BORRIERO, FRANCESCO [S10/150] Violin: Schio, 1854   6,200/7,440 NS

BOSSI, GIUSEPPE (attributed to) [B11/81] Violin (Dario D'Attili)   5,010/8,350
$4,801   £2,875   DM8,021   ¥583,596

BOULANGEOT, JULES CAMILLE [P11/60] Good Violin in immediate playing condition, w/case: Brussels, 1929   2,520/3,360
$3,671   £2,185   DM6,118   ¥438,726

BOULLANGIER, CHARLES [B6/106] Fine Violin: London   10,020/16,700 NS

BOULLANGIER, CHARLES [B11/149] Fine Violin: London   8,350/11,690 NS

BOULLANGIER, CHARLES [C4/130] English Violin
1,670/2,505
$3,265   £1,955   DM6,061   ¥436,825

BOULLANGIER, CHARLES [P11/95] Good Violin that will gleam when cleaned: London, 1886
3,360/5,040
$6,182   £3,680   DM10,304   ¥738,907

BOYES, ARNOLD [S1117/388] Violin: Leeds, 1974
5,010/6,680 NS

BRETON [B5/227] Violin   244/326
$169   £104   DM300   ¥22,659

BRETON [C11/329] French Violin w/case, 2 bows
1,336/2,004
$1,344   £805   DM2,246   ¥163,407

BRETON [C11/357] French Violin   835/1,169 NS

BRETON [C11/370] French Half-Size Violin 501/668
$768   £460   DM1,283   ¥93,375

BRETON [P11/45] Good French Violin in immediate playing condition, w/case: c. 1800 (J. & A. Beare, London, March 17, 1969)   1,680/2,520
$3,091   £1,840   DM5,152   ¥369,454

BRETON BREVETE [Bf7/10353] French Violin: c. 1940   700/1,200 NS

BRIGGS, JAMES WILLIAM [B3/157] Violin: Glasgow, 1897   6,696/10,044 NS

BRIGGS, JAMES WILLIAM [B6/103] Good Violin: Glasgow, 1897   5,010/6,680 NS

BRIGGS, JAMES WILLIAM [B10/158] Good Violin: Glasgow, 1897   5,100/6,800 NS

BROWN, JAMES [S3/255] Violin w/case: London, c. 1820 (D.R. Hill, Great Missenden, April 15, 1994)   5,022/8,370 NS

BROWN, JAMES [S6/125] Violin: London, 1789
7,425/9,075 NS

BROWN, JAMES [S1117/141] Violin w/case: London, c. 1820 (D.R. Hill, Great Missenden, April 15, 1994)   3,006/4,175 NS

BRULLO, LORENZO R. [Bf7/10483] Good American Violin w/case: El Cajon, California, 1980
1,200/1,600 NS

BRYANT, L.D. [Sk11/307] American Violin w/case, 3 bows: Boston, 1917   800/1,200
$489   £293   DM826   ¥59,628

BUCKMAN, GEORGE H. [C4/215] English Violin w/case, bow   1,169/1,670
$1,632   £977   DM3,029   ¥218,301

BULLARD, OLIN [Sk11/434] American Violin w/case, bow: Bridgeport, 1918   1,600/1,800
$920   £552   DM1,555   ¥112,240

BYROM, JOHN [P4/73] Good English Violin in immediate playing condition: Liverpool, 1890
6,668/8,335
$7,668   £4,600   DM14,205   ¥1,024,098

CALLIER, FRANK [Sk5/386] American Violin w/case: St Louis, Missouri   600/800
$690   £414   DM1,228   ¥91,756

CAMILLI, CAMILLO [B11/91] Very Fine Italian Violin in an exceptional state of preservation: Mantova, 1739   83,500/116,900
$134,435   £80,500   DM224,595   ¥16,340,695

CAMILLI, CAMILLO (attributed to) [Bf9/4608] Good Italian Violin w/case, 2 bows: Mantua, c. 1750 (Emil Hermann, January 13, 1930)   14,000/18,000
$16,000   £9,600   DM27,040   ¥2,129,120

CANTOV, JULIUS (attributed to) [P12/47] Good Violin w/case, bow: Germany, 1896   668/835
$845   £506   DM1,397   ¥98,822

CAPELA, DOMINGOS [S1117/11] Violin w/case: Anta Espinho, 1956   4,676/5,845 NS

CAPELLINI, VIRGILIO [S3/341] Violin w/case: Cremona, 1953   3,348/5,022 NS

CAPICCHIONI, MARIO [S1117/33] Violin w/case, cover: Rimini, 1976   10,020/13,360
$9,603   £5,750   DM16,043   ¥1,167,193

CAPPA, GIOFFREDO [S6/135] Violin w/case, bow: Saluzzo, c. 1860 (Herbert Moritz Monnig, Ebingen, April 5, 1976)   82,500/99,000 NS

CARCASSI, LORENZO [Bf2/4180] Fine Violin: Florence, c. 1750 (David Jones, January 26, 1994)
25,000/35,000
$14,375   £8,798   DM26,105   ¥1,785,088

CARCASSI, LORENZO & TOMMASO [B6/122] Very Fine Italian Violin: Florence, 1747 (W.E. Hill & Sons)   58,450/75,150 NS

CARCASSI, LORENZO & TOMMASO [B11/126]
Very Fine Italian Violin: Florence, 1747 (W.E. Hill &
Sons)   50,100/66,800
$49,933   £29,900   DM83,421   ¥6,069,401

CARCASSI, LORENZO & TOMMASO
[S1117/373] Violin w/case: Florence, 1765 (L.P.
Balmforth & Son, Leeds, December 1970)
                                       50,100/66,800
$48,013   £28,750   DM80,213   ¥5,835,963

CARLETTI, CARLO [C11/182] Italian Violin w/case,
2 bows   8,350/11,690
$10,563   £6,325   DM17,647   ¥1,283,912

CARLETTI, CARLO (attributed to) [S10/67] Violin
w/case   2,480/3,720 NS

CARLETTI, GABRIELE [S10/66] Violin: Pieve di
Cento, 1984 (maker's, September 1, 1997)
                                    3,720/4,960 NS

CARLETTI, GENUZIO [S6/16] Violin w/case: Pieve
di Cento, 1936   3,300/4,950
$4,744   £2,875   DM8,539   ¥684,106

CARLETTI, GENUZIO (ascribed to) [Sk11/206]
Modern Italian Violin: Pieve di Cento, 1956
                                    4,500/5,500
$4,888   £2,933   DM8,260   ¥596,275

CARTWRIGHT, CHARLES D. [Sk5/419] American
Violin w/case, 2 bows: Berlin, Massachusetts
                                    1,200/1,400 NS

CARTWRIGHT, CHARLES D. [Sk11/361] American
Violin w/case, 2 bows: Berlin, Massachusetts
                                    800/1,200 NS

CARY, ALPHONSE [S3/46] Violin w/case: London or
Newbury, 1890   2,511/3,348 NS

CARY, ALPHONSE [S1117/392] Violin w/case: 1890
                                    1,670/2,505 NS

CASTAGNERI, ANDREA [S1117/393] Violin
w/case, 2 bows: Paris, c. 1745   10,020/13,360 NS

CASTELLO, PAOLO [S1117/370] Violin w/double
case: Genoa, 1779 (Rembert Wurlitzer, New York,
July 2, 1952)   33,400/41,750 NS

CASTELLO, PAOLO [Sk11/77] Italian Violin w/case:
Genoa, 1778 (W.E. Hill & Sons, London, January 8,
1917)   8,000/12,000
$10,350   £6,210   DM17,492   ¥1,262,700

CAUSSIN, F.N. [B11/135] Violin   3,340/5,010 NS

CAUSSIN, FRANCOIS [B11/137] English Violin:
London, 1917   4,175/5,010 NS

CAUSSIN, FRANCOIS (attributed to) [P12/31]
French Violin in immediate playing condition, w/case,
bow: c. 1880   835/1,002
$960   £575   DM1,587   ¥112,298

CAVALLI, ARISTIDE [B3/162] Italian Violin:
Cremona, 1905   3,348/5,022
$2,310   £1,380   DM4,274   ¥307,864

CAVALLI, ARISTIDE [S1117/48] Violin w/case:
Cremona, 1920   1,670/3,340
$3,073   £1,840   DM5,134   ¥373,502

CAVALLO, LUIGI [S10/4] Child's Violin: Noceto,
1851   1,860/3,100 NS

CAVANI, VINCENZO [Sk11/80] Modern Italian
Violin: 1936   6,000/8,000 NS

CELONIATO, GIOVANNI FRANCESCO [S6/35]
Violin w/case: Turin, c. 1720   62,700/74,250 NS

CERRUTI, RICARDO [B6/78] Violin
                                    6,680/10,020 NS

CERUTI, ENRICO [C11/212] Fine Italian Violin
w/case, bow   41,750/50,100 NS

CERUTI, ENRICO (ascribed to) [S1117/143] Violin
w/double case (L.P. Balmforth, Leeds, January 23,
1969)   10,020/13,360
$31,688   £18,975   DM52,940   ¥3,851,735

CERUTI, GIOVANNI BATTISTA (attributed to)
[Bf9/4596] Violin w/case   1,700/2,250
$1,610   £966   DM2,721   ¥214,243

CHANNON, FREDERICK WILLIAM [B11/75]
Violin: 1925   4,175/5,845
$4,321   £2,588   DM7,219   ¥525,237

CHANOT [P4/36] Fine Mute Violin in good condition, w/case: c. 1890   1,667/2,501 NS

CHANOT, GEORGE [B11/132] Fine French Violin:
Paris, 1848   20,040/25,050
$40,331   £24,150   DM67,379   ¥4,902,209

CHANOT, GEORGE [P4/94] Good French Violin
with old table restorations, w/case, 2 bows: Paris,
1858   25,005/33,340 NS

CHANOT, GEORGE [P11/58] Good French Violin
with old table restorations, w/case, cover, 2 bows:
Paris, 1858   20,160/25,200 NS

CHANOT, GEORGE ADOLPH (workshop of)
[Sk11/94] Violin w/case: Manchester, 1899
                                    3,500/5,500
$4,600   £2,760   DM7,774   ¥561,200

CHANOT, GEORGES [Bf2/4174] Fine and Handsome Violin w/case: Paris, c. 1850 (Dario D'Attili,
April 23, 1985)   20,000/25,000
$32,200   £19,706   DM58,475   ¥3,998,596

CHANOT, GEORGES (II) [S3/24] Violin w/case:
Paris, 1840   2,009/2,678
$1,925   £1,150   DM3,562   ¥256,554

CHANOT, JOSEPH ANTHONY [S1117/9] Violin:
London, 1910   7,515/9,185 NS

CHANOT FAMILY (MEMBER OF) [S1117/148]
Mute Violin: England, c. 1900   1,670/2,505 NS

CHAPPUY (attributed to) [B2/117] French Violin
                                    820/1,148
$679   £414   DM1,235   ¥85,756

CHAPPUY, NICOLAS AUGUSTIN [Bf9/4611]
French Violin w/case, bow: Paris, 1870   2,000/3,000
$1,840   £1,104   DM3,110   ¥244,849

CHAPPUY, NICOLAS AUGUSTIN [S10/18] Violin:
Mirecourt, c. 1780   1,240/1,860 NS

CHAPPUY, NICOLAS AUGUSTIN [Sk5/128] French
Violin w/case: Paris, c. 1775   1,800/2,200
$2,875   £1,725   DM5,118   ¥382,317

CHERPITEL, L. [Bf9/4612] Good French Violin:
Mirecourt, 1925   4,000/5,500 NS

CHEVRIER, CLAUDE [S1117/50] Violin w/case,
bow, cover: Mirecourt, mid 19th C.   1,670/2,505 NS

CHEVRIER, CLAUDE [Sk5/303] French Violin:
Mirecourt   800/1,200
$1,093   £656   DM1,945   ¥145,281

CHIOCCHI, GAETANO [P4/77] Fine, Handsome,
and Rare Italian Violin in immediate playing condition, w/case: Padua, 1872 (J. & A. Beare, London,
December 9, 1997)   30,006/36,674 NS

CHIPOT-VUILLAUME [C11/200] French Violin
w/case, bow   1,670/2,505
$2,113   £1,265   DM3,529   ¥256,782

CHIPOT-VUILLAUME (workshop of) [Bf9/4613]
French Violin: Mirecourt, c. 1895   1,400/2,000
$1,380   £828   DM2,332   ¥183,637

CHIPOT-VUILLAUME (workshop of) [Sk11/209]
French Violin   800/1,200
$1,955   £1,173   DM3,304   ¥238,510

CIOFFI, A. [B11/66] Neapolitan Violin
                                 1,670/20,040 NS

COCKER, LAWRENCE [C11/147] English Violin
w/case, bow   1,670/2,505
$2,113   £1,265   DM3,529   ¥256,782

COFFMANN, C.R. [Bf7/10470] Interesing American
Violin: c. 1930   300/500 NS

COLAPIETRO, FRANCESCO [C11/152] Italian
Violin   5,010/6,680 NS

COLIN, JEAN BAPTISTE [C11/167] French Violin
w/case, 2 bows   835/1,336
$1,440   £862   DM2,405   ¥174,977

COLIN, JEAN BAPTISTE [C11/177] French Violin
                                 1,002/1,336 NS

COLIN, JEAN BAPTISTE [C11/350] French Violin
                                   835/1,336
$1,247   £747   DM2,084   ¥151,634

COLIN, JEAN BAPTISTE [Sk11/365] French Violin:
1905   600/800
$920   £552   DM1,555   ¥112,240

COLLIN-MEZIN (attributed to) [P11/27] French
Violin in immediate playing condition, w/case: 1949
                                 2,520/3,024 NS

COLLIN-MEZIN (workshop of) [Bf9/4585] French
Violin w/case: Paris, c. 1895   2,000/4,000
$1,150   £690   DM1,944   ¥153,031

COLLIN-MEZIN (workshop of) [Bf9/4604] French
Violin w/case: Mirecourt, c. 1900   2,250/2,750 NS

COLLIN-MEZIN, CH.J.B. [B3/127] French Violin:
Paris, 1892   3,348/5,022
$4,620   £2,760   DM8,548   ¥615,728

COLLIN-MEZIN, CH.J.B. [B3/141] French Violin:
Paris   2,511/3,348 NS

COLLIN-MEZIN, CH.J.B. [B3/172] French Violin:
Paris, 1892   3,348/5,022
$3,850   £2,300   DM7,123   ¥513,107

COLLIN-MEZIN, CH.J.B. [B3/196] French Violin:
Paris, 1889   6,696/10,044
$7,700   £4,600   DM14,246   ¥1,026,214

COLLIN-MEZIN, CH.J.B. [B5/268] Violin
                                 1,956/2,445 NS

COLLIN-MEZIN, CH.J.B. [B7/132] Violin
                                 1,650/2,475 NS

COLLIN-MEZIN, CH.J.B. [C4/142] French Violin
w/case   3,006/4,175
$3,457   £2,070   DM6,417   ¥462,521

COLLIN-MEZIN, CH.J.B. [C4/166] French Violin
                                 3,006/4,175
$4,609   £2,760   DM8,556   ¥616,694

COLLIN-MEZIN, CH.J.B. [C4/195] French Violin
w/case   3,006/4,175
$3,649   £2,185   DM6,774   ¥488,216

COLLIN-MEZIN, CH.J.B. [P4/85] Good French
Violin requiring modest table restoration: Paris, 1893
                                 3,334/5,001
$3,451   £2,070   DM6,392   ¥460,844

COLLIN-MEZIN, CH.J.B. [P4/142] Good French
Violin in good condition: Paris (maker's)
                                 1,667/2,501 NS

COLLIN-MEZIN, CH.J.B. [S3/10] Violin w/case:
Mirecourt, c. 1920   3,013/4,185 NS

COLLIN-MEZIN, CH.J.B. [S3/254] Violin w/case:
Mirecourt, 1920   2,511/3,348
$2,503   £1,495   DM4,630   ¥333,520

COLLIN-MEZIN, CH.J.B. [S6/33] Violin: Paris,
1892 (Wilhelm Heckenthaler, April 18, 1991)
                                 4,125/5,775 NS

COLLIN-MEZIN, CH.J.B. [Sk11/121] French Violin:
1884   2,500/3,500
$4,255   £2,553   DM7,191   ¥519,110

COLLIN-MEZIN, CH.J.B. [Sk11/208] French Violin:
1880   2,200/2,400
$3,565   £2,139   DM6,025   ¥434,930

COLLIN-MEZIN, CH.J.B. (workshop of) [Sk11/419]
French Violin w/case   1,200/1,400
$1,610   £966   DM2,721   ¥196,420

COLLIN-MEZIN, CH.J.B. (FILS) [B11/117] French
Violin: Paris, 1892   3,340/5,010
$3,649   £2,185   DM6,096   ¥443,533

COLLIN-MEZIN, CH.J.B. (FILS) [S1117/1] Violin
w/case, bow: Paris, 1888 (L.P. Balmforth, Leeds,
November 1971)   4,175/5,845
$4,801   £2,875   DM8,021   ¥583,596

COLLIN-MEZIN, CH.J.B. (FILS) [S1117/62] Violin:
Paris, 1892 (Wilhelm Heckenthaler, April 18, 1991)
                                 3,340/5,010 NS

COLLIN-MEZIN, CH.J.B. (FILS) [S1117/371]
Violin: Paris, 1891   3,340/5,010
$3,457   £2,070   DM5,775   ¥420,189

COLLIN-MEZIN, CH.J.B. (FILS) (attributed to)
[P12/81] Good French Violin with minor restorable
blemishes: 1911   835/1,002 NS

COLT, E.W. [Bf7/10416] Violin: c. 1927
                800/1,200 NS

CONIA, STEFANO [S3/249] Violin: Cremona, 1993
(maker's, July 24, 1993)   5,859/7,533
$6,160   £3,680   DM11,397   ¥820,971

CONIA, STEFANO [S6/138] Violin: Tatabanya,
1971   3,300/4,950 NS

CONNELAN, MICHAEL [P12/216] Violin requiring
minor regluing: Polstead, 1989   334/501
$384   £230   DM635   ¥44,919

CONTINO, ALFREDO [S6/21] Violin w/case:
Naples, c. 1920   16,500/24,750
$18,975   £11,500   DM34,155   ¥2,736,425

CORDANUS, J. [B6/92] Italian Violin: Genoa,
c. 1770 (W.E. Hill & Sons)   20,040/25,050 NS

CORDANUS, J. [B11/118] Italian Violin: Genoa,
c. 1760 (W.E. Hill & Sons)   13,360/20,040
$24,967   £14,950   DM41,711   ¥3,034,701

CORNELLISSEN, MARTEN [C4/164] Violin w/case
                5,010/6,680 NS

CORSINI, GIORGIO [S3/5] Violin: Rome, 1976
                3,348/5,022 NS

COSSU, FRANCESCO [B3/156] Violin: 1970
                1,674/2,511 NS

COSSU, FRANCESCO [B6/111] Italian Violin: 1970
                1,670/25,050 NS

COUCH, C.M. [Sk5/275] American Violin w/case:
1927   400/600
$345   £207   DM614   ¥45,878

COUTURIEUX, M. [C11/318] French Violin w/case
                1,169/1,670
$768   £460   DM1,283   ¥93,375

CRASKE, GEORGE [B3/122] Good English Violin
                3,348/5,022
$3,850   £2,300   DM7,123   ¥513,107

CRASKE, GEORGE [B3/143] English Violin
                3,348/5,022
$5,005   £2,990   DM9,260   ¥667,039

CRASKE, GEORGE [B6/118] English Violin
                5,010/8,350
$5,762   £3,450   DM10,316   ¥792,741

CRASKE, GEORGE [S3/4] Violin w/case: c. 1860
                5,022/6,696
$6,160   £3,680   DM11,397   ¥820,971

CRASKE, GEORGE [S3/260] Violin w/case:
Stockport, 1830   3,348/5,022
$5,390   £3,220   DM9,972   ¥718,350

CRASKE, GEORGE [S6/38] Violin w/case, bow:
c. 1860   3,300/4,950
$3,416   £2,070   DM6,148   ¥492,557

CRASKE, GEORGE [S6/133] Violin: c. 1860
                4,125/5,775 NS

CRASKE, GEORGE [S1117/2] Violin w/case, bow:
Stockport, 1860   4,175/5,845
$4,993   £2,990   DM8,342   ¥606,940

CRASKE, GEORGE [S1117/378] Violin w/case:
Stockport, c. 1850   2,505/3,340 NS

CRASKE, GEORGE [Sk11/68] Good English Violin
                4,000/6,000
$5,463   £3,278   DM9,232   ¥666,425

CREMONINI, VIRGILIO [B6/81] Violin: 1995
                2,505/4,175 NS

CURLETTO, ANSELMO [S10/39] Violin: Turin,
1958 (maker's, October 10, 1963) 18,600/24,800 NS

CURLETTO, ANSELMO [S10/118] Violin w/bow:
Turin, 1960 (maker's, November 1963)
                18,600/24,800 NS

CUYPERS, JOHANNES [P4/63] Fine and Handsome
Dutch Violin with skillful old table restorations: The
Hague, 1782 (L.P. Balmforth & Son, Leeds, April
1971)   25,005/33,340
$28,756   £17,250   DM53,268   ¥3,840,368

CUYPERS, JOHANNES [P4/95] Fine and Handsome
Dutch Violin in immediate playing condition: The
Hague, 1797 (W.E. Hill & Sons, Buckinghamshire,
May 25, 1976)   33,340/41,675
$38,341   £23,000   DM71,024   ¥5,120,490

CUYPERS, JOHANNES FRANCIS [S1117/383]
Violin w/double case, cover: Amsterdam, 1812
(Johann Stüber, The Hague, December 3, 1954)
                20,040/25,050
$19,205   £11,500   DM32,085   ¥2,334,385

CUYPERS, JOHANNES THEODORUS [S1117/136]
Violin: The Hague, 1765 (W.E. Hill & Sons, London,
February 17, 1939)   30,060/41,750
$28,808   £17,250   DM48,128   ¥3,501,578

DAHLEN, FRANS WALDEMAR [S1117/4] Violin
w/case: Gothenburg, 1946   1,336/2,004
$1,344   £805   DM2,246   ¥163,407

DAHLEN, FRANS WALDEMAR [S1117/60] Violin
w/case: Gothenburg, 1951   1,336/2,004
$2,113   £1,265   DM3,529   ¥256,782

DALL'AGLIO, GIUSEPPE [Bf9/4588] Violin w/case
                4,500/6,000 NS

DALLA COSTA, PIETRO ANTONIO (attributed to)
[Sk11/102] Fine Italian Violin w/case: Treviso, 1760
                18,000/22,000
$20,700   £12,420   DM34,983   ¥2,525,400

DALLINGER, SEBASTIAN [P11/39] Good Violin in
immediate playing condition: Wien, 1790
                4,200/5,880 NS

DARBY [B7/220] Violin   2,475/3,300 NS

DARBEY, GEORGE [S3/2] Violin w/case: Bristol, 1893   3,348/5,022
$2,888   £1,725   DM5,342   ¥384,830

DARCHE, HILAIRE [C4/158] Good Belgian Violin
                                        8,350/11,690
$11,523   £6,900   DM21,390   ¥1,541,736

DARCHE, HILAIRE [S3/264] Violin w/case: Brussels, 1913   6,696/8,370 NS

DARCHE, NICHOLAS [Bf2/4173] Violin w/case, violin, bass bow (Rudolph Wurlitzer Co., December 3, 1947)   2,000/3,000
$1,610   £985   DM2,924   ¥199,930

DE BARBIERI, PAOLO [Bf9/4595] Very Fine Violin: Genoa, 1928   16,000/20,000 NS

DEBLAYE, ALBERT [C11/194] French Violin
                                        1,670/2,004
$1,921   £1,150   DM3,209   ¥233,439

DEBLAYE, ALBERT (attributed to) [P4/151] Good Violin in good condition: Mirecourt, c. 1920
                                        1,000/1,334 NS

DE COMBLE, AMBROISE [P4/59] Good Violin requiring restoration, w/case: Tournay, 1757
                                        5,001/6,668
$7,668   £4,600   DM14,205   ¥1,024,098

DEGANI, EUGENIO [B11/147] Fine Italian Violin: Venice, 1898 (W.E. Hill & Sons)   20,040/25,050
$32,649   £19,550   DM54,545   ¥3,968,455

DEGANI, EUGENIO [P11/32] Good Violin with minor restorable table blemishes, w/case, bow: Venice, 1897   16,800/25,200
$28,014   £16,675   DM46,690   ¥3,348,173

DEGANI, GIULIO [B11/77] Fine Italian Violin
                                        20,040/25,050
$24,006   £14,375   DM40,106   ¥2,917,981

DEGANI, GIULIO [C4/169] Italian Violin w/case, 2 bows   16,700/20,040
$17,285   £10,350   DM32,085   ¥2,312,604

DEGANI, GIULIO [C11/186] Italian Violin w/case
                                        16,700/20,040
$21,126   £12,650   DM35,294   ¥2,567,824

DEGANI, GIULIO [P4/56] Fine and Handsome Italian Violin in immediate playing condition, w/case: Venice, 1915   10,002/13,336
$10,927   £6,555   DM20,242   ¥1,459,340

DELEPLANQUE, GERARD J. [B3/165] French Violin retaining the original neck and fingerboard: Lille, 1784   2,511/3,348
$2,599   £1,553   DM4,808   ¥346,347

DEL LUNGO, ALFREDO [S10/1] Violin: Florence, 1942   1,860/3,100
$1,783   £1,035   DM2,875   ¥209,875

DERAZEY, H. [B11/146] Fine French Violin
                                        10,020/13,360 NS

DERAZEY, HONORE [B3/186] Very Fine French Violin   20,088/25,110 NS

DERAZEY, HONORE [S6/8] Violin w/case, bow: Mirecourt, c. 1880   3,300/4,950
$3,416   £2,070   DM6,148   ¥492,557

DERAZEY, HONORE [S1117/14] Violin w/case: Mirecourt, c. 1840 (L.P. Balmforth & Son, Leeds, November 15, 1972)   10,020/13,360
$15,364   £9,200   DM25,668   ¥1,867,508

DERAZEY, HONORE (workshop of) [Sk11/90] French Violin w/case: Mirecourt   1,800/2,200
$1,840   £1,104   DM3,110   ¥224,480

DERAZEY, JUSTIN [B3/154] Fine French Violin
                                        2,511/3,348
$3,273   £1,955   DM6,055   ¥436,141

DERAZEY, JUSTIN [B11/129] Violin
                                        2,505/3,340 NS

DERAZEY, JUSTIN [C4/181] French Violin
                                        4,175/5,010
$4,801   £2,875   DM8,913   ¥642,390

DERAZEY, JUSTIN [S3/275] Violin w/case: Mirecourt, c. 1880   4,185/5,859 NS

DERAZEY, JUSTIN (attributed to) [P11/98] Good French Violin in good condition, w/case, bow: c. 1870
                                        2,016/2,520 NS

DERAZEY FAMILY (MEMBER OF) [P11/42] French Violin in immediate playing condition: c. 1870 (Gilles Chancereul, Paris, May 27, 1997)
                                        6,720/7,560 NS

DESIATO, GIUSEPPE (attributed to) [Sk5/402] Violin w/case, 2 bows (John Chapin, San Francisco, September 8, 1952)   2,800/3,200
$3,220   £1,932   DM5,732   ¥428,196

DESIATO, VINCENZO (attributed to) [S1117/369] Violin w/case, bow: c. 1925   2,338/3,006 NS

DE TOPPANI, ANGELO [S1117/367] Violin: Rome, 1741 (Dario D'Attili, Winter Garden, Florida, July 14, 1993)   11,690/13,360
$7,490   £4,485   DM12,513   ¥910,410

DE ZORZI, VALENTINO [B3/185] Fine Florentine Violin: 1906   20,088/25,110 NS

DE ZORZI, VALENTINO [Sk5/57] Italian Violin w/case: Florence, 1890   6,000/8,000
$14,950   £8,970   DM26,611   ¥1,988,051

DICKENSON, EDWARD [C4/132] English Violin
                                        1,169/1,670
$1,344   £805   DM2,496   ¥179,869

DIEUDONNE, AMEDEE [Bf2/4179] Violin: Mirecourt, 1925   2,700/3,000 NS

DIEUDONNE, AMEDEE [Bf9/4598] French Violin w/case, cover   1,900/2,500
$1,725   £1,035   DM2,915   ¥229,546

DIEUDONNE, AMEDEE [C11/202] French Violin
                                        1,670/2,004 NS

DIEUDONNE, AMEDEE [P10/59] Fine and Handsome French Violin in immediate playing condition, w/case, bow stick: 1937   3,400/5,100
$4,106   £2,415   DM6,690   ¥483,193

DIEUDONNE, AMEDEE [S6/27] Violin: Mirecourt, 1948 (maker's)   3,300/4,950
$2,846   £1,725   DM5,123   ¥410,464

DIEUDONNE, AMEDEE [Sk5/117] French Violin: 1925   2,200/2,400
$2,300   £1,380   DM4,094   ¥305,854

DIEUDONNE, AMEDEE (attributed to) [P10/82] Good French Violin in good condition: Mirecourt, 1948   2,040/3,060
$1,916   £1,127   DM3,122   ¥225,490

DIEUDONNE, AMEDEE (attributed to) [P12/54] Good French Violin: 1934   2,505/3,340 NS

DOBRITCHCOV, FILIP [Bf9/4592] Good Modern Violin w/case, cover   2,500/3,500
$2,588   £1,553   DM4,373   ¥344,319

DOLLING, ROBERT A. [Sk11/84] Violin w/case: Markneukirchen, c. 1925   1,000/1,500
$1,495   £897   DM2,527   ¥182,390

DORELLI, GIOVANNI (ascribed to) [S1117/145] Violin with later head (L.P. Balmforth & Son, Leeds, October 2, 1967)   3,340/5,010 NS

DROZEN, F.X. [S3/22] Violin w/case: Turnov, 1945   1,004/1,339 NS

DUKE, RICHARD [B11/124] English Violin: London, c. 1780 (W.E. Hill & Sons)   8,350/11,690 NS

DUKE, RICHARD [C11/198] English Violin
                                                   5,010/6,680
$4,993   £2,990   DM8,342   ¥606,940

DUKE, RICHARD [P4/51] English Violin in immediate playing condition, w/case: London   2,501/3,334
$4,218   £2,530   DM7,813   ¥563,254

DVORAK, JAN BAPTISTA [S3/37] Violin w/case: Prague, 1886   3,348/5,022
$5,390   £3,220   DM9,972   ¥718,350

DYKES, ARTHUR WILLIAM [P10/61] Good English Violin in good condition, w/case, bow: Leeds, 1901
                                                   850/1,020 NS

DYKES, ARTHUR WILLIAM [P12/27] Good English Violin in good condition, w/case, bow: Leeds, 1901
                                                   835/1,002
$1,229   £736   DM2,031   ¥143,741

DYKES, GEORGE [C11/138] English Violin w/case, bow   2,004/2,505
$4,609   £2,760   DM7,700   ¥560,252

EBERLE, JOHANN ULRICH [S3/47] Violin w/case, 2 bows: Prague, 1767   8,370/11,718
$9,240   £5,520   DM17,095   ¥1,231,457

EBERLE, JOHANN ULRICH [S6/126] Violin: Prague, c. 1760   3,300/4,950 NS

EBERLE, JOHANN ULRICH [S6/142] Violin w/case, cover, 2 bows: Prague, 1757   6,600/9,900 NS

EBERLE, TOMASO [B11/104] Fine Neapolitan Violin: c. 1780   41,750/58,450
$65,297   £39,100   DM109,089   ¥7,936,909

EKSTRAND, GUSTAF [S3/7] Violin w/case, bow: Stockholm, 1932   3,348/5,022 NS

ERBA, PAOLO [S10/147] Violin: Mariano Comense, c. 1910   6,200/8,680 NS

ESPOSITO, RAFFAELE (attributed to) [Bf7/10485] Violin   1,200/1,800
$1,093   £666   DM1,945   ¥151,770

EWAN, DAVID [P12/240] Violin w/three-valve cornet: Scotland, 1906   251/334 NS

EWBANK, HENRY [Sk5/232] American Violin: Sterling, Illinois, 1947   400/600
$345   £207   DM614   ¥45,878

FABRICATORE, GENNARO [Bf2/4143] Violin w/case: Naples, 1799 (Dario D'Attili, July 10, 1990)
                                                   12,000/18,000 NS

FABRICATORE, GENNARO [Bf9/4590] Violin w/case, cover: Naples, 1799 (Dario D'Attile, July 10, 1990)   10,000/15,000 NS

FABRICATORE, GENNARO [S10/74] Violin: Naples, c. 1810   9,300/12,400 NS

FAGNOLA, ANNIBALE [P11/35] Italian Violin in immediate playing condition, w/case: Turin, 1910
                                                   36,960/42,000 NS

FAGNOLA, ANNIBALE (attributed to) [P4/65] Good Violin in immediate playing condition, w/double case   13,336/20,004 NS

FAGNOLA, ANNIBALE (attributed to) [P11/74] Good Violin in immediate playing condition, w/double case   10,080/11,760 NS

FAGNOLA, ANNIBALE (attributed to) [S10/148] Violin w/case: Piedmont, c. 1920   6,200/9,300
$12,121   £7,038   DM19,550   ¥1,427,150

FAGNOLA, H. [B11/138] Very Fine Italian Violin: Turin, 1931 (W.E. Hill & Sons)   41,750/58,450
$72,979   £43,700   DM121,923   ¥8,870,663

FALISSE, A. [P4/121] Good Violin in immediate playing condition: Brussels, 1929   5,001/6,668 NS

FARLEY, CHARLES E. [Sk5/258] American Violin w/case: 1886   600/800
$575   £345   DM1,024   ¥76,464

FAROTTI, CELESTE [S10/47] Violin w/case: Milan, 1909   6,200/9,300
$17,112   £9,936   DM27,600   ¥2,014,800

FENDT, BERNARD [Sk11/100] Fine English Violin w/case: London, c. 1810 (Kenneth Warren & Son, Chicago, November 28, 1986)   15,000/20,000 NS

FENDT, FRANCOIS (attributed to) [P4/102] Interesting French Violin in immediate playing condition: Paris, c. 1790   6,668/8,335 NS

FENT, FRANCOIS [S3/359] Violin: Paris, c. 1770 (William Lewis & Son, Chicago, June 5, 1950)
                                                   5,022/8,370
$4,235   £2,530   DM7,835   ¥564,418

FICKER, JOHANN CHRISTIAN [C11/203] German
Violin w/case, 2 bows   1,670/2,505
$2,113   £1,265   DM3,529   ¥256,782

FICKER, JOHANN GOTTLOB [Sk11/462] Violin
w/case: Markneukirchen, c. 1750   800/1,200
$1,840   £1,104   DM3,110   ¥224,480

FILIPPI, VITTORIO [S3/41] Violin w/case: Frascati,
1976 (maker's, November 4, 1997)   2,846/3,348
$3,080   £1,840   DM5,698   ¥410,486

FIORINI, GIUSEPPE (ascribed to) [S6/37] Violin
(Dario D'Attili, Durmont, November 10, 1992)
                                        16,500/24,750 NS

FISCHER, RAY [Bf7/10516] American Violin:
c. 1988   900/1,300 NS

FORST, HANS (workshop of) [Sk5/376] Child's
Violin: Mittenwald   1,200/1,400 NS

FORST, HANS (workshop of) [Sk11/408] Child's
Violin: Mittenwald   700/900
$978   £587   DM1,652   ¥119,255

FORSTER, WILLIAM [B11/103] English Violin
                                        5,010/8,350
$7,298   £4,370   DM12,192   ¥887,066

FORSTER, WILLIAM [P11/68] Violin with some
varnish loss on table, w/case, bow: London, c. 1790
(Phillips Son & Neale, August 21, 1979)
                                        3,360/5,040 NS

FOSCHI, GIORGIO [S3/33] Violin w/case: Carate
Brianza, 1974   5,022/6,696
$5,005   £2,990   DM9,260   ¥667,039

FREDI, RODOLFO [B3/144] Italian Violin: Rome,
1932   6,696/10,044
$4,235   £2,530   DM7,835   ¥564,418

FURBER [C4/227] English Violin   668/1,002 NS

GABRIELLI, GIOVANNI BATTISTA [S1117/49]
Violin w/double case, cover: Florence, c. 1770 (W.E.
Hill & Sons, London, September 24, 1957)
                                        41,750/58,450
$38,410   £23,000   DM64,170   ¥4,668,770

GADDA, GAETANO (attributed to) [C11/171]
Italian Violin w/case (Karl Roy, Mittenwald, April 12,
1995)   10,020/13,360 NS

GAFFINO, JOSEPH (attributed to) [Bf2/4169]
French Violin: Paris, late 19th C.   6,000/8,000 NS

GAGGINI (ascribed to) [P11/62] Violin in good condition, w/case: c. 1940   2,520/3,360
$2,898   £1,725   DM4,830   ¥346,363

GAGGINI, PIETRO (attributed to) [B3/182] Violin:
Nice, 1933   3,348/5,022 NS

GAGGINI, PIETRO (attributed to) [B6/95] Violin:
Nice, 1933   2,505/3,340 NS

GAGGINI, PIETRO (attributed to) [B11/136] Violin:
Nice, 1933   2,505/3,340 NS

GAGLIANO, ALESSANDRO [C4/200] Fine Italian
Violin (Kenneth Warren & Son, Ltd., Chicago,
October 5, 1979)   80,160/91,850 NS

GAGLIANO, FERDINAND [S3/266] Violin w/case:
Naples, c. 1780 (Emil Hjorth & Sønner, Copenhagen,
April 23, 1963)   75,330/92,070 NS

GAGLIANO, FERDINAND [S3/353] Violin w/case:
Naples, late 18th C.   30,132/40,176
$25,026   £14,950   DM46,300   ¥3,335,196

GAGLIANO, FERDINAND (attributed to) [Sk11/91]
Fine Neapolitan Violin: c. 1774 (Lyon & Healy,
Chicago, September 10, 1948)   35,000/45,000
$44,850   £26,910   DM75,797   ¥5,471,700

GAGLIANO, GIUSEPPE & ANTONIO [S6/151]
Violin w/case, cover: Naples, c. 1800
                                        66,000/99,000 NS

GAGLIANO, JOHANNES (attributed to) [Sk5/418]
Neapolitan Violin: c. 1800 (Dykes & Sons, London,
May 23, 1929)   5,000/7,000
$6,900   £4,140   DM12,282   ¥917,562

GAGLIANO, JOSEPH [C11/208] Italian Violin
w/case   50,100/66,800 NS

GAGLIANO, NICOLA [S3/34] Violin w/case:
Naples, 1752 (Caressa & Français, Paris, February
27, 1922)   66,960/100,440 NS

GAGLIANO, NICOLA [S3/240] Violin w/case:
Naples, c. 1740 (Helmut Möckel, Bonn, March 24,
1958)   75,330/100,440
$87,215   £52,100   DM161,354   ¥11,622,989

GAGLIANO, NICOLA [S6/41] Violin w/case:
Naples, c. 1750 (Hammmig & Co., Berlin, July 16,
1923)   99,000/132,000
$100,485   £60,900   DM180,873   ¥14,491,155

GAGLIANO, NICOLA [S6/134] Violin w/case:
Naples, c. 1760 (Hamilton Caswell, Bristol, June 11,
1992)   66,000/82,500
$71,445   £43,300   DM128,601   ¥10,303,235

GAGLIANO, NICOLA [S1117/66] Violin w/case:
Naples, 1752 (Caressa & Français, Paris, February
27, 1922)   58,450/75,150
$72,311   £43,300   DM120,807   ¥8,789,467

GAGLIANO, NICOLA (attributed to) [B3/147] Fine
Neapolitan Violin w/copy of same violin made by
Bernard Millant in 1954 (Maucotel & Deschamp)
                                        30,132/41,850
$25,026   £14,950   DM46,300   ¥3,335,196

GAGLIANO, NICOLO (II) [B3/198] Neapolitan
Violin: c. 1820–30 (J. & A. Beare, 1996)
                                        50,220/66,960 NS

GAGLIANO, RAFFAELE & ANTONIO (II)
[B6/116] Fine Italian Violin: Naples
                                        30,060/41,750 NS

GAGLIANO, RAFFAELE & ANTONIO (II)
(attributed to) [B11/114] Fine Neapolitan Violin
                                        20,040/25,050
$30,728   £18,400   DM51,336   ¥3,735,016

GAGLIANO FAMILY (MEMBER OF) [B3/183] Fine
Neapolitan Violin: Naples, c. 1800 (Henry Werro)
                                        33,480/50,220
$34,652   £20,700   DM64,108   ¥4,617,963

GAIBISSO, GIOVANNI BATTISTA [S10/117] Violin: Alassio, 1958   9,300/12,400 NS

GAIDA, GIOVANNI [B3/159] Fine Italian Violin
    13,392/20,088 NS

GALLA, ANTON [S6/6] Violin: 1956   2,310/2,970
$2,277   £1,380   DM4,099   ¥328,371

GALLA, ANTON [Sk5/65] Violin w/case: 1952
    2,500/3,500
$2,760   £1,656   DM4,913   ¥367,025

GAND, ADOLPHE CHARLES [C11/136] French Violin w/case   5,010/6,680 NS

GAND BROS. [C11/185] Fine French Violin w/case
    16,700/25,050
$19,205   £11,500   DM32,085   ¥2,334,385

GAND BROS. [P11/37] Fine and Handsome French Violin in good condition, w/case, cover: Paris, 1858
    10,080/11,760
$10,626   £6,325   DM17,710   ¥1,269,997

GAND & BERNARDEL [C11/207] French Violin w/case   10,020/13,360
$11,523   £6,900   DM19,251   ¥1,400,631

GAND & BERNARDEL [Sk11/72] Good French Violin w/case, bow: Paris, 1890   12,000/15,000
$16,100   £9,660   DM27,209   ¥1,964,200

GARTNER, EUGEN [S3/35] Violin w/case: Stuttgart, 1937   3,013/4,185 NS

GEISSENHOF, FRANZ [B11/105] Fine Violin: c. 1790   13,360/20,040
$20,165   £12,075   DM33,689   ¥2,451,104

GEISSENHOF, FRANZ [P4/83] Violin with some old restored blemishes, w/case: Vienna, 1804
    6,668/8,335 NS

GEISSENHOF, FRANZ [S1117/69] Violin w/case: Vienna, 1804   5,010/8,350
$5,377   £3,220   DM8,984   ¥653,628

GEMUNDER, AUGUST & SONS [Sk5/71] American Violin: New York, 1890   2,800/3,200 NS

GEMUNDER, AUGUST & SONS [Sk5/222] German Violin w/case, 2 bows   500/700
$575   £345   DM1,024   ¥76,464

GEMUNDER, AUGUST & SONS [Sk11/116] American Violin: New York, c. 1890   1,800/2,200 NS

GEMUNDER, GEORGE (SR.) [Bf2/4121] Fine Violin w/case: New York, 1888   10,000/12,000 NS

GENOVA, GIOVANNI BATTISTA [S6/152] Violin: Turin or Alessandria, c. 1770   39,600/46,200 NS

GIORDANI, ENRICO [S10/21] Violin w/case: Genoa, 1936   1,860/3,100 NS

GIORGIS, NICOLAUS [B6/88] Rare Italian Violin: Turin, 1732   8,350/11,690
$8,642   £5,175   DM15,473   ¥1,189,112

GIRARDI, MARIO [S10/0] Violin: Vicenza, 1918 (Roberto Lanaro, Padua, March 20, 1998)
    3,720/4,960 NS

GLASS, FRIEDRICH AUGUST [Bf7/10423] Good German Violin w/case: c. 1900   400/800
$403   £246   DM716   ¥55,915

GLENISTER, WILLIAM [S3/280] Violin: London, 1906   2,344/3,013 NS

GLENISTER, WILLIAM [S6/9] Violin w/case, violin bow, violoncello bow: London, 1924   2,310/2,970
$2,277   £1,380   DM4,099   ¥328,371

GLIER, ROBERT [Sk5/299] American Violin w/case, bow: Cincinnati, Ohio, 1914   1,400/1,600
$1,495   £897   DM2,661   ¥198,805

GOULD, JOHN ALFRED [Bf2/4118] Fine Violin: Boston, 1909   7,000/8,000 NS

GOULD, JOHN ALFRED [Bf9/4587] Fine American Violin w/case: Boston, 1909   6,500/7,500 NS

GOULDING & CO. [P11/93] Fine and Handsome English Violin in immediate playing condition, w/case: London, c. 1790   1,344/2,016
$2,318   £1,380   DM3,864   ¥277,090

GRAGNANI, ANTONIO [S6/157] Child's Violin with original neck, adjusted at heel: Livorno, c. 1780
    4,950/8,250
$7,970   £4,830   DM14,345   ¥1,149,299

GRANCINO, GIOVANNI [P4/106] Fine and Handsome Italian Violin in immediate playing condition, w/case: Milan, 1707 (W.E. Hill & Sons, London, March 6, 1951)   58,345/75,015 NS

GRANCINO, GIOVANNI [S3/246] Violin w/case: Milan, c. 1700   100,440/133,920 NS

GRANCINO, GIOVANNI [S1117/47] Violin w/case, cover: Milan, c. 1700   75,150/100,200 NS

GRATER, THOMAS [B5/188] Violin   815/1,141
$787   £483   DM1,401   ¥105,743

GUADAGNINI, FELICE [S6/25] Violin w/case: Turin, 1835   66,000/99,000
$56,925   £34,500   DM102,465   ¥8,209,275

GUADAGNINI, FRANCESCO [S3/251] Violin w/case: Turin, 1903   28,458/33,480 NS

GUADAGNINI, FRANCESCO [S1117/23] Violin w/case: Turin, 1903   23,380/30,060 NS

GUADAGNINI, GIOVANNI BATTISTA [Sk11/123] Important Italian Violin w/case: Parma, c. 1761 (Emil Herrmann, New York, January 31, 1950)
    140,000/160,000 NS

GUADAGNINI, GIUSEPPE (attributed to) [B3/146] Italian Violin: 1779   11,718/16,740 NS

GUADAGNINI, GIUSEPPE (attributed to) [P11/85] Italian Violin in good condition, w/case: Pavia, c. 1800   67,200/100,800 NS

GUADAGNINI FAMILY (MEMBER OF) [Bf2/4181] Very Fine Violin, two lower pins on back not original, w/case, bow: Parma, c. 1770 (Erich Lachmann, April 20, 1948)   35,000/50,000 NS

GUADAGNINI FAMILY (MEMBER OF) (ascribed to) [C11/180] Violin (Fridolin Hamma, Stuttgart, January 16, 1969)　　　16,700/25,050
$103,540　£62,000　DM172,980　¥12,585,380

GUADO, LORENZO FRASSINO [S6/3] Violin: Cremona, 1974　　　2,475/3,300
$3,795　£2,300　DM6,831　¥547,285

GUADO, LORENZO FRASSINO (attributed to) [P11/91] Good Contemporary Violin in good condition: Castelleone, 1994　　　2,520/3,360 NS

GUARNERI, ANDREA [C11/216] Fine Italian Violin w/double case, bow (Max Möller & Zoon, Amsterdam, September 10, 1966)　　167,000/217,100
$149,465　£89,500　DM249,705　¥18,167,605

GUARNERI, ANDREA [S3/23] Violin w/case, 2 bows: Cremona, c. 1645　　58,590/75,330
$105,629　£63,100　DM195,421　¥14,076,979

GUARNERI, GIUSEPPE (FILIUS ANDREAE) [S1117/366] Violin w/case: Cremona, 1703
　　　167,000/250,500
$278,055 £166,500　DM464,535　¥33,797,835

GUARNERI, JOSEPH (DEL GESU) [S6/30] Violin w/case: Cremona, 1726　660,000/990,000 NS

GUARNERI, PIETRO (OF VENICE) [S3/29] Violin w/case: Venice, 1729 (Rembert Wurlitzer, New York, March 24, 1953)　　418,500/502,200 NS

GUERRA, EVASIO EMILE [S6/31] Violin w/case: Turin, 194　　　11,650/23,100
$15,180　£9,200　DM27,324　¥2,189,140

GUERSAN, LOUIS [C4/192] French Violin with replacement scroll, w/case　　3,340/4,175
$3,457　£2,070　DM6,417　¥462,521

GUERSAN, LOUIS (attributed to) [B11/121] Violin: Paris, c. 1780　　8,350/11,690 NS

GUIDANTE, GIOVANNI FLORENO (attributed to) [C4/156] Italian Violin w/case, bow (Erich Lachmann, New York, March 28, 1928)　　20,040/25,050
$24,967　£14,950　DM46,345　¥3,340,428

HADDEN, ROBERT [P4/129] Good Scottish Violin in immediate playing condition: Edinburgh, 1894
　　　583/750
$690　£414　DM1,278　¥92,169

HAMM, JOHANN GOTTFRIED (workshop of) [Bf7/10421] German Violin that has been revarnished, w/case: c. 1810　　300/500
$173　£105　DM307　¥23,964

HARDIE, MATTHEW [P11/26] Fine and Handsome Violin in immediate playing condition: Edinburgh, c. 1810　　　3,360/5,040
$3,864　£2,300　DM6,440　¥461,817

HARDIE, MATTHEW [S1117/46] Violin w/double case: Edinburgh, 1802 (W.E. Hill & Sons, London, November 20, 1970)　　6,680/10,020 NS

HARDIE, MATTHEW (attributed to) [P4/53] Good Violin with minor blemishes: Edinburgh, c. 1800
　　　6,668/10,002 NS

HARRIS, CHARLES [P11/66] English Violin in good condition, w/case: 1835　　5,880/7,560
$7,728　£4,600　DM12,880　¥923,634

HART & SON [Sk5/125] English Violin w/case: London, 1928　　　2,200/2,400
$3,335　£2,001　DM5,936　¥443,488

HAVEMANN, CARL FRIEDRICH [C11/488] German Violin
$210　£126　DM352　¥25,577

HEATON, WILLIAM [B5/165] Violin　815/1,141 NS

HEATON, WILLIAM [B7/134] Violin: Leeds, 1888
　　　660/990
$797　£483　DM1,415　¥110,554

HEBERLEIN, G.F. (JR.) [Sk11/108] German Violin w/case, bow: 1925　　1,200/1,400
$978　£587　DM1,652　¥119,255

HEBERLEIN, HEINRICH TH. (JR.) [Sk5/286] German Violin w/case　　　400/600
$805　£483　DM1,433　¥107,049

HEBERLEIN, HEINRICH TH. (JR.) [Sk11/207] Violin w/case: Markneukirchen　　1,600/1,800
$2,530　£1,518　DM4,276　¥308,660

HEBERLEIN, HEINRICH TH. (JR.) [Sk11/335] Violin w/case, bow: Markneukirchen, 1927　250/350
$805　£483　DM1,360　¥98,210

HEBERLEIN, HEINRICH TH. (JR.) (workshop of) [Sk5/137] Violin w/case, bow: Markeneukirchen
　　　1,400/1,600
$1,380　£828　DM2,456　¥183,512

HEBERLEIN, HEINRICH TH. (JR.) (workshop of) [Sk5/292] German Violin w/case, 2 bows　800/1,200
$1,380　£828　DM2,456　¥183,512

HEBERLEIN, HEINRICH TH. (JR.) (workshop of) [Sk5/293] German Violin w/case, bow　800/1,200
$748　£449　DM1,331　¥99,403

HEINEL, OSKAR BERNHARD [Sk11/332] Violin w/case: Markneukirchen　　1,000/1,500
$805　£483　DM1,360　¥98,210

HEINEL, OSKAR ERICH [S3/16] Violin w/case: Markneukirchen, c. 1950　　1,674/2,511
$2,695　£1,610　DM4,986　¥359,175

HEINEL, OSKAR ERICH [S3/242] Violin w/case: Markneukirchen, c. 1950　　2,511/3,348 NS

HEINEL, OSKAR ERICH [S1117/38] Violin w/case: Markneukirchen, c. 1950　　1,336/2,004 NS

HEINICKE, MATHIAS [C4/163] German Violin
　　　3,340/4,175 NS

HEINICKE, MATHIAS [S3/267] Violin w/case: Wildstein bei Eger, 1933　　2,511/3,348 NS

HEL, J. [B11/83] Fine Violin　　13,360/20,040
$16,324　£9,775　DM27,272　¥1,984,227

HEL, JOSEPH [P4/71] Fine and Handsome French Violin in immediate playing condition, w/case: Lille, 1896　　　20,004/30,006 NS

HEL, JOSEPH [P11/50] Fine and Handsome French Violin in immediate playing condition, w/case: Lille, 1896   116,800/25,200 NS

HEL, JOSEPH (attributed to) [P4/118] Fine and Handsome French Violin in immediate playing condition: Lille, 1888   13,336/15,003
$16,295   £9,775   DM30,185   ¥2,176,208

HEL, PIERRE JEAN HENRI [S6/15] Violin w/case: Lille, 1903   13,200/19,800 NS

HEL, PIERRE JOSEPH [B3/137] Fine French Violin: 1887   11,718/16,740 NS

HEL, PIERRE JOSEPH [S6/144] Violin w/case, 2 bows: Lille, 1887   9,900/13,200 NS

HEL, PIERRE JOSEPH [S1117/17] Violin w/case: Lille, 1893   13,360/20,040
$14,404   £8,625   DM24,064   ¥1,750,789

HENDERSON, F.V. [Sk5/264] Contemporary American Violin w/case: Seattle, Washington, 1987
                                          500/700
$518   £311   DM921   ¥68,817

HENNING, GUSTAV [Sk11/435] American Violin w/case: Malden, Massachusetts, 1914   800/1,200
$690   £414   DM1,166   ¥84,180

HENTSCHEL, JOHANN JOSEPH [C11/161] Violin w/case, bow   2,505/3,340 NS

HERBRIG, CHARLES EDWARD [Bf2/4117] Violin: St. Paul, 1927   1,000/1,400
$805   £493   DM1,462   ¥99,965

HERMANN (workshop of) [Bf7/10519] German Violin w/case: c. 1950   300/500
$196   £119   DM348   ¥27,159

HERTL, ANTON [B2/125] Violin   1,312/1,968 NS

HERTL, ANTON [B5/185] Violin   978/1,630 NS

HERTL, ANTON [B7/151] Violin   825/1,155
$854   £518   DM1,516   ¥118,451

HESKETH [B11/145] Violin   2,505/4,175
$4,993   £2,990   DM8,342   ¥606,940

HESKETH, THOMAS EARLE [B11/90] Violin
                                        3,340/6,680
$7,298   £4,370   DM12,192   ¥887,066

HESKETH, THOMAS EARLE [S3/38] Violin w/case: Manchester, 1907   1,674/2,344
$1,733   £1,035   DM3,205   ¥230,898

HEYLIGERS, MATHIJS [C11/191] Violin (maker's, Cremona, December 10, 1987)   5,010/6,680 NS

HILL, JOSEPH [B6/102] English Violin: c. 1770
                                        5,010/8,350 NS

HILL, JOSEPH [S1117/28] Violin: London, 1768 (Olympic Galleries, Leeds, January 26, 1968)
                                        5,845/8,350
$8,066   £4,830   DM13,476   ¥980,442

HILL, W.E. & SONS [P4/75] Fine and Handsome English Violin in immediate playing condition, w/case: London, 1895   10,002/13,336 NS

HILL, W.E. & SONS [P4/76] Fine and Handsome English Violin in immediate playing condition: London, 1905   13,336/20,004 NS

HILL, W.E. & SONS [P4/82] Fine and Handsome Violin in immediate playing condition, w/case: London, 1918   6,668/10,002 NS

HILL, W.E. & SONS [S1117/20] Violin w/case: London, 1900   10,020/13,360
$9,987   £5,980   DM16,684   ¥1,213,880

HJORTH, KNUD [C4/190] Good Violin w/case
                                        5,010/6,680 NS

HOLDER, T. J. (attributed to) [P4/146] Good French Violin in good condition, w/case: c. 1920
                                        5,835/7,502 NS

HOLDER, THOMAS (attributed to) [P11/102] Good French Violin in good condition, w/case, cover: c. 1920   5,880/7,560 NS

HOLST, JOHANNES (attributed to) [P10/58] Violin in good condition, w/case, bow: 1929
                                        1,020/1,190 NS

HOLST, JOHANNES (attributed to) [P12/61] Violin in good condition, w/case, bow: 1929   835/1,002
$883   £529   DM1,460   ¥103,314

HOPF [B2/124] Violin with later scroll   410/574
$358   £219   DM652   ¥45,260

HOPF (attributed to) [P12/62] Good Klingenthal Violin, skillfully restored, w/case, cover: c. 1780
                                          668/835
$691   £414   DM1,143   ¥80,854

HOPF, DAVID [Sk11/350] Saxon Violin w/case: Klingenthal, c. 1800   1,200/1,400
$1,380   £828   DM2,332   ¥168,360

HOPF FAMILY (MEMBER OF) [P12/223] Saxon Violin with later scroll, w/bow: c. 1770   367/468
$1,536   £920   DM2,539   ¥179,676

HORNSTEINER [B5/204] German Violin   326/489
$394   £242   DM700   ¥52,872

HORNSTEINER (ascribed to) [C11/330] German Violin w/case   1,336/2,004
$1,344   £805   DM2,246   ¥163,407

HORNSTEINER (workshop of) [Bf7/10415] Good German Violin w/case: c. 1840   600/900
$345   £210   DM614   ¥47,927

HOYER, FRIEDRICH [P4/160] Saxon Violin with minor, restorable blemishes, w/case, bow: Klingenthal, 1875   500/667
$537   £322   DM994   ¥71,687

HUDSON, GEORGE [S3/368] Violin w/case: Skegness, 1902   2,511/3,348 NS

HUDSON, GEORGE WULME [P4/96] Fine and Handsome English Violin in immediate playing condition   10,002/13,336 NS

HUMS, ALBIN [Sk5/268] German Violin w/case: Markneukirchen, 1952   800/1,200
$1,035   £621   DM1,842   ¥137,634

HUNGER, C.F. [C11/131] German Violin w/case,
bow   1,670/2,505
$3,073   £1,840   DM5,134   ¥373,502

JACOBS, H. [B11/84] Fine Violin: Amsterdam,
c. 1690 (Jacques Français)   30,060/41,750
$28,808   £17,250   DM48,128   ¥3,501,578

JACQUEMIN, RENE (workshop of) [Sk5/337]
French Violin w/case: 1947   600/800
$863   £518   DM1,535   ¥114,695

JAMIESON [P12/53] Good Violin in good condition,
w/case, bow: Scotland, c. 1835   835/1,002 NS

JAUCK, JOHANNES (ascribed to) [P4/150]
Interesting Violin with some old table restoration,
w/case, bow: Graz, c. 1760   2,501/3,334
$2,876   £1,725   DM5,327   ¥384,037

JIROWSKY, HANS [S6/141] Violin: Vienna, 1935
                                   2,475/3,300 NS

JOMBAR, PAUL (attributed to) [P10/36] Fine and
Handsome French Violin in immediate playing
condition, w/case, bow: 1899   2,550/3,400 NS

JOMBAR, PAUL (attributed to) [P12/43] Fine and
Handsome French Violin in immediate playing
condition, w/case, bow: 1899   1,670/2,505
$2,881   £1,725   DM4,761   ¥336,893

JORIO, VINCENZO (ascribed to) [C4/159]
Neapolitan Violin w/case: c. 1860   8,350/11,690 NS

JUZEK, JOHN [Sk11/347] Czech Violin w/case,
2 bows: Prague, 1920   200/300
$546   £328   DM923   ¥66,643

KARNER, BARTHOLOMAUS [S1117/151] Violin
w/case, bow: Mittenwald, 1763   1,169/1,670
$960   £575   DM1,604   ¥116,719

KARNER, BARTHOLOMAUS (II) [S3/367] Violin
w/case: Mittenwald, 1797   2,511/3,348 NS

KAUL, PAUL [C4/188] French Violin w/case
                                   6,680/10,020 NS

KAUL, PAUL [Sk11/87] French Violin w/case: Paris,
1940   2,200/2,400
$2,990   £1,794   DM5,053   ¥364,780

KENNEDY, THOMAS [P4/79] Fine and Handsome
Violin in immediate playing condition, w/case:
London, c. 1835   7,502/9,169 NS

KENNEDY, THOMAS [S6/149] Violin with repaired
head, w/case, bow: London, 1813 (Violinateljé Gefle,
Gävle, April 16, 1997)   11,550/16,500 NS

KESSLER, W. AUGUST (JR.) [C4/136] German
Violin   3,006/3,674
$3,457   £2,070   DM6,417   ¥462,521

KLINTH, ALBERT W. [Sk5/234] Contemporary
American Violin w/case, 2 bows: Grand Rapids,
Michigan, 1960   250/350
$431   £259   DM768   ¥57,348

KLOTZ, AEGIDIUS (I) [S3/346] Violin w/case:
Mittenwald, late 18th C.   3,348/5,022
$4,235   £2,530   DM7,835   ¥564,418

KLOTZ, AEGIDIUS (I) [S1117/65] Violin w/case:
Mittenwald, c. 1790   4,175/5,845
$3,841   £2,300   DM6,417   ¥466,877

KLOTZ, AEGIDIUS (II) [S6/122] Violin: Mittenwald,
c. 1770   3,300/4,950
$3,795   £2,300   DM6,831   ¥547,285

KLOTZ, AEGIDIUS (II) [Sk11/78] Good Violin
w/case, 2 bows: Mittenwald   3,000/5,000
$4,255   £2,553   DM7,191   ¥519,110

KLOTZ, AEGIDIUS (II) (attributed to) [C11/172]
German Violin   5,010/6,680 NS

KLOTZ, CARL FREDRICH (attributed to)
[Bf9/4621] Good German Violin: Mittenwald,
c. 1795   3,000/5,000 NS

KLOTZ, GEORG (II) [S6/17] Violin w/double case:
Mittenwald, c. 1770   9,900/11,550 NS

KLOTZ, JOHANN CARL [Bf2/4139] Violin w/case:
Mittenwald, c. 1770   2,500/3,000
$2,875   £1,760   DM5,221   ¥357,018

KLOTZ, JOSEPH (attributed to) [Sk11/442] Good
Violin w/case, bow: Mittenwald (Wagner & George,
Chicago, April 4, 1938)   5,000/6,000
$4,025   £2,415   DM6,802   ¥491,050

KLOTZ, MATHIAS (I) [Bf9/4617] Violin: Mittenwald, c. 1760   3,500/4,500 NS

KLOTZ, MATHIAS (I) [S3/370] Violin w/case, bow:
Mittenwald, c. 1770   5,859/7,533 NS

KLOTZ, MATHIAS (I) (attributed to) [B11/122]
Good German Violin   3,340/5,010 NS

KLOTZ, MATHIAS (II) [S1117/129] Violin w/case,
cover, 2 bows: Mittenwald, c. 1770   4,175/5,845 NS

KLOTZ, SEBASTIAN [B3/125] German Violin
                                   3,348/5,022 NS

KLOTZ, SEBASTIAN [B6/110] German Violin
                                   1,670/2,505
$2,497   £1,495   DM4,470   ¥343,521

KLOTZ, SEBASTIAN [S6/150] Violin: Mittenwald,
c. 1765   9,900/11,550 NS

KLOTZ, SEBASTIAN [Sk5/122] South German
Violin: Mittenwald, 1767 (William Lewis & Son,
Chicago, October 29, 1959)   4,000/6,000
$4,255   £2,553   DM7,574   ¥565,830

KLOTZ, SEBASTIAN (II) [S3/354] Violin w/case:
Mittenwald, c. 1800   4,185/5,859 NS

KLOTZ, SEBASTIAN (II) [S1117/44] Violin w/case:
Mittenwald, c. 1800   4,175/5,845
$3,457   £2,070   DM5,775   ¥420,189

KLOTZ FAMILY (MEMBER OF) [B6/130] Violin
                                   3,006/4,175 NS

KLOTZ FAMILY (MEMBER OF) [C11/130] German
Violin w/case: c. 1770   2,338/3,006
$3,073   £1,840   DM5,134   ¥373,502

KLOTZ FAMILY (MEMBER OF) [C11/157] German
Three-Quarter-Size Violin w/case, bow   1,503/2,004
$1,824   £1,092   DM3,047   ¥221,665

KLOTZ FAMILY (MEMBER OF) [S3/50] Violin
w/case: Mittenwald, c. 1800   5,022/6,696 NS

KLOTZ FAMILY (MEMBER OF) [S1117/31] Violin
w/case: Mittenwald, c. 1800   2,505/4,175 NS

KNOPF, HENRY RICHARD [Bf9/4605] Good
American Violin w/case, 2 bows: New York, 1927
                                     1,500/3,000
$3,163   £1,898   DM5,345   ¥420,834

KNOPF, HENRY RICHARD [Sk11/69] American
Violin: New York, 1917   1,800/2,200
$2,875   £1,725   DM4,859   ¥350,750

KNORR, ALBERT [Sk5/72] Good Markneukirchen
Violin w/case: c. 1910   1,800/2,200
$3,738   £2,243   DM6,653   ¥497,013

KOCH, FRANZ JOSEPH [Bf2/4177] Violin w/case,
2 bows: Dresden, 1920 (maker's, August 26, 1925)
                                     1,000/1,600
$1,150   £704   DM2,088   ¥142,807

KRELL, ALBERT [Bf9/4583] Good American Violin:
Cincinnati, c. 1815   1,400/2,200
$1,840   £1,104   DM3,110   ¥244,849

KRINER, JOSEPH [B5/242] Violin: late 18th C.
                                     978/1,304 NS

KRINER, JOSEPH [B7/131] Violin: late 18th C.
                                     660/825 NS

KRIZ, FRANTISEK [C4/128] Czech Violin
                                     4,175/5,010 NS

KRUMBHOLZ, LORENZ [C11/133] Dutch Violin
w/case   3,006/4,175
$7,298   £4,370   DM12,192   ¥887,066

KUDANOWSKI, JAN [B5/194] Violin
                                     1,630/2,445 NS

KUDANOWSKI, JAN [B7/208] Violin: 1973
                                     1,320/1,980
$1,328   £805   DM2,359   ¥184,256

KUDANOWSKI, JAN [S6/19] Violin: Birmingham,
1980   1,980/2,640
$2,087   £1,265   DM3,757   ¥301,007

KUDANOWSKI, JAN [S1117/10] Violin:
Birmingham, 1980   2,338/3,006 NS

KVAMME, MAGNE [Sk5/276] Contemporary
Norwegian Violin w/case: 1976   800/1,200
$575   £345   DM1,024   ¥76,464

LABERTE, MARC [Sk5/404] French Violin w/case
                                     2,800/3,200
$2,875   £1,725   DM5,118   ¥382,317

LABERTE-MAGNIE [P4/57] Good Violin in good
condition: Mirecourt, c. 1930   5,001/6,668 NS

LABERTE-MAGNIE [P12/37] Good Violin in good
condition: Mirecourt   2,505/3,340 NS

LAFLEUR, J. [B5/205] Violin   652/978
$937   £575   DM1,668   ¥125,885

LAMBERT [B3/166] Fine French Violin: c. 1790
                                     2,511/3,348
$3,080   £1,840   DM5,698   ¥410,486

LANGE, H. FRANCIS [Sk5/374] Contemporary
German Violin: 1966   250/350
$748   £449   DM1,331   ¥99,403

LARCHER, JEAN [C4/154] French Violin
                                     1,670/2,004
$1,921   £1,150   DM3,565   ¥256,956

LARCHER, JEAN [C11/333] French Violin
                                     1,169/1,503
$1,344   £805   DM2,246   ¥163,407

LATTERELL, GEORGE [Bf2/4113] American Violin:
Paynesville, 1922   1,500/1,800
$1,380   £845   DM2,506   ¥171,368

LAURENT, EMILE [S1117/5] Violin w/case, bow:
Brussels, 1910   4,175/5,845
$7,682   £4,600   DM12,834   ¥933,754

LEAVITT, F.A. [Sk5/281] American Violin w/case,
2 bows: East Weymouth, Massachusetts, 1911
                                     600/800
$518   £311   DM921   ¥68,817

LECCHI, GUISEPPE [C4/167] Italian Violin w/case
                                     15,030/20,040 NS

LECHI, ANTONIO [B3/140] Violin: Cremona, 1921
                                     670/1,004
$770   £460   DM1,425   ¥102,621

LECHI, ANTONIO [P4/162] Good Violin in immediate playing condition   1,167/1,500
$1,572   £943   DM2,912   ¥209,940

LEE, PERCY [B11/123] Violin   3,340/5,010
$4,609   £2,760   DM7,700   ¥560,252

LEWIS, WILLIAM & SON [Bf7/10496] German
Violin in immediate playing condition, w/case
                                     400/500 NS

LINDORFER, WILLI [S3/263] Violin w/case:
Weimar, c. 1950   10,044/13,392 NS

LIPPOLD, CARL FREDERICK (attributed to)
[S10/17] Violin: Markneukirchen   744/930 NS

LONGMAN [B2/102] English Violin   328/492
$566   £345   DM1,029   ¥71,463

LONGMAN, LUKEY & CO. [C11/343] English
Violin in Baroque condition, w/case 668/1,002
$768   £460   DM1,283   ¥93,375

LOTT, JOHN FREDERICK (attributed to) [S3/278]
Violin w/case, bow: England, mid 19th C.
                                     6,696/10,044 NS

LOWENDALL [P12/74] Violin in good condition
w/case, bow: Berlin, c. 1900   300/400 NS

LOWENDALL [P12/251] Good German Violin in
good condition, w/2 cases, 2 bows, violin: Dresden,
c. 1900   251/334 NS

LOWENDALL, LOUIS [P11/92] Good Violin in
good condition, w/case, 2 bows: Berlin, 1893
                                     840/1,008
$966   £575   DM1,610   ¥115,454

LUCCI, GIUSEPPE [Bf2/4167] Fine and Handsome Violin w/case: Rome, 1987 (maker's, October 2, 1989)   10,000/15,000
$8,625   £5,279   DM15,663   ¥1,071,053

LUCCI, GIUSEPPE [S3/15] Violin w/case: Rome, 1989 (maker's)   11,718/16,740
$12,513   £7,475   DM23,150   ¥1,667,598

LUFF, WILLIAM H. [S3/328] Violin w/case: Dorset, 1971   6,696/10,044
$6,930   £4,140   DM12,822   ¥923,593

LUPOT, NICOLAS [C11/215] Fine French Violin (Jean-Jacques Rampal, Paris, March 31, 1998)
                                            83,500/116,900
$103,540   £62,000   DM172,980   ¥12,585,380

LUPOT, NICOLAS [S1117/41] Violin w/case: Paris, 1809   91,850/116,900
$134,769   £80,700   DM225,153   ¥16,381,293

LUTZ, IGNAZ [Sk11/119] Good American Violin w/case, 2 bows: San Francisco, 1927   2,500/3,500
$4,485   £2,691   DM7,580   ¥547,170

MAAG, HENRY [Bf2/4122] Violin: Glendale, California, 1953   800/1,200 NS

MAAG, HENRY [Bf2/4123] Violin: Glendale, California, 1965   300/400
$173   £106   DM313   ¥21,421

MAAG, HENRY [Bf2/4124] Violin: Glendale, California, 1960   300/400 NS

MAAG, HENRY [Bf2/4125] Violin: Prescott, Arizona, 1959   300/400 NS

MAAG, HENRY [Bf2/4126] Violin: Prescott, Arizona, 1976   200/300 NS

MAAG, HENRY [Bf2/4127] Violin: Glendale, California, 1958   300/400
$173   £106   DM313   ¥21,421

MAAG, HENRY [Bf2/4128] Violin: Glendale, California, 1960   300/400
$161   £99   DM292   ¥19,993

MAAG, HENRY [Bf2/4129] Violin: Prescott, Arizona, 1975   300/400 NS

MAAG, HENRY [Bf2/4130] Violin: Glendale, California, 1968   200/300
$150   £91   DM271   ¥18,565

MAAG, HENRY [Bf2/4131] Violin: Prescott, Arizona, 1977   400/500 NS

MAAG, HENRY [Bf2/4132] Violin: Glendale, California, 1958   500/600 NS

MAAG, HENRY [Bf2/4133] Violin: Glendale, California, 1954   400/500 NS

MAAG, HENRY [Bf2/4134] Violin: Prescott, Arizona, 1969   500/600 NS

MAAG, HENRY [Bf2/4135] Violin: Glendale, California, 1953   500/600 NS

MAAG, HENRY [Bf2/4136] Violin: Glendale, California, 1954   500/600 NS

MAAG, HENRY [Bf2/4137] Violin: Prescott, Arizona, 1975   600/700 NS

MAAG, HENRY [Bf7/10352] American Violin: Prescott, Arizona   300/400 NS

MAAG, HENRY [Bf7/10357] American Violin: Glendale, California, 1958   500/600
$460   £281   DM819   ¥63,903

MAAG, HENRY [Bf7/10359] American Violin: Glendale, California, 1954   300/400 NS

MAAG, HENRY [Bf7/10364] American Violin: Prescott, Arizona, 1977   300/400 NS

MAAG, HENRY [Bf7/10401] American Violin: Prescott, Arizona, 1975   200/300 NS

MAAG, HENRY [Bf7/10404] American Violin: 1959   200/300 NS

MAAG, HENRY [Bf7/10410] American Violin: Glendale, California, 1953   500/600 NS

MAAG, HENRY [Bf7/10411] American Violin: Prescott, Arizona, 1959   150/250
$115   £70   DM205   ¥15,976

MAAG, HENRY [Bf7/10414] American Violin: Glendale, California, 1960   200/300 NS

MAAG, HENRY [Bf7/10420] American Violin: Glendale, California, 1954   300/400 NS

MAAG, HENRY [Bf7/10495] American Violin: Prescott, Arizona, 1975   400/500 NS

MAAG, HENRY [Bf7/10526] American Violin: Glendale, California, 1959   300/400 NS

MACCARTHY, J.L.T. [P12/45] Good Violin in immediate playing condition: Cambridge, England, 1923
                                            1,002/1,169 NS

MACVEAN, ALEXANDER [C4/221] Scottish Violin w/case, 2 bows   1,002/1,336 NS

MAGGINI, GIOVANNI PAOLO [S1117/359] Violin with later head, w/case: Brescia, c. 1600 (W.E. Hill & Sons, London, November 19, 1924)
                                            91,850/108,550 NS

MAGGINI, GIOVANNI PAOLO [S1117/51] Violin w/case: Brescia, 1632   25,050/33,400 NS

MAGNIERE, GABRIEL [B6/129] French Violin
                                            1,002/1,336
$1,344   £805   DM2,407   ¥184,973

MAGNIERE, GABRIEL [C11/195] French Violin w/case, bow   1,336/2,004
$1,536   £920   DM2,567   ¥186,751

MAGNIERE, GABRIEL [S3/8] Violin w/case, bow: Mirecourt, 1893   1,339/2,009 NS

MANDELLI, CAMILLO [Bf9/4599] Good Italian Violin w/case: Milan, c. 1935 (John L. Rossi, January 16, 1998)   22,500/27,500
$23,000   £13,800   DM38,870   ¥3,060,610

MANGENOT, AMATI [S1117/63] Violin w/case: Bordeaux, mid 20th C.   3,340/5,010 NS

MANGENOT, AMATI [Sk11/73] Good French
Violin w/case, bow: Bordeaux, 1927 2,800/3,200 NS

MANTEGAZZA, PIETRO GIOVANNI [Bf2/4178]
Fine Violin w/case: Milan, c. 1790 (Dario D'Attili,
March 10, 1983)   25,000/30,000 NS

MANTEGAZZA, PIETRO GIOVANNI [Bf9/4616]
Fine Violin w/case, cover: Milan, c. 17909 (Dario
D'Attili, March, 10, 1983)   20,000/25,000
$20,125   £12,075   DM34,011   ¥2,678,034

MARCHETTI, ENRICO [S3/241] Violin w/case:
Turin, c. 1925   23,436/26,784 NS

MARCHETTI, ENRICO [S10/144] Violin: Turin,
1927 (maker's, September 15, 1928)
                                        12,400/15,500 NS

MARCONCINI, JOSEPH [S10/139] Violin: Ferrara,
1839 (Atelier Gerber, Lausanne, January 24, 1994)
                                        49,600/62,000 NS

MARCONCINI, JOSEPH (attributed to) [Sk11/109]
Violin w/case (Joseph Settin, New York, May 13,
1967)   12,000/14,000 NS

MARDULA, FRANCISZEK & STANISLAW
[Sk11/337] Polish Violin w/case: Zakopane, 1989
(maker's)   1,500/2,000 NS

MARIANI (attributed to) [B11/113] Violin
                                        3,340/5,010 NS

MARSIGLIESE, BIAGIO [S10/68] Violin w/case:
Rome, 1930   1,240/1,860 NS

MARTIN [P4/174] Interesting English Violin:
London, c. 1790   667/1,000 NS

MARTIN, E. [Sk11/331] Child's Saxon Violin w/case
                                        350/450
$403   £242   DM680   ¥49,105

MARTIN, E. (workshop of) [Sk5/304] Violin w/case,
bow: Markneukirchen   600/800
$460   £276   DM819   ¥61,171

MARTIN, E. (workshop of) [Sk11/421] Violin
w/case, bow: Markneukirchen, c. 1925   600/800
$345   £207   DM583   ¥42,090

MAURIZI, FRANCESCO [B6/82] Italian Violin:
Appignano, c. 1850 (D.R. Hill)   13,360/20,040
$14,980   £8,970   DM26,820   ¥2,061,127

MAURIZI, FRANCESCO [S1117/56] Violin:
Appignano, c. 1830 (L.P. Balmforth & Sons, Leeds,
November 15, 1972)   8,350/11,690
$23,046   £13,800   DM38,502   ¥2,801,262

MAYSON, WALTER H. [C4/220] English Violin
                                        835/1,169
$768   £460   DM1,426   ¥102,782

MAYSON, WALTER H. [C11/148] English Violin
w/case   1,002/1,336 NS

MAYSON, WALTER H. [P10/23] Fine and Handsome English Violin in immediate playing condition:
Manchester, 1898   680/850
$782   £460   DM1,274   ¥92,037

MEINEL, OSKAR [Sk5/324] German Violin: 1966
                                        800/1,200
$920   £552   DM1,638   ¥122,342

MEISEL, JOHANN GEORG [Sk5/351] Violin
w/case, bow: c. 1780   600/800
$575   £345   DM1,024   ¥76,464

MEISEL, KARL [Sk11/346] German Violin w/case,
2 bows   250/350
$259   £155   DM437   ¥31,568

MEISEL, KARL (workshop of) [Sk5/375] German
Violin w/case, bow   600/800
$633   £380   DM1,126   ¥84,110

MEISEL, KARL (workshop of) [Sk5/401] Violin
w/case: Markneukirchen, 1923   1,400/1,600
$920   £552   DM1,638   ¥122,342

MELEGARI, MICHELE & PIETRO [S10/12] Violin
w/case: Turin, c. 1860   12,400/18,600 NS

MELZL, JOHANN GEORG [S6/11] Violin w/case,
2 bows: Straubing, 1855   990/1,320 NS

MENNESSON, EMILE [B5/277] Violin 2,445/1,956
$2,062   £1,265   DM3,669   ¥276,946

MENZINGER, GUSTAV [Sk5/219] German Violin
w/case, bow   1,400/1,500
$1,380   £828   DM2,456   ¥183,512

MERCIOLLE, JULES (workshop of) [Bf2/4162]
Good French Violin: Paris, c. 1930 4,000/6,000 NS

MERCIOLLE, JULES (workshop of) [Sk5/66] Good
French Violin: Paris   2,400/2,600
$2,415   £1,449   DM4,299   ¥321,147

MERMILLOT, MAURICE [C4/155] French Violin
                                        3,340/4,175
$3,457   £2,070   DM6,417   ¥462,521

MICHETTI, PLINIO [S10/0] Violin: Turin, 1930
                                        12,400/18,600
$14,973   £8,694   DM24,150   ¥1,762,950

MICHETTI, PLINIO [Sk11/70] Modern Italian
Violin: Turin, 1926   5,000/7,000
$7,475   £4,485   DM12,633   ¥911,950

MILITELLA, MARIANO [Sk11/439] Violin:
Rosario, c. 1926   3,500/4,500 NS

MINNOZZI, MARCO [B6/83] Violin 2,505/4,175
$2,881   £1,725   DM5,158   ¥396,371

MIREMONT, CLAUDE AUGUSTIN [C11/127]
French Violin w/case, bow   4,175/5,845
$4,801   £2,875   DM8,021   ¥583,596

MIREMONT, CLAUDE AUGUSTIN [S1117/6]
Violin: Paris, 1874   5,010/8,350
$12,483   £7,475   DM20,855   ¥1,517,350

MOINEL, DANIEL [C4/124] French Violin
                                        1,169/1,670
$1,344   £805   DM2,496   ¥179,869

MOINEL & CHERPITEL [S3/351] Violin w/case:
Paris, 1929   5,022/6,696 NS

MOITESSIER, LOUIS [B5/206] Violin 815/1,141 NS

MONK, JOHN KING [Sk5/229] English Violin
w/case: Lewisham, England, 1908   800/1,200
$460   £276   DM819   ¥61,171

MONNIG, FRITZ [S6/23] Violin: Vienna, 1930
2,475/3,300 NS

MONZINO, ANTONIO [B3/151] Italian Violin
6,696/10,044 NS

MONZINO & FIGLI [B6/79] Italian Violin
2,505/3,340 NS

MONZINO & FIGLI [B10/78] Italian Violin
2,040/2,550
$1,955   £1,150   DM3,151   ¥241,753

MORASSI, GIOVANNI BATTISTA [C11/181] Italian
Violin (maker's, Cremona, November 10, 1994)
5,845/7,515 NS

MORITZ, ALFRED [P12/52] Good German Violin
in good condition, w/case, bow: c. 1900   668/835
$730   £437   DM1,206   ¥85,346

MORLOT [B5/236] French Violin   978/1,630
$1,031   £633   DM1,834   ¥138,473

MORTIMER, JOHN WILLIAM [P10/183] Violin in
good condition: Cardiff, 1918   425/595
$430   £253   DM701   ¥50,620

MOSHER, ALEX H. [Bf2/4120] Violin w/case:
Watertown, New York, 1920   1,400/1,800 NS

MOSHER, ALEX H. [Bf7/10506] Good American
Violin w/case: Watertown, New York, 1920
1,200/1,600 NS

MOUGENOT, GEORGES [P10/54] Fine and Handsome Violin in immediate playing condition, w/case:
c. 1920   2,040/2,550
$2,346   £1,380   DM3,823   ¥276,110

MOUGENOT, GEORGES [S6/7] Violin: Brussels,
1892   4,950/8,250
$4,744   £2,875   DM8,539   ¥684,106

MOUGENOT, LEON [P12/39] Good Violin in good
condition, w/case, bow: 1920   1,336/1,670
$2,113   £1,265   DM3,491   ¥247,055

MOUGENOT, LEON (attributed to) [P11/51]
Violin in good condition, w/bow: Gauche, 1905
2,016/2,520
$2,705   £1,610   DM4,508   ¥323,272

MOZZANI, LUIGI [S3/358] Violin: Cento, 1927
5,022/6,696 NS

MOZZANI, LUIGI [S3/361] Violin: mid 20th C.
3,348/5,022
$2,310   £1,380   DM4,274   ¥307,864

MOZZANI, LUIGI (workshop of) [Sk11/111] Italian
Violin: 1928   5,500/6,500 NS

MUMBY, ERNEST [S1117/8] Violin w/2 cases,
violin, bow: Tottenham, 1924   2,004/3,006 NS

MUNCHER, ROMEDIO (workshop of) [Sk5/120]
Violin w/case, bow: Cremona, 1925   3,000/4,000 NS

MUTTI, VITTORIO [Bf9/4622] Italian Violin w/case:
Mantua, c. 1940   1,500/2,000 NS

NEUMANN, ADOLPH (workshop of) [Sk5/238]
Child's German Violin w/case, bow   300/500
$345   £207   DM614   ¥45,878

NEUNER, LUDWIG [C4/259] German Violin
334/668
$364   £218   DM676   ¥48,710

NEUNER, MATHIAS [B7/199] Violin   660/825
$664   £403   DM1,179   ¥92,128

NEUNER, MATHIAS [B10/128] Violin w/violin
680/1,020
$743   £437   DM1,197   ¥91,866

NEUNER, MATHIAS [B5/175] Violin 815/1,141 NS

NEUNER, MATHIAS [Sk11/395] Violin w/case:
Mittenwald, 1881   200/300
$345   £207   DM583   ¥42,090

NEUNER & HORNSTEINER [B2/118] German
Violin   328/492
$528   £322   DM961   ¥66,699

NEUNER & HORNSTEINER [P4/49] Good Violin
in good playing condition, w/case, 2 bows:
Mittenwald, c. 1880   667/1,000
$1,438   £863   DM2,663   ¥192,018

NEUNER & HORNSTEINER [P4/135] Violin in
good condition, w/case, bow: Mittenwald, c. 1880
750/1,084
$863   £518   DM1,598   ¥115,211

NEUNER & HORNSTEINER [P4/161] Violin in
immediate playing condition, w/case: Mittenwald,
c. 1890   834/1,167 NS

NEUNER & HORNSTEINER [P10/195] Violin with
restored table blemishes: Mittenwald, c. 1880
595/680 NS

NEUNER & HORNSTEINER [P11/214] Violin with
minor restorable blemishes, w/case, bow: Mittenwald,
c. 1880   504/672 NS

NEUNER & HORNSTEINER [P12/73] Good Violin
in good condition, w/case, bow: Mittenwald, c. 1890
668/835
$768   £460   DM1,270   ¥89,838

NEUNER & HORNSTEINER [P12/233] Violin:
Mittenwald, c. 1880   501/585 NS

NEUNER & HORNSTEINER (workshop of)
[Sk5/306] Mittenwald Violin: c. 1880   600/800
$748   £449   DM1,331   ¥99,403

NEUNER & HORNSTEINER (workshop of)
[Sk5/322] Mittenwald Violin   800/1,200 NS

NEUNER & HORNSTEINER (workshop of)
[Sk5/333] Mittenwald Violin w/case, bow 800/1,200
$460   £276   DM819   ¥61,171

NEUNER & HORNSTEINER (workshop of)
[Sk11/427] Violin: Mittenwald   400/500
$288   £173   DM486   ¥35,075

NICOLAS, DIDIER (L'AINE) [B2/81] Good Violin
820/1,148
$1,226   £748   DM2,231   ¥154,837

NICOLAS, DIDIER (L'AINE) [B3/128] French Violin
3,013/3,683 NS

NICOLAS, DIDIER (L'AINE) [B6/117] French Violin:
Mirecourt   1,670/2,505 NS

NICOLAS, DIDIER (L'AINE) [B11/87] Violin (Daniel
Moinel)   2,505/3,340 NS

NICOLAS, DIDIER (L'AINE) [Bf2/4168] Violin:
Mirecourt, c. 1810   3,500/5,000 NS

NICOLAS, DIDIER (L'AINE) [Bf9/4615] Violin:
Mirecourt, c. 1810   3,000/4,000 NS

NICOLAS, DIDIER (L'AINE) [C11/163] French
Violin w/case   3,340/4,175 NS

NICOLAS, DIDIER (L'AINE) [P10/56] Good French
Violin in immediate playing condition: c. 1790
                                                     680/850
$704   £414   DM1,147   ¥82,833

NICOLAS, DIDIER (L'AINE) [S3/39] Violin with
painted back, w/case: Mirecourt, c. 1820 1,004/1,674
$963   £575   DM1,781   ¥128,277

NICOLAS, DIDIER (L'AINE) [S1117/70] Violin:
Mirecourt, c. 1820   1,670/2,505
$3,841   £2,300   DM6,417   ¥466,877

NICOLAS, DIDIER (L'AINE) [Sk5/373] French
Violin w/case, bow: Mirecourt   600/800
$748   £449   DM1,331   ¥99,403

NICOLAS, DIDIER (L'AINE) [Sk11/368] Violin:
Mirecourt   500/700
$489   £293   DM826   ¥59,628

NICOLAS, DIDIER (L'AINE) (workshop of)
[Sk5/233] French Violin: c. 1875   800/1,200
$1,093   £656   DM1,945   ¥145,281

NOBILE, FRANCESCO (attributed to) [B3/161]
Italian Violin: Rome, c. 1790   8,370/11,718
$4,620   £2,760   DM8,548   ¥615,728

NUPIERI, GIUSEPPE [Sk11/97] Contemporary
Italian Violin w/case, bow: Rome, 1974   1,000/1,500
$1,150   £690   DM1,944   ¥140,300

NUPIERI, GIUSEPPE [Sk11/120] Modern Italian
Violin w/case: 1975   800/1,200
$1,495   £897   DM2,527   ¥182,390

NUPIERI, GIUSEPPE [S1117/390] Violin: Rome,
1979 (maker's, March 12, 1992)   1,670/2,505
$1,152   £690   DM1,925   ¥140,063

ODDONE, CARLO GIUSEPPE [C11/187] Italian
Violin w/case   33,400/41,750
$26,887   £16,100   DM44,919   ¥3,268,139

ODDONE, CARLO GIUSEPPE [S10/41] Violin:
Turin, 1930   49,600/62,000 NS

OLIVIER & BISCH [B6/101] French Violin
                                            2,004/2,505
$2,305   £1,380   DM4,126   ¥317,096

ORNATI, GIUSEPPE [C4/170] Italian Violin
                                          30,060/36,740 NS

ORSELLI, ENRICO [S10/16] Violin: Pesaro, 1952
                                            4,340/6,200
$6,061   £3,519   DM9,775   ¥713,575

OWEN, JOHN W. [P11/53] Good English Violin
w/case: Leeds, c. 1900   2,520/3,360
$3,864   £2,300   DM6,440   ¥461,817

PACHEREL, PIERRE [S1117/363] Violin w/case:
Nice, 1840 (Emil Hjorth & Sønner, Copenhagen,
November 2, 1981)   25,050/33,400
$26,887   £16,100   DM44,919   ¥3,268,139

PAINE, ARTHUR [Sk5/295] American Violin w/case:
Pittsfield, Massachusetts   1,400/1,600
$1,840   £1,104   DM3,275   ¥244,683

PAINE, THOMAS D. [Sk5/335] American Violin
w/case, bow: 1878   400/800
$288   £173   DM512   ¥38,232

PALLAVER, GIOVANNI [S10/5] Violin: Verona,
1978   3,720/4,960 NS

PAMPHILON, EDWARD [B3/173] Rare English
Violin: London, 1680   5,022/8,370 NS

PANORMO, VINCENZO [S10/143] Violin: c. 1790
(Giancarlo Francesconi, Milan, June 24, 1998)
                                          15,500/21,700 NS

PANORMO, VINCENZO [S1117/42] Violin w/case,
2 bows: Paris, c. 1760 (W.E. Hill & Sons, London,
May 25, 1943)   25,050/33,400
$38,410   £23,000   DM64,170   ¥4,668,770

PAOLETTI, SILVIO VEZIO [S3/261] Violin: Florence, c. 1945 (Carlo Vettori, Florence)   5,022/6,696
$4,620   £2,760   DM8,548   ¥615,728

PARESCHI, GAETANO [B3/148] Italian Violin:
Ferrara, 1953   1,674/2,511 NS

PARESCHI, GAETANO [B7/161] Italian Violin:
Ferrara, 1953   990/1,650 NS

PARESCHI, GAETANO [S10/137] Violin: Ferrara,
1938   9,300/12,400 NS

PARESCHI, GAETANO [S1117/387] Violin: Ferrara,
19764,175/5,845 NS

PARKER, DANIEL [P4/78] Fine, Handsome, and
Rare English Violin in immediate playing condition:
London, c. 1720 (J. & A. Beare, London, April 5,
1990)   53,344/63,346 NS

PASSAURO-ZUCCARO, RAYMOND [Sk11/312]
Baroque-Style Violin w/case, Baroque-style bow
                                            1,200/1,400
$1,265   £759   DM2,138   ¥154,330

PASSAURO-ZUCCARO, RAYMOND [Sk11/313]
Baroque-Style Violin w/case   800/1,200
$805   £483   DM1,360   ¥98,210

PAULSEN, P.C. [S3/269] Violin: Chicago, 1898
                                            2,344/3,013 NS

PEDRAZZINI, GIUSEPPE [B3/171] Fine Milanese
Violin: 1936   25,110/30,132 NS

PEDRAZZINI, GIUSEPPE [B3/192] Very Fine Italian
Violin: Milan, 1924   33,480/50,220 NS

PEDRAZZINI, GIUSEPPE [B6/90] Fine Italian
Violin: Milan, 1924   33,400/41,750
$46,092   £27,600   DM82,524   ¥6,341,928

PEDRAZZINI, GIUSEPPE [B11/125] Fine Italian
Violin: Milan, 1920   30,060/41,750
$57,615   £34,500   DM96,255   ¥7,003,155

PEDRAZZINI, GIUSEPPE [P4/72] Fine and Handsome Italian Violin in immediate playing condition:
Milan, 1910 (W.E. Hill & Sons, London, September
21, 1964)   41,675/50,010 NS

PEDRAZZINI, GIUSEPPE [P4/80] Good Italian
Violin in immediate playing condition: w/case,
2 bows: Milan, 1948   20,004/26,672 NS

PEDRAZZINI, GIUSEPPE [P10/35] Good Italian
Violin in immediate playing condition, w/case, bow:
Milan, 1948   13,600/20,400 NS

PEDRAZZINI, GIUSEPPE (ascribed to) [S3/3] Violin
                                   6,696/10,044 NS

PEDRAZZINI, GIUSEPPE (attributed to) [Sk11/458]
Fine Violin w/case: Milan, 1931 (Michael A. Baum-
gartner, Basel, March 13, 1995)   18,000/22,000 NS

PELLACANI, GIUSEPPE (attributed to) [B11/143]
Violin (Primavera-Caellini)   6,680/10,020 NS

PERRY, THOMAS & WM. WILKINSON [C4/162]
Good Irish Violin   5,010/6,680 NS

PERRY & WILKINSON [B3/132] Good Irish Violin:
Dublin, 1820   1,674/2,511
$1,925   £1,150   DM3,562   ¥256,554

PERRY & WILKINSON [Bf2/4165] Good Violin:
Dublin 1813   4,000/5,000
$4,025   £2,463   DM7,309   ¥499,825

PETERS, WILLIAM L. [Sk11/318] American Violin
w/case, 2 bows: Worcester, Massachusetts, 1891
                                   1,200/1,400
$1,610   £966   DM2,721   ¥196,420

PFRETZSCHNER [Bf7/10497] German Violin in
immediate playing condition, w/case: c. 1950
                                   500/700 NS

PFRETZSCHNER, E.R. [Bf7/10356] Three-Quarter-
Size Violin w/case   110/150
$92   £56   DM164   ¥12,781

PFRETZSCHNER, G.A. (workshop of) [Sk11/410]
German Violin   200/300
$201   £121   DM340   ¥24,553

PICKSTONE, HARRY [P10/176] Good Contemporary Violin in good condition: Birmingham, 1980
                                   255/425
$332   £196   DM542   ¥39,116

PICKSTONE, HARRY [P12/229] Good Contemporary Violin in good condition: Birmingham, 1980
                                   200/251
$230   £138   DM381   ¥26,951

PIERCE, WILLIAM [Sk11/324] American Violin
w/case: Allentown, Pennsylvania, 1940   200/300
$403   £242   DM680   ¥49,105

PIEROTTE, JULES [C4/145] French Violin
                                   1,169/1,503 NS

PIERRAY, CLAUDE [Bf9/4602] Good French Violin
w/case: Paris, 1751 (Jacques Français, July 15, 1998)
                                   6,000/8,000
$5,750   £3,450   DM9,718   ¥765,153

PILAR, VLADIMIR [S6/131] Violin: Hradec Kralove,
1947   2,475/3,300
$2,467   £1,495   DM4,440   ¥355,735

PINEAU, JOSEPH [Sk5/336] American Violin w/case,
bow   600/800
$690   £414   DM1,228   ¥91,756

PIROT, CLAUDE [Bf9/45600] Fine French Violin
w/case, cover: Paris, 1923 (Rudolph Wurlitzer Co.,
October 30, 1943)   12,000/15,000
$17,250   £10,350   DM29,153   ¥2,295,458

PIVA, GIOVANNI [S10/43] Violin: Genoa, 1897
                                   2,170/2,790 NS

POGGI, ANSALDO [S6/24] Violin w/case: Bologna,
1931   33,000/41,250
$34,155   £20,700   DM61,479   ¥4,925,565

POIRSON, ELOPHE [Sk5/114] Fine French Violin
w/case: Lyon, France, 1890 (William Moennig & Son,
Philadelphia, January 11, 1971)   16,000/18,000
$15,525   £9,315   DM27,635   ¥2,064,514

POLITI, RAUL [S6/146] Violin w/case: Rome, 1967
                                   6,600/9,900
$6,641   £4,025   DM11,954   ¥957,749

POLLASTRI, GAETANO [S3/337] Violin w/case:
Bologna, 1955 (maker's, September 19, 1955)
                                   13,392/20,088 NS

POLLASTRI, GAETANO [S1117/45] Violin w/case:
Bologna, 1955 (maker's, September 19, 1955)
                                   11,690/15,030 NS

POLLASTRI, GAETANO (ascribed to) [Sk5/119]
Violin   8,000/12,000
$10,925   £6,555   DM19,447   ¥1,452,807

POSTIGLIONE, VINCENZO [Bf2/4170] Fine Violin
w/case: Naples, late 19th C. (Dario D'Attili, April 26,
1996)   24,000/28,000
$23,000   £14,076   DM41,768   ¥2,856,140

POSTIGLIONE, VINCENZO [S3/239] Violin w/case:
Naples, 1879   50,220/66,960
$43,315   £25,875   DM80,135   ¥5,772,454

POSTIGLIONE, VINCENZO [S10/52] Violin:
Naples, 1907   24,800/37,200
$24,955   £14,490   DM40,250   ¥2,938,250

POSTIGLIONE, VINCENZO [Sk11/101] Neapolitan
Violin: 1907   16,000/18,000 NS

POSTIGLIONE, VINCENZO & GIOVANNI
PISTUCCI [S10/120] Violin: Naples, 1899
                                   37,200/49,600 NS

POWLOSKI, PATRICIA [Bf2/4114] Violin: Portland,
1990   2,500/3,000 NS

POWLOSKI-BANCHERO, PATRICIA [Sk5/56]
American Violin: Portland, Oregon, 1990
1,800/2,200
$1,840   £1,104   DM3,275   ¥244,683

PRAGA, EUGENIO [S6/28] Violin w/case: Genoa,
1899 (Giovanni Longiaru, New York, March 12,
1953)   9,900/13,200
$8,539   £5,175   DM15,370   ¥1,231,391

PRESSENDA, GIOVANNI FRANCESCO [B3/177]
Italian Violin: Turin, 1827   50,220/83,700 NS

PRIESTNALL, JOHN [C4/335] English Violin
w/case, bow   501/668
$538   £322   DM998   ¥71,948

PROKOP, LADISLAV (II) [S6/12] Violin: Chrudim,
1941   3,300/4,950 NS

PUGLISI, MICHELANGELO [S3/369] Violin: first
half of the 20th C.   6,696/8,370 NS

PUGLISI, REALE [S3/274] Violin: Catania, c. 1930
4,185/5,859
$3,850   £2,300   DM7,123   ¥513,107

PUSKAS, JOSEPH [Bf2/4115] Fine American Violin
w/case: Los Angeles, 1970   3,500/4,500
$2,875   £1,760   DM5,221   ¥357,018

PUSKAS, JOSEPH [Bf9/4579] Fine American Violin
w/case: Los Angeles, 1970   3,500/4,500
$3,450   £2,070   DM5,831   ¥459,092

PYNE, GEORGE [B5/261] Violin   1,630/2,445
$4,874   £2,990   DM8,671   ¥654,601

QUENOIL, VICTOR [Bf2/4148] Good French
Violin: Massy, c. 1940   5,000/7,000 NS

RAE, JOHN [S3/363] Violin w/case: London, 1914
1,004/1,339 NS

RAVIZZA, CARLO [S10/70] Violin: Milan, 1903
4,960/6,200 NS

REICHEL, E.O. [Sk11/328] Violin w/case, bow:
Markneukirchen, 1923   400/500
$460   £276   DM777   ¥56,120

REICHEL, J.G. (attributed to) [P11/94] Violin in immediate playing condition: c. 1800   1,344/1,512 NS

REICHERT, EDUARD [Sk5/329] German Violin
w/case   300/500
$575   £345   DM1,024   ¥76,464

REICHERT, EDUARD [Sk11/330] Child's Violin
w/case, bow: Dresden, 1911   250/350
$431   £259   DM729   ¥52,613

REICHERT, EDUARD [Sk11/333] German Violin
w/case, bow: Dresden, 1911   200/300
$316   £190   DM534   ¥38,583

REICHERT, EDUARD (workshop of) [Sk5/387]
German Violin w/case, bow   400/600
$489   £293   DM870   ¥64,994

REMY, JEAN MATHURIN [S6/32] Violin w/case,
cover, 2 bows: Paris, c. 1840   3,300/4,950 NS

RESUCHE, CHARLES (attributed to) [P4/122] Fine
French Violin in immediate playing condition: Lyons,
c. 1890   2,501/3,334
$3,834   £2,300   DM7,102   ¥512,049

RICHARDSON, ARTHUR [B11/76] Fine Violin:
1944   5,010/8,350
$7,682   £4,600   DM12,834   ¥933,754

RICHARDSON, ARTHUR [S1117/7] Violin w/case:
Crediton, 1927   5,010/8,350 NS

RINALDI, MARENGO ROMANUS (ascribed to)
[S1117/386] Violin: Turin, c. 1915 (Giuseppe Lucci,
Rome, April 16, 1976)   25,050/33,400
$23,046   £13,800   DM38,502   ¥2,801,262

RIVOLTA, GIACOMO [S10/51] Violin: Milan, 1835
11,160/14,880 NS

ROBINSON, WILLIAM [B3/150] English Violin:
London, 1933   1,674/2,511 NS

ROBINSON, WILLIAM [B6/85] English Violin:
London, 1933   1,503/2,004
$1,728   £1,035   DM3,095   ¥237,822

ROBINSON, WILLIAM [P11/86] Good Violin in
playing condition, w/case: London, 1956
1,680/2,520 NS

ROBINSON, WILLIAM [S3/42] Violin w/case, bow:
Plumstead, 1929   2,511/4,185
$4,235   £2,530   DM7,835   ¥564,418

ROCCA, ENRICO [Bf2/4171] Fine and Handsome
Violin w/case: Genoa, c. 1898 (Erich Lachmann, Los
Angeles, November 21, 1952)   50,000/55,000
$29,900   £18,299   DM54,298   ¥3,712,982

ROCCA, JOSEPH (attributed to) [Bf9/4614] Fine
Violin: c. 1850 (Joseph Hornsteiner, March 1, 1922)
35,000/50,000
$28,750   £17,250   DM48,588   ¥3,825,763

ROCCA, JOSEPH (workshop of) [S10/72] Violin
w/case, 2 bows: mid 19th C.   18,600/24,800 NS

ROCCHI, SESTO [S3/327] Violin w/case: Reggio
Emilia, 1979   10,044/11,718
$14,438   £8,625   DM26,712   ¥1,924,151

ROCCHI, SESTO [S10/9] Violin: San Polo d'Enza,
1968 (maker's, April 11, 1973)   17,360/21,700 NS

ROCCHI, SESTO [S10/73] Violin: San Polo d'Enza,
1978   11,160/14,880 NS

ROCCHI, SESTO [S10/142] Violin: San Polo d'Enza,
1974   11,160/14,880
$10,339   £6,003   DM16,675   ¥1,217,275

ROCCHI, SESTO [S1117/54] Violin: San Polo
d'Enza, 1981   8,350/11,690
$8,642   £5,175   DM14,438   ¥1,050,473

ROOT-DUERER [Bf7/10484] Swiss Violin w/case:
1905   300/500
$316   £193   DM563   ¥43,933

ROSADONI, GIOVANNI [S3/44] Violin: Pavia, 1949
5,022/6,696
$5,005   £2,990   DM9,260   ¥667,039

ROSCHER, CHRISTIAN HEINRICH WILHELM [Sk5/73] German Violin w/case, 3 bows: 1871
2,800/3,200
$3,220   £1,932   DM5,732   ¥428,196

ROSSI, GIUSEPPE [S10/138] Violin w/case: Rome, 1919   9,300/12,400 NS

ROTH (attributed to) [P11/78] Violin in good condition, w/case: c. 1920   2,520/3,360
$3,671   £2,185   DM6,118   ¥438,726

ROTH, ERNST HEINRICH [C11/150] German Violin w/case   2,004/2,505
$2,113   £1,265   DM3,529   ¥256,782

ROTH, ERNST HEINRICH [P4/50] Good Violin in good condition, w/case, bow: Markneukirchen, c. 1950   1,000/1,167 NS

ROTH, ERNST HEINRICH [S6/5] Violin: Markneukirchen, 1924   3,300/4,950 NS

ROTH, ERNST HEINRICH [Sk5/112] Markneukirchen Violin w/case: 1931   1,600/1,800
$3,105   £1,863   DM5,527   ¥412,903

ROTH, ERNST HEINRICH [Sk5/405] Markneukirchen Violin w/case: 1925   1,600/1,800
$2,300   £1,380   DM4,094   ¥305,854

ROTH, ERNST HEINRICH [Sk11/71] Violin w/case, bow: Markneukirchen, 1929   1,800/2,200
$2,415   £1,449   DM4,081   ¥294,630

ROTH, ERNST HEINRICH [Sk11/93] German Violin w/case: 1954   800/1,200
$1,093   £656   DM1,846   ¥133,285

ROTH, ERNST HEINRICH [Sk11/303] German Violin w/case, bow: Bubenreuth-Erlangen, 1959   1,200/1,400 NS

ROTH, ERNST HEINRICH (workshop of) [Sk5/307] German Violin   300/500
$460   £276   DM819   ¥61,171

ROTH & LEDERER [Sk11/334] German Violin w/case   200/300
$518   £311   DM875   ¥63,135

ROVESCALLI, MANLIO [S10/27] Violin: Milan, 1927   9,300/11,160 NS

RUBUS, RIGART [B5/178] Russian Violin   130/195
$206   £127   DM367   ¥27,695

RUBUS, RIGART [Bf7/10413] Russian Violin w/case: c. 1850   200/400
$115   £70   DM205   ¥15,976

RUGGIERI, FRANCESCO [S6/36] Violin w/case: Cremona, 1960   33,000/49,500 NS

RUGGIERI, FRANCESCO [S1117/57] Violin w/case: Cremona, c. 1660 (Carl Mächler, Zurich, March 27, 1970)   100,200/133,600
$151,302   £90,600   DM252,774   ¥18,390,894

RUSHWORTH & DREAPER [B5/171] Violin
1,630/2,445 NS

SALOMON, J.B. [P11/23] Good French Violin in good condition: Paris, c. 1760   6,720/8,400
$7,728   £4,600   DM12,880   ¥923,634

SALOMON, J.B. [P11/46] French Violin with skillful old table and varnish restoration: Paris, c. 1760
2,520/3,360
$3,478   £2,070   DM5,796   ¥415,635

SALOMON, JEAN BAPTISTE DESHAYES [S6/130] Violin w/case, cover: Paris, c. 1740
11,550/16,500 NS

SALVADORI, GIUSEPPE [Bf9/4601] Italian Violin w/case: Pistoja, 1863   2,500/3,500 NS

SANINO, V. [B11/134] Very Fine Italian Violin: Naples   30,060/41,750 NS

SANNINO, VINCENZO [B3/170] Fine Italian Violin
30,132/41,850
$34,652   £20,700   DM64,108   ¥4,617,963

SANNINO, VINCENZO [Bf9/4581] Fine Italian Violin: Naples, 1900   35,000/45,000
$61,900   £37,140   DM104,611   ¥8,237,033

SANNINO, VINCENZO [S3/356] Violin: South Italy, c. 1910   8,370/11,718 NS

SANTAGIULIANA, GIACINTO [S1117/389] Violin: Vicenza, 1825 (Carlo Vettori, Florence, 1994)
16,700/23,380 NS

SCARAMPELLA, STEFANO [B3/131] Fine Italian Violin: Mantova, 1895   46,872/58,590
$53,903   £32,200   DM99,723   ¥7,183,498

SCARAMPELLA, STEFANO [B11/119] Very Fine Violin: Brescia, 1908 (Hans Weisshar)
58,450/75,150 NS

SCARAMPELLA, STEFANO (ascribed to) [Sk5/113] Modern Italian Violin w/case   12,000/14,000
$9,200   £5,520   DM16,376   ¥1,223,416

SCARAMPELLA, STEFANO (attributed to) [B3/139] Italian Violin   20,088/25,110 NS

SCARAMPELLA, STEFANO (attributed to) [B6/99] Italian Violin: Brescia   13,360/20,040
$14,404   £8,625   DM25,789   ¥1,981,853

SCHETELIG, ERNST [S3/262] Violin w/case: Markneukirchen, 1910 (Oskar Erich Heinel, Markneukirchen, February 20, 1951)   1,674/2,511 NS

SCHETELIG, ERNST [S1117/21] Violin w/case: Markneukirchen, 1910 (Oskar Erich Heinel, Markneukirchen, February 20, 1951)   1,336/2,004 NS

SCHLOSSER, HERMANN [C11/388] German Violin w/case, bow   501/668
$615   £368   DM1,027   ¥74,700

SCHMIDT, ERNST REINHOLD [Sk5/352] Saxon Violin w/case, bow: Markneukirchen   1,200/1,400
$2,070   £1,242   DM3,685   ¥275,269

SCHMIDT, E.R. & CO. [C11/466] German Violin
NS

SCHMIDT, REINHOLD [Sk5/253] Saxon Violin
w/case: Markeneukirchen   800/1,200
$1,150   £690   DM2,047   ¥152,927

SCHROETTER, A. [Bf7/10409] Half-Size Violin
w/case   170/250 NS

SCHROETTER, A. [Bf7/10493] Three-Quarter-Size
Violin w/case, bow   100/150
$92   £56   DM164   ¥12,781

SCHUSTER, MAX K. [S3/276] Violin w/case:
Markneukirchen, early 20th C.   3,013/4,185
$3,850   £2,300   DM7,123   ¥513,107

SCHUSTER, MAX K. [Sk5/411] Violin:
Markneukirchen   1,400/1,600
$1,380   £828   DM2,456   ¥183,512

SCIALE, GIUSEPPE [S1117/138] Violin w/case:
Rome, 1828 (L.P. Balmforth, Leeds, November 1970)
                                        25,050/33,400
$23,046   £13,800   DM38,502   ¥2,801,262

SCOGGINS, MICHAEL GENE [Sk11/441]
Contemporary American Violin: Salt Lake City, 1989
                                          2,000/3,000
$2,415   £1,449   DM4,081   ¥294,630

SDERCI, IGINO [S10/38] Violin w/case: Florence,
1950 (Carlo Vettori, Florence)   15,500/21,700 NS

SDERCI, IGINO [S1117/61] Violin w/case: Florence,
1952   10,020/13,360
$13,444   £8,050   DM22,460   ¥1,634,070

SDERCI, LUCIANO [S3/30] Violin: Florence, 1952
                                       16,740/20,088
$11,551   £6,900   DM21,369   ¥1,539,321

SEITZ, NICOLAS [B2/89] German Violin:
Mittenwald, 1825   984/1,640
$1,282   £782   DM2,333   ¥161,983

SERAPHIN, SANCTUS [C11/209] Italian Violin
(Henry Werro, Bern, January 17, 1940)
                                       66,800/100,200 NS

SGARABOTTO, GAETANO [C4/199] Italian Violin
                                       30,060/36,740
$36,490   £21,850   DM67,735   ¥4,882,164

SGARABOTTO, GAETANO [B3/123] Very Fine
Italian Violin: Parma, 1930 (H. Brandvig, Portland)
                                       30,132/41,850 NS

SGARABOTTO, GAETANO [B6/98] Fine Italian
Violin: Parma, 1930 (H. Brandvig, Portland)
                                       25,050/33,400 NS

SGARABOTTO, GAETANO [S3/21] Violin w/case,
bow: Brescia, 1954 (maker's, August 6, 1954)
                                       33,480/41,850
$33,689   £20,125   DM62,327   ¥4,489,686

SGARABOTTO, GAETANO [S3/265] Violin w/case:
North Italy, c. 1925   41,850/58,590 NS

SGARABOTTO, GAETANO [Sk11/82] Good
Modern Italian Violin: Parma, 1930   16,000/18,000
$26,450   £15,870   DM44,701   ¥3,226,900

SGARABOTTO, GAETANO (attributed to)
[P11/63A] Violin in immediate playing condition,
w/case   10,080/11,760
$5,796   £3,450   DM9,660   ¥692,726

SGARABOTTO, GAETANO (attributed to)
[S10/155] Violin: c. 1950   12,400/15,500
$12,834   £7,452   DM20,700   ¥1,511,100

SGARABOTTO, GAETANO (attributed to)
[Sk11/437A] Modern Italian Violin w/case: Parma,
1950   8,000/12,000
$8,625   £5,175   DM14,576   ¥1,052,250

SGARBI, ANTONIO [S6/34] Violin w/case, bow:
Palermo, 1912   4,125/5,775
$3,795   £2,300   DM6,831   ¥547,285

SHIPMAN, MARGARET [Bf9/4591] American
Violin: Los Angeles, 1983   1,800/2,250
$2,300   £1,380   DM3,887   ¥306,061

SIEGA, IGINIO [S10/63] Violin w/case: Venice,
c. 1925   15,500/18,600 NS

SILVESTRE, HIPPOLYTE [S1117/34] Violin w/case:
Lyon, 1863   10,020/13,360
$15,364   £9,200   DM25,668   ¥1,867,508

SILVESTRE, HIPPOLYTE CHRETIEN [S3/329]
Violin w/case: Lyon, 1882 (Silvestre & Maucotel,
Paris, January 10, 1929)   20,088/26,784 NS

SILVESTRE, HIPPOLYTE CHRETIEN [S1117/133]
Violin w/case, cover: Lyon, 1882 (Silvestre &
Maucotel, Paris, January 10, 1929)   13,360/20,040
$13,444   £8,050   DM22,460   ¥1,634,070

SILVESTRE, HIPPOLYTE CHRETIEN (attributed to)
[Sk5/111] Good French Violin w/case: Lyon, France,
1883 (N.V. Josef Vedral, The Hague, January 15,
1929)   6,000/8,000
$6,613   £3,968   DM11,770   ¥879,330

SILVESTRE, PIERRE [S1117/360] Violin w/double
case: Lyon, 1850 (W.E. Hill & Sons, London,
November 9, 1966)   25,050/33,400 NS

SIMONAZZI, AMADEO [S1117/368] Violin
w/double case: Reggio Emilia, 1945   4,950/8,250
$6,154   £3,685   DM10,281   ¥748,018

SIMONIN, CHARLES (attributed to) [P4/62] French
Violin in immediate playing condition, w/case:
c. 1850   10,836/12,503 NS

SIMONIN, CHARLES (attributed to) [P11/61]
French Violin in immediate playing condition, w/case:
c. 1850   8,400/10,080 NS

SIMPSON, JAMES & JOHN [Bf9/4603] English
Violin w/case, bow: London, c. 1785   2,000/3,000
$2,588   £1,553   DM4,373   ¥344,319

SMILLIE, ALEXANDER [B11/94] Violin
                                       3,006/4,175
$4,993   £2,990   DM8,342   ¥606,940

SMILLIE, ALEXANDER [C11/140] Scottish Violin
w/case   1,002/1,336
$1,247   £747   DM2,084   ¥151,634

SMITH, JOHN [B7/184] Violin: 1917
1,320/1,980 NS

SMITH, JOHN [B5/248] Violin: 1917
1,630/2,445 NS

SMITH, JOHN [P10/39] Good Violin in immediate playing condition, w/case: Falkirk, Scotland, 1896
1,020/1,190
$1,134   £667   DM1,848   ¥133,453

SMITH, JOHN [P12/35] Good Violin in good condition, w/case: Scotland, 1896   1,002/1,169
$1,632   £978   DM2,698   ¥190,906

SMITH, THOMAS [Sk11/339] American Violin w/case, bow: Cambridge, 1861   300/500
$201   £121   DM340   ¥24,553

SNEIDER, JOSEPH [S10/157] Violin w/case: Pavia, c. 1705   18,600/24,800 NS

SNEIDER, JOSEPH (attributed to) [Bf9/4620] Good Italian Violin: c. 1730 (Frank Passa, August 18, 1975)
15,000/19,000
$16,100   £9,660   DM27,209   ¥2,142,427

SOFFRITTI, ETTORE [S6/153] Violin w/case: North Italy, c. 1920   29,700/36,300 NS

SOLFERINO, REMO [S10/13] Violin: Mantua, 1929
3,720/4,960 NS

SOLIANI, ANGELO [C4/197] Good Italian Violin (William Lewis, Lincolnwood, March 30, 1970)
33,400/41,750 NS

SORSANO, SPIRITO [B6/100] Fine Italian Violin: 1725   50,100/66,800
$53,774   £32,200   DM96,278   ¥7,398,916

SPIDLEN, OTAKAR FRANTISEK [S3/344] Violin: Prague, 1939   1,339/2,009
$3,850   £2,300   DM7,123   ¥513,107

SPIDLEN, PREMYSL OTAKAR [S6/145] Violin w/case, cover: Prague, 1955   6,600/9,900 NS

SQUIER, VICTOR CARROLL [C11/149] American Violin w/case   1,336/2,004 NS

SQUIRE, V.C. [Sk5/278] American Violin: Battle Creek, Michigan   500/600
$374   £224   DM665   ¥49,701

STADLMANN, JOHANN JOSEPH (attributed to) [P12/38] Violin in immediate playing condition, w/case: Vienna, 1770   1,670/2,505 NS

STAINER, JACOB [C11/188] Very Fine Violin (Rudolph Wurlitzer Co., New York, May 15, 1948)
63,460/75,150
$57,615   £34,500   DM96,255   ¥7,003,155

STANLEY, C.F. [Sk5/271] American Violin w/case, bow   1,200/1,400
$1,840   £1,104   DM3,275   ¥244,683

STEFANINI, GIUSEPPE [S3/12] Violin: Brescia, 1972
5,022/8,370
$8,470   £5,060   DM15,671   ¥1,128,835

STIRRAT, DAVID [S3/340] Violin w/case: Edinburgh, 1819   8,370/11,718 NS

STIRRAT, DAVID [S1117/381] Violin w/case: Edinburgh, 1819   5,845/8,350 NS

STORIONI, CARLO [P12/34] Good Violin in good condition, w/case, cover: 1897   1,336/1,503
$1,536   £920   DM2,539   ¥179,676

STOSS, IGNAZ GEORG [S3/1] Violin: St. Pölten, c. 1810   1,004/1,339
$1,348   £805   DM2,493   ¥179,587

STRADIVARI, ANTONIO [C4/173] Very Fine Italian Violin w/case (Rembert Wurlitzer, New York, January 31, 1958)   1,085,500/1,419,500
$1,582,325£947,500   DM2,937,250   ¥211,709,400

STRADIVARI, ANTONIO [C11/189] Important Cremonese Violin (William Lewis & Son, Chicago, April 14, 1958)   835,000/1,169,000
$884,265   £529,500   DM1,477,305   ¥107,483,205

STRAUB, JOSEPH [S1117/13] Violin: Röthenbach, c. 1805 (Walter Hamma, Stuttgart, March 8, 1987)
4,676/5,845
$5,377   £3,220   DM8,984   ¥653,628

STRNAD, CASPAR [S1117/377] Violin w/case: Prague, c. 1820   11,690/16,700
$11,523   £6,900   DM19,251   ¥1,400,631

STUMPEL, H.C. [Sk5/231] German Violin   400/600
$403   £242   DM716   ¥53,524

SUZUKI [B2/79] 3/4-Size Violin   66/98
$104   £63   DM189   ¥13,102

TARANTINO, GIUSEPPE [S10/71] Violin: Naples, 1900   6,200/9,300
$6,417   £3,726   DM10,350   ¥755,550

TARR, THOMAS [B5/159] Violin   1,630/2,445 NS

TARR, THOMAS [B7/189] Violin: Sheffield
1,155/1,650
$1,176   £713   DM2,089   ¥163,199

TARR, WILLIAM [C4/122] English Seven-Eighths-Size Violin w/case   2,338/3,006 NS

TECCHLER, DAVID [P4/58] Italian Violin in immediate playing condition, w/case, bow: Rome, 1705
20,004/25,005
$23,005   £13,800   DM42,614   ¥3,072,294

TESTORE, CARLO ANTONIO [Bf9/4607] Good Italian Violin: Milan, c. 1750 (Jacques Français, July 15, 1998)   30,000/40,000 NS

TESTORE, CARLO ANTONIO [S1117/64] Violin: Milan, mid 18th C.   46,760/58,450
$30,728   £18,400   DM51,336   ¥3,735,016

TESTORE, CARLO ANTONIO [S1117/130] Violin w/case: Milan, c. 1735 (L.P. Balmforth & Son, Leeds, October 30, 1965)   30,060/41,750 NS

TESTORE, CARLO ANTONIO (attributed to) [B6/114] Fine Violin   30,060/41,750 NS

TESTORE, CARLO ANTONIO (attributed to) [B11/96] Fine Violin   20,040/25,050
$16,324   £9,775   DM27,272   ¥1,984,227

TESTORE FAMILY (MEMBER OF) [C4/194] Italian
Violin w/case   8,350/11,690
$11,523   £6,900   DM21,390   ¥1,541,736

THIBOUT, JACQUES PIERRE [C4/168] Good
French Violin w/case   15,030/20,040 NS

THIBOUVILLE-LAMY, J. [B5/293] Violin 815/1,141
$1,218   £748   DM2,168   ¥163,650

THIBOUVILLE-LAMY, J. [C4/273] French Violin
                                        334/501
$384   £230   DM713   ¥51,391

THIBOUVILLE-LAMY, J. [C4/278] French Violin
                                      835/1,169
$922   £552   DM1,711   ¥123,339

THIBOUVILLE-LAMY, J. [C4/302] French Quarter-
Size Violin
$538   £322   DM998   ¥71,948

THIBOUVILLE-LAMY, J. [C4/307] French Violin
$307   £184   DM570   ¥41,113

THIBOUVILLE-LAMY, J. [C11/404] French Half-
Size Violin w/case   334/501
$307   £184   DM513   ¥37,350

THIBOUVILLE-LAMY, J. [P4/159] Good Violin in
good condition: Mirecourt, c. 1910   667/834 NS

THIBOUVILLE-LAMY, J. [P4/165] Good Violin in
immediate playing condition, w/case: Mirecourt,
c. 1910   834/1,000 NS

THIBOUVILLE-LAMY, J. [P10/21] Good French
Violin in immediate playing condition, w/case, cover,
bow: c. 1900   1,020/1,190
$1,134   £667   DM1,848   ¥133,453

THIBOUVILLE-LAMY, J. [P10/155] Good Violin in
good condition: Mirecourt, c. 1910   340/510 NS

THIBOUVILLE-LAMY, J. [P10/157] Good Small-Size
Violin in good condition, w/case, bow: Mirecourt,
c. 1900   255/340
$371   £219   DM605   ¥43,717

THIBOUVILLE-LAMY, J. [P10/158] Good Small-Size
Violin in good condition, w/case, bow: Mirecourt,
c. 1900   170/340
$274   £161   DM446   ¥32,213

THIBOUVILLE-LAMY, J. [P10/161] Good Violin in
good condition: Mirecourt, c. 1910   680/850 NS

THIBOUVILLE-LAMY, J. [P10/173] Violin in good
condition: Mirecourt, c. 1880   340/510 NS

THIBOUVILLE-LAMY, J. [P10/174] French Violin in
good condition: Mirecourt, c. 1900   510/680
$684   £403   DM1,115   ¥80,532

THIBOUVILLE-LAMY, J. [P10/191] French Violin in
good condition: c. 1900   340/425
$352   £207   DM573   ¥41,417

THIBOUVILLE-LAMY, J. [P11/65] Good French
Violin in immediate playing condition: Paris, c. 1900
                                      1,008/1,176 NS

THIBOUVILLE-LAMY, J. [P12/69] Good French
Violin in good condition: c. 1900   668/835 NS

THIBOUVILLE-LAMY, J. [P12/77] Good French
Violin in good condition, w/case: c. 1900   835/1,002
$960   £575   DM1,587   ¥112,298

THIBOUVILLE-LAMY, J. [P12/171] Good Small-Size
French Violin: c. 1900   334/501
$480   £288   DM793   ¥56,149

THIBOUVILLE-LAMY, J. [P12/181] Violin in good
condition: Mirecourt, c. 1900   434/534 NS

THIBOUVILLE-LAMY, J. [P12/201] Good Violin in
good condition: Mirecourt, c. 1910   668/835 NS

THIBOUVILLE-LAMY, J. [P12/222] Violin w/small-
size violin: Mirecourt, c. 1900   334/501 NS

THIBOUVILLE-LAMY, J. [P12/235] Good Violin in
good condition: Mirecourt, c. 1910   334/501 NS

THIBOUVILLE-LAMY, J. [P12/245] Violin in good
condition: Mirecourt, c. 1900   418/501 NS

THIBOUVILLE-LAMY, J. [P12/248] Violin in good
condition: Mirecourt, c. 1900   334/418 NS

THIBOUVILLE-LAMY, J. [P12/249] Violin in good
condition: Mirecourt, c. 1880   167/334
$173   £104   DM286   ¥20,214

THIBOUVILLE-LAMY, J. (workshop of) [Sk5/273]
French Violin w/case   600/800
$805   £483   DM1,433   ¥107,049

THIBOUVILLE-LAMY, J. (workshop of) [Sk5/394]
French Violin   250/350
$316   £190   DM563   ¥42,055

THIR, MATHIAS [S6/121] Violin w/violin: Vienna,
c. 1790   2,970/3,630
$4,175   £2,530   DM7,514   ¥602,014

THIR, MATHIAS [S6/127] Violin: Vienna, 1775
                                      2,970/4,125
$4,934   £2,990   DM8,880   ¥711,471

THOMASSIN [S6/139] Violin w/case, cover, 2 bows:
France, 1835 (L.P. Balmforth & Son, September 24,
1960)   4,125/5,775
$8,349   £5,060   DM15,028   ¥1,204,027

THOMPSON, CHARLES & SAMUEL [B5/193]
Violin   815/1,141
$787   £483   DM1,401   ¥105,743

THOMPSON, CHARLES & SAMUEL [C11/193]
English Violin w/case   1,837/2,505
$2,689   £1,610   DM4,492   ¥326,814

THOMPSON, CHARLES & SAMUEL [P10/60]
English Violin with restorable blemishes: c. 1770
                                      680/1,020 NS

THOMPSON, CHARLES & SAMUEL [P12/217]
English Violin with restorable blemishes: c. 1770
                                        501/668 NS

THOMPSON, E.A. [Bf7/10408] Unique American
Violin w/case: Minneapolis, 1995   500/700
$288   £175   DM512   ¥39,940

TILLER, WILFRED [B5/214] Violin   652/978
$656   £403   DM1,167   ¥88,119

TIPPER, J.W. [P12/66] English Violin in good condition, w/case, bow: Derby, 1918   835/1,002
$1,191   £713   DM1,968   ¥139,249

TONONI, CARLO [S3/49] Violin w/case: Venice, c. 1720   33,480/41,850 NS

TONONI, GIOVANNI (attributed to) [Sk11/113] Italian Violin w/case: Bologna, c. 1696 (Kenneth Warren & Son, Chicago, May 13, 1974)
18,000/22,000 NS

TWEEDALE, CHARLES L. [B7/191] Violin
990/1,650
$949   £575   DM1,685   ¥131,612

TWEEDALE, CHARLES L. [P4/152] Good Violin in immediate playing condition, w/case, bow: Weston, 1926   2,000/3,001 NS

UDALRICUS, JOHANNES (attributed to) [P11/28] Violin with skillful old restorations, w/case: Prague, 1744   3,360/5,040 NS

ULCIGRAI, NICOLO [S1117/374] Violin w/case, 2 bows: Venice, 1953   3,340/5,010 NS

URFF, WILLIAM [Sk11/414] American Violin w/case, bow: Philadelphia, 1889   400/600
$431   £259   DM729   ¥52,613

UTILI, NICOLO [S10/8] Eccentric Violin: Castelbolognese, c. 1925   6,200/8,680 NS

UTILI, NICOLO [S10/48] Decorative Violin w/case, 2 bows: Castelbolognese, 1908   3,100/3,720 NS

UTILI, NICOLO [S10/121] Violin w/case: Castelbolognese, 1914   12,400/18,600 NS

VACCARI, RAFFAELLO [Bf2/4150] Fine Italian Violin: Parma, 1949 (Harry Duffy, Del Mar, California, November 22, 1997)   8,000/10,000 NS

VACCARI, RAFFAELLO [Bf9/4584] Italian Violin: Parma, 1949 (Harry Duffy, Del Mar, California, November 22, 1997)   8,000/10,000 NS

VAN DER GEEST, JACOB JAN [P4/74] Good Violin in immediate playing condition: Johannesburg, 1956
5,835/7,502 NS

VAN DER GEEST, JACOB JAN [P11/104] Good Violin in immediate playing condition   2,016/2,520
$3,091   £1,840   DM5,152   ¥369,454

VAN DER GEEST, JACOB JAN [S1117/384] Violin: c. 1930   3,006/4,175 NS

VAN HOOF, ALPHONS [S3/25] Violin: Antwerp, 1924   6,696/10,044
$6,930   £4,140   DM12,822   ¥923,593

VENTAPANE, LORENZO (ascribed to) [S1117/144] Violin w/double case: Naples, early 19th C. (L.P. Balmforth, Leeds, November 15, 1972)
33,400/50,100 NS

VENTAPANE, PASQUALE [S3/257] Violin w/case: Naples, c. 1870   4,185/5,859 NS

VENTAPANE, PASQUALE [S1117/131] Violin w/case: Naples, c. 1870   3,340/4,175
$4,033   £2,415   DM6,738   ¥490,221

VENTURINI, LUCIANO [C11/173] Italian Violin
3,340/4,175 NS

UTILI, NICOLO [S10/121] Violin w/case: Castelbolognese, 1914   12,400/18,600 NS

VETTORI, CARLO [S10/153] Violin: Florence, 1982
3,720/4,960 NS

VETTORI, CARLO [S1117/24] Violin: Florence, 1995 (maker's, August 25, 1998)   4,175/6,680
$3,457   £2,070   DM5,775   ¥420,189

VETTORI, DARIO [S10/141] Violin w/double case: Florence, 1946   9,300/12,400 NS

VETTORI, PAULO [Sk5/64] Italian Violin: Florence, 1978   3,000/4,000
$4,313   £2,588   DM7,676   ¥573,476

VICKERS, J.E. [P12/214] Contemporary Violin in good condition, w/case   418/501 NS

VILLA, LUIGI [S1117/196] Violin: Cesano Maderno, 1976   2,004/2,672 NS

VILLA, LUIGI [S1117/198] Violin: Cesano Maderno, 1970   2,004/2,672
$1,824   £1,092   DM3,047   ¥221,665

VILLA, LUIGI [S1117/201] Violin: Cesano Maderno, 1990   2,004/2,672 NS

VILLA, LUIGI [S1117/202] Violin: Cesano Maderno, 1976   2,004/2,672
$1,824   £1,092   DM3,047   ¥221,665

VILLA, LUIGI [S1117/204] Violin: Cesano Maderno, 1979   2,004/2,672 NS

VILLA, LUIGI [S1117/207] Violin: Cesano Maderno, 1977   2,004/2,672 NS

VILLA, LUIGI [S1117/208] Violin: Cesano Maderno, 1975   2,004/2,672 NS

VILLA, LUIGI [S1117/211] Violin: Cesano Maderno, 1975   3,340/5,010
$3,073   £1,840   DM5,134   ¥373,502

VILLA, LUIGI [S1117/212] Violin: Cesano Maderno, 1985   2,004/2,672 NS

VILLA, LUIGI [S1117/215] Violin: Cesano Maderno, 1988   2,338/2,672 NS

VILLA, LUIGI [S1117/216] Violin: Cesano Maderno, 1984   2,004/2,672
$1,824   £1,092   DM3,047   ¥221,665

VILLA, LUIGI [S1117/217] Violin: Cesano Maderno, 1973   2,004/2,672 NS

VILLA, LUIGI [S1117/220] Violin: Cesano Maderno, 1973   1,670/2,338 NS

VILLA, LUIGI [S1117/223] Violin: Cesano Maderno, 1987   2,505/3,006 NS

VILLA, LUIGI [S1117/225] Violin: Cesano Maderno, 1975   2,004/2,672 NS

VILLA, LUIGI [S1117/227] Violin: Cesano Maderno, 1988   2,505/3,006 NS

VILLA, LUIGI [S1117/228] Violin: Cesano Maderno, 1987   2,505/3,340 NS

VILLA, LUIGI [S1117/230] Violin: Cesano Maderno, 1978   3,340/5,010 NS

VILLA, LUIGI [S1117/231] Violin: Cesano Maderno, 1978   3,006/4,175 NS

VILLA, LUIGI [S1117/234] Violin: Cesano Maderno, 1985   2,505/3,340 NS

VILLA, LUIGI [S1117/235] Violin: Cesano Maderno, 1987   2,505/3,340 NS

VILLA, LUIGI [S1117/237] Violin: Cesano Maderno, 1983   3,340/5,010 NS

VILLA, LUIGI [S1117/238] Violin: Cesano Maderno, 1974   2,004/2,338 NS

VILLA, LUIGI [S1117/239] Violin: Cesano Maderno, 1986   2,505/3,340 NS

VILLA, LUIGI [S1117/240] Violin: Cesano Maderno, 1976   2,004/2,338 NS

VINACCIA, GAETANO [Bf2/4155] Very Fine Violin w/case: Naples, 1829 (Harry Duffy, Del Mar, California, November 23, 1997)   25,000/30,000 NS

VINACCIA, GENNARO [S3/372] Violin w/case: Naples, c. 1760   11,718/16,740
$11,551   £6,900   DM21,369   ¥1,539,321

VINCENT, ALFRED [S1117/135] Violin: London, 1924   5,845/6,680 NS

VISTOLI, LUIGI [S10/152] Violin w/case: Lugo, 1945   3,720/4,960 NS

VOIGT, JOHANN GEORG [C4/228] German Violin w/case   501/668
$768   £460   DM1,426   ¥102,782

VOIGT, PAUL [B5/154] Violin   978/1,304
$900   £552   DM1,601   ¥120,849

VUILLAUME, JEAN BAPTISTE [B3/164] Violin   3,006/4,185 NS

VUILLAUME, JEAN BAPTISTE [C4/171] Fine French Violin   46,760/58,450
$53,774   £32,200   DM99,820   ¥7,194,768

VUILLAUME, JEAN BAPTISTE [C11/214] Fine French Violin w/case   58,450/66,800
$64,963   £38,900   DM108,531   ¥7,896,311

VUILLAUME, JEAN BAPTISTE [S3/245] Violin w/case: Paris, 1861 (Marcel Vatelot, Paris, May 8, 1944)   50,220/83,700 NS

VUILLAUME, JEAN BAPTISTE [S6/1] "St. Cecile" Model Violin w/case: Mirecourt, 1844   4,950/8,250 NS

VUILLAUME, JEAN BAPTISTE [S1117/396] Violin w/case: Paris, 1861 (Marcel Vatelot, Paris, May 8, 1944)   33,400/50,100
$34,569   £20,700   DM57,753   ¥4,201,893

VUILLAUME, JEAN BAPTISTE (workshop of) [B6/84] Very Fine French Violin: Paris, c. 1860   20,040/25,050 NS

VUILLAUME, JEAN BAPTISTE (workshop of) [Sk5/108] French Violin w/case   18,000/22,000 NS

VUILLAUME, NICOLAS [P4/47] Good French Violin: Mirecourt, c. 1860   1,000/1,334 NS

VUILLAUME, NICOLAS [S6/40] Violin: Mirecourt, c. 1860 (Danial Schranz, Thun, June 1, 1994)   8,250/11,550 NS

VUILLAUME, NICOLAS FRANCOIS [Bf2/4145] Very Fine Violin: Mirecourt, 1862 16,000/20,000 NS

VUILLAUME, NICOLAS FRANCOIS [S1117/68] Violin w/case, bow: Brussels, c. 1875 11,690/15,030
$12,483   £7,475   DM20,855   ¥1,517,350

VUILLAUME, SEBASTIAN [C4/175] French Violin w/case   4,676/5,845 NS

WADE, H.F. [Sk5/270] American Violin w/case, bow   600/800
$690   £414   DM1,228   ¥91,756

WARWICK, A. [P10/72] English Violin in good condition, w/case, cover: Portsmouth, 1933   2,040/2,550 NS

WARWICK, A. [P12/56] English Violin in good condition, w/case, cover: Portsmouth, 1933 1,336/2,004
$1,191   £713   DM1,968   ¥139,249

WATSON, FRANK [C11/317] English Violin   1,169/1,503
$2,305   £1,380   DM3,850   ¥280,126

WATT, WALTER [C11/345] English Violin w/case   835/1,169
$1,440   £862   DM2,405   ¥174,977

WEBB, R.J. [P11/64] Good English Violin in good condition: London, 1949   5,880/7,560
$6,569   £3,910   DM10,948   ¥785,089

WEBSTER, GEORGE [P10/43] Violin in immediate playing condition: Aberdeen, 1958   1,190/1,360
$1,212   £713   DM1,975   ¥142,657

WELLER, FREDERICK [C4/222] English Violin w/case, bow   835/1,336
$1,632   £977   DM3,029   ¥218,301

WESTON, A.T. [Bf2/4116] Violin: Minneapolis, 1940   1,000/1,400
$863   £528   DM1,566   ¥107,105

WHITMARSH, EMANUEL [S3/253] Violin w/case, bow: London, c. 1900   1,674/2,511 NS

WIDHALM, MARTIN LEOPOLD [S1117/26] Violin w/case, bow: Nuremberg, 1805   8,350/11,690
$9,603   £5,750   DM16,043   ¥1,167,193

WILD, ANDREA (ascribed to) [C11/344] German Violin w/case   668/1,002 NS

WILKANOWSKI, W. [Sk11/338] American Violin w/case: New York   250/350
$518   £311   DM875   ¥63,135

WILLARD, ELI A. [Sk11/336] American Violin w/case: Boston, 1884   400/500
$489   £293   DM826   ¥59,628

WILLIAMS, F.C. [Bf9/4586] Fine American Violin
w/case: Elkhart, Indiana   1,600/2,400
$920   £552   DM1,555   ¥122,424

WINTERLING, GEORG [S3/11] Violin w/case, bow:
Hamburg, 1914   8,370/11,718
$8,085   £4,830   DM14,959   ¥1,077,525

WITHERS, GEORGE & SONS [P4/86] Good
English Violin with minor restorable blemishes,
w/case, bow: London, 1912   2,000/3,001 NS

WITHERS, GEORGE & SONS [P10/22] Good
English Violin with minor restorable blemishes,
w/case, bow: London, 1912   1,020/1,190
$1,329   £782   DM2,166   ¥156,463

WOLFF BROS. [P11/185] Good German Violin with
minor table blemish, w/case: 1890   672/840 NS

WOLFF BROS. [P12/194] Good German Violin in
good condition: 1894   501/668
$576   £345   DM952   ¥67,379

WOOD, OTIS W. [Sk5/357] American Violin w/case,
2 bows: 1907   400/500
$431   £259   DM768   ¥57,348

WULME-HUDSON, GEORGE [B11/111] Violin:
London, 1924   6,680/10,020
$7,682   £4,600   DM12,834   ¥933,754

WULME-HUDSON, GEORGE [B11/139] Violin:
London, 1919   6,680/10,020
$9,410   £5,635   DM15,722   ¥1,143,849

WULME-HUDSON, GEORGE [S3/286] Violin:
Walthamstow, 1897   1,339/2,009 NS

WURLITZER CO., RUDOLPH [Sk5/225] German
Violin w/case, bow   400/500
$403   £242   DM716   ¥53,524

VIOLIN BOW

ADAM (attributed to) [C4/32] French Silver Violin
Bow   6,680/10,020
$6,338   £3,795   DM11,765   ¥847,955

ADAM (attributed to) [C11/32] Silver Violin Bow
                                          8,350/11,690 NS

ALVEY, BRIAN [C4/380] Silver Violin Bow
                                             668/1,002 NS

ASHMEAD, RALPH [Bf2/4042] Transitional
American Violin Bow   1,200/1,400 NS

AUBRY, JOSEPH [S1117/424] Silver Violin Bow with
original lapping: Le Havre, c. 1930   1,002/1,336
$960   £575   DM1,604   ¥116,719

AUDINOT, JACQUES [S3/230] Silver Violin Bow:
Paris   1,172/1,674
$1,155   £690   DM2,137   ¥153,932

BASTIEN, E. [S3/193] Silver Violin Bow w/bow:
c. 1900   1,339/1,674
$1,348   £805   DM2,493   ¥179,587

BAUSCH [B5/70] Nickel Violin Bow   163/815
$150   £92   DM267   ¥20,142

BAUSCH [B7/56] Silver Violin Bow   660/990 NS

BAUSCH, LUDWIG [Sk5/151] Silver Violin Bow
                                             800/1,200
$690   £414   DM1,228   ¥91,756

BAUSCH, LUDWIG & SOHN [S3/198] Silver Violin
Bow: Leipzig, c. 1900   502/837
$673   £402   DM1,245   ¥89,682

BAUSCH, LUDWIG & SOHN [S6/57] Silver Violin
Bow: Leipzig, late 19th C.   990/1,320
$949   £575   DM1,708   ¥136,821

BAUSCH, LUDWIG & SOHN [S6/77] Silver Violin
Bow: Leipzig, c. 1900   990/1,320 NS

BAUSCH, OTTO [Bf7/10476] Silver Violin Bow
(David Jones)   800/1,300
$805   £491   DM1,433   ¥111,831

BAZIN [B2/50] Silver Violin Bow   820/1,148 NS

BAZIN [B2/52] Silver Violin Bow   1,312/1,640
$1,320   £805   DM2,402   ¥166,748

BAZIN [B3/22] Good Silver Violin Bow
                                          2,511/3,348 NS

BAZIN [B3/37] Nickel and Ivory Violin Bow without
hair, and with a later ivory button   670/1,004 NS

BAZIN [B7/63] Nickel and Ivory Violin Bow with
later ivory button, lacking hair   330/495
$380   £230   DM674   ¥52,645

BAZIN [B7/86] Nickel Violin Bow   495/660 NS

BAZIN [B5/67] Silver Violin Bow   489/815
$525   £322   DM934   ¥70,495

BAZIN [B5/78] Nickel Violin Bow   652/978 NS

BAZIN [B6/13] Good Silver Violin Bow
                                          1,670/2,505 NS

BAZIN [B10/30] Good Silver Violin Bow
                                          1,020/1,360 NS

BAZIN [S3/81] Silver Violin Bow: Mirecourt, c. 1930
                                          1,674/2,511 NS

BAZIN (workshop of) [Bf2/4089] Silver Violin Bow
                                          1,400/1,800 NS

BAZIN (workshop of) [S1117/407] Ivory Violin Bow:
Mircourt, c. 1940   2,004/2,672
$2,113   £1,265   DM3,529   ¥256,782

BAZIN, CHARLES [Bf2/4074] Silver Violin Bow
                                          2,250/2,750
$1,265   £774   DM2,297   ¥157,088

BAZIN, CHARLES [Sk5/170] Silver Violin Bow without hair   800/1,200
$1,093   £656   DM1,945   ¥145,281

BAZIN, CHARLES NICHOLAS [C4/6] Nickel Violin
Bow without hair (Jean-François Raffin, Paris,
October 5, 1997)   1,336/2,004 NS

BAZIN, CHARLES NICHOLAS [C11/55] Silver
Violin Bow without hair (Jean-François Raffin, Paris,
November 24, 1997)   1,336/2,004
$2,305   £1,380   DM3,850   ¥280,126

BAZIN, CHARLES NICHOLAS [S3/234] Silver
Violin Bow: Mirecourt, c. 1910   1,674/2,511 NS

BAZIN, CHARLES NICHOLAS [S6/56] Silver Violin
Bow: Mirecourt, early 20th C.   1,155/1,650
$1,233   £747   DM2,219   ¥177,749

BAZIN, CHARLES NICHOLAS [S10/33] Silver
Violin Bow: Mirecourt, c. 1900   1,550/2,170
$1,569   £911   DM2,530   ¥184,690

BAZIN, CHARLES NICHOLAS [S1117/164] Silver
Violin Bow: Mirecourt, c. 1900   1,002/1,336
$1,152   £690   DM1,925   ¥140,063

BAZIN, CHARLES NICHOLAS [S1117/422] Silver
Violin Bow w/bow: Mirecourt, c. 1900
                              1,336/1,670 NS

BAZIN, LOUIS [C4/64] Silver Violin Bow
                              2,004/2,505
$2,305   £1,380   DM4,278   ¥308,347

BAZIN, LOUIS [C11/15] Silver Violin Bow
                              2,505/3,006
$2,881   £1,725   DM4,813   ¥350,158

BAZIN, LOUIS [C11/54] Silver Violin Bow
                              1,336/1,670
$1,632   £977   DM2,726   ¥198,321

BAZIN, LOUIS [P11/117] French Nickel Violin Bow
without hair: c. 1940 (Jean-François Raffin, Paris,
June 10, 1998)   1,344/1,512 NS

BAZIN, LOUIS [Sk5/163] Nickel Violin Bow
                              450/650
$633   £380   DM1,126   ¥84,110

BAZIN, LOUIS (II) [S3/101] Ivory Violin Bow with
later adjuster: Mirecourt, c. 1920   1,004/1,339
$347   £207   DM641   ¥46,180

BAZIN FAMILY (MEMBER OF) [S6/59] Silver
Violin Bow without hair: Mirecourt, c. 1920
                              990/1,320
$1,612   £977   DM2,902   ¥232,477

BAZIN FAMILY (MEMBER OF) [S6/62] Silver
Violin Bow: Mirecourt, late 20th C.   990/1,320 NS

BAZIN FAMILY (MEMBER OF) (attributed to)
[S10/30] Silver Violin Bow with later frog, w/3 bows:
late 19th C.   1,984/2,232 NS

BEARE, JOHN & ARTHUR [B6/10] Silver Violin
Bow   1,336/2,004 NS

BEARE, JOHN & ARTHUR [C11/34] Silver Violin
Bow   1,670/2,505
$1,921   £1,150   DM3,209   ¥233,439

BERNARDEL, LEON [B3/17] Silver Violin Bow:
c. 1900   586/837
$539   £322   DM997   ¥71,835

BERNARDEL, LEON [B11/14] Silver Violin Bow
                              1,002/1,336 NS

BETTS [C4/26] Transitional Ivory Violin Bow
                              2,004/2,505
$2,497   £1,495   DM4,635   ¥334,043

BOLLINGER, JOSEPH [Bf9/4514] Good Silver
Violin Bow (Kenneth Warren & Sons, November 23,
1981)   1,000/1,500
$920   £552   DM1,555   ¥122,424

BOUVIN, JEAN [Bf2/4098] Silver Violin Bow
                              700/900 NS

BRAMBACH, P. OTTO [Bf9/4504] Silver Violin Bow
                              700/1,000 NS

BRYANT [B3/55] Ivory Violin Bow   1,004/1,674 NS

BRYANT [B6/25] Ivory Violin Bow   668/1,002 NS

BULTITUDE, ARTHUR RICHARD [B2/56]
Baroque-Style Ivory Violin Bow   492/820
$453   £276   DM824   ¥57,171

BULTITUDE, ARTHUR RICHARD [B6/36] Silver
and Tortoiseshell Violin Bow   1,670/2,505
$1,536   £920   DM2,751   ¥211,398

BULTITUDE, ARTHUR RICHARD [Bf9/4516]
Good Gold and Tortoiseshell Violin Bow 2,750/3,500
$3,163   £1,898   DM5,345   ¥420,834

BULTITUDE, ARTHUR RICHARD [S3/75] Gold
and Blonde-Tortoiseshell Violin Bow: Hawkhurst,
1953   3,013/4,185
$2,888   £1,725   DM5,342   ¥384,830

BULTITUDE, ARTHUR RICHARD [S3/109]
Chased-Gold and Blonde-Tortoiseshell Violin Bow:
Hawkhurst, 1965   4,687/5,859
$5,390   £3,220   DM9,972   ¥718,350

BULTITUDE, ARTHUR RICHARD [S1117/417]
Gold and Blonde-Tortoiseshell Violin Bow:
Hawkhurst, 1966 (Walter Hamma, Stuttgart, May
22, 1987)   4,175/5,010
$4,225   £2,530   DM7,059   ¥513,565

BUTHOD, CHARLES LOUIS [B5/94] Silver Violin
Bow   652/978
$1,125   £690   DM2,001   ¥151,062

BYROM, H. [B6/21] Silver Violin Bow   501/835
$691   £414   DM1,238   ¥95,129

BYRON, J. [B3/62] Silver Violin Bow   670/1,004 NS

CALLIER, FRANK [Sk11/261] American Silver
Violin Bow   250/350
$345   £207   DM583   ¥42,090

CARESSA, ALBERT [C11/226] Nickel Violin Bow
                              668/1,002 NS

CHARDON, ANDRE [B3/41] Three-Quarter-Size
Silver Violin Bow (B. Millant)   837/1,339
$1,579   £943   DM2,920   ¥210,374

CLASQUIN, G. [S1117/190] Silver Violin Bow
w/bow: Paris, c. 1920   1,169/1,670 NS

CLASQUIN, G. [Sk5/141] Silver Violin Bow
                              1,800/2,200
$2,185   £1,311   DM3,889   ¥290,561

CLAUDOT, ALBERT [S1117/418] Silver Violin Bow:
Paris, c. 1950   1,002/1,336 NS

CLUTTERBUCK, JOHN [S3/80] Silver Violin Bow:
Bicester, 1995   1,004/1,339
$1,058   £632   DM1,957   ¥140,993

COLAS, PROSPER [B6/26] Silver Violin Bow
                                         1,336/2,004 NS

COLAS, PROSPER [S3/213] Silver Violin Bow without hair: Paris, c. 1900   670/1,004
$693   £414   DM1,282   ¥92,359

COLLIN-MEZIN [C4/1] Silver Violin Bow
                                         2,004/2,505 NS

COLLIN-MEZIN [C4/24] Silver Violin Bow
                                         2,338/3,006 NS

COLLIN-MEZIN [C4/50] Silver Violin Bow
                                         2,338/3,006 NS

COLLIN-MEZIN [C4/65] Silver Violin Bow
                                         2,505/3,340 NS

COLLIN-MEZIN [C11/58] Silver Violin Bow
                                         2,004/2,505
$2,113   £1,265   DM3,529   ¥256,782

COLLIN-MEZIN [C11/233] Nickel Violin Bow
                                         668/1,002 NS

COLLIN-MEZIN, CH.J.B. [S1117/119] Silver Violin
Bow: Mirecourt, c. 1900   1,002/1,336
$960   £575   DM1,604   ¥116,719

COLLIN-MEZIN, CH.J.B. [S1117/410] Silver Violin
Bow: Paris, c. 1900   1,169/1,670
$1,575   £943   DM2,631   ¥191,420

COLLIN-MEZIN, CH.J.B. (FILS) [S10/123] Nickel
Violin Bow: Mirecourt, c. 1920   930/1,240 NS

CUNIOT-HURY [B3/59] Silver Violin Bow without
hair   1,004/1,339 NS

CUNIOT-HURY [Bf9/4519] Fine Silver Violin Bow
(Kenneth Warren & Sons, June 11, 1987) 1,200/1,600
$1,610   £966   DM2,721   ¥214,243

CUNIOT-HURY [C4/12] Silver Violin Bow
                                         1,169/1,670
$1,632   £977   DM3,029   ¥218,301

CUNIOT-HURY [C4/53] Silver Violin Bow without
hair   1,336/1,670
$2,113   £1,265   DM3,922   ¥282,652

CUNIOT-HURY [C11/3] Silver Violin Bow with
partial hair   1,336/1,670
$1,440   £862   DM2,405   ¥174,977

CUNIOT-HURY, EUGENE [B11/18A] Silver Violin
Bow   4,175/5,845 NS

CUNIOT-HURY, EUGENE [S3/66] Silver Violin Bow:
Mirecourt, c. 1900   502/837
$616   £368   DM1,140   ¥82,097

DARBEY, GEORGE [C4/19] Engraved Gold Violin
Bow   1,670/2,004 NS

DARCHE, HILAIRE [C4/38] Silver Violin Bow
                                         835/1,336
$1,344   £805   DM2,496   ¥179,869

DARCHE, HILAIRE [C4/84] Silver Violin Bow
                                         835/1,169
$960   £575   DM1,783   ¥128,478

DARCHE, HILAIRE [S3/57] Silver Violin Bow with
repaired head: Brussels, c. 1910   1,674/2,511
$1,733   £1,035   DM3,205   ¥230,898

DARCHE, HILAIRE [S6/45] Silver Violin Bow:
Brussels, early 20th C.   990/1,320
$1,612   £977   DM2,902   ¥232,477

DARCHE, HILAIRE [S10/61] Silver Violin Bow:
Brussels, c. 1900   930/1,240
$214   £124   DM345   ¥25,185

DIDIER, PAUL [Bf2/4038] Silver Violin Bow
                                         1,000/1,500 NS

DIDIER, PAUL [Bf9/4501] Violin Bow
                                         1,000/1,500 NS

DITER BROTHERS [S3/70] Silver Violin Bow:
c. 1910   670/1,004 NS

DODD [B3/26] Bone Violin Bow   837/1,172 NS

DODD [B3/57] Violin Bow   837/1,172 NS

DODD [B7/87] Nickel Violin Bow with head
separated from stick   660/990 NS

DODD [C4/14] Silver and Tortoiseshell Violin Bow
                                         1,670/2,505 NS

DODD [C4/46] Ivory Violin Bow without hair
                                         1,336/2,004 NS

DODD [C11/20] Silver and Tortoiseshell Violin Bow
                                         1,336/1,670
$1,344   £805   DM2,246   ¥163,407

DODD (attributed to) [C4/70] Violin Bow with
replacement adjuster   1,169/1,503 NS

DODD, J. [C11/66] Ivory Violin Bow without hair
                                         1,002/1,336
$960   £575   DM1,604   ¥116,719

DODD, JAMES [Bf2/4075] Silver Violin Bow
                                         1,800/2,500 NS

DODD, JAMES [S1117/159] Silver Violin Bow:
London, c. 1830   3,340/5,010 NS

DODD, JOHN [Bf2/4058] Very Fine Ivory Violin
Bow   2,500/3,000
$4,025   £2,463   DM7,309   ¥499,825

DODD, JOHN [Bf2/4081] Fine Gold and Ivory
Violin Bow   5,000/6,000 NS

DODD, JOHN [Bf9/4525] Fine Silver and Ivory
Violin Bow   5,000/6,000
$5,175   £3,105   DM8,746   ¥688,637

DODD, JOHN [Sk11/243] Silver Violin Bow
                                         1,600/1,800
$1,265   £759   DM2,138   ¥154,330

DODD FAMILY (MEMBER OF) [Sk5/157] Silver
English Violin Bow   800/1,200 NS

DOLLING, HEINZ [B5/83] Nickel Violin Bow
98/163
$169   £104   DM300   ¥22,659

DOLLING, HEINZ [S10/55] Silver Violin Bow:
Saxony, c. 1960   434/620 NS

DOLLING, HEINZ [S1117/186] Silver Violin Bow
668/1,002 NS

DORFLER, EGIDIUS [Bf9/4513] Chased-Gold and
Ivory Violin Bow   1,300/1,800
$1,150   £690   DM1,944   ¥153,031

DOTSCHKAIL, R. [Bf2/4048] Gold and Ebony
Violin Bow   1,400/1,700 NS

DOTSCHKAIL, R. [Bf2/4049] Tortoiseshell and
Silver Violin Bow   1,500/2,000 NS

DUCHAINE [Bf2/4076] Rare Transitional Violin
Bow (François Raffin, February 24, 1997)
2,500/3,250 NS

DUPUY [B3/24] Silver and Ivory Violin Bow
3,348/5,022 NS

DUPUY [B6/19] Silver and Ivory Violin Bow
2,505/3,340 NS

DUPUY [B10/34] Silver and Ivory Violin Bow
1,700/2,550
$1,760   £1,035   DM2,836   ¥217,578

DUPUY, GEORGE [Bf9/4521] Good Silver Violin
Bow (David N. Jones, July 30, 1992) 1,300/1,800 NS

ENEL, CHARLES [C4/87] Silver Violin Bow
1,169/1,503
$1,344   £805   DM2,496   ¥179,869

ENEL, CHARLES [S10/131] Silver Violin Bow: Paris,
c. 1920   1,860/2,480
$570   £331   DM920   ¥67,160

EURY, NICOLAS [S3/62A] Silver Violin Bow: Paris,
c. 1820   6,696/10,044
$7,508   £4,485   DM13,890   ¥1,000,559

FAROTTO, CELESTINO [S10/60] Silver Violin Bow:
Milan, c. 1946   620/930 NS

FETIQUE, CHARLES [B6/20] Silver Violin Bow
without hair   1,670/2,505 NS

FETIQUE, CHARLES [S1117/111] Silver Violin Bow:
Mirecourt, c. 1925   3,340/5,010
$863   £517   DM1,442   ¥104,946

FETIQUE, JULES [Sk11/147] Gold and Tortoiseshell
Violin Bow (Jacques Français, New York, March 9,
1961)   6,000/7,000
$5,750   £3,450   DM9,718   ¥701,500

FETIQUE, MARCEL [S3/65] Silver and Ivory Violin
Bow: Paris or Mirecourt, c. 1930   3,348/5,022 NS

FETIQUE, VICTOR [B6/42] Silver Violin Bow (Jean-
François Raffin)   4,676/5,845 NS

FETIQUE, VICTOR [Bf2/4082] Rare Ivory Violin
Bow   6,000/7,000
$7,475   £4,575   DM13,575   ¥928,246

FETIQUE, VICTOR [Bf9/4524] Good Silver Violin
Bow   2,500/3,200
$5,175   £3,105   DM8,746   ¥688,637

FETIQUE, VICTOR [C11/28] Silver Violin Bow
3,340/5,010 NS

FETIQUE, VICTOR [C11/39] Nickel Violin Bow
without lapping   2,338/3,006
$2,689   £1,610   DM4,492   ¥326,814

FETIQUE, VICTOR [C11/40] Silver Violin Bow
(Jean-François Raffin, Paris, December 15, 1997)
4,676/5,845
$5,377   £3,220   DM8,984   ¥653,628

FETIQUE, VICTOR [C11/47] Engraved Gold Violin
Bow without hair   6,680/10,020
$7,298   £4,370   DM12,192   ¥887,066

FETIQUE, VICTOR [P4/201] Good Silver Violin
Bow: Paris   3,334/4,168 NS

FETIQUE, VICTOR [P11/144] Good Silver Violin
Bow: Paris   3,024/3,696
$3,478   £2,070   DM5,796   ¥415,635

FETIQUE, VICTOR [S3/78] Silver Violin Bow: Paris,
early 20th C.   4,687/5,859 NS

FETIQUE, VICTOR [S3/100] Silver Violin Bow:
Paris, early 20th C.   3,348/5,022
$4,620   £2,760   DM8,548   ¥615,728

FETIQUE, VICTOR [S1117/440] Silver Violin Bow
with repaired stick and head: Paris, c. 1910
3,340/5,010 NS

FETIQUE, VICTOR (attributed to) [B11/19] Very
Fine Gold and Tortoiseshell Violin Bow
8,350/11,690 NS

FETIQUE, VICTOR (workshop of) [Sk5/79] Violin
Bow   1,200/1,400
$978   £587   DM1,740   ¥129,988

FINKEL [B2/57] Ivory Violin Bow   656/984 NS

FINKEL [B5/71] Ivory Violin Bow   489/815 NS

FINKEL [B7/51] Ivory Violin Bow   330/495
$304   £184   DM539   ¥42,116

FINKEL, JOHANNES S. [B3/44] Gold and Tortoiseshell Violin Bow   2,511/3,348 NS

FINKEL, JOHANNES S. [S3/235] Chased-Gold and
Tortoiseshell Violin Bow: Brienz, c. 1980 2,511/3,013
$2,695   £1,610   DM4,986   ¥359,175

FINKEL, JOHANNES S. [S3/236] Chased-Gold and
Tortoiseshell Violin Bow: Brienz, c. 1980
2,511/3,013 NS

FINKEL, SIEGFRIED [Sk11/227] Silver and Tortoiseshell Violin Bow   3,000/4,000 NS

FLEURY, H. [B5/84] Nickel Violin Bow   98/163
$169   £104   DM300   ¥22,659

FRANCAIS, LUCIEN [S3/190] Silver Violin Bow:
Nancy, mid 20th C.   3,013/4,185 NS

FRANCAIS, LUCIEN [S1117/157] Silver Violin Bow: Nancy, mid 20th C.   2,004/2,672
$1,921   £1,150   DM3,209   ¥233,439

GAND & BERNARDEL [C4/10] Silver Violin Bow
                                                  1,670/2,505 NS

GAND & BERNARDEL [C4/13] Nickel Violin Bow
                                                  1,169/1,670 NS

GAND & BERNARDEL [Sk11/153] Good Violin Bow   1,600/1,800 NS

GEROME, ROGER [C4/44] Silver Violin Bow
                                                  1,002/1,336
$1,152   £690   DM2,139   ¥154,174

GEROME, ROGER [C4/369] Nickel Violin Bow without hair (Jean-François Raffin, Paris, December 1, 1997)   835/1,169
$960   £575   DM1,783   ¥128,478

GEROME, ROGER [C11/1] Gold and Tortoiseshell Violin Bow   2,505/3,340 NS

GEROME, ROGER [C11/63] Gold and Tortoiseshell Violin Bow   2,505/3,340 NS

GREEN, HOWARD [C11/236] Silver Violin Bow
                                                      501/668
$730   £437   DM1,219   ¥88,707

GREEN, HOWARD [C11/243] Gold Violin Bow
                                                    668/1,002
$691   £414   DM1,155   ¥84,038

GREEN, HOWARD [C11/254] Gold Violin Bow
                                                    668/1,002
$691   £414   DM1,155   ¥84,038

GREEN, HOWARD [S3/307] Gold Violin Bow: London, c. 1995   837/1,172
$963   £575   DM1,781   ¥128,277

GRUNKE, RICHARD [Sk11/241] Silver Violin Bow
                                                  1,000/1,200
$920   £552   DM1,555   ¥112,240

HART & SON [P11/122] Silver Violin Bow or viola bow: London   1,176/1,512
$1,932   £1,150   DM3,220   ¥230,909

HAWKES & SON [B7/52] Silver Violin Bow 248/330
$266   £161   DM472   ¥36,851

HEL, PIERRE JOSEPH [S1117/73] Silver Violin Bow: c. 1900   2,505/4,175 NS

HERMANN, EMIL [Bf7/10474] Good Silver Violin Bow   700/900
$1,265   £772   DM2,252   ¥175,734

HERNOULT, HENRI (attributed to) [C11/23] Silver Violin Bow   2,004/3,006
$1,921   £1,150   DM3,209   ¥233,439

HERRMANN, A. [B6/16] Nickel Violin Bow
                                                      334/501 NS

HERRMANN, A. [B10/45] Nickel Violin Bow
                                                      255/340
$293   £173   DM473   ¥36,263

HERRMANN, EMIL [Bf2/4037] Silver Violin Bow
                                                    700/1,000 NS

HERRMANN, EMIL [Bf2/4041] Silver Violin Bow
                                                  1,000/1,500 NS

HILL, WILLIAM EBSWORTH [Sk11/133] Silver Violin Bow without hair or wrap   1,400/1,600
$1,380   £828   DM2,332   ¥168,360

HILL, W.E. & SONS [B2/47] Silver Violin Bow
                                                      984/1,640
$1,301   £794   DM2,368   ¥164,366

HILL, W.E. & SONS [B3/7] Very Fine Gold and Tortoiseshell Violin Bow   5,022/8,370
$7,700   £4,600   DM14,246   ¥1,026,214

HILL, W.E. & SONS [B3/9] Silver Violin Bow
                                                  1,674/2,511 NS

HILL, W.E. & SONS [B3/16] Silver Violin Bow
                                                  1,674/2,511
$1,925   £1,150   DM3,562   ¥256,554

HILL, W.E. & SONS [B3/30] Silver and Ivory Violin Bow   1,674/2,511
$1,925   £1,150   DM3,562   ¥256,554

HILL, W.E. & SONS [B3/31] Fine Silver and Tortoiseshell Violin Bow   3,348/5,022
$3,658   £2,185   DM6,767   ¥487,452

HILL, W.E. & SONS [B3/47] Silver Violin Bow
                                                  1,339/2,009
$1,444   £863   DM2,671   ¥192,415

HILL, W.E. & SONS [B3/53] Silver Violin Bow
                                                      837/1,172
$1,829   £1,093   DM3,383   ¥243,726

HILL, W.E. & SONS [B5/75] Silver Violin Bow
                                                      652/978 NS

HILL, W.E. & SONS [B5/95] Silver Violin Bow
                                                  1,304/1,956
$1,500   £920   DM2,668   ¥201,416

HILL, W.E. & SONS [B5/97] Silver Violin Bow
                                                  1,141/1,630
$1,312   £805   DM2,335   ¥176,239

HILL, W.E. & SONS [B6/17] Silver Violin Bow
                                                  1,336/2,004
$1,824   £1,093   DM3,267   ¥251,035

HILL, W.E. & SONS [B6/35] Silver Violin Bow
                                                  1,670/2,505
$2,401   £1,438   DM4,298   ¥330,309

HILL, W.E. & SONS [B10/28] Silver Violin Bow
                                                      680/1,020
$821   £483   DM1,323   ¥101,536

HILL, W.E. & SONS [B11/13] Gold and Tortoiseshell Violin Bow   3,340/5,010 $3,457
£2,070   DM5,775   ¥420,189

HILL, W.E. & SONS [B11/16] Gold and Ebony Violin Bow   3,340/5,010
$3,457   £2,070   DM5,775   ¥420,189

HILL, W.E. & SONS [B11/27] Silver Violin Bow
                                                  1,670/2,505
$1,921   £1,150   DM3,209   ¥233,439

HILL, W.E. & SONS [B11/8] Silver Violin Bow
3,340/5,010 NS

HILL, W.E. & SONS [C4/2] Silver Violin Bow with partial hair   1,670/2,338
$2,305   £1,380   DM4,278   ¥308,347

HILL, W.E. & SONS [C4/9] Silver Violin Bow
2,004/3,006
$2,305   £1,380   DM4,278   ¥308,347

HILL, W.E. & SONS [C4/55] Silver Violin Bow with partial hair   2,004/2,505
$2,689   £1,610   DM4,991   ¥359,738

HILL, W.E. & SONS [C4/56] Silver Violin Bow
2,505/3,340
$3,265   £1,955   DM6,061   ¥436,825

HILL, W.E. & SONS [C4/72] Silver Violin Bow
1,169/1,670
$1,632   £977   DM3,029   ¥218,301

HILL, W.E. & SONS [C11/4] Silver Violin Bow without lapping or hair   835/1,169
$863   £517   DM1,442   ¥104,946

HILL, W.E. & SONS [C11/16] Silver Violin Bow
3,006/3,674
$3,073   £1,840   DM5,134   ¥373,502

HILL, W.E. & SONS [C11/22] Silver Violin Bow
835/1,336
$1,344   £805   DM2,246   ¥163,407

HILL, W.E. & SONS [C11/52] Silver Violin Bow
1,336/1,670
$1,824   £1,092   DM3,047   ¥221,665

HILL, W.E. & SONS [C11/59A] Silver Violin Bow
1,670/2,505
$1,921   £1,150   DM3,209   ¥233,439

HILL, W.E. & SONS [C11/61] Silver Violin Bow without lapping   1,002/1,336
$1,728   £1,035   DM2,888   ¥210,095

HILL, W.E. & SONS [C11/67] Silver Violin Bow
1,336/1,670
$1,344   £805   DM2,246   ¥163,407

HILL, W.E. & SONS [P4/185] Gold Violin Bow:
London   2,501/3,334 NS

HILL, W.E. & SONS [P4/199] Good Silver Violin Bow: London   1,667/2,501
$1,917   £1,150   DM3,551   ¥256,025

HILL, W.E. & SONS [P11/109] Good Silver Violin Bow: London   1,680/2,520
$1,932   £1,150   DM3,220   ¥230,909

HILL, W.E. & SONS [P11/120] Silver Violin Bow: London   1,680/2,520
$2,512   £1,495   DM4,186   ¥300,181

HILL, W.E. & SONS [P11/124] Silver Violin Bow: London   1,344/2,016
$1,893   £1,127   DM3,156   ¥226,290

HILL, W.E. & SONS [P11/128] Silver Violin Bow: London   1,680/2,520
$2,125   £1,265   DM3,542   ¥253,999

HILL, W.E. & SONS [S3/52] Ivory Violin Bow: London, c. 1920   2,344/3,013
$2,503   £1,495   DM4,630   ¥333,520

HILL, W.E. & SONS [S3/58] Silver Violin Bow: London, 1943   1,004/1,339
$1,733   £1,035   DM3,205   ¥230,898

HILL, W.E. & SONS [S3/62] Silver Violin Bow: London, 1927   1,674/2,344
$2,310   £1,380   DM4,274   ¥307,864

HILL, W.E. & SONS [S3/63] Silver Violin Bow: London, c. 1925   2,009/2,511
$3,273   £1,955   DM6,055   ¥436,141

HILL, W.E. & SONS [S3/105] Silver Violin Bow: c. 1920   1,339/2,009
$1,733   £1,035   DM3,205   ¥230,898

HILL, W.E. & SONS [S3/200] Chased-Gold Violin Bow: London, 1964   2,511/3,348
$3,080   £1,840   DM5,698   ¥410,486

HILL, W.E. & SONS [S3/221] Silver and Tortoiseshell Violin Bow: London, 1952   2,009/2,678 $2,695
£1,610   DM4,986   ¥359,175

HILL, W.E. & SONS [S3/232] Gold and Tortoise-shell Violin Bow: London, c. 1970   4,185/5,859
$6,160   £3,680   DM11,397   ¥820,971

HILL, W.E. & SONS [S3/289] Silver Violin Bow: London, c. 1930   1,339/167
$1,443   £862   DM2,670   ¥192,304

HILL, W.E. & SONS [S3/297] Silver Violin Bow: London, c. 1935   1,339/1,674
$1,828   £1,092   DM3,382   ¥243,614

HILL, W.E. & SONS [S6/47] Silver Violin Bow: London, c. 1920   1,650/2,310 NS

HILL, W.E. & SONS [S6/75] Silver Violin Bow with repaired handle: London, c. 1930   660/990
$949   £575   DM1,708   ¥136,821

HILL, W.E. & SONS [S10/134] Silver and Tortoise-shell Violin Bow: London, c. 1935   1,860/2,480
$1,996   £1,159   DM3,220   ¥235,060

HILL, W.E. & SONS [S1117/71] Silver and Tortoise-shell "Fleur-de-Lys" Violin Bow: London, 1965
2,505/3,340
$3,649   £2,185   DM6,096   ¥443,533

HILL, W.E. & SONS [S1117/75] Silver Violin Bow: London, c. 1910   2,505/3,340
$3,265   £1,955   DM5,454   ¥396,845

HILL, W.E. & SONS [S1117/120] Silver Violin Bow without hair: London, 1937   1,002/1,336
$1,824   £1,092   DM3,047   ¥221,665

HILL, W.E. & SONS [S1117/127] Silver Violin Bow: London, 1949   1,670/2,505
$2,113   £1,265   DM3,529   ¥256,782

HILL, W.E. & SONS [S1117/409] Chased-Gold Violin Bow: London, 1971   2,505/3,340
$2,305   £1,380   DM3,850   ¥280,126

HILL, W.E. & SONS [S1117/441] Silver Violin Bow: London, c. 1910   2,004/2,672
$3,265   £1,955   DM5,454   ¥396,845

HILL, W.E. & SONS [Sk5/81] Silver Violin Bow without wrap or hair   2,000/3,000
$2,645   £1,587   DM4,708   ¥351,732

HILL, W.E. & SONS [Sk5/144] Silver Violin Bow   1,800/2,200
$2,185   £1,311   DM3,889   ¥290,561

HILL, W.E. & SONS [Sk11/140] Ivory and Silver Violin Bow   2,000/2,500
$2,530   £1,518   DM4,276   ¥308,660

HILL, W.E. & SONS [Sk11/145] Silver Violin Bow   1,600/1,800
$1,610   £966   DM2,721   ¥196,420

HILL, W.E. & SONS [Sk11/149] Gold and Tortoise-shell Violin Bow   3,000/5,000
$3,450   £2,070   DM5,831   ¥420,900

HILL, W.E. & SONS [Sk11/232] Silver Violin Bow   1,600/1,800
$2,875   £1,725   DM4,859   ¥350,750

HOUFFLACK, G. [B3/14] French Silver Violin Bow   1,674/2,511
$1,829   £1,093   DM3,383   ¥243,726

HOYER, C.A. [B7/60] Silver Violin Bow 660/990 NS

HOYER, C.A. [B10/31] Silver Violin Bow   510/850 NS

HOYER, OTTO [B7/66] Silver Violin Bow 330/660
$493   £299   DM876   ¥68,438

HOYER, OTTO [Bf7/10480] Good Silver Violin Bow   800/1,300
$1,150   £702   DM2,047   ¥159,758

HOYER, OTTO A. [C4/407] Silver Violin Bow   334/501
$538   £322   DM998   ¥71,948

HOYER, OTTO [Sk5/80] Silver Violin Bow   800/1,200
$1,265   £759   DM2,252   ¥168,220

HOYER, OTTO A. [Sk5/91] Silver Violin Bow without hair or wrap   800/1,200
$1,150   £690   DM2,047   ¥152,927

HOYER, OTTO A. [Sk5/160] Silver Violin Bow   400/600
$518   £311   DM921   ¥68,817

HOYER, OTTO A. [Sk5/161] Silver Violin Bow   600/800
$575   £345   DM1,024   ¥76,464

HOYER, OTTO A. [Sk5/171] Silver Violin Bow   800/1,200
$920   £552   DM1,638   ¥122,342

HOYER, OTTO A. [S10/34] Silver Violin Bow: Markneukirchen, c. 1930   930/1,240 NS

HUSSON, AUGUST [S10/129] Silver Violin Bow: Mirecourt, c. 1900   1,240/1,550
$856   £497   DM1,380   ¥100,740

HUSSON, AUGUST [S1117/402] Silver Violin Bow with original lapping: Paris, c. 1910   1,670/2,505
$3,073   £1,840   DM5,134   ¥373,502

HUSSON, CHARLES CLAUDE [B3/27] Silver Violin Bow   502/670
$1,155   £690   DM2,137   ¥153,932

HUSSON, CHARLES CLAUDE [S10/127] Silver Violin Bow: Mirecourt, c. 1900   1,240/1,550
$713   £414   DM1,150   ¥83,950

HUSSON, CHARLES CLAUDE [S1117/182] Silver Violin Bow: Paris, c. 1890   1,169/1,670 NS

JOMBAR, PAUL [B3/62A] Nickel Violin Bow   837/1,172 NS

JOMBAR, PAUL [S10/62] Silver Violin Bow: Paris, c. 1920   1,860/2,480 NS

KITTEL, NICOLAUS (attributed to) [Bf2/4079] Fine Silver Violin Bow   3,500/4,500
$2,588   £1,584   DM4,699   ¥321,316

KNOPF (workshop of) [Sk5/82] Silver Violin Bow   400/600
$748   £449   DM1,331   ¥99,403

KNOPF, HEINRICH [B3/21] Silver Violin Bow: c. 1870   502/670
$1,155   £690   DM2,137   ¥153,932

KNOPF, HEINRICH [S3/195] Silver Violin Bow: Berlin, c. 1870   1,172/1,674
$1,155   £690   DM2,137   ¥153,932

KNOPF, HEINRICH [S3/295] Silver Violin Bow w/bow: Berlin, c. 1870   670/1,004
$616   £368   DM1,140   ¥82,097

KNOPF, HEINRICH [S1117/438] Silver Violin Bow with original lapping: Berlin, c. 1880 1,336/2,004 NS

KNOPF, HENRY RICHARD [S10/128] Silver Violin Bow: New York, c. 1920   620/930 NS

KOVANDA, FRANK [S3/206] Silver Violin Bow: Los Angeles, c. 1950   502/837 NS

KUEHNL, EMIL [B3/63] Gold Violin Bow   NS

KUEHNL, EMIL [B11/21] Gold Violin Bow 334/501
$115   £69   DM193   ¥14,006

LABERTE [C11/224] Nickel Violin Bow (Jean-François Raffin, Paris, June 14, 1998) 835/1,169 NS

LABERTE [P11/121] Silver French Violin Bow without hair: c. 1950 (Jean-François Raffin, Paris, June 10, 1998)   1,344/1,512 NS

LABERTE, MARC [B5/73] Nickel Violin Bow   244/326
$187   £115   DM334   ¥25,177

LABERTE, MARC [S3/209] Silver Violin Bow: Mirecourt, c. 1920   1,004/1,339 NS

LABERTE, MARC [S3/305] Silver Violin Bow: Mirecourt, c. 1930   502/837
$270   £161   DM499   ¥35,917

LABERTE, MARC [S10/124] Silver Violin Bow:
Mirecourt, c. 1920   620/930
$357   £207   DM575   ¥41,975

LAFLEUR, JOSEPH RENE [C11/43] Nickel Violin
Bow (Jean-François Raffin, Paris, June 12, 1996)
                                        3,340/4,175
$3,841   £2,300   DM6,417   ¥466,877

LAMBERT, N. [S6/68] Silver Violin Bow with original lapping but without hair: Paris, early 20th C.
                                        990/1,320
$1,518   £920   DM2,732   ¥218,914

LAMY, A. [B3/74] Silver Violin Bow
                                        6,696/10,044 NS

LAMY, A. [B3/75] Fine Silver Violin Bow (Jean-
François Raffin)   7,533/10,044
$9,240   £5,520   DM17,095   ¥1,231,457

LAMY, A. [B11/4] Silver Violin Bow   4,175/5,845
$4,225   £2,530   DM7,059   ¥513,565

LAMY, A. [B11/23] Violin Bow: Paris, c. 1870
                                        6,680/10,020
$12,483   £7,475   DM20,855   ¥1,517,350

LAMY, ALFRED [C4/30] Silver Violin Bow
                                        4,175/5,010
$4,801   £2,875   DM8,913   ¥642,390

LAMY, ALFRED [C11/29] Silver Violin Bow
                                        5,010/6,680 NS

LAMY, ALFRED [C11/45] Silver Violin Bow
                                        5,010/6,680
$7,682   £4,600   DM12,834   ¥933,754

LAMY, ALFRED (attributed to) [Bf2/4057] Silver
Violin Bow   2,000/2,500
$1,265   £774   DM2,297   ¥157,088

LAMY, ALFRED JOSEPH [Bf9/4522] Good Silver
Violin Bow (David N. Jones, July 17, 1992)
                                        3,000/4,000
$3,450   £2,070   DM5,831   ¥459,092

LAMY, ALFRED JOSEPH [S3/60] Silver Violin Bow:
Paris, c. 1890   3,348/5,022 NS

LAMY, ALFRED JOSEPH [S3/298] Silver Violin Bow
without hair: Paris, c. 1890   2,511/3,348
$1,348   £805   DM2,493   ¥179,587

LAMY, ALFRED JOSEPH [S6/53] Silver Violin Bow
repaired stick: Paris, c. 1890   3,300/4,950
$4,175   £2,530   DM7,514   ¥602,014

LAMY, ALFRED JOSEPH [S6/66] Gold and Ivory
Violin Bow w/bow box: Paris, c. 1890
                                        9,900/13,200 NS

LAMY, ALFRED JOSEPH [S1117/160] Silver Violin
Bow: Paris, c. 1890   3,340/5,010
$1,344   £805   DM2,246   ¥163,407

LAMY, ALFRED JOSEPH [S1117/176] Silver Violin
Bow with original lapping: Paris, c. 1890
                                        8,350/11,690
$13,444   £8,050   DM22,460   ¥1,634,070

LAMY, ALFRED JOSEPH [S1117/177] Silver Violin
Bow: Paris, c. 1890   6,680/10,020 NS

LAMY, ALFRED JOSEPH [S1117/411] Silver Violin
Bow: Paris, c. 1900   5,010/6,680
$5,762   £3,450   DM9,626   ¥700,316

LAMY, ALFRED JOSEPH [S1117/415] Silver Violin
Bow: Paris, c. 1900   2,300/3,450 NS

LAMY, ALFRED JOSEPH [S1117/427] Silver Violin
Bow: Paris, c. 1890   5,845/8,350
$6,914   £4,140   DM11,551   ¥840,379

LAMY, HIPPOLYTE CAMILLE [S1117/166] Silver
Violin Bow with original lapping: Paris, c. 1890
                                        4,175/5,845 NS

LAPIERRE, MARCEL [C4/82] Silver Violin Bow
                                        1,002/1,503
$1,344   £805   DM2,496   ¥179,869

LAPIERRE, MARCEL [P11/140] Good French Silver
Violin Bow (Jean-François Raffin, Paris, December 1,
1997)   1,344/2,016
$1,584   £943   DM2,640   ¥189,345

LAPIERRE, MARCEL [Sk11/139] Silver Violin Bow
                                        1,800/2,200
$1,265   £759   DM2,138   ¥154,330

LAURY, N. [B2/48] Silver Violin Bow   1,312/1,968
$1,697   £1,035   DM3,088   ¥214,390

LECCHI, BERNARDO GIUSEPPE [S10/122] Gold
and Tortoiseshell Violin Bow: Genoa, c. 1945
                                        1,860/2,480 NS

LEICHT, MAX [S3/304] Silver Violin Bow:
Hohendorf, c. 1920   670/1,004
$673   £402   DM1,245   ¥89,682

LOTTE, FRANCOIS [B3/35] Silver Violin Bow
                                        1,339/2,009 NS

LOTTE, FRANCOIS [C4/81] Silver Violin Bow
(Jean-François Raffin, Paris, December 1, 1997)
                                        2,338/3,006 NS

LOTTE, FRANCOIS [C4/370] Nickel Violin Bow
(Jean-François Raffin, Paris, December 1, 1997)
                                        1,169/1,503
$1,344   £805   DM2,496   ¥179,869

LOTTE, FRANCOIS [C11/6] Silver Violin Bow with
partial hair   1,336/1,67
$1,536   £920   DM2,567   ¥186,751

LOTTE, FRANCOIS [P11/135] Silver Violin Bow
(Jean-François Raffin, Paris, December 1, 1997)
                                        1,344/2,016
$1,546   £920   DM2,576   ¥184,727

LOTTE, FRANCOIS [S3/216] Silver Violin Bow:
Mirecourt, c. 1920   1,172/1,507
$1,155   £690   DM2,137   ¥153,932

LOTTE, FRANCOIS [S1117/81] Silver Violin Bow
without hair but with extra lapping   668/835
$1,344   £805   DM2,246   ¥163,407

LOTTE, FRANCOIS [S1117/118] Silver Violin Bow
w/bow: Mirecourt, c. 1920   1,002/1,336
$2,305   £1,380   DM3,850   ¥280,126

LOTTE, FRANCOIS [Sk5/148] Nickel Violin Bow
800/1,200
$2,070   £1,242   DM3,685   ¥275,269

LOTTE, ROGER [C11/230] Silver Violin Bow
668/1,002 NS

LOTTE, ROGER-FRANCOIS [C4/54] Silver Violin
Bow (Jean-François Raffin, Paris, October 4, 1997)
2,004/2,505
$2,305   £1,380   DM4,278   ¥308,347

LOTTE, ROGER-FRANCOIS [P11/116] French
Silver Violin Bow: c. 1970 (Jean-François Raffin,
Paris, October 4, 1997)   1,680/2,016
$1,777   £1,058   DM2,962   ¥212,436

LUPOT [B6/7] Silver Violin Bow (B. Millant)
5,845/8,350 NS

LUPOT [Bf9/4520] Good Silver Violin Bow
2,500/3,500
$2,300   £1,380   DM3,887   ¥306,061

MAGNIERE, GABRIEL [Bf2/4050] Silver Violin Bow
1,000/1,500 NS

MAIRE, N. (workshop of) [B11/33] Gold and Nickel
Violin Bow   5,010/8,350
$5,762   £3,450   DM9,626   ¥700,316

MAIRE, NICOLAS [B6/31] Silver Violin Bow: Paris,
c. 1860   9,185/10,855 NS

MAIRE, NICOLAS [S3/224] Silver Violin Bow: Paris,
mid 19th C. (Jean-Jacques Millant, Paris, March 3,
1989)   11,718/13,392
$18,288   £10,925   DM33,835   ¥2,437,258

MAIRE, NICOLAS [S1117/175] Gold and Tortoiseshell Violin Bow: Paris, mid 19th C. (Walter Hamma,
Stuttgart, February 24, 1987)   13,360/16,700
$19,205   £11,500   DM32,085   ¥2,334,385

MALINE, GUILLAUME [B3/5] Very Fine Silver
Violin Bow: Paris, c. 1830 (Etienne Vatelot, Paris)
16,740/25,110 NS

MALINE, GUILLAUME [B3/6] Very Fine Silver
Violin Bow: Paris, c. 1830   20,088/25,110 NS

MALINE, GUILLAUME [Sk11/150] Silver Violin
Bow (Etienne Vatelot, Paris, November 18, 1993)
14,000/16,000
$11,500   £6,900   DM19,435   ¥1,403,000

MALINE, GUILLAUME (workshop of) [B3/34]
Silver Violin Bow (Jean-François Raffin)
3,348/5,022 NS

MARTIN, JEAN JOSEPH [C11/18] Silver Violin Bow
2,505/3,340 NS

MARTIN, JEAN JOSEPH [P4/204] Good French
Nickel Violin Bow: c. 1880 (Jean-François Raffin,
Paris, November 3, 1997)   2,000/3,001
$2,300   £1,380   DM4,261   ¥307,229

MARTIN, JEAN JOSEPH [S1117/169] Silver and
Tortoiseshell Violin Bow: c. 1880 (Gilles Duhaut,
Mirecourt, March 14, 1998)   2,004/3,006
$4,417   £2,645   DM7,380   ¥536,909

MAUCOTEL & DESCHAMPS [S3/59] Silver Violin
Bow: Paris, c. 1930   1,339/2,009
$347   £207   DM641   ¥46,180

MCGILL, A. [Bf7/10481] Good Silver Violin Bow in
perfect condition   800/1,400 NS

MCGILL, A. [Bf7/10511] Good Silver Violin Bow in
perfect condition   800/1,400 NS

MEINEL, F. [B5/82] Nickel-Mounted Violin Bow
244/326 NS

MENNESSON, EMILE [S3/222] Silver Violin Bow:
Mirecourt, c. 1880   502/837 NS

METTAL, WALTER [Bf2/4091] Ivory Violin Bow
500/700 NS

METTAL, WALTER [Bf2/4092] Ivory Violin Bow
600/800 NS

METTAL, WALTER [Bf2/4093] Tortoiseshell and
Silver Violin Bow   600/900
$690   £422   DM1,253   ¥85,684

MOHR, RODNEY D. [Sk5/97] Silver Violin Bow
500/700
$690   £414   DM1,228   ¥91,756

MOLLER & ZOON [S3/83] Silver Violin Bow:
Amsterdam, c. 1925   1,004/1,339
$1,635   £977   DM3,026   ¥217,959

MONNIG, A. HERMANN [S3/201] Silver Violin
Bow: Markneukirchen, c. 1910   1,004/1,339 NS

MORIZOT (attributed to) [P4/209] Good French
Silver Violin Bow with skillful old restoration
2,501/3,334 NS

MORIZOT, LOUIS [Bf9/4505] Good Silver Violin
Bow   1,500/2,200 NS

MORIZOT, LOUIS [C4/16] Silver Violin Bow (Jean-
François Raffin, Paris, October 4, 1992) 2,004/2,338
$1,632   £977   DM3,029   ¥218,301

MORIZOT, LOUIS [C4/60] Silver Violin Bow
2,004/2,672 NS

MORIZOT, LOUIS [C4/371] Nickel Violin Bow
without hair   668/1,002
$615   £368   DM1,141   ¥82,226

MORIZOT, LOUIS [C11/219] Nickel Violin Bow
668/1,002
$768   £460   DM1,283   ¥93,375

MORIZOT, LOUIS [S6/71] Silver Violin Bow:
Mirecourt, c. 1930   3,300/4,950 NS

MORIZOT, LOUIS (II) [S3/220] Gold and Tortoiseshell Violin Bow with spliced head: Mirecourt, mid
20th C.   1,004/1,339 NS

MORIZOT, LOUIS (II) [S1117/416] Silver Violin
Bow: Mirecourt, c. 1930   2,505/3,340 NS

MORIZOT, LOUIS (II) [S1117/419] Silver Violin
Bow with minor damage to head: Mirecourt, mid
20th C.   2,004/2,505
$1,824   £1,092   DM3,047   ¥221,665

MORIZOT (FRERES), LOUIS [C11/225] Nickel
Violin Bow (Jean-François Raffin, Paris, June 10,
1998)   1,336/1,670
$1,344   £805   DM2,246   ¥163,407

MORIZOT (FRERES), LOUIS [Sk5/87] Silver Violin
Bow (Jean-François Raffin, Paris, September 2, 1997)
                                         1,200/1,400
$1,150   £690   DM2,047   ¥152,927

MORIZOT FAMILY [Sk5/92] Silver French Violin
Bow with tinsel wrap   1,800/2,200
$2,530   £1,518   DM4,503   ¥336,439

MORIZOT FAMILY [Sk11/154] Silver Violin Bow
with original tinsel wrap   1,200/1,400
$1,265   £759   DM2,138   ¥154,330

MORIZOT FAMILY [Sk11/253] Silver Violin Bow
                                         1,400/1,600 NS

MORIZOT FAMILY [Sk11/262] Silver Violin Bow
without hair   800/1,200
$978   £587   DM1,652   ¥119,255

NURNBERGER (workshop of) [Sk5/89] Silver Violin
Bow   800/1,200
$1,265   £759   DM2,252   ¥168,220

NURNBERGER, ALBERT [B3/38] Silver Violin Bow
                                         1,674/2,511
$1,925   £1,150   DM3,562   ¥256,554

NURNBERGER, ALBERT [B11/1] Very Fine Gold
Violin Bow   5,010/6,680 NS

NURNBERGER, ALBERT [Bf2/1403] Silver Violin
Bow   1,400/1,800
$1,495   £915   DM2,715   ¥185,649

NURNBERGER, ALBERT [Bf2/4046] Tortoiseshell
and Gold Violin Bow   1,500/2,000 NS

NURNBERGER, ALBERT [Bf2/4097] Fine Silver
Violin Bow   1,500/2,000 NS

NURNBERGER, ALBERT [Bf2/4100] Silver Violin
Bow   1,400/1,700
$1,495   £915   DM2,715   ¥185,649

NURNBERGER, ALBERT [Bf9/4508] Silver and
Tortoiseshell Violin Bow   1,200/1,700
$1,093   £656   DM1,846   ¥145,379

NURNBERGER, ALBERT [Bf9/4518] Silver Violin
Bow   1,000/1,600
$1,035   £621   DM1,749   ¥137,727

NURNBERGER, ALBERT [C4/5] Silver Violin Bow
                                         1,336/2,004
$1,536   £920   DM2,852   ¥205,565

NURNBERGER, ALBERT [C11/5] Silver Violin Bow
                                         668/835
$1,728   £1,035   DM2,888   ¥210,095

NURNBERGER, ALBERT [C11/217] Silver Violin
Bow   1,169/1,670
$960   £575   DM1,604   ¥116,719

NURNBERGER, ALBERT [C11/223] Silver Violin
Bow without hair   334/501
$960   £575   DM1,604   ¥116,719

NURNBERGER, ALBERT [C11/248] Silver Violin
Bow   501/668 NS

NURNBERGER, ALBERT [C11/250] Silver Violin
Bow   585/752
$576   £345   DM963   ¥70,032

NURNBERGER, ALBERT [C11/266] Silver Violin
Bow   501/668 NS

NURNBERGER, ALBERT [C11/270] Gold Violin
Bow   1,002/1,503
$1,055   £632   DM1,763   ¥128,290

NURNBERGER, ALBERT [Sk5/168] Silver Violin
Bow, frog and adjuster not original   400/600
$546   £328   DM972   ¥72,640

NURNBERGER, ALBERT [Sk11/142] Silver Violin
Bow   800/1,200
$1,093   £656   DM1,846   ¥133,285

NURNBERGER, ALBERT [Sk11/157] Silver Violin
Bow   500/600
$805   £483   DM1,360   ¥98,210

NURNBERGER, ALBERT (workshop of) [Bf2/4096]
Violin Bow   1,000/1,500 NS

NURNBERGER, CHRISTIAN ALBERT [S1117/191]
Silver Violin Bow: c. 1970 (maker's, Berlin)
                                         1,336/2,004
$1,536   £920   DM2,567   ¥186,751

NURNBERGER, KARL ALBERT [S3/51] Gold
Violin Bow: Markneukirchen   2,009/2,678
$2,695   £1,610   DM4,986   ¥359,175

NURNBERGER, KARL ALBERT [S3/79] Silver
Violin Bow without lapping: Markneukirchen, mid
20th C.   1,004/1,339
$1,635   £977   DM3,026   ¥217,959

NURNBERGER, KARL ALBERT [S3/110] Nickel
Violin Bow without hair: Markneukirchen, mid
20th C.   502/837
$865   £517   DM1,601   ¥115,338

NURNBERGER, KARL ALBERT [S3/211] Silver
Violin Bow   1,339/1,674
$1,635   £977   DM3,026   ¥217,959

NURNBERGER, KARL ALBERT [S3/228]
Silver Violin Bow: Markneukirchen, c. 1930
                                         1,004/1,339 NS

NURNBERGER, KARL ALBERT [S3/231] Silver
Violin Bow: Markneukirchen   1,339/2,009
$1,348   £805   DM2,493   ¥179,587

NURNBERGER, KARL ALBERT [S6/44] Silver
Violin Bow: Markneukirchen, c. 1930   1,650/2,310
$1,518   £920   DM2,732   ¥218,914

NURNBERGER, KARL ALBERT [S10/133] Silver
Violin Bow: Markneukirchen, c. 1930   930/1,240 NS

NURNBERGER, KARL ALBERT [S1117/72] Gold
Violin Bow: Markneukirchen, ca. 1960   1,670/2,505
$3,457   £2,070   DM5,775   ¥420,189

NURNBERGER, KARL ALBERT [S1117/121] Silver
Violin Bow: Markneukirchen, c. 1930   1,336/1,670
$1,824   £1,092   DM3,047   ¥221,665

NURNBERGER, KARL ALBERT [S1117/154] Silver
Violin Bow   1,336/2,004
$1,536   £920   DM2,567   ¥186,751

NURNBERGER, KARL ALBERT [S1117/170] Silver
Violin Bow: Markneukirchen, c. 1930   1,002/1,336
$960   £575   DM1,604   ¥116,719

NURNBERGER, KARL ALBERT [S1117/185] Silver
Violin Bow   1,336/2,004
$2,689   £1,610   DM4,492   ¥326,814

NURNBERGER, KARL ALBERT [S1117/437] Silver
Violin Bow: Markneukirchen   1,336/2,004
$1,344   £805   DM2,246   ¥163,407

OUCHARD, BERNARD [S10/136] Silver Violin
Bow: Geneva, c. 1950   806/3,100 NS

OUCHARD, EMILE [B3/27A] Silver Violin Bow
                                             3,348/5,022 NS

OUCHARD, EMILE [B6/44] Silver Violin Bow
                                             2,505/3,340 NS

OUCHARD, EMILE [C4/29] Silver Violin Bow
                                             3,340/4,175 NS

OUCHARD, EMILE [C4/47] Silver Violin Bow
                                             2,338/3,006
$3,265   £1,955   DM6,061   ¥436,825

OUCHARD, EMILE [C11/10] Silver Violin Bow
                                             2,004/2,505
$3,265   £1,955   DM5,454   ¥396,845

OUCHARD, EMILE [C11/42] Silver Violin Bow
                                             2,505/3,340
$3,457   £2,070   DM5,775   ¥420,189

OUCHARD, EMILE [P4/212] Nickel Violin Bow
(Jean-François Raffin, Paris, May 5, 1997)
                                             1,167/1,334
$1,495   £897   DM2,770   ¥199,699

OUCHARD, EMILE [S3/113] Silver Violin Bow:
Mirecourt, c. 1920 (Claude Lebet, La Chaux-de-
Fonds, May 9, 1997)   2,511/3,348
$5,005   £2,990   DM9,260   ¥667,039

OUCHARD, EMILE [Sk11/137] Silver Violin Bow
                                             3,200/3,400 NS

OUCHARD, EMILE [Sk11/144] Silver Violin Bow
                                             3,000/4,000
$6,038   £3,623   DM10,203   ¥736,575

OUCHARD, EMILE A. [B3/51] Silver Violin Bow
                                             4,185/5,859 NS

OUCHARD, EMILE A. [S3/196] Silver Violin Bow:
c. 1925   1,004/1,339
$519   £310   DM960   ¥69,158

OUCHARD, EMILE FRANCOIS [S3/95] Silver
Violin Bow with later adjuster: Mirecourt, c. 1920
                                             2,009/2,678
$2,118   £1,265   DM3,918   ¥282,209

OUCHARD, EMILE FRANCOIS [S1117/112] Silver
Violin Bow: Mirecourt, c. 1920   1,169/1,670
$2,689   £1,610   DM4,492   ¥326,814

OUCHARD, EMILE FRANCOIS [S10/58] Silver
Violin Bow: Mirecourt, c. 1920   2,480/3,720 NS

OUDINOT [B6/41] Gold Violin Bow 1,503/2,004 NS

PAJEOT [S6/65] Gold and Tortoiseshell Violin Bow:
Paris, c. 1830   9,900/13,200
$11,765   £7,130   DM21,176   ¥1,696,584

PAJEOT, ETIENNE [B3/66] Fine Silver Violin Bow
(J. Roda, 1966)   6,696/10,044 NS

PAJEOT, ETIENNE [B6/37] Silver Violin Bow
(J. Roda, 1966)   5,010/6,680 NS

PAJEOT, ETIENNE [B11/31] Silver Violin Bow
(J. Roda, 1966)   5,010/6,680 NS

PAJEOT, ETIENNE [Bf2/4080] Fine and Rare Ivory
Violin Bow in a fine state of preservation
                                             9,000/11,000
$9,775   £5,982   DM17,751   ¥1,213,860

PAJEOT, ETIENNE [S3/226] Silver Violin Bow: Paris,
c. 1840   5,859/8,370 NS

PAJEOT, ETIENNE [Sk5/95] Silver Violin Bow:
c. 1840 (Paul Childs, Montrose, July 3, 1997)
                                             7,000/9,000
$6,900   £4,140   DM12,282   ¥917,562

PAJEOT, ETIENNE [Sk11/210] Fine Nickel Violin
Bow: c. 1830 (Bernard Millant, October 18, 1995)
                                             10,000/12,000
$13,800   £8,280   DM23,322   ¥1,683,600

PAJEOT, LOUIS SIMON [B6/30] Bone and Silver
Violin Bow   9,185/10,855 NS

PANORMO, LOUIS [S1117/174] Silver Violin Bow:
London, c. 1840   1,002/1,336
$960   £575   DM1,604   ¥116,719

PAULUS, GUNTER A. [C4/67] Gold and Tortoiseshell Violin Bow   1,169/1,670
$1,344   £805   DM2,496   ¥179,869

PECATTE, C. [B11/15] Silver Violin Bow
                                             5,845/9,185 NS

PECCATTE, D. & HENRY, J. [B6/29] Fine Nickel
Violin Bow: Paris, c. 1860 (Jean-François Raffin)
                                             6,680/10,020
$7,682   £4,600   DM13,754   ¥1,056,988

PECCATTE, DOMINIQUE [B3/68] Self-Rehairing
Silver Violin Bow modified for normal use; shaft
spliced under lapping: Paris, c. 1850 5,022/8,370 NS

PECCATTE, DOMINIQUE (ascribed to) [P4/179]
Fine, Handsome, and Interesting Violin Bow
                                             13,336/20,004 NS

PENZEL, K. GERHARD [S3/291] Silver Violin Bow:
Germany, c. 1960   1,004/1,339 NS

PERSOIS [C4/80] Silver Violin Bow (William Lewis
& Son, Chicago, January 19, 1965)   20,040/23,380
$20,165   £12,075   DM37,433   ¥2,698,038

PFRETZSCHNER [B5/93] Silver Violin Bow 489/815
$469   £288   DM834   ¥62,942

PFRETZSCHNER, G.A. [Bf9/4509] Chased Silver
Violin Bow (David N. Jones, July 30, 1992)

			1,200/1,500
$1,380	£828	DM2,332	¥183,637

PFRETZSCHNER, G.A. [Bf9/4511] Gold and Ebony
Violin Bow   700/1,300

$690	£414	DM1,166	¥91,818

PFRETZSCHNER, H.R. [B2/51] Silver Violin Bow

			656/984
$660	£403	DM1,201	¥83,374

PFRETZSCHNER, H.R. [B2/58] Silver Violin Bow
820/1,148 NS

PFRETZSCHNER, H.R. [B3/48] Silver Violin Bow

			670/1,004
$674	£403	DM1,247	¥89,794

PFRETZSCHNER, H.R. [Bf2/4065] Silver Violin
Bow   1,400/1,700

$863	£528	DM1,566	¥107,105

PFRETZSCHNER, H.R. [Bf9/4523] Fine Silver Violin
Bow, frog possibly later   2,000/2,500

$1,840	£1,104	DM3,110	¥244,849

PFRETZSCHNER, H.R. [C11/251] Silver Violin Bow

			585/752
$671	£402	DM1,122	¥81,602

PFRETZSCHNER, H.R. [C11/258] Silver Violin Bow

			585/752
$768	£460	DM1,283	¥93,375

PFRETZSCHNER, H.R. [S3/212] Nickel Violin Bow
1,339/2,009 NS

PFRETZSCHNER, H.R. [S3/229] Silver Violin Bow:
Markneukirchen   1,004/1,339 NS

PFRETZSCHNER, H.R. [S1117/76] Silver Violin
Bow: Markneukirchen   835/1,169

$3,073	£1,840	DM5,134	¥373,502

PFRETZSCHNER, H.R. [S1117/122] Nickel Violin
Bow   1,002/1,336 NS

PFRETZSCHNER, H.R. [S1117/156] Silver Violin
Bow   668/1,002

$922	£552	DM1,540	¥112,050

PFRETZSCHNER, H.R. [S1117/404] Silver Violin
Bow w/violoncello bow: Markneukirchen, c. 1930
1,336/2,004 NS

PFRETZSCHNER, H.R. [Sk11/158] Silver Violin
Bow   1,000/1,500

$1,035	£621	DM1,749	¥126,270

PFRETZSCHNER, H.R. (workshop of) [Sk11/237]
Engraved Silver Violin Bow without hair   400/500

$489	£293	DM826	¥59,628

PFRETZSCHNER, W.A. [S3/322] Silver Violin Bow:
Markneukirchen, early 20th C.   837/1,172

$770	£460	DM1,425	¥102,621

PILLOT [C4/36] Silver Violin Bow with partial hair
835/1,169

$1,728	£1,035	DM3,209	¥231,260

POIRSON [B3/42A] Nickel Violin Bow without hair
and with a later button   1,004/1,674 NS

POIRSON, JUSTIN [P11/112] Silver Violin Bow:
Paris (Jean-François Raffin, Paris, March 17, 1997)
4,200/5,040 NS

POIRSON, JUSTIN [S6/46] Silver Violin Bow without hair: Paris, c. 1900   1,320/1,980 NS

PRAGA, EUGENIO [S10/56] Silver Violin Bow:
Genoa, c. 1890   868/1,116 NS

PRAGER, AUGUST EDWIN [B10/48A] Gold Violin
Bow   850/1,190

$1,564	£920	DM2,521	¥193,402

PRAGER, AUGUST EDWIN [C4/405] Silver Violin
Bow   334/501

$576	£345	DM1,070	¥77,087

PRAGER, AUGUST EDWIN [S3/310] Gold and
Tortoiseshell Violin Bow w/bow box: Marknew-
kirchen, c. 1930   2,009/2,678

$2,310	£1,380	DM4,274	¥307,864

PRAGER, AUGUST EDWIN [S3/311] Gold Violin
Bow w/bow box: Markneukirchen, c. 1930

			1,674/2,511
$1,925	£1,150	DM3,562	¥256,554

PRAGER, AUGUST EDWIN [S3/312] Gold Portrait
Violin Bow w/bow box: Markneukirchen, c. 1930
2,009/2,678 NS

PRAGER, AUGUST EDWIN [S3/313] Gold Portrait
Violin Bow w/bow box: Markneukirchen
2,009/2,678 NS

PRAGER, AUGUST EDWIN [S3/314] Gold Portrait
Violin Bow: Markneukirchen   2,009/2,678 NS

PRAGER, AUGUST EDWIN [S3/315] Silver Violin
Bow: Markneukirchen   837/1,172

$963	£575	DM1,781	¥128,277

PRAGER, AUGUST EDWIN [S3/318] Nickel Violin
Bow without hair or lapping: Markneukirchen
670/1,004 NS

PRAGER, AUGUST EDWIN [S6/84] Silver Portrait
Violin Bow   1,155/1,650

$1,898	£1,150	DM3,416	¥273,643

PRAGER, AUGUST EDWIN [S1117/82] Gold
Portrait Violin Bow: Markneukirchen   1,336/2,004

$1,344	£805	DM2,246	¥163,407

PRAGER, AUGUST EDWIN [S1117/165] Silver
Violin Bow: Markneukirchen, c. 1930   1,002/1,336

$960	£575	DM1,604	¥116,719

PRAGER, AUGUST EDWIN [S1117/171] Gold
Portrait Violin Bow w/bow box: Markneukirchen,
c. 1930   1,336/2,004

$1,344	£805	DM2,246	¥163,407

PRAGER, AUGUST EDWIN [S1117/189] Gold
Portrait Violin Bow w/bow box   1,336/2,004

$1,824	£1,092	DM3,047	¥221,665

PRAGER, GUSTAV [C11/227] Silver Violin Bow
835/1,169 NS

PRAGER, GUSTAV OSKAR [S1117/405] Silver
Violin Bow: Markneukirchen   668/1,002
$922   £552   DM1,540   ¥112,050

PRELL, HERMAN WILHELM [Bf2/4090] Gold and
Tortoiseshell Violin Bow   1,700/2,000 NS

PRELL, HERMAN WILHELM [P11/139] Part-Gold
Violin Bow   588/756
$985   £587   DM1,642   ¥117,763

PRELL, HERMAN WILHELM [S3/296] Silver Violin
Bow: Markneukirchen, c. 1920   1,004/1,339 NS

RAU, AUGUST [S3/321] Gold Violin Bow:
Markneukirchen   670/1,004
$963   £575   DM1,781   ¥128,277

ROBICHAUD [C11/37] Silver Violin Bow
                                            1,336/1,670
$1,536   £920   DM2,567   ¥186,751

ROLLAND [C11/41] Gold and Tortoiseshell Violin
Bow   2,505/3,340
$5,762   £3,450   DM9,626   ¥700,316

SARTORY, EUGENE [B3/4] Silver Violin Bow: Paris,
c. 1920   8,370/11,71
$16,363   £9,775   DM30,273   ¥2,180,705

SARTORY, EUGENE [B3/72] Extremely Fine Silver
Violin Bow   13,392/16,740
$15,401   £9,200   DM28,492   ¥2,052,428

SARTORY, EUGENE [B7/77A] Silver Violin Bow
with repaired head   1,650/2,475
$1,898   £1,150   DM3,370   ¥263,224

SARTORY, EUGENE [B11/12] Silver Violin Bow
                                           6,680/10,020
$7,298   £4,370   DM12,192   ¥887,066

SARTORY, EUGENE [C11/31] Silver Violin Bow
                                          6,680/8,350 NS

SARTORY, EUGENE [P4/176] Good Silver Violin
Bow: Paris (Gilles Chancereul, Paris, October 30,
1997)   7,502/9,169
$8,627   £5,175   DM15,980   ¥1,152,110

SARTORY, EUGENE [P10/84] Silver Violin Bow:
Paris   8,500/10,200 NS

SARTORY, EUGENE [P12/94] Silver Violin Bow:
Paris   6,680/8,350 NS

SARTORY, EUGENE [S3/111] Silver Violin Bow:
Paris, c. 1925   5,859/8,370 NS

SARTORY, EUGENE [S6/43] Silver Violin Bow:
Paris, c. 1930   4,950/8,250
$9,108   £5,520   DM16,394   ¥1,313,484

SARTORY, EUGENE [S6/51] Silver Exhibition Violin
Bow without lapping: Paris, 1908   6,600/9,900
$11,006   £6,670   DM19,810   ¥1,587,127

SARTORY, EUGENE [S6/52] Silver Violin Bow with
original lapping: Paris, c. 1920   9,900/13,200
$12,524   £7,590   DM22,542   ¥1,806,041

SARTORY, EUGENE [S6/80] Silver Violin Bow with
repaired head: Paris, c. 1920   3,300/4,950 NS

SARTORY, EUGENE [S6/82] Violin Bow: Paris,
c. 1920   3,300/4,950
$3,226   £1,955   DM5,806   ¥465,192

SARTORY, EUGENE [S10/132] Silver Violin Bow
with later adjuster: Paris, c. 1920   2,480/3,100 NS

SARTORY, EUGENE [S1117/428] Silver Violin Bow:
Paris, c. 1905   6,680/10,020
$9,987   £5,980   DM16,684   ¥1,213,880

SARTORY, EUGENE [S1117/431] Silver Violin Bow
w/bow box: Paris, c. 1910   8,350/11,690 NS

SARTORY, EUGENE [Sk5/84] Silver Violin Bow
without hair: Paris   1,500/2,000
$4,140   £2,484   DM7,369   ¥550,537

SARTORY, EUGENE [Sk5/156] Silver Violin Bow
                                             800/1,200
$920   £552   DM1,638   ¥122,342

SARTORY, EUGENE (attributed to) [C11/50] French
Silver Violin Bow   1,670/2,505
$2,689   £1,610   DM4,492   ¥326,814

SARTORY, EUGENE (workshop of) [B3/50] Silver
Violin Bow (J.F. Raffin, Paris, 1997)   2,511/3,348
$3,658   £2,185   DM6,767   ¥487,452

SCHICKER, HORST [C4/381] Silver Violin Bow
                                            418/585 NS

SCHMIDT, HANS KARL [Sk11/151] Gold and
Tortoiseshell Violin Bow   3,500/4,500 NS

SCHMITT, LUCIEN [S6/78] Silver Violin Bow:
Grenoble, mid 20th C.   1,155/1,485
$1,518   £920   DM2,732   ¥218,914

SCHUSTER, ADOLF [Bf2/1401] Silver Violin Bow
                                            700/900 NS

SCHUSTER, ADOLF [C4/86] Silver Violin Bow
                                           835/1,169 NS

SCHUSTER, MAX K. [Sk5/90] Gold and Ebony
Violin Bow   800/1,200
$1,035   £621   DM1,842   ¥137,634

SEIFERT, LOTHAR [C4/383] Gold Violin Bow
                                            835/1,169
$1,055   £632   DM1,959   ¥141,214

SEIFERT, LOTHAR [S1117/425] Gold and Ivory
Violin Bow   2,004/2,505 NS

SERDET, PAUL [S10/135] Silver Violin Bow:
Mirecourt, c. 1930   620/992 NS

SILVESTRE & MAUCOTEL [B3/38A] Silver Violin
Bow   837/1,172 NS

SILVESTRE & MAUCOTEL [Bf2/1402] Silver Violin
Bow   2,500/3,000 NS

SILVESTRE & MAUCOTEL [Bf2/4040] Silver Violin
Bow   2,000/2,500 NS

SILVESTRE & MAUCOTEL [S10/57] Silver Violin
Bow: Mirecourt, c. 1900   1,550/1,860 NS

SIMON, PAUL [S6/73] Silver Self-Rehairing Violin
Bow, semi-converted, with minor damage to head:
Paris, c. 1840   3,300/4,125
$3,795   £2,300   DM6,831   ¥547,285

SIMON, PAUL [Sk5/150] Silver Violin Bow: Paris,
c. 1865   6,000/8,000
$6,325   £3,795   DM11,259   ¥841,098

SIMON, PAUL (attributed to) [Sk5/83] Fine Gold and
Tortoiseshell Violin Bow   4,000/6,000
$4,140   £2,484   DM7,369   ¥550,537

TAYLOR, MALCOLM [S3/54] Gold Violin Bow:
Barnstaple   1,339/2,009 NS

THIBOUVILLE-LAMY, J. [S3/112] Silver Violin
Bow: Mirecourt, c. 1890   502/837
$462   £276   DM855   ¥61,573

THIBOUVILLE-LAMY, J. [S3/191] Silver and Ivory
Violin Bow: Mirecourt, c. 1900   1,004/1,339
$519   £310   DM960   ¥69,158

THIBOUVILLE-LAMY, J. [S3/197] Silver Violin Bow
w/bow: Mirecourt, c. 1900   670/1,004 NS

THIBOUVILLE-LAMY, J. [S6/74] Silver Violin Bow:
Mirecourt, c. 1870   660/990 NS

THOMASSIN, C. [B3/20] Silver Violin Bow
                                     1,004/1,674
$1,059   £633   DM1,959   ¥141,104

THOMASSIN, C. [B3/39] Fine Silver Violin Bow
                                     4,185/5,859 NS

THOMASSIN, C. [B6/9] Silver Violin Bow
                                     3,340/5,010 NS

THOMASSIN, C. [B10/42] Silver Violin Bow
                                     1,700/2,550
$1,662   £978   DM2,678   ¥205,490

THOMASSIN, CLAUDE [B3/56] Fine Silver Violin
Bow   5,022/6,696 NS

THOMASSIN, CLAUDE [C4/42] Gold Violin Bow
                                     1,670/2,338
$1,728   £1,035   DM3,209   ¥231,260

THOMASSIN, CLAUDE [P11/129] Good Silver
Violin Bow with minor restored blemish: Paris (Jean-
François Raffin, Paris, September 13, 1998)
                                     2,520/3,024
$2,898   £1,725   DM4,830   ¥346,363

THOMASSIN, CLAUDE [S3/72] Silver Violin Bow:
Paris, c. 1920   2,511/3,348
$5,198   £3,105   DM9,616   ¥692,694

THOMASSIN, CLAUDE [S3/192] Silver Violin Bow:
Paris, c. 1920   1,674/2,511 NS

THOMASSIN, CLAUDE [S6/42] Silver Violin Bow:
Mirecourt, early 20th C.   1,320/1,980
$4,364   £2,645   DM7,856   ¥629,378

THOMASSIN, CLAUDE [S10/125] Silver Violin
Bow: Mirecourt, c. 1910   1,550/2,170
$713   £414   DM1,150   ¥83,950

THOMASSIN, CLAUDE [Sk5/147] Silver Violin Bow
                                     1,800/2,200
$2,645   £1,587   DM4,708   ¥351,732

TOURTE, FRANCOIS [Bf2/4086] Fine and Rare
Silver Violin Bow in a good state of preservation
                                     40,000/50,000 NS

TOURTE, FRANCOIS (ascribed to) [P4/178] Silver
Violin Bow with restorations   16,670/25,005 NS

TOURTE, FRANCOIS XAVIER [S3/56] Silver Violin
Bow with later ebony adjuster and without hair:
Paris, c. 1810   30,132/41,850 NS

TUBBS [B5/96] Silver Violin Bow   978/1,630
$1,312   £805   DM2,335   ¥176,239

TUBBS [B7/73] Silver Violin Bow with later frog
                                     660/990
$664   £403   DM1,179   ¥92,128

TUBBS, ALFRED [B11/34] Rare Silver Violin Bow
                                     3,340/5,010 NS

TUBBS, JAMES [B3/8] Extremely Fine and Rare Gold
and Tortoiseshell Violin Bow: London, c. 1860
                                     8,370/11,718
$11,551   £6,900   DM21,369   ¥1,539,321

TUBBS, JAMES [B3/32] Fine Silver Violin Bow
                                     4,185/5,859
$5,005   £2,990   DM9,260   ¥667,039

TUBBS, JAMES [B3/33] Silver Violin Bow
                                     2,511/3,348
$2,888   £1,725   DM5,342   ¥384,830

TUBBS, JAMES [B7/59] Silver Violin Bow without
hair   2,475/3,300
$1,803   £1,093   DM3,201   ¥250,062

TUBBS, JAMES [B11/6] Silver Violin Bow
                                     4,175/5,845 NS

TUBBS, JAMES [B11/7] Silver Violin Bow
                                     3,006/4,175 NS

TUBBS, JAMES [B11/32] Silver Violin Bow
                                     5,010/8,350 NS

TUBBS, JAMES [C4/25] Silver Violin Bow
                                     3,340/4,175 NS

TUBBS, JAMES [P4/183] Fine and Handsome Silver
Violin Bow: London   4,168/5,835 NS

TUBBS, JAMES [P4/184] Fine and Handsome Silver
Violin Bow: London   4,168/5,835 NS

TUBBS, JAMES [P4/186] Good Silver Violin Bow:
London   3,334/5,001
$3,642   £2,185   DM6,747   ¥486,447

TUBBS, JAMES [S3/68] Silver Violin Bow: London,
c. 1890 (Joseph Roda, Riverside, Illinois, October 18,
1967)   3,013/4,185
$3,273   £1,955   DM6,055   ¥436,141

TUBBS, JAMES [S3/89] Silver Violin Bow: London,
c. 1900   5,859/8,370
$6,353   £3,795   DM11,753   ¥846,627

TUBBS, JAMES [S3/99] Silver Violin Bow: London, c. 1900   1,674/2,511 NS

TUBBS, JAMES [S3/215] Silver Violin Bow: London, c. 1880   2,511/3,348
$5,005   £2,990   DM9,260   ¥667,039

TUBBS, JAMES [S6/83] Silver Violin Bow with repaired head: London, c. 1900   1,650/3,300 NS

TUBBS, JAMES [S1117/77] Silver Violin Bow: London, c. 1900   4,175/5,845 NS

TUBBS, JAMES [S1117/109] Silver Violin Bow: London, c. 1890   3,006/3,340 NS

TUBBS, JAMES [S1117/178] Silver Violin Bow: London, c. 1890   6,680/10,020 NS

TUBBS, JAMES [S1117/179] Silver Violin Bow with original lapping: London, c. 1890   5,010/8,350
$5,377   £3,220   DM8,984   ¥653,628

TUBBS, JAMES [S1117/180] Silver Violin Bow: London, c. 1900   1,169/1,670
$1,152   £690   DM1,925   ¥140,063

TUBBS, JAMES [S1117/401] Silver Violin Bow: London, c. 1900   5,010/6,680
$5,377   £3,220   DM8,984   ¥653,628

TUBBS, JAMES [S1117/420] Silver Violin Bow with original lapping: London, c. 1900   2,505/3,340
$4,609   £2,760   DM7,700   ¥560,252

TUBBS, JAMES [Sk11/143] Silver Violin Bow   2,800/3,200
$2,990   £1,794   DM5,053   ¥364,780

TUBBS, JAMES [Sk11/245] Silver Violin Bow   2,500/3,500
$2,875   £1,725   DM4,859   ¥350,750

TUBBS, WILLIAM [C4/39] Silver Violin Bow with replacement adjuster   1,336/2,004 NS

TUBBS, WILLIAM [C11/21] Silver Violin Bow   1,002/1,670 NS

TUBBS, WILLIAM (attributed to) [P4/181] Gold Violin Bow with later frog: London   2,000/2,501
$2,109   £1,265   DM3,906   ¥281,627

UEBEL, K. WERNER [C4/382] Silver Violin Bow   418/585 NS

ULLMANN, GIORGIO [S3/194] Silver Violin Bow: Milan, c. 1930   670/1,004 NS

ULLMANN, GIORGIO [S10/126] Silver Violin Bow: Milan, c. 1920   930/1,550
$856   £497   DM1,380   ¥100,740

ULLMANN, GIORGIO [S1117/406] Silver Violin Bow: Milan, c. 1930   668/1,002 NS

VAN DER MEER, KAREL [S3/69] Silver Violin Bow with damaged stick and repaired head: Amsterdam, c. 1900   502/837 NS

VAN DER MEER, KAREL [S1117/125] Silver Violin Bow: Amsterdam, c. 1900   334/501 NS

VICKERS, J.E. [P12/125] Violin Bow w/violoncello bow   334/501 NS

VIDOUDEZ, PIERRE [Bf9/4515] Fine Silver and Tortoiseshell Violin Bow in a very good state of preservation   1,600/2,250
$2,588   £1,553   DM4,373   ¥344,319

VIDOUDEZ, PIERRE [S3/323] Silver Violin Bow: Geneva, c. 1960   1,674/2,511
$480   £287   DM889   ¥64,027

VIDOUDEZ, PIERRE [S1117/78] Gold and Tortoiseshell Violin Bow: Geneva, c. 1960   4,175/5,845 NS

VIGNERON, A. [B3/67] Silver Violin Bow with a later button (Jean-François Raffin)   4,185/5,859 NS

VIGNERON, ANDRE [B6/40] Silver Violin Bow (Jean-François Raffin)   3,340/4,175
$3,841   £2,300   DM6,877   ¥528,494

VIGNERON, ANDRE [B11/20] Silver Violin Bow   4,175/5,845 NS

VIGNERON, ANDRE [B11/22] Silver Violin Bow   5,845/9,185
$6,722   £4,025   DM11,230   ¥817,035

VIGNERON, ANDRE [C11/17] Silver Violin Bow   3,006/4,175
$4,225   £2,530   DM7,059   ¥513,565

VIGNERON, ANDRE [S6/55] Silver Violin Bow with repaired head: Paris, late 19th C.   1,320/1,980
$2,846   £1,725   DM5,123   ¥410,464

VIGNERON, JOSEPH ARTHUR [Bf9/4506] Good Silver Violin Bow   3,500/4,250 NS

VIGNERON, JOSEPH ARTHUR [C4/28] Silver Violin Bow   3,340/4,175 NS

VIGNERON, JOSEPH ARTHUR [C4/31] Silver Violin Bow   5,010/6,680 NS

VIGNERON, JOSEPH ARTHUR [C4/76] Silver Violin Bow   5,010/6,680
$4,801   £2,875   DM8,913   ¥642,390

VIGNERON, JOSEPH ARTHUR [C11/24] Silver Violin Bow   3,006/4,175
$3,265   £1,955   DM5,454   ¥396,845

VIGNERON, JOSEPH ARTHUR [C11/33] Silver Violin Bow   2,004/3,006 NS

VIGNERON, JOSEPH ARTHUR [S3/102] Silver Violin Bow: Paris, c. 1900   1,339/2,009
$2,310   £1,380   DM4,274   ¥307,864

VIGNERON, JOSEPH ARTHUR [S6/58] Silver Violin Bow: Paris, c. 1890   2,970/3,630
$5,123   £3,105   DM9,222   ¥738,835

VIGNERON, JOSEPH ARTHUR [S1117/110] Silver Violin Bow, w/bow box, extra lapping: Paris, c. 1890   835/1,169
$863   £517   DM1,442   ¥104,946

VIGNERON, JOSEPH ARTHUR [S1117/399] Silver Violin Bow: Paris, c. 1900   4,175/5,845 NS

VIGNERON, JOSEPH ARTHUR [S1117/430] Silver Violin Bow w/bow box: Paris, c. 1890   5,010/8,350
$7,682   £4,600   DM12,834   ¥933,754

VIGNERON, JOSEPH ARTHUR [Sk5/78] Silver
Violin Bow   1,800/2,200
$1,093   £656   DM1,945   ¥145,281

VIGNERON, JOSEPH ARTHUR [Sk5/100] Silver
Violin Bow with tinsel wrap, without hair: Paris
                                          2,200/2,400
$2,990   £1,794   DM5,322   ¥397,610

VIGNERON, JOSEPH ARTHUR [Sk11/127] Silver
Violin Bow   2,800/3,200
$2,415   £1,449   DM4,081   ¥294,630

VOIGT, ARNOLD [B2/59] Silver Violin Bow
                                          656/984
$1,320   £805   DM2,402   ¥166,748

VOIGT, ARNOLD [C4/408] Nickel Violin Bow
                                          334/418 NS

VOIGT, ARNOLD [C11/220] Silver Violin Bow
                                          501/835
$730   £437   DM1,219   ¥88,707

VOIGT, ARNOLD [C11/246] Silver Violin Bow without hair, w/bow   668/1,002
$807   £483   DM1,348   ¥98,044

VOIGT, ARNOLD [S1117/163] Silver Violin Bow:
Markneukirchen, c. 1930   835/1,169 NS

VOIGT, ARNOLD [S1117/426] Ivory Violin Bow:
c. 1930   835/1,169
$768   £460   DM1,283   ¥93,375

VOIRIN, FRANCOIS NICOLAS [B3/29] Fine Nickel
Violin Bow fitted with a replica frog, w/original frog
                                          5,859/7,533 NS

VOIRIN, FRANCOIS NICOLAS [B3/73] Very Fine
Silver Violin Bow (Jean-François Raffin) 7,533/10,044
$8,663   £5,175   DM16,027   ¥1,154,491

VOIRIN, FRANCOIS NICOLAS [B11/10] Very Fine
Gold and Tortoiseshell Violin Bow   13,360/20,040
$14,404   £8,625   DM24,064   ¥1,750,789

VOIRIN, FRANCOIS NICOLAS [B11/11] Silver
Violin Bow   1,670/3,340
$2,305   £1,380   DM3,850   ¥280,126

VOIRIN, FRANCOIS NICOLAS [P4/191] Fine and
Handsome French Silver Violin Bow: Paris
                                          5,835/7,502 NS

VOIRIN, FRANCOIS NICOLAS [P4/193] Silver
Violin Bow with minor wear at thumb position: Paris
                                          4,168/5,835 NS

VOIRIN, FRANCOIS NICOLAS [Bf9/4507] Silver
Violin Bow   2,500/3,250 NS

VOIRIN, FRANCOIS NICOLAS [C4/40] Silver
Violin Bow (Jean-François Raffin, Paris, December 1,
1997)   2,672/3,340
$3,265   £1,955   DM6,061   ¥436,825

VOIRIN, FRANCOIS NICOLAS [C11/30] Silver
Violin Bow   5,010/6,680
$7,682   £4,600   DM12,834   ¥933,754

VOIRIN, FRANCOIS NICOLAS [S3/108] Silver
Violin Bow: Paris, c. 1870   1,674/2,511
$1,925   £1,150   DM3,562   ¥256,554

VOIRIN, FRANCOIS NICOLAS [S3/225] Silver
Violin Bow: Paris, c. 1880 (Jean-Jacques Raffin, Paris,
March 24, 1996)   6,696/8,370 NS

VOIRIN, FRANCOIS NICOLAS [S3/90] Gold and
Ivory Exhibition Violin Bow: Paris, 1878
                                          10,044/13,392
$17,326   £10,350   DM32,054   ¥2,308,982

VOIRIN, FRANCOIS NICOLAS [S6/64] Gold and
Tortoiseshell Violin Bow with damaged head: Paris,
c. 1875   4,125/5,775 NS

VOIRIN, FRANCOIS NICOLAS [S1117/168] Silver
Violin Bow with replacement adjuster: Paris, c. 1870
                                          3,340/5,010 NS

VOIRIN, FRANCOIS NICOLAS [S1117/423] Silver
Violin Bow: Paris, c. 1870   5,010/6,680 NS

VOIRIN, FRANCOIS NICOLAS (ascribed to)
[P11/118] Nickel Violin Bow   3,360/5,040 NS

VOIRIN, J. [B2/49] Nickel Violin Bow 984/1,312 NS

VOIRIN, J. [B5/99] Nickel Violin Bow   978/1,630
$1,031   £633   DM1,834   ¥138,473

VOIRIN, J. [B11/5] Silver Violin Bow
                                          7,515/10,855 NS

VOIRIN, JOSEPH [S1117/442] Silver Violin Bow:
Paris, c. 1860   2,004/2,505 NS

VUILLAUME, JEAN BAPTISTE [C4/27] Rare Steel
Violin Bow   3,340/5,010 NS

VUILLAUME, JEAN BAPTISTE [C4/57] Silver Violin
Bow   2,505/3,340
$2,305   £1,380   DM4,278   ¥308,347

VUILLAUME, JEAN BAPTISTE [C11/27] Rare Steel
Violin Bow   3,006/3,674
$3,841   £2,300   DM6,417   ¥466,877

VUILLAUME, JEAN BAPTISTE [C11/57] Silver
Violin Bow converted from a self-rehairing bow
                                          2,672/3,340
$5,762   £3,450   DM9,626   ¥700,316

VUILLAUME, JEAN BAPTISTE [B10/43] Fine Silver
Violin Bow   5,100/8,500 NS

VUILLAUME, JEAN BAPTISTE [Bf2/4078] Rare
Metal Violin Bow   2,500/3,000
$1,495   £915   DM2,715   ¥185,649

VUILLAUME, JEAN BAPTISTE [S3/73] Silver Violin
Bow: Paris, c. 1840   2,511/3,348
$1,155   £690   DM2,137   ¥153,932

VUILLAUME, JEAN BAPTISTE [S3/223] Silver
Portrait Violin Bow: Paris, mid 19th C.
                                          6,696/10,044 NS

VUILLAUME, JEAN BAPTISTE [S1117/162] Silver
Violin Bow w/bow box: Paris, c. 1850
                                          5,845/7,515 NS

VUILLAUME, JEAN BAPTISTE [Sk5/75] Good Silver
French Violin Bow: Paris   8,000/12,000
$7,763   £4,658   DM13,817   ¥1,032,257

VUILLAUME, JEAN BAPTISTE [Sk5/138] Silver
Violin Bow: Paris   2,800/3,200
$2,875   £1,725   DM5,118   ¥382,317

VUILLAUME, JEAN BAPTISTE [Sk5/149] Silver
Violin Bow, repaired at the head   800/1,200
$1,840   £1,104   DM3,275   ¥244,683

WATSON, WILLIAM [C4/34] Silver Violin Bow
                                           1,169/1,670
$1,344   £805   DM2,496   ¥179,869

WATSON, WILLIAM [Sk5/98] Silver Violin Bow:
London   1,400/1,600
$1,840   £1,104   DM3,275   ¥244,683

WEICHOLD [B2/55] Nickel Violin Bow without hair,
w/another violin bow   164/328
$283   £173   DM515   ¥35,732

WEICHOLD [B5/74] Nickel Violin Bow   489/652
$469   £288   DM834   ¥62,942

WEICHOLD [B5/79] Silver Violin Bow   652/978 NS

WEICHOLD [B7/78] Silver Violin Bow   330/660
$721   £437   DM1,280   ¥100,025

WEICHOLD [B7/84] Silver Violin Bow   495/660
$474   £288   DM842   ¥65,806

WEICHOLD [C11/237] Silver Violin Bow 835/1,169
$863   £517   DM1,442   ¥104,946

WEICHOLD, RICHARD [B3/58] Silver Violin Bow
                                           670/1,004
$770   £460   DM1,425   ¥102,621

WEICHOLD, RICHARD [Bf2/4085] Fine Silver
Violin Bow   1,000/1,600
$1,725   £1,056   DM3,133   ¥214,211

WEICHOLD, RICHARD [Bf7/10512] Silver Violin
Bow   800/1,200 NS

WEICHOLD, RICHARD [S3/218] Silver Violin Bow:
Dresden   670/1,004
$963   £575   DM1,781   ¥128,277

WEICHOLD, RICHARD [S1117/436] Silver Violin
Bow: Dresden, c. 1890   668/1,002
$807   £483   DM1,348   ¥98,044

WEICHOLD, RICHARD [Sk5/139] Silver Violin Bow
without hair   600/800
$1,035   £621   DM1,842   ¥137,634

WEICHOLD, RICHARD [Sk5/146] Silver Violin Bow
                                           800/1,200 NS

WEICHOLD, RICHARD [Sk11/238] Silver Violin
Bow without hair   250/350
$1,725   £1,035   DM2,915   ¥210,450

WEICHOLD, RICHARD [Sk11/254] Silver Violin
Bow   600/800
$489   £293   DM826   ¥59,628

WERNER, EMIL [C11/60] Gold Violin Bow
                                           1,336/2,004 NS

WILSON, GARNER [C4/63] Gold Violin Bow
                                           1,169/1,503 NS

WUNDERLICH, FRIEDRICH [S1117/113] Silver
Violin Bow: Leipzig, c. 1930   334/501
$807   £483   DM1,348   ¥98,044

YOUNG, DAVID RUSSELL [Bf9/4512] Gold Violin
Bow   1,800/2,500 NS

ZABINSKI, ROGER ALFONS [Sk5/152] Silver
Violin Bow: Minneapolis, Minnesota   500/700
$546   £328   DM972   ¥72,640

ZABINSKI, ROGER ALFONS [Sk5/153] Silver
Violin Bow: Minneapolis, Minnesota   500/700
$518   £311   DM921   ¥68,817

VIOLONCELLO

ALBERTI, FERDINANDO (attributed to) [Bf9/4582]
Good Child's Violoncello   3,000/5,000 NS

APPARUT, GEORGES (workshop of) [P10/122] Fine
and Handsome French Violoncello in good condition:
1929   8,500/10,200 NS

APPARUT, GEORGES (workshop of) [P12/156] Fine
and Handsome French Violoncello in good condition:
1929   7,515/8,350 NS

BACZYNSKI, LADISLAUS [S3/145] Violoncello
w/cover: Lwów, 1910   4,185/5,022 NS

BAILLY, CHARLES [S1117/341] Violoncello w/case:
Mirecourt, 1924   5,845/7,515
$6,914   £4,140   DM11,551   ¥840,379

BANDINI, MARIO [S3/153] Violoncello w/cover:
Ravenna, 1978   5,859/8,370
$6,738   £4,025   DM12,465   ¥897,937

BERNARDEL, AUGUST SEBASTIEN PHILIPPE
[S1117/349] Violoncello w/case: Paris, 1849
                                           58,450/83,500
$61,289   £36,700   DM102,393   ¥7,449,733

BERNARDEL, LEON [S6/107] Violoncello w/case:
Paris, 1901   24,750/29,700
$22,770   £13,800   DM40,986   ¥3,283,710

BETTS, JOHN [S3/162] Violoncello w/case: London,
c. 1785   16,740/25,110 NS

BETTS, JOHN [S1117/337] Violoncello: London,
c. 1780   5,010/8,350 NS

BISIACH (workshop of) [S6/108] Violoncello w/case:
Milan, c. 1890   33,000/41,250
$37,950   £23,000   DM68,310   ¥5,472,850

CALCAGNI, BERNARDO [Bf2/4110] Rare and
Exceptional Violoncello: Genoa, 1737 (J. & A. Beare,
London, October 3, 1983)   140,000/150,000
$156,500   £95,778   DM284,204   ¥19,434,170

CARCASSI, TOMMASO [Bf2/4106] Very Fine
Violoncello w/case: Florence, c. 1750
                                           60,000/70,000 NS

CHAROTTE, VICTOR JOSEPH [S1117/345]
Violoncello: Mirecourt, 1904   3,340/5,010
$3,457   £2,070   DM5,775   ¥420,189

COLLIN-MEZIN, CH.J.B. [S3/163] Violoncello
w/case: Mirecourt, 1952   3,683/4,687 NS

COLLIN-MEZIN, CH.J.B. (III) [S1117/344]
Violoncello w/case: Mirecourt, 1952   2,505/3,340
$2,305   £1,380   DM3,850   ¥280,126

CUISSET, A. [B3/105] Good Belgian Violoncello:
Brussels   8,370/11,718 NS

CUISSET, A. [B6/68] Good Belgian Violoncello:
Brussels   6,680/10,020 NS

CUISSET, A. [B11/48] Good Belgian Violoncello:
Brussels   6,680/10,020 NS

DARCHE, HILAIRE [C4/113] Violoncello
11,690/15,030 NS

DECONET, MICHAEL [S6/102] Violoncello, head
possibly by another hand: Venice, c. 1750 (W.E. Hill
& Sons, June 3, 1932)   396,000/462,000 NS

DERAZEY, JUSTIN [Bf2/4107] Good French
Violoncello: Mirecourt, c. 1860   16,000/18,000 NS

DODD, THOMAS [B3/107] English Violoncello:
London, c. 1830   10,044/13,392 NS

DODD, THOMAS [B3/111] Very Fine English
Violoncello: London, c. 1820 (W.E. Hill & Sons,
London, 1920)   41,850/58,590 NS

DODD, THOMAS [B6/67] Very Fine English
Violoncello: London, c. 1820 (W.E. Hill & Sons,
London, 1925)   41,750/58,450 NS

DODD, THOMAS [B11/53] Very Fine English
Violoncello: London, c. 1820 (W.E. Hill & Sons,
London, 1925)   41,750/58,450 NS

DOLLENZ, GIOVANNI [S10/84] Violoncello:
Trieste, 1855   18,600/24,800 NS

DOLLING, HERMANN (JR.) [S6/104] Violoncello
w/case: c. 1900   2,475/4,125
$2,846   £1,725   DM5,123   ¥410,464

EMERY, JULIAN [P11/167] Fine and Handsome
Violoncello in pristine condition, w/case: Wales, 1998
5,040/6,720
$5,796   £3,450   DM9,660   ¥692,726

ENZENSPERGER, BERNARD (II) [S3/158]
Violoncello w/case, bow: Vienna, 1854 6,696/10,044
$7,315   £4,370   DM13,534   ¥974,903

FARINA, ERMINIO [S1117/351] Violoncello w/case:
Milan, c. 1910   30,060/36,740
$32,649   £19,550   DM54,545   ¥3,968,455

FAROTTI, CELESTE [Sk5/39] Fine and Rare
Violoncello w/case: Milan, 1912   40,000/60,000
$68,500   £41,100   DM121,930   ¥9,109,130

FORSTER, SIMON ANDREW [B11/60] Fine English
Violoncello: London, c. 1830   33,400/41,750
$38,410   £23,000   DM64,170   ¥4,668,770

FORSTER, WILLIAM [B3/97] Very Fine English
Violoncello (W.E. Hill & Sons, London)
41,850/58,590
$46,202   £27,600   DM85,477   ¥6,157,284

FORSTER, WILLIAM [P4/266] Fine and Handsome
English Violoncello in immediate playing condition,
w/case: London, 1790   25,005/33,340
$28,756   £17,250   DM53,268   ¥3,840,368

FORSTER, WILLIAM (II) [S1117/357] Violoncello
w/case: London, 1780 (Wm. Moennig & Son,
Philadelphia, May 1, 1961)   30,060/41,750
$30,728   £18,400   DM51,336   ¥3,735,016

FUCHS, WENZEL [Sk5/43] Contemporary German
Violoncello w/case: Eltersdorf, Germany, 1954
2,200/2,400
$2,990   £1,794   DM5,322   ¥397,610

FURBER (FAMILY OF) [S6/110] Violoncello:
England, early 19th C.   4,950/8,250 NS

GAND BROS. [P4/267] Fine and Handsome French
Violoncello in immediate playing condition, w/cover:
Paris, c. 1860   50,010/66,680 NS

GAND BROS. [P11/163] Fine and Handsome French
Violoncello in immediate playing condition, w/cover:
Paris, c. 1860   50,400/67,200 NS

GILBERT, JEFFREY J. [S3/152] Violoncello w/case:
Peterborough, 1927   9,207/12,555 NS

GILBERT, JEFFREY JAMES [S1117/346] Violoncello
w/case: Peterborough, 1927   6,680/8,350 NS

GOULDING & CO. [S6/101] Violoncello w/bow:
England, early 19th C.   3,300/4,950
$14,801   £8,970   DM26,641   ¥2,134,412

GRANCINO, GIOVANNI [B11/54] Very Fine and
Important Italian Violoncello: Milan, c. 1700
167,000/250,500
$307,280 £184,000   DM513,360   ¥37,350,160

HAIDE, JAY [S1117/352] Violoncello: Berkeley, 1997
3,340/5,010 NS

HAMMIG, W.H. [B11/51A] Fine German Violoncello
10,020/13,360 NS

HARDIE, MATTHEW [P11/160] Violoncello in
immediate playing condition: Edinburgh, c. 1810
16,800/25,200
$18,354   £10,925   DM30,590   ¥2,193,631

HELMER, JOANES GEORGIUS (ascribed to)
[C11/284] Violoncello w/soft case   2,505/3,340
$2,497   £1,495   DM4,171   ¥303,470

HILL, HENRY LOCKEY [B11/47] Fine English
Violoncello: London, c. 1820 (J. & A. Beare)
23,380/30,060 NS

HILL, JOSEPH (ascribed to) [S6/115] Violoncello
w/case: England, late 18th C. (Kenneth Warren,
Chicago, May 6, 1953)   6,600/9,900
$6,641   £4,025   DM11,954   ¥957,749

HILL, LOCKEY [B3/108] English Violoncello:
London, c. 1800   6,696/10,044
$8,470   £5,060   DM15,671   ¥1,128,835

HORNSTEINER [B2/74] German Violoncello
2,460/3,280
$3,961   £2,415   DM7,206   ¥500,243

KENNEDY, THOMAS [B11/52] Fine English
Violoncello: London, c. 1830　　　25,050/33,400
$46,092　£27,600　　DM77,004　　¥5,602,524

KLOTZ, AEGIDIUS (I) [B3/93] German Violoncello:
Mittenwald, 18th C.　　　　　　　3,348/5,022
$3,465　£2,070　　DM6,411　　¥461,796

KLOTZ, SEBASTIAN (II) (attributed to) [S3/146]
Violoncello w/case: Mittenwald, early 19th C.
　　　　　　　　　　　　　　5,022/6,696 NS

KLOTZ FAMILY (MEMBER OF) [Sk11/193]
Eighteenth-Century Violoncello w/case: Mittenwald
　　　　　　　　　　　　　　7,000/9,000 NS

LECAVELLE, FRANCOIS [C11/111] French
Violoncello　　　　　　　　　5,010/5,845
$5,377　£3,220　　DM8,984　　¥653,628

LONGMAN & BRODERIP [S6/116] Violoncello:
London, late 18th C.　　　　　6,600/9,900
$6,072　£3,680　　DM10,930　　¥875,656

LONGMAN, LUKEY & CO. [S3/156] Violoncello:
London, c. 1770　　　　　13,392/20,088 NS

LONGMAN, LUKEY & CO. [S1117/348]
Violoncello: London, c. 1770　　10,020/13,360 NS

LOWENDALL, LOUIS [B3/99] Good German
Violoncello　　　　　　　　1,339/2,009
$1,540　£920　　DM2,849　　¥205,243

MEINEL, OSKAR [Sk5/37] German Violoncello:
1937　　　　　　　　　　　1,200/1,400
$2,875　£1,725　　DM5,118　　¥382,317

MESSORI, PIETRO [B2/67] Italian Violoncello:
Modena, 1909　　　　　　　1,640/2,460
$3,018　£1,840　　DM5,491　　¥381,138

MORASSI, GIOVANNI BATTISTA [P4/260] Italian
Violoncello in immediate playing condition:
Cremona, 1971　　　　　　20,004/30,006
$23,005　£13,800　　DM42,614　　¥3,072,294

MOUGENOT, LEON [C11/115] French Violoncello
　　　　　　　　　　　　　8,350/11,690 NS

NEUNER & HORNSTEINER [B5/121] Good
German Violoncello　　　　　978/1,630 NS

NEUNER & HORNSTEINER [B7/107] Good
German Violoncello　　　　　743/825
$759　£460　　DM1,348　　¥105,289

NEUNER & HORNSTEINER [P4/279] Violoncello
in immediate playing condition, w/case: Mittenwald,
c. 1880　　　　　　　　　4,168/5,835
$4,409　£2,645　　DM8,168　　¥588,856

NEUNER & HORNSTEINER [P4/282] Violoncello
with restored table blemishes, w/case, bow:
Mittenwald, 1882　　　　　5,001/6,668 NS

NEUNER & HORNSTEINER [P11/172] Violoncello
in immediate playing condition, w/case: Mittenwald,
1882　　　　　　　　　　2,520/3,360
$2,705　£1,610　　DM4,508　　¥323,272

NORMAN, BARAK [B2/75] Rare Half-Size English
Violoncello decorated with ornamental purfling:
London, 1719　　　　　　　2,460/3,280
$3,018　£1,840　　DM5,491　　¥381,138

PANORMO, VINCENZO (attributed to) [P4/261]
Violoncello with skillful repairs on back: London,
c. 1805　　　　　　　　　6,668/8,335
$7,668　£4,600　　DM14,205　　¥1,024,098

PEDRAZZINI, GIUSEPPE [B11/46] Fine Italian
Violoncello in an exceptional state of preservation:
Milan, 1922　　　　　　　41,750/58,450
$61,456　£36,800　　DM102,672　　¥7,470,032

PETERNELLA, JAGO [B6/71] Italian Violoncello:
Venice, 1925　　　　　　　10,020/13,360 NS

PFRETZSCHNER (workshop of) [Sk11/190] German
Violoncello w/soft case　　　600/800
$1,380　£828　　DM2,332　　¥168,360

PFRETZSCHNER (workshop of) [Sk11/198] German
Violoncello w/soft case　　　400/600
$575　£345　　DM972　　¥70,150

PIATTELLINI, A. [B11/59] Fine Italian Violoncello
w/case: Florence, 1772　　　33,400/50,100
$57,615　£34,500　　DM96,255　　¥7,003,155

PICCAGLIANI (workshop of) [S1117/342]
Violoncello w/case: mid 20th C.　4,676/5,845 NS

POGGI, ANSALDO [S3/141] Violoncello w/case:
Bologna, 1933　　　　　　50,220/66,960
$79,850　£47,700　　DM147,727　　¥10,641,393

PRESSENDA, GIOVANNI FRANCESCO [S3/135]
Violoncello w/case: Turin, 1854　334,800/435,240
$343,170　£205,000　　DM634,885　　¥45,733,450

PRINCE, W.B. [S3/138] Violoncello w/case, 2 bows:
London, 1915　　　　　　　5,022/8,370
$5,775　£3,450　　DM10,685　　¥769,661

REGAZZONI, DANTE PAOLO [S3/160] Violoncello: Cortenova Valsassina, 1960　5,022/8,370
$3,850　£2,300　　DM7,123　　¥513,107

RICHARDSON, ARTHUR [P11/161] Good Violoncello in good condition: Crediton, Devon, 1926
　　　　　　　　　　　　　6,720/8,400 NS

RIECHERS, AUGUST (attributed to) [P4/273] Good
German Violoncello requiring minor restoration,
w/cover: Hanover, 1868　　　2,000/3,001
$3,259　£1,955　　DM6,037　　¥435,242

RIVOLTA, GIACOMO (attributed to) [C11/125]
Italian Violoncello (Max Möller, Amsterdam,
February 14, 1964)　　　　30,060/36,740
$49,933　£29,900　　DM83,421　　¥6,069,401

ROTH, ERNST HEINRICH [C11/94] German
Violoncello w/case, bow　　3,340/5,010
$6,146　£3,680　　DM10,267　　¥747,003

SCARAMPELLA, STEFANO [S1117/350] Violoncello w/cover: Mantua, 1924　66,800/83,500 NS

SCARAMPELLA, STEFANO (ascribed to)
[S1117/343] Violoncello: c. 1930 (Walter Hamma,
Stuttgart, June 14, 1985)　　25,050/33,400 NS

SCIORILLI, LUIGI [S1117/336] Violoncello: Rome, 1994 (maker's, October 24, 1994)   1,670/3,340
$2,113   £1,265   DM3,529   ¥256,782

SILVESTRE, HIPPOLYTE CHRETIEN [Sk5/49] Good French Violoncello w/soft case: Lyon, 1881
18,000/22,000
$36,800   £22,080   DM65,504   ¥4,893,664

SMITH, THOMAS [C11/123] Good English Violoncello w/case   10,020/13,360 NS

SMITH, THOMAS [S6/113] Violoncello w/case, cover, bow: London, c. 1785 (W.E. Hill & Sons, London, March 19, 1912)   6,600/9,900 NS

TESTORE, CARLO ANTONIO [S10/98] Violoncello w/case: Milan, c. 1740 (Celestino Farotto, Milan, April 18, 1972)   49,600/62,000 NS

TESTORE, CARLO GIUSEPPE [C4/116] Fine Italian Violoncello w/case (Hug & Co., Zurich, June 5, 1953)   116,900/150,300
$158,650   £95,000   DM294,500   ¥21,226,800

THIBOUVILLE-LAMY, J. [B5/133] Violoncello
2,445/3,260 NS

THIBOUVILLE-LAMY, J. [C11/296] French Violoncello w/case, bow   835/1,169
$2,113   £1,265   DM3,529   ¥256,782

THIBOUVILLE-LAMY, J. [P11/180] Violoncello w/case: Mirecourt, c. 1920   840/1,176 NS

THIBOUVILLE-LAMY, J. (workshop of) [Sk5/47] Child's French Violoncello   500/700
$575   £345   DM1,024   ¥76,464

THOMPSON, ROBERT (attributed to) [P4/271] Old English Violoncello in a good state of restoration, w/cover: London, 1758   1,334/2,000
$2,971   £1,783   DM5,504   ¥396,838

VENTAPANE, LORENZO (attributed to) [B11/58] Italian Violoncello (Jacques Français)
33,400/50,100 NS

VILLA, LUIGI [S1117/209] Violoncello: Cesano Maderno, 1985   5,845/7,515 NS

VILLA, LUIGI [S1117/210] Violoncello: Cesano Maderno, 1989   5,845/7,515 NS

VILLA, LUIGI [S1117/214] Violoncello: Cesano Maderno, 1985   5,010/8,350 NS

VILLA, LUIGI [S1117/219] Violoncello: Cesano Maderno, 1988   5,010/8,350 NS

VILLA, LUIGI [S1117/221] Violoncello: Cesano Maderno, 1990   6,680/8,350 NS

VILLA, LUIGI [S1117/224] Violoncello: Cesano Maderno, 1993   7,515/10,855 NS

VILLA, LUIGI [S1117/226] Violoncello: Cesano Maderno, 1984   5,010/8,350 NS

VILLA, LUIGI [S1117/229] Violoncello: Cesano Maderno, 1987   5,845/8,350 NS

VILLA, LUIGI [S1117/233] Violoncello: Cesano Maderno, 1978   5,010/8,350 NS

VILLA, LUIGI [S1117/236] Violoncello: Cesano Maderno, 1976   6,680/10,020 NS

VUILLAUME, JEAN BAPTISTE [Bf2/4111] Very Fine Violoncello: Paris, c. 1860 (Helmuth Keller, November 28, 1974)   120,000/130,000 NS

VUILLAUME, JEAN BAPTISTE [S3/140] Violoncello w/cover, 2 bows: Paris, 1846   58,590/75,330
$68,634   £41,000   DM126,977   ¥9,146,690

WAMSLEY, PETER [B6/59] English Violoncello: London, c. 1730   25,050/33,400 NS

WAMSLEY, PETER [B11/45] Violoncello: London, c. 1750   20,040/25,050 NS

VIOLONCELLO BOW

ALVEY, BRIAN [B5/114] Child's Violoncello Bow
652/978 NS

ALVEY, BRIAN [B7/96] Child's Violoncello Bow
495/660 NS

ALVEY, BRIAN [B10/48] Child's Violoncello Bow
255/425
$274   £161   DM441   ¥33,845

BAILEY, G.E. [B7/79] Silver Violoncello Bow
990/1,650 NS

BAILEY, G.E. [B10/47] Silver Violoncello Bow
850/1,190
$743   £437   DM1,197   ¥91,866

BAZIN [B3/84] Silver Violoncello Bow   3,348/5,022
$3,465   £2,070   DM6,411   ¥461,796

BAZIN (attributed to) [P12/97] Silver Violoncello Bow requiring rehairing   2,505/3,340 NS

BAZIN, CHARLES NICHOLAS [C11/9] Silver Violoncello Bow   3,340/4,175
$4,225   £2,530   DM7,059   ¥513,565

BAZIN, CHARLES NICHOLAS [S6/70] Silver Violoncello Bow: Mirecourt, c. 1900 1,650/2,310 NS

BAZIN, CHARLES NICHOLAS [S10/76] Silver Violoncello Bow: Mirecourt, c. 1900   1,860/3,100
$570   £331   DM920   ¥67,160

BAZIN, CHARLES NICHOLAS [S10/104] Silver Violoncello Bow: Mirecourt, c. 1900   1,860/2,480
$1,070   £621   DM1,725   ¥125,925

BAZIN, CHARLES NICHOLAS [S1117/79] Silver Violoncello Bow: Mirecourt, c. 1910   1,169/1,670
$1,728   £1,035   DM2,888   ¥210,095

BAZIN, LOUIS [C4/18] Silver Violoncello Bow (Jean-François Raffin, June 5, 1996)   1,670/2,004 NS

BAZIN, LOUIS (workshop of) [P10/93] Good French Nickel Violoncello Bow (Gilles Duhaut, June 1998)
850/1,020 NS

BAZIN, LOUIS (workshop of) [P12/119] Good Nickel Violoncello Bow (Gilles Duhaut, June 1998)
668/835
$768   £460   DM1,270   ¥89,838

BEARE, JOHN & ARTHUR [B2/62] Nickel
Violoncello Bow with later nickel button   492/820
$849   £518   DM1,544   ¥107,195

BEARE & SON [B3/83] Silver Violoncello Bow
                                    1,004/1,674
$1,155   £690   DM2,137   ¥153,932

BECHINI, RENZO [S10/83] Silver Violoncello Bow:
Paris, c. 1980   1,860/2,480 NS

BERNARDEL, GUSTAVE [B5/110] Silver Violoncello
Bow   978/1,304
$1,462   £897   DM2,601   ¥196,380

BERNARDEL, GUSTAVE [Bf2/4052] Silver
Violoncello Bow   2,500/3,000
$2,875   £1,760   DM5,221   ¥357,018

BERNARDEL, LEON [S3/202] Silver Violoncello
Bow: Paris, c. 1900   1,339/2,009 NS

BERNARDEL, LEON [S3/219] Silver Violoncello
Bow: Paris, c. 1920   1,339/2,009
$1,733   £1,035   DM3,205   ¥230,898

BERNARDEL, LEON [S10/102] Silver Violoncello
Bow: Paris, c. 1910   930/1,240
$428   £248   DM690   ¥50,370

BOURGUIGNON, MAURICE [S3/325] Silver
Violoncello Bow: Brussels   1,674/2,511
$2,118   £1,265   DM3,918   ¥282,209

BRYANT, PERCIVAL WILFRED [S3/324] Silver
Violoncello Bow: Brighton, c. 1945   1,674/2,511
$1,540   £920   DM2,849   ¥205,243

CARESSA, ALBERT [S1117/115] Silver Violoncello
Bow: Paris, c. 1920   2,004/2,672
$1,152   £690   DM1,925   ¥140,063

CHANOT & CHARDON [S1117/83] Silver
Violoncello Bow: Paris, c. 1930   3,006/4,175 NS

CHERPITEL, MOINEL [Bf2/4051] Silver Violoncello
Bow   2,000/2,500 NS

COLAS, PROSPER [Sk11/220] Silver Violoncello
Bow, frog and adjuster not original   1,200/1,400 NS

CUNIOT-HURY [C4/37] Nickel Violoncello Bow
                                    1,169/1,503 NS

DAVIS [C4/15] Ivory Violoncello Bow without hair
                                    2,004/2,505
$2,497   £1,495   DM4,635   ¥334,043

DODD [B3/89] Fine Silver Violoncello Bow
                                    6,696/10,044
$6,930   £4,140   DM12,822   ¥923,593

DODD [B3/90] Extremely Fine Gold and Tortoiseshell Violoncello Bow   8,370/11,718
$7,700   £4,600   DM14,246   ¥1,026,214

DODD [B5/116] Nickel Violoncello Bow   652/978
$1,031   £633   DM1,834   ¥138,473

DODD [B11/24] Swan-Headed Ivory Violoncello
Bow   4,175/5,845
$7,682   £4,600   DM12,834   ¥933,754

DODD [C11/49] Silver Violoncello Bow   3,006/3,674
$6,722   £4,025   DM11,230   ¥817,035

DODD, JOHN [Bf2/4072] Fine Silver Violoncello
Bow   2,500/3,000
$2,588   £1,584   DM4,699   ¥321,316

DODD, JOHN [S6/67] Ivory Violoncello Bow: Kew,
early 19th C.   4,620/5,775
$5,503   £3,335   DM9,905   ¥793,563

DUPUY, GEORGE [S6/69] Silver Violoncello Bow:
Paris, c. 1930   1,320/1,980
$1,612   £977   DM2,902   ¥232,477

FETIQUE, VICTOR [B11/17] Violoncello Bow
                                    6,680/10,020 NS

FETIQUE, VICTOR [S3/61] Silver Violoncello Bow
with repaired head: Paris, early 20th C.   1,004/1,339
$2,310   £1,380   DM4,274   ¥307,864

FETIQUE, VICTOR [S1117/103] Silver Violoncello
Bow: Paris, c. 1910   6,680/10,020
$8,066   £4,830   DM13,476   ¥980,442

FETIQUE, VICTOR [S1117/117] Silver Violoncello
Bow, frog and adjuster by another hand: Paris,
c. 1920   2,672/3,674
$2,881   £1,725   DM4,813   ¥350,158

FINKEL, JOHANNES S. [S3/238] Chased-Gold and
Tortoiseshell Violoncello Bow: Brienz, c. 1975
                                    3,348/5,022 NS

FRANCAIS, EMILE [S3/67] Silver Violoncello Bow:
Paris, c. 1950   1,674/2,511
$1,502   £897   DM2,778   ¥200,112

GAND BROS. [S10/108] Silver Violoncello Bow with
later frog: Paris, c. 1860   2,480/3,720
$2,496   £1,449   DM4,025   ¥293,825

GEROME, ROGER [Sk11/223] Silver Violoncello
Bow without hair or wrap   1,600/1,800
$1,725   £1,035   DM2,915   ¥210,450

GILLET, LOUIS [S1117/107] Silver Violoncello Bow
c. 1940   3,340/5,010
$5,762   £3,450   DM9,626   ¥700,316

GRANDCHAMP, ERIC [S3/53] Silver Violoncello
Bow: Geneva, c. 1980   837/1,172
$1,540   £920   DM2,849   ¥205,243

GRUNKE [B11/39A] Silver Violoncello Bow
                                    2,004/2,505 NS

HILL, W.E. & SONS [B2/61] Silver Violoncello Bow
                                    1,312/1,968 NS

HILL, W.E. & SONS [B3/80] Silver Violoncello Bow
                                    3,013/4,185 NS

HILL, W.E. & SONS [B5/112] Silver Violoncello Bow
with broken head   1,141/1,467 $1,125
£690   DM2,001   ¥151,062

HILL, W.E. & SONS [B5/115] Silver Violoncello Bow
                      978/1,630 $1,031
£633   DM1,834   ¥138,473

HILL, W.E. & SONS [B6/51] Silver Violoncello Bow
2,505/3,340
$2,497   £1,495   DM4,470   ¥343,521

HILL, W.E. & SONS [C11/261] Silver Violoncello
Bow without hair or lapping, w/bow   334/418
$326   £195   DM544   ¥39,583

HILL, W.E. & SONS [P10/91] Violoncello Bow
requiring rehairing   765/935
$860   £506   DM1,402   ¥101,240

HILL, W.E. & SONS [P11/131] Silver Violoncello
Bow: London   1,008/1,176 NS

HILL, W.E. & SONS [S3/77] Silver Violoncello Bow:
London, c. 1940   2,511/3,348
$5,005   £2,990   DM9,260   ¥667,039

HILL, W.E. & SONS [S3/82] Silver Violoncello Bow:
London, 1938   1,674/2,511
$1,733   £1,035   DM3,205   ¥230,898

HILL, W.E. & SONS [S1117/95] Silver Violoncello
Bow: London, c. 1940   3,340/5,010
$3,457   £2,070   DM5,775   ¥420,189

HILL, W.E. & SONS [S1117/105] Silver Violoncello
Bow: London, c. 1930   2,505/3,340
$3,841   £2,300   DM6,417   ¥466,877

JOMBAR, PAUL [S1117/158] Silver Violoncello
Bow: Paris, c. 1910   1,336/2,004
$192   £115   DM321   ¥23,344

LAMY, A. [B11/36A] Very Fine Gold and Tortoiseshell Violoncello Bow (Bernard Millant)
13,360/16,700 NS

LAMY, ALFRED [Sk11/214] Fine Silver Violoncello
Bow   7,000/9,000 NS

LAMY, ALFRED [Sk11/215] Fine Silver Violoncello
Bow   4,000/5,000 NS

LAMY, ALFRED JOSEPH [S3/92] Silver Violoncello
Bow w/bow box: Paris, c. 1890 (Pierre Vidoudez,
Geneva, February 14, 1973)   8,370/11,718
$7,700   £4,600   DM14,246   ¥1,026,214

LAMY, ALFRED JOSEPH [S3/93] Silver Violoncello
Bow w/bow box: Paris, c. 1890 (Pierre Vidoudez,
Geneva, February 13, 1973)   6,696/10,044
$6,160   £3,680   DM11,397   ¥820,971

LAMY, ALFRED JOSEPH [S1117/89] Gold Violoncello Bow, frog probably later: Paris, c. 1890
10,020/13,360
$9,603   £5,750   DM16,043   ¥1,167,193

LAMY, ALFRED JOSEPH [S1117/94] Silver Violoncello Bow: Paris, c. 1890   5,845/7,515 NS

LAMY, ALFRED JOSEPH [S1117/98] Silver Violoncello Bow with original lapping: Paris, c. 1910
5,010/8,350 NS

LAMY, ALFRED JOSEPH [S1117/99] Silver Violoncello Bow with original lapping: Paris, c. 1890
6,680/10,020
$9,603   £5,750   DM16,043   ¥1,167,193

LAMY, ALFRED JOSEPH [S1117/100] Silver Violoncello Bow with original lapping: Paris, c. 1890
6,680/10,020
$8,066   £4,830   DM13,476   ¥980,442

LAMY, ALFRED JOSEPH [S1117/101] Silver Violoncello Bow: Paris, c. 1890   6,680/10,020 NS

LAMY, ALFRED JOSEPH [S1117/102] Silver Violoncello Bow: Paris, c. 1890   6,680/10,020 NS

LAMY, ALFRED JOSEPH [S1117/435] Silver Violoncello Bow: Paris, c. 1900   1,670/2,505
$2,497   £1,495   DM4,171   ¥303,470

LAMY, ALFRED JOSEPH [S1117/88] Gold and
Tortoiseshell Violoncello Bow: Paris, c. 1890
25,050/33,400 NS

LAMY, JULES [C4/73] Silver Violoncello Bow
5,010/6,680 NS

LAMY, JULES [C11/64] Silver Violoncello Bow
3,340/5,010 NS

LAPIERRE, MARCEL [Bf2/4053] Silver and Ivory
Violoncello Bow   2,500/3,000 NS

LEE, JOHN NORWOOD [C4/59] Gold and Ivory
Violoncello Bow   1,670/2,505 NS

LEE, JOHN NORWOOD [C11/19] Gold and Ivory
Violoncello Bow   1,670/2,505 NS

LOTTE, FRANCOIS [S3/64] Silver Violoncello Bow:
Mirecourt, c. 1910   1,004/1,339
$809   £483   DM1,496   ¥107,752

LOTTE, FRANCOIS [S10/103] Silver Violoncello
Bow: Mirecourt, c. 1950   930/1,240
$428   £248   DM690   ¥50,370

LOTTE, ROGER-FRANCOIS [C4/51] Silver Violoncello Bow with partial hair   1,670/2,505
$2,689   £1,610   DM4,991   ¥359,738

LOTTE, ROGER-FRANCOIS [S3/71] Silver Violoncello Bow w/bow box   1,339/1,674
$2,695   £1,610   DM4,986   ¥359,175

LOTTE, ROGER-FRANCOIS [S6/81] Silver and
Ivory Violoncello Bow   1,320/1,980 NS

MALINE, GUILLAUME [B11/25] Silver Violoncello
Bow: Paris, c. 1860   8,350/11,690 NS

MARTIN, JEAN JOSEPH [S3/290] Silver Violoncello
Bow: Paris, c. 1890   2,511/3,348
$673   £402   DM1,245   ¥89,682

MOINEL & CHERPITEL [S3/74] Silver Violoncello
Bow: Paris, c. 1900   1,004/1,339
$1,540   £920   DM2,849   ¥205,243

MORIZOT, LOUIS [C4/33] Silver Violoncello Bow
(Jean-François Raffin, Paris, August 8, 1997)
1,670/2,004 NS

MORIZOT, LOUIS [C4/35] Silver Violoncello Bow
1,002/1,336
$1,344   £805   DM2,496   ¥179,869

MORIZOT, LOUIS [C4/49] Silver Violoncello Bow
2,672/3,340 NS

MORIZOT, LOUIS [C4/364] Three-Quarter-Size
Nickel Violoncello Bow without hair   668/1,002
$576   £345   DM1,070   ¥77,087

MORIZOT (FRERES), LOUIS [P11/113] French
Silver Violoncello Bow: c. 1950 (Jean-François Raffin,
Paris, June 14, 1998)   2,520/3,024 NS

MORIZOT FAMILY [Sk11/217] Silver Violoncello
Bow   1,500/1,600
$1,380   £828   DM2,332   ¥168,360

NEUDORFER, RUDOLPH [B5/113] Silver-Mounted
Violoncello Bow   652/978 NS

NEUDORFER, RUDOLPH [B7/95] Silver Violoncello Bow   330/495
$342   £207   DM607   ¥47,380

NURNBERGER, ALBERT [C4/66] Silver and
Tortoiseshell Violoncello Bow   2,505/3,340 NS

NURNBERGER, ALBERT [C11/26] Silver and
Tortoiseshell Violoncello Bow   2,505/3,340
$2,881   £1,725   DM4,813   ¥350,158

NURNBERGER, ALBERT [Sk11/221] Silver
Violoncello Bow   1,200/1,400 NS

NURNBERGER, KARL ALBERT [S1117/433] Silver
Violoncello Bow: Markneukirchen, c. 1960
                                  1,670/2,505 NS

OUCHARD, EMILE (FILS) (attributed to) [P4/177]
Elegant Gold Violoncello Bow   11,669/15,003 NS

OUCHARD, EMILE (FILS) (attributed to) [P11/108]
Good Silver Violoncello Bow requiring rehairing
                                      3,360/5,040
$6,569   £3,910   DM10,948   ¥785,089

OUCHARD, EMILE A. [S1117/181] Nickel
Violoncello Bow: Mirecourt, c. 1925   1,670/2,505
$2,881   £1,725   DM4,813   ¥350,158

PAJEOT, ETIENNE [S6/54] Silver Violoncello Bow:
Paris, c. 1845   5,775/6,600
$12,334   £7,475   DM22,201   ¥1,778,676

PAQUOTTE, PLACIDE [S1117/114] Silver Violoncello Bow: Paris, c. 1895   1,002/1,336
$2,497   £1,495   DM4,171   ¥303,470

PAULUS, JOHANNES O. [C4/83] Silver Violoncello
Bow   835/1,169
$960   £575   DM1,783   ¥128,478

PECATTE, CHARLES [B6/32] Silver Violoncello
Bow   3,340/5,010 NS

PECATTE, CHARLES [B6/33] Silver Violoncello
Bow   10,020/16,700
$10,563   £6,325   DM18,912   ¥1,453,359

PECATTE, CHARLES [B10/50] Silver Violoncello
Bow with later button   2,550/3,400 NS

PECATTE, CHARLES [S1117/104] Silver Violoncello Bow: Paris, c. 1890   5,010/6,680
$7,682   £4,600   DM12,834   ¥933,754

PECCATTE, FRANCOIS (workshop of) [B11/38A]
Fine Silver Violoncello Bow   2,505/4,175
$3,073   £1,840   DM5,134   ¥373,502

PECCATTE, FRANCOIS & DOMINIQUE [B3/88]
Silver Violoncello Bow with later ebony button
(B. Millant)   13,392/20,088
$13,476   £8,050   DM24,931   ¥1,795,875

PECCATTE FAMILY (MEMBER OF) [P4/192]
French Silver Violoncello Bow with later frog and
without hair: c. 1850 (Jean-François Raffin, Paris,
October 30, 1997)   2,501/3,334
$3,067   £1,840   DM5,682   ¥409,639

PFRETZSCHNER, H.R. [C4/58] Gold Violoncello
Bow   2,004/2,505
$2,689   £1,610   DM4,991   ¥359,738

PFRETZSCHNER, H.R. [S6/48] Gold Violoncello
Bow: Markneukirchen, c. 1950   1,650/2,310
$1,518   £920   DM2,732   ¥218,914

PFRETZSCHNER, H.R. [S1117/80] Silver Violoncello Bow: Markneukirchen   1,169/1,503
$1,152   £690   DM1,925   ¥140,063

PFRETZSCHNER, H.R. [S1117/90] Silver Violoncello Bow w/2 bows   1,670/2,338
$3,073   £1,840   DM5,134   ¥373,502

POIRSON, JUSTIN [S10/105] Silver Violoncello
Bow: Paris, c. 1900   1,860/2,480
$570   £331   DM920   ¥67,160

POIRSON, JUSTIN [Sk11/211] Good Silver
Violoncello Bow   5,000/6,000 NS

PRAGER, AUGUST EDWIN [S3/316] Nickel
Violoncello Bow w/violin bow, violoncello bow:
Markneukirchen   502/837
$1,117   £667   DM2,066   ¥148,801

PRAGER, AUGUST EDWIN [S3/317] Silver
Violoncello Bow: Markneukirchen   1,172/1,674 NS

PRAGER, AUGUST EDWIN [S3/319] Silver
Violoncello Bow: Markneukirchen   1,172/1,674 NS

PRAGER, AUGUST EDWIN [S3/320] Silver
Violoncello Bow: Markneukirchen   1,172/1,674 NS

PRAGER, AUGUST EDWIN [S1117/193] Silver
Violoncello Bow w/violin bow, violoncello bow
                                  1,670/2,505 NS

PRAGER, AUGUST EDWIN [S1117/439] Silver
Violoncello Bow: Markneukirchen   1,002/1,336 NS

RETFORD, WILLIAM C. [B3/87] Silver Violoncello
Bow   2,511/3,348
$4,813   £2,875   DM8,904   ¥641,384

ROLLAND, BENOIT [S10/82] Gold Violoncello
Bow: Paris, c. 1980   2,480/3,100
$2,852   £1,656   DM4,600   ¥335,800

SARTORY, EUGENE [B3/91] Very Fine Gold
Violoncello Bow   20,088/25,110
$21,176   £12,650   DM39,177   ¥2,822,089

SARTORY, EUGENE [C4/75] Silver Violoncello Bow
                                      3,340/4,175
$3,841   £2,300   DM7,130   ¥513,912

SARTORY, EUGENE [S1117/85] Silver Violoncello Bow with original lapping: Paris, c. 1920
13,360/20,040
$23,046   £13,800   DM38,502   ¥2,801,262

SARTORY, EUGENE [S1117/86] Silver Violoncello Bow: Paris, c. 1900
11,690/16,700
$11,523   £6,900   DM19,251   ¥1,400,631

SARTORY, EUGENE [Sk11/213] Good Silver Violoncello Bow (Jean-François Raffin, Paris, October 22, 1997)
5,000/7,000
$5,750   £3,450   DM9,718   ¥701,500

SCHUSTER, GOTHARD [Sk5/104] Good Silver Violoncello Bow
1,200/1,400 NS

SCHUSTER, GOTHARD [Sk11/271] Silver Violoncello Bow
800/1,200
$805   £483   DM1,360   ¥98,210

SIMON (attributed to) [B3/81] Silver Violoncello Bow with later nickel button
4,185/5,859 NS

SIMON, PAUL [Bf2/4055] Fine Silver Violoncello Bow
5,000/6,000 NS

SIMON, PAUL [S10/75] Silver Violoncello Bow: mid 19th C.
1,240/1,860 NS

SIMON BROS. [C11/56] Nickel Violoncello Bow
2,004/2,505 NS

STENGEL, V. [B5/106] Nickel-Mounted Violoncello Bow
130/196
$159   £98   DM283   ¥21,400

THIBOUVILLE-LAMY, J. [C11/53] Silver Violoncello Bow
1,002/1,503 NS

TUBBS, JAMES [S1117/91] Silver Violoncello Bow: London, c. 1900
5,010/8,350
$9,218   £5,520   DM15,401   ¥1,120,505

VIGNERON, A. [B11/9] Silver Violoncello Bow
6,680/10,020 NS

VIGNERON, ANDRE [B6/39] Silver Violoncello Bow (Jean-François Raffin)
8,350/11,690 NS

VIGNERON, JOSEPH ARTHUR [Bf2/4054] Fine Silver Violoncello Bow (Bernard Sabatier, September 17, 1997)
5,500/6,500 NS

VIGNERON, JOSEPH ARTHUR [S1117/106] Silver Violoncello Bow: Paris, c. 1890
1,670/2,505
$3,073   £1,840   DM5,134   ¥373,502

VOIRIN, FRANCOIS NICOLAS [Sk11/212] Silver Violoncello Bow
2,200/2,600 NS

VOIRIN, FRANCOIS NICOLAS [S1117/92] Silver Violoncello Bow with original lapping: Paris, c. 1875
5,010/6,680 NS

VOIRIN, FRANCOIS NICOLAS [S1117/184] Silver Violoncello Bow: Paris, c. 1860
1,670/2,505
$1,536   £920   DM2,567   ¥186,751

VOIRIN, FRANCOIS NICOLAS [S1117/400] Silver Violoncello Bow: Paris, c. 1875
5,010/6,680
$5,377   £3,220   DM8,984   ¥653,628

VOIRIN, FRANCOIS NICOLAS [S1117/412] Silver Violoncello Bow: Paris, c. 1870
2,505/3,340 NS

VUILLAUME, JEAN BAPTISTE [S3/302] Silver Violoncello Bow: Paris, mid 19th C.   4,185/5,859 NS

VUILLAUME, JEAN BAPTISTE [S1117/87] Silver Violoncello Bow with original lapping: Paris, c. 1865
11,690/16,700
$11,523   £6,900   DM19,251   ¥1,400,631

VUILLAUME, JEAN BAPTISTE [S1117/172] Violoncello Bow: Paris, c. 1860
835/1,169
$768   £460   DM1,283   ¥93,375

VUILLAUME, JEAN BAPTISTE [S1117/194] Silver Violoncello Bow: Paris, c. 1850   3,340/4,175 NS

WEICHOLD, RICHARD [B11/40A] Silver Violoncello Bow
668/1,002
$615   £368   DM1,027   ¥74,700

WITHERS, GEORGE & SONS [P11/147] Part-Silver Violoncello Bow: London   672/840 NS

ZITHER

PUGH, JOHANNES [S1104/306] Bowed Zither w/case, bow, 2 bowed zithers: Altona, late 19th C.
531/830
$476   £287   DM792   ¥55,489

SCHUSTER, CARL GOTTLOB (JR.) [P4/33] Concert Zither with some cracks on the table, w/case, accessories: Markneukirchen, c. 1900   500/667
$575   £345   DM1,065   ¥76,807

ZITHER-BANJO

CAMMEYER, ALFRED D. [B2/44] Five-String Zither-Banjo
246/410
$339   £207   DM618   ¥42,878

Five-Year Summary

sales by
item and
maker

HOW TO READ THE SUMMARY
BY ITEM AND MAKER

Beginning on the next page, you will find the five-year Summary by Item and Maker, with monetary values expressed in dollars, Deutsche marks, pounds sterling, and yen. This section summarizes the more detailed data found in the first part of the guide (the Item-by-Item Listings) and combines it with auction information from the preceding four years. Hence you will find a brief overview of the items offered from 1994 through 1998, arranged alphabetically by item—viola, violin, violoncello, etc.—and, within each item category, by maker. Items that have been offered as being "attributed to" or "ascribed to" a particular maker are shown separately from those identified as "by" that maker. (You may find inconsistencies in the way names have been given—a first initial in one case, a full name in the next. These problems have been raised and discussed in the Introduction.)

In the second column, you will find a numeric count of the items by that maker that were offered at auction during the 1994–1998 period. To the immediate right is the count of those items that were actually sold. If none sold, you will see a zero here. (If you are looking for information on a particular maker and cannot find the name, it is because no items by that maker were offered at auction during this period.)

In the next three columns are monetary values. First is the lowest sale price of an item by that maker, then the highest, and finally the average. If only one item was sold, you will find the same number in all three columns. Please use extreme caution in assessing these monetary values. From a purely statistical point of view, they are almost completely unreliable. Nonetheless, they can be construed, within narrow limits, as reflective of the current market. This is also a good place to repeat what was said earlier: this guide does not reflect upon the playing qualities or the physical condition of the items offered at auction. The only way to assess these factors is through personal experience.

Maker	Items Bid	Sold	Selling Prices Low	High	Avg

ACCORDION

Maker	Bid	Sold	Low	High	Avg
CASALI	1	0			
HOHNER	1	0			
SCANDALLI	1	0			
SOPRANI, PAOLO	1	0			

ÆOLA

WHEATSTONE & CO., C.	3	3	$1,061	$2,252	$1,655
			DM1,561	DM4,016	DM2,683
			£690	£1,380	£1,016
			¥112,580	¥294,809	¥197,035

ARPANETTA

KARP, JOHANN	1	1	$11,836	$11,836	$11,836
			DM19,679	DM19,679	DM19,679
			£7,130	£7,130	£7,130
			¥1,378,514	¥1,378,514	¥1,378,514

BAGPIPES

COULLIE, THOMAS	1	1	$2,720	$2,720	$2,720
			DM4,074	DM4,074	DM4,074
			£1,610	£1,610	£1,610
			¥302,744	¥302,744	¥302,744
HARDIE, R.G.	1	0			
HEDWORTH, WILLIAM	1	1	$2,332	$2,332	$2,332
			DM3,492	DM3,492	DM3,492
			£1,380	£1,380	£1,380
			¥259,495	¥259,495	¥259,495
HENDERSON, PETER	1	1	$2,181	$2,181	$2,181
			DM3,080	DM3,080	DM3,080
			£1,380	£1,380	£1,380
			¥194,631	¥194,631	¥194,631
LAWRIE, R.G.	1	1	$778	$778	$778
			DM1,312	DM1,312	DM1,312
			£483	£483	£483
			¥95,568	¥95,568	¥95,568
REID, ROBERT	5	4	$1,149	$5,440	$3,242
			DM1,936	DM8,149	DM4,844
			£713	£3,220	£1,961
			¥141,076	¥605,489	¥356,816
REID, ROBIN	3	1	$877	$877	$877
			DM1,354	DM1,354	DM1,354
			£552	£552	£552
			¥87,438	¥87,438	¥87,438
ROBERTSON	1	1	$6,765	$6,765	$6,765
			DM10,122	DM10,122	DM10,122
			£4,025	£4,025	£4,025
			¥754,607	¥754,607	¥754,607
ROBERTSON (attributed to)	1	0			

BANDURRIA

ANDRADE, JOAO MIGUEL	1	1	$324	$324	$324
			DM538	DM538	DM538
			£195	£195	£195
			¥37,701	¥37,701	¥37,701

Maker	Items		Selling Prices		
	Bid	Sold	Low	High	Avg

BANJEAURINE

HAYNES CO., JOHN C.	1	0			

BANJO

Maker	Bid	Sold	Low	High	Avg
ABBOTT, J.	2	1	$164	$164	$164
			DM287	DM287	DM287
			£98	£98	£98
			¥20,954	¥20,954	¥20,954
BACON BANJO CO.	1	1	$431	$431	$431
			DM649	DM649	DM649
			£262	£262	£262
			¥48,205	¥48,205	¥48,205
BACON & DAY	4	3	$144	$978	$431
			DM243	DM1,652	DM730
			£86	£587	£258
			¥17,538	¥119,255	¥52,738
BARNES & MULLINS	1	0			
CHAMBERLAIN, J.	1	1	$501	$501	$501
			DM897	DM897	DM897
			£299	£299	£299
			¥58,156	¥58,156	¥58,156
DALLAS, D.E.	2	1	$212	$212	$212
			DM312	DM312	DM312
			£138	£138	£138
			¥22,516	¥22,516	¥22,516
DALLAS, J.E.	1	1	$348	$348	$348
			DM534	DM534	DM534
			£230	£230	£230
			¥37,082	¥37,082	¥37,082
DANIELS, J.	1	1	$159	$159	$159
			DM234	DM234	DM234
			£104	£104	£104
			¥16,887	¥16,887	¥16,887
DOBSON, E.C.	1	1	$150	$150	$150
			DM221	DM221	DM221
			£98	£98	£98
			¥15,949	¥15,949	¥15,949
DOBSON, E.D.W.G.	1	1	$345	$345	$345
			DM583	DM583	DM583
			£207	£207	£207
			¥42,090	¥42,090	¥42,090
DOBSON, GEORGE	1	1	$230	$230	$230
			DM389	DM389	DM389
			£138	£138	£138
			¥28,060	¥28,060	¥28,060
DORE BROS.	1	0			
EPIPHONE	1	1	$690	$690	$690
			DM1,166	DM1,166	DM1,166
			£414	£414	£414
			¥84,180	¥84,180	¥84,180
ESSEX, CLIFFORD	6	4	$373	$556	$430
			DM565	DM937	DM727
			£230	£345	£264
			¥36,343	¥68,263	¥50,520

Maker	Items		Selling Prices		
	Bid	Sold	Low	High	Avg
FAIRBANKS CO., A.C.	1	1	$3,163	$3,163	$3,163
			DM5,345	DM5,345	DM5,345
			£1,898	£1,898	£1,898
			¥420,834	¥420,834	¥420,834
FAIRBANKS & COLE	4	3	$173	$374	$249
			DM249	DM632	DM391
			£113	£224	£156
			¥17,466	¥45,598	¥27,813
FRAMUS	1	1	$256	$256	$256
			DM387	DM387	DM387
			£157	£157	£157
			¥24,866	¥24,866	¥24,866
GIBSON CO.	2	2	$1,085	$2,070	$1,578
			DM1,636	DM3,115	DM2,376
			£666	£1,257	£961
			¥105,204	¥231,385	¥168,294
GREY & SONS, JOHN	2	1	$604	$604	$604
			DM1,098	DM1,098	DM1,098
			£368	£368	£368
			¥76,228	¥76,228	¥76,228
HANDEL, J.T.C.	1	1	$141	$141	$141
			DM208	DM208	DM208
			£92	£92	£92
			¥15,011	¥15,011	¥15,011
HAYNES CO., JOHN C.	2	1	$150	$150	$150
			DM253	DM253	DM253
			£90	£90	£90
			¥18,239	¥18,239	¥18,239
JEDSON	2	2	$338	$380	$359
			DM573	DM674	DM623
			£207	£230	£219
			¥39,226	¥52,645	¥45,935
KEECH	1	1	$178	$178	$178
			DM268	DM268	DM268
			£109	£109	£109
			¥17,215	¥17,215	¥17,215
LANGE, WILLIAM L.	3	3	$201	$1,725	$786
			DM303	DM2,596	DM1,183
			£122	£1,047	£477
			¥22,496	¥192,821	¥87,840
LOCKE, G.S.	1	1	$316	$316	$316
			DM534	DM534	DM534
			£190	£190	£190
			¥38,583	¥38,583	¥38,583
LUDWIG	5	4	$144	$748	$476
			DM223	DM1,279	DM780
			£92	£442	£286
			¥14,132	¥92,825	¥54,409
LYON & HEALY	1	1	$132	$132	$132
			DM240	DM240	DM240
			£81	£81	£81
			¥16,675	¥16,675	¥16,675
MANSFIELD, E.B.	1	1	$518	$518	$518
			DM875	DM875	DM875
			£311	£311	£311
			¥63,135	¥63,135	¥63,135

Maker	Items		Selling Prices		
	Bid	Sold	Low	High	Avg
MORRISON, JAMES A.	1	1	$460	$460	$460
			DM777	DM777	DM777
			£276	£276	£276
			¥56,120	¥56,120	¥56,120
PARAMOUNT	1	1	$2,565	$2,565	$2,565
			DM3,867	DM3,867	DM3,867
			£1,573	£1,573	£1,573
			¥248,663	¥248,663	¥248,663
RELIANCE	1	1	$143	$143	$143
			DM203	DM203	DM203
			£90	£90	£90
			¥12,722	¥12,722	¥12,722
SHELTONE	1	1	$112	$112	$112
			DM196	DM196	DM196
			£69	£69	£69
			¥13,521	¥13,521	¥13,521
SIMSON & CO., J.K.	2	1	$130	$130	$130
			DM179	DM179	DM179
			£81	£81	£81
			¥10,834	¥10,834	¥10,834
SLINGERLAND (attributed to)	1	0			
STEWART, S.S.	6	4	$271	$611	$423
			DM472	DM980	DM668
			£161	£397	£271
			¥31,091	¥69,519	¥46,915
TEMLETT, W.	2	2	$223	$637	$430
			DM331	DM937	DM634
			£144	£414	£279
			¥24,118	¥67,548	¥45,833
THOMPSON & ODELL	2	2	$201	$230	$216
			DM340	DM346	DM343
			£121	£140	£130
			¥24,553	¥25,709	¥25,131
TURNER, JOHN ALVEY	2	2	$209	$290	$249
			DM371	DM506	DM438
			£127	£173	£150
			¥28,955	¥36,977	¥32,966
TURNER, WILLIAM	1	0			
VEGA COMPANY	12	10	$115	$5,980	$1,177
			DM166	DM8,647	DM1,775
			£75	£3,906	£757
			¥11,644	¥605,475	¥123,918
WARD & SON	1	1	$168	$168	$168
			DM247	DM247	DM247
			£109	£109	£109
			¥17,825	¥17,825	¥17,825
WASHBURN, GEORGE	1	1	$1,644	$1,644	$1,644
			DM2,538	DM2,538	DM2,538
			£1,035	£1,035	£1,035
			¥163,947	¥163,947	¥163,947
WEAVER	1	1	$196	$196	$196
			DM315	DM315	DM315
			£115	£115	£115
			¥24,175	¥24,175	¥24,175
WELTTON	1	1	$132	$132	$132
			DM240	DM240	DM240
			£81	£81	£81
			¥16,675	¥16,675	¥16,675

Maker	Items		Selling Prices		
	Bid	Sold	Low	High	Avg
WILKES, F.C.	1	1	$180	$180	$180
			DM275	DM275	DM275
			£115	£115	£115
			¥20,073	¥20,073	¥20,073
WINDER, J.G.	1	1	$262	$262	$262
			DM456	DM456	DM456
			£161	£161	£161
			¥31,693	¥31,693	¥31,693
WINDSOR	1	1	$1,880	$1,880	$1,880
			DM3,183	DM3,183	DM3,183
			£1,150	£1,150	£1,150
			¥217,920	¥217,920	¥217,920

BANJO-GUITAR

Maker	Items		Selling Prices		
	Bid	Sold	Low	High	Avg
VEGA COMPANY	1	1	$1,035	$1,035	$1,035
			DM1,771	DM1,771	DM1,771
			£612	£612	£612
			¥128,526	¥128,526	¥128,526

BANJO-MANDOLIN

Maker	Items		Selling Prices		
	Bid	Sold	Low	High	Avg
TIERI	1	1	$86	$86	$86
			DM148	DM148	DM148
			£51	£51	£51
			¥10,711	¥10,711	¥10,711

BANJOLELE

Maker	Items		Selling Prices		
	Bid	Sold	Low	High	Avg
DALLAS, J.E.	1	1	$151	$151	$151
			DM275	DM275	DM275
			£92	£92	£92
			¥19,057	¥19,057	¥19,057
FORMBY, GEORGE	1	1	$289	$289	$289
			DM519	DM519	DM519
			£172	£172	£172
			¥33,408	¥33,408	¥33,408

BARITONE

Maker	Items		Selling Prices		
	Bid	Sold	Low	High	Avg
BUNDY	1	1	$184	$184	$184
			DM328	DM328	DM328
			£112	£112	£112
			¥25,561	¥25,561	¥25,561

BASS GUITAR

Maker	Items		Selling Prices		
	Bid	Sold	Low	High	Avg
FENDER	3	2	$525	$972	$748
			DM911	DM1,685	DM1,298
			£322	£575	£449
			¥60,823	¥123,550	¥92,186
GIBSON CO.	1	1	$806	$806	$806
			DM1,399	DM1,399	DM1,399
			£495	£495	£495
			¥93,406	¥93,406	¥93,406
GOODFELLOW CO.	1	0			
GRETSCH	1	0			
HOFNER	4	2	$18	$70	$44
			DM27	DM108	DM68
			£12	£46	£29
			¥1,920	¥7,679	¥4,799

Maker	Items		Selling Prices		
	Bid	Sold	Low	High	Avg
HOFNER, KARL	2	1	$700	$700	$700
			DM1,213	DM1,213	DM1,213
			£414	£414	£414
			¥88,956	¥88,956	¥88,956
JOURDAN	1	0			
RICKENBACKER	1	0			

BASSOON

Maker	Bid	Sold	Low	High	Avg
ADLER & CO., OSCAR	1	1	$2,051	$2,051	$2,051
			DM3,590	DM3,590	DM3,590
			£1,265	£1,265	£1,265
			¥247,877	¥247,877	¥247,877
BESSON & CO.	1	1	$288	$288	$288
			DM476	DM476	DM476
			£173	£173	£173
			¥33,689	¥33,689	¥33,689
BILTON	2	0			
BOOSEY & CO.	1	0			
BUCHNER, F.	1	1	$3,259	$3,259	$3,259
			DM6,037	DM6,037	DM6,037
			£1,955	£1,955	£1,955
			¥435,242	¥435,242	¥435,242
BUFFET CRAMPON & CO.	2	2	$262	$463	$363
			DM467	DM781	DM624
			£161	£288	£224
			¥35,248	¥56,886	¥46,067
CABART	1	1	$425	$425	$425
			DM636	DM636	DM636
			£253	£253	£253
			¥47,432	¥47,432	¥47,432
CHAPPELL, S.A.	1	1	$254	$254	$254
			DM360	DM360	DM360
			£161	£161	£161
			¥26,243	¥26,243	¥26,243
CRAMPON & CO.	1	1	$351	$351	$351
			DM498	DM498	DM498
			£225	£225	£225
			¥35,675	¥35,675	¥35,675
CUVILLIER (ascribed to)	1	1	$271	$271	$271
			DM405	DM405	DM405
			£161	£161	£161
			¥30,184	¥30,184	¥30,184
DE LUIGI, GIACOMO	1	1	$1,527	$1,527	$1,527
			DM2,539	DM2,539	DM2,539
			£920	£920	£920
			¥177,873	¥177,873	¥177,873
FELCHLIN, JOSEF KARL	1	1	$993	$993	$993
			DM1,650	DM1,650	DM1,650
			£598	£598	£598
			¥115,617	¥115,617	¥115,617
GALANDER	1	0			
HASENEIER, H.F.	1	1	$1,121	$1,121	$1,121
			DM1,955	DM1,955	DM1,955
			£690	£690	£690
			¥135,827	¥135,827	¥135,827

Maker	Items		Selling Prices		
	Bid	Sold	Low	High	Avg
HAWKES & SON	3	3	$168	$509	$331
			DM177	DM719	DM443
			£104	£322	£207
			¥12,813	¥45,414	¥28,180
HECKEL	11	5	$1,845	$14,098	$5,546
			DM2,764	DM23,871	DM9,393
			£1,092	£8,625	£3,403
			¥205,340	¥1,634,403	¥659,365
HIRSBRUNNER FAMILY (MEMBER OF)	2	2	$1,622	$3,054	$2,338
			DM2,697	DM5,078	DM3,887
			£977	£1,840	£1,409
			¥188,893	¥355,746	¥272,319
HOLLER	1	1	$1,196	$1,196	$1,196
			DM1,836	DM1,836	DM1,836
			£782	£782	£782
			¥130,545	¥130,545	¥130,545
HORAK, JOHANN WENZEL	1	1	$2,708	$2,708	$2,708
			DM4,209	DM4,209	DM4,209
			£1,725	£1,725	£1,725
			¥266,513	¥266,513	¥266,513
KEY, THOMAS	1	1	$397	$397	$397
			DM617	DM617	DM617
			£253	£253	£253
			¥39,089	¥39,089	¥39,089
KOHLERT & SONS	1	1	$672	$672	$672
			DM989	DM989	DM989
			£437	£437	£437
			¥71,301	¥71,301	¥71,301
KOHLERT'S SOHNE, V.	1	1	$382	$382	$382
			DM635	DM635	DM635
			£230	£230	£230
			¥44,468	¥44,468	¥44,468
LAFLEUR	1	1	$279	$279	$279
			DM383	DM383	DM383
			£173	£173	£173
			¥23,217	¥23,217	¥23,217
LARSHOF, JACOB GEORG	1	1	$1,635	$1,635	$1,635
			DM2,317	DM2,317	DM2,317
			£1,035	£1,035	£1,035
			¥167,353	¥167,353	¥167,353
LINTON MANUFACTURING CO.	1	1	$147	$147	$147
			DM217	DM217	DM217
			£96	£96	£96
			¥15,623	¥15,623	¥15,623
LUDWIG, FRANZ	1	1	$1,527	$1,527	$1,527
			DM2,539	DM2,539	DM2,539
			£920	£920	£920
			¥177,873	¥177,873	¥177,873
METZLER & CO.	1	0			
MILHOUSE, WILLIAM	8	3	$751	$1,749	$1,406
			DM1,339	DM2,857	DM2,271
			£460	£1,035	£843
			¥98,270	¥200,107	¥164,333
MONNIG, FRITZ	1	1	$5,263	$5,263	$5,263
			DM8,912	DM8,912	DM8,912
			£3,220	£3,220	£3,220
			¥610,177	¥610,177	¥610,177

Maker	Items		Selling Prices		
	Bid	Sold	Low	High	Avg
PARKER, JOHN	1	1	$725	$725	$725
			DM1,206	DM1,206	DM1,206
			£437	£437	£437
			¥84,490	¥84,490	¥84,490
RUDALL, CARTE & CO.	1	0			
SAVARY	1	0			
SAVARY, J.N. (JEUNE)	2	1	$789	$789	$789
			DM1,337	DM1,337	DM1,337
			£483	£483	£483
			¥91,527	¥91,527	¥91,527
SAVARY, JEAN NICHOLAS	2	0			
SCHREIBER	4	4	$1,266	$1,671	$1,469
			DM1,944	DM2,565	DM2,255
			£828	£1,093	£960
			¥138,224	¥182,379	¥160,301
TAYLOR, R.	1	0			
TRIEBERT	1	1	$1,055	$1,055	$1,055
			DM1,620	DM1,620	DM1,620
			£690	£690	£690
			¥115,187	¥115,187	¥115,187
TRIEBERT & SONS, GUILLAUME	2	2	$458	$1,689	$1,074
			DM762	DM3,012	DM1,887
			£276	£1,035	£656
			¥53,362	¥221,107	¥137,234
WOOD & IVY	2	0			

BIWA

Maker	Items		Selling Prices		
	Bid	Sold	Low	High	Avg
SHIGEMASA, TOKUKUNI MATAEIMON (ascribed to)	1	1	$578	$578	$578
			DM898	DM898	DM898
			£368	£368	£368
			¥56,856	¥56,856	¥56,856

BUGLE

Maker	Items		Selling Prices		
	Bid	Sold	Low	High	Avg
BESSON, FONTAINE	1	0			
CLEMENTI & CO.	1	1	$4,025	$4,025	$4,025
			DM6,802	DM6,802	DM6,802
			£2,415	£2,415	£2,415
			¥535,607	¥535,607	¥535,607
EBERSOHN, J.F.	1	1	$2,908	$2,908	$2,908
			DM4,107	DM4,107	DM4,107
			£1,840	£1,840	£1,840
			¥259,508	¥259,508	¥259,508
FIRTH HALL & POND	1	1	$3,163	$3,163	$3,163
			DM5,345	DM5,345	DM5,345
			£1,898	£1,898	£1,898
			¥420,834	¥420,834	¥420,834
HIGHAM, JOSEPH	2	1	$161	$161	$161
			DM246	DM246	DM246
			£104	£104	£104
			¥15,917	¥15,917	¥15,917
LOGIER, JOHN BERNHARD	1	1	$3,163	$3,163	$3,163
			DM5,345	DM5,345	DM5,345
			£1,898	£1,898	£1,898
			¥420,834	¥420,834	¥420,834

Maker	Items		Selling Prices		
	Bid	Sold	Low	High	Avg
PACE, CHARLES	2	0			
SANDBACH, W.	1	1	$1,183	$1,183	$1,183
			DM1,692	DM1,692	DM1,692
			£748	£748	£748
			¥118,842	¥118,842	¥118,842
SAURLE, MICHAEL	1	0			
WHITE & CO., H.N.	1	0			

BUGLET

KEAT & SONS, H.	1	0			

CECILIUM

DE GROMBARD, ARTHUR QUENTIN	1	0			

CHAMBER BASS

BAJONI, LUIGI	1	1	$62,186	$62,186	$62,186
			DM87,004	DM87,004	DM87,004
			£38,900	£38,900	£38,900
			¥5,259,786	¥5,259,786	¥5,259,786
DOLLING, HERMANN (JR.)	1	1	$5,257	$5,257	$5,257
			DM9,119	DM9,119	DM9,119
			£3,105	£3,105	£3,105
			¥666,364	¥666,364	¥666,364
GILKES, SAMUEL	1	0			
HILL, JOSEPH (ascribed to)	1	0			
PALLOTTA, PIETRO (attributed to)	1	0			
SCHULZ, AUGUST (attributed to)	1	1	$2,927	$2,927	$2,927
			DM4,154	DM4,154	DM4,154
			£1,840	£1,840	£1,840
			¥271,676	¥271,676	¥271,676

CHANTER

GLEN, DAVID	1	0			

CHITARONNE

BUCHENBERG, MATTHAUS	1	1	$4,694	$4,694	$4,694
			DM7,296	DM7,296	DM7,296
			£2,990	£2,990	£2,990
			¥461,955	¥461,955	¥461,955

CHURCH BASS

PRENTISS, HENRY	1	1	$1,265	$1,265	$1,265
			DM1,827	DM1,827	DM1,827
			£806	£806	£806
			¥109,739	¥109,739	¥109,739
PRESCOTT, ABRAHAM	2	2	$489	$690	$589
			DM758	DM998	DM878
			£313	£451	£382
			¥48,049	¥69,863	¥58,956

Maker	Items		Selling Prices		
	Bid	Sold	Low	High	Avg

CITTERN

Maker	Bid	Sold	Low	High	Avg
BRODERIP & WILKINSON	1	1	$730	$730	$730
			DM1,219	DM1,219	DM1,219
			£437	£437	£437
			¥88,707	¥88,707	¥88,707
HINTZ, FREDERICK	1	1	$623	$623	$623
			DM1,053	DM1,053	DM1,053
			£418	£418	£418
			¥66,044	¥66,044	¥66,044
LIESSEM, R.	1	1	$867	$867	$867
			DM1,303	DM1,303	DM1,303
			£518	£518	£518
			¥96,545	¥96,545	¥96,545
RUTHERFORD	1	1	$1,252	$1,252	$1,252
			DM1,882	DM1,882	DM1,882
			£748	£748	£748
			¥139,454	¥139,454	¥139,454

CLARINET

Maker	Bid	Sold	Low	High	Avg
ALBERT, E.J.	1	1	$992	$992	$992
			DM1,542	DM1,542	DM1,542
			£632	£632	£632
			¥97,644	¥97,644	¥97,644
ALBERT, EUGENE A.	1	1	$764	$764	$764
			DM1,270	DM1,270	DM1,270
			£460	£460	£460
			¥88,936	¥88,936	¥88,936
AMMANN, ULRICH	2	1	$6,491	$6,491	$6,491
			DM10,792	DM10,792	DM10,792
			£3,910	£3,910	£3,910
			¥755,959	¥755,959	¥755,959
ASHTON, JOHN	2	2	$489	$805	$647
			DM758	DM1,248	DM1,003
			£313	£515	£414
			¥48,049	¥79,140	¥63,594
ASTOR & CO.	1	0			
ASTOR & CO., GEORGE	1	1	$2,363	$2,363	$2,363
			DM3,337	DM3,337	DM3,337
			£1,495	£1,495	£1,495
			¥210,850	¥210,850	¥210,850
BARFOOT, CHARLES SMITH	1	1	$472	$472	$472
			DM669	DM669	DM669
			£299	£299	£299
			¥48,347	¥48,347	¥48,347
BAUMANN	1	1	$1,680	$1,680	$1,680
			DM2,793	DM2,793	DM2,793
			£1,012	£1,012	£1,012
			¥195,660	¥195,660	¥195,660
BETTONEY, H.	1	1	$259	$259	$259
			DM437	DM437	DM437
			£161	£161	£161
			¥31,856	¥31,856	¥31,856
BILLING, FRIEDRICH	1	1	$992	$992	$992
			DM1,542	DM1,542	DM1,542
			£632	£632	£632
			¥97,644	¥97,644	¥97,644

Maker	Items		Selling Prices		
	Bid	Sold	Low	High	Avg
BILTON	5	3	$460	$1,725	$882
			DM676	DM2,915	DM1,429
			£276	£1,035	£537
			¥48,785	¥229,546	¥109,940
BILTON, RICHARD	2	2	$618	$638	$628
			DM873	DM1,138	DM1,005
			£391	£391	£391
			¥55,145	¥83,529	¥69,337
BLACKMAN	1	0			
BOOSEY & CO.	7	2	$94	$254	$174
			DM167	DM360	DM264
			£58	£161	£109
			¥12,284	¥26,243	¥19,263
BOOSEY & HAWKES	22	16	$74	$3,452	$657
			DM125	DM4,891	DM989
			£46	£2,185	£422
			¥9,102	¥353,301	¥70,377
BRAUN	1	1	$587	$587	$587
			DM945	DM945	DM945
			£345	£345	£345
			¥72,526	¥72,526	¥72,526
BRONSEL, T.	1	1	$201	$201	$201
			DM375	DM375	DM375
			£127	£127	£127
			¥23,758	¥23,758	¥23,758
BUESCHER	3	3	$77	$230	$154
			DM128	DM409	DM259
			£46	£140	£97
			¥9,338	¥31,952	¥19,325
BUFFET	1	1	$82	$82	$82
			DM116	DM116	DM116
			£52	£52	£52
			¥8,435	¥8,435	¥8,435
BUFFET & CO.	1	1	$99	$99	$99
			DM149	DM149	DM149
			£61	£61	£61
			¥9,564	¥9,564	¥9,564
BUFFET CRAMPON & CO.	5	2	$218	$1,055	$637
			DM309	DM1,763	DM1,036
			£138	£632	£385
			¥22,494	¥128,290	¥75,392
BUTLER, GEORGE	1	1	$291	$291	$291
			DM412	DM412	DM412
			£184	£184	£184
			¥29,752	¥29,752	¥29,752
CADET	1	0			
CHRISTIANI	1	1	$576	$576	$576
			DM1,070	DM1,070	DM1,070
			£345	£345	£345
			¥77,087	¥77,087	¥77,087
CLEMENTI & CO.	3	2	$348	$417	$382
			DM534	DM591	DM563
			£230	£264	£247
			¥37,082	¥42,687	¥39,884
CONN, C.G.	1	0			

Maker	Items		Selling Prices		
	Bid	Sold	Low	High	Avg
CONN USA	1	1	$278	$278	$278
			DM468	DM468	DM468
			£173	£173	£173
			¥34,131	¥34,131	¥34,131
CRAMPON & CO.	1	1	$242	$242	$242
			DM424	DM424	DM424
			£150	£150	£150
			¥29,295	¥29,295	¥29,295
D'ALMAINE & CO.	2	2	$425	$699	$562
			DM721	DM1,048	DM884
			£286	£414	£350
			¥45,127	¥77,849	¥61,488
DAVIS	1	1	$52	$52	$52
			DM80	DM80	DM80
			£35	£35	£35
			¥5,562	¥5,562	¥5,562
DISTIN, HENRY	1	1	$133	$133	$133
			DM221	DM221	DM221
			£80	£80	£80
			¥15,467	¥15,467	¥15,467
DISTIN & CO.	1	1	$800	$800	$800
			DM1,229	DM1,229	DM1,229
			£529	£529	£529
			¥85,288	¥85,288	¥85,288
ELKHART	1	1	$132	$132	$132
			DM240	DM240	DM240
			£81	£81	£81
			¥16,675	¥16,675	¥16,675
FINGERHUTH, CHRISTIAN	1	1	$1,240	$1,240	$1,240
			DM2,062	DM2,062	DM2,062
			£747	£747	£747
			¥144,425	¥144,425	¥144,425
GARRETT, RICHARD	1	1	$581	$581	$581
			DM824	DM824	DM824
			£368	£368	£368
			¥59,503	¥59,503	¥59,503
GAUTROT (AINE)	1	0			
GEROCK, CHRISTOPHER	2	1	$378	$378	$378
			DM584	DM584	DM584
			£238	£238	£238
			¥37,708	¥37,708	¥37,708
GEROCK & WOLF	1	1	$632	$632	$632
			DM893	DM893	DM893
			£403	£403	£403
			¥53,968	¥53,968	¥53,968
GILMER & CO.	1	1	$131	$131	$131
			DM233	DM233	DM233
			£81	£81	£81
			¥17,624	¥17,624	¥17,624
GOODLAD & CO.	1	1	$283	$283	$283
			DM515	DM515	DM515
			£173	£173	£173
			¥35,732	¥35,732	¥35,732
GOULDING	1	1	$846	$846	$846
			DM1,432	DM1,432	DM1,432
			£518	£518	£518
			¥98,064	¥98,064	¥98,064

Maker	Items		Selling Prices		
	Bid	Sold	Low	High	Avg
GOULDING & CO.	2	2	$383	$730	$557
			DM710	DM1,219	DM965
			£230	£437	£334
			¥51,205	¥88,707	¥69,956
GOULDING & D'ALMAINE	2	1	$635	$635	$635
			DM900	DM900	DM900
			£402	£402	£402
			¥65,001	¥65,001	¥65,001
GOULDING D'ALMAINE POTTER	1	1	$542	$542	$542
			DM766	DM766	DM766
			£345	£345	£345
			¥46,258	¥46,258	¥46,258
GRAFTON	1	1	$502	$502	$502
			DM903	DM903	DM903
			£299	£299	£299
			¥58,075	¥58,075	¥58,075
GRAS, J.	1	0			
GRAVES, SAMUEL	1	1	$1,064	$1,064	$1,064
			DM1,649	DM1,649	DM1,649
			£681	£681	£681
			¥104,577	¥104,577	¥104,577
GREEN, J.	1	1	$546	$546	$546
			DM789	DM789	DM789
			£348	£348	£348
			¥47,387	¥47,387	¥47,387
GRETSCH	2	1	$163	$163	$163
			DM232	DM232	DM232
			£104	£104	£104
			¥16,871	¥16,871	¥16,871
HALL, WILLIAM	1	1	$173	$173	$173
			DM267	DM267	DM267
			£110	£110	£110
			¥16,958	¥16,958	¥16,958
HALL & SON, WILLIAM	1	1	$230	$230	$230
			DM409	DM409	DM409
			£140	£140	£140
			¥31,952	¥31,952	¥31,952
HASENEIER, H.F.	1	1	$1,431	$1,431	$1,431
			DM2,379	DM2,379	DM2,379
			£862	£862	£862
			¥166,659	¥166,659	¥166,659
HAWKES & SON	3	2	$383	$391	$387
			DM637	DM717	DM677
			£230	£242	£236
			¥45,356	¥46,018	¥45,687
HEROUARD	1	1	$245	$245	$245
			DM347	DM347	DM347
			£157	£157	£157
			¥24,893	¥24,893	¥24,893
JEHRING FAMILY (MEMBER OF)	1	0			
KEY, THOMAS	2	1	$480	$480	$480
			DM681	DM681	DM681
			£304	£304	£304
			¥49,155	¥49,155	¥49,155
KLEMM & BRO.	1	1	$920	$920	$920
			DM1,555	DM1,555	DM1,555
			£552	£552	£552
			¥122,424	¥122,424	¥122,424

Maker	Items		Selling Prices		
	Bid	Sold	Low	High	Avg
KOHLER & SON	1	1	$1,336	$1,336	$1,336
			DM2,222	DM2,222	DM2,222
			£805	£805	£805
			¥155,639	¥155,639	¥155,639
KOHLERT, VINCENZ FERARIUS	1	0			
KOHLERT & SONS	1	1	$103	$103	$103
			DM160	DM160	DM160
			£66	£66	£66
			¥10,194	¥10,194	¥10,194
KRUSPE, C.	1	0			
LAFLEUR, J.R. & SON	1	1	$546	$546	$546
			DM781	DM781	DM781
			£345	£345	£345
			¥54,850	¥54,850	¥54,850
LEBLANC	3	0			
LEBLANC, GEORGES	2	0			
LEDUC	1	1	$58	$58	$58
			DM102	DM102	DM102
			£35	£35	£35
			¥7,988	¥7,988	¥7,988
LEFEVRE	1	1	$2,123	$2,123	$2,123
			DM3,604	DM3,604	DM3,604
			£1,430	£1,430	£1,430
			¥225,637	¥225,637	¥225,637
LEWIN BROS.	2	0			
LILLE, J. GRAS A	1	0			
LINTON MANUFACTURING CO.	1	0			
MARTIN	2	2	$161	$259	$210
			DM226	DM401	DM313
			£101	£166	£133
			¥13,657	¥25,438	¥19,547
MARTIN BROS.	2	1	$575	$575	$575
			DM972	DM972	DM972
			£345	£345	£345
			¥76,515	¥76,515	¥76,515
MEINEL, CLEMENS	1	1	$764	$764	$764
			DM1,270	DM1,270	DM1,270
			£460	£460	£460
			¥88,936	¥88,936	¥88,936
METZLER & CO.	4	4	$247	$496	$358
			DM376	DM825	DM584
			£150	£299	£217
			¥22,716	¥57,809	¥40,915
MEYER, KARL	1	1	$176	$176	$176
			DM284	DM284	DM284
			£104	£104	£104
			¥21,758	¥21,758	¥21,758
MILLER, GEORGE	2	2	$816	$2,673	$1,744
			DM1,222	DM4,444	DM2,833
			£483	£1,610	£1,047
			¥90,823	¥311,277	¥201,050
MOLLENHAUER, JOHANN ANDREAS	1	1	$438	$438	$438
			DM729	DM729	DM729
			£264	£264	£264
			¥51,042	¥51,042	¥51,042

Maker	Items Bid	Sold	Selling Prices Low	High	Avg
MONNIG GEBRUDER	1	1	$1,718 DM2,857 £1,035 ¥200,107	$1,718 DM2,857 £1,035 ¥200,107	$1,718 DM2,857 £1,035 ¥200,107
NICHOLSON, CHARLES	1	1	$151 DM275 £92 ¥19,057	$151 DM275 £92 ¥19,057	$151 DM275 £92 ¥19,057
NOBLET, N.	1	0			
ORSI, ROMEO	1	0			
PAN-AMERICAN	1	0			
PASK, JOHN	1	1	$611 DM1,016 £368 ¥71,149	$611 DM1,016 £368 ¥71,149	$611 DM1,016 £368 ¥71,149
PAYNE, GEORGE	1	1	$509 DM719 £322 ¥45,414	$509 DM719 £322 ¥45,414	$509 DM719 £322 ¥45,414
PEACHEY, G.	1	1	$385 DM579 £230 ¥42,909	$385 DM579 £230 ¥42,909	$385 DM579 £230 ¥42,909
POTTER, HENRY	3	2	$309 DM437 £196 ¥29,408	$353 DM486 £219 ¥31,867	$331 DM461 £207 ¥30,637
POTTER, SAMUEL	1	1	$461 DM762 £276 ¥53,903	$461 DM762 £276 ¥53,903	$461 DM762 £276 ¥53,903
PURDAY	1	0			
RAMPONE, AGOSTINO	1	1	$1,336 DM2,222 £805 ¥155,639	$1,336 DM2,222 £805 ¥155,639	$1,336 DM2,222 £805 ¥155,639
REILLY, J.	1	1	$492 DM756 £322 ¥53,754	$492 DM756 £322 ¥53,754	$492 DM756 £322 ¥53,754
ROTTENBURGH, G.A.	1	1	$1,128 DM1,863 £690 ¥139,676	$1,128 DM1,863 £690 ¥139,676	$1,128 DM1,863 £690 ¥139,676
ROUSTAGNEQ	1	1	$1,718 DM2,857 £1,035 ¥200,107	$1,718 DM2,857 £1,035 ¥200,107	$1,718 DM2,857 £1,035 ¥200,107
RUDALL, CARTE & CO.	1	1	$226 DM382 £138 ¥26,150	$226 DM382 £138 ¥26,150	$226 DM382 £138 ¥26,150
RUDALL, ROSE, CARTE & CO.	1	0			
SCHENKELAARS, H.	1	0			

Maker	Items		Selling Prices		
	Bid	Sold	Low	High	Avg
SCHUSTER & CO., G.	1	1	$1,107	$1,107	$1,107
			DM1,841	DM1,841	DM1,841
			£667	£667	£667
			¥128,958	¥128,958	¥128,958
SELMER	9	7	$161	$1,633	$666
			DM227	DM2,773	DM1,115
			£101	£1,100	£442
			¥14,277	¥173,567	¥72,514
SELMER, HENRI	8	4	$168	$5,814	$1,714
			DM177	DM8,238	DM2,469
			£104	£3,680	£1,078
			¥12,813	¥595,034	¥177,376
SELMER BUNDY	2	1	$115	$115	$115
			DM205	DM205	DM205
			£70	£70	£70
			¥15,976	¥15,976	¥15,976
STIEGLER, MAX	1	1	$1,127	$1,127	$1,127
			DM1,591	DM1,591	DM1,591
			£713	£713	£713
			¥100,559	¥100,559	¥100,559
SYMPHONY	1	1	$163	$163	$163
			DM277	DM277	DM277
			£110	£110	£110
			¥17,357	¥17,357	¥17,357
THIBOUVILLE	1	1	$230	$230	$230
			DM409	DM409	DM409
			£140	£140	£140
			¥31,952	¥31,952	¥31,952
THIBOUVILLE-LAMY, J.	4	3	$61	$316	$150
			DM94	DM563	DM260
			£40	£193	£93
			¥6,489	¥43,933	¥19,841
TOMSCHIK, MARTIN	1	0			
TRIEBERT	1	1	$180	$180	$180
			DM275	DM275	DM275
			£115	£115	£115
			¥20,073	¥20,073	¥20,073
UHLMANN, JOHANN TOBIAS	1	1	$1,431	$1,431	$1,431
			DM2,379	DM2,379	DM2,379
			£862	£862	£862
			¥166,659	¥166,659	¥166,659
WHITELY	1	1	$805	$805	$805
			DM1,360	DM1,360	DM1,360
			£483	£483	£483
			¥107,121	¥107,121	¥107,121
WILLIAMS, E.G.	1	1	$800	$800	$800
			DM1,129	DM1,129	DM1,129
			£506	£506	£506
			¥71,365	¥71,365	¥71,365
WINNEN, JEAN	1	1	$311	$311	$311
			DM466	DM466	DM466
			£184	£184	£184
			¥34,599	¥34,599	¥34,599
WOLF & CO., ROBERT	2	2	$316	$509	$412
			DM476	DM719	DM597
			£194	£322	£258
			¥30,605	¥45,414	¥38,009

Maker	Items Bid	Sold	Selling Prices Low	High	Avg
WOOD, JAMES	1	1	$232 DM417 £138 ¥26,804	$232 DM417 £138 ¥26,804	$232 DM417 £138 ¥26,804
WOOD, JAMES & SON	1	1	$125 DM206 £75 ¥14,599	$125 DM206 £75 ¥14,599	$125 DM206 £75 ¥14,599
WOOD & IVY	3	3	$649 DM975 £391 ¥61,633	$1,380 DM2,332 £828 ¥183,637	$907 DM1,462 £552 ¥106,955
WREDE, H.	1	1	$319 DM567 £196 ¥42,801	$319 DM567 £196 ¥42,801	$319 DM567 £196 ¥42,801
WURLITZER, FRITZ	1	0			
YAMAHA	1	0			

CLAVICHORD

Maker	Bid	Sold	Low	High	Avg
DOLMETSCH, ARNOLD	3	3	$2,544 DM3,604 £1,610 ¥260,327	$7,555 DM12,635 £5,060 ¥802,865	$4,625 DM7,519 £3,067 ¥488,208
GOUGH, HUGH PERCIVAL HENRY	1	1	$1,222 DM1,960 £794 ¥139,037	$1,222 DM1,960 £794 ¥139,037	$1,222 DM1,960 £794 ¥139,037
HERZ, ERIC	1	1	$2,185 DM3,341 £1,437 ¥230,299	$2,185 DM3,341 £1,437 ¥230,299	$2,185 DM3,341 £1,437 ¥230,299
PALAZZI, NICOLA	1	1	$11,658 DM17,462 £6,900 ¥1,297,476	$11,658 DM17,462 £6,900 ¥1,297,476	$11,658 DM17,462 £6,900 ¥1,297,476

CLAVIOLINE

Maker	Bid	Sold	Low	High	Avg
SELMER, HENRI	1	0			

COMPAGNON

Maker	Bid	Sold	Low	High	Avg
THIBOUVILLE-LAMY, J.	1	1	$382 DM547 £242 ¥38,395	$382 DM547 £242 ¥38,395	$382 DM547 £242 ¥38,395

CONCERTINA

Maker	Bid	Sold	Low	High	Avg
BOSTOCK	1	1	$2,513 DM3,759 £1,495 ¥280,283	$2,513 DM3,759 £1,495 ¥280,283	$2,513 DM3,759 £1,495 ¥280,283
CASE, GEORGE	3	2	$160 DM264 £98 ¥19,787	$544 DM815 £322 ¥60,549	$352 DM539 £210 ¥40,168

| Maker | Items | | Selling Prices | | |
	Bid	Sold	Low	High	Avg
CHIDLEY, ROCK	6	1	$380	$380	$380
			DM674	DM674	DM674
			£230	£230	£230
			¥52,645	¥52,645	¥52,645
CRABB, HENRY	2	2	$807	$2,905	$1,856
			DM1,497	DM5,169	DM3,333
			£483	£1,783	£1,133
			¥107,922	¥390,243	¥249,082
JEFFRIES	6	6	$1,055	$4,481	$3,352
			DM1,959	DM7,843	DM5,591
			£632	£2,910	£2,085
			¥141,214	¥568,331	¥403,921
JEFFRIES, CHARLES	19	18	$178	$4,660	$2,922
			DM252	DM8,159	DM4,799
			£112	£2,875	£1,804
			¥15,832	¥563,356	¥333,020
JONES	1	1	$1,710	$1,710	$1,710
			DM2,613	DM2,613	DM2,613
			£1,093	£1,093	£1,093
			¥190,696	¥190,696	¥190,696
JONES, GEORGE	3	2	$1,220	$1,783	$1,501
			DM2,175	DM3,179	DM2,677
			£748	£1,093	£920
			¥159,688	¥233,391	¥196,540
JONES, WILLIAM H.	1	1	$1,215	$1,215	$1,215
			DM2,118	DM2,118	DM2,118
			£748	£748	£748
			¥147,145	¥147,145	¥147,145
LACHENAL	47	35	$59	$1,482	$471
			DM95	DM2,499	DM756
			£35	£920	£295
			¥7,253	¥182,034	¥53,132
LACHENAL, LOUIS	4	2	$261	$321	$291
			DM275	DM476	DM375
			£161	£207	£184
			¥19,931	¥34,730	¥27,331
LACHENAL & CO.	29	18	$91	$1,501	$650
			DM141	DM2,677	DM1,039
			£58	£920	£403
			¥9,108	¥196,540	¥72,042
METZLER & CO.	1	1	$80	$80	$80
			DM117	DM117	DM117
			£52	£52	£52
			¥8,444	¥8,444	¥8,444
PARISH, THOMAS	1	1	$261	$261	$261
			DM401	DM401	DM401
			£173	£173	£173
			¥27,811	¥27,811	¥27,811
PEAKE, J.	2	1	$151	$151	$151
			DM225	DM225	DM225
			£98	£98	£98
			¥16,400	¥16,400	¥16,400
VICKERS	1	1	$508	$508	$508
			DM819	DM819	DM819
			£299	£299	£299
			¥62,856	¥62,856	¥62,856

Maker	Items		Selling Prices		
	Bid	Sold	Low	High	Avg
VICKERS, J.J. & SONS	1	1	$1,521	$1,521	$1,521
			DM2,325	DM2,325	DM2,325
			£978	£978	£978
			¥150,324	¥150,324	¥150,324
WHEATSTONE, C.	49	40	$114	$2,846	$720
			DM194	DM5,054	DM1,159
			£77	£1,725	£450
			¥12,150	¥394,835	¥78,941
WHEATSTONE, C. (attributed to)	2	1	$783	$783	$783
			DM825	DM825	DM825
			£483	£483	£483
			¥59,793	¥59,793	¥59,793
WHEATSTONE & CO., C.	43	33	$200	$4,963	$914
			DM283	DM8,252	DM1,442
			£126	£2,990	£573
			¥18,530	¥578,087	¥99,239
WOODWARD	1	1	$72	$72	$72
			DM110	DM110	DM110
			£46	£46	£46
			¥8,029	¥8,029	¥8,029

CORNET

Maker	Items		Selling Prices		
	Bid	Sold	Low	High	Avg
ANTON (SR.), EBERHARD	1	0			
BESSON	4	4	$123	$3,250	$1,146
			DM189	DM5,051	DM1,803
			£81	£2,070	£721
			¥13,438	¥319,815	¥117,275
BESSON & CO.	2	2	$173	$466	$319
			DM307	DM698	DM503
			£104	£276	£190
			¥22,939	¥51,899	¥37,419
BOOSEY & CO.	4	2	$85	$805	$445
			DM140	DM1,360	DM750
			£52	£483	£267
			¥10,476	¥107,121	¥58,799
BOOSEY & HAWKES	4	2	$97	$457	$277
			DM149	DM702	DM425
			£63	£299	£181
			¥10,559	¥49,914	¥30,236
CONN, C.G.	1	1	$748	$748	$748
			DM1,331	DM1,331	DM1,331
			£449	£449	£449
			¥99,403	¥99,403	¥99,403
CONN USA	1	1	$690	$690	$690
			DM1,166	DM1,166	DM1,166
			£414	£414	£414
			¥91,818	¥91,818	¥91,818
CORTON	2	0			
DISTIN, HENRY	3	2	$805	$1,243	$1,024
			DM1,231	DM1,788	DM1,509
			£530	£805	£667
			¥84,847	¥126,176	¥105,511
DUPONT, M.	1	1	$92	$92	$92
			DM164	DM164	DM164
			£56	£56	£56
			¥12,781	¥12,781	¥12,781

Maker	Items		Selling Prices		
	Bid	Sold	Low	High	Avg
GLASSL, EGIDIUS	1	1	$802	$802	$802
			DM1,333	DM1,333	DM1,333
			£483	£483	£483
			¥93,383	¥93,383	¥93,383
GRAVES, J.G.	1	1	$113	$113	$113
			DM206	DM206	DM206
			£69	£69	£69
			¥14,293	¥14,293	¥14,293
HAWKES & SON	1	1	$256	$256	$256
			DM478	DM478	DM478
			£161	£161	£161
			¥30,237	¥30,237	¥30,237
HOFLIEFERVNT, F. ALTRICHTER	2	1	$210	$210	$210
			DM324	DM324	DM324
			£132	£132	£132
			¥20,949	¥20,949	¥20,949
HULLER, EMMANUEL	1	1	$1,145	$1,145	$1,145
			DM1,904	DM1,904	DM1,904
			£690	£690	£690
			¥133,405	¥133,405	¥133,405
KOHLER	2	2	$1,789	$2,738	$2,263
			DM3,344	DM5,118	DM4,231
			£1,127	£1,725	£1,426
			¥211,662	¥323,972	¥267,817
LAFLEUR, J.R. & SON	3	0			
LYON & HEALY	1	1	$916	$916	$916
			DM1,524	DM1,524	DM1,524
			£552	£552	£552
			¥106,724	¥106,724	¥106,724
MORITZ, C.W.	1	0			
OLDS & SON	1	1	$690	$690	$690
			DM1,166	DM1,166	DM1,166
			£414	£414	£414
			¥91,818	¥91,818	¥91,818
SCHUSTER & CO., G.	1	1	$690	$690	$690
			DM1,166	DM1,166	DM1,166
			£414	£414	£414
			¥91,818	¥91,818	¥91,818
STAR	1	1	$1,265	$1,265	$1,265
			DM2,238	DM2,238	DM2,238
			£764	£764	£764
			¥164,324	¥164,324	¥164,324
WHITE & CO., H.N.	1	1	$115	$115	$115
			DM176	DM176	DM176
			£76	£76	£76
			¥12,121	¥12,121	¥12,121
WOODS & CO.	2	1	$77	$77	$77
			DM116	DM116	DM116
			£46	£46	£46
			¥8,624	¥8,624	¥8,624
WURLITZER CO., RUDOLPH	1	1	$144	$144	$144
			DM256	DM256	DM256
			£86	£86	£86
			¥19,116	¥19,116	¥19,116

Maker	Items		Selling Prices		
	Bid	Sold	Low	High	Avg

CORNOPEAN

KOHLER, JOHN	1	1	$6,217	$6,217	$6,217
			DM9,313	DM9,313	DM9,313
			£3,680	£3,680	£3,680
			¥691,987	¥691,987	¥691,987

CYMBALUM

SCHUNDA, JOSEF V.	1	0			

DOUBLE BASS

BALLANTYNE, ROBERT	1	1	$1,880	$1,880	$1,880
			DM2,819	DM2,819	DM2,819
			£1,150	£1,150	£1,150
			¥181,884	¥181,884	¥181,884
BERGONZI, NICOLO	1	1	$124,369	$124,369	$124,369
			DM215,166	DM215,166	DM215,166
			£76,300	£76,300	£76,300
			¥14,191,800	¥14,191,800	¥14,191,800
CUNE, RENE	1	1	$4,520	$4,520	$4,520
			DM6,946	DM6,946	DM6,946
			£2,990	£2,990	£2,990
			¥482,063	¥482,063	¥482,063
DERAZEY, JUSTIN	1	1	$13,530	$13,530	$13,530
			DM20,243	DM20,243	DM20,243
			£8,050	£8,050	£8,050
			¥1,509,214	¥1,509,214	¥1,509,214
FENDT, BERNARD	1	1	$35,514	$35,514	$35,514
			DM56,854	DM56,854	DM56,854
			£23,100	£23,100	£23,100
			¥3,594,914	¥3,594,914	¥3,594,914
FENDT, BERNARD SIMON	1	1	$36,708	$36,708	$36,708
			DM66,009	DM66,009	DM66,009
			£21,850	£21,850	£21,850
			¥4,243,926	¥4,243,926	¥4,243,926
GARIMBERTI, FERDINANDO	1	1	$17,621	$17,621	$17,621
			DM26,012	DM26,012	DM26,012
			£11,500	£11,500	£11,500
			¥1,873,362	¥1,873,362	¥1,873,362
GILKES, WILLIAM	1	1	$25,367	$25,367	$25,367
			DM40,610	DM40,610	DM40,610
			£16,500	£16,500	£16,500
			¥2,567,796	¥2,567,796	¥2,567,796
HAMMIG, JOHANN CHRISTIAN	1	0			
HAWKES & SON	1	1	$8,304	$8,304	$8,304
			DM11,559	DM11,559	DM11,559
			£5,175	£5,175	£5,175
			¥700,571	¥700,571	¥700,571
HERRMANN, KARL (workshop of)	2	0			
JACQUOT (ascribed to)	1	1	$4,455	$4,455	$4,455
			DM7,535	DM7,535	DM7,535
			£2,990	£2,990	£2,990
			¥472,420	¥472,420	¥472,420
PILLEMENT, FRANCOIS	2	1	$12,617	$12,617	$12,617
			DM21,345	DM21,345	DM21,345
			£7,935	£7,935	£7,935
			¥1,563,195	¥1,563,195	¥1,563,195

Maker	Items		Selling Prices		
	Bid	Sold	Low	High	Avg
POLLMAN	2	2	$4,420	$8,746	$6,583
			DM6,525	DM15,163	DM10,844
			£2,875	£5,175	£4,025
			¥470,856	¥1,111,952	¥791,404
RIVIERE & HAWKES	1	1	$6,088	$6,088	$6,088
			DM9,746	DM9,746	DM9,746
			£3,960	£3,960	£3,960
			¥616,271	¥616,271	¥616,271
TARR, WILLIAM (attributed to)	1	1	$11,838	$11,838	$11,838
			DM17,847	DM17,847	DM17,847
			£7,260	£7,260	£7,260
			¥1,147,675	¥1,147,675	¥1,147,675
VILLA, LUIGI	3	3	$5,377	$9,218	$6,786
			DM8,984	DM15,401	DM11,337
			£3,220	£5,520	£4,063
			¥653,628	¥1,120,505	¥824,816

DOUBLE BASS BOW

Maker	Items		Selling Prices		
	Bid	Sold	Low	High	Avg
BAILEY, G.E.	1	1	$1,019	$1,019	$1,019
			DM1,718	DM1,718	DM1,718
			£633	£633	£633
			¥125,148	¥125,148	¥125,148
BRYANT, PERCIVAL WILFRED	5	5	$1,840	$2,437	$2,026
			DM2,872	DM4,216	DM3,254
			£1,178	£1,495	£1,282
			¥183,816	¥278,070	¥220,127
BULTITUDE, ARTHUR RICHARD	1	1	$1,475	$1,475	$1,475
			DM2,054	DM2,054	DM2,054
			£920	£920	£920
			¥124,704	¥124,704	¥124,704
DEVOIVRE, JEROME	1	0			
DODD	1	1	$2,913	$2,913	$2,913
			DM4,401	DM4,401	DM4,401
			£1,955	£1,955	£1,955
			¥308,519	¥308,519	¥308,519
DUPUY	1	1	$2,020	$2,020	$2,020
			DM3,100	DM3,100	DM3,100
			£1,265	£1,265	£1,265
			¥198,031	¥198,031	¥198,031
FETIQUE, VICTOR	3	3	$2,766	$5,991	$4,481
			DM3,851	DM8,844	DM6,934
			£1,725	£3,910	£2,837
			¥233,820	¥636,943	¥468,504
HILL, W.E. & SONS	1	1	$387	$387	$387
			DM578	DM578	DM578
			£230	£230	£230
			¥43,120	¥43,120	¥43,120
KLING, AIME	1	1	$657	$657	$657
			DM985	DM985	DM985
			£402	£402	£402
			¥63,580	¥63,580	¥63,580
KOVANDA, FRANK	1	1	$583	$583	$583
			DM985	DM985	DM985
			£391	£391	£391
			¥61,778	¥61,778	¥61,778

Maker	Items		Selling Prices		
	Bid	Sold	Low	High	Avg
LAMY, ALFRED	1	1	$2,632	$2,632	$2,632
			DM3,946	DM3,946	DM3,946
			£1,610	£1,610	£1,610
			¥254,638	¥254,638	¥254,638
LAPIERRE	2	0			
LAPIERRE, MARCEL	2	2	$1,687	$2,875	$2,281
			DM2,919	DM4,327	DM3,623
			£1,035	£1,745	£1,390
			¥192,510	¥321,368	¥256,939
LENOBLE, AUGUSTE	2	1	$3,998	$3,998	$3,998
			DM5,647	DM5,647	DM5,647
			£2,530	£2,530	£2,530
			¥356,824	¥356,824	¥356,824
LOTTE, FRANCOIS	1	1	$1,018	$1,018	$1,018
			DM1,633	DM1,633	DM1,633
			£661	£661	£661
			¥115,864	¥115,864	¥115,864
MORIZOT, LOUIS	2	1	$1,840	$1,840	$1,840
			DM3,180	DM3,180	DM3,180
			£1,137	£1,137	£1,137
			¥233,192	¥233,192	¥233,192
MORIZOT, LOUIS (II)	1	1	$1,828	$1,828	$1,828
			DM3,382	DM3,382	DM3,382
			£1,092	£1,092	£1,092
			¥243,614	¥243,614	¥243,614
OUCHARD, EMILE FRANCOIS	1	1	$1,785	$1,785	$1,785
			DM2,676	DM2,676	DM2,676
			£1,092	£1,092	£1,092
			¥172,711	¥172,711	¥172,711
PFRETZSCHNER, H.R.	2	1	$778	$778	$778
			DM1,145	DM1,145	DM1,145
			£506	£506	£506
			¥82,559	¥82,559	¥82,559
RAU, AUGUST	1	1	$1,344	$1,344	$1,344
			DM2,246	DM2,246	DM2,246
			£805	£805	£805
			¥163,407	¥163,407	¥163,407
SCHMITT, JEAN-FREDERIC	1	1	$940	$940	$940
			DM1,409	DM1,409	DM1,409
			£575	£575	£575
			¥90,942	¥90,942	¥90,942
SCHUSTER, ADOLPH CURT	1	1	$845	$845	$845
			DM1,296	DM1,296	DM1,296
			£529	£529	£529
			¥82,813	¥82,813	¥82,813
SIEFERT, W.	1	0			
TARR, THOMAS	1	1	$1,089	$1,089	$1,089
			DM1,533	DM1,533	DM1,533
			£690	£690	£690
			¥111,319	¥111,319	¥111,319
TEMPLE, WILLIAM	1	1	$271	$271	$271
			DM382	DM382	DM382
			£172	£172	£172
			¥27,749	¥27,749	¥27,749
THOMASSIN, CLAUDE	1	1	$792	$792	$792
			DM1,169	DM1,169	DM1,169
			£517	£517	£517
			¥84,220	¥84,220	¥84,220

Maker	Items		Selling Prices		
	Bid	Sold	Low	High	Avg
ULLMANN, GIORGIO	1	1	$881	$881	$881
			DM1,301	DM1,301	DM1,301
			£575	£575	£575
			¥93,668	¥93,668	¥93,668
VICKERS, J.E.	6	5	$282	$551	$367
			DM416	DM845	DM574
			£184	£345	£230
			¥28,517	¥54,008	¥38,886
VIGNERON, ANDRE	1	1	$2,198	$2,198	$2,198
			DM3,520	DM3,520	DM3,520
			£1,430	£1,430	£1,430
			¥222,542	¥222,542	¥222,542
VOIGT, ARNOLD	1	1	$602	$602	$602
			DM902	DM902	DM902
			£368	£368	£368
			¥58,203	¥58,203	¥58,203
WANKA, HERBERT	1	1	$1,139	$1,139	$1,139
			DM1,718	DM1,718	DM1,718
			£690	£690	£690
			¥129,030	¥129,030	¥129,030
WERNER, ERICH	1	1	$528	$528	$528
			DM961	DM961	DM961
			£322	£322	£322
			¥66,699	¥66,699	¥66,699

DRUM

WINDSOR	1	0			

DULCIMER

EBBLEWHITE	1	0			

DULCITONE

MACHELL, THOMAS	1	1	$168	$168	$168
			DM268	DM268	DM268
			£109	£109	£109
			¥16,947	¥16,947	¥16,947

EDEOPHONE

LACHENAL & CO.	7	4	$782	$1,651	$1,209
			DM1,300	DM2,472	DM1,915
			£471	£977	£736
			¥91,063	¥183,715	¥139,580

ENGLISH HORN

ALBERT, JACQUES	1	1	$820	$820	$820
			DM864	DM864	DM864
			£506	£506	£506
			¥62,640	¥62,640	¥62,640
BOOSEY & HAWKES	2	2	$739	$861	$800
			DM1,134	DM1,436	DM1,285
			£483	£575	£529
			¥80,631	¥88,383	¥84,507
FORNARI, ANDREAS	2	0			

Maker	Items		Selling Prices		
	Bid	Sold	Low	High	Avg
HOWARD	1	1	$1,091	$1,091	$1,091
			DM1,674	DM1,674	DM1,674
			£713	£713	£713
			¥119,026	¥119,026	¥119,026
LOREE, F.	1	1	$993	$993	$993
			DM1,650	DM1,650	DM1,650
			£598	£598	£598
			¥115,617	¥115,617	¥115,617
LOUIS	2	2	$1,091	$1,196	$1,143
			DM1,674	DM1,836	DM1,755
			£713	£782	£748
			¥119,026	¥130,545	¥124,785
TRIEBERT & SONS, GUILLAUME	3	3	$3,054	$9,759	$6,774
			DM5,078	DM17,402	DM11,955
			£1,840	£5,980	£4,140
			¥355,746	¥1,277,507	¥871,984
ZIEGLER, I.	1	1	$3,818	$3,818	$3,818
			DM6,348	DM6,348	DM6,348
			£2,300	£2,300	£2,300
			¥444,682	¥444,682	¥444,682

EPINETTE DES VOSGES

Maker	Items		Selling Prices		
LAMBERT, A.	1	1	$476	$476	$476
			DM792	DM792	DM792
			£287	£287	£287
			¥55,489	¥55,489	¥55,489

EUPHONIUM

Maker	Items		Selling Prices		
BESSON	2	1	$457	$457	$457
			DM702	DM702	DM702
			£299	£299	£299
			¥49,914	¥49,914	¥49,914
BOOSEY & HAWKES	2	2	$457	$563	$510
			DM702	DM864	DM783
			£299	£368	£334
			¥49,914	¥61,433	¥55,673

FIFE

Maker	Items		Selling Prices		
ADLEF	1	1	$112	$112	$112
			DM153	DM153	DM153
			£69	£69	£69
			¥9,287	¥9,287	¥9,287
HAWKES & SON	1	0			
MILHOUSE, WILLIAM	1	1	$191	$191	$191
			DM317	DM317	DM317
			£115	£115	£115
			¥22,234	¥22,234	¥22,234
ROSE & CO.	1	0			
SIMPSON	1	1	$142	$142	$142
			DM253	DM253	DM253
			£86	£86	£86
			¥19,742	¥19,742	¥19,742
WOLF & FIGG	1	1	$113	$113	$113
			DM174	DM174	DM174
			£75	£75	£75
			¥12,052	¥12,052	¥12,052

Maker	Items		Selling Prices		
	Bid	Sold	Low	High	Avg

FLAGEOLET

Maker	Bid	Sold	Low	High	Avg
BAINBRIDGE, WILLIAM	9	9	$243 DM360 £161 ¥25,957	$3,271 DM4,620 £2,070 ¥291,947	$1,274 DM1,887 £796 ¥124,907
BAINBRIDGE & WOOD	7	7	$328 DM554 £220 ¥34,760	$3,627 DM6,031 £2,185 ¥422,448	$1,115 DM1,835 £689 ¥125,445
BUHNER & KELLER	1	1	$955 DM1,587 £575 ¥111,171	$955 DM1,587 £575 ¥111,171	$955 DM1,587 £575 ¥111,171
BUTHOD & THIBOUVILLE	1	1	$938 DM1,673 £575 ¥122,837	$938 DM1,673 £575 ¥122,837	$938 DM1,673 £575 ¥122,837
CAMP, WILLIAM	1	1	$578 DM898 £368 ¥56,856	$578 DM898 £368 ¥56,856	$578 DM898 £368 ¥56,856
CARD, W.	1	1	$289 DM519 £172 ¥33,408	$289 DM519 £172 ¥33,408	$289 DM519 £172 ¥33,408
CLEMENTI & CO.	1	1	$981 DM1,386 £621 ¥87,584	$981 DM1,386 £621 ¥87,584	$981 DM1,386 £621 ¥87,584
HASTRICK	3	2	$635 DM900 £402 ¥65,001	$763 DM1,081 £483 ¥78,098	$699 DM991 £443 ¥71,550
LAMBERT, JEAN NICOLAS	1	1	$955 DM1,587 £575 ¥111,171	$955 DM1,587 £575 ¥111,171	$955 DM1,587 £575 ¥111,171
LAUSSEDAT	1	0			
MARGUERITAT	1	1	$1,240 DM2,062 £747 ¥144,425	$1,240 DM2,062 £747 ¥144,425	$1,240 DM2,062 £747 ¥144,425
PROWSE	1	1	$197 DM333 £132 ¥20,856	$197 DM333 £132 ¥20,856	$197 DM333 £132 ¥20,856
PROWSE & CO., KEITH	2	2	$363 DM513 £230 ¥32,439	$712 DM1,267 £437 ¥95,672	$538 DM890 £334 ¥64,056
SATZGER	1	0			
SIMPSON	2	2	$172 DM267 £110 ¥16,991	$533 DM766 £345 ¥54,075	$352 DM517 £228 ¥35,533

Maker	Items		Selling Prices		
	Bid	Sold	Low	High	Avg

Maker	Bid	Sold	Low	High	Avg
SIMPSON, JOHN	3	2	$237	$955	$596
			DM444	DM1,587	DM1,015
			£150	£575	£362
			¥28,078	¥111,171	¥69,624

FLUGELHORN

Maker	Bid	Sold	Low	High	Avg
BESSON & CO.	1	1	$575	$575	$575
			DM972	DM972	DM972
			£345	£345	£345
			¥76,515	¥76,515	¥76,515
LOW, JACOB	1	1	$1,909	$1,909	$1,909
			DM3,174	DM3,174	DM3,174
			£1,150	£1,150	£1,150
			¥222,341	¥222,341	¥222,341
OTTO, FRANZ	1	1	$916	$916	$916
			DM1,524	DM1,524	DM1,524
			£552	£552	£552
			¥106,724	¥106,724	¥106,724
SCHUSTER & CO.	1	1	$633	$633	$633
			DM1,069	DM1,069	DM1,069
			£380	£380	£380
			¥84,167	¥84,167	¥84,167

FLUTE

Maker	Bid	Sold	Low	High	Avg
ADLER, F.O.	1	1	$186	$186	$186
			DM256	DM256	DM256
			£115	£115	£115
			¥15,478	¥15,478	¥15,478
ALEXANDER GEBRUDER	1	1	$458	$458	$458
			DM762	DM762	DM762
			£276	£276	£276
			¥53,362	¥53,362	¥53,362
ARMSTRONG, W.T.	1	0			
ARMSTRONG CO.	2	1	$354	$354	$354
			DM522	DM522	DM522
			£230	£230	£230
			¥37,668	¥37,668	¥37,668
ARTILEY	2	1	$177	$177	$177
			DM284	DM284	DM284
			£115	£115	£115
			¥17,897	¥17,897	¥17,897
ASTOR & CO.	1	1	$764	$764	$764
			DM1,270	DM1,270	DM1,270
			£460	£460	£460
			¥88,936	¥88,936	¥88,936
BACON & HART	1	0			
BAINBRIDGE & WOOD	3	2	$224	$2,294	$1,259
			DM391	DM3,524	DM1,958
			£138	£1,495	£817
			¥27,165	¥251,144	¥139,154
BARRET & GRANIER	1	1	$327	$327	$327
			DM555	DM555	DM555
			£220	£220	£220
			¥34,713	¥34,713	¥34,713

Maker	Items		Selling Prices		
	Bid	Sold	Low	High	Avg
BERCIOUX, EUGENE	1	1	$1,783	$1,783	$1,783
			DM3,179	DM3,179	DM3,179
			£1,093	£1,093	£1,093
			¥233,391	¥233,391	¥233,391
BERNAREGGI, FRANCISCO	1	1	$1,454	$1,454	$1,454
			DM2,059	DM2,059	DM2,059
			£920	£920	£920
			¥148,758	¥148,758	¥148,758
BETTONEY, H.	1	1	$431	$431	$431
			DM668	DM668	DM668
			£276	£276	£276
			¥42,396	¥42,396	¥42,396
BEUKERS, WILLEM	3	0			
BILTON	3	2	$219	$351	$285
			DM409	DM498	DM454
			£138	£225	£182
			¥25,918	¥35,675	¥30,796
BILTON, RICHARD	3	1	$582	$582	$582
			DM821	DM821	DM821
			£368	£368	£368
			¥51,902	¥51,902	¥51,902
BLESSING	1	1	$209	$209	$209
			DM321	DM321	DM321
			£138	£138	£138
			¥22,249	¥22,249	¥22,249
BLUME, JOHANN CHRISTIAN	2	2	$631	$1,026	$829
			DM981	DM1,646	DM1,313
			£402	£667	£535
			¥62,109	¥103,802	¥82,955
BOEHM & MENDLER	3	3	$7,497	$13,151	$10,769
			DM11,303	DM18,667	DM15,811
			£4,598	£8,437	£6,645
			¥726,861	¥1,337,720	¥1,120,686
BOIE, FRIEDRICH	1	1	$1,314	$1,314	$1,314
			DM2,343	DM2,343	DM2,343
			£805	£805	£805
			¥171,972	¥171,972	¥171,972
BONNEVILLE	2	0			
BOOSEY & CO.	4	3	$307	$583	$418
			DM434	DM873	DM607
			£196	£345	£257
			¥26,213	¥64,874	¥42,759
BOOSEY & HAWKES	15	9	$74	$474	$201
			DM125	DM714	DM306
			£46	£290	£126
			¥9,102	¥45,907	¥21,092
BUFFET	3	2	$156	$309	$233
			DM240	DM556	DM398
			£104	£184	£144
			¥16,687	¥35,738	¥26,213
BUFFET CRAMPON & CO.	3	2	$220	$1,577	$899
			DM352	DM2,239	DM1,296
			£143	£1,012	£578
			¥22,254	¥160,457	¥91,355
BUHNER & KELLER	1	1	$2,889	$2,889	$2,889
			DM4,490	DM4,490	DM4,490
			£1,840	£1,840	£1,840
			¥284,280	¥284,280	¥284,280

Maker	Items		Selling Prices		
	Bid	Sold	Low	High	Avg
BUTLER	1	1	$1,228	$1,228	$1,228
			DM1,908	DM1,908	DM1,908
			£782	£782	£782
			¥120,819	¥120,819	¥120,819
BUTLER, GEORGE	1	1	$103	$103	$103
			DM184	DM184	DM184
			£63	£63	£63
			¥13,512	¥13,512	¥13,512
BUTTON & CO.	1	1	$134	$134	$134
			DM201	DM201	DM201
			£80	£80	£80
			¥14,998	¥14,998	¥14,998
CABART	8	2	$103	$195	$149
			DM108	DM286	DM197
			£63	£127	£95
			¥7,830	¥20,640	¥14,235
CAHUSAC	5	2	$271	$1,128	$699
			DM433	DM1,910	DM1,171
			£176	£690	£433
			¥27,390	¥130,752	¥79,071
CAHUSAC, THOMAS	4	3	$120	$816	$486
			DM203	DM1,222	DM742
			£75	£483	£301
			¥14,790	¥90,823	¥53,745
CAHUSAC, THOMAS (SR.)	1	1	$2,544	$2,544	$2,544
			DM3,594	DM3,594	DM3,594
			£1,610	£1,610	£1,610
			¥227,070	¥227,070	¥227,070
CARLSSON, P.A.	1	1	$2,167	$2,167	$2,167
			DM3,367	DM3,367	DM3,367
			£1,380	£1,380	£1,380
			¥213,210	¥213,210	¥213,210
CLEMENTI & CO.	5	2	$318	$945	$631
			DM554	DM1,335	DM944
			£196	£598	£397
			¥38,484	¥84,340	¥61,412
CLINTON & CO.	1	1	$142	$142	$142
			DM227	DM227	DM227
			£92	£92	£92
			¥14,318	¥14,318	¥14,318
COLAS, PROSPER	1	0			
COLLARD & COLLARD	1	1	$618	$618	$618
			DM873	DM873	DM873
			£391	£391	£391
			¥55,145	¥55,145	¥55,145
COLONIEU, MARIUS HENRY	3	1	$264	$264	$264
			DM480	DM480	DM480
			£161	£161	£161
			¥33,350	¥33,350	¥33,350
CONN USA	1	1	$485	$485	$485
			DM841	DM841	DM841
			£287	£287	£287
			¥61,668	¥61,668	¥61,668
CORTELLINI	1	1	$1,300	$1,300	$1,300
			DM2,020	DM2,020	DM2,020
			£828	£828	£828
			¥127,926	¥127,926	¥127,926

Maker	Items		Selling Prices		
	Bid	Sold	Low	High	Avg
COUESNON	1	0			
CRONE, GOTTLEIB	1	0			
CUVILLIER	1	1	$1,145	$1,145	$1,145
			DM1,904	DM1,904	DM1,904
			£690	£690	£690
			¥133,405	¥133,405	¥133,405
D'ALMAINE & CO.	4	3	$98	$308	$195
			DM166	DM437	DM310
			£66	£195	£123
			¥10,428	¥31,530	¥21,529
DALE, COCKERILL & CO.	1	1	$1,362	$1,362	$1,362
			DM1,924	DM1,924	DM1,924
			£862	£862	£862
			¥121,574	¥121,574	¥121,574
DODD	1	1	$72	$72	$72
			DM110	DM110	DM110
			£46	£46	£46
			¥8,029	¥8,029	¥8,029
DOLLARD	1	1	$722	$722	$722
			DM1,122	DM1,122	DM1,122
			£460	£460	£460
			¥71,070	¥71,070	¥71,070
DOLLING FAMILY (MEMBER OF)	1	1	$840	$840	$840
			DM1,397	DM1,397	DM1,397
			£506	£506	£506
			¥97,830	¥97,830	¥97,830
DROUET	3	2	$1,009	$2,113	$1,561
			DM1,617	DM3,529	DM2,573
			£656	£1,265	£960
			¥102,012	¥256,782	¥179,397
DROUET, LOUIS	5	4	$622	$6,217	$3,303
			DM931	DM9,313	DM4,990
			£368	£3,680	£1,990
			¥69,199	¥691,987	¥357,713
DUBOIS & COUTURIER	2	1	$573	$573	$573
			DM952	DM952	DM952
			£345	£345	£345
			¥66,702	¥66,702	¥66,702
ELKHART	5	0			
EMBACH, LUDWIG	1	0			
EULER, AUGUST ANTON	1	1	$618	$618	$618
			DM875	DM875	DM875
			£391	£391	£391
			¥63,222	¥63,222	¥63,222
FIRTH, HALL & POND	5	5	$230	$518	$364
			DM356	DM802	DM567
			£138	£331	£234
			¥22,611	¥51,514	¥38,623
FISCHER, CARL	1	1	$115	$115	$115
			DM205	DM205	DM205
			£70	£70	£70
			¥15,976	¥15,976	¥15,976
FORNARI	1	0			
FRENCH, G.	1	1	$283	$283	$283
			DM418	DM418	DM418
			£184	£184	£184
			¥30,127	¥30,127	¥30,127

Maker	Items Bid	Sold	Selling Prices Low	High	Avg
FRERE, HEROUARD	1	1	$691	$691	$691
			DM975	DM975	DM975
			£437	£437	£437
			¥61,633	¥61,633	¥61,633
FREYER & MARTIN	2	0			
FREYER, JOHANN GOTTLIEB	1	1	$2,471	$2,471	$2,471
			DM3,796	DM3,796	DM3,796
			£1,610	£1,610	£1,610
			¥270,462	¥270,462	¥270,462
GARRETT	1	1	$230	$230	$230
			DM385	DM385	DM385
			£138	£138	£138
			¥28,013	¥28,013	¥28,013
GAUTROT (AINE)	1	0			
GEDNEY, CALEB	1	1	$5,451	$5,451	$5,451
			DM7,723	DM7,723	DM7,723
			£3,450	£3,450	£3,450
			¥557,844	¥557,844	¥557,844
GEHRING	1	1	$6,706	$6,706	$6,706
			DM10,302	DM10,302	DM10,302
			£4,370	£4,370	£4,370
			¥734,112	¥734,112	¥734,112
GEMEINHARDT	3	2	$212	$309	$260
			DM381	DM556	DM468
			£126	£184	£155
			¥24,473	¥35,738	¥30,106
GEROCK, CHRISTOPHER	9	5	$293	$3,250	$1,115
			DM504	DM5,051	DM1,702
			£195	£2,070	£709
			¥30,329	¥319,815	¥110,247
GEROCK, ASTOR & CO.	1	1	$1,444	$1,444	$1,444
			DM2,245	DM2,245	DM2,245
			£920	£920	£920
			¥142,140	¥142,140	¥142,140
GLIER, JOHANN WILHELM	1	1	$1,909	$1,909	$1,909
			DM3,174	DM3,174	DM3,174
			£1,150	£1,150	£1,150
			¥222,341	¥222,341	¥222,341
GODEFROY, CLAIR	3	3	$2,181	$5,088	$3,582
			DM3,080	DM7,208	DM5,513
			£1,380	£3,220	£2,223
			¥194,631	¥520,655	¥372,447
GODEFROY, CLAIR (AINE)	5	3	$676	$2,291	$1,434
			DM1,205	DM3,809	DM2,412
			£414	£1,380	£866
			¥88,443	¥266,809	¥170,297
GOLDING & CO.	2	1	$169	$169	$169
			DM243	DM243	DM243
			£109	£109	£109
			¥17,124	¥17,124	¥17,124
GOODLAD, JOHN DUNKIN	1	1	$381	$381	$381
			DM539	DM539	DM539
			£241	£241	£241
			¥38,968	¥38,968	¥38,968
GOODLAD & CO.	1	1	$840	$840	$840
			DM1,397	DM1,397	DM1,397
			£506	£506	£506
			¥97,830	¥97,830	¥97,830

| Maker | Items | | Selling Prices | | |
	Bid	Sold	Low	High	Avg
GOOZMAN, J.P.	1	0			
GOTTFRIED, AUGUST LEHNHOLD	1	1	$327	$327	$327
			DM463	DM463	DM463
			£207	£207	£207
			¥33,471	¥33,471	¥33,471
GOULDING & CO.	6	4	$291	$691	$426
			DM504	DM975	DM640
			£172	£437	£268
			¥32,525	¥61,633	¥43,006
GOULDING & D'ALMAINE	3	3	$135	$836	$490
			DM236	DM1,181	DM780
			£81	£529	£303
			¥17,256	¥74,609	¥52,810
GOULDING D'ALMAINE POTTER	5	4	$535	$1,300	$843
			DM821	DM2,020	DM1,329
			£322	£828	£523
			¥51,902	¥127,926	¥88,313
GRENSER, CARL AUGUSTIN (I)	4	2	$2,362	$9,994	$6,178
			DM3,347	DM14,159	DM8,753
			£1,495	£6,325	£3,910
			¥241,733	¥1,022,715	¥632,224
GRENSER, JOHANN HEINRICH	2	0			
GREVE, ANDREAS	1	0			
HALE, JOHN	1	0			
HALL, WILLIAM	1	1	$288	$288	$288
			DM512	DM512	DM512
			£173	£173	£173
			¥38,232	¥38,232	¥38,232
HALLETT, BENJAMIN	1	1	$3,382	$3,382	$3,382
			DM5,415	DM5,415	DM5,415
			£2,200	£2,200	£2,200
			¥342,373	¥342,373	¥342,373
HAMMIG, PHILIP	2	1	$1,999	$1,999	$1,999
			DM2,832	DM2,832	DM2,832
			£1,265	£1,265	£1,265
			¥204,543	¥204,543	¥204,543
HANN, RICHARD	1	0			
HARRIS	1	1	$437	$437	$437
			DM625	DM625	DM625
			£276	£276	£276
			¥43,880	¥43,880	¥43,880
HAWKES & SON	5	3	$210	$409	$306
			DM299	DM562	DM392
			£135	£253	£191
			¥21,405	¥34,051	¥26,078
HAYNES CO., WILLIAM S.	3	3	$863	$2,070	$1,514
			DM1,319	DM3,685	DM2,488
			£567	£1,242	£956
			¥90,908	¥275,269	¥178,623
HAYNES & CO.	3	3	$1,265	$2,185	$1,648
			DM2,187	DM3,777	DM2,849
			£782	£1,350	£1,019
			¥160,320	¥276,916	¥208,902
HILL, HENRY	1	1	$488	$488	$488
			DM870	DM870	DM870
			£299	£299	£299
			¥63,875	¥63,875	¥63,875

JOHANNES CUYPERS
Fine and Handsome Dutch Violin:
The Hague, 1797
Phillips, April 2, 1998, Lot 95

GIOVANNI GRANCINO
*Very Fine and Important Italian
Violoncello: Milan, c. 1700
Bonhams, November 18, 1998, Lot 54*

JOHANN SEELOS
Bass Viola da Gamba: Linz, 1691
Sotheby's, November 4, 1998, Lot 153

ANTONIO STRADIVARI
Important Cremonese Violin
Christie's, November 18, 1998, Lot 189

GAGLIANO FAMILY (member of)
Fine Neapolitan Violin: Naples, c. 1800
Bonhams, March 31, 1998, Lot 183

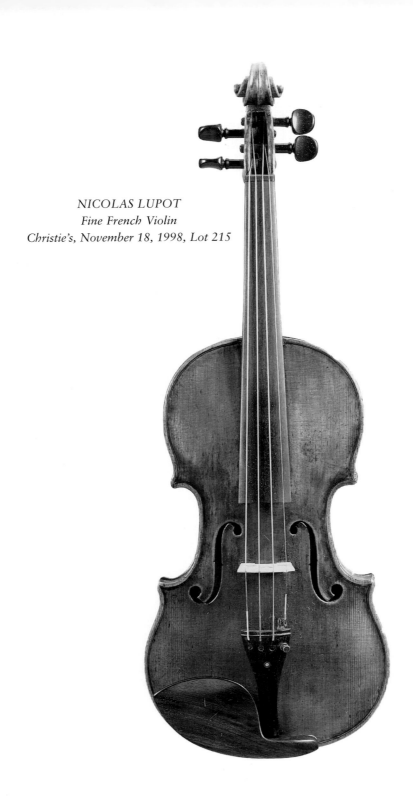

NICOLAS LUPOT
Fine French Violin
Christie's, November 18, 1998, Lot 215

HIPPOLYTE CHRETIEN SILVESTRE
Good French Violoncello: Lyon, 1881
Skinner, May 3, 1998, Lot 49

BERNARDO CALCAGNI
Rare and Exceptional Violoncello:
Genoa, 1737
Butterfields', February 9, 1998, Lot 4110

Maker	Items		Selling Prices		
	Bid	Sold	Low	High	Avg
HILL, HENRY LOCKEY	1	1	$836	$836	$836
			DM1,181	DM1,181	DM1,181
			£529	£529	£529
			¥74,609	¥74,609	¥74,609
HODSOLL, WILLIAM	1	1	$397	$397	$397
			DM617	DM617	DM617
			£253	£253	£253
			¥39,089	¥39,089	¥39,089
HUSSON & BUTHOD	1	1	$300	$300	$300
			DM535	DM535	DM535
			£184	£184	£184
			¥39,308	¥39,308	¥39,308
INGRAM, THOMAS WILLIAM	1	0			
JACOBS, HENDRIK	1	1	$30,728	$30,728	$30,728
			DM57,040	DM57,040	DM57,040
			£18,400	£18,400	£18,400
			¥4,111,296	¥4,111,296	¥4,111,296
JAMES, TREVOR J.	5	1	$130	$130	$130
			DM219	DM219	DM219
			£81	£81	£81
			¥15,928	¥15,928	¥15,928
JULLIOT, DJALMA	1	0			
KAUFFMANN, ANDREW	2	1	$1,606	$1,606	$1,606
			DM2,447	DM2,447	DM2,447
			£1,035	£1,035	£1,035
			¥178,124	¥178,124	¥178,124
KEY, THOMAS	1	1	$945	$945	$945
			DM1,339	DM1,339	DM1,339
			£598	£598	£598
			¥96,693	¥96,693	¥96,693
KING MUSICAL INSTRUMENT CO.	1	0			
KIRST, FRIEDRICH GABRIEL AUGUST	2	2	$27,082	$38,851	$32,967
			DM42,090	DM62,185	DM52,137
			£17,250	£25,300	£21,275
			¥2,665,125	¥3,920,235	¥3,292,680
KLINGSON	1	0			
KNOCHENHAUER, AUGUST T.A.	1	1	$2,544	$2,544	$2,544
			DM3,604	DM3,604	DM3,604
			£1,610	£1,610	£1,610
			¥260,327	¥260,327	¥260,327
KOCH, FRANZ JOSEPH	1	1	$2,907	$2,907	$2,907
			DM4,119	DM4,119	DM4,119
			£1,840	£1,840	£1,840
			¥297,517	¥297,517	¥297,517
KOCH, S.	2	2	$1,260	$4,009	$2,635
			DM1,926	DM6,665	DM4,296
			£805	£2,415	£1,610
			¥140,513	¥466,916	¥303,714
KOHLER, JOHN	1	0			
KUSDER, HENRY	1	1	$3,284	$3,284	$3,284
			DM5,904	DM5,904	DM5,904
			£1,955	£1,955	£1,955
			¥379,720	¥379,720	¥379,720
LAFLEUR, J.R. & SON	2	1	$817	$817	$817
			DM1,157	DM1,157	DM1,157
			£517	£517	£517
			¥83,596	¥83,596	¥83,596

| Maker | Items | | Selling Prices | | |
	Bid	Sold	Low	High	Avg
LAMY, J.T.	1	0			
LANGLOIS, A.M.	2	1	$678	$678	$678
			DM1,033	DM1,033	DM1,033
			£437	£437	£437
			¥75,208	¥75,208	¥75,208
LARSHOF, JACOB GEORG	1	1	$920	$920	$920
			DM1,475	DM1,475	DM1,475
			£598	£598	£598
			¥93,064	¥93,064	¥93,064
LAWSON	4	3	$699	$939	$839
			DM1,048	DM1,460	DM1,322
			£414	£598	£514
			¥77,849	¥102,277	¥90,839
LEBLANC	1	0			
LEBRET	2	1	$816	$816	$816
			DM1,222	DM1,222	DM1,222
			£483	£483	£483
			¥90,823	¥90,823	¥90,823
LEBRET, LOUIS LEON JOSEPH	1	1	$382	$382	$382
			DM635	DM635	DM635
			£230	£230	£230
			¥44,468	¥44,468	¥44,468
LEROUX (AINE)	3	1	$509	$509	$509
			DM719	DM719	DM719
			£322	£322	£322
			¥45,414	¥45,414	¥45,414
LEWISCH, M.	1	1	$509	$509	$509
			DM721	DM721	DM721
			£322	£322	£322
			¥52,065	¥52,065	¥52,065
LOT, LOUIS	6	5	$967	$9,694	$3,526
			DM1,686	DM16,971	DM5,907
			£575	£5,980	£2,197
			¥123,257	¥1,171,781	¥413,395
LUVONI, UBALDO	2	1	$612	$612	$612
			DM916	DM916	DM916
			£362	£362	£362
			¥68,070	¥68,070	¥68,070
MAHILLON, C.	1	1	$535	$535	$535
			DM889	DM889	DM889
			£322	£322	£322
			¥62,255	¥62,255	¥62,255
MARTIN, A.	1	0			
MARTIN, JEAN-FRANCOIS	1	1	$690	$690	$690
			DM978	DM978	DM978
			£437	£437	£437
			¥70,660	¥70,660	¥70,660
MARTIN BROS.	2	1	$1,943	$1,943	$1,943
			DM2,910	DM2,910	DM2,910
			£1,150	£1,150	£1,150
			¥216,246	¥216,246	¥216,246
MATEKI	1	1	$2,452	$2,452	$2,452
			DM4,461	DM4,461	DM4,461
			£1,495	£1,495	£1,495
			¥309,674	¥309,674	¥309,674

Maker	Items		Selling Prices		
	Bid	Sold	Low	High	Avg
MCNEILL, JOHN	1	1	$618	$618	$618
			DM873	DM873	DM873
			£391	£391	£391
			¥55,145	¥55,145	¥55,145
METZLER	7	3	$128	$178	$152
			DM228	DM272	DM243
			£78	£115	£97
			¥16,694	¥19,792	¥17,730
METZLER, VALENTIN	4	1	$407	$407	$407
			DM610	DM610	DM610
			£241	£241	£241
			¥45,318	¥45,318	¥45,318
METZLER & CO.	5	4	$112	$488	$351
			DM200	DM841	DM580
			£69	£330	£223
			¥15,106	¥56,505	¥38,279
MILHOUSE, WILLIAM	4	4	$400	$1,565	$808
			DM566	DM2,603	DM1,265
			£253	£943	£500
			¥40,909	¥182,320	¥87,562
MILLEREAU	3	1	$329	$329	$329
			DM508	DM508	DM508
			£207	£207	£207
			¥32,789	¥32,789	¥32,789
MILLHOUSE	3	1	$327	$327	$327
			DM463	DM463	DM463
			£207	£207	£207
			¥33,741	¥33,741	¥33,741
MILLIGAN	1	1	$400	$400	$400
			DM665	DM665	DM665
			£241	£241	£241
			¥46,595	¥46,595	¥46,595
MOLLENHAUER & SONS, J.	2	1	$261	$261	$261
			DM275	DM275	DM275
			£161	£161	£161
			¥19,931	¥19,931	¥19,931
MONZANI	5	3	$773	$1,444	$1,037
			DM1,288	DM2,245	DM1,700
			£460	£920	£644
			¥92,363	¥142,140	¥114,223
MONZANI, TEBALDO	4	2	$708	$858	$783
			DM1,135	DM1,427	DM1,281
			£460	£517	£489
			¥71,588	¥99,957	¥85,772
MONZANI & CO.	18	15	$285	$3,841	$830
			DM411	DM6,417	DM1,275
			£184	£2,300	£519
			¥25,951	¥466,877	¥88,413
MURAMATSU	1	0			
NAUST	1	1	$26,098	$26,098	$26,098
			DM45,692	DM45,692	DM45,692
			£16,100	£16,100	£16,100
			¥3,154,795	¥3,154,795	¥3,154,795
NEDDERMANN, JOHANN ADOPH	2	1	$764	$764	$764
			DM1,270	DM1,270	DM1,270
			£460	£460	£460
			¥88,936	¥88,936	¥88,936

Maker	Items		Selling Prices		
	Bid	Sold	Low	High	Avg
NICHOLSON, CHARLES	1	1	$1,933	$1,933	$1,933
			DM2,892	DM2,892	DM2,892
			£1,150	£1,150	£1,150
			¥215,602	¥215,602	¥215,602
OPPENHEIM, H.	1	1	$802	$802	$802
			DM1,333	DM1,333	DM1,333
			£483	£483	£483
			¥93,383	¥93,383	¥93,383
OTTEN, JOHN	2	2	$282	$394	$338
			DM502	DM703	DM602
			£173	£242	£207
			¥36,851	¥51,592	¥44,221
OTTO, JOHANN GEORG	1	0			
PAN-AMERICAN	1	0			
PARKER, JOHN	1	1	$618	$618	$618
			DM873	DM873	DM873
			£391	£391	£391
			¥55,145	¥55,145	¥55,145
PAXMAN BROS.	1	0			
PEARSON	1	1	$947	$947	$947
			DM1,428	DM1,428	DM1,428
			£581	£581	£581
			¥91,814	¥91,814	¥91,814
PHILLIPS	1	0			
PHIPPS & CO.	1	0			
POTTER	9	4	$217	$378	$316
			DM337	DM588	DM473
			£138	£241	£203
			¥21,321	¥37,235	¥31,994
POTTER, HENRY	1	1	$224	$224	$224
			DM391	DM391	DM391
			£138	£138	£138
			¥27,165	¥27,165	¥27,165
POTTER, RICHARD	5	5	$763	$3,353	$1,724
			DM1,078	DM5,151	DM2,687
			£483	£2,185	£1,095
			¥68,121	¥367,056	¥190,022
POTTER, RICHARD (attributed to)	1	1	$2,399	$2,399	$2,399
			DM3,624	DM3,624	DM3,624
			£1,610	£1,610	£1,610
			¥254,074	¥254,074	¥254,074
POTTER, WILLIAM HENRY	18	13	$102	$1,534	$614
			DM172	DM2,384	DM956
			£63	£977	£379
			¥12,515	¥150,947	¥64,988
PROSER	3	2	$773	$1,107	$940
			DM1,157	DM1,841	DM1,499
			£460	£667	£564
			¥86,241	¥128,958	¥107,599
PROWSE	1	0			
PROWSE, JOSEPH	1	1	$509	$509	$509
			DM719	DM719	DM719
			£322	£322	£322
			¥45,414	¥45,414	¥45,414

| Maker | Items | | Selling Prices | | |
	Bid	Sold	Low	High	Avg
PROWSE, THOMAS	7	7	$327	$1,093	$676
			DM463	DM1,846	DM1,038
			£207	£656	£413
			¥33,471	¥145,379	¥76,459
PROWSE & CO., KEITH	1	1	$601	$601	$601
			DM1,071	DM1,071	DM1,071
			£368	£368	£368
			¥78,616	¥78,616	¥78,616
ROBINSON	1	1	$149	$149	$149
			DM204	DM204	DM204
			£92	£92	£92
			¥12,382	¥12,382	¥12,382
ROESSLER, HEINZ	2	1	$469	$469	$469
			DM837	DM837	DM837
			£288	£288	£288
			¥61,419	¥61,419	¥61,419
ROSE, J.M.	1	1	$3,053	$3,053	$3,053
			DM4,798	DM4,798	DM4,798
			£1,955	£1,955	£1,955
			¥306,210	¥306,210	¥306,210
RUDALL & ROSE	18	15	$442	$4,880	$1,974
			DM653	DM8,701	DM3,163
			£288	£2,990	£1,233
			¥47,074	¥638,754	¥217,970
RUDALL, CARTE & CO.	58	39	$73	$4,963	$724
			DM126	DM8,252	DM1,157
			£50	£2,990	£449
			¥7,582	¥578,087	¥78,202
RUDALL, ROSE, CARTE & CO.	7	7	$469	$2,815	$1,140
			DM797	DM5,020	DM1,788
			£288	£1,725	£714
			¥57,079	¥368,512	¥130,226
SAX, CHARLES JOSEPH	1	1	$1,544	$1,544	$1,544
			DM2,187	DM2,187	DM2,187
			£977	£977	£977
			¥157,975	¥157,975	¥157,975
SCHAEFFER, EVETTE	1	1	$840	$840	$840
			DM1,397	DM1,397	DM1,397
			£506	£506	£506
			¥97,830	¥97,830	¥97,830
SCHMIDT	1	1	$945	$945	$945
			DM1,335	DM1,335	DM1,335
			£598	£598	£598
			¥84,340	¥84,340	¥84,340
SCHOTT, B. (FILS)	1	1	$573	$573	$573
			DM952	DM952	DM952
			£345	£345	£345
			¥66,702	¥66,702	¥66,702
SCHUCHART	1	1	$1,352	$1,352	$1,352
			DM2,431	DM2,431	DM2,431
			£805	£805	£805
			¥156,355	¥156,355	¥156,355
SCHUCHART, CHARLES	2	2	$727	$3,453	$2,090
			DM1,027	DM4,877	DM2,952
			£460	£2,185	£1,323
			¥64,877	¥308,166	¥186,521

Maker	Items		Selling Prices		
	Bid	Sold	Low	High	Avg
SCHUCHART, JOHN JUST	1	0			
SEEGER, ALFRED	2	0			
SEIDEL, AUGUST	1	1	$363	$363	$363
			DM515	DM515	DM515
			£230	£230	£230
			¥37,190	¥37,190	¥37,190
SELMER	1	0			
SICCAMA, ABEL	5	2	$305	$1,145	$725
			DM508	DM1,904	DM1,206
			£184	£690	£437
			¥35,575	¥133,405	¥84,490
SIGGANIA	1	1	$287	$287	$287
			DM460	DM460	DM460
			£187	£187	£187
			¥29,102	¥29,102	¥29,102
SIMPSON	1	1	$4,235	$4,235	$4,235
			DM6,507	DM6,507	DM6,507
			£2,760	£2,760	£2,760
			¥463,650	¥463,650	¥463,650
SIMPSON, JOHN	2	2	$350	$1,805	$1,078
			DM524	DM2,806	DM1,665
			£207	£1,150	£679
			¥38,924	¥177,675	¥108,300
SIMPSON, JOHN OR ANN	1	0			
STANESBY, THOMAS	2	2	$9,706	$14,536	$12,121
			DM14,911	DM20,594	DM17,753
			£6,325	£9,200	£7,763
			¥1,062,530	¥1,487,585	¥1,275,058
STARK	1	1	$473	$473	$473
			DM667	DM667	DM667
			£299	£299	£299
			¥42,170	¥42,170	¥42,170
SZEPESSY, BELA	1	1	$8,818	$8,818	$8,818
			DM16,336	DM16,336	DM16,336
			£5,290	£5,290	£5,290
			¥1,177,713	¥1,177,713	¥1,177,713
THIBOUVILLE, MARTIN (L'AINE)	1	1	$764	$764	$764
			DM1,270	DM1,270	DM1,270
			£460	£460	£460
			¥88,936	¥88,936	¥88,936
THIBOUVILLE-LAMY, J.	2	2	$54	$436	$245
			DM77	DM618	DM348
			£35	£276	£155
			¥5,624	¥44,628	¥25,126
THORSEN, NIELS CHRISTENSEN	1	1	$960	$960	$960
			DM1,604	DM1,604	DM1,604
			£575	£575	£575
			¥116,719	¥116,719	¥116,719
THURGOOD, G.J.	1	1	$1,636	$1,636	$1,636
			DM2,310	DM2,310	DM2,310
			£1,035	£1,035	£1,035
			¥145,973	¥145,973	¥145,973
TULOU, JEAN-LOUIS	3	1	$756	$756	$756
			DM1,158	DM1,158	DM1,158
			£483	£483	£483
			¥84,293	¥84,293	¥84,293

Maker	Items		Selling Prices		
	Bid	Sold	Low	High	Avg
UEBEL	1	1	$189	$189	$189
			DM279	DM279	DM279
			£123	£123	£123
			¥20,144	¥20,144	¥20,144
VAN GULIK, D.	1	1	$1,090	$1,090	$1,090
			DM1,545	DM1,545	DM1,545
			£690	£690	£690
			¥111,569	¥111,569	¥111,569
WALLIS, JOSEPH & SON	2	1	$472	$472	$472
			DM669	DM669	DM669
			£299	£299	£299
			¥48,347	¥48,347	¥48,347
WALLIS, JOSEPH & SONS	1	1	$763	$763	$763
			DM1,078	DM1,078	DM1,078
			£483	£483	£483
			¥68,121	¥68,121	¥68,121
WARREN, I.	1	1	$836	$836	$836
			DM1,181	DM1,181	DM1,181
			£529	£529	£529
			¥74,609	¥74,609	¥74,609
WAYLETT, HENRY	1	1	$4,153	$4,153	$4,153
			DM6,454	DM6,454	DM6,454
			£2,645	£2,645	£2,645
			¥408,653	¥408,653	¥408,653
WEISSE, JOHANN W.	1	1	$1,625	$1,625	$1,625
			DM2,525	DM2,525	DM2,525
			£1,035	£1,035	£1,035
			¥159,908	¥159,908	¥159,908
WELSH, THOMAS	1	1	$526	$526	$526
			DM937	DM937	DM937
			£322	£322	£322
			¥68,789	¥68,789	¥68,789
WHEATSTONE, C.	1	1	$237	$237	$237
			DM444	DM444	DM444
			£150	£150	£150
			¥28,078	¥28,078	¥28,078
WHITAKER & CO.	1	0			
WILLIAMS, E.G.	1	1	$329	$329	$329
			DM493	DM493	DM493
			£195	£195	£195
			¥36,668	¥36,668	¥36,668
WILLIS, JOHN	2	0			
WOOD, JAMES & SON	2	1	$1,049	$1,049	$1,049
			DM1,744	DM1,744	DM1,744
			£632	£632	£632
			¥122,191	¥122,191	¥122,191
WOOD & IVY	3	1	$381	$381	$381
			DM538	DM538	DM538
			£241	£241	£241
			¥33,990	¥33,990	¥33,990
WYLDE, HENRY	4	3	$535	$2,332	$1,180
			DM816	DM3,492	DM1,795
			£345	£1,380	£721
			¥59,375	¥259,495	¥128,959

Maker	Items		Selling Prices		
	Bid	Sold	Low	High	Avg
XAVER, FRANZ	1	1	$1,541	$1,541	$1,541
			DM2,316	DM2,316	DM2,316
			£920	£920	£920
			¥171,636	¥171,636	¥171,636
XAVER, FRANZ (attributed to)	1	0			
YAMAHA	6	5	$247	$1,075	$553
			DM423	DM1,733	DM903
			£150	£633	£333
			¥30,284	¥132,964	¥67,020
ZIEGLER, I.	1	1	$812	$812	$812
			DM1,261	DM1,261	DM1,261
			£517	£517	£517
			¥79,877	¥79,877	¥79,877

FLUTE D'AMORE

Maker	Items		Selling Prices		
MONZANI, TEBALDO	1	1	$1,635	$1,635	$1,635
			DM2,317	DM2,317	DM2,317
			£1,035	£1,035	£1,035
			¥167,353	¥167,353	¥167,353
MONZANI & CO.	1	1	$1,817	$1,817	$1,817
			DM2,574	DM2,574	DM2,574
			£1,150	£1,150	£1,150
			¥185,948	¥185,948	¥185,948

FLUTE/PICCOLO

Maker	Items		Selling Prices		
NICHOLSON	2	1	$224	$224	$224
			DM236	DM236	DM236
			£138	£138	£138
			¥17,084	¥17,084	¥17,084

FRENCH HORN

Maker	Items		Selling Prices		
BOOSEY & HAWKES	1	0			
DALLAS	1	0			
GREY & SONS, JOHN	1	0			
KNOPF	2	0			
MAHILLON, C.	1	1	$496	$496	$496
			DM825	DM825	DM825
			£299	£299	£299
			¥57,809	¥57,809	¥57,809
MAINZ, ALEXANDER	1	0			
STOWASSER, ADOLF	1	0			

GALOUBET

Maker	Items		Selling Prices		
LONG	1	1	$1,069	$1,069	$1,069
			DM1,777	DM1,777	DM1,777
			£644	£644	£644
			¥124,511	¥124,511	¥124,511

GIRAFFENFLUGEL

Maker	Items		Selling Prices		
SCHEHL, KARL	3	0			

Maker	Items Bid	Sold	Low	Selling Prices High	Avg
GLOCKENSPIEL					
FERRIER, R.	1	0			
PREMIER	1	1	$282	$282	$282
			DM477	DM477	DM477
			£173	£173	£173
			¥32,688	¥32,688	¥32,688
GUITAR					
ABBOTT	1	1	$750	$750	$750
			DM1,302	DM1,302	DM1,302
			£460	£460	£460
			¥86,889	¥86,889	¥86,889
ALBERTINI, ALFREDO	5	0			
ARAM, KEVIN	1	1	$3,749	$3,749	$3,749
			DM6,509	DM6,509	DM6,509
			£2,300	£2,300	£2,300
			¥434,447	¥434,447	¥434,447
ARIA	1	1	$124	$124	$124
			DM182	DM182	DM182
			£81	£81	£81
			¥13,134	¥13,134	¥13,134
AUBRY, JACQUES	1	0			
BARRY	1	1	$1,336	$1,336	$1,336
			DM2,222	DM2,222	DM2,222
			£805	£805	£805
			¥155,639	¥155,639	¥155,639
BELLEGRANDE	1	1	$1,199	$1,199	$1,199
			DM1,812	DM1,812	DM1,812
			£805	£805	£805
			¥127,037	¥127,037	¥127,037
BERNABE, PAULINO	2	0			
BERTET, JOSEPH R. (attributed to)	1	0			
BERWIND, J.	1	1	$1,380	$1,380	$1,380
			DM2,332	DM2,332	DM2,332
			£828	£828	£828
			¥168,360	¥168,360	¥168,360
BODY, HANS	3	1	$118	$118	$118
			DM167	DM167	DM167
			£75	£75	£75
			¥12,184	¥12,184	¥12,184
BOOSEY & CO.	1	1	$1,456	$1,456	$1,456
			DM2,181	DM2,181	DM2,181
			£862	£862	£862
			¥162,090	¥162,090	¥162,090
BOUCHET, ROBERT	3	3	$26,476	$30,912	$28,847
			DM42,465	DM55,568	DM49,525
			£17,193	£18,400	£17,614
			¥3,012,470	¥3,706,508	¥3,430,936
BOULLANGIER, CHARLES	1	0			
BOULLANGIER, CHARLES (attributed to)	5	1	$280	$280	$280
			DM295	DM295	DM295
			£173	£173	£173
			¥21,355	¥21,355	¥21,355

Maker	Items		Selling Prices		
	Bid	Sold	Low	High	Avg
BOULLANGIER, G.	1	1	$168	$168	$168
			DM248	DM248	DM248
			£109	£109	£109
			¥17,888	¥17,888	¥17,888
BURNS	2	1	$1,125	$1,125	$1,125
			DM1,953	DM1,953	DM1,953
			£690	£690	£690
			¥130,334	¥130,334	¥130,334
BUTLER	1	1	$89	$89	$89
			DM137	DM137	DM137
			£58	£58	£58
			¥8,843	¥8,843	¥8,843
CAMACHO, RODOLFO	1	0			
CAMACHO, VICENTE	3	1	$1,635	$1,635	$1,635
			DM2,317	DM2,317	DM2,317
			£1,035	£1,035	£1,035
			¥167,353	¥167,353	¥167,353
CHIQUITA	1	1	$1,125	$1,125	$1,125
			DM1,953	DM1,953	DM1,953
			£690	£690	£690
			¥130,334	¥130,334	¥130,334
COLUMBIAN	2	2	$131	$225	$178
			DM228	DM391	DM309
			£81	£138	£109
			¥15,206	¥26,067	¥20,636
CONDE, HERMANOS	4	2	$1,083	$1,264	$1,174
			DM1,684	DM1,964	DM1,824
			£690	£805	£748
			¥106,605	¥124,373	¥115,489
CONTRERAS, MANUEL	6	1	$1,845	$1,845	$1,845
			DM3,200	DM3,200	DM3,200
			£1,092	£1,092	£1,092
			¥234,638	¥234,638	¥234,638
D'ANGELICO	1	0			
D'ANGELICO, JOHN	3	1	$14,375	$14,375	$14,375
			DM22,281	DM22,281	DM22,281
			£9,200	£9,200	£9,200
			¥1,413,206	¥1,413,206	¥1,413,206
DA CUNHA MELLO, JOAQUIM	1	1	$316	$316	$316
			DM490	DM490	DM490
			£202	£202	£202
			¥31,091	¥31,091	¥31,091
DANELECTRO	1	0			
DE LA CHICA, MANUEL	1	1	$1,986	$1,986	$1,986
			DM3,087	DM3,087	DM3,087
			£1,265	£1,265	£1,265
			¥195,443	¥195,443	¥195,443
DEL PILAR, GUILLERMO	1	0			
DE SOTO Y SOLARES, MANUEL	2	2	$297	$909	$603
			DM409	DM1,283	DM846
			£184	£575	£380
			¥24,765	¥81,096	¥52,930
DITSON, OLIVER	1	1	$690	$690	$690
			DM996	DM996	DM996
			£440	£440	£440
			¥59,858	¥59,858	¥59,858

Maker	Items		Selling Prices		
	Bid	Sold	Low	High	Avg
DOBRO	5	4	$403	$1,062	$700
			DM582	DM1,909	DM1,146
			£263	£632	£434
			¥40,753	¥122,753	¥79,905
DREAPER	2	1	$487	$487	$487
			DM846	DM846	DM846
			£299	£299	£299
			¥56,478	¥56,478	¥56,478
DUBOIS (FILS)	2	1	$1,817	$1,817	$1,817
			DM2,574	DM2,574	DM2,574
			£1,150	£1,150	£1,150
			¥185,948	¥185,948	¥185,948
EPIPHONE	4	3	$546	$1,052	$715
			DM790	DM1,493	DM1,069
			£328	£675	£453
			¥55,308	¥107,024	¥76,325
ESPINOSA, JULIAN	1	1	$580	$580	$580
			DM1,042	DM1,042	DM1,042
			£345	£345	£345
			¥67,009	¥67,009	¥67,009
ESTRUCH, JUAN	1	0			
FABRICATORE, GENNARO	4	3	$937	$2,570	$1,506
			DM1,513	DM3,883	DM2,341
			£575	£1,725	£966
			¥108,612	¥272,222	¥164,427
FABRICATORE, GIOVANNI BATTISTA	2	1	$1,783	$1,783	$1,783
			DM2,875	DM2,875	DM2,875
			£1,035	£1,035	£1,035
			¥209,875	¥209,875	¥209,875
FAVILLA, HERK (workshop of)	1	1	$288	$288	$288
			DM433	DM433	DM433
			£175	£175	£175
			¥32,137	¥32,137	¥32,137
FENDER	13	10	$289	$4,910	$1,070
			DM433	DM6,969	DM1,659
			£172	£3,150	£671
			¥32,247	¥499,445	¥114,916
FERNANDEZ, ARCANGEL	3	2	$5,377	$15,347	$10,362
			DM8,984	DM23,851	DM16,417
			£3,220	£9,775	£6,498
			¥653,628	¥1,510,238	¥1,081,933
FISCHER, CARL	2	1	$535	$535	$535
			DM889	DM889	DM889
			£322	£322	£322
			¥62,255	¥62,255	¥62,255
FLEESON, MARTIN	1	0			
FLETA & SONS, IGNACIO	2	2	$19,090	$20,645	$19,867
			DM31,740	DM36,812	DM34,276
			£11,500	£12,650	£12,075
			¥2,223,410	¥2,702,420	¥2,462,915
FLETA, IGNACIO	3	1	$26,432	$26,432	$26,432
			DM39,018	DM39,018	DM39,018
			£17,250	£17,250	£17,250
			¥2,810,042	¥2,810,042	¥2,810,042
FRIEDERICH, DANIEL	1	1	$12,719	$12,719	$12,719
			DM18,020	DM18,020	DM18,020
			£8,050	£8,050	£8,050
			¥1,301,637	¥1,301,637	¥1,301,637

| Maker | Items | | Selling Prices | | |
---	Bid	Sold	Low	High	Avg
FRITH, STEPHEN	1	0			
FUSSINGER, J.T.	1	1	$1,166	$1,166	$1,166
			DM1,746	DM1,746	DM1,746
			£690	£690	£690
			¥129,748	¥129,748	¥129,748
GAND, CHARLES	1	0			
GARCIA, ENRIQUE	2	0			
GARCIA, JOAQUIN	1	0			
GERARD, J.H.	2	0			
GIBSON, WILLIAM	1	1	$1,049	$1,049	$1,049
			DM1,744	DM1,744	DM1,744
			£632	£632	£632
			¥122,191	¥122,191	¥122,191
GIBSON CO.	32	24	$184	$9,644	$1,921
			DM328	DM13,689	DM2,949
			£112	£6,187	£1,200
			¥25,561	¥980,974	¥203,842
GOUDOT	1	0			
GRETSCH	5	4	$2,812	$6,561	$4,874
			DM4,882	DM11,391	DM8,462
			£1,725	£4,025	£2,990
			¥325,835	¥760,282	¥564,781
GRUMMIT	1	0			
GUADAGNINI, FRANCESCO (ascribed to)	1	1	$1,610	$1,610	$1,610
			DM2,755	DM2,755	DM2,755
			£952	£952	£952
			¥199,930	¥199,930	¥199,930
GUILD	1	0			
HAGSTROM	1	0			
HAMER	1	0			
HANDEL, J.T.C.	2	0			
HAUSER, HERMANN	3	1	$13,122	$13,122	$13,122
			DM22,782	DM22,782	DM22,782
			£8,050	£8,050	£8,050
			¥1,520,565	¥1,520,565	¥1,520,565
HAUSER, HERMANN (II)	1	1	$21,146	$21,146	$21,146
			DM31,214	DM31,214	DM31,214
			£13,800	£13,800	£13,800
			¥2,248,034	¥2,248,034	¥2,248,034
HAYNES CO., JOHN C.	1	0			
HENRY, NICOLAS	1	0			
HENSE, DIETER	1	1	$675	$675	$675
			DM1,214	DM1,214	DM1,214
			£402	£402	£402
			¥78,080	¥78,080	¥78,080
HERNANDEZ, MANUEL & VICTORIANO AGUADO	1	1	$18,354	$18,354	$18,354
			DM32,994	DM32,994	DM32,994
			£10,925	£10,925	£10,925
			¥2,121,963	¥2,121,963	¥2,121,963
HERNANDEZ, SANTOS	4	1	$1,762	$1,762	$1,762
			DM2,601	DM2,601	DM2,601
			£1,150	£1,150	£1,150
			¥187,336	¥187,336	¥187,336
HERNANDEZ, SOBRINOS SANTOS	1	0			

Maker	Items		Selling Prices		
	Bid	Sold	Low	High	Avg
HOFNER	6	2	$44	$134	$89
			DM68	DM201	DM134
			£29	£80	£54
			¥4,799	¥14,998	¥9,899
HOFNER, KARL	2	2	$244	$412	$328
			DM423	DM716	DM570
			£150	£253	£201
			¥28,239	¥47,789	¥38,014
HOPF, DIETER	1	0			
HOWELL, T.	1	1	$2,037	$2,037	$2,037
			DM3,267	DM3,267	DM3,267
			£1,323	£1,323	£1,323
			¥231,728	¥231,728	¥231,728
HUSSON, BUTHOD & THIBOUVILLE	3	1	$619	$619	$619
			DM911	DM911	DM911
			£403	£403	£403
			¥65,672	¥65,672	¥65,672
IBANEZ	1	1	$428	$428	$428
			DM652	DM652	DM652
			£276	£276	£276
			¥47,500	¥47,500	¥47,500
JONES, A.H.	1	1	$382	$382	$382
			DM588	DM588	DM588
			£253	£253	£253
			¥40,790	¥40,790	¥40,790
JONES, EDWARD B.	1	0			
KIMBARA	1	1	$112	$112	$112
			DM195	DM195	DM195
			£69	£69	£69
			¥13,033	¥13,033	¥13,033
KONO, MASARU	1	1	$967	$967	$967
			DM1,329	DM1,329	DM1,329
			£598	£598	£598
			¥80,485	¥80,485	¥80,485
LACOTE	3	1	$1,273	$1,273	$1,273
			DM1,873	DM1,873	DM1,873
			£828	£828	£828
			¥135,096	¥135,096	¥135,096
LACOTE, RENE	2	2	$2,786	$3,114	$2,950
			DM4,712	DM5,267	DM4,990
			£1,870	£2,090	£1,980
			¥295,460	¥330,220	¥312,840
LACOTE, RENE (attributed to)	1	0			
LARSON (workshop of)	1	0			
LARSON BROS.	1	0			
LEVIN GOLIATH	1	1	$412	$412	$412
			DM716	DM716	DM716
			£253	£253	£253
			¥47,789	¥47,789	¥47,789
LIESSEM, R.	2	1	$992	$992	$992
			DM1,542	DM1,542	DM1,542
			£632	£632	£632
			¥97,644	¥97,644	¥97,644
LION, ARTHUR	1	1	$374	$374	$374
			DM665	DM665	DM665
			£228	£228	£228
			¥51,921	¥51,921	¥51,921

Maker	Items		Selling Prices		
	Bid	Sold	Low	High	Avg
LONGMAN & BRODERIP	3	2	$1,145	$5,727	$3,436
			DM1,904	DM9,522	DM5,713
			£690	£3,450	£2,070
			¥133,405	¥667,023	¥400,214
LUTZEMBERGER	1	0			
MACCAFERRI	1	1	$233	$233	$233
			DM329	DM329	DM329
			£146	£146	£146
			¥20,638	¥20,638	¥20,638
MAIRE, FRANCAIS	1	1	$1,360	$1,360	$1,360
			DM2,037	DM2,037	DM2,037
			£805	£805	£805
			¥151,372	¥151,372	¥151,372
MANN	1	0			
MANZANERO, FELIX	1	0			
MARCHAL	2	1	$590	$590	$590
			DM822	DM822	DM822
			£368	£368	£368
			¥49,882	¥49,882	¥49,882
MARCHAL, PIERRE PAUL	1	0			
MARCHAND	1	1	$713	$713	$713
			DM1,272	DM1,272	DM1,272
			£437	£437	£437
			¥93,356	¥93,356	¥93,356
MARTIN	5	3	$537	$5,637	$2,368
			DM821	DM8,309	DM3,518
			£345	£3,680	£1,541
			¥53,055	¥601,202	¥248,740
MARTIN, CHRISTIAN FREDERICK	4	3	$1,035	$2,622	$1,909
			DM1,604	DM3,928	DM2,882
			£662	£1,552	£1,157
			¥101,751	¥291,838	¥208,325
MARTIN, E.	1	0			
MARTIN & CO., C.F.	29	26	$345	$16,100	$3,486
			DM590	DM27,209	DM5,756
			£204	£9,660	£2,107
			¥42,842	¥1,964,200	¥411,176
MARZAL, JESUS	1	0			
MAST, BLAISE	1	0			
MAST, JOSEPH LAURENT	1	1	$1,360	$1,360	$1,360
			DM2,037	DM2,037	DM2,037
			£805	£805	£805
			¥151,372	¥151,372	¥151,372
MATHIEU, MARESCHAL	1	0			
MOITESSIER, LOUIS	1	0			
MONTRON (attributed to)	1	0			
MONZINO, ANTONIO	1	1	$690	$690	$690
			DM1,166	DM1,166	DM1,166
			£414	£414	£414
			¥84,180	¥84,180	¥84,180
MOSELEY, SEMI	1	1	$288	$288	$288
			DM512	DM512	DM512
			£175	£175	£175
			¥39,940	¥39,940	¥39,940

Maker	Items		Selling Prices		
	Bid	Sold	Low	High	Avg
MUSSER, D.	1	1	$6,748	$6,748	$6,748
			DM11,716	DM11,716	DM11,716
			£4,140	£4,140	£4,140
			¥782,005	¥782,005	¥782,005
NADERMAN, JEAN-HENRI	1	0			
NATIONAL	14	11	$259	$11,500	$2,920
			DM443	DM16,606	DM4,527
			£153	£7,327	£1,825
			¥32,132	¥997,625	¥300,814
PADILLA, JUAN ROMAIN	1	1	$103	$103	$103
			DM108	DM108	DM108
			£63	£63	£63
			¥7,830	¥7,830	¥7,830
PANORMO	2	2	$2,050	$2,347	$2,199
			DM2,160	DM3,648	DM2,904
			£1,265	£1,495	£1,380
			¥156,601	¥230,978	¥193,789
PANORMO, LOUIS	18	17	$599	$4,582	$2,173
			DM951	DM7,618	DM3,419
			£391	£2,760	£1,345
			¥60,599	¥533,618	¥240,216
PERFUMO, JUAN	1	1	$1,595	$1,595	$1,595
			DM2,845	DM2,845	DM2,845
			£978	£978	£978
			¥208,823	¥208,823	¥208,823
PETERSEN, HAROLD	9	5	$264	$688	$447
			DM390	DM1,164	DM709
			£172	£462	£288
			¥28,169	¥72,996	¥47,669
PETITJEAN (L'AINE)	2	0			
PIRETTI, ENRICO	1	0			
PONS FAMILY (MEMBER OF)	1	1	$3,109	$3,109	$3,109
			DM4,656	DM4,656	DM4,656
			£1,840	£1,840	£1,840
			¥345,994	¥345,994	¥345,994
PRESTON, JOHN	2	1	$638	$638	$638
			DM1,138	DM1,138	DM1,138
			£391	£391	£391
			¥83,529	¥83,529	¥83,529
RAMIREZ	1	1	$1,217	$1,217	$1,217
			DM1,870	DM1,870	DM1,870
			£805	£805	£805
			¥129,786	¥129,786	¥129,786
RAMIREZ, JOSE	9	6	$881	$2,899	$1,755
			DM1,298	DM5,210	DM2,816
			£575	£1,725	£1,088
			¥93,938	¥335,047	¥192,701
RAMIREZ, JOSE (workshop of)	1	1	$1,840	$1,840	$1,840
			DM2,769	DM2,769	DM2,769
			£1,117	£1,117	£1,117
			¥205,675	¥205,675	¥205,675
RAMIREZ, JOSE (I)	1	0			
RAMIREZ, JOSE (III)	6	2	$1,714	$2,999	$2,357
			DM2,664	DM5,207	DM3,936
			£1,092	£1,840	£1,466
			¥168,714	¥347,558	¥258,136

Maker	Items		Selling Prices		
	Bid	Sold	Low	High	Avg
RAMIREZ, MANUEL	3	1	$4,229	$4,229	$4,229
			DM6,243	DM6,243	DM6,243
			£2,760	£2,760	£2,760
			¥449,607	¥449,607	¥449,607
RAUCHE, MICHAEL	1	0			
REGAL CO.	1	1	$259	$259	$259
			DM461	DM461	DM461
			£158	£158	£158
			¥35,946	¥35,946	¥35,946
RHOUDLOFF, H.	1	1	$1,527	$1,527	$1,527
			DM2,539	DM2,539	DM2,539
			£920	£920	£920
			¥177,873	¥177,873	¥177,873
RICKENBACKER	2	2	$637	$4,686	$2,662
			DM1,107	DM8,136	DM4,621
			£391	£2,875	£1,633
			¥73,856	¥543,059	¥308,457
ROCA, ALEJANDRO	2	0			
ROCA, ALEJANDRO & BROS.	1	0			
ROMANILLOS, JOSE	2	1	$8,435	$8,435	$8,435
			DM14,645	DM14,645	DM14,645
			£5,175	£5,175	£5,175
			¥977,506	¥977,506	¥977,506
ROUDHLOFF, D. & A.	2	1	$758	$758	$758
			DM1,179	DM1,179	DM1,179
			£483	£483	£483
			¥74,624	¥74,624	¥74,624
ROUDHLOFF, D. & A. (attributed to)	1	1	$1,519	$1,519	$1,519
			DM2,634	DM2,634	DM2,634
			£897	£897	£897
			¥192,505	¥192,505	¥192,505
RUBIO, DAVID	1	0			
RUBIO, JOSE	1	0			
SALOMON (attributed to)	1	0			
SCHERZER	1	0			
SCHMIDT & MAUL	1	1	$748	$748	$748
			DM1,279	DM1,279	DM1,279
			£442	£442	£442
			¥92,825	¥92,825	¥92,825
SELMER	1	1	$7,890	$7,890	$7,890
			DM11,200	DM11,200	DM11,200
			£5,062	£5,062	£5,062
			¥802,600	¥802,600	¥802,600
SELMER, HENRI	1	1	$21,252	$21,252	$21,252
			DM38,203	DM38,203	DM38,203
			£12,650	£12,650	£12,650
			¥2,457,010	¥2,457,010	¥2,457,010
SEMPLE, TREVOR	1	0			
SENSIER	2	1	$73	$73	$73
			DM103	DM103	DM103
			£46	£46	£46
			¥7,498	¥7,498	¥7,498
SENTCHORDI, BROS.	1	1	$542	$542	$542
			DM842	DM842	DM842
			£345	£345	£345
			¥53,303	¥53,303	¥53,303

| Maker | Items | | Selling Prices | | |
	Bid	Sold	Low	High	Avg
SILVERTONE	3	2	$104	$345	$224
			DM184	DM614	DM399
			£63	£210	£137
			¥14,378	¥47,927	¥31,153
SIMPLICIO, FRANCISCO	2	2	$4,639	$5,163	$4,901
			DM6,941	DM7,189	DM7,065
			£2,760	£3,220	£2,990
			¥436,465	¥517,445	¥476,955
SIMPLICIO, FRANCISCO & MIGUEL	2	1	$3,816	$3,816	$3,816
			DM5,406	DM5,406	DM5,406
			£2,415	£2,415	£2,415
			¥390,491	¥390,491	¥390,491
SIMPLICIO, MIGUEL	1	1	$5,524	$5,524	$5,524
			DM8,329	DM8,329	DM8,329
			£3,388	£3,388	£3,388
			¥535,582	¥535,582	¥535,582
SMALLMAN, GREG	1	0			
STAUFFER (attributed to)	1	0			
STAUFFER, ANTON	1	0			
STAUFFER, JOHANN GEORG	2	1	$1,456	$1,456	$1,456
			DM2,082	DM2,082	DM2,082
			£920	£920	£920
			¥146,267	¥146,267	¥146,267
STROMBERG, CHARLES AND ELMER	1	1	$10,350	$10,350	$10,350
			DM17,709	DM17,709	DM17,709
			£6,122	£6,122	£6,122
			¥1,285,263	¥1,285,263	¥1,285,263
STROMBERG, ELMER	1	1	$18,400	$18,400	$18,400
			DM31,096	DM31,096	DM31,096
			£11,040	£11,040	£11,040
			¥2,244,800	¥2,244,800	¥2,244,800
TAYMAR	2	1	$200	$200	$200
			DM283	DM283	DM283
			£127	£127	£127
			¥20,620	¥20,620	¥20,620
THIBOUVILLE-LAMY, J.	1	1	$562	$562	$562
			DM976	DM976	DM976
			£345	£345	£345
			¥65,167	¥65,167	¥65,167
THOMSON	1	1	$934	$934	$934
			DM1,629	DM1,629	DM1,629
			£575	£575	£575
			¥113,189	¥113,189	¥113,189
VEGA COMPANY	3	3	$345	$2,990	$1,275
			DM583	DM5,053	DM2,154
			£207	£1,794	£765
			¥42,090	¥364,780	¥155,499
VELASQUEZ, JOSE LUIS	1	1	$115	$115	$115
			DM205	DM205	DM205
			£70	£70	£70
			¥15,976	¥15,976	¥15,976
VENTAPANE, PASQUALE	1	0			
VILLA, LUIGI	1	0			
VINACCIA, GAETANO	2	1	$1,229	$1,229	$1,229
			DM2,079	DM2,079	DM2,079
			£825	£825	£825
			¥130,350	¥130,350	¥130,350

Maker	Items		Selling Prices		
	Bid	Sold	Low	High	Avg
VINACCIA, GENNARO & ACHILLE	1	0			
VOX	1	1	$562	$562	$562
			DM976	DM976	DM976
			£345	£345	£345
			¥65,167	¥65,167	¥65,167
WASHBURN	1	0			
WOODFIELD, PHILIP	1	0			
YAMAHA	1	1	$811	$811	$811
			DM1,459	DM1,459	DM1,459
			£483	£483	£483
			¥93,813	¥93,813	¥93,813
ZEMAITIS, A.G. (TONY)	1	0			

GUITAR-HARP

Maker	Items		Selling Prices		
LEVIEN, MORDAUNT	1	1	$485	$485	$485
			DM726	DM726	DM726
			£287	£287	£287
			¥53,967	¥53,967	¥53,967

GUITAR-LUTE

Maker	Items		Selling Prices		
HAUSER, HERMANN	1	1	$1,093	$1,093	$1,093
			DM1,846	DM1,846	DM1,846
			£656	£656	£656
			¥133,285	¥133,285	¥133,285

GUITARRA

Maker	Items		Selling Prices		
ANDRADE, JOAO MIGUEL	1	1	$182	$182	$182
			DM337	DM337	DM337
			£109	£109	£109
			¥24,322	¥24,322	¥24,322

HARMONICA

Maker	Items		Selling Prices		
HOHNER	1	0			

HARP

Maker	Items		Selling Prices		
AOYAMA	1	1	$592	$592	$592
			DM892	DM892	DM892
			£363	£363	£363
			¥57,384	¥57,384	¥57,384
BANKS, BENJAMIN	1	1	$1,431	$1,431	$1,431
			DM2,379	DM2,379	DM2,379
			£862	£862	£862
			¥166,659	¥166,659	¥166,659
DELVEAU	1	1	$3,864	$3,864	$3,864
			DM6,440	DM6,440	DM6,440
			£2,300	£2,300	£2,300
			¥461,817	¥461,817	¥461,817
ERARD, J.	1	1	$1,076	$1,076	$1,076
			DM1,668	DM1,668	DM1,668
			£644	£644	£644
			¥122,560	¥122,560	¥122,560
ERARD, SEBASTIAN	24	21	$1,211	$6,185	$3,382
			DM1,935	DM10,699	DM5,374
			£787	£3,680	£2,100
			¥122,398	¥693,393	¥372,276

| Maker | Items | | Selling Prices | | |
	Bid	Sold	Low	High	Avg
ERARD, SEBASTIAN & PIERRE	15	13	$163	$12,751	$4,429
			DM280	DM21,252	DM7,493
			£110	£7,590	£2,680
			¥16,849	¥1,523,996	¥524,946
ERARD & CIE.	2	1	$4,200	$4,200	$4,200
			DM6,983	DM6,983	DM6,983
			£2,530	£2,530	£2,530
			¥489,150	¥489,150	¥489,150
ERAT, I. & I.	3	2	$2,167	$3,003	$2,585
			DM3,367	DM5,354	DM4,361
			£1,380	£1,840	£1,610
			¥213,210	¥393,079	¥303,145
ERAT, J.	1	0			
GROSJEAN, SCHWIESO & CO.	2	2	$448	$2,012	$1,230
			DM747	DM2,856	DM1,801
			£299	£1,265	£782
			¥45,959	¥186,777	¥116,368
HOLDERNESSE, CHARLES	2	2	$1,336	$6,217	$3,777
			DM2,222	DM9,313	DM5,767
			£805	£3,680	£2,243
			¥155,639	¥691,987	¥423,813
LIGHT, EDWARD	4	3	$661	$1,311	$995
			DM1,015	DM2,218	DM1,680
			£437	£880	£646
			¥70,455	¥139,040	¥114,053
MOFFAT, J.W.	1	0			
MORLEY, JOHN	2	0			
MUIR CO.	1	0			
MUIR WOOD & CO.	1	1	$2,820	$2,820	$2,820
			DM4,658	DM4,658	DM4,658
			£1,725	£1,725	£1,725
			¥349,190	¥349,190	¥349,190
NADERMAN FAMILY (MEMBER OF)	1	0			
NADERMANN, HENRY	1	1	$9,603	$9,603	$9,603
			DM16,043	DM16,043	DM16,043
			£5,750	£5,750	£5,750
			¥1,167,193	¥1,167,193	¥1,167,193
PLEYEL, WOLFE, LYON & CO.	1	1	$3,271	$3,271	$3,271
			DM4,634	DM4,634	DM4,634
			£2,070	£2,070	£2,070
			¥334,707	¥334,707	¥334,707
RENAULT & CHATELAIN	1	1	$5,036	$5,036	$5,036
			DM7,045	DM7,045	DM7,045
			£3,150	£3,150	£3,150
			¥425,921	¥425,921	¥425,921
SCHWIESO, J.	2	2	$1,427	$3,018	$2,222
			DM2,025	DM4,342	DM3,184
			£897	£1,955	£1,426
			¥132,442	¥306,427	¥219,434
SEROUET, E.	1	1	$1,032	$1,032	$1,032
			DM1,841	DM1,841	DM1,841
			£633	£633	£633
			¥135,121	¥135,121	¥135,121
STUMPFF, J.C.	1	0			
VENTURA, A.B. (attributed to)	1	1	$2,291	$2,291	$2,291
			DM3,809	DM3,809	DM3,809
			£1,380	£1,380	£1,380
			¥266,809	¥266,809	¥266,809

Maker	Items		Selling Prices		
	Bid	Sold	Low	High	Avg

HARP-LUTE

BARRY	1	0			
CLEMENTI & CO.	1	0			
LIGHT, EDWARD	1	1	$840	$840	$840
			DM1,397	DM1,397	DM1,397
			£506	£506	£506
			¥97,830	¥97,830	¥97,830

HARPSICHORD

BACKERS, AMERICUS	2	1	$67,565	$67,565	$67,565
			DM120,474	DM120,474	DM120,474
			£41,400	£41,400	£41,400
			¥8,844,282	¥8,844,282	¥8,844,282
DOWD, WILLIAM	1	1	$18,400	$18,400	$18,400
			DM32,550	DM32,550	DM32,550
			£11,110	£11,110	£11,110
			¥2,390,160	¥2,390,160	¥2,390,160
FABRI, FILIPPO	1	1	$14,444	$14,444	$14,444
			DM22,448	DM22,448	DM22,448
			£9,200	£9,200	£9,200
			¥1,421,400	¥1,421,400	¥1,421,400
FRY, E.V.	1	1	$3,672	$3,672	$3,672
			DM5,495	DM5,495	DM5,495
			£2,185	£2,185	£2,185
			¥409,644	¥409,644	¥409,644
HERZ, ERIC	1	1	$2,300	$2,300	$2,300
			DM3,517	DM3,517	DM3,517
			£1,513	£1,513	£1,513
			¥242,420	¥242,420	¥242,420
KIRCKMAN, JACOB	1	1	$48,748	$48,748	$48,748
			DM75,762	DM75,762	DM75,762
			£31,050	£31,050	£31,050
			¥4,797,225	¥4,797,225	¥4,797,225
KIRCKMAN, JACOB & ABRAHAM	1	1	$173,512	$173,512	$173,512
			DM259,903	DM259,903	DM259,903
			£102,700	£102,700	£102,700
			¥19,311,708	¥19,311,708	¥19,311,708
PLEYEL	1	1	$5,345	$5,345	$5,345
			DM8,887	DM8,887	DM8,887
			£3,220	£3,220	£3,220
			¥622,555	¥622,555	¥622,555
RUCKERS, ANDREAS	1	1	$141,410	$141,410	$141,410
			DM200,346	DM200,346	DM200,346
			£89,500	£89,500	£89,500
			¥14,471,613	¥14,471,613	¥14,471,613
SABERINO, P. GASPARRO	1	1	$25,277	$25,277	$25,277
			DM39,284	DM39,284	DM39,284
			£16,100	£16,100	£16,100
			¥2,487,450	¥2,487,450	¥2,487,450
SHUDI, BURKAT & BROADWOOD, JOHN	1	1	$104,746	$104,746	$104,746
			DM174,156	DM174,156	DM174,156
			£63,100	£63,100	£63,100
			¥12,199,754	¥12,199,754	¥12,199,754

HELICON

DE CART FRERES, FERDINAND & LOUIS	1	0			

Maker	Items		Selling Prices		
	Bid	Sold	Low	High	Avg

HORN

Maker	Bid	Sold	Low	High	Avg
BESSON	3	2	$97	$114	$106
			DM149	DM176	DM162
			£63	£75	£69
			¥10,559	¥12,479	¥11,519
BOOSEY & CO.	1	1	$156	$156	$156
			DM255	DM255	DM255
			£92	£92	£92
			¥18,407	¥18,407	¥18,407
BOOSEY & HAWKES	2	2	$211	$457	$334
			DM324	DM702	DM513
			£138	£299	£219
			¥23,037	¥49,914	¥36,476
CERVENY & SOHNE, V.F.	1	1	$764	$764	$764
			DM1,270	DM1,270	DM1,270
			£460	£460	£460
			¥88,936	¥88,936	¥88,936
GROSS & BRAMBACH	1	1	$1,813	$1,813	$1,813
			DM3,014	DM3,014	DM3,014
			£1,092	£1,092	£1,092
			¥211,127	¥211,127	¥211,127
HAAS, JOHANN WILHELM	1	1	$3,606	$3,606	$3,606
			DM6,098	DM6,098	DM6,098
			£2,420	£2,420	£2,420
			¥382,360	¥382,360	¥382,360
HAWKES & SON	1	1	$357	$357	$357
			DM551	DM551	DM551
			£225	£225	£225
			¥35,613	¥35,613	¥35,613
KNOPF	1	1	$324	$324	$324
			DM495	DM495	DM495
			£207	£207	£207
			¥36,132	¥36,132	¥36,132
KOHLERT'S SOHNE, V.	1	1	$458	$458	$458
			DM762	DM762	DM762
			£276	£276	£276
			¥53,362	¥53,362	¥53,362
KRETZSCHMANN, CHARLES	1	0			
LAPINI	1	1	$403	$403	$403
			DM680	DM680	DM680
			£242	£242	£242
			¥53,561	¥53,561	¥53,561
MULLER, C.A.	1	1	$535	$535	$535
			DM889	DM889	DM889
			£322	£322	£322
			¥62,255	¥62,255	¥62,255
PERINET, FRANCOIS	1	1	$1,189	$1,189	$1,189
			DM1,711	DM1,711	DM1,711
			£771	£771	£771
			¥120,768	¥120,768	¥120,768
POTTER, HENRY	3	0			
SCHOPPER, ROBERT	1	0			
WEBER, CARL AUGUST	1	1	$1,049	$1,049	$1,049
			DM1,744	DM1,744	DM1,744
			£632	£632	£632
			¥122,191	¥122,191	¥122,191

| Maker | Items | | Selling Prices | | |
---	Bid	Sold	Low	High	Avg
ZEDLITZ, EDUARD	1	1	$764	$764	$764
			DM1,270	DM1,270	DM1,270
			£460	£460	£460
			¥88,936	¥88,936	¥88,936

HURDY-GURDY

COLSON, NICOLAS	1	1	$1,413	$1,413	$1,413
			DM2,088	DM2,088	DM2,088
			£920	£920	£920
			¥150,635	¥150,635	¥150,635
LOUVET, PIERRE	1	0			
MASSETY	1	1	$4,543	$4,543	$4,543
			DM6,436	DM6,436	DM6,436
			£2,875	£2,875	£2,875
			¥464,870	¥464,870	¥464,870
PAJEOT (FILS)	1	1	$1,635	$1,635	$1,635
			DM2,317	DM2,317	DM2,317
			£1,035	£1,035	£1,035
			¥167,353	¥167,353	¥167,353
PAJOT	1	0			

KIT

PERRY	1	1	$2,332	$2,332	$2,332
			DM4,043	DM4,043	DM4,043
			£1,380	£1,380	£1,380
			¥291,180	¥291,180	¥291,180
PERRY, THOMAS	1	0			

LUTE

BARRY	1	0			
CHALLEN, CHRISTOPHER	1	1	$3,036	$3,036	$3,036
			DM5,391	DM5,391	DM5,391
			£1,840	£1,840	£1,840
			¥421,158	¥421,158	¥421,158
DOLMETSCH, ARNOLD	4	1	$1,267	$1,267	$1,267
			DM1,335	DM1,335	DM1,335
			£782	£782	£782
			¥96,808	¥96,808	¥96,808
GOFF, THOMAS	1	1	$1,457	$1,457	$1,457
			DM2,183	DM2,183	DM2,183
			£863	£863	£863
			¥162,185	¥162,185	¥162,185
GORRETT, JOHN	1	1	$526	$526	$526
			DM891	DM891	DM891
			£322	£322	£322
			¥61,018	¥61,018	¥61,018
GUGGENBERGER, ANTON	1	0			
HARWOOD, IAN	1	0			
HARWOOD, JOHN	2	1	$186	$186	$186
			DM196	DM196	DM196
			£115	£115	£115
			¥14,236	¥14,236	¥14,236
HAUSER, HERMANN	1	0			

| Maker | Items | | Selling Prices | | |
	Bid	Sold	Low	High	Avg
HOLMES, HENRY H.	1	1	$348	$348	$348
			DM607	DM607	DM607
			£207	£207	£207
			¥44,373	¥44,373	¥44,373
JAKOB, RICHARD	1	0			
JORDAN, HANS	1	0			
KAROUBI, J.	1	0			
RIECHE, J.G.	1	1	$580	$580	$580
			DM963	DM963	DM963
			£385	£385	£385
			¥60,356	¥60,356	¥60,356
TIEFFENBRUCKER, WENDELIN ("VENERE")	1	0			
VINCENT, WILLIAM M.	1	1	$354	$354	$354
			DM567	DM567	DM567
			£230	£230	£230
			¥35,794	¥35,794	¥35,794
WHITEMAN, DAVID	1	1	$540	$540	$540
			DM825	DM825	DM825
			£345	£345	£345
			¥60,220	¥60,220	¥60,220

MANDO-CELLO

GIBSON CO.	1	1	$1,380	$1,380	$1,380
			DM2,361	DM2,361	DM2,361
			£816	£816	£816
			¥171,368	¥171,368	¥171,368

MANDOLA

GARGANO, FRANCESCO	1	1	$368	$368	$368
			DM552	DM552	DM552
			£218	£218	£218
			¥40,993	¥40,993	¥40,993

MANDOLIN

ABBOTT	1	1	$171	$171	$171
			DM261	DM261	DM261
			£109	£109	£109
			¥19,070	¥19,070	¥19,070
BANONI	1	1	$189	$189	$189
			DM294	DM294	DM294
			£121	£121	£121
			¥18,690	¥18,690	¥18,690
BOHMANN, JOSEPH	2	1	$115	$115	$115
			DM205	DM205	DM205
			£70	£70	£70
			¥15,976	¥15,976	¥15,976
CALACE	1	1	$1,388	$1,388	$1,388
			DM2,357	DM2,357	DM2,357
			£935	£935	£935
			¥147,532	¥147,532	¥147,532
CALACE, GIUSEPPE	2	2	$4,857	$14,092	$9,474
			DM7,276	DM20,774	DM14,025
			£2,875	£9,200	£6,038
			¥540,615	¥1,503,004	¥1,021,810

| Maker | Items | | Selling Prices | | |
	Bid	Sold	Low	High	Avg
CALACE, NICOLA & RAFFAELLE	2	2	$2,347	$2,363	$2,355
			DM3,337	DM3,648	DM3,492
			£1,495	£1,495	£1,495
			¥210,850	¥230,978	¥220,914
CALACE, RAFFAELE	1	1	$1,534	$1,534	$1,534
			DM2,841	DM2,841	DM2,841
			£920	£920	£920
			¥204,820	¥204,820	¥204,820
CALACE & FIGLIO, RAFFAELE	2	2	$2,628	$3,378	$3,003
			DM4,685	DM6,024	DM5,354
			£1,610	£2,070	£1,840
			¥343,944	¥442,214	¥393,079
CAPONETTO, LUIGI	2	1	$168	$168	$168
			DM177	DM177	DM177
			£104	£104	£104
			¥12,813	¥12,813	¥12,813
CAPPIELLO, V. & G.	3	1	$113	$113	$113
			DM201	DM201	DM201
			£69	£69	£69
			¥14,740	¥14,740	¥14,740
CASELLA, M.	1	1	$782	$782	$782
			DM1,202	DM1,202	DM1,202
			£518	£518	£518
			¥83,434	¥83,434	¥83,434
CECCHERINI, UMBERTO	5	4	$154	$482	$319
			DM254	DM863	DM529
			£92	£288	£198
			¥17,968	¥55,919	¥35,411
DALLAS, J.E.	1	1	$230	$230	$230
			DM338	DM338	DM338
			£150	£150	£150
			¥24,392	¥24,392	¥24,392
DEL PERUGIA, FERNANDO	2	2	$452	$1,212	$832
			DM801	DM1,955	DM1,378
			£278	£704	£491
			¥55,148	¥142,715	¥98,932
DE MEGLIO, GIOVANNI	6	6	$149	$657	$335
			DM157	DM1,171	DM541
			£92	£403	£207
			¥11,389	¥85,986	¥39,152
DE MEGLIO, VINCENZO	1	1	$343	$343	$343
			DM485	DM485	DM485
			£219	£219	£219
			¥29,297	¥29,297	¥29,297
DE MEGLIO & FIGLIO	4	4	$230	$710	$425
			DM426	DM1,015	DM640
			£138	£449	£267
			¥30,723	¥71,305	¥45,508
DOBRO	2	2	$287	$985	$636
			DM405	DM1,391	DM898
			£180	£618	£399
			¥25,444	¥87,359	¥56,401
EMBERGHER, LUIGI	1	1	$8,018	$8,018	$8,018
			DM13,331	DM13,331	DM13,331
			£4,830	£4,830	£4,830
			¥933,832	¥933,832	¥933,832

Maker	Items		Selling Prices		
	Bid	Sold	Low	High	Avg
ESSEX, CLIFFORD	2	2	$241	$597	$419
			DM406	DM1,044	DM725
			£150	£368	£259
			¥29,581	¥72,110	¥50,845
FAIRBANKS CO., A.C.	1	1	$460	$460	$460
			DM713	DM713	DM713
			£294	£294	£294
			¥45,223	¥45,223	¥45,223
FANGA, LUIGI	1	0			
FERRARI & CO	4	3	$321	$433	$368
			DM476	DM809	DM626
			£207	£273	£233
			¥34,730	¥51,197	¥43,054
FILANO, DONATO	1	0			
GAROZZO, C.	1	1	$1,217	$1,217	$1,217
			DM1,870	DM1,870	DM1,870
			£805	£805	£805
			¥129,786	¥129,786	¥129,786
GIBSON CO.	24	22	$345	$3,335	$1,086
			DM590	DM5,636	DM1,752
			£204	£2,001	£668
			¥42,842	¥406,870	¥123,568
GRIMALDI, EMILIO	1	1	$4,504	$4,504	$4,504
			DM8,032	DM8,032	DM8,032
			£2,760	£2,760	£2,760
			¥589,619	¥589,619	¥589,619
HOWE, ELIAS	1	1	$518	$518	$518
			DM875	DM875	DM875
			£311	£311	£311
			¥63,135	¥63,135	¥63,135
IBANEZ	1	1	$707	$707	$707
			DM1,044	DM1,044	DM1,044
			£460	£460	£460
			¥75,337	¥75,337	¥75,337
KAY	1	1	$92	$92	$92
			DM164	DM164	DM164
			£56	£56	£56
			¥12,781	¥12,781	¥12,781
LYON & HEALY	1	1	$150	$150	$150
			DM266	DM266	DM266
			£91	£91	£91
			¥20,769	¥20,769	¥20,769
MAGLIONI, GENNARO	1	1	$169	$169	$169
			DM286	DM286	DM286
			£104	£104	£104
			¥19,613	¥19,613	¥19,613
MANFREDI, GIUSEPPE	2	1	$2,137	$2,137	$2,137
			DM3,201	DM3,201	DM3,201
			£1,265	£1,265	£1,265
			¥237,871	¥237,871	¥237,871
MARTELLO, CARLOS	2	1	$400	$400	$400
			DM614	DM614	DM614
			£265	£265	£265
			¥42,644	¥42,644	¥42,644
MARTIN & CO., C.F.	3	3	$316	$403	$355
			DM490	DM689	DM587
			£202	£238	£216
			¥31,091	¥49,982	¥41,054

153

Maker	Items		Selling Prices		
	Bid	Sold	Low	High	Avg
MEGLIO & FIGLIO	1	1	$445	$445	$445
			DM750	DM750	DM750
			£276	£276	£276
			¥54,610	¥54,610	¥54,610
MOLINARI, GIUSEPPE	1	1	$5,255	$5,255	$5,255
			DM9,370	DM9,370	DM9,370
			£3,220	£3,220	£3,220
			¥687,889	¥687,889	¥687,889
MONZINO, ANTONIO	1	1	$1,164	$1,164	$1,164
			DM2,075	DM2,075	DM2,075
			£713	£713	£713
			¥152,318	¥152,318	¥152,318
NAPOLI, DOMENICO BANONI	1	1	$891	$891	$891
			DM1,322	DM1,322	DM1,322
			£575	£575	£575
			¥96,474	¥96,474	¥96,474
PECORARO, P.	1	1	$675	$675	$675
			DM1,201	DM1,201	DM1,201
			£414	£414	£414
			¥90,637	¥90,637	¥90,637
PERRETTI, FRANCESCO & SON	3	2	$243	$371	$307
			DM374	DM625	DM499
			£161	£230	£196
			¥25,957	¥45,509	¥35,733
PRESBLER, GIUSEPPE	1	0			
PUGLISI, GIUSEPPE	3	2	$288	$2,440	$1,364
			DM433	DM4,350	DM2,392
			£175	£1,495	£835
			¥32,137	¥319,377	¥175,757
ROCCA, ENRICO	1	0			
ROMANILLOS, JOSE	2	1	$1,079	$1,079	$1,079
			DM1,510	DM1,510	DM1,510
			£675	£675	£675
			¥91,269	¥91,269	¥91,269
SALVINO & CO., A.	1	1	$618	$618	$618
			DM1,111	DM1,111	DM1,111
			£368	£368	£368
			¥71,477	¥71,477	¥71,477
STEWART, S.S.	1	1	$431	$431	$431
			DM729	DM729	DM729
			£259	£259	£259
			¥52,613	¥52,613	¥52,613
THIBOUVILLE-LAMY, J.	1	1	$298	$298	$298
			DM476	DM476	DM476
			£194	£194	£194
			¥30,129	¥30,129	¥30,129
TONELLI, PIETRO	1	1	$231	$231	$231
			DM414	DM414	DM414
			£138	£138	£138
			¥26,841	¥26,841	¥26,841
VARANO, MICHELE	2	1	$446	$446	$446
			DM661	DM661	DM661
			£288	£288	£288
			¥48,237	¥48,237	¥48,237
VATIANI, PAOLO	1	1	$74	$74	$74
			DM125	DM125	DM125
			£46	£46	£46
			¥9,102	¥9,102	¥9,102

Maker	Items		Selling Prices		
	Bid	Sold	Low	High	Avg
VEGA COMPANY	2	1	$518	$518	$518
			DM748	DM748	DM748
			£338	£338	£338
			¥52,397	¥52,397	¥52,397
VINACCIA, ANTONIO	2	2	$2,864	$9,927	$6,395
			DM4,761	DM16,505	DM10,633
			£1,725	£5,980	£3,853
			¥333,512	¥1,156,173	¥744,842
VINACCIA, GENNARO	1	0			
VINACCIA, GENNARO & ACHILLE	1	1	$3,997	$3,997	$3,997
			DM5,663	DM5,663	DM5,663
			£2,530	£2,530	£2,530
			¥409,086	¥409,086	¥409,086
VINACCIA, GIOVANNI	1	1	$2,724	$2,724	$2,724
			DM3,859	DM3,859	DM3,859
			£1,725	£1,725	£1,725
			¥281,175	¥281,175	¥281,175
VINACCIA, GIUSEPPE	1	1	$789	$789	$789
			DM1,337	DM1,337	DM1,337
			£483	£483	£483
			¥91,527	¥91,527	¥91,527
VINACCIA BROS.	2	2	$4,721	$6,537	$5,629
			DM6,689	DM9,262	DM7,975
			£2,990	£4,140	£3,565
			¥487,370	¥674,820	¥581,095
WASHBURN	2	2	$150	$316	$233
			DM266	DM563	DM415
			£91	£193	£142
			¥20,769	¥43,933	¥32,351

MANDOLIN-LYRE

Maker	Items		Selling Prices		
	Bid	Sold	Low	High	Avg
CALACE FRATELLI	1	1	$1,035	$1,035	$1,035
			DM1,749	DM1,749	DM1,749
			£621	£621	£621
			¥126,270	¥126,270	¥126,270

MANDOLINO

Maker	Items		Selling Prices		
	Bid	Sold	Low	High	Avg
FONTANELLI, GIOVANNI GIUSEPPE	1	1	$2,496	$2,496	$2,496
			DM4,025	DM4,025	DM4,025
			£1,449	£1,449	£1,449
			¥293,825	¥293,825	¥293,825
NONEMACHER, CRISTIANO	1	1	$6,872	$6,872	$6,872
			DM11,426	DM11,426	DM11,426
			£4,140	£4,140	£4,140
			¥800,428	¥800,428	¥800,428

MARTINSHORN

Maker	Items				
	Bid	Sold			
MARTIN, MAX BERNHARDT	1	0			

MELLOPHONE

Maker	Items				
	Bid	Sold			
HOLTON & CO.	1	0			
PEPPER	1	0			
YORK	1	0			

	Items		Selling Prices		
Maker	Bid	Sold	Low	High	Avg

NORMAPHON

WUNDERLICH	1	1	$5,463 DM9,232 £3,278 ¥726,895	$5,463 DM9,232 £3,278 ¥726,895	$5,463 DM9,232 £3,278 ¥726,895

OBOE

ADLER, FREDERIC GUILLAUME	2	0			
ALBERT, J.	1	1	$97 DM143 £63 ¥10,320	$97 DM143 £63 ¥10,320	$97 DM143 £63 ¥10,320
ALBERT, JACQUES	1	1	$327 DM463 £207 ¥33,471	$327 DM463 £207 ¥33,471	$327 DM463 £207 ¥33,471
ANCIUTI, JOHANNES MARIA	1	0			
ASTOR & CO., GEORGE	3	2	$407 DM610 £241 ¥45,318	$3,436 DM5,713 £2,070 ¥400,214	$1,922 DM3,162 £1,156 ¥222,766
BAHRMAN	1	1	$2,362 DM3,347 £1,495 ¥241,733	$2,362 DM3,347 £1,495 ¥241,733	$2,362 DM3,347 £1,495 ¥241,733
BAUER, JEAN	1	0			
BAUR, JAKOB	1	1	$2,907 DM4,119 £1,840 ¥297,517	$2,907 DM4,119 £1,840 ¥297,517	$2,907 DM4,119 £1,840 ¥297,517
BOEKHOUT, THOMAS (attributed to)	1	1	$1,769 DM2,837 £1,150 ¥178,969	$1,769 DM2,837 £1,150 ¥178,969	$1,769 DM2,837 £1,150 ¥178,969
BOOSEY & HAWKES	5	3	$317 DM486 £207 ¥34,556	$422 DM648 £276 ¥46,075	$358 DM549 £234 ¥39,035
BUFFET	2	2	$242 DM255 £150 ¥18,507	$2,628 DM4,685 £1,610 ¥343,944	$1,435 DM2,470 £880 ¥181,226
BUISSON, F.	3	1	$334 DM562 £207 ¥40,958	$334 DM562 £207 ¥40,958	$334 DM562 £207 ¥40,958
CAHUSAC, THOMAS (SR.)	2	2	$1,714 DM2,664 £1,092 ¥168,714	$3,634 DM5,149 £2,300 ¥371,896	$2,674 DM3,907 £1,696 ¥270,305
COLLIER, THOMAS	1	0			
CRONE, JOHANN AUGUST	1	1	$1,999 DM2,832 £1,265 ¥204,543	$1,999 DM2,832 £1,265 ¥204,543	$1,999 DM2,832 £1,265 ¥204,543

Maker	Items		Selling Prices		
	Bid	Sold	Low	High	Avg
DELUSSE, CHRISTOPHER	2	2	$3,754	$9,759	$6,756
			DM6,693	DM17,402	DM12,047
			£2,300	£5,980	£4,140
			¥491,349	¥1,277,507	¥884,428
ELKHART	1	0			
ENGELHARD, JOHANN FRIEDRICH	1	0			
GEDNEY, CALEB	1	1	$3,529	$3,529	$3,529
			DM5,422	DM5,422	DM5,422
			£2,300	£2,300	£2,300
			¥386,375	¥386,375	¥386,375
GOLDE, CARL	2	1	$6,606	$6,606	$6,606
			DM9,895	DM9,895	DM9,895
			£3,910	£3,910	£3,910
			¥735,236	¥735,236	¥735,236
GRENSER, CARL AUGUSTIN (I)	2	2	$5,088	$18,768	$11,928
			DM7,208	DM33,465	DM20,336
			£3,220	£11,500	£7,360
			¥520,655	¥2,456,745	¥1,488,700
GRUNDMANN & FLOT	1	1	$826	$826	$826
			DM1,472	DM1,472	DM1,472
			£506	£506	£506
			¥108,097	¥108,097	¥108,097
GUERINI	1	0			
GULIELMINETTI	1	1	$2,137	$2,137	$2,137
			DM3,201	DM3,201	DM3,201
			£1,265	£1,265	£1,265
			¥237,871	¥237,871	¥237,871
HAWKES & CO.	1	1	$93	$93	$93
			DM156	DM156	DM156
			£58	£58	£58
			¥11,377	¥11,377	¥11,377
HAWKES & SON	2	1	$132	$132	$132
			DM203	DM203	DM203
			£86	£86	£86
			¥14,398	¥14,398	¥14,398
HECKEL	1	1	$827	$827	$827
			DM1,400	DM1,400	DM1,400
			£506	£506	£506
			¥95,885	¥95,885	¥95,885
HOE, JOHANN WOLFGANG	1	1	$10,686	$10,686	$10,686
			DM16,007	DM16,007	DM16,007
			£6,325	£6,325	£6,325
			¥1,189,353	¥1,189,353	¥1,189,353
HORAK & SOHN, W.	1	1	$1,909	$1,909	$1,909
			DM3,174	DM3,174	DM3,174
			£1,150	£1,150	£1,150
			¥222,341	¥222,341	¥222,341
HOWARTH	1	1	$535	$535	$535
			DM816	DM816	DM816
			£345	£345	£345
			¥59,375	¥59,375	¥59,375
HOWARTH & CO.	1	1	$336	$336	$336
			DM587	DM587	DM587
			£207	£207	£207
			¥40,562	¥40,562	¥40,562

Maker	Items		Selling Prices		
	Bid	Sold	Low	High	Avg
HULLER, G.H.	1	1	$382 DM635 £230 ¥44,468	$382 DM635 £230 ¥44,468	$382 DM635 £230 ¥44,468
KATTOFEN, AMMON	1	1	$382 DM635 £230 ¥44,468	$382 DM635 £230 ¥44,468	$382 DM635 £230 ¥44,468
KOHLERT & SONS	1	1	$150 DM267 £92 ¥20,142	$150 DM267 £92 ¥20,142	$150 DM267 £92 ¥20,142
KRUSPE, FRIEDRICH WILHELM	1	1	$2,137 DM3,201 £1,265 ¥237,871	$2,137 DM3,201 £1,265 ¥237,871	$2,137 DM3,201 £1,265 ¥237,871
LAFLEUR, J.R. & SON	1	1	$150 DM267 £92 ¥20,142	$150 DM267 £92 ¥20,142	$150 DM267 £92 ¥20,142
LOREE, F.	6	4	$818 DM1,170 £517 ¥82,196	$1,548 DM2,376 £1,012 ¥168,940	$1,261 DM1,830 £791 ¥130,941
LOREE, FRANCOIS	2	0			
LOUIS	5	2	$469 DM663 £299 ¥40,090	$719 DM1,006 £450 ¥60,846	$594 DM835 £375 ¥50,468
LUDWIG, FRANZ	2	2	$3,436 DM5,713 £2,070 ¥400,214	$4,582 DM7,618 £2,760 ¥533,618	$4,009 DM6,665 £2,415 ¥466,916
LUDWIG & MARTINKA	2	2	$1,456 DM2,181 £862 ¥162,090	$4,963 DM8,252 £2,990 ¥578,087	$3,210 DM5,217 £1,926 ¥370,089
METZLER & CO.	1	1	$363 DM515 £230 ¥37,190	$363 DM515 £230 ¥37,190	$363 DM515 £230 ¥37,190
MILHOUSE, RICHARD	1	1	$3,627 DM6,031 £2,185 ¥422,448	$3,627 DM6,031 £2,185 ¥422,448	$3,627 DM6,031 £2,185 ¥422,448
MILHOUSE, WILLIAM	2	2	$909 DM1,287 £575 ¥92,974	$2,726 DM3,850 £1,725 ¥243,289	$1,817 DM2,569 £1,150 ¥168,131
MOENNIG, OTTO	1	0			
MOLLENHAUER, CONRAD	1	0			
MONNIG, OTTO	2	2	$764 DM1,270 £460 ¥88,936	$802 DM1,333 £483 ¥93,383	$783 DM1,301 £472 ¥91,160

Maker	Items		Selling Prices		
	Bid	Sold	Low	High	Avg
MONNIG GEBRUDER	4	1	$179	$179	$179
			DM295	DM295	DM295
			£109	£109	£109
			¥22,115	¥22,115	¥22,115
MORTON & SONS, A.	2	1	$180	$180	$180
			DM275	DM275	DM275
			£115	£115	£115
			¥20,073	¥20,073	¥20,073
MORTON, ALFRED	1	1	$155	$155	$155
			DM231	DM231	DM231
			£92	£92	£92
			¥17,248	¥17,248	¥17,248
OMS	1	1	$8,160	$8,160	$8,160
			DM12,223	DM12,223	DM12,223
			£4,830	£4,830	£4,830
			¥908,233	¥908,233	¥908,233
PANORMO, VINCENZO	1	0			
PARADIS	1	1	$86	$86	$86
			DM132	DM132	DM132
			£57	£57	£57
			¥9,091	¥9,091	¥9,091
PINDER, HEINRICH FRANZ EDUARD	1	1	$916	$916	$916
			DM1,524	DM1,524	DM1,524
			£552	£552	£552
			¥106,724	¥106,724	¥106,724
REICHENBACHER, ERNST	1	1	$1,943	$1,943	$1,943
			DM2,910	DM2,910	DM2,910
			£1,150	£1,150	£1,150
			¥216,246	¥216,246	¥216,246
RICHTERS, HENDRIK	1	1	$22,522	$22,522	$22,522
			DM40,158	DM40,158	DM40,158
			£13,800	£13,800	£13,800
			¥2,948,094	¥2,948,094	¥2,948,094
ROESSLER, HEINZ	1	1	$432	$432	$432
			DM770	DM770	DM770
			£265	£265	£265
			¥56,505	¥56,505	¥56,505
ROTTENBURGH, JOANNES HYACINTHUS (I)	1	1	$24,398	$24,398	$24,398
			DM43,505	DM43,505	DM43,505
			£14,950	£14,950	£14,950
			¥3,193,769	¥3,193,769	¥3,193,769
RUDALL, CARTE & CO.	3	2	$132	$334	$233
			DM223	DM562	DM392
			£81	£207	£144
			¥15,254	¥40,958	¥28,106
SATTLER, CARL WILHELM	1	1	$7,507	$7,507	$7,507
			DM13,386	DM13,386	DM13,386
			£4,600	£4,600	£4,600
			¥982,698	¥982,698	¥982,698
SCHLEGEL, JEREMIAS	2	1	$1,240	$1,240	$1,240
			DM2,062	DM2,062	DM2,062
			£747	£747	£747
			¥144,425	¥144,425	¥144,425
SELMER	1	1	$169	$169	$169
			DM286	DM286	DM286
			£104	£104	£104
			¥19,613	¥19,613	¥19,613

Maker	Items		Selling Prices		
	Bid	Sold	Low	High	Avg
SHARPE, JOHN	2	2	$622	$1,527	$1,074
			DM931	DM2,539	DM1,735
			£368	£920	£644
			¥69,199	¥177,873	¥123,536
SIMPSON, JOHN	1	0			
STANESBY, THOMAS SR. AND JR.	1	1	$11,261	$11,261	$11,261
			DM20,079	DM20,079	DM20,079
			£6,900	£6,900	£6,900
			¥1,474,047	¥1,474,047	¥1,474,047
STARK	1	1	$196	$196	$196
			DM319	DM319	DM319
			£115	£115	£115
			¥23,009	¥23,009	¥23,009
STEHLE	1	1	$1,049	$1,049	$1,049
			DM1,744	DM1,744	DM1,744
			£632	£632	£632
			¥122,191	¥122,191	¥122,191
THIBOUVILLE-LAMY, J.	1	1	$182	$182	$182
			DM260	DM260	DM260
			£115	£115	£115
			¥18,283	¥18,283	¥18,283
TRIEBERT	1	0			
TRIEBERT & SONS, GUILLAUME	1	1	$1,622	$1,622	$1,622
			DM2,697	DM2,697	DM2,697
			£977	£977	£977
			¥188,893	¥188,893	¥188,893
TRIEBERT & COUESNON	1	1	$1,454	$1,454	$1,454
			DM2,059	DM2,059	DM2,059
			£920	£920	£920
			¥148,758	¥148,758	¥148,758
UHLMANN, JOHANN TOBIAS	1	1	$2,291	$2,291	$2,291
			DM3,809	DM3,809	DM3,809
			£1,380	£1,380	£1,380
			¥266,809	¥266,809	¥266,809
WEYGANDT, T.J.	1	1	$6,109	$6,109	$6,109
			DM10,157	DM10,157	DM10,157
			£3,680	£3,680	£3,680
			¥711,491	¥711,491	¥711,491

OPHICLEIDE

Maker	Items		Selling Prices		
	Bid	Sold	Low	High	Avg
BONNEL	1	1	$2,064	$2,064	$2,064
			DM3,681	DM3,681	DM3,681
			£1,265	£1,265	£1,265
			¥270,242	¥270,242	¥270,242
HENRI	1	0			
SMITH, HENRY	3	1	$1,167	$1,167	$1,167
			DM1,835	DM1,835	DM1,835
			£748	£748	£748
			¥117,080	¥117,080	¥117,080

ORGAN

Maker	Items		Selling Prices		
	Bid	Sold	Low	High	Avg
HANCOCK, JAMES GRANGE	1	1	$16,353	$16,353	$16,353
			DM23,168	DM23,168	DM23,168
			£10,350	£10,350	£10,350
			¥1,673,533	¥1,673,533	¥1,673,533

Maker	Items		Selling Prices		
	Bid	Sold	Low	High	Avg

Maker	Bid	Sold	Low	High	Avg
STUMPHLER, JOHANN STEPHAN (ascribed to)	1	0			
WILLIS, HENRY	1	0			

PHONO-FIDDLE

Maker	Bid	Sold	Low	High	Avg
EVANS & CO., GEORGE	1	1	$840 DM1,397 £506 ¥97,830	$840 DM1,397 £506 ¥97,830	$840 DM1,397 £506 ¥97,830
HOWSON, A.T.	6	5	$131 DM228 £81 ¥14,772	$447 DM783 £276 ¥54,082	$231 DM389 £143 ¥26,422
STROH, CHARLES	1	1	$687 DM1,143 £414 ¥80,043	$687 DM1,143 £414 ¥80,043	$687 DM1,143 £414 ¥80,043
STROVIOL	2	2	$180 DM276 £115 ¥20,070	$248 DM364 £161 ¥26,269	$214 DM320 £138 ¥23,169

PIANINO

Maker	Bid	Sold	Low	High	Avg
CHAPPELL	1	1	$13,600 DM20,372 £8,050 ¥1,513,722	$13,600 DM20,372 £8,050 ¥1,513,722	$13,600 DM20,372 £8,050 ¥1,513,722

PIANO

Maker	Bid	Sold	Low	High	Avg
ASTOR & HORWOOD	1	1	$909 DM1,287 £575 ¥92,974	$909 DM1,287 £575 ¥92,974	$909 DM1,287 £575 ¥92,974
BECHSTEIN	2	1	$2,609 DM4,167 £1,694 ¥263,627	$2,609 DM4,167 £1,694 ¥263,627	$2,609 DM4,167 £1,694 ¥263,627
BERNHARDT, P.	1	1	$6,756 DM12,047 £4,140 ¥884,428	$6,756 DM12,047 £4,140 ¥884,428	$6,756 DM12,047 £4,140 ¥884,428
BLAND & WELLER	2	1	$999 DM1,415 £632 ¥102,191	$999 DM1,415 £632 ¥102,191	$999 DM1,415 £632 ¥102,191
BLUTHNER	3	2	$1,618 DM2,263 £1,012 ¥136,836	$2,141 DM3,262 £1,380 ¥237,498	$1,879 DM2,763 £1,196 ¥187,167
BOSENDORFER	1	1	$387,500 DM685,488 £233,973 ¥50,336,250	$387,500 DM685,488 £233,973 ¥50,336,250	$387,500 DM685,488 £233,973 ¥50,336,250
BROADWOOD, JOHN	1	1	$2,104 DM2,987 £1,350 ¥214,048	$2,104 DM2,987 £1,350 ¥214,048	$2,104 DM2,987 £1,350 ¥214,048

| Maker | Items | | Selling Prices | | |
	Bid	Sold	Low	High	Avg
BROADWOOD, JOHN (attributed to)	1	1	$1,062	$1,062	$1,062
			DM1,702	DM1,702	DM1,702
			£690	£690	£690
			¥107,381	¥107,381	¥107,381
BROADWOOD, JOHN & SONS	4	2	$2,346	$2,362	$2,354
			DM3,347	DM4,183	DM3,765
			£1,438	£1,495	£1,466
			¥241,733	¥307,093	¥274,413
BUNTLEBART, GABRIEL	1	1	$1,863	$1,863	$1,863
			DM2,977	DM2,977	DM2,977
			£1,210	£1,210	£1,210
			¥188,305	¥188,305	¥188,305
CHALLEN & HOLLIS	2	0			
CLEMENTI, MUZIO	6	5	$464	$1,835	$1,197
			DM694	DM2,746	DM1,828
			£276	£1,092	£745
			¥51,744	¥204,728	¥126,555
CLEMENTI & CO.	2	0			
COLLARD & COLLARD	2	1	$2,291	$2,291	$2,291
			DM3,809	DM3,809	DM3,809
			£1,380	£1,380	£1,380
			¥266,809	¥266,809	¥266,809
EDWARDS, WILLIAM	1	1	$3,003	$3,003	$3,003
			DM5,354	DM5,354	DM5,354
			£1,840	£1,840	£1,840
			¥393,079	¥393,079	¥393,079
GANER, CHRISTOPHER	2	1	$916	$916	$916
			DM1,469	DM1,469	DM1,469
			£595	£595	£595
			¥104,177	¥104,177	¥104,177
GANER, CHRISTOPHER (attributed to)	1	1	$188	$188	$188
			DM335	DM335	DM335
			£115	£115	£115
			¥24,567	¥24,567	¥24,567
HAXBY, THOMAS	2	2	$1,240	$2,854	$2,047
			DM2,062	DM4,350	DM3,206
			£747	£1,840	£1,294
			¥144,425	¥316,664	¥230,544
KIRCKMAN, JACOB & ABRAHAM	1	0			
KLEIN, F.A.	1	0			
LONGMAN, JAMES	1	1	$1,641	$1,641	$1,641
			DM2,951	DM2,951	DM2,951
			£977	£977	£977
			¥189,763	¥189,763	¥189,763
LONGMAN & CO.	2	1	$1,240	$1,240	$1,240
			DM2,062	DM2,062	DM2,062
			£747	£747	£747
			¥144,425	¥144,425	¥144,425
LONGMAN & BRODERIP	11	8	$960	$2,720	$1,775
			DM1,604	DM4,168	DM2,854
			£575	£1,610	£1,057
			¥116,719	¥302,744	¥203,871
LONGMAN, CLEMENTI & CO.	1	1	$1,408	$1,408	$1,408
			DM2,510	DM2,510	DM2,510
			£863	£863	£863
			¥184,256	¥184,256	¥184,256
MORNINGTON, ROBERT	1	0			

Maker	Items		Selling Prices		
	Bid	Sold	Low	High	Avg
PHILLIPS, W.	1	1	$1,222 DM1,960 £794 ¥139,037	$1,222 DM1,960 £794 ¥139,037	$1,222 DM1,960 £794 ¥139,037
POHLMAN, JOHANNES	2	1	$1,689 DM3,012 £1,035 ¥221,107	$1,689 DM3,012 £1,035 ¥221,107	$1,689 DM3,012 £1,035 ¥221,107
PRESTON, THOMAS	2	1	$1,145 DM1,904 £690 ¥133,405	$1,145 DM1,904 £690 ¥133,405	$1,145 DM1,904 £690 ¥133,405
ROLFE, WILLIAM & SONS	2	0			
ROLFE & CO., WILLIAM	1	0			
STEINWAY & SONS	2	2	$2,877 DM4,026 £1,800 ¥243,383	$7,826 DM12,502 £5,082 ¥790,881	$5,352 DM8,264 £3,441 ¥517,132
STEINWEG, GROTRIAN	1	1	$3,156 DM4,480 £2,025 ¥321,072	$3,156 DM4,480 £2,025 ¥321,072	$3,156 DM4,480 £2,025 ¥321,072
STODART, M. & W.	1	1	$618 DM1,111 £368 ¥71,477	$618 DM1,111 £368 ¥71,477	$618 DM1,111 £368 ¥71,477
STODART, WILLIAM	1	0			
STODART, WILLIAM & SON	1	1	$6,606 DM9,895 £3,910 ¥735,236	$6,606 DM9,895 £3,910 ¥735,236	$6,606 DM9,895 £3,910 ¥735,236
TOMLINSON & CO., WILLIAM	1	0			
WEBLEN, ALEXANDER	1	0			

PIANOFORTE

Maker	Items		Selling Prices		
	Bid	Sold	Low	High	Avg
BROADWOOD, JOHN	3	1	$8,910 DM13,461 £5,980 ¥943,704	$8,910 DM13,461 £5,980 ¥943,704	$8,910 DM13,461 £5,980 ¥943,704
BROADWOOD, JOHN & SONS	7	5	$1,909 DM3,174 £1,150 ¥222,341	$27,201 DM40,744 £16,100 ¥3,027,444	$11,943 DM17,902 £7,337 ¥1,263,570
COLLARD & COLLARD	1	1	$3,245 DM5,396 £1,955 ¥377,980	$3,245 DM5,396 £1,955 ¥377,980	$3,245 DM5,396 £1,955 ¥377,980
CRISI, VINCENZO	1	1	$9,759 DM17,402 £5,980 ¥1,277,507	$9,759 DM17,402 £5,980 ¥1,277,507	$9,759 DM17,402 £5,980 ¥1,277,507
EHLERS, JOACHIM	1	0			
FIRTH & HALL	1	1	$920 DM1,638 £552 ¥122,342	$920 DM1,638 £552 ¥122,342	$920 DM1,638 £552 ¥122,342

Maker	Items Bid	Sold	Selling Prices Low	High	Avg
GRAF, CONRAD	2	2	$26,275 DM46,851 £16,100 ¥3,439,443	$38,859 DM58,206 £23,000 ¥4,324,920	$32,567 DM52,529 £19,550 ¥3,882,182
HANCOCK, CRANG	1	1	$22,941 DM35,245 £14,950 ¥2,511,436	$22,941 DM35,245 £14,950 ¥2,511,436	$22,941 DM35,245 £14,950 ¥2,511,436
HAWKINS, JOHN ISAAC	1	1	$34,362 DM57,132 £20,700 ¥4,002,138	$34,362 DM57,132 £20,700 ¥4,002,138	$34,362 DM57,132 £20,700 ¥4,002,138
LONGMAN & BRODERIP	1	1	$17,830 DM31,792 £10,925 ¥2,333,908	$17,830 DM31,792 £10,925 ¥2,333,908	$17,830 DM31,792 £10,925 ¥2,333,908
LONGMAN, CLEMENTI & CO.	1	0			
SOUTHWELL, WILLIAM	1	1	$50,554 DM78,568 £32,200 ¥4,974,900	$50,554 DM78,568 £32,200 ¥4,974,900	$50,554 DM78,568 £32,200 ¥4,974,900
STEIN, JOHANN ANDREAS	1	1	$76,872 DM115,147 £45,500 ¥8,555,820	$76,872 DM115,147 £45,500 ¥8,555,820	$76,872 DM115,147 £45,500 ¥8,555,820
STEIN, MATTHAUS ANDREAS	1	1	$27,201 DM40,744 £16,100 ¥3,027,444	$27,201 DM40,744 £16,100 ¥3,027,444	$27,201 DM40,744 £16,100 ¥3,027,444
STODART, M. & W.	1	0			

PICCOLO

Maker	Items Bid	Sold	Selling Prices Low	High	Avg
BESSON & CO.	1	1	$207 DM342 £127 ¥25,607	$207 DM342 £127 ¥25,607	$207 DM342 £127 ¥25,607
BUTLER	1	1	$150 DM248 £92 ¥18,623	$150 DM248 £92 ¥18,623	$150 DM248 £92 ¥18,623
GAND, CHARLES	1	0			
GOULDING & CO.	1	1	$188 DM335 £115 ¥24,567	$188 DM335 £115 ¥24,567	$188 DM335 £115 ¥24,567
HAMMIG, PHILIP	1	1	$1,635 DM2,317 £1,035 ¥167,353	$1,635 DM2,317 £1,035 ¥167,353	$1,635 DM2,317 £1,035 ¥167,353
HAWKES & SON	1	1	$158 DM167 £98 ¥12,101	$158 DM167 £98 ¥12,101	$158 DM167 £98 ¥12,101
HAYNES CO., WILLIAM S.	1	1	$382 DM635 £230 ¥44,468	$382 DM635 £230 ¥44,468	$382 DM635 £230 ¥44,468

Maker	Items		Selling Prices		
	Bid	Sold	Low	High	Avg
HAYNES & CO.	1	1	$748	$748	$748
			DM1,292	DM1,292	DM1,292
			£462	£462	£462
			¥94,734	¥94,734	¥94,734
JAHN, M.A.	1	0			
KING MUSICAL INSTRUMENT CO.	1	0			
KRUSPE, C.	1	0			
LEFT, JACK	1	0			
LOT, LOUIS	6	2	$414	$581	$498
			DM683	DM824	DM753
			£253	£368	£311
			¥51,215	¥59,503	¥55,359
MONZANI	1	1	$714	$714	$714
			DM1,087	DM1,087	DM1,087
			£460	£460	£460
			¥79,166	¥79,166	¥79,166
RITTERSHAUSEN, E.	1	1	$150	$150	$150
			DM221	DM221	DM221
			£98	£98	£98
			¥15,949	¥15,949	¥15,949
RUDALL, CARTE & CO.	9	5	$122	$317	$202
			DM202	DM486	DM319
			£75	£207	£129
			¥15,132	¥34,556	¥23,028
SELMER	1	0			
SKOUSBOE, HENNING ANDERSEN	1	1	$581	$581	$581
			DM824	DM824	DM824
			£368	£368	£368
			¥59,503	¥59,503	¥59,503
THIBOUVILLE-LAMY, J.	1	1	$56	$56	$56
			DM95	DM95	DM95
			£35	£35	£35
			¥6,538	¥6,538	¥6,538
WALLIS, JOSEPH	2	1	$725	$725	$725
			DM1,206	DM1,206	DM1,206
			£437	£437	£437
			¥84,490	¥84,490	¥84,490
YAMAHA	1	0			

POCHETTE

Maker	Items		Selling Prices		
	Bid	Sold	Low	High	Avg
AMAN, GEORG	2	1	$4,880	$4,880	$4,880
			DM8,701	DM8,701	DM8,701
			£2,990	£2,990	£2,990
			¥638,754	¥638,754	¥638,754
BAADER, J. (workshop of)	1	1	$978	$978	$978
			DM1,471	DM1,471	DM1,471
			£593	£593	£593
			¥109,265	¥109,265	¥109,265
BETTS, JOHN	1	1	$642	$642	$642
			DM1,115	DM1,115	DM1,115
			£380	£380	£380
			¥81,444	¥81,444	¥81,444
BETTS, JOHN (attributed to)	1	0			

Maker	Items		Selling Prices		
	Bid	Sold	Low	High	Avg
JAY, HENRY (attributed to)	1	1	$2,783	$2,783	$2,783
			DM4,375	DM4,375	DM4,375
			£1,783	£1,783	£1,783
			¥279,191	¥279,191	¥279,191
WORLE, MATHIAS	1	1	$4,888	$4,888	$4,888
			DM8,363	DM8,363	DM8,363
			£2,891	£2,891	£2,891
			¥606,930	¥606,930	¥606,930

QUINTON

Maker	Items		Selling Prices		
	Bid	Sold	Low	High	Avg
GUERSAN, LOUIS	2	2	$4,663	$4,673	$4,668
			DM6,985	DM8,106	DM7,545
			£2,760	£2,760	£2,760
			¥518,990	¥592,324	¥555,657
GUERSAN, LOUIS (attributed to)	1	0			

RACKET BASSOON

Maker	Items		Selling Prices		
	Bid	Sold	Low	High	Avg
BIZEY, CHARLES	1	0			

RECORDER

Maker	Items		Selling Prices		
	Bid	Sold	Low	High	Avg
ANCIUTI, JOHANNES MARIA	1	1	$12,638	$12,638	$12,638
			DM19,642	DM19,642	DM19,642
			£8,050	£8,050	£8,050
			¥1,243,725	¥1,243,725	¥1,243,725
AULOS	1	1	$35	$35	$35
			DM52	DM52	DM52
			£23	£23	£23
			¥3,753	¥3,753	¥3,753
DENNER, JOHANN CHRISTOPH	2	0			
DOLMETSCH, ARNOLD	2	2	$177	$2,889	$1,533
			DM284	DM4,490	DM2,387
			£115	£1,840	£978
			¥17,897	¥284,280	¥151,088
EICHENTOPF, JOHANN HEINRICH	1	1	$20,645	$20,645	$20,645
			DM36,812	DM36,812	DM36,812
			£12,650	£12,650	£12,650
			¥2,702,420	¥2,702,420	¥2,702,420
GAHN, JOHANN B.	2	1	$16,249	$16,249	$16,249
			DM25,254	DM25,254	DM25,254
			£10,350	£10,350	£10,350
			¥1,599,075	¥1,599,075	¥1,599,075
HOHNER	1	1	$9	$9	$9
			DM13	DM13	DM13
			£6	£6	£6
			¥938	¥938	¥938
OBERLENDER, JOHANN WILHELM (I)	1	0			
RIPPERT, JEAN JACQUES	2	1	$17,181	$17,181	$17,181
			DM28,566	DM28,566	DM28,566
			£10,350	£10,350	£10,350
			¥2,001,069	¥2,001,069	¥2,001,069
STANESBY, THOMAS	2	1	$40,801	$40,801	$40,801
			DM61,116	DM61,116	DM61,116
			£24,150	£24,150	£24,150
			¥4,541,166	¥4,541,166	¥4,541,166

Maker	Items		Selling Prices		
	Bid	Sold	Low	High	Avg
STANESBY, THOMAS JR.	1	1	$20,999	$20,999	$20,999
			DM34,914	DM34,914	DM34,914
			£12,650	£12,650	£12,650
			¥2,445,751	¥2,445,751	¥2,445,751
VON HUENE, FRIEDRICH	1	1	$1,610	$1,610	$1,610
			DM2,866	DM2,866	DM2,866
			£966	£966	£966
			¥214,098	¥214,098	¥214,098

ROTHPHONE

Maker	Bid	Sold	Low	High	Avg
BOTTALI, A.M.	1	1	$2,291	$2,291	$2,291
			DM3,809	DM3,809	DM3,809
			£1,380	£1,380	£1,380
			¥266,809	¥266,809	¥266,809
BOTTALI FRATELLI, A.M.	2	2	$3,054	$6,109	$4,582
			DM5,078	DM10,157	DM7,618
			£1,840	£3,680	£2,760
			¥355,746	¥711,491	¥533,618

SARRUSOPHONE

Maker	Bid	Sold	Low	High	Avg
CONN, C.G.	1	0			
ORSI, ROMEO	1	0			
RAMPONE	1	1	$5,345	$5,345	$5,345
			DM8,887	DM8,887	DM8,887
			£3,220	£3,220	£3,220
			¥622,555	¥622,555	¥622,555

SAW

Maker	Bid	Sold	Low	High	Avg
FELDMANN, C.	1	1	$56	$56	$56
			DM94	DM94	DM94
			£34	£34	£34
			¥6,574	¥6,574	¥6,574
SANDVICKENS, JERNVERKS A.B.	1	1	$133	$133	$133
			DM221	DM221	DM221
			£80	£80	£80
			¥15,467	¥15,467	¥15,467

SAXHORN

Maker	Bid	Sold	Low	High	Avg
DISTIN, HENRY	1	1	$1,234	$1,234	$1,234
			DM1,958	DM1,958	DM1,958
			£805	£805	£805
			¥124,762	¥124,762	¥124,762
KLEMM & BRO.	1	1	$3,163	$3,163	$3,163
			DM5,345	DM5,345	DM5,345
			£1,898	£1,898	£1,898
			¥420,834	¥420,834	¥420,834
ZOEBISCH & SONS, C.A.	1	1	$802	$802	$802
			DM1,333	DM1,333	DM1,333
			£483	£483	£483
			¥93,383	¥93,383	¥93,383

SAXOPHONE

Maker	Bid	Sold	Low	High	Avg
BEAUGNIER	1	0			
BEUSCHER, PAUL	1	0			

Maker	Items		Selling Prices		
	Bid	Sold	Low	High	Avg
BLESSING	2	0			
BOOSEY & HAWKES	1	0			
BUESCHER	15	10	$149	$1,260	$507
			DM261	DM1,926	DM790
			£92	£805	£320
			¥18,027	¥140,513	¥56,823
BUFFET CRAMPON & CO.	1	0			
CABART	2	1	$338	$338	$338
			DM573	DM573	DM573
			£207	£207	£207
			¥39,226	¥39,226	¥39,226
COHN	2	2	$522	$695	$608
			DM801	DM1,069	DM935
			£345	£460	£403
			¥55,623	¥74,164	¥64,893
CONN, C.G.	15	11	$271	$981	$510
			DM314	DM1,784	DM845
			£161	£598	£314
			¥22,778	¥123,870	¥60,622
COUESNON	4	3	$176	$669	$487
			DM281	DM945	DM715
			£114	£414	£310
			¥17,803	¥67,192	¥46,905
DEARMAN	1	1	$215	$215	$215
			DM358	DM358	DM358
			£143	£143	£143
			¥22,418	¥22,418	¥22,418
DUBOIS, RAYMOND	1	1	$259	$259	$259
			DM437	DM437	DM437
			£161	£161	£161
			¥31,856	¥31,856	¥31,856
ELKHART	2	2	$241	$429	$335
			DM402	DM657	DM529
			£161	£276	£219
			¥24,747	¥42,444	¥33,596
ELKHART BAND INSTRUMENT CO.	1	0			
GRAFTON	13	12	$574	$2,141	$1,306
			DM810	DM3,262	DM2,003
			£360	£1,380	£815
			¥50,889	¥237,498	¥139,872
GUENOT	3	1	$130	$130	$130
			DM208	DM208	DM208
			£85	£85	£85
			¥13,181	¥13,181	¥13,181
HAWKES & SON	6	5	$130	$447	$279
			DM228	DM783	DM482
			£81	£276	£170
			¥15,774	¥54,082	¥34,947
HULLER, G.H.	1	1	$916	$916	$916
			DM1,524	DM1,524	DM1,524
			£552	£552	£552
			¥106,724	¥106,724	¥106,724
KEILWERTH, JULIUS	1	0			
KING MUSICAL INSTRUMENT CO.	1	0			

Maker	Items Bid	Sold	Selling Prices Low	High	Avg
LAFLEUR	7	2	$395 DM595 £242 ¥38,256	$533 DM766 £345 ¥54,075	$464 DM681 £294 ¥46,166
MARTIN BAND INSTRUMENT CO.	1	0			
OEHLER, OSKAR	2	0			
ORSI, ROMEO	1	0			
SAX, ADOLPHE	5	4	$484 DM774 £315 ¥48,959	$2,252 DM4,016 £1,380 ¥294,809	$1,162 DM1,953 £726 ¥138,982
SELMER	15	12	$336 DM494 £219 ¥35,650	$2,632 DM4,456 £1,610 ¥305,089	$1,369 DM2,214 £883 ¥151,210
SELMER, HENRI	5	2	$1,817 DM2,574 £1,150 ¥185,948	$2,260 DM3,473 £1,495 ¥241,031	$2,038 DM3,024 £1,323 ¥213,490
SELMER BUNDY	1	1	$150 DM266 £91 ¥20,769	$150 DM266 £91 ¥20,769	$150 DM266 £91 ¥20,769
STRASSER MARIGAUX	1	1	$161 DM287 £98 ¥22,366	$161 DM287 £98 ¥22,366	$161 DM287 £98 ¥22,366
STRASSER, MARIGAUX, LEMAIRE	1	1	$630 DM963 £403 ¥70,256	$630 DM963 £403 ¥70,256	$630 DM963 £403 ¥70,256
THIBOUVILLE-LAMY, J.	4	2	$155 DM270 £92 ¥19,721	$408 DM687 £253 ¥50,059	$281 DM478 £173 ¥34,890

SERPENT

Maker	Items Bid	Sold	Selling Prices Low	High	Avg
CRAMER, JOHN	1	0			
MONK, CHRISTOPHER	1	1	$1,009 DM1,759 £621 ¥122,244	$1,009 DM1,759 £621 ¥122,244	$1,009 DM1,759 £621 ¥122,244
PRETTY, F.	1	1	$2,922 DM4,108 £1,840 ¥260,783	$2,922 DM4,108 £1,840 ¥260,783	$2,922 DM4,108 £1,840 ¥260,783
PRETTY, F. (attributed to)	1	1	$2,056 DM3,584 £1,265 ¥249,015	$2,056 DM3,584 £1,265 ¥249,015	$2,056 DM3,584 £1,265 ¥249,015
PRETTY, ROBERT	1	1	$2,277 DM4,043 £1,380 ¥315,868	$2,277 DM4,043 £1,380 ¥315,868	$2,277 DM4,043 £1,380 ¥315,868

Maker	Items		Selling Prices		
	Bid	Sold	Low	High	Avg
WOLF & CO., ROBERT	1	1	$4,200	$4,200	$4,200
			DM6,983	DM6,983	DM6,983
			£2,530	£2,530	£2,530
			¥489,150	¥489,150	¥489,150

SOUSAPHONE

Maker	Bid	Sold	Low	High	Avg
BESSON	1	1	$805	$805	$805
			DM1,433	DM1,433	DM1,433
			£491	£491	£491
			¥111,831	¥111,831	¥111,831
DE PRINS GEBRUDER	1	0			

SPINET

Maker	Bid	Sold	Low	High	Avg
BARTON (ascribed to)	1	0			
BARTON, GEORGE	1	0			
DOLMETSCH, ARNOLD	1	1	$5,055	$5,055	$5,055
			DM7,857	DM7,857	DM7,857
			£3,220	£3,220	£3,220
			¥497,490	¥497,490	¥497,490
HITCHCOCK, THOMAS (YOUNGER)	2	1	$16,353	$16,353	$16,353
			DM23,168	DM23,168	DM23,168
			£10,350	£10,350	£10,350
			¥1,673,533	¥1,673,533	¥1,673,533
KEENE, STEPHEN	1	1	$50,554	$50,554	$50,554
			DM78,568	DM78,568	DM78,568
			£32,200	£32,200	£32,200
			¥4,974,900	¥4,974,900	¥4,974,900
SHEAN, CHRISTIAN	1	0			
SISON, BENJAMIN	1	0			
SMITH, WILLIAM	1	1	$17,395	$17,395	$17,395
			DM26,027	DM26,027	DM26,027
			£10,350	£10,350	£10,350
			¥1,940,418	¥1,940,418	¥1,940,418
STEWART, N.	1	1	$9,894	$9,894	$9,894
			DM14,619	DM14,619	DM14,619
			£6,440	£6,440	£6,440
			¥1,054,447	¥1,054,447	¥1,054,447
WEBER, FERDINAND	1	1	$23,315	$23,315	$23,315
			DM34,924	DM34,924	DM34,924
			£13,800	£13,800	£13,800
			¥2,594,952	¥2,594,952	¥2,594,952

STRING QUARTET

Maker	Bid	Sold	Low	High	Avg
CANDI, CESARE	1	1	$121,131	$121,131	$121,131
			DM181,619	DM181,619	DM181,619
			£74,100	£74,100	£74,100
			¥11,719,656	¥11,719,656	¥11,719,656
CANDI, ORESTE	1	1	$109,965	$109,965	$109,965
			DM154,112	DM154,112	DM154,112
			£69,000	£69,000	£69,000
			¥9,693,465	¥9,693,465	¥9,693,465

SUSAPHONE

Maker	Bid	Sold	Low	High	Avg
PAXMAN BROS.	1	0			

Maker	Items		Selling Prices		
	Bid	Sold	Low	High	Avg

SYMPHONIUM

WHEATSTONE, C.	2	2	$2,889	$3,651	$3,270
			DM4,490	DM5,610	DM5,050
			£1,840	£2,415	£2,128
			¥284,280	¥389,358	¥336,819

TAROGATO

| MOGYOROSSY, G.Y. | 1 | 0 | | | |

TIMPANI

HAWKES & SON	1	1	$505	$505	$505
			DM757	DM757	DM757
			£299	£299	£299
			¥56,224	¥56,224	¥56,224
HIGHAM, JOSEPH	1	0			

TIPLE

MARTIN & CO., C.F.	2	2	$259	$431	$345
			DM437	DM738	DM588
			£155	£255	£205
			¥31,568	¥53,553	¥42,560

TROMBONE

BESSON	3	3	$79	$106	$91
			DM122	DM156	DM138
			£52	£69	£59
			¥8,639	¥11,258	¥9,832
BOOSEY & CO.	1	1	$403	$403	$403
			DM680	DM680	DM680
			£242	£242	£242
			¥53,561	¥53,561	¥53,561
BOOSEY & HAWKES	6	6	$160	$585	$288
			DM270	DM976	DM465
			£98	£391	£188
			¥19,198	¥60,100	¥30,904
BURGER, JULIUS MAX	1	1	$428	$428	$428
			DM712	DM712	DM712
			£258	£258	£258
			¥49,882	¥49,882	¥49,882
COUESNON	1	1	$335	$335	$335
			DM460	DM460	DM460
			£207	£207	£207
			¥27,860	¥27,860	¥27,860
COURTOIS, ANTOINE (FILS)	3	1	$485	$485	$485
			DM726	DM726	DM726
			£287	£287	£287
			¥53,967	¥53,967	¥53,967
DE CART FRERES, FERDINAND & LOUIS	1	1	$840	$840	$840
			DM1,397	DM1,397	DM1,397
			£506	£506	£506
			¥97,830	¥97,830	¥97,830
FICKHERT, WILHELM	1	0			

Maker	Items		Selling Prices		
	Bid	*Sold*	*Low*	*High*	*Avg*
HAWKES & SON	2	2	$84	$119	$101
			DM147	DM183	DM165
			£52	£75	£63
			¥10,187	¥11,841	¥11,014
LAFLEUR	1	1	$54	$54	$54
			DM82	DM82	DM82
			£35	£35	£35
			¥5,306	¥5,306	¥5,306
RIVIERE & HAWKES	1	0			
ROUSSEAU, A.F.	1	1	$611	$611	$611
			DM1,016	DM1,016	DM1,016
			£368	£368	£368
			¥71,149	¥71,149	¥71,149
RUDALL, CARTE & CO.	1	1	$188	$188	$188
			DM318	DM318	DM318
			£115	£115	£115
			¥21,792	¥21,792	¥21,792
SENECAUT, PIERRE	1	1	$878	$878	$878
			DM1,460	DM1,460	DM1,460
			£529	£529	£529
			¥102,277	¥102,277	¥102,277
VAN ENGELEN, H.	1	0			
WHITE & CO., H.N.	1	0			
ZELENKA, ANTONIN	1	1	$420	$420	$420
			DM698	DM698	DM698
			£253	£253	£253
			¥48,915	¥48,915	¥48,915

TROMPE DE CHASSE

Maker	Items		Selling Prices		
GAUTROT (AINE)	1	1	$916	$916	$916
			DM1,524	DM1,524	DM1,524
			£552	£552	£552
			¥106,724	¥106,724	¥106,724

TRUMPET

Maker	Items		Selling Prices		
BESSON	2	2	$281	$387	$334
			DM432	DM594	DM513
			£184	£253	£219
			¥30,716	¥42,235	¥36,476
BESSON, FONTAINE	1	1	$56	$56	$56
			DM95	DM95	DM95
			£35	£35	£35
			¥6,538	¥6,538	¥6,538
BEUSCHER, PAUL	2	1	$34	$34	$34
			DM53	DM53	DM53
			£22	£22	£22
			¥3,398	¥3,398	¥3,398
BOOSEY & HAWKES	1	1	$62	$62	$62
			DM95	DM95	DM95
			£40	£40	£40
			¥6,719	¥6,719	¥6,719
COURTURIER, ERNST ALBERT	1	1	$748	$748	$748
			DM1,263	DM1,263	DM1,263
			£449	£449	£449
			¥99,470	¥99,470	¥99,470

Maker	Items Bid	Sold	Low	Selling Prices High	Avg
DE CLERCQ, L.	1	1	$535 DM889 £322 ¥62,255	$535 DM889 £322 ¥62,255	$535 DM889 £322 ¥62,255
HAWKES & SON	1	1	$74 DM102 £46 ¥6,191	$74 DM102 £46 ¥6,191	$74 DM102 £46 ¥6,191
HOLTON	1	1	$115 DM166 £73 ¥9,976	$115 DM166 £73 ¥9,976	$115 DM166 £73 ¥9,976
KERNER, IGNAZ	1	1	$4,333 DM6,734 £2,760 ¥426,420	$4,333 DM6,734 £2,760 ¥426,420	$4,333 DM6,734 £2,760 ¥426,420
KIEL, KRULL & BOLLMANN	1	1	$370 DM588 £242 ¥37,429	$370 DM588 £242 ¥37,429	$370 DM588 £242 ¥37,429
MAINZ, ALEXANDER	2	1	$1,173 DM1,911 £690 ¥138,055	$1,173 DM1,911 £690 ¥138,055	$1,173 DM1,911 £690 ¥138,055
OTTO, FRANZ	1	1	$878 DM1,460 £529 ¥102,277	$878 DM1,460 £529 ¥102,277	$878 DM1,460 £529 ¥102,277
SCHULLER, LUHABEN	1	1	$1,635 DM2,317 £1,035 ¥167,353	$1,635 DM2,317 £1,035 ¥167,353	$1,635 DM2,317 £1,035 ¥167,353
WOLF, AUGUST	1	0			

TUBA

Maker	Items Bid	Sold	Low	Selling Prices High	Avg
BESSON & CO.	2	1	$188 DM335 £115 ¥24,567	$188 DM335 £115 ¥24,567	$188 DM335 £115 ¥24,567
BOOSEY & HAWKES	5	5	$158 DM243 £104 ¥17,278	$668 DM1,026 £437 ¥72,951	$429 DM659 £281 ¥46,843
HALARI	1	0			
HAWKES & SON	2	1	$141 DM234 £94 ¥14,658	$141 DM234 £94 ¥14,658	$141 DM234 £94 ¥14,658
SUDRE, FRANCOIS	1	0			

UKULELE

Maker	Items Bid	Sold	Low	Selling Prices High	Avg
ALOHA	1	1	$288 DM512 £175 ¥39,940	$288 DM512 £175 ¥39,940	$288 DM512 £175 ¥39,940
GIBSON CO.	2	2	$179 DM274 £115 ¥17,685	$295 DM416 £185 ¥26,151	$237 DM345 £150 ¥21,918

Maker	Items Bid	Sold	Low	Selling Prices High	Avg
KUMALAE	2	2	$150 DM266 £91 ¥20,769	$201 DM344 £119 ¥24,991	$176 DM305 £105 ¥22,880
MARTIN, CHRISTIAN FREDERICK	1	1	$138 DM199 £88 ¥11,972	$138 DM199 £88 ¥11,972	$138 DM199 £88 ¥11,972
MARTIN & CO., C.F.	3	3	$374 DM632 £224 ¥45,598	$690 DM1,181 £408 ¥85,684	$566 DM931 £346 ¥64,488

UNION PIPE

Maker	Items Bid	Sold	Low	Selling Prices High	Avg
ROBERTSON, HUGH	1	1	$7,636 DM12,696 £4,600 ¥889,364	$7,636 DM12,696 £4,600 ¥889,364	$7,636 DM12,696 £4,600 ¥889,364

VIELLE

Maker	Items Bid	Sold	Low	High	Avg
COLSON	1	0			

VIHUELA

Maker	Items Bid	Sold	Low	Selling Prices High	Avg
DOLMETSCH, ARNOLD	2	1	$999 DM1,415 £632 ¥102,191	$999 DM1,415 £632 ¥102,191	$999 DM1,415 £632 ¥102,191

VIOL

Maker	Items Bid	Sold	Low	Selling Prices High	Avg
CAPICCHIONI, MARINO	1	0			
CARLETTI, NATALE	1	0			
CASTAGNERI, ANDREA	2	1	$3,109 DM4,656 £1,840 ¥345,994	$3,109 DM4,656 £1,840 ¥345,994	$3,109 DM4,656 £1,840 ¥345,994
CROSS, H. CHARLES (attributed to)	1	1	$839 DM884 £518 ¥64,064	$839 DM884 £518 ¥64,064	$839 DM884 £518 ¥64,064
EBERLE, JOHANN ULRICH (attributed to)	1	0			
FIORINI, RAFFAELE	1	0			
GAND, CHARLES FRANCOIS	1	1	$6,181 DM9,893 £4,025 ¥623,674	$6,181 DM9,893 £4,025 ¥623,674	$6,181 DM9,893 £4,025 ¥623,674
GAGLIANO, FERDINAND	1	1	$10,322 DM18,406 £6,325 ¥1,351,210	$10,322 DM18,406 £6,325 ¥1,351,210	$10,322 DM18,406 £6,325 ¥1,351,210
GOLDT, JACOBUS HEINRICH	1	1	$46,764 DM66,148 £29,900 ¥4,748,389	$46,764 DM66,148 £29,900 ¥4,748,389	$46,764 DM66,148 £29,900 ¥4,748,389
GUGGENBERGER, ANTON	1	0			

Maker	Items		Selling Prices		
	Bid	Sold	Low	High	Avg

JORDAN, HANS	1	1	$955 DM1,587 £575 ¥111,171	$955 DM1,587 £575 ¥111,171	$955 DM1,587 £575 ¥111,171
KESSLER, DIETRICH	1	1	$1,002 DM1,795 £598 ¥116,311	$1,002 DM1,795 £598 ¥116,311	$1,002 DM1,795 £598 ¥116,311
LEE, PERCY	1	0			
PIERRAY, CLAUDE	1	1	$38,157 DM54,060 £24,150 ¥3,904,910	$38,157 DM54,060 £24,150 ¥3,904,910	$38,157 DM54,060 £24,150 ¥3,904,910
ROTA, JOANNES (attributed to)	1	0			
ROY, KARL	1	0			
SEELOS, JOHANN	1	1	$36,271 DM60,306 £21,850 ¥4,224,479	$36,271 DM60,306 £21,850 ¥4,224,479	$36,271 DM60,306 £21,850 ¥4,224,479
SMITH, HENRY	1	0			
STEBER, ERNST	1	0			
UDALRICUS, JOHANNES (attributed to)	2	1	$822 DM1,433 £506 ¥99,606	$822 DM1,433 £506 ¥99,606	$822 DM1,433 £506 ¥99,606
UEBEL, WOLFGANG	1	1	$1,043 DM1,603 £690 ¥111,245	$1,060 DM1,696 £690 ¥106,915	$1,052 DM1,650 £690 ¥109,080
VISTOLI, LUIGI	1	1	$978 DM1,633 £652 ¥102,452	$978 DM1,633 £652 ¥102,452	$978 DM1,633 £652 ¥102,452

VIOL BOW

BRYANT (attributed to)	1	1	$634 DM895 £403 ¥63,850	$634 DM895 £403 ¥63,850	$634 DM895 £403 ¥63,850
TUBBS, JAMES (attributed to)	2	1	$809 DM1,449 £483 ¥93,944	$809 DM1,449 £483 ¥93,944	$809 DM1,449 £483 ¥93,944

VIOLA

ALBANELLI, FRANCO	2	0			
AMATI, ANTONIO & GIROLAMO	1	0			
AMATI, DOM NICOLO	1	0			
AMELOT	1	1	$3,220 DM5,381 £2,149 ¥337,488	$3,220 DM5,381 £2,149 ¥337,488	$3,220 DM5,381 £2,149 ¥337,488
ANTONIAZZI, ROMEO	2	0			

Maker	Items Bid	Sold	Selling Prices Low	High	Avg
ARASSI, ENZO	1	1	$5,175 DM7,788 £3,141 ¥578,462	$5,175 DM7,788 £3,141 ¥578,462	$5,175 DM7,788 £3,141 ¥578,462
ARCANGELI, ULDERICO	1	0			
AREZIO, CLAUDIO	4	1	$4,397 DM6,751 £2,875 ¥479,944	$4,397 DM6,751 £2,875 ¥479,944	$4,397 DM6,751 £2,875 ¥479,944
ARTMANN, GEORG VALENTIN	1	0			
ASCHAUER, LEO (workshop of)	1	1	$1,610 DM2,690 £1,074 ¥168,744	$1,610 DM2,690 £1,074 ¥168,744	$1,610 DM2,690 £1,074 ¥168,744
ASHFORD, LAWRENCE	1	0			
ATKINSON, WILLIAM	1	1	$2,383 DM3,339 £1,495 ¥210,025	$2,383 DM3,339 £1,495 ¥210,025	$2,383 DM3,339 £1,495 ¥210,025
AVERNA, GESUALDO	1	0			
AYERS, PAUL	1	0			
BADALASSI, PIERO (attributed to)	1	1	$3,319 DM4,622 £2,070 ¥280,584	$3,319 DM4,622 £2,070 ¥280,584	$3,319 DM4,622 £2,070 ¥280,584
BAILLY, PAUL	1	0			
BAILLY, PAUL (ascribed to)	1	1	$6,340 DM9,578 £4,255 ¥671,482	$6,340 DM9,578 £4,255 ¥671,482	$6,340 DM9,578 £4,255 ¥671,482
BAILLY, PAUL (attributed to)	1	0			
BAILLY, PAUL (workshop of)	1	1	$2,645 DM4,100 £1,693 ¥260,030	$2,645 DM4,100 £1,693 ¥260,030	$2,645 DM4,100 £1,693 ¥260,030
BANKS FAMILY (MEMBER OF)	2	0			
BARBIERI, BRUNO	9	2	$2,846 DM5,123 £1,725 ¥410,464	$5,175 DM7,483 £3,380 ¥523,969	$4,011 DM6,303 £2,553 ¥467,216
BARBIERI, ENZO	3	2	$2,990 DM4,724 £1,914 ¥298,701	$3,220 DM5,088 £2,061 ¥321,678	$3,105 DM4,906 £1,987 ¥310,190
BARBIERI, PAOLO	1	0			
BARGELLI, G.	2	0			
BARKER, J.	1	1	$1,585 DM2,337 £1,035 ¥169,088	$1,585 DM2,337 £1,035 ¥169,088	$1,585 DM2,337 £1,035 ¥169,088
BARNABETTI, GERONIMO	1	1	$2,131 DM3,592 £1,323 ¥261,674	$2,131 DM3,592 £1,323 ¥261,674	$2,131 DM3,592 £1,323 ¥261,674

Maker	Items		Selling Prices		
	Bid	Sold	Low	High	Avg
BARTON, JOHN	1	1	$1,817	$1,817	$1,817
			DM2,567	DM2,567	DM2,567
			£1,150	£1,150	£1,150
			¥162,193	¥162,193	¥162,193
BARTON, JOHN EDWARD	1	0			
BARZONI, FRANCOIS	5	5	$1,252	$2,944	$1,890
			DM1,924	DM4,981	DM3,094
			£828	£1,852	£1,208
			¥133,494	¥364,746	¥212,973
BASTON, VICTOR	2	1	$466	$466	$466
			DM491	DM491	DM491
			£288	£288	£288
			¥35,591	¥35,591	¥35,591
BEARD, JOHN	4	1	$920	$920	$920
			DM1,475	DM1,475	DM1,475
			£598	£598	£598
			¥93,064	¥93,064	¥93,064
BELLAROSA, VITTORIO	1	0			
BERNARDEL, GUSTAVE	2	0			
BERNARDEL, GUSTAVE ADOLPHE	1	0			
BERTHOLINI, NICOLAS	1	1	$1,700	$1,700	$1,700
			DM2,541	DM2,541	DM2,541
			£1,035	£1,035	£1,035
			¥163,558	¥163,558	¥163,558
BERTOLAZZI, GIACINTO	2	0			
BETTS	3	1	$15,159	$15,159	$15,159
			DM26,282	DM26,282	DM26,282
			£8,970	£8,970	£8,970
			¥1,892,670	¥1,892,670	¥1,892,670
BETTS, JOHN	7	4	$2,557	$11,064	$6,301
			DM3,595	DM15,406	DM9,009
			£1,610	£6,900	£3,970
			¥228,185	¥935,281	¥560,193
BEYER, GEORGE W.	2	1	$690	$690	$690
			DM1,166	DM1,166	DM1,166
			£414	£414	£414
			¥84,180	¥84,180	¥84,180
BICKLE, PAUL	1	1	$785	$785	$785
			DM1,368	DM1,368	DM1,368
			£483	£483	£483
			¥95,079	¥95,079	¥95,079
BIGNAMI, OTELLO	2	0			
BILLOLET, LOUIS	1	0			
BIRD, RICHMOND HENRY (attributed to)	1	0			
BISIACH, LEANDRO	1	0			
BISIACH, LEANDRO (JR.)	1	1	$6,854	$6,854	$6,854
			DM11,592	DM11,592	DM11,592
			£4,600	£4,600	£4,600
			¥726,800	¥726,800	¥726,800
BISSOLOTTI, TIZIANO	1	1	$1,955	$1,955	$1,955
			DM2,827	DM2,827	DM2,827
			£1,277	£1,277	£1,277
			¥197,944	¥197,944	¥197,944
BISSOLOTTI, VINCENZO	1	1	$2,070	$2,070	$2,070
			DM3,498	DM3,498	DM3,498
			£1,242	£1,242	£1,242
			¥275,455	¥275,455	¥275,455

Maker	Items		Selling Prices		
	Bid	Sold	Low	High	Avg
BLANCHARD, PAUL	3	2	$5,532	$15,771	$10,651
			DM7,703	DM26,681	DM17,192
			£3,450	£9,919	£6,684
			¥467,641	¥1,953,994	¥1,210,817
BLANCHI, ALBERTO	2	0			
BOIANCIUC, ROMAN	1	1	$1,387	$1,387	$1,387
			DM2,485	DM2,485	DM2,485
			£828	£828	£828
			¥161,046	¥161,046	¥161,046
BONNETT, CHRIS	1	0			
BOTTAJO, VINCENZO JOANNES	1	0			
BOUETTE, MAURICE	1	1	$3,353	$3,353	$3,353
			DM5,151	DM5,151	DM5,151
			£2,185	£2,185	£2,185
			¥367,056	¥367,056	¥367,056
BOULLANGIER, CHARLES	5	2	$7,951	$19,376	$13,663
			DM11,747	DM28,564	DM20,155
			£5,175	£12,650	£8,913
			¥847,323	¥2,066,631	¥1,456,977
BOULLANGIER, CHARLES (attributed to)	1	1	$3,129	$3,129	$3,129
			DM4,809	DM4,809	DM4,809
			£2,070	£2,070	£2,070
			¥333,736	¥333,736	¥333,736
BOURGUIGNON, MAURICE	1	0			
BOYES, ARNOLD	1	1	$1,708	$1,708	$1,708
			DM2,577	DM2,577	DM2,577
			£1,035	£1,035	£1,035
			¥193,545	¥193,545	¥193,545
BRETON BREVETE	2	2	$1,629	$4,073	$2,851
			DM2,613	DM6,533	DM4,573
			£1,058	£2,645	£1,852
			¥185,383	¥463,457	¥324,420
BRUCKNER, WILHELM	1	1	$2,294	$2,294	$2,294
			DM3,524	DM3,524	DM3,524
			£1,495	£1,495	£1,495
			¥251,144	¥251,144	¥251,144
BUCHANAN, DOUGLAS MORRICE	1	0			
BUCKMAN, GEORGE H.	1	1	$1,310	$1,310	$1,310
			DM2,347	DM2,347	DM2,347
			£782	£782	£782
			¥152,099	¥152,099	¥152,099
BUTHOD	3	1	$3,091	$3,091	$3,091
			DM5,557	DM5,557	DM5,557
			£1,840	£1,840	£1,840
			¥357,383	¥357,383	¥357,383
BUTHOD, CHARLES LOUIS	1	1	$3,271	$3,271	$3,271
			DM4,620	DM4,620	DM4,620
			£2,070	£2,070	£2,070
			¥291,947	¥291,947	¥291,947
CANDI, CESARE	1	0			
CAPELA, ANTONIO	10	5	$5,290	$7,475	$6,195
			DM7,639	DM12,633	DM9,549
			£3,370	£4,485	£3,940
			¥458,908	¥994,698	¥649,852
CAPELA, D.	1	0			
CAPELA, DOMINGOS	1	0			

Maker	Items Bid	Sold	Low	Selling Prices High	Avg
CAPELLI, ALDO	1	0			
CAPICCHIONI, MARINO	3	2	$25,816	$27,209	$26,513
			DM35,946	DM47,173	DM41,560
			£16,100	£16,100	£16,100
			¥2,182,323	¥3,397,100	¥2,789,711
CAPPELLARO, A.	1	0			
CARCASSI, LORENZO & TOMMASO	1	0			
CARESSA & FRANCAIS	2	1	$11,138	$11,138	$11,138
			DM16,826	DM16,826	DM16,826
			£7,475	£7,475	£7,475
			¥1,179,630	¥1,179,630	¥1,179,630
CARLETTI, CARLO	4	2	$9,718	$19,550	$14,634
			DM14,358	DM28,269	DM21,314
			£6,325	£12,770	£9,548
			¥1,035,618	¥1,979,438	¥1,507,528
CARLETTI, GENUZIO	3	1	$4,664	$4,664	$4,664
			DM8,087	DM8,087	DM8,087
			£2,760	£2,760	£2,760
			¥582,360	¥582,360	¥582,360
CASINI, SERAFINO	1	0			
CASTELLI, CESARE	2	0			
CASTELLO, PAOLO	1	1	$23,972	$23,972	$23,972
			DM33,379	DM33,379	DM33,379
			£14,950	£14,950	£14,950
			¥2,026,443	¥2,026,443	¥2,026,443
CAUSSIN FAMILY (MEMBER OF)	1	1	$3,992	$3,992	$3,992
			DM5,622	DM5,622	DM5,622
			£2,530	£2,530	£2,530
			¥408,170	¥408,170	¥408,170
CAVALAZZI, ANTONIO	1	0			
CAVALINI, DINO	1	0			
CAVANI, GIOVANNI	1	1	$23,000	$23,000	$23,000
			DM33,258	DM33,258	DM33,258
			£15,024	£15,024	£15,024
			¥2,328,750	¥2,328,750	¥2,328,750
CAVANI, V.	1	0			
CAVANI, VINCENZO	3	2	$3,450	$9,087	$6,268
			DM5,451	DM12,835	DM9,143
			£2,208	£5,750	£3,979
			¥344,655	¥810,963	¥577,809
CE, GIORGIO	1	1	$1,955	$1,955	$1,955
			DM2,827	DM2,827	DM2,827
			£1,277	£1,277	£1,277
			¥197,944	¥197,944	¥197,944
CERUTI, GIUSEPPE (ascribed to)	1	1	$14,610	$14,610	$14,610
			DM20,542	DM20,542	DM20,542
			£9,200	£9,200	£9,200
			¥1,298,792	¥1,298,792	¥1,298,792
CHADWICK, JOHN	1	1	$975	$975	$975
			DM1,378	DM1,378	DM1,378
			£621	£621	£621
			¥83,264	¥83,264	¥83,264
CHANOT, FRANCOIS	1	1	$2,300	$2,300	$2,300
			DM3,326	DM3,326	DM3,326
			£1,502	£1,502	£1,502
			¥232,875	¥232,875	¥232,875

Maker	Items		Selling Prices		
	Bid	Sold	Low	High	Avg
CHANOT, JOSEPH ANTHONY (attributed to)	1	1	$5,375 DM7,537 £3,450 ¥543,040	$5,375 DM7,537 £3,450 ¥543,040	$5,375 DM7,537 £3,450 ¥543,040
CHEVRIER (attributed to)	3	0			
CHEVRIER, ANDRE	1	0			
COCKER, LAWRENCE	6	3	$1,327 DM2,128 £863 ¥134,227	$2,922 DM4,108 £1,840 ¥259,758	$1,970 DM2,849 £1,246 ¥178,092
COLIN, JEAN BAPTISTE	1	1	$2,444 DM3,664 £1,495 ¥236,449	$2,444 DM3,664 £1,495 ¥236,449	$2,444 DM3,664 £1,495 ¥236,449
COLLENOT, LOUIS	1	1	$2,471 DM3,792 £1,610 ¥270,496	$2,471 DM3,792 £1,610 ¥270,496	$2,471 DM3,792 £1,610 ¥270,496
COLLIN-MEZIN, CH.J.B.	6	4	$1,291 DM1,797 £805 ¥109,116	$7,417 DM11,872 £4,830 ¥748,409	$5,066 DM7,610 £3,191 ¥478,099
COLLIN-MEZIN, CH.J.B. (attributed to)	1	1	$5,641 DM9,317 £3,450 ¥698,380	$5,641 DM9,317 £3,450 ¥698,380	$5,641 DM9,317 £3,450 ¥698,380
CONIA, STEFANO	4	1	$5,762 DM9,626 £3,450 ¥700,316	$5,762 DM9,626 £3,450 ¥700,316	$5,762 DM9,626 £3,450 ¥700,316
CONIA, STEFANO (workshop of)	1	1	$3,335 DM5,573 £2,225 ¥349,541	$3,335 DM5,573 £2,225 ¥349,541	$3,335 DM5,573 £2,225 ¥349,541
CONTAVALLI, PRIMO	1	1	$3,680 DM6,219 £2,208 ¥448,960	$3,680 DM6,219 £2,208 ¥448,960	$3,680 DM6,219 £2,208 ¥448,960
CONTIN, MARIO	1	1	$6,344 DM9,364 £4,140 ¥674,410	$6,344 DM9,364 £4,140 ¥674,410	$6,344 DM9,364 £4,140 ¥674,410
COOPER, HUGH W.	1	1	$2,582 DM3,595 £1,610 ¥218,232	$2,582 DM3,595 £1,610 ¥218,232	$2,582 DM3,595 £1,610 ¥218,232
COPELAND, JOSEPH N.	1	0			
COPLERE, JEAN	1	1	$1,495 DM2,527 £897 ¥182,390	$1,495 DM2,527 £897 ¥182,390	$1,495 DM2,527 £897 ¥182,390
COSTA, FELIX MORI (ascribed to)	1	1	$9,200 DM14,260 £5,888 ¥904,452	$9,200 DM14,260 £5,888 ¥904,452	$9,200 DM14,260 £5,888 ¥904,452

Maker	Items Bid	Sold	Low	Selling Prices High	Avg
CRASKE, GEORGE	8	7	$2,889 DM5,177 £1,725 ¥335,513	$10,592 DM14,893 £6,670 ¥1,020,217	$5,933 DM8,931 £3,733 ¥600,933
CRASKE, GEORGE (attributed to)	2	1	$4,748 DM6,676 £2,990 ¥423,773	$4,748 DM6,676 £2,990 ¥423,773	$4,748 DM6,676 £2,990 ¥423,773
CROSS, H. CHARLES	2	2	$466 DM491 £288 ¥35,591	$652 DM687 £403 ¥49,827	$559 DM589 £345 ¥42,709
CROSS, NATHANIEL	1	1	$30,441 DM48,732 £19,800 ¥3,081,355	$30,441 DM48,732 £19,800 ¥3,081,355	$30,441 DM48,732 £19,800 ¥3,081,355
CURLETTO, ANSELMO	1	0			
CURTIN, JOSEPH	1	0			
DA FIESOLE, GIANPIERO	1	1	$4,180 DM5,904 £2,645 ¥373,043	$4,180 DM5,904 £2,645 ¥373,043	$4,180 DM5,904 £2,645 ¥373,043
DA FIESOLE, MINO	1	0			
DE BARBIERI, PAOLO	1	0			
DE JONG, MATTHIJS	1	0			
DE SOUZA, COSMO	1	0			
DE VITOR, PIETRO PAOLO (attributed to)	1	1	$55,028 DM83,042 £33,350 ¥6,236,450	$55,028 DM83,042 £33,350 ¥6,236,450	$55,028 DM83,042 £33,350 ¥6,236,450
DEARLOVE, MARK WILLIAM	1	1	$3,651 DM5,610 £2,415 ¥389,358	$3,651 DM5,610 £2,415 ¥389,358	$3,651 DM5,610 £2,415 ¥389,358
DEBLAYE, ALBERT	1	1	$3,384 DM5,074 £2,070 ¥327,391	$3,384 DM5,074 £2,070 ¥327,391	$3,384 DM5,074 £2,070 ¥327,391
DELEPLANQUE, GERARD J.	1	1	$3,479 DM5,205 £2,070 ¥388,084	$3,479 DM5,205 £2,070 ¥388,084	$3,479 DM5,205 £2,070 ¥388,084
DERAZEY, JUSTIN	1	1	$8,460 DM12,684 £5,175 ¥818,478	$8,460 DM12,684 £5,175 ¥818,478	$8,460 DM12,684 £5,175 ¥818,478
DERAZEY, JUSTIN (workshop of)	1	1	$3,816 DM5,391 £2,415 ¥340,604	$3,816 DM5,391 £2,415 ¥340,604	$3,816 DM5,391 £2,415 ¥340,604
DEROUX, AUGUST S.	1	1	$8,625 DM13,627 £5,520 ¥861,637	$8,625 DM13,627 £5,520 ¥861,637	$8,625 DM13,627 £5,520 ¥861,637
DEROUX, SEBASTIEN AUGUSTE	1	1	$7,728 DM13,892 £4,600 ¥893,458	$7,728 DM13,892 £4,600 ¥893,458	$7,728 DM13,892 £4,600 ¥893,458

| Maker | Items | | Selling Prices | | |
	Bid	Sold	Low	High	Avg
DEVONEY, FRANK	1	1	$2,462	$2,462	$2,462
			DM3,781	DM3,781	DM3,781
			£1,610	£1,610	£1,610
			¥268,769	¥268,769	¥268,769
DICKSON, JOHN (attributed to)	1	1	$4,710	$4,710	$4,710
			DM6,652	DM6,652	DM6,652
			£2,990	£2,990	£2,990
			¥474,313	¥474,313	¥474,313
DIDIER, MARIUS	2	0			
DIEUDONNE, AMEDEE	1	0			
DIGIUNI, LUIGI	4	2	$1,837	$3,769	$2,803
			DM3,089	DM6,679	DM4,884
			£1,150	£2,314	£1,732
			¥225,472	¥459,569	¥342,521
DIX, DAVID	1	1	$918	$918	$918
			DM1,409	DM1,409	DM1,409
			£575	£575	£575
			¥90,014	¥90,014	¥90,014
DOBBS, HARRY	2	1	$1,011	$1,011	$1,011
			DM1,415	DM1,415	DM1,415
			£633	£633	£633
			¥85,522	¥85,522	¥85,522
DODD, THOMAS	1	1	$21,379	$21,379	$21,379
			DM37,065	DM37,065	DM37,065
			£12,650	£12,650	£12,650
			¥2,669,150	¥2,669,150	¥2,669,150
DODDS, EDWARD	1	1	$5,499	$5,499	$5,499
			DM8,820	DM8,820	DM8,820
			£3,571	£3,571	£3,571
			¥625,667	¥625,667	¥625,667
DOUBLEDAY, MILES	1	0			
DUKE, RICHARD	5	4	$1,944	$3,649	$3,037
			DM3,370	DM6,096	DM4,969
			£1,150	£2,185	£1,869
			¥247,101	¥443,533	¥355,024
DVORAK, JAN BAPTISTA	1	0			
EBERLE, EUGENE	1	1	$7,682	$7,682	$7,682
			DM12,834	DM12,834	DM12,834
			£4,600	£4,600	£4,600
			¥933,754	¥933,754	¥933,754
EDLER, ERNEST	1	0			
EMERY, JULIAN	4	0			
ENEL, CHARLES	1	0			
ERDESZ, OTTO ALEXANDER	1	0			
ERICIAN, MARTIN	1	0			
EVE, J.C.	1	1	$2,336	$2,336	$2,336
			DM4,053	DM4,053	DM4,053
			£1,380	£1,380	£1,380
			¥296,162	¥296,162	¥296,162
FABIANI, ANTONIO (ascribed to)	1	0			
FAGNOLA, ANNIBALE	2	0			
FAGNOLA, ANNIBALE (workshop of)	1	0			
FAIRFAX, ANNELEEN	1	0			
FANTIN, DOMENICO	1	0			

Maker	Items		Selling Prices		
	Bid	Sold	Low	High	Avg
FARLEY, CHARLES E.	1	1	$690 DM998 £451 ¥69,863	$690 DM998 £451 ¥69,863	$690 DM998 £451 ¥69,863
FAROTTI, CELESTE	1	1	$4,225 DM7,843 £2,530 ¥565,303	$4,225 DM7,843 £2,530 ¥565,303	$4,225 DM7,843 £2,530 ¥565,303
FAROTTO, CELESTE	5	4	$4,025 DM5,812 £2,564 ¥349,169	$6,613 DM10,235 £4,350 ¥764,635	$5,353 DM8,419 £3,339 ¥592,832
FENDT, BERNARD SIMON	2	0			
FENDT, BERNARD SIMON JR.	1	1	$13,800 DM23,322 £8,280 ¥1,683,600	$13,800 DM23,322 £8,280 ¥1,683,600	$13,800 DM23,322 £8,280 ¥1,683,600
FENG, BING HUI	1	0			
FERRONI, FERDINANDO	2	1	$2,645 DM4,470 £1,587 ¥322,690	$2,645 DM4,470 £1,587 ¥322,690	$2,645 DM4,470 £1,587 ¥322,690
FERWERDA, J.D.	1	1	$4,597 DM7,359 £2,990 ¥465,316	$4,597 DM7,359 £2,990 ¥465,316	$4,597 DM7,359 £2,990 ¥465,316
FICHTL, JOHANN ULRICH	1	1	$1,910 DM3,080 £1,109 ¥224,840	$1,910 DM3,080 £1,109 ¥224,840	$1,910 DM3,080 £1,109 ¥224,840
FIORINI, RAFFAELE	1	1	$59,606 DM87,988 £38,900 ¥6,336,849	$59,606 DM87,988 £38,900 ¥6,336,849	$59,606 DM87,988 £38,900 ¥6,336,849
FIRATI, PIETRO (ascribed to)	1	1	$6,325 DM9,993 £4,048 ¥631,868	$6,325 DM9,993 £4,048 ¥631,868	$6,325 DM9,993 £4,048 ¥631,868
FLETA, IGNACIO	1	1	$5,693 DM10,247 £3,450 ¥820,928	$5,693 DM10,247 £3,450 ¥820,928	$5,693 DM10,247 £3,450 ¥820,928
FLEURY, BENOIT	2	1	$15,902 DM23,495 £10,350 ¥1,694,647	$15,902 DM23,495 £10,350 ¥1,694,647	$15,902 DM23,495 £10,350 ¥1,694,647
FLORENTIN, N.	1	1	$1,380 DM2,077 £838 ¥154,256	$1,380 DM2,077 £838 ¥154,256	$1,380 DM2,077 £838 ¥154,256
FONTANA, ALFREDO	1	1	$2,126 DM3,181 £1,265 ¥237,162	$2,126 DM3,181 £1,265 ¥237,162	$2,126 DM3,181 £1,265 ¥237,162
FORSTER	3	1	$4,225 DM7,843 £2,530 ¥565,303	$4,225 DM7,843 £2,530 ¥565,303	$4,225 DM7,843 £2,530 ¥565,303

Maker	Items Bid	Items Sold	Selling Prices Low	Selling Prices High	Selling Prices Avg
FORSTER, WILLIAM	7	5	$3,208	$18,453	$7,287
			DM4,761	DM25,688	DM10,722
			£2,070	£11,500	£4,544
			¥347,305	¥1,556,824	¥706,250
FORSTER, WILLIAM (workshop of)	1	1	$3,529	$3,529	$3,529
			DM5,422	DM5,422	DM5,422
			£2,300	£2,300	£2,300
			¥386,375	¥386,375	¥386,375
FORSTER, WILLIAM (II)	7	3	$5,410	$12,650	$9,649
			DM9,728	DM21,379	DM15,480
			£3,220	£7,590	£5,903
			¥625,421	¥1,543,300	¥1,093,970
FOSCHI, GIORGIO	1	0			
FOSCHINI, GIOVANNI	3	1	$3,887	$3,887	$3,887
			DM6,739	DM6,739	DM6,739
			£2,300	£2,300	£2,300
			¥494,201	¥494,201	¥494,201
FUERST, GEORG	1	1	$20,679	$20,679	$20,679
			DM31,005	DM31,005	DM31,005
			£12,650	£12,650	£12,650
			¥2,000,724	¥2,000,724	¥2,000,724
GABRIELLI, GIOVANNI BATTISTA	1	1	$46,000	$46,000	$46,000
			DM66,516	DM66,516	DM66,516
			£30,047	£30,047	£30,047
			¥4,657,500	¥4,657,500	¥4,657,500
GABRIELLI, GIOVANNI BATTISTA (workshop of)	1	1	$30,360	$30,360	$30,360
			DM45,816	DM45,816	DM45,816
			£18,400	£18,400	£18,400
			¥3,440,800	¥3,440,800	¥3,440,800
GADDA, GAETANO	1	1	$14,539	$14,539	$14,539
			DM20,535	DM20,535	DM20,535
			£9,200	£9,200	£9,200
			¥1,297,540	¥1,297,540	¥1,297,540
GADDA, MARIO	1	1	$7,166	$7,166	$7,166
			DM10,050	DM10,050	DM10,050
			£4,600	£4,600	£4,600
			¥724,054	¥724,054	¥724,054
GAGLIANO, ANTONIO	1	0			
GAGLIANO FAMILY (MEMBER OF)	1	0			
GALLA, ANTON	1	1	$4,832	$4,832	$4,832
			DM7,230	DM7,230	DM7,230
			£2,875	£2,875	£2,875
			¥539,005	¥539,005	¥539,005
GALLACHER	1	1	$930	$930	$930
			DM1,489	DM1,489	DM1,489
			£605	£605	£605
			¥94,153	¥94,153	¥94,153
GAND & BERNARDEL	3	1	$18,288	$18,288	$18,288
			DM33,835	DM33,835	DM33,835
			£10,925	£10,925	£10,925
			¥2,437,258	¥2,437,258	¥2,437,258
GARDINI, ATHOS	1	0			
GARIMBERTI, F.	1	0			
GARTNER, EUGEN	1	1	$7,360	$7,360	$7,360
			DM12,451	DM12,451	DM12,451
			£4,629	£4,629	£4,629
			¥911,864	¥911,864	¥911,864

Maker	Items		Selling Prices		
	Bid	Sold	Low	High	Avg
GAVINIES, FRANCOIS	1	1	$13,739	$13,739	$13,739
			DM20,254	DM20,254	DM20,254
			£8,970	£8,970	£8,970
			¥1,465,429	¥1,465,429	¥1,465,429
GEISSENHOF, FRANZ	1	1	$14,719	$14,719	$14,719
			DM24,903	DM24,903	DM24,903
			£9,258	£9,258	£9,258
			¥1,823,728	¥1,823,728	¥1,823,728
GIANOTTI, ALFREDO	3	2	$6,325	$7,431	$6,878
			DM10,822	DM11,916	DM11,369
			£3,741	£4,830	£4,286
			¥751,669	¥785,439	¥768,554
GILBERT, JEFFREY J.	3	2	$1,371	$2,867	$2,119
			DM2,318	DM4,020	DM3,169
			£920	£1,840	£1,380
			¥145,360	¥289,622	¥217,491
GILKES, SAMUEL	1	1	$20,779	$20,779	$20,779
			DM31,053	DM31,053	DM31,053
			£12,650	£12,650	£12,650
			¥1,999,042	¥1,999,042	¥1,999,042
GILKES, SAMUEL (attributed to)	1	1	$1,363	$1,363	$1,363
			DM2,364	DM2,364	DM2,364
			£805	£805	£805
			¥172,761	¥172,761	¥172,761
GIRAUD, FRANCO	1	1	$1,388	$1,388	$1,388
			DM2,357	DM2,357	DM2,357
			£935	£935	£935
			¥147,532	¥147,532	¥147,532
GIULIANI, R.G.	1	0			
GLAESEL, LUDWIG	1	1	$1,725	$1,725	$1,725
			DM2,725	DM2,725	DM2,725
			£1,104	£1,104	£1,104
			¥172,327	¥172,327	¥172,327
GLOOR, ADOLF	2	1	$860	$860	$860
			DM1,499	DM1,499	DM1,499
			£529	£529	£529
			¥104,134	¥104,134	¥104,134
GOFTON, ROBERT	1	0			
GOLDSMITH, WILLIAM	1	1	$2,820	$2,820	$2,820
			DM4,228	DM4,228	DM4,228
			£1,725	£1,725	£1,725
			¥272,826	¥272,826	¥272,826
GORRIE, ANDREW	1	1	$951	$951	$951
			DM1,350	DM1,350	DM1,350
			£598	£598	£598
			¥88,295	¥88,295	¥88,295
GOTTI, A.	1	0			
GOTTI, ANSELMO	1	1	$4,543	$4,543	$4,543
			DM6,417	DM6,417	DM6,417
			£2,875	£2,875	£2,875
			¥405,481	¥405,481	¥405,481
GOTZ, CONRAD	3	2	$658	$848	$753
			DM935	DM1,519	DM1,227
			£414	£506	£460
			¥61,127	¥98,417	¥79,772
GOULDING	2	0			

Maker	Items		Selling Prices		
	Bid	Sold	Low	High	Avg
GOUVERNEL, PIERRE	2	1	$2,643 DM3,902 £1,725 ¥281,004	$2,643 DM3,902 £1,725 ¥281,004	$2,643 DM3,902 £1,725 ¥281,004
GRABNER, KARL HEINZ JOACHIM	1	1	$575 DM831 £376 ¥58,219	$575 DM831 £376 ¥58,219	$575 DM831 £376 ¥58,219
GRANCINO, FRANCESCO & GIOVANNI	1	1	$166,135 DM280,980 £111,500 ¥17,617,000	$166,135 DM280,980 £111,500 ¥17,617,000	$166,135 DM280,980 £111,500 ¥17,617,000
GRANDJON, JULES (FILS)	1	1	$4,383 DM6,163 £2,760 ¥389,637	$4,383 DM6,163 £2,760 ¥389,637	$4,383 DM6,163 £2,760 ¥389,637
GRUBAUGH, JOSEPH & SIGRUN SEIFERT	1	1	$6,325 DM9,993 £4,048 ¥631,868	$6,325 DM9,993 £4,048 ¥631,868	$6,325 DM9,993 £4,048 ¥631,868
GUADAGNINI, GIUSEPPE (ascribed to)	1	0			
GUADAGNINI, PAOLO	1	1	$36,800 DM58,144 £23,552 ¥3,676,320	$36,800 DM58,144 £23,552 ¥3,676,320	$36,800 DM58,144 £23,552 ¥3,676,320
GUASTALLA, DANTE (attributed to)	2	0			
GUERRA, ALBERTO	1	1	$6,762 DM12,160 £4,025 ¥781,776	$6,762 DM12,160 £4,025 ¥781,776	$6,762 DM12,160 £4,025 ¥781,776
GUERRA, ALBERTO (ascribed to)	3	2	$1,495 DM2,606 £920 ¥181,102	$1,495 DM2,606 £920 ¥181,102	$1,495 DM2,606 £920 ¥181,102
GUERSAN, LOUIS	1	1	$17,265 DM24,386 £10,925 ¥1,540,829	$17,265 DM24,386 £10,925 ¥1,540,829	$17,265 DM24,386 £10,925 ¥1,540,829
GUICCIARDI, GIANCARLO	2	1	$12,681 DM17,910 £8,050 ¥1,276,996	$12,681 DM17,910 £8,050 ¥1,276,996	$12,681 DM17,910 £8,050 ¥1,276,996
HAAHTI, NICOLIEN	2	1	$3,887 DM5,743 £2,530 ¥414,247	$3,887 DM5,743 £2,530 ¥414,247	$3,887 DM5,743 £2,530 ¥414,247
HALLETT, L.C.	1	1	$863 DM1,539 £529 ¥113,010	$863 DM1,539 £529 ¥113,010	$863 DM1,539 £529 ¥113,010
HALLIDAY, R.L.	1	1	$1,091 DM1,674 £713 ¥119,026	$1,091 DM1,674 £713 ¥119,026	$1,091 DM1,674 £713 ¥119,026
HAMMOND, JOHN	2	0			

| Maker | Items | | Selling Prices | | |
---	Bid	Sold	Low	High	Avg
HARRILD, PAUL V.	4	1	$1,478 DM2,271 £978 ¥157,597	$1,478 DM2,271 £978 ¥157,597	$1,478 DM2,271 £978 ¥157,597
HARRIS, CHARLES	4	2	$3,693 DM6,402 £2,185 ¥469,491	$4,225 DM7,059 £2,530 ¥513,565	$3,959 DM6,730 £2,358 ¥491,528
HARRIS, RICHARD	1	0			
HART, J. (ascribed to)	1	1	$3,427 DM5,796 £2,300 ¥363,400	$3,427 DM5,796 £2,300 ¥363,400	$3,427 DM5,796 £2,300 ¥363,400
HAWKES & SON	1	1	$2,950 DM4,108 £1,840 ¥249,408	$2,950 DM4,108 £1,840 ¥249,408	$2,950 DM4,108 £1,840 ¥249,408
HEBERLEIN	1	1	$2,875 DM4,327 £1,745 ¥321,368	$2,875 DM4,327 £1,745 ¥321,368	$2,875 DM4,327 £1,745 ¥321,368
HEBERLEIN, HEINRICH TH. (JR.)	1	1	$2,881 DM4,813 £1,725 ¥350,158	$2,881 DM4,813 £1,725 ¥350,158	$2,881 DM4,813 £1,725 ¥350,158
HEESOM, EDWARD	1	1	$5,141 DM8,694 £3,450 ¥545,100	$5,141 DM8,694 £3,450 ¥545,100	$5,141 DM8,694 £3,450 ¥545,100
HEL, JOSEPH	1	0			
HESKETH, THOMAS EARLE	2	1	$10,060 DM14,278 £6,325 ¥933,886	$10,060 DM14,278 £6,325 ¥933,886	$10,060 DM14,278 £6,325 ¥933,886
HIGHFIELD	1	0			
HIGHFIELD, IAN	1	1	$1,892 DM3,202 £1,190 ¥234,479	$1,892 DM3,202 £1,190 ¥234,479	$1,892 DM3,202 £1,190 ¥234,479
HILL, HENRY LOCKEY (attributed to)	1	1	$3,434 DM5,743 £2,300 ¥364,939	$3,434 DM5,743 £2,300 ¥364,939	$3,434 DM5,743 £2,300 ¥364,939
HILL, JOSEPH	11	7	$5,036 DM7,124 £3,220 ¥511,365	$23,101 DM42,739 £13,800 ¥3,078,642	$10,588 DM18,170 £6,468 ¥1,280,000
HILL, JOSEPH (attributed to)	3	1	$16,373 DM29,335 £9,775 ¥1,901,238	$16,373 DM29,335 £9,775 ¥1,901,238	$16,373 DM29,335 £9,775 ¥1,901,238
HILL, JOSEPH & SONS	1	1	$3,887 DM5,743 £2,530 ¥414,247	$3,887 DM5,743 £2,530 ¥414,247	$3,887 DM5,743 £2,530 ¥414,247

Maker	Items		Selling Prices		
	Bid	Sold	Low	High	Avg
HILL, LOCKEY	1	1	$3,850	$3,850	$3,850
			DM7,123	DM7,123	DM7,123
			£2,300	£2,300	£2,300
			¥513,107	¥513,107	¥513,107
HILL, WILLIAM	2	1	$6,574	$6,574	$6,574
			DM9,244	DM9,244	DM9,244
			£4,140	£4,140	£4,140
			¥586,762	¥586,762	¥586,762
HILL, W.E. & SONS	2	0			
HOFNER, KARL	1	0			
HOING, CLIFFORD A.	2	1	$5,081	$5,081	$5,081
			DM7,155	DM7,155	DM7,155
			£3,220	£3,220	£3,220
			¥519,489	¥519,489	¥519,489
HOLLY, FLOYD	2	1	$895	$895	$895
			DM1,265	DM1,265	DM1,265
			£562	£562	£562
			¥79,443	¥79,443	¥79,443
HOLT, ROBERT	1	1	$230	$230	$230
			DM333	DM333	DM333
			£150	£150	£150
			¥23,288	¥23,288	¥23,288
HORLEIN, KARL ADAM	1	0			
HOWE, ROBERT	1	1	$963	$963	$963
			DM1,781	DM1,781	DM1,781
			£575	£575	£575
			¥128,277	¥128,277	¥128,277
HUBER, JOHANN GEORG	1	1	$9,373	$9,373	$9,373
			DM16,215	DM16,215	DM16,215
			£5,750	£5,750	£5,750
			¥1,069,500	¥1,069,500	¥1,069,500
HUNGER, C.F.	2	1	$2,537	$2,537	$2,537
			DM4,061	DM4,061	DM4,061
			£1,650	£1,650	£1,650
			¥256,780	¥256,780	¥256,780
HUSSON	1	0			
HUSSON FAMILY (MEMBER OF)	1	1	$8,642	$8,642	$8,642
			DM14,438	DM14,438	DM14,438
			£5,175	£5,175	£5,175
			¥1,050,473	¥1,050,473	¥1,050,473
ISTAVAN, KONYA	1	1	$1,353	$1,353	$1,353
			DM2,166	DM2,166	DM2,166
			£880	£880	£880
			¥136,949	¥136,949	¥136,949
JACQUEMIN, RENE	2	0			
JACQUOT, CHARLES	1	1	$11,500	$11,500	$11,500
			DM18,170	DM18,170	DM18,170
			£7,360	£7,360	£7,360
			¥1,148,850	¥1,148,850	¥1,148,850
JACQUOT, CHARLES (attributed to)	2	1	$5,435	$5,435	$5,435
			DM7,676	DM7,676	DM7,676
			£3,450	£3,450	£3,450
			¥547,284	¥547,284	¥547,284
JACQUOT, PIERRE CHARLES (attributed to)	3	0			

Maker	Items		Selling Prices		
	Bid	Sold	Low	High	Avg
JAIS, ANTON	2	1	$1,610	$1,610	$1,610
			DM2,924	DM2,924	DM2,924
			£985	£985	£985
			¥199,930	¥199,930	¥199,930
JAIS, JOHANN	1	0			
JAURA, WILHELM THOMAS	1	0			
JOHNSON, MOIRA	1	1	$1,134	$1,134	$1,134
			DM1,610	DM1,610	DM1,610
			£713	£713	£713
			¥105,274	¥105,274	¥105,274
JOHNSON, W.A.	1	1	$1,342	$1,342	$1,342
			DM2,052	DM2,052	DM2,052
			£863	£863	£863
			¥132,639	¥132,639	¥132,639
JOMBAR, PAUL	1	0			
JUZEK, JOHN (workshop of)	1	1	$920	$920	$920
			DM1,330	DM1,330	DM1,330
			£601	£601	£601
			¥93,150	¥93,150	¥93,150
KAUL, PAUL	1	1	$6,914	$6,914	$6,914
			DM12,834	DM12,834	DM12,834
			£4,140	£4,140	£4,140
			¥925,042	¥925,042	¥925,042
KENNEDY, THOMAS	3	1	$3,890	$3,890	$3,890
			DM6,227	DM6,227	DM6,227
			£2,530	£2,530	£2,530
			¥393,729	¥393,729	¥393,729
KENNEDY, THOMAS (attributed to)	1	1	$3,887	$3,887	$3,887
			DM5,743	DM5,743	DM5,743
			£2,530	£2,530	£2,530
			¥414,247	¥414,247	¥414,247
KLOTZ, AEGIDIUS (II)	1	1	$4,801	$4,801	$4,801
			DM8,021	DM8,021	DM8,021
			£2,875	£2,875	£2,875
			¥583,596	¥583,596	¥583,596
KLOTZ, JOSEPH (attributed to)	2	1	$4,609	$4,609	$4,609
			DM7,700	DM7,700	DM7,700
			£2,760	£2,760	£2,760
			¥560,252	¥560,252	¥560,252
KOBERLING, JOHANN	1	0			
KONYA, LAJOS	2	1	$978	$978	$978
			DM1,673	DM1,673	DM1,673
			£578	£578	£578
			¥121,386	¥121,386	¥121,386
KRAUSS, KARL	1	1	$684	$684	$684
			DM1,045	DM1,045	DM1,045
			£437	£437	£437
			¥76,278	¥76,278	¥76,278
KUCZER, JOHN T.	1	1	$2,185	$2,185	$2,185
			DM3,155	DM3,155	DM3,155
			£1,392	£1,392	£1,392
			¥189,549	¥189,549	¥189,549
KUDANOWSKI, JAN	2	1	$2,744	$2,744	$2,744
			DM3,894	DM3,894	DM3,894
			£1,725	£1,725	£1,725
			¥254,696	¥254,696	¥254,696

Maker	Items		Selling Prices		
	Bid	Sold	Low	High	Avg
KUSTER, FREDERICK	1	1	$920	$920	$920
			DM1,574	DM1,574	DM1,574
			£544	£544	£544
			¥114,246	¥114,246	¥114,246
LABERTE, MARC	5	3	$489	$6,958	$2,712
			DM870	DM10,411	DM4,170
			£298	£4,140	£1,617
			¥67,897	¥776,167	¥311,940
LABERTE, MARC (workshop of)	3	3	$1,265	$1,725	$1,418
			DM1,961	DM2,596	DM2,224
			£810	£1,047	£900
			¥124,362	¥192,821	¥149,922
LABERTE-HUMBERT BROS.	2	1	$3,707	$3,707	$3,707
			DM5,689	DM5,689	DM5,689
			£2,415	£2,415	£2,415
			¥405,744	¥405,744	¥405,744
LABRAM, LEONARD	1	1	$1,502	$1,502	$1,502
			DM2,692	DM2,692	DM2,692
			£897	£897	£897
			¥174,467	¥174,467	¥174,467
LAMBERTON, JAMES	1	0			
LANARO, ALOISIUS	2	0			
LANARO, UMBERTO	5	2	$3,850	$4,355	$4,103
			DM6,133	DM7,123	DM6,628
			£2,300	£2,760	£2,530
			¥445,276	¥513,107	¥479,192
LANDOLFI, CARLO FERDINANDO	1	0			
LANGONET, ALFRED CHARLES	3	0			
LANT, ERNEST FRANCIS	2	1	$1,118	$1,118	$1,118
			DM1,178	DM1,178	DM1,178
			£690	£690	£690
			¥85,419	¥85,419	¥85,419
LASSI, ENZO (attributed to)	2	1	$3,386	$3,386	$3,386
			DM5,025	DM5,025	DM5,025
			£2,185	£2,185	£2,185
			¥366,599	¥366,599	¥366,599
LAURENT, EMILE	2	0			
LECLERC, JOSEPH NICOLAS	1	1	$10,592	$10,592	$10,592
			DM16,253	DM16,253	DM16,253
			£6,900	£6,900	£6,900
			¥1,159,269	¥1,159,269	¥1,159,269
LEE, PERCY	3	2	$5,654	$6,580	$6,117
			DM8,354	DM9,865	DM9,109
			£3,680	£4,025	£3,853
			¥602,541	¥636,594	¥619,568
LEONI, GUIDO	2	0			
LEROUX, PIERRE	1	1	$4,243	$4,243	$4,243
			DM6,793	DM6,793	DM6,793
			£2,760	£2,760	£2,760
			¥429,522	¥429,522	¥429,522
LODGE, JOHN	1	1	$576	$576	$576
			DM963	DM963	DM963
			£345	£345	£345
			¥70,032	¥70,032	¥70,032

Maker	Items		Selling Prices		
	Bid	Sold	Low	High	Avg
LONGMAN & BRODERIP	1	1	$2,037	$2,037	$2,037
			DM3,267	DM3,267	DM3,267
			£1,323	£1,323	£1,323
			¥231,728	¥231,728	¥231,728
LOWENDALL	1	1	$1,427	$1,427	$1,427
			DM2,025	DM2,025	DM2,025
			£897	£897	£897
			¥132,442	¥132,442	¥132,442
LUCA, IOAN	1	1	$963	$963	$963
			DM1,726	DM1,726	DM1,726
			£575	£575	£575
			¥111,838	¥111,838	¥111,838
LUCCI, GIUSEPPE	4	1	$8,698	$8,698	$8,698
			DM13,014	DM13,014	DM13,014
			£5,175	£5,175	£5,175
			¥970,209	¥970,209	¥970,209
LUFF, WILLIAM H.	3	1	$16,390	$16,390	$16,390
			DM27,720	DM27,720	DM27,720
			£11,000	£11,000	£11,000
			¥1,738,000	¥1,738,000	¥1,738,000
MAAG, HENRY	2	1	$219	$219	$219
			DM389	DM389	DM389
			£133	£133	£133
			¥30,354	¥30,354	¥30,354
MACHOLD, OSKAR	1	1	$1,236	$1,236	$1,236
			DM1,896	DM1,896	DM1,896
			£805	£805	£805
			¥135,248	¥135,248	¥135,248
MAGNIERE, GABRIEL	1	1	$3,870	$3,870	$3,870
			DM6,206	DM6,206	DM6,206
			£2,513	£2,513	£2,513
			¥440,284	¥440,284	¥440,284
MALLER, ANTON	1	0			
MANGIACASALE, SALVATORE	1	0			
MANTEGAZZA, PIETRO GIOVANNI	1	1	$85,170	$85,170	$85,170
			DM158,100	DM158,100	DM158,100
			£51,000	£51,000	£51,000
			¥11,395,440	¥11,395,440	¥11,395,440
MARAVIGLIA, FRANCESCO	1	1	$4,943	$4,943	$4,943
			DM7,585	DM7,585	DM7,585
			£3,220	£3,220	£3,220
			¥540,992	¥540,992	¥540,992
MARAVIGLIA, GUIDO	2	0			
MARCHETTI, ABBONDIO (attributed to)	1	0			
MARCHETTI, ENRICO	1	1	$21,379	$21,379	$21,379
			DM37,065	DM37,065	DM37,065
			£12,650	£12,650	£12,650
			¥2,669,150	¥2,669,150	¥2,669,150
MARTINI, ORESTE	2	2	$4,252	$9,713	$6,982
			DM6,362	DM15,546	DM10,954
			£2,530	£6,325	£4,428
			¥474,324	¥980,059	¥727,192
MASTERS, JOHN	1	1	$1,725	$1,725	$1,725
			DM2,951	DM2,951	DM2,951
			£1,020	£1,020	£1,020
			¥214,211	¥214,211	¥214,211
MAUCOTEL & DESCHAMPS	1	0			

Maker	Items		Selling Prices		
	Bid	Sold	Low	High	Avg
MAUSSIELL, LEONHARD	3	0			
MELLONI, SETTIMO	1	0			
MENNESSON, EMILE	1	0			
MERRETT, H.W.	2	1	$542	$542	$542
			DM766	DM766	DM766
			£345	£345	£345
			¥46,258	¥46,258	¥46,258
MEYER, MAGNUS ANDREAS	1	1	$3,995	$3,995	$3,995
			DM6,759	DM6,759	DM6,759
			£2,513	£2,513	£2,513
			¥495,012	¥495,012	¥495,012
MILNES, JOHN	1	0			
MINO DA FIESOLE	1	0			
MOCHALOV, ALEXANDER	1	1	$3,266	$3,266	$3,266
			DM4,600	DM4,600	DM4,600
			£2,070	£2,070	£2,070
			¥333,957	¥333,957	¥333,957
MOLLER, MAX (II)	1	1	$12,721	$12,721	$12,721
			DM17,968	DM17,968	DM17,968
			£8,050	£8,050	£8,050
			¥1,135,348	¥1,135,348	¥1,135,348
MONK, JOHN KING	1	0			
MONNIG, KURT	1	1	$4,658	$4,658	$4,658
			DM6,532	DM6,532	DM6,532
			£2,990	£2,990	£2,990
			¥470,635	¥470,635	¥470,635
MORASSI, GIOVANNI BATTISTA	1	0			
MORETTI, EGIDO	1	0			
MORIZOT, RENE	1	1	$1,212	$1,212	$1,212
			DM2,101	DM2,101	DM2,101
			£717	£717	£717
			¥151,287	¥151,287	¥151,287
MOUGENOT, LEON	1	1	$2,570	$2,570	$2,570
			DM3,883	DM3,883	DM3,883
			£1,725	£1,725	£1,725
			¥272,222	¥272,222	¥272,222
MOUGENOT, LEON (workshop of)	1	1	$1,725	$1,725	$1,725
			DM3,071	DM3,071	DM3,071
			£1,035	£1,035	£1,035
			¥229,390	¥229,390	¥229,390
MOZZANI, LUIGI	1	1	$8,460	$8,460	$8,460
			DM12,684	DM12,684	DM12,684
			£5,175	£5,175	£5,175
			¥818,478	¥818,478	¥818,478
MUELLER, KARL	1	1	$345	$345	$345
			DM596	DM596	DM596
			£213	£213	£213
			¥43,724	¥43,724	¥43,724
NEEDHAM, HOWARD	1	1	$2,070	$2,070	$2,070
			DM2,993	DM2,993	DM2,993
			£1,352	£1,352	£1,352
			¥209,588	¥209,588	¥209,588
NEUNER, LUDWIG	1	0			
NEUNER & HORNSTEINER	6	5	$1,265	$4,626	$2,646
			DM1,829	DM7,827	DM4,513
			£826	£2,910	£1,617
			¥128,081	¥573,172	¥319,801

Maker	Items		Selling Prices		
	Bid	Sold	Low	High	Avg
NEUNER & HORNSTEINER (workshop of)	2	2	$633	$1,610	$1,121
			DM952	DM2,866	DM1,909
			£384	£966	£675
			¥70,701	¥214,098	¥142,399
NIGGEL, SYMPERT	1	1	$4,428	$4,428	$4,428
			DM8,192	DM8,192	DM8,192
			£2,645	£2,645	£2,645
			¥590,073	¥590,073	¥590,073
NOLLI, FRANCO	2	1	$1,500	$1,500	$1,500
			DM2,301	DM2,301	DM2,301
			£977	£977	£977
			¥164,146	¥164,146	¥164,146
NORMAN, BARAK	1	1	$1,692	$1,692	$1,692
			DM2,537	DM2,537	DM2,537
			£1,035	£1,035	£1,035
			¥163,696	¥163,696	¥163,696
NOVELLI, NATALE	1	0			
NOWAK, STEFFEN	1	1	$3,688	$3,688	$3,688
			DM5,135	DM5,135	DM5,135
			£2,300	£2,300	£2,300
			¥311,760	¥311,760	¥311,760
NUPIERI, GIUSEPPE	7	5	$1,030	$1,629	$1,287
			DM1,782	DM2,783	DM2,209
			£621	£1,058	£799
			¥117,552	¥204,043	¥154,771
NURNBERGER, WILHELM	1	1	$1,062	$1,062	$1,062
			DM1,909	DM1,909	DM1,909
			£632	£632	£632
			¥122,753	¥122,753	¥122,753
NUTI, CANO	2	1	$2,118	$2,118	$2,118
			DM3,251	DM3,251	DM3,251
			£1,380	£1,380	£1,380
			¥231,854	¥231,854	¥231,854
ODOARDI, GIUSEPPE	2	1	$3,618	$3,618	$3,618
			DM6,411	DM6,411	DM6,411
			£2,222	£2,222	£2,222
			¥441,186	¥441,186	¥441,186
ODOARDI, GIUSEPPE (ascribed to)	1	1	$17,285	$17,285	$17,285
			DM28,877	DM28,877	DM28,877
			£10,350	£10,350	£10,350
			¥2,100,947	¥2,100,947	¥2,100,947
ODOARDI, GIUSEPPE (attributed to)	1	0			
ORNATI, GIUSEPPE	1	1	$24,705	$24,705	$24,705
			DM37,956	DM37,956	DM37,956
			£16,100	£16,100	£16,100
			¥2,704,623	¥2,704,623	¥2,704,623
ORZELLI, JOSEPH	1	0			
PADDAY, A.L.	1	0			
PADEWET, CARL	1	1	$1,273	$1,273	$1,273
			DM1,873	DM1,873	DM1,873
			£828	£828	£828
			¥135,096	¥135,096	¥135,096
PALLOTTA, PIETRO	1	1	$50,164	$50,164	$50,164
			DM70,347	DM70,347	DM70,347
			£32,200	£32,200	£32,200
			¥5,068,377	¥5,068,377	¥5,068,377
PALMER	1	0			

Maker	Items		Selling Prices		
	Bid	Sold	Low	High	Avg
PANORMO, VINCENZO (ascribed to)	1	1	$33,350	$33,350	$33,350
			DM51,692	DM51,692	DM51,692
			£21,344	£21,344	£21,344
			¥3,278,638	¥3,278,638	¥3,278,638
PANORMO, VINCENZO (attributed to)	1	1	$21,379	$21,379	$21,379
			DM37,065	DM37,065	DM37,065
			£12,650	£12,650	£12,650
			¥2,718,106	¥2,718,106	¥2,718,106
PARESCHI, GAETANO	3	2	$4,025	$4,589	$4,307
			DM6,359	DM7,762	DM7,061
			£2,576	£3,080	£2,828
			¥402,097	¥486,640	¥444,369
PAUL, ADAM D.	2	1	$1,181	$1,181	$1,181
			DM1,874	DM1,874	DM1,874
			£771	£771	£771
			¥119,415	¥119,415	¥119,415
PEAT, RICHARD	1	1	$782	$782	$782
			DM1,202	DM1,202	DM1,202
			£518	£518	£518
			¥83,434	¥83,434	¥83,434
PERRIN, E.J. (FILS)	1	1	$2,899	$2,899	$2,899
			DM4,094	DM4,094	DM4,094
			£1,840	£1,840	£1,840
			¥291,885	¥291,885	¥291,885
PERRY, L.A.	5	4	$880	$1,199	$1,032
			DM1,433	DM1,902	DM1,647
			£518	£782	£656
			¥98,433	¥121,197	¥107,811
PERRY, THOMAS	2	1	$6,900	$6,900	$6,900
			DM11,806	DM11,806	DM11,806
			£4,081	£4,081	£4,081
			¥856,842	¥856,842	¥856,842
PETERNELLA, JAGO	1	0			
PEVERE, ERNESTO (ascribed to)	1	1	$3,575	$3,575	$3,575
			DM6,048	DM6,048	DM6,048
			£2,248	£2,248	£2,248
			¥442,905	¥442,905	¥442,905
PFRETZSCHNER, E.R. (workshop of)	1	1	$374	$374	$374
			DM639	DM639	DM639
			£221	£221	£221
			¥46,412	¥46,412	¥46,412
PHILLIPS, HAROLD	1	0			
PICCAGLIANI, ARMANDO	2	0			
PICKERING, NORMAN	1	1	$805	$805	$805
			DM1,360	DM1,360	DM1,360
			£483	£483	£483
			¥98,210	¥98,210	¥98,210
PILLEMENT, FRANCOIS	1	0			
PIZZOLINI, MARIO	2	0			
PLOWRIGHT, DENIS G.	2	1	$895	$895	$895
			DM943	DM943	DM943
			£552	£552	£552
			¥68,335	¥68,335	¥68,335
PROCAK, MYRON	1	0			
PUSKAS, JOSEPH	1	0			

Maker	Items		Selling Prices		
	Bid	Sold	Low	High	Avg
QUENOIL, CHARLES	1	1	$3,738	$3,738	$3,738
			DM6,395	DM6,395	DM6,395
			£2,211	£2,211	£2,211
			¥464,123	¥464,123	¥464,123
RAABS, GOTTFRIED (workshop of)	1	1	$863	$863	$863
			DM1,441	DM1,441	DM1,441
			£576	£576	£576
			¥90,399	¥90,399	¥90,399
RADIGHIERI, OTELLO	1	0			
RAYMOND, ROBERT JOHN	2	2	$642	$1,460	$1,051
			DM952	DM2,730	DM1,841
			£414	£920	£667
			¥69,461	¥172,785	¥121,123
READ, JOHN R.W.	1	0			
REITER, JOHANN	1	1	$1,845	$1,845	$1,845
			DM2,569	DM2,569	DM2,569
			£1,150	£1,150	£1,150
			¥155,682	¥155,682	¥155,682
REMY, JEAN MATHURIN	1	1	$1,817	$1,817	$1,817
			DM2,567	DM2,567	DM2,567
			£1,150	£1,150	£1,150
			¥162,193	¥162,193	¥162,193
RENOUX, F.	1	0			
RICHARDSON, ARTHUR	7	2	$2,237	$3,084	$2,660
			DM2,356	DM4,660	DM3,508
			£1,380	£2,070	£1,725
			¥170,837	¥326,667	¥248,752
RINALDI, GIOFREDO BENEDETTO (ascribed to)	3	0			
RINALDI, MARENGO ROMANUS (ascribed to)	1	1	$17,250	$17,250	$17,250
			DM24,909	DM24,909	DM24,909
			£10,990	£10,990	£10,990
			¥1,496,438	¥1,496,438	¥1,496,438
RITTER	1	1	$789	$789	$789
			DM1,190	DM1,190	DM1,190
			£484	£484	£484
			¥76,512	¥76,512	¥76,512
RITTER, HERMANN	2	1	$460	$460	$460
			DM819	DM819	DM819
			£276	£276	£276
			¥61,171	¥61,171	¥61,171
ROBERTSON, P.	2	1	$413	$413	$413
			DM649	DM649	DM649
			£265	£265	£265
			¥41,428	¥41,428	¥41,428
ROBINSON, WILLIAM	5	4	$2,820	$4,225	$3,576
			DM4,658	DM7,076	DM5,918
			£1,725	£2,530	£2,185
			¥347,737	¥513,565	¥430,014
ROCCHI, S.	1	0			
RODENBERG, KOR	1	0			
RONIG, ADOLF	1	0			
ROSADONI, GIOVANNI	2	1	$2,319	$2,319	$2,319
			DM3,470	DM3,470	DM3,470
			£1,380	£1,380	£1,380
			¥258,722	¥258,722	¥258,722

Maker	Items		Selling Prices		
	Bid	Sold	Low	High	Avg
ROSSI, GIUSEPPE	2	1	$6,765 DM10,122 £4,025 ¥754,607	$6,765 DM10,122 £4,025 ¥754,607	$6,765 DM10,122 £4,025 ¥754,607
ROSSI, STELIO	2	2	$5,444 DM7,666 £3,450 ¥556,595	$6,768 DM10,147 £4,140 ¥654,782	$6,106 DM8,907 £3,795 ¥605,689
ROTH, ERNST HEINRICH	4	2	$941 DM1,354 £610 ¥95,533	$1,119 DM1,582 £713 ¥95,600	$1,030 DM1,468 £661 ¥95,566
ROTH, ERNST HEINRICH (workshop of)	1	1	$920 DM1,574 £544 ¥114,246	$920 DM1,574 £544 ¥114,246	$920 DM1,574 £544 ¥114,246
RUDDIMAN, JOSEPH	1	1	$2,178 DM3,066 £1,380 ¥222,638	$2,178 DM3,066 £1,380 ¥222,638	$2,178 DM3,066 £1,380 ¥222,638
RUPING, HENRY	2	1	$403 DM615 £265 ¥42,424	$403 DM615 £265 ¥42,424	$403 DM615 £265 ¥42,424
RUTH, BENJAMIN WARREN	1	1	$2,300 DM3,935 £1,360 ¥285,614	$2,300 DM3,935 £1,360 ¥285,614	$2,300 DM3,935 £1,360 ¥285,614
SALF	1	0			
SANDERSON, DERICK	2	1	$1,153 DM1,787 £690 ¥131,314	$1,153 DM1,787 £690 ¥131,314	$1,153 DM1,787 £690 ¥131,314
SAUNDERS, WILFRED G.	1	1	$3,266 DM4,600 £2,070 ¥333,957	$3,266 DM4,600 £2,070 ¥333,957	$3,266 DM4,600 £2,070 ¥333,957
SAVELL, KELVIN	1	1	$431 DM721 £288 ¥45,199	$431 DM721 £288 ¥45,199	$431 DM721 £288 ¥45,199
SCARAMPELLA, STEFANO	1	1	$78,857 DM111,382 £49,900 ¥7,037,746	$78,857 DM111,382 £49,900 ¥7,037,746	$78,857 DM111,382 £49,900 ¥7,037,746
SCARAMPELLA, STEFANO (attributed to)	3	1	$1,075 DM1,519 £675 ¥95,416	$1,075 DM1,519 £675 ¥95,416	$1,075 DM1,519 £675 ¥95,416
SCHMITT, LUCIEN	1	1	$5,775 DM10,685 £3,450 ¥769,661	$5,775 DM10,685 £3,450 ¥769,661	$5,775 DM10,685 £3,450 ¥769,661
SCOLARI, GIORGIO	2	2	$6,530 DM10,713 £3,910 ¥793,691	$7,128 DM10,909 £4,255 ¥793,817	$6,829 DM10,811 £4,083 ¥793,754

Maker	Items		Selling Prices		
	Bid	Sold	Low	High	Avg
SDERCI, IGINO	3	2	$6,900	$6,900	$6,900
			DM9,977	DM11,530	DM10,754
			£4,507	£4,604	£4,556
			¥698,625	¥723,189	¥710,907
SDERCI, LUCIANO	1	1	$9,200	$9,200	$9,200
			DM14,536	DM14,536	DM14,536
			£5,888	£5,888	£5,888
			¥919,080	¥919,080	¥919,080
SEGAMIGLIA, GIUSTINO	1	0			
SERDET, PAUL	1	1	$19,205	$19,205	$19,205
			DM35,650	DM35,650	DM35,650
			£11,500	£11,500	£11,500
			¥2,569,560	¥2,569,560	¥2,569,560
SGARABOTTO, GAETANO	1	1	$25,180	$25,180	$25,180
			DM35,618	DM35,618	DM35,618
			£16,100	£16,100	£16,100
			¥2,556,825	¥2,556,825	¥2,556,825
SGARABOTTO, GAETANO (attributed to)	1	0			
SGARABOTTO, PIETRO	1	1	$17,680	$17,680	$17,680
			DM28,304	DM28,304	DM28,304
			£11,500	£11,500	£11,500
			¥1,789,676	¥1,789,676	¥1,789,676
SHEPHERD, WILLIAM N.	1	1	$924	$924	$924
			DM1,427	DM1,427	DM1,427
			£582	£582	£582
			¥92,175	¥92,175	¥92,175
SICCARDI, SERGIO	1	0			
SIMONAZZI, AMADEO	1	0			
SIRLETO	1	0			
SMITH, ARTHUR E.	2	2	$10,651	$16,740	$13,696
			DM16,346	DM24,711	DM20,528
			£6,670	£10,925	£8,798
			¥1,044,162	¥1,779,693	¥1,411,928
SMITH, THOMAS	1	0			
SMITH, THOMAS (attributed to)	1	0			
SOLOMON, GIMPEL	1	1	$1,892	$1,892	$1,892
			DM3,202	DM3,202	DM3,202
			£1,190	£1,190	£1,190
			¥234,479	¥234,479	¥234,479
SOMNY, JOSEPH MAURICE	1	1	$2,796	$2,796	$2,796
			DM4,896	DM4,896	DM4,896
			£1,725	£1,725	£1,725
			¥338,014	¥338,014	¥338,014
SONZOGNI, UMBERTO	1	1	$2,300	$2,300	$2,300
			DM3,517	DM3,517	DM3,517
			£1,513	£1,513	£1,513
			¥242,420	¥242,420	¥242,420
STADLMANN, MICHAEL IGNAZ	2	0			
STAINER, JACOB	1	1	$67,106	$67,106	$67,106
			DM113,531	DM113,531	DM113,531
			£42,205	£42,205	£42,205
			¥8,314,385	¥8,314,385	¥8,314,385
STANTINGER, M.W.	1	1	$5,662	$5,662	$5,662
			DM8,815	DM8,815	DM8,815
			£3,630	£3,630	£3,630
			¥560,690	¥560,690	¥560,690

Maker	Items		Selling Prices		
	Bid	Sold	Low	High	Avg
STEFANINI, GIUSEPPE	1	0			
STEFANINI, GIUSEPPE (attributed to)	1	0			
STELZNER, DR. ALFRED	1	1	$2,875	$2,875	$2,875
			DM4,157	DM4,157	DM4,157
			£1,878	£1,878	£1,878
			¥291,094	¥291,094	¥291,094
STORIONI, CARLO	2	1	$1,933	$1,933	$1,933
			DM3,372	DM3,372	DM3,372
			£1,150	£1,150	£1,150
			¥246,514	¥246,514	¥246,514
STORIONI, LORENZO	3	2	$70,073	$90,672	$80,372
			DM97,569	DM135,505	DM116,537
			£43,700	£55,200	£49,450
			¥5,923,448	¥8,723,090	¥7,323,269
STYLES, HAROLD LEICESTER	2	1	$1,237	$1,237	$1,237
			DM1,827	DM1,827	DM1,827
			£805	£805	£805
			¥131,806	¥131,806	¥131,806
SUNDERLAND, EDWARD ELLIOTT	1	1	$194	$194	$194
			DM308	DM308	DM308
			£127	£127	£127
			¥19,605	¥19,605	¥19,605
TARR, AUBREY J.	1	0			
TAYLERSON, PETE	2	0			
TAYLOR, ERIC	3	1	$1,126	$1,126	$1,126
			DM2,008	DM2,008	DM2,008
			£690	£690	£690
			¥147,405	¥147,405	¥147,405
THIBOUVILLE-LAMY, J.	15	12	$839	$4,206	$1,878
			DM884	DM7,115	DM3,091
			£518	£2,645	£1,169
			¥64,064	¥521,065	¥210,198
THIR, ANTON	1	1	$10,281	$10,281	$10,281
			DM17,388	DM17,388	DM17,388
			£6,900	£6,900	£6,900
			¥1,090,200	¥1,090,200	¥1,090,200
THIR FAMILY (MEMBER OF)	1	0			
THOMPSON, CHARLES & SAMUEL	5	2	$1,028	$3,470	$2,249
			DM1,553	DM4,879	DM3,216
			£690	£2,185	£1,438
			¥108,889	¥308,463	¥208,676
THOMPSON, CHARLES & SAMUEL (attributed to)	1	1	$11,433	$11,433	$11,433
			DM17,553	DM17,553	DM17,553
			£7,475	£7,475	£7,475
			¥1,247,854	¥1,247,854	¥1,247,854
TRIBBY, SCOTT L.	1	1	$2,415	$2,415	$2,415
			DM4,174	DM4,174	DM4,174
			£1,492	£1,492	£1,492
			¥306,065	¥306,065	¥306,065
TRIMBOLI, PIETRO	1	0			
TRIMBOLI, PIETRO (ascribed to)	1	1	$2,462	$2,462	$2,462
			DM3,781	DM3,781	DM3,781
			£1,610	£1,610	£1,610
			¥268,769	¥268,769	¥268,769

Maker	Items Bid	Sold	Selling Prices Low	High	Avg
TURCSAK, TIBOR GABOR	1	1	$1,932 DM3,473 £1,150 ¥223,365	$1,932 DM3,473 £1,150 ¥223,365	$1,932 DM3,473 £1,150 ¥223,365
VACCARI, RAFFAELLO	1	0			
VAN DER GEEST, JACOB JAN (attributed to)	2	0			
VAN DER GRINTEN, JOOST	2	0			
VATILIOTIS, C.A.	1	1	$2,444 DM3,920 £1,587 ¥278,074	$2,444 DM3,920 £1,587 ¥278,074	$2,444 DM3,920 £1,587 ¥278,074
VAVRA, JAN BAPTISTA	1	1	$2,178 DM3,066 £1,380 ¥222,638	$2,178 DM3,066 £1,380 ¥222,638	$2,178 DM3,066 £1,380 ¥222,638
VETTORI, CARLO	2	1	$3,105 DM4,748 £2,043 ¥327,267	$3,105 DM4,748 £2,043 ¥327,267	$3,105 DM4,748 £2,043 ¥327,267
VETTORI, PAULO	1	0			
VICKERS	1	0			
VICKERS, J.E.	3	2	$505 DM880 £311 ¥61,122	$827 DM1,269 £541 ¥90,229	$666 DM1,074 £426 ¥75,676
VILLA, LUIGI	2	1	$1,824 DM3,047 £1,092 ¥221,665	$1,824 DM3,047 £1,092 ¥221,665	$1,824 DM3,047 £1,092 ¥221,665
VILLAUME, GUSTAVE EUGENE	1	1	$3,884 DM5,959 £2,530 ¥425,065	$3,884 DM5,959 £2,530 ¥425,065	$3,884 DM5,959 £2,530 ¥425,065
VINCENT, MAURICE	1	1	$478 DM766 £311 ¥48,322	$478 DM766 £311 ¥48,322	$478 DM766 £311 ¥48,322
VOIGT (attributed to)	2	0			
VOIGT, E.R. & SON	3	2	$2,650 DM3,916 £1,610 ¥282,441	$2,721 DM4,717 £1,725 ¥345,941	$2,686 DM4,317 £1,668 ¥314,191
VOIGT, PAUL	3	0			
VOIGT, WERNER (workshop of)	1	1	$2,530 DM3,658 £1,653 ¥256,163	$2,530 DM3,658 £1,653 ¥256,163	$2,530 DM3,658 £1,653 ¥256,163
VOLLER BROTHERS (attributed to)	1	0			
VUILLAUME (workshop of)	1	1	$14,517 DM20,443 £9,200 ¥1,484,254	$14,517 DM20,443 £9,200 ¥1,484,254	$14,517 DM20,443 £9,200 ¥1,484,254
VUILLAUME, JEAN BAPTISTE	3	2	$14,128 DM22,613 £9,200 ¥1,425,540	$20,298 DM28,256 £12,650 ¥1,712,506	$17,213 DM25,434 £10,925 ¥1,569,023

Maker	Items Bid	Sold	Low	Selling Prices High	Avg
VUILLAUME, NICOLAS FRANCOIS	1	1	$4,243 DM6,793 £2,760 ¥429,522	$4,243 DM6,793 £2,760 ¥429,522	$4,243 DM6,793 £2,760 ¥429,522
WAGNER, JOSEPH	1	1	$2,122 DM3,396 £1,380 ¥214,761	$2,122 DM3,396 £1,380 ¥214,761	$2,122 DM3,396 £1,380 ¥214,761
WALKER, JOHN	1	1	$2,444 DM4,138 £1,495 ¥283,297	$2,444 DM4,138 £1,495 ¥283,297	$2,444 DM4,138 £1,495 ¥283,297
WARD, ROBERT	1	1	$1,239 DM2,067 £828 ¥127,271	$1,239 DM2,067 £828 ¥127,271	$1,239 DM2,067 £828 ¥127,271
WARD, ROD	1	1	$743 DM1,197 £437 ¥91,866	$743 DM1,197 £437 ¥91,866	$743 DM1,197 £437 ¥91,866
WATSON, FRANK	1	1	$2,919 DM4,882 £1,955 ¥310,198	$2,919 DM4,882 £1,955 ¥310,198	$2,919 DM4,882 £1,955 ¥310,198
WELLER, FREDERICK	2	1	$918 DM1,409 £575 ¥90,014	$918 DM1,409 £575 ¥90,014	$918 DM1,409 £575 ¥90,014
WELLER, FREDERICK (attributed to)	1	1	$1,224 DM1,874 £782 ¥136,475	$1,224 DM1,874 £782 ¥136,475	$1,224 DM1,874 £782 ¥136,475
WELLS, DANIEL	1	1	$1,955 DM3,089 £1,251 ¥195,304	$1,955 DM3,089 £1,251 ¥195,304	$1,955 DM3,089 £1,251 ¥195,304
WHITE, WILFRED	2	1	$1,461 DM2,256 £920 ¥145,731	$1,461 DM2,256 £920 ¥145,731·	$1,461 DM2,256 £920 ¥145,731
WHITMAN, EUGENE	1	1	$546 DM790 £357 ¥55,308	$546 DM790 £357 ¥55,308	$546 DM790 £357 ¥55,308
WHITMARSH, E.	2	1	$904 DM1,389 £598 ¥96,413	$904 DM1,389 £598 ¥96,413	$904 DM1,389 £598 ¥96,413
WHITMARSH, EDWIN	1	0			
WHITMARSH, EMANUEL	1	1	$3,105 DM4,365 £1,955 ¥275,993	$3,105 DM4,365 £1,955 ¥275,993	$3,105 DM4,365 £1,955 ¥275,993
WILKINSON, JOHN	3	3	$2,649 DM4,240 £1,725 ¥267,289	$7,520 DM11,275 £4,600 ¥727,536	$5,674 DM8,623 £3,642 ¥573,584

Maker	Items Bid	Items Sold	Selling Prices Low	Selling Prices High	Avg
WILLER, JOANNES MICHAEL	1	0			
WITHERS, GEORGE & SONS	1	0			
WOLFF BROS.	2	1	$482	$482	$482
			DM722	DM722	DM722
			£287	£287	£287
			¥53,807	¥53,807	¥53,807
WOODWARD, CECIL F.	5	4	$317	$635	$429
			DM504	DM1,007	DM680
			£207	£414	£279
			¥32,082	¥64,163	¥43,330
WULME-HUDSON, GEORGE (attributed to)	3	0			
ZANI, ALDO	1	1	$4,600	$4,600	$4,600
			DM6,642	DM6,642	DM6,642
			£2,931	£2,931	£2,931
			¥399,050	¥399,050	¥399,050
ZANOLI, FRANCESCO	1	0			

VIOLA BOW

Maker	Items Bid	Items Sold	Selling Prices Low	Selling Prices High	Avg
BAUSCH	6	2	$293	$309	$301
			DM473	DM539	DM506
			£173	£184	£178
			¥36,263	¥39,442	¥37,853
BAUSCH, LUDWIG	1	1	$863	$863	$863
			DM1,535	DM1,535	DM1,535
			£518	£518	£518
			¥114,695	¥114,695	¥114,695
BAZIN	3	3	$1,529	$4,081	$3,153
			DM2,163	DM7,123	DM5,454
			£978	£2,415	£1,898
			¥155,236	¥513,107	¥392,636
BAZIN, CHARLES	3	3	$1,495	$2,990	$2,358
			DM2,498	DM4,373	DM3,732
			£998	£1,953	£1,501
			¥156,691	¥344,319	¥267,916
BAZIN, CHARLES NICHOLAS	2	1	$3,674	$3,674	$3,674
			DM6,177	DM6,177	DM6,177
			£2,300	£2,300	£2,300
			¥450,945	¥450,945	¥450,945
BAZIN, LOUIS	3	3	$901	$2,726	$1,995
			DM1,525	DM3,850	DM2,899
			£605	£1,725	£1,275
			¥95,590	¥243,289	¥193,357
BAZIN, LOUIS (ascribed to)	1	0			
BECHINI, RENZO	1	0			
BERNARDEL, LEON	1	1	$1,093	$1,093	$1,093
			DM1,984	DM1,984	DM1,984
			£669	£669	£669
			¥135,667	¥135,667	¥135,667
BEUSCHER, PAUL	1	1	$2,028	$2,028	$2,028
			DM2,824	DM2,824	DM2,824
			£1,265	£1,265	£1,265
			¥171,468	¥171,468	¥171,468
BLONDELET, EMILE (workshop of)	1	1	$1,840	$1,840	$1,840
			DM2,814	DM2,814	DM2,814
			£1,211	£1,211	£1,211
			¥193,936	¥193,936	¥193,936

Maker	Items		Selling Prices		
	Bid	Sold	Low	High	Avg
BOLANDER, JOHN	1	1	$978	$978	$978
			DM1,633	DM1,633	DM1,633
			£652	£652	£652
			¥102,452	¥102,452	¥102,452
BOUVIN, JEAN	3	3	$575	$805	$709
			DM830	DM1,248	DM1,052
			£366	£515	£453
			¥49,881	¥79,140	¥64,622
BRISTOW, S.E.	1	1	$1,390	$1,390	$1,390
			DM2,063	DM2,063	DM2,063
			£897	£897	£897
			¥150,499	¥150,499	¥150,499
BRYANT	1	1	$1,930	$1,930	$1,930
			DM2,701	DM2,701	DM2,701
			£1,208	£1,208	£1,208
			¥163,270	¥163,270	¥163,270
BRYANT, PERCIVAL WILFRED	2	2	$2,068	$2,256	$2,162
			DM3,101	DM3,382	DM3,241
			£1,265	£1,380	£1,323
			¥200,072	¥218,261	¥209,167
BULTITUDE, ARTHUR RICHARD	15	12	$875	$3,468	$2,392
			DM1,516	DM5,212	DM3,620
			£518	£2,070	£1,510
			¥109,193	¥386,181	¥249,546
BUTHOD, CHARLES LOUIS	1	1	$1,150	$1,150	$1,150
			DM1,758	DM1,758	DM1,758
			£757	£757	£757
			¥121,210	¥121,210	¥121,210
CALLIER, FRANK	1	1	$1,725	$1,725	$1,725
			DM2,725	DM2,725	DM2,725
			£1,104	£1,104	£1,104
			¥172,327	¥172,327	¥172,327
CHALUPETZKY, F.	1	0			
CLUTTERBUCK, JOHN	1	1	$1,033	$1,033	$1,033
			DM1,549	DM1,549	DM1,549
			£632	£632	£632
			¥99,957	¥99,957	¥99,957
COCKER, L.	2	2	$460	$475	$467
			DM643	DM668	DM655
			£288	£299	£293
			¥38,874	¥42,377	¥40,626
COCKER, LAWRENCE	1	1	$735	$735	$735
			DM1,127	DM1,127	DM1,127
			£460	£460	£460
			¥72,011	¥72,011	¥72,011
COLAS, PROSPER	1	1	$2,300	$2,300	$2,300
			DM4,094	DM4,094	DM4,094
			£1,380	£1,380	£1,380
			¥305,854	¥305,854	¥305,854
COLLIN-MEZIN, CH.J.B. (III)	1	1	$2,544	$2,544	$2,544
			DM3,594	DM3,594	DM3,594
			£1,610	£1,610	£1,610
			¥227,070	¥227,070	¥227,070
CUNIOT-HURY, EUGENE	1	0			
DEBLAYE, ALBERT	1	1	$937	$937	$937
			DM1,622	DM1,622	DM1,622
			£575	£575	£575
			¥106,950	¥106,950	¥106,950

Maker	Items		Selling Prices		
	Bid	Sold	Low	High	Avg
DITER BROTHERS	1	0			
DODD	3	2	$1,349	$1,676	$1,512
			DM1,908	DM2,574	DM2,241
			£863	£1,092	£977
			¥136,973	¥183,444	¥160,208
DODD, J.	2	0			
DODD, JOHN	2	1	$3,196	$3,196	$3,196
			DM4,792	DM4,792	DM4,792
			£1,955	£1,955	£1,955
			¥309,203	¥309,203	¥309,203
DODD FAMILY (MEMBER OF)	2	1	$2,530	$2,530	$2,530
			DM3,869	DM3,869	DM3,869
			£1,664	£1,664	£1,664
			¥266,662	¥266,662	¥266,662
DOE, ROGER	1	0			
DOLLING, HEINZ	1	1	$633	$633	$633
			DM967	DM967	DM967
			£416	£416	£416
			¥66,666	¥66,666	¥66,666
DOLLING, KURT	3	2	$730	$759	$744
			DM1,145	DM1,355	DM1,250
			£437	£460	£449
			¥86,020	¥97,643	¥91,832
DORFLER, EGIDIUS	1	0			
DUGAD, ANDRE	1	1	$1,536	$1,536	$1,536
			DM2,567	DM2,567	DM2,567
			£920	£920	£920
			¥186,751	¥186,751	¥186,751
DUPUY, PHILIPPE	1	1	$1,636	$1,636	$1,636
			DM2,310	DM2,310	DM2,310
			£1,035	£1,035	£1,035
			¥145,973	¥145,973	¥145,973
DURRSCHMIDT, OTTO	1	1	$1,422	$1,422	$1,422
			DM2,560	DM2,560	DM2,560
			£862	£862	£862
			¥205,113	¥205,113	¥205,113
DURRSCHMIDT, OTTO (workshop of)	1	1	$690	$690	$690
			DM1,153	DM1,153	DM1,153
			£460	£460	£460
			¥72,319	¥72,319	¥72,319
DURRSCHMIDT, WILLI CARL	1	1	$1,426	$1,426	$1,426
			DM2,300	DM2,300	DM2,300
			£828	£828	£828
			¥167,900	¥167,900	¥167,900
ENEL, CHARLES	1	1	$1,610	$1,610	$1,610
			DM2,544	DM2,544	DM2,544
			£1,030	£1,030	£1,030
			¥160,839	¥160,839	¥160,839
FETIQUE, JULES	1	1	$1,344	$1,344	$1,344
			DM2,496	DM2,496	DM2,496
			£805	£805	£805
			¥179,869	¥179,869	¥179,869
FETIQUE, VICTOR	3	1	$4,801	$4,801	$4,801
			DM8,596	DM8,596	DM8,596
			£2,875	£2,875	£2,875
			¥660,618	¥660,618	¥660,618

Maker	Items		Selling Prices		
	Bid	Sold	Low	High	Avg
FINKEL, JOHANN S.	2	2	$1,060	$3,304	$2,182
			DM1,696	DM5,728	DM3,712
			£690	£1,955	£1,323
			¥106,915	¥412,505	¥259,710
FINKEL, JOHANNES S.	2	0			
FLEISHER, HARRY	1	1	$633	$633	$633
			DM1,093	DM1,093	DM1,093
			£391	£391	£391
			¥80,160	¥80,160	¥80,160
GAND & BERNARDEL	2	2	$2,472	$3,693	$3,082
			DM3,957	DM6,402	DM5,180
			£1,610	£2,185	£1,898
			¥249,469	¥461,035	¥355,252
GAUDE, PHILIPPE	1	1	$2,722	$2,722	$2,722
			DM3,833	DM3,833	DM3,833
			£1,725	£1,725	£1,725
			¥278,298	¥278,298	¥278,298
GAULARD	1	0			
GEROME, ROGER	1	1	$1,725	$1,725	$1,725
			DM2,638	DM2,638	DM2,638
			£1,135	£1,135	£1,135
			¥181,815	¥181,815	¥181,815
GILLET, LOUIS	1	1	$2,300	$2,300	$2,300
			DM3,634	DM3,634	DM3,634
			£1,472	£1,472	£1,472
			¥229,770	¥229,770	¥229,770
GOTZ, CONRAD (workshop of)	1	1	$690	$690	$690
			DM998	DM998	DM998
			£451	£451	£451
			¥69,863	¥69,863	¥69,863
GRANIER, DENIS	2	0			
HART & SON	1	1	$2,645	$2,645	$2,645
			DM4,420	DM4,420	DM4,420
			£1,765	£1,765	£1,765
			¥277,222	¥277,222	¥277,222
HEL, PIERRE JOSEPH	1	0			
HERMANN, LOTHAR	1	1	$425	$425	$425
			DM742	DM742	DM742
			£253	£253	£253
			¥54,233	¥54,233	¥54,233
HERRMANN, EMIL	1	0			
HERRMANN, LOTHAR	2	2	$713	$1,348	$1,030
			DM1,150	DM2,493	DM1,822
			£414	£805	£610
			¥83,950	¥179,587	¥131,769
HILL, W.E. & SONS	49	44	$707	$6,611	$3,058
			DM1,044	DM10,145	DM4,742
			£460	£4,140	£1,926
			¥75,318	¥648,100	¥324,094
HUSSON, AUGUST	2	2	$3,177	$3,196	$3,187
			DM4,792	DM4,876	DM4,834
			£1,955	£2,070	£2,013
			¥309,203	¥347,781	¥328,492
KUN, JOSEPH	1	0			

Maker	Items Bid	Sold	Selling Prices Low	High	Avg
LABERTE, MARC	3	2	$1,632	$2,181	$1,906
			DM3,029	DM3,080	DM3,054
			£977	£1,380	£1,179
			¥194,631	¥218,301	¥206,466
LAMY, ALFRED	1	1	$24,522	$24,522	$24,522
			DM39,256	DM39,256	DM39,256
			£15,950	£15,950	£15,950
			¥2,482,203	¥2,482,203	¥2,482,203
LAPIERRE	1	1	$1,567	$1,567	$1,567
			DM2,182	DM2,182	DM2,182
			£978	£978	£978
			¥132,498	¥132,498	¥132,498
LAPIERRE, MARCEL	8	6	$1,059	$3,092	$2,030
			DM1,627	DM4,627	DM3,092
			£690	£1,840	£1,250
			¥115,912	¥344,963	¥221,080
LAUXERROIS, JEAN-PAUL	1	1	$1,527	$1,527	$1,527
			DM2,449	DM2,449	DM2,449
			£991	£991	£991
			¥173,696	¥173,696	¥173,696
LAVELLO, JEAN	1	0			
LIU, LLOYD	1	1	$1,265	$1,265	$1,265
			DM1,934	DM1,934	DM1,934
			£832	£832	£832
			¥133,331	¥133,331	¥133,331
LOTTE, FRANCOIS	3	1	$853	$853	$853
			DM1,287	DM1,287	DM1,287
			£517	£517	£517
			¥96,679	¥96,679	¥96,679
LOTTE, ROGER	8	7	$1,366	$2,178	$1,598
			DM2,160	DM3,066	DM2,484
			£859	£1,380	£999
			¥153,582	¥222,638	¥181,154
MAIRE, N. (attributed to)	1	1	$4,960	$4,960	$4,960
			DM8,339	DM8,339	DM8,339
			£3,105	£3,105	£3,105
			¥608,776	¥608,776	¥608,776
MAIRE, NICOLAS	2	1	$18,453	$18,453	$18,453
			DM25,688	DM25,688	DM25,688
			£11,500	£11,500	£11,500
			¥1,556,824	¥1,556,824	¥1,556,824
MAIRE, NICOLAS (attributed to)	1	1	$3,176	$3,176	$3,176
			DM4,880	DM4,880	DM4,880
			£2,070	£2,070	£2,070
			¥347,737	¥347,737	¥347,737
MALINE, GUILLAUME	1	0			
MALINE, NICOLAS	1	1	$13,245	$13,245	$13,245
			DM21,199	DM21,199	DM21,199
			£8,625	£8,625	£8,625
			¥1,336,444	¥1,336,444	¥1,336,444
MALINE, NICOLAS (attributed to)	1	1	$6,146	$6,146	$6,146
			DM10,267	DM10,267	DM10,267
			£3,680	£3,680	£3,680
			¥747,003	¥747,003	¥747,003
MANGENOT, PAUL	1	0			

Maker	Items		Selling Prices		
	Bid	Sold	Low	High	Avg
MAW, JOHN	1	1	$1,065	$1,065	$1,065
			DM1,533	DM1,533	DM1,533
			£690	£690	£690
			¥108,151	¥108,151	¥108,151
MILLANT, JEAN-JACQUES	1	1	$5,775	$5,775	$5,775
			DM10,685	DM10,685	DM10,685
			£3,450	£3,450	£3,450
			¥769,661	¥769,661	¥769,661
MOENNIG, WILLIAM (workshop of)	1	1	$546	$546	$546
			DM913	DM913	DM913
			£365	£365	£365
			¥57,252	¥57,252	¥57,252
MOINEL, DANIEL	1	0			
MOINEL & CHERPITEL	1	1	$1,502	$1,502	$1,502
			DM2,405	DM2,405	DM2,405
			£977	£977	£977
			¥152,045	¥152,045	¥152,045
MOINIER, ALAIN	2	1	$1,265	$1,265	$1,265
			DM1,904	DM1,904	DM1,904
			£768	£768	£768
			¥141,402	¥141,402	¥141,402
MOLLER, MAX	1	1	$1,921	$1,921	$1,921
			DM3,565	DM3,565	DM3,565
			£1,150	£1,150	£1,150
			¥256,956	¥256,956	¥256,956
MORIZOT	2	1	$1,762	$1,762	$1,762
			DM2,601	DM2,601	DM2,601
			£1,150	£1,150	£1,150
			¥187,336	¥187,336	¥187,336
MORIZOT, C.	1	0			
MORIZOT, LOUIS	10	8	$919	$3,479	$2,576
			DM1,286	DM5,205	DM3,840
			£575	£2,070	£1,625
			¥77,747	¥388,084	¥260,931
MORIZOT, LOUIS (attributed to)	1	1	$975	$975	$975
			DM1,686	DM1,686	DM1,686
			£598	£598	£598
			¥111,228	¥111,228	¥111,228
MORIZOT, LOUIS (II)	2	2	$2,888	$3,785	$3,336
			DM5,342	DM6,404	DM5,873
			£1,725	£2,381	£2,053
			¥384,830	¥468,959	¥426,894
NEUDORFER	1	1	$978	$978	$978
			DM1,495	DM1,495	DM1,495
			£643	£643	£643
			¥103,029	¥103,029	¥103,029
NEUVEVILLE, G.C.	1	0			
NURNBERGER, ALBERT	7	7	$978	$3,220	$1,822
			DM1,495	DM5,088	DM2,844
			£632	£2,061	£1,137
			¥94,774	¥321,678	¥189,770
NURNBERGER, CHRISTIAN ALBERT	1	1	$2,103	$2,103	$2,103
			DM3,558	DM3,558	DM3,558
			£1,323	£1,323	£1,323
			¥260,533	¥260,533	¥260,533

Maker	Items Bid	Sold	Selling Prices Low	High	Avg
NURNBERGER, FRANZ ALBERT (II)	1	1	$2,181	$2,181	$2,181
			DM3,080	DM3,080	DM3,080
			£1,380	£1,380	£1,380
			¥194,631	¥194,631	¥194,631
NURNBERGER, KARL ALBERT	3	2	$1,312	$2,996	$2,154
			DM2,270	DM4,422	DM3,346
			£805	£1,955	£1,380
			¥149,730	¥318,471	¥234,101
PAESOLD, RODERICH	3	3	$569	$1,328	$863
			DM859	DM2,004	DM1,311
			£345	£805	£531
			¥64,515	¥150,535	¥94,295
PAJEOT, ETIENNE	3	1	$2,819	$2,819	$2,819
			DM4,162	DM4,162	DM4,162
			£1,840	£1,840	£1,840
			¥299,738	¥299,738	¥299,738
PAJEOT, LOUIS SIMON	1	1	$3,770	$3,770	$3,770
			DM6,376	DM6,376	DM6,376
			£2,530	£2,530	£2,530
			¥399,740	¥399,740	¥399,740
PFRETZSCHNER, BERTHOLD	1	1	$795	$795	$795
			DM1,272	DM1,272	DM1,272
			£517	£517	£517
			¥80,458	¥80,458	¥80,458
PFRETZSCHNER, H.R.	1	1	$2,291	$2,291	$2,291
			DM3,382	DM3,382	DM3,382
			£1,495	£1,495	£1,495
			¥243,537	¥243,537	¥243,537
PIERNOT, MARIE LOUIS	2	0			
POIRSON, JUSTIN	1	1	$1,955	$1,955	$1,955
			DM3,030	DM3,030	DM3,030
			£1,251	£1,251	£1,251
			¥192,196	¥192,196	¥192,196
PRAGER, AUGUST EDWIN	4	4	$1,265	$2,213	$1,634
			DM1,934	DM3,081	DM2,531
			£832	£1,380	£1,027
			¥133,331	¥194,120	¥166,658
PRAGER, GUSTAV	1	1	$792	$792	$792
			DM1,169	DM1,169	DM1,169
			£517	£517	£517
			¥84,220	¥84,220	¥84,220
RAGUSE, DOUGLAS	1	1	$1,093	$1,093	$1,093
			DM1,826	DM1,826	DM1,826
			£729	£729	£729
			¥114,505	¥114,505	¥114,505
REICHEL, AUGUST	1	0			
RETFORD, WILLIAM C.	1	1	$5,143	$5,143	$5,143
			DM8,648	DM8,648	DM8,648
			£3,220	£3,220	£3,220
			¥631,323	¥631,323	¥631,323
RICHAUME, ANDRE	2	1	$12,558	$12,558	$12,558
			DM20,930	DM20,930	DM20,930
			£7,475	£7,475	£7,475
			¥1,500,905	¥1,500,905	¥1,500,905
ROTH, ERNST HEINRICH	1	1	$305	$305	$305
			DM489	DM489	DM489
			£198	£198	£198
			¥34,659	¥34,659	¥34,659

Maker	Items		Selling Prices		
	Bid	Sold	Low	High	Avg
SALCHOW, WILLIAM	2	2	$1,495	$1,725	$1,610
			DM2,286	DM2,494	DM2,390
			£984	£1,127	£1,055
			¥157,573	¥174,656	¥166,115
SARTORY, EUGENE	12	9	$4,610	$23,101	$11,337
			DM6,419	DM42,739	DM18,019
			£2,875	£13,800	£7,066
			¥389,701	¥3,078,642	¥1,197,065
SARTORY, EUGENE (workshop of)	1	1	$7,188	$7,188	$7,188
			DM10,393	DM10,393	DM10,393
			£4,695	£4,695	£4,695
			¥727,734	¥727,734	¥727,734
SCHICKER, HORST	2	1	$461	$461	$461
			DM856	DM856	DM856
			£276	£276	£276
			¥61,669	¥61,669	¥61,669
SCHMIDT, C. HANS CARL	1	1	$1,898	$1,898	$1,898
			DM2,864	DM2,864	DM2,864
			£1,150	£1,150	£1,150
			¥215,050	¥215,050	¥215,050
SCHMIDT, HANS KARL	1	1	$2,138	$2,138	$2,138
			DM3,706	DM3,706	DM3,706
			£1,265	£1,265	£1,265
			¥271,811	¥271,811	¥271,811
SCHUSTER, ADOLPH CURT	2	2	$1,255	$1,495	$1,375
			DM1,878	DM2,527	DM2,203
			£747	£897	£822
			¥140,048	¥182,390	¥161,219
SCHUSTER, ALBERT	1	1	$1,035	$1,035	$1,035
			DM1,842	DM1,842	DM1,842
			£621	£621	£621
			¥137,634	¥137,634	¥137,634
SEIFERT, LOTHAR	2	2	$576	$2,888	$1,732
			DM1,070	DM5,342	DM3,206
			£345	£1,725	£1,035
			¥77,087	¥384,830	¥230,959
SERDET, PAUL	1	1	$2,827	$2,827	$2,827
			DM4,177	DM4,177	DM4,177
			£1,840	£1,840	£1,840
			¥301,271	¥301,271	¥301,271
SIMON (workshop of)	1	0			
SIRDEVAN, JOHN	1	1	$546	$546	$546
			DM789	DM789	DM789
			£348	£348	£348
			¥47,387	¥47,387	¥47,387
SUSS, JOHANN CHRISTIAN	1	1	$2,363	$2,363	$2,363
			DM3,337	DM3,337	DM3,337
			£1,495	£1,495	£1,495
			¥210,850	¥210,850	¥210,850
TAYLOR, MALCOLM	5	4	$669	$1,944	$1,360
			DM987	DM2,872	DM2,092
			£437	£1,265	£886
			¥71,393	¥207,124	¥141,069
THIBOUVILLE-LAMY, J.	4	0			
THOMACHOT, STEPHANE	1	0			

Maker	Items Bid	Sold	Selling Prices Low	High	Avg
THOMASSIN, CLAUDE	3	2	$2,185	$4,025	$3,105
			DM3,160	DM5,812	DM4,486
			£1,427	£2,564	£1,996
			¥221,231	¥349,169	¥285,200
THOMASSIN, CLAUDE (attributed to)	1	0			
THOMASSIN, VICTOR	1	1	$3,529	$3,529	$3,529
			DM5,422	DM5,422	DM5,422
			£2,300	£2,300	£2,300
			¥386,375	¥386,375	¥386,375
TUA, SILVIO	2	0			
TUBBS (ascribed to)	1	1	$916	$916	$916
			DM1,353	DM1,353	DM1,353
			£598	£598	£598
			¥97,415	¥97,415	¥97,415
TUBBS, C.E. (attributed to)	1	1	$2,570	$2,570	$2,570
			DM3,883	DM3,883	DM3,883
			£1,725	£1,725	£1,725
			¥272,222	¥272,222	¥272,222
TUBBS, JAMES	13	12	$922	$18,173	$7,170
			DM1,711	DM25,669	DM10,608
			£552	£11,500	£4,479
			¥123,339	¥1,621,926	¥727,145
UEBEL, K. WERNER	1	1	$1,265	$1,265	$1,265
			DM1,934	DM1,934	DM1,934
			£832	£832	£832
			¥133,331	¥133,331	¥133,331
UEBEL, KLAUS W.	1	0			
VICTOR, T.	1	0			
VIDOUDEZ, PIERRE	2	1	$3,785	$3,785	$3,785
			DM6,404	DM6,404	DM6,404
			£2,381	£2,381	£2,381
			¥468,959	¥468,959	¥468,959
VIGNERON, ANDRE	2	2	$5,308	$6,722	$6,015
			DM8,511	DM11,230	DM9,871
			£3,450	£4,025	£3,738
			¥536,906	¥817,035	¥676,971
VIGNERON, ARTHUR	1	1	$6,179	$6,179	$6,179
			DM8,728	DM8,728	DM8,728
			£3,910	£3,910	£3,910
			¥551,455	¥551,455	¥551,455
VIGNERON, JOSEPH ARTHUR	1	1	$6,722	$6,722	$6,722
			DM12,478	DM12,478	DM12,478
			£4,025	£4,025	£4,025
			¥899,346	¥899,346	¥899,346
VITALE, GIUSEPPE	1	0			
VOIGT, ARNOLD	3	1	$358	$358	$358
			DM547	DM547	DM547
			£230	£230	£230
			¥35,370	¥35,370	¥35,370
VOIRIN, FRANCOIS NICOLAS	1	1	$4,025	$4,025	$4,025
			DM6,726	DM6,726	DM6,726
			£2,686	£2,686	£2,686
			¥421,860	¥421,860	¥421,860
WATSON, D.	1	1	$4,801	$4,801	$4,801
			DM8,021	DM8,021	DM8,021
			£2,875	£2,875	£2,875
			¥583,596	¥583,596	¥583,596

| Maker | Items | | Selling Prices | | |
---	Bid	Sold	Low	High	Avg
WEIDHAAS, PAUL	1	1	$1,262	$1,262	$1,262
			DM2,189	DM2,189	DM2,189
			£747	£747	£747
			¥157,617	¥157,617	¥157,617
WERNER, E.	2	1	$580	$580	$580
			DM1,012	DM1,012	DM1,012
			£345	£345	£345
			¥73,954	¥73,954	¥73,954
WILSON, GARNER	8	5	$623	$2,191	$1,364
			DM1,053	DM3,156	DM2,088
			£418	£1,380	£847
			¥66,044	¥226,290	¥143,702
WITHERS, EDWARD	1	1	$1,004	$1,004	$1,004
			DM1,877	DM1,877	DM1,877
			£633	£633	£633
			¥118,790	¥118,790	¥118,790
WITHERS, GEORGE & SONS	1	1	$2,758	$2,758	$2,758
			DM3,858	DM3,858	DM3,858
			£1,725	£1,725	£1,725
			¥233,242	¥233,242	¥233,242
ZOPHEL, ERNST WILLY	1	1	$1,025	$1,025	$1,025
			DM1,642	DM1,642	DM1,642
			£667	£667	£667
			¥103,801	¥103,801	¥103,801

VIOLIN

| Maker | Items | | Selling Prices | | |
---	Bid	Sold	Low	High	Avg
ACHNER, PHILIP (attributed to)	1	1	$4,596	$4,596	$4,596
			DM6,430	DM6,430	DM6,430
			£2,875	£2,875	£2,875
			¥388,737	¥388,737	¥388,737
ACOULON, ALFRED (attributed to)	4	1	$2,050	$2,050	$2,050
			DM2,160	DM2,160	DM2,160
			£1,265	£1,265	£1,265
			¥156,601	¥156,601	¥156,601
ACOULON, ALFRED (FILS)	1	1	$1,373	$1,373	$1,373
			DM2,137	DM2,137	DM2,137
			£880	£880	£880
			¥135,925	¥135,925	¥135,925
AERTS	1	0			
AERTS, MARCEL	1	1	$2,527	$2,527	$2,527
			DM4,380	DM4,380	DM4,380
			£1,495	£1,495	£1,495
			¥321,231	¥321,231	¥321,231
AIRETON, EDMUND	1	1	$2,913	$2,913	$2,913
			DM4,927	DM4,927	DM4,927
			£1,955	£1,955	£1,955
			¥308,890	¥308,890	¥308,890
ALBANELLI, FRANCO	8	4	$2,990	$5,901	$4,194
			DM4,916	DM8,216	DM6,363
			£1,794	£3,680	£2,593
			¥364,780	¥498,817	¥422,415
ALBANI, GIUSEPPE	1	1	$9,450	$9,450	$9,450
			DM13,348	DM13,348	DM13,348
			£5,980	£5,980	£5,980
			¥843,401	¥843,401	¥843,401

Maker	Items		Selling Prices		
	Bid	Sold	Low	High	Avg
ALBANI, JOSEPH	1	1	$18,092	$18,092	$18,092
			DM32,057	DM32,057	DM32,057
			£11,109	£11,109	£11,109
			¥2,205,930	¥2,205,930	¥2,205,930
ALBANI, MATHIAS (ascribed to)	1	1	$16,187	$16,187	$16,187
			DM22,897	DM22,897	DM22,897
			£10,350	£10,350	£10,350
			¥1,643,673	¥1,643,673	¥1,643,673
ALBANI, MATHIAS (attributed to)	2	0			
ALBANI, MATTEO	1	1	$16,822	$16,822	$16,822
			DM28,460	DM28,460	DM28,460
			£10,580	£10,580	£10,580
			¥2,084,260	¥2,084,260	¥2,084,260
ALBANI, MICHAEL	1	0			
ALBERT, CHARLES F.	5	1	$690	$690	$690
			DM1,069	DM1,069	DM1,069
			£442	£442	£442
			¥67,834	¥67,834	¥67,834
ALBERT, J.	1	1	$1,610	$1,610	$1,610
			DM2,783	DM2,783	DM2,783
			£995	£995	£995
			¥204,043	¥204,043	¥204,043
ALBERTI, FERDINANDO	1	0			
ALBERTI, FERDINANDO (attributed to)	1	0			
ALDRIC, JEAN FRANCOIS	2	2	$21,808	$22,036	$21,922
			DM30,803	DM33,818	DM32,311
			£13,800	£13,800	£13,800
			¥1,946,311	¥2,160,335	¥2,053,323
ALDRIC, JEAN FRANCOIS (attributed to)	6	1	$5,401	$5,401	$5,401
			DM8,269	DM8,269	DM8,269
			£3,450	£3,450	£3,450
			¥602,094	¥602,094	¥602,094
ALF, GREGG	5	3	$9,200	$20,562	$14,038
			DM13,846	DM34,776	DM22,533
			£5,585	£13,800	£9,145
			¥1,028,376	¥2,180,400	¥1,520,362
ALLEN, JOSEPH S.	1	1	$3,335	$3,335	$3,335
			DM5,936	DM5,936	DM5,936
			£2,001	£2,001	£2,001
			¥443,488	¥443,488	¥443,488
ALLETSEE, PAULUS (attributed to)	1	1	$3,738	$3,738	$3,738
			DM5,715	DM5,715	DM5,715
			£2,459	£2,459	£2,459
			¥393,933	¥393,933	¥393,933
ALLISON, JOHN L.	1	1	$518	$518	$518
			DM921	DM921	DM921
			£311	£311	£311
			¥68,817	¥68,817	¥68,817
ALTAVILLA, ARMANDO	10	6	$3,872	$13,122	$7,566
			DM5,392	DM22,701	DM12,183
			£2,415	£8,050	£4,785
			¥327,348	¥1,497,300	¥803,974
ALVANI, GAETANO	1	1	$9,424	$9,424	$9,424
			DM14,238	DM14,238	DM14,238
			£6,325	£6,325	£6,325
			¥998,148	¥998,148	¥998,148

| Maker | Items | | Selling Prices | | |
	Bid	Sold	Low	High	Avg
AMATI, ANTONIO & GIROLAMO	2	2	$86,863	$94,581	$90,722
			DM139,058	DM174,981	DM157,019
			£56,500	£56,500	£56,500
			¥8,792,756	¥12,604,585	¥10,698,671
AMATI, DOM NICOLO	2	2	$6,325	$42,251	$24,288
			DM9,672	DM75,647	DM42,659
			£4,161	£25,300	£14,731
			¥666,655	¥5,813,434	¥3,240,045
AMATI, GIROLAMO (II)	1	1	$26,503	$26,503	$26,503
			DM39,158	DM39,158	DM39,158
			£17,250	£17,250	£17,250
			¥2,824,412	¥2,824,412	¥2,824,412
AMATI, NICOLO	4	0			
AMATI FAMILY (MEMBER OF)	1	0			
AMATI, ANTONIO & GIROLAMO	2	2	$86,863	$94,581	$90,722
			DM139,058	DM174,981	DM157,019
			£56,500	£56,500	£56,500
			¥8,792,756	¥12,604,585	¥10,698,671
AMATI, DOM NICOLO	2	2	$6,325	$42,251	$24,288
			DM9,672	DM75,647	DM42,659
			£4,161	£25,300	£14,731
			¥666,655	¥5,813,434	¥3,240,045
AMATI, GIROLAMO (II)	1	1	$26,503	$26,503	$26,503
			DM39,158	DM39,158	DM39,158
			£17,250	£17,250	£17,250
			¥2,824,412	¥2,824,412	¥2,824,412
AMATI, NICOLO	4	0			
AMATI FAMILY (MEMBER OF)	1	0			
AMIGHETTI, CLAUDIO	6	4	$1,660	$5,750	$3,984
			DM2,311	DM9,445	DM6,230
			£1,035	£3,491	£2,408
			¥140,292	¥685,474	¥439,879
ANASTASIO, VINCENZO	3	1	$3,504	$3,504	$3,504
			DM4,878	DM4,878	DM4,878
			£2,185	£2,185	£2,185
			¥296,172	¥296,172	¥296,172
ANDERSEN, CARL	2	1	$539	$539	$539
			DM847	DM847	DM847
			£345	£345	£345
			¥54,037	¥54,037	¥54,037
ANDERSON, A.	1	0			
ANDREWS, EDWARD	1	1	$374	$374	$374
			DM652	DM652	DM652
			£230	£230	£230
			¥45,276	¥45,276	¥45,276
ANDREWS, M.H.	1	1	$431	$431	$431
			DM738	DM738	DM738
			£255	£255	£255
			¥53,553	¥53,553	¥53,553
ANGARD, MAXIME	1	1	$855	$855	$855
			DM1,372	DM1,372	DM1,372
			£555	£555	£555
			¥97,326	¥97,326	¥97,326
ANGERER, FRANZ	1	1	$1,955	$1,955	$1,955
			DM3,379	DM3,379	DM3,379
			£1,208	£1,208	£1,208
			¥247,767	¥247,767	¥247,767

Maker	Items Bid	Sold	Low	Selling Prices High	Avg
ANTONELLI, G.	2	1	$1,131	$1,131	$1,131
			DM2,004	DM2,004	DM2,004
			£694	£694	£694
			¥137,871	¥137,871	¥137,871
ANTONIAZZI (workshop of)	1	0			
ANTONIAZZI, GAETANO	1	1	$11,684	$11,684	$11,684
			DM20,704	DM20,704	DM20,704
			£7,175	£7,175	£7,175
			¥1,424,663	¥1,424,663	¥1,424,663
ANTONIAZZI, RICCARDO	9	7	$6,914	$21,416	$13,738
			DM11,551	DM39,177	DM22,201
			£4,140	£12,650	£8,477
			¥840,379	¥2,822,089	¥1,587,057
ANTONIAZZI, ROMEO	12	10	$4,900	$33,922	$19,633
			DM8,682	DM60,108	DM33,234
			£3,009	£20,829	£11,931
			¥597,439	¥4,136,119	¥2,293,447
ANTONIAZZI, ROMEO (ascribed to)	2	1	$7,991	$7,991	$7,991
			DM13,519	DM13,519	DM13,519
			£5,026	£5,026	£5,026
			¥990,024	¥990,024	¥990,024
ANTONIAZZI, ROMEO (attributed to)	2	1	$29,900	$29,900	$29,900
			DM47,242	DM47,242	DM47,242
			£19,136	£19,136	£19,136
			¥2,987,010	¥2,987,010	¥2,987,010
ANTONIAZZI, ROMEO (workshop of)	3	1	$10,925	$10,925	$10,925
			DM18,463	DM18,463	DM18,463
			£6,555	£6,555	£6,555
			¥1,332,850	¥1,332,850	¥1,332,850
APPARUT, G.	1	0			
APPARUT, GEORGES	9	7	$1,467	$4,686	$3,106
			DM2,422	DM8,107	DM5,220
			£897	£2,875	£1,886
			¥181,579	¥535,526	¥360,873
APPARUT, GEORGES (attributed to)	1	1	$1,769	$1,769	$1,769
			DM2,837	DM2,837	DM2,837
			£1,150	£1,150	£1,150
			¥178,969	¥178,969	¥178,969
ARASSI, ENZO	2	0			
ARASSI, ENZO (workshop of)	1	1	$3,738	$3,738	$3,738
			DM6,316	DM6,316	DM6,316
			£2,243	£2,243	£2,243
			¥455,975	¥455,975	¥455,975
ARBUCKLE, WILLIAM	1	1	$1,917	$1,917	$1,917
			DM3,551	DM3,551	DM3,551
			£1,150	£1,150	£1,150
			¥256,025	¥256,025	¥256,025
ARBUCKLE, WILLIAM (attributed to)	1	1	$283	$283	$283
			DM418	DM418	DM418
			£184	£184	£184
			¥30,127	¥30,127	¥30,127
ARCANGELI, LORENZO	2	1	$21,202	$21,202	$21,202
			DM31,326	DM31,326	DM31,326
			£13,800	£13,800	£13,800
			¥2,259,529	¥2,259,529	¥2,259,529

| Maker | Items | | Selling Prices | | |
	Bid	Sold	Low	High	Avg
ARCANGELI, ULDERICO	3	1	$22,770	$22,770	$22,770
			DM34,362	DM34,362	DM34,362
			£13,800	£13,800	£13,800
			¥2,580,600	¥2,580,600	¥2,580,600
ARCANGELI, ULDERICO (attributed to)	1	1	$6,146	$6,146	$6,146
			DM10,267	DM10,267	DM10,267
			£3,680	£3,680	£3,680
			¥747,003	¥747,003	¥747,003
ARDERN, JOB	10	5	$870	$2,415	$1,670
			DM1,517	DM3,593	DM2,585
			£518	£1,577	£1,060
			¥110,931	¥254,901	¥184,770
AREY, ISAIAH H.	1	1	$1,610	$1,610	$1,610
			DM2,690	DM2,690	DM2,690
			£1,074	£1,074	£1,074
			¥168,744	¥168,744	¥168,744
ARMBRUSTER, ADOLF	1	1	$730	$730	$730
			DM1,132	DM1,132	DM1,132
			£437	£437	£437
			¥83,165	¥83,165	¥83,165
ASHFORD, LAWRENCE (attributed to)	2	1	$974	$974	$974
			DM1,496	DM1,496	DM1,496
			£644	£644	£644
			¥103,829	¥103,829	¥103,829
ASKEW, JOHN	2	2	$971	$1,589	$1,280
			DM1,491	DM2,438	DM1,965
			£633	£1,035	£834
			¥106,253	¥173,890	¥140,072
ASSUNTO, CARLONI	1	1	$1,128	$1,128	$1,128
			DM1,910	DM1,910	DM1,910
			£690	£690	£690
			¥130,752	¥130,752	¥130,752
ATKINSON, WILLIAM	20	10	$1,606	$4,250	$2,604
			DM2,400	DM7,247	DM4,323
			£978	£2,530	£1,604
			¥154,471	¥507,999	¥294,674
AUBRY, JOSEPH	3	1	$4,060	$4,060	$4,060
			DM6,230	DM6,230	DM6,230
			£2,645	£2,645	£2,645
			¥444,386	¥444,386	¥444,386
AUCIELLO, LUIGI	1	1	$4,470	$4,470	$4,470
			DM7,750	DM7,750	DM7,750
			£2,645	£2,645	£2,645
			¥558,095	¥558,095	¥558,095
AUDINOT, JUSTIN (attributed to)	1	1	$1,880	$1,880	$1,880
			DM3,106	DM3,106	DM3,106
			£1,150	£1,150	£1,150
			¥232,793	¥232,793	¥232,793
AUDINOT, NESTOR	7	5	$4,718	$13,223	$10,034
			DM6,644	DM22,176	DM15,734
			£2,990	£8,800	£6,360
			¥482,383	¥1,390,400	¥1,064,742
AUDINOT, NESTOR (ascribed to)	1	0			
AUDINOT, NESTOR (attributed to)	1	1	$4,673	$4,673	$4,673
			DM8,106	DM8,106	DM8,106
			£2,760	£2,760	£2,760
			¥592,324	¥592,324	¥592,324

Maker	Items		Selling Prices		
	Bid	Sold	Low	High	Avg
AZZOLA, LUIGI	3	0			
BAADER & CO. (workshop of)	1	1	$460	$460	$460
			DM769	DM769	DM769
			£307	£307	£307
			¥48,213	¥48,213	¥48,213
BAADER, J. (workshop of)	1	1	$546	$546	$546
			DM972	DM972	DM972
			£328	£328	£328
			¥72,640	¥72,640	¥72,640
BADARELLO, CARLO	2	2	$6,906	$9,179	$8,043
			DM9,754	DM14,086	DM11,920
			£4,370	£5,980	£5,175
			¥616,332	¥1,004,700	¥810,516
BAILLY, CHARLES	7	3	$1,692	$3,084	$2,423
			DM2,537	DM4,660	DM3,938
			£1,035	£2,070	£1,533
			¥163,696	¥332,832	¥274,398
BAILLY, CHARLES (attributed to)	1	1	$2,512	$2,512	$2,512
			DM4,186	DM4,186	DM4,186
			£1,495	£1,495	£1,495
			¥300,181	¥300,181	¥300,181
BAILLY, CHARLES (workshop of)	1	1	$2,185	$2,185	$2,185
			DM3,889	DM3,889	DM3,889
			£1,311	£1,311	£1,311
			¥290,561	¥290,561	¥290,561
BAILLY, JENNY	4	3	$1,590	$1,942	$1,813
			DM2,349	DM2,980	DM2,674
			£1,035	£1,265	£1,169
			¥169,465	¥212,533	¥184,076
BAILLY, PAUL	29	19	$1,169	$11,138	$6,489
			DM1,635	DM18,636	DM10,225
			£731	£7,475	£4,041
			¥98,841	¥1,307,256	¥686,772
BAILLY, PAUL (attributed to)	4	3	$1,704	$5,131	$2,981
			DM2,618	DM8,228	DM4,917
			£1,127	£3,335	£1,909
			¥181,701	¥519,009	¥327,446
BAILLY, PAUL (workshop of)	1	1	$4,025	$4,025	$4,025
			DM6,887	DM6,887	DM6,887
			£2,381	£2,381	£2,381
			¥499,825	¥499,825	¥499,825
BAILLY, RENE	1	1	$1,380	$1,380	$1,380
			DM2,456	DM2,456	DM2,456
			£828	£828	£828
			¥183,512	¥183,512	¥183,512
BAKER, CALVIN	1	1	$2,645	$2,645	$2,645
			DM4,100	DM4,100	DM4,100
			£1,693	£1,693	£1,693
			¥260,030	¥260,030	¥260,030
BALAZS, ISTVAN	2	2	$1,610	$1,955	$1,783
			DM2,866	DM3,379	DM3,123
			£966	£1,208	£1,087
			¥214,098	¥247,767	¥230,932
BALBO, FRANCESCO	1	1	$1,475	$1,475	$1,475
			DM2,054	DM2,054	DM2,054
			£920	£920	£920
			¥124,704	¥124,704	¥124,704
BALDANTONI, GIUSEPPE	1	0			

Maker	Items		Selling Prices		
	Bid	Sold	Low	High	Avg
BALDANTONI, GIUSEPPE (ascribed to)	1	1	$20,088	$20,088	$20,088
			DM28,245	DM28,245	DM28,245
			£12,650	£12,650	£12,650
			¥1,785,838	¥1,785,838	¥1,785,838
BALDONI, DANTE	1	1	$8,166	$8,166	$8,166
			DM11,499	DM11,499	DM11,499
			£5,175	£5,175	£5,175
			¥834,893	¥834,893	¥834,893
BALESTRIERI, TOMMASO	8	3	$113,611	$137,724	$125,765
			DM175,345	DM211,364	DM194,421
			£69,700	£86,250	£78,150
			¥10,627,016	¥13,502,093	¥12,364,436
BALL, HARVEY	1	1	$1,150	$1,150	$1,150
			DM1,944	DM1,944	DM1,944
			£690	£690	£690
			¥140,300	¥140,300	¥140,300
BALLANTYNE, ROBERT	2	1	$714	$714	$714
			DM1,209	DM1,209	DM1,209
			£437	£437	£437
			¥82,810	¥82,810	¥82,810
BALLERINI, PIETRO	1	0			
BANKS, BENJAMIN	11	5	$1,687	$10,870	$6,035
			DM2,919	DM15,351	DM9,248
			£1,035	£6,900	£3,910
			¥192,510	¥1,094,568	¥637,976
BANKS, JAMES & HENRY	5	3	$3,220	$13,708	$9,804
			DM5,566	DM23,184	DM17,307
			£1,990	£9,200	£6,222
			¥408,087	¥1,670,214	¥1,177,300
BAPT, JOHN	1	1	$3,382	$3,382	$3,382
			DM5,415	DM5,415	DM5,415
			£2,200	£2,200	£2,200
			¥342,373	¥342,373	¥342,373
BARBE, F. (attributed to)	3	0			
BARBE, FRANCOIS	2	1	$2,368	$2,368	$2,368
			DM3,569	DM3,569	DM3,569
			£1,452	£1,452	£1,452
			¥229,535	¥229,535	¥229,535
BARBE, JACQUES (SR.)	1	1	$460	$460	$460
			DM795	DM795	DM795
			£284	£284	£284
			¥58,298	¥58,298	¥58,298
BARBE, TELESPHORE AMABLE	2	1	$4,801	$4,801	$4,801
			DM8,021	DM8,021	DM8,021
			£2,875	£2,875	£2,875
			¥583,596	¥583,596	¥583,596
BARBE FAMILY (MEMBER OF)	2	0			
BARBIERI, BRUNO	6	5	$2,705	$9,131	$5,740
			DM4,864	DM12,839	DM9,215
			£1,610	£5,750	£3,604
			¥312,710	¥873,540	¥604,741
BARBIERI, BRUNO (attributed to)	2	1	$5,616	$5,616	$5,616
			DM7,931	DM7,931	DM7,931
			£3,565	£3,565	£3,565
			¥565,527	¥565,527	¥565,527

Maker	Items		Selling Prices		
	Bid	Sold	Low	High	Avg
BARBIERI, ENZO	6	2	$3,448	$3,795	$3,621
			DM4,855	DM5,882	DM5,369
			£2,185	£2,429	£2,307
			¥352,510	¥373,086	¥362,798
BARNBURNS, A.F.	1	1	$1,752	$1,752	$1,752
			DM2,439	DM2,439	DM2,439
			£1,093	£1,093	£1,093
			¥148,086	¥148,086	¥148,086
BARNES & MULLINS	1	1	$570	$570	$570
			DM981	DM981	DM981
			£385	£385	£385
			¥58,973	¥58,973	¥58,973
BARREL	1	0			
BARRETT, JOHN	8	5	$794	$3,518	$2,117
			DM1,123	DM5,401	DM3,140
			£506	£2,300	£1,356
			¥67,845	¥383,955	¥207,949
BARRI, ROBERT	2	1	$556	$556	$556
			DM855	DM855	DM855
			£368	£368	£368
			¥59,331	¥59,331	¥59,331
BARTON, GEORGE	6	2	$192	$3,882	$2,037
			DM357	DM5,964	DM3,160
			£115	£2,530	£1,323
			¥25,696	¥425,012	¥225,354
BARTON FAMILY	2	1	$940	$940	$940
			DM1,591	DM1,591	DM1,591
			£575	£575	£575
			¥108,960	¥108,960	¥108,960
BARZONI, FRANCOIS	21	13	$918	$2,820	$1,572
			DM1,409	DM4,228	DM2,400
			£575	£1,725	£1,009
			¥90,014	¥272,826	¥158,886
BARZONI, FRANCOIS (attributed to)	2	1	$1,390	$1,390	$1,390
			DM2,063	DM2,063	DM2,063
			£897	£897	£897
			¥150,499	¥150,499	¥150,499
BASILE, PIETRO	1	1	$2,824	$2,824	$2,824
			DM4,334	DM4,334	DM4,334
			£1,840	£1,840	£1,840
			¥309,138	¥309,138	¥309,138
BASSOT, JOSEPH	3	2	$2,899	$7,728	$5,314
			DM4,338	DM13,892	DM9,115
			£1,725	£4,600	£3,163
			¥323,403	¥893,458	¥608,431
BASSOT, JOSEPH (attributed to)	1	1	$2,920	$2,920	$2,920
			DM5,066	DM5,066	DM5,066
			£1,725	£1,725	£1,725
			¥370,202	¥370,202	¥370,202
BASTIEN, E.	1	0			
BATCHELDER, A.M.	1	1	$431	$431	$431
			DM729	DM729	DM729
			£259	£259	£259
			¥52,613	¥52,613	¥52,613
BAUER, JEAN	3	1	$4,252	$4,252	$4,252
			DM6,362	DM6,362	DM6,362
			£2,530	£2,530	£2,530
			¥474,324	¥474,324	¥474,324

Maker	Items Bid	Sold	Selling Prices Low	High	Avg
BAUR, ADOLF	5	3	$4,590	$6,415	$5,672
			DM7,043	DM9,623	DM8,552
			£2,990	£4,025	£3,642
			¥502,350	¥608,490	¥558,764
BAUR, MARTIN	1	1	$1,475	$1,475	$1,475
			DM2,054	DM2,054	DM2,054
			£920	£920	£920
			¥124,704	¥124,704	¥124,704
BAUR, T.	1	0			
BAYEUR	1	0			
BAZIN, GUSTAVE	1	0			
BAZIN, GUSTAVE (attributed to)	1	0			
BEARD, JOHN	4	2	$425	$877	$651
			DM681	DM1,233	DM957
			£276	£552	£414
			¥42,953	¥78,235	¥60,594
BEARE & SON	1	1	$3,089	$3,089	$3,089
			DM4,364	DM4,364	DM4,364
			£1,955	£1,955	£1,955
			¥275,727	¥275,727	¥275,727
BECCHINI, RENZO	2	0			
BECKER, ROBERT	1	1	$3,000	$3,000	$3,000
			DM4,609	DM4,609	DM4,609
			£1,955	£1,955	£1,955
			¥328,418	¥328,418	¥328,418
BEDOCCHI, MARIO	3	1	$10,350	$10,350	$10,350
			DM15,577	DM15,577	DM15,577
			£6,283	£6,283	£6,283
			¥1,156,923	¥1,156,923	¥1,156,923
BEEBE, E.W.	1	1	$748	$748	$748
			DM1,292	DM1,292	DM1,292
			£462	£462	£462
			¥94,734	¥94,734	¥94,734
BEEMAN, HENRY W.	2	1	$796	$796	$796
			DM1,277	DM1,277	DM1,277
			£518	£518	£518
			¥80,536	¥80,536	¥80,536
BELLAFONTANA, LORENZO	4	2	$5,998	$8,085	$7,042
			DM10,378	DM14,959	DM12,668
			£3,680	£4,830	£4,255
			¥684,480	¥1,077,525	¥881,002
BELLAFONTANA, LORENZO (ascribed to)	1	1	$1,759	$1,759	$1,759
			DM2,700	DM2,700	DM2,700
			£1,150	£1,150	£1,150
			¥191,978	¥191,978	¥191,978
BELLAROSA, VITTORIO	3	2	$9,775	$11,485	$10,630
			DM16,520	DM16,968	DM16,744
			£5,865	£7,475	£6,670
			¥1,192,550	¥1,223,912	¥1,208,231
BELLAROSA, VITTORIO (attributed to)	1	1	$4,206	$4,206	$4,206
			DM7,115	DM7,115	DM7,115
			£2,645	£2,645	£2,645
			¥521,065	¥521,065	¥521,065
BELLIVEAU, LEANDER	1	1	$345	$345	$345
			DM498	DM498	DM498
			£220	£220	£220
			¥29,929	¥29,929	¥29,929

Maker	Items		Selling Prices		
	Bid	Sold	Low	High	Avg
BELLOSIO, ANSELMO	1	0			
BELTRAMI, GIUSEPPE	3	2	$2,310	$12,483	$7,397
			DM4,274	DM20,855	DM12,565
			£1,380	£7,475	£4,428
			¥307,864	¥1,517,350	¥912,607
BENOZZATI, GIROLAMO	2	0			
BENOZZATI, GIROLAMO (attributed to)	1	1	$1,885	$1,885	$1,885
			DM3,339	DM3,339	DM3,339
			£1,157	£1,157	£1,157
			¥229,784	¥229,784	¥229,784
BERGER, KARL AUGUST	2	2	$1,380	$4,025	$2,703
			DM2,306	DM6,887	DM4,596
			£921	£2,381	£1,651
			¥144,638	¥499,825	¥322,231
BERGONZI, MICHAEL ANGELO	1	1	$113,543	$113,543	$113,543
			DM167,607	DM167,607	DM167,607
			£74,100	£74,100	£74,100
			¥12,070,964	¥12,070,964	¥12,070,964
BERGONZI, RICCARDO	1	1	$4,991	$4,991	$4,991
			DM8,050	DM8,050	DM8,050
			£2,898	£2,898	£2,898
			¥587,650	¥587,650	¥587,650
BERNADEO, LEON	1	1	$4,057	$4,057	$4,057
			DM5,649	DM5,649	DM5,649
			£2,530	£2,530	£2,530
			¥342,936	¥342,936	¥342,936
BERNARD, ANDRE	1	1	$2,471	$2,471	$2,471
			DM3,792	DM3,792	DM3,792
			£1,610	£1,610	£1,610
			¥270,496	¥270,496	¥270,496
BERNARD, ANDRE (attributed to)	1	0			
BERNARDEL (workshop of)	2	2	$3,565	$28,194	$15,880
			DM6,025	DM41,619	DM23,822
			£2,139	£18,400	£10,270
			¥434,930	¥2,997,378	¥1,716,154
BERNARDEL, AUGUST SEBASTIEN & ERNEST AUGUST	1	0			
BERNARDEL, AUGUST SEBASTIEN PHILIPPE	9	4	$19,550	$25,082	$22,473
			DM33,815	DM38,749	DM35,634
			£11,730	£16,100	£14,001
			¥2,435,370	¥2,841,656	¥2,602,743
BERNARDEL, AUGUST SEBASTIEN PHILIPPE (attributed to)	4	0			
BERNARDEL, GUSTAVE	5	1	$17,996	$17,996	$17,996
			DM27,618	DM27,618	DM27,618
			£11,270	£11,270	£11,270
			¥1,764,273	¥1,764,273	¥1,764,273
BERNARDEL, GUSTAVE (Workshop of)	1	1	$546	$546	$546
			DM944	DM944	DM944
			£338	£338	£338
			¥69,229	¥69,229	¥69,229
BERNARDEL, GUSTAVE ADOLPHE	2	0			
BERNARDEL, LEON	16	11	$1,320	$6,295	$2,952
			DM2,246	DM9,626	DM4,565
			£805	£4,025	£1,819
			¥163,407	¥700,316	¥324,407

Maker	Items		Selling Prices		
	Bid	Sold	Low	High	Avg
BERNARDEL, LEON (attributed to)	3	1	$1,026	$1,026	$1,026
			DM1,571	DM1,571	DM1,571
			£656	£656	£656
			¥114,398	¥114,398	¥114,398
BERNARDEL, LEON (workshop of)	2	2	$1,150	$1,840	$1,495
			DM1,944	DM3,180	DM2,562
			£690	£1,137	£913
			¥140,300	¥233,192	¥186,746
BERTELLI, LUIGI	1	1	$1,382	$1,382	$1,382
			DM1,925	DM1,925	DM1,925
			£862	£862	£862
			¥116,842	¥116,842	¥116,842
BERTOLAZZI, GIACINTO	2	1	$5,654	$5,654	$5,654
			DM10,018	DM10,018	DM10,018
			£3,472	£3,472	£3,472
			¥689,353	¥689,353	¥689,353
BETTS	9	1	$332	$332	$332
			DM536	DM536	DM536
			£196	£196	£196
			¥41,098	¥41,098	¥41,098
BETTS (ascribed to)	1	0			
BETTS, EDWARD	1	1	$1,075	$1,075	$1,075
			DM1,519	DM1,519	DM1,519
			£675	£675	£675
			¥95,416	¥95,416	¥95,416
BETTS, JOHN	16	11	$321	$16,124	$5,894
			DM583	DM22,612	DM8,575
			£196	£10,350	£3,734
			¥40,496	¥1,629,121	¥622,168
BETTS, JOHN (workshop of)	2	1	$8,824	$8,824	$8,824
			DM12,346	DM12,346	DM12,346
			£5,520	£5,520	£5,520
			¥746,376	¥746,376	¥746,376
BEUSCHER, PAUL (attributed to)	3	2	$1,188	$1,233	$1,211
			DM1,819	DM2,209	DM2,014
			£736	£759	£748
			¥132,461	¥143,152	¥137,806
BEUSCHER, PAUL (workshop of)	1	1	$1,725	$1,725	$1,725
			DM3,071	DM3,071	DM3,071
			£1,035	£1,035	£1,035
			¥229,390	¥229,390	¥229,390
BEYER, HERMANN	1	0			
BEYER, NEUMANN	1	0			
BIANCHI, CHRISTOPHER	1	0			
BIANCHI, NICOLO	2	2	$3,256	$5,264	$4,260
			DM5,506	DM7,892	DM6,699
			£2,185	£3,220	£2,703
			¥345,230	¥509,275	¥427,253
BIANCHI, PASQUALE	1	1	$863	$863	$863
			DM1,535	DM1,535	DM1,535
			£526	£526	£526
			¥119,818	¥119,818	¥119,818
BIGGAM, JOHN	2	0			
BIMBI, BARTOLOMEO	2	0			
BIMBI, BARTOLOMEO (ascribed to)	1	1	$7,538	$7,538	$7,538
			DM13,357	DM13,357	DM13,357
			£4,629	£4,629	£4,629
			¥919,138	¥919,138	¥919,138

Maker	Items		Selling Prices		
	Bid	Sold	Low	High	Avg
BIMBI, BARTOLOMEO (attributed to)	2	0			
BINI, LUCIANO	2	1	$2,062	$2,062	$2,062
			DM3,567	DM3,567	DM3,567
			£1,265	£1,265	£1,265
			¥235,290	¥235,290	¥235,290
BIRD, RICHMOND HENRY	3	1	$3,778	$3,778	$3,778
			DM5,646	DM5,646	DM5,646
			£2,300	£2,300	£2,300
			¥363,462	¥363,462	¥363,462
BIRD, RICHMOND HENRY (attributed to)	3	3	$970	$4,945	$2,830
			DM1,524	DM7,914	DM4,582
			£621	£3,220	£1,855
			¥97,267	¥498,939	¥289,970
BISCH, PAUL (workshop of)	1	1	$1,725	$1,725	$1,725
			DM3,071	DM3,071	DM3,071
			£1,035	£1,035	£1,035
			¥229,390	¥229,390	¥229,390
BISIACH (attributed to)	1	0			
BISIACH (workshop of)	1	1	$14,752	$14,752	$14,752
			DM20,541	DM20,541	DM20,541
			£9,200	£9,200	£9,200
			¥1,247,042	¥1,247,042	¥1,247,042
BISIACH, CARLO	7	4	$21,191	$28,750	$25,667
			DM33,919	DM49,694	DM41,204
			£13,800	£17,765	£16,045
			¥2,138,310	¥3,643,631	¥2,835,502
BISIACH, LEANDRO	16	9	$7,161	$44,200	$24,898
			DM12,689	DM70,760	DM39,493
			£4,397	£28,750	£15,660
			¥873,181	¥4,474,190	¥2,666,804
BISIACH, LEANDRO (attributed to)	2	1	$12,563	$12,563	$12,563
			DM18,797	DM18,797	DM18,797
			£7,475	£7,475	£7,475
			¥1,401,413	¥1,401,413	¥1,401,413
BISIACH, LEANDRO (workshop of)	1	1	$25,300	$25,300	$25,300
			DM38,077	DM38,077	DM38,077
			£15,358	£15,358	£15,358
			¥2,828,034	¥2,828,034	¥2,828,034
BISIACH, LEANDRO (JR.)	2	1	$21,379	$21,379	$21,379
			DM37,065	DM37,065	DM37,065
			£12,650	£12,650	£12,650
			¥2,669,150	¥2,669,150	¥2,669,150
BISIACH, LEANDRO (JR.) (workshop of)	2	1	$12,061	$12,061	$12,061
			DM21,372	DM21,372	DM21,372
			£7,406	£7,406	£7,406
			¥1,470,620	¥1,470,620	¥1,470,620
BISIACH, LEANDRO & GIACOMO	4	1	$32,586	$32,586	$32,586
			DM52,265	DM52,265	DM52,265
			£21,160	£21,160	£21,160
			¥3,707,655	¥3,707,655	¥3,707,655
BISIACH, LEANDRO & GIACOMO (workshop of)	1	1	$26,450	$26,450	$26,450
			DM38,247	DM38,247	DM38,247
			£17,277	£17,277	£17,277
			¥2,678,063	¥2,678,063	¥2,678,063

| Maker | Items | | Selling Prices | | |
	Bid	Sold	Low	High	Avg
BISIACH, LEANDRO (II) & GIACOMO	3	1	$26,565 DM47,817 £16,100 ¥3,830,995	$26,565 DM47,817 £16,100 ¥3,830,995	$26,565 DM47,817 £16,100 ¥3,830,995
BISIACH FAMILY (MEMBER OF) (attributed to)	2	1	$13,138 DM21,896 £7,820 ¥1,570,178	$13,138 DM21,896 £7,820 ¥1,570,178	$13,138 DM21,896 £7,820 ¥1,570,178
BITTNER, ALOIS	1	1	$2,898 DM5,210 £1,725 ¥335,047	$2,898 DM5,210 £1,725 ¥335,047	$2,898 DM5,210 £1,725 ¥335,047
BLACK, JAMES	1	1	$462 DM664 £299 ¥46,865	$462 DM664 £299 ¥46,865	$462 DM664 £299 ¥46,865
BLANCHARD, PAUL	4	3	$11,454 DM16,908 £7,475 ¥1,217,685	$14,122 DM21,671 £9,200 ¥1,545,692	$12,409 DM19,428 £8,165 ¥1,332,979
BLANCHARD, PAUL (attributed to)	2	0			
BLANCHARD, PAUL (workshop of)	1	1	$6,997 DM12,130 £4,140 ¥873,540	$6,997 DM12,130 £4,140 ¥873,540	$6,997 DM12,130 £4,140 ¥873,540
BLANCHI, ALBERTO	6	4	$5,831 DM10,109 £3,450 ¥741,302	$12,908 DM19,706 £8,050 ¥1,235,560	$9,800 DM15,199 £6,268 ¥1,001,176
BLANCHI, ALBERTO (attributed to)	1	1	$9,909 DM15,888 £6,440 ¥1,002,225	$9,909 DM15,888 £6,440 ¥1,002,225	$9,909 DM15,888 £6,440 ¥1,002,225
BLONDELET, EMILE	9	8	$1,424 DM2,661 £897 ¥168,466	$3,006 DM5,189 £1,955 ¥342,240	$2,213 DM3,642 £1,384 ¥241,527
BLONDELET, H. EMILE	20	9	$1,256 DM1,880 £748 ¥140,141	$3,498 DM6,065 £2,185 ¥444,781	$2,305 DM3,667 £1,416 ¥258,310
BLONDELET, H. EMILE (attributed to)	1	1	$1,812 DM2,559 £1,150 ¥182,428	$1,812 DM2,559 £1,150 ¥182,428	$1,812 DM2,559 £1,150 ¥182,428
BLONDELET, H. EMILE (workshop of)	1	1	$1,150 DM1,922 £767 ¥120,531	$1,150 DM1,922 £767 ¥120,531	$1,150 DM1,922 £767 ¥120,531
BLYTH, WILLIAMSON	1	1	$576 DM882 £368 ¥64,223	$576 DM882 £368 ¥64,223	$576 DM882 £368 ¥64,223
BLYTH, WILLIAMSON (attributed to)	1	1	$452 DM695 £299 ¥48,206	$452 DM695 £299 ¥48,206	$452 DM695 £299 ¥48,206

Maker	Items Bid	Sold	Low	Selling Prices High	Avg
BOCQUAY, JACQUES	4	3	$2,820 DM4,228 £1,725 ¥272,826	$17,285 DM32,085 £10,350 ¥2,312,604	$9,557 DM16,934 £5,942 ¥1,164,643
BODOR, JOHN JR.	1	1	$2,875 DM5,118 £1,725 ¥382,317	$2,875 DM5,118 £1,725 ¥382,317	$2,875 DM5,118 £1,725 ¥382,317
BOERNER, LAWRENCE E.	2	0			
BOFILL, SALVATORE	1	1	$8,694 DM15,629 £5,175 ¥1,005,140	$8,694 DM15,629 £5,175 ¥1,005,140	$8,694 DM15,629 £5,175 ¥1,005,140
BOLLER, MICHAEL (ascribed to)	1	0			
BONDANELLI, CHIARISSIMO	1	1	$2,249 DM3,892 £1,380 ¥256,680	$2,249 DM3,892 £1,380 ¥256,680	$2,249 DM3,892 £1,380 ¥256,680
BONNAVENTURE, G. (attributed to)	1	1	$1,596 DM2,770 £943 ¥202,377	$1,596 DM2,770 £943 ¥202,377	$1,596 DM2,770 £943 ¥202,377
BONNEL, CHARLES	1	0			
BONNEL, EMILE	3	1	$2,540 DM3,578 £1,610 ¥259,745	$2,540 DM3,578 £1,610 ¥259,745	$2,540 DM3,578 £1,610 ¥259,745
BOOSEY & HAWKES (workshop of)	1	1	$1,233 DM1,860 £747 ¥139,689	$1,233 DM1,860 £747 ¥139,689	$1,233 DM1,860 £747 ¥139,689
BOOTH, WILLIAM (II)	1	1	$3,448 DM4,855 £2,185 ¥352,510	$3,448 DM4,855 £2,185 ¥352,510	$3,448 DM4,855 £2,185 ¥352,510
BOQUAY, JACQUES	2	2	$6,694 DM9,867 £4,370 ¥713,927	$15,456 DM27,793 £9,200 ¥1,786,916	$11,075 DM18,830 £6,785 ¥1,250,421
BORGHI, PIETRO	1	1	$5,807 DM8,177 £3,680 ¥593,702	$5,807 DM8,177 £3,680 ¥593,702	$5,807 DM8,177 £3,680 ¥593,702
BORRIERO, FRANCESCO	1	0			
BOSI, CARLO (attributed to)	2	1	$4,397 DM6,751 £2,875 ¥479,944	$4,397 DM6,751 £2,875 ¥479,944	$4,397 DM6,751 £2,875 ¥479,944
BOSSI, GIUSEPPE (attributed to)	1	1	$4,801 DM8,021 £2,875 ¥583,596	$4,801 DM8,021 £2,875 ¥583,596	$4,801 DM8,021 £2,875 ¥583,596
BOTTOMLEY, THOMAS (attributed to)	2	1	$983 DM1,405 £621 ¥98,730	$983 DM1,405 £621 ¥98,730	$983 DM1,405 £621 ¥98,730

Maker	Items		Selling Prices		
	Bid	Sold	Low	High	Avg
BOTTURI, BENVENUTO (ascribed to)	1	1	$704	$704	$704
			DM1,080	DM1,080	DM1,080
			£460	£460	£460
			¥76,791	¥76,791	¥76,791
BOULANGEOT, EMILE	7	4	$966	$5,624	$3,142
			DM1,737	DM9,729	DM5,133
			£575	£3,450	£1,940
			¥111,682	¥641,700	¥333,102
BOULANGEOT, JULES CAMILLE	1	1	$3,671	$3,671	$3,671
			DM6,118	DM6,118	DM6,118
			£2,185	£2,185	£2,185
			¥438,726	¥438,726	¥438,726
BOULANGIER, C.	1	0			
BOULLANGIER, CHARLES	12	6	$2,570	$32,990	$10,938
			DM4,347	DM46,233	DM16,680
			£1,725	£20,700	£6,843
			¥272,550	¥2,908,040	¥1,124,035
BOULLANGIER, CHARLES (attributed to)	2	1	$2,340	$2,340	$2,340
			DM3,583	DM3,583	DM3,583
			£1,495	£1,495	£1,495
			¥260,907	¥260,907	¥260,907
BOURGUIGNON, MAURICE	1	0			
BOUTSON, PIERRE	1	1	$163	$163	$163
			DM280	DM280	DM280
			£110	£110	£110
			¥16,849	¥16,849	¥16,849
BOWLER, ARTHUR	3	2	$3,448	$4,725	$4,086
			DM4,855	DM6,674	DM5,765
			£2,185	£2,990	£2,588
			¥352,510	¥421,701	¥387,106
BOYES, ARNOLD	1	0			
BOYLAN, KERRY	1	1	$1,542	$1,542	$1,542
			DM2,311	DM2,311	DM2,311
			£943	£943	£943
			¥149,145	¥149,145	¥149,145
BOYLE, W.F.	1	1	$355	$355	$355
			DM535	DM535	DM535
			£218	£218	£218
			¥34,430	¥34,430	¥34,430
BRAN, MARSINO	1	1	$1,410	$1,410	$1,410
			DM2,081	DM2,081	DM2,081
			£920	£920	£920
			¥149,869	¥149,869	¥149,869
BRANDNER, JOHANN	1	1	$529	$529	$529
			DM780	DM780	DM780
			£345	£345	£345
			¥56,201	¥56,201	¥56,201
BRAUND, FREDERICK T.	5	4	$756	$1,601	$1,362
			DM1,155	DM2,341	DM1,973
			£483	£1,035	£868
			¥84,308	¥168,871	¥136,931
BRETON	6	4	$169	$3,091	$1,343
			DM300	DM5,152	DM2,245
			£104	£1,840	£802
			¥22,659	¥369,454	¥162,224

Maker	Items		Selling Prices		
	Bid	Sold	Low	High	Avg
BRETON (workshop of)	4	3	$431	$633	$537
			DM649	DM952	DM812
			£262	£384	£335
			¥48,205	¥70,701	¥58,827
BRETON, FRANCOIS	1	0			
BRETON, FRANCOIS (workshop of)	5	4	$460	$920	$647
			DM664	DM1,574	DM1,058
			£293	£544	£399
			¥39,905	¥114,246	¥73,118
BRETON BREVETE	1	0			
BRETON FAMILY (MEMBER OF)	1	1	$1,588	$1,588	$1,588
			DM2,769	DM2,769	DM2,769
			£978	£978	£978
			¥192,421	¥192,421	¥192,421
BRIGGS, JAMES WILLIAM	14	8	$1,316	$5,900	$4,172
			DM2,174	DM9,979	DM6,504
			£805	£3,960	£2,686
			¥162,955	¥625,680	¥430,414
BRIGGS, MARTIN	1	1	$160	$160	$160
			DM230	DM230	DM230
			£104	£104	£104
			¥16,223	¥16,223	¥16,223
BRODERIP & WILKINSON	2	1	$1,085	$1,085	$1,085
			DM1,636	DM1,636	DM1,636
			£666	£666	£666
			¥105,204	¥105,204	¥105,204
BROLIO, V. STEPHANO	2	0			
BROSCHI, CARLO	1	1	$2,638	$2,638	$2,638
			DM4,675	DM4,675	DM4,675
			£1,620	£1,620	£1,620
			¥321,698	¥321,698	¥321,698
BROUGHTON, LEONARD W.	1	1	$488	$488	$488
			DM841	DM841	DM841
			£330	£330	£330
			¥50,548	¥50,548	¥50,548
BROWN, J.	3	3	$672	$1,759	$1,186
			DM989	DM2,700	DM1,827
			£437	£1,150	£774
			¥71,301	¥191,978	¥125,782
BROWN, JAMES	4	1	$3,498	$3,498	$3,498
			DM6,065	DM6,065	DM6,065
			£2,070	£2,070	£2,070
			¥444,781	¥444,781	¥444,781
BRUCKNER, E. (attributed to)	1	0			
BRUCKNER, ERICH (attributed to)	1	1	$790	$790	$790
			DM1,304	DM1,304	DM1,304
			£483	£483	£483
			¥97,773	¥97,773	¥97,773
BRUGERE, CHARLES GEORGES	3	1	$2,399	$2,399	$2,399
			DM4,057	DM4,057	DM4,057
			£1,610	£1,610	£1,610
			¥254,380	¥254,380	¥254,380
BRUGERE, CHARLES GEORGES (workshop of)	1	1	$2,256	$2,256	$2,256
			DM3,382	DM3,382	DM3,382
			£1,380	£1,380	£1,380
			¥218,261	¥218,261	¥218,261

| | Items | | Selling Prices | | |
Maker	Bid	Sold	Low	High	Avg
BRULLO, LORENZO R.	1	0			
BRUNEAU, SIMON	1	1	$2,185	$2,185	$2,185
			DM3,777	DM3,777	DM3,777
			£1,350	£1,350	£1,350
			¥276,916	¥276,916	¥276,916
BRUNO, CARLO	3	1	$9,373	$9,373	$9,373
			DM16,215	DM16,215	DM16,215
			£5,750	£5,750	£5,750
			¥1,069,500	¥1,069,500	¥1,069,500
BRUNO, CARLO (workshop of)	2	2	$805	$1,265	$1,035
			DM1,162	DM1,827	DM1,495
			£513	£806	£659
			¥69,834	¥109,739	¥89,786
BRYANT, GEORGE E.	1	1	$748	$748	$748
			DM1,159	DM1,159	DM1,159
			£478	£478	£478
			¥73,487	¥73,487	¥73,487
BRYANT, L.D.	1	1	$489	$489	$489
			DM826	DM826	DM826
			£293	£293	£293
			¥59,628	¥59,628	¥59,628
BUBENIK, JOHANN	1	1	$2,213	$2,213	$2,213
			DM3,081	DM3,081	DM3,081
			£1,380	£1,380	£1,380
			¥187,056	¥187,056	¥187,056
BUCCI, MARIANO	1	1	$11,322	$11,322	$11,322
			DM15,920	DM15,920	DM15,920
			£7,130	£7,130	£7,130
			¥1,006,563	¥1,006,563	¥1,006,563
BUCHSTETTER, GABRIEL DAVID	2	1	$4,907	$4,907	$4,907
			DM6,931	DM6,931	DM6,931
			£3,105	£3,105	£3,105
			¥437,920	¥437,920	¥437,920
BUCKMAN, GEORGE H.	4	3	$1,500	$1,632	$1,574
			DM2,301	DM3,029	DM2,626
			£977	£1,035	£996
			¥161,071	¥218,301	¥181,172
BULLARD, OLIN	2	2	$920	$920	$920
			DM1,426	DM1,555	DM1,490
			£552	£589	£570
			¥90,445	¥112,240	¥101,343
BURGESS, DAVID	1	1	$7,475	$7,475	$7,475
			DM11,810	DM11,810	DM11,810
			£4,784	£4,784	£4,784
			¥746,752	¥746,752	¥746,752
BUTHOD	4	4	$829	$1,641	$1,146
			DM1,375	DM2,951	DM1,923
			£550	£977	£712
			¥86,223	¥189,763	¥128,233
BUTHOD (workshop of)	1	1	$1,610	$1,610	$1,610
			DM2,783	DM2,783	DM2,783
			£995	£995	£995
			¥204,043	¥204,043	¥204,043
BUTHOD, CHARLES LOUIS	2	2	$357	$2,648	$1,502
			DM544	DM4,063	DM2,303
			£230	£1,725	£978
			¥39,583	¥289,817	¥164,700

Maker	Items Bid	Sold	Low	High	Avg
BUTLER, AVA LUCILE	1	1	$2,645 DM3,825 £1,728 ¥267,806	$2,645 DM3,825 £1,728 ¥267,806	$2,645 DM3,825 £1,728 ¥267,806
BYROM, JOHN	1	1	$7,668 DM14,205 £4,600 ¥1,024,098	$7,668 DM14,205 £4,600 ¥1,024,098	$7,668 DM14,205 £4,600 ¥1,024,098
CAHUSAC	7	3	$442 DM709 £288 ¥44,742	$1,427 DM2,175 £920 ¥158,332	$977 DM1,598 £613 ¥108,609
CAHUSAC (attributed to)	2	2	$723 DM1,206 £483 ¥74,241	$1,604 DM2,380 £1,035 ¥173,652	$1,163 DM1,793 £759 ¥123,947
CAHUSAC, THOMAS (SR.)	1	1	$2,471 DM3,792 £1,610 ¥270,496	$2,471 DM3,792 £1,610 ¥270,496	$2,471 DM3,792 £1,610 ¥270,496
CAHUSAC, WILLIAM MAURICE	1	0			
CAIL, LOUIS	1	1	$920 DM1,353 £598 ¥97,570	$920 DM1,353 £598 ¥97,570	$920 DM1,353 £598 ¥97,570
CAIRNS, PETER	2	1	$338 DM602 £207 ¥44,221	$338 DM602 £207 ¥44,221	$338 DM602 £207 ¥44,221
CALACE, CAVALIERE RAFFAELE (attributed to)	1	1	$1,955 DM2,827 £1,277 ¥197,944	$1,955 DM2,827 £1,277 ¥197,944	$1,955 DM2,827 £1,277 ¥197,944
CALACE, GIUSEPPE	1	1	$4,255 DM6,144 £2,711 ¥369,121	$4,255 DM6,144 £2,711 ¥369,121	$4,255 DM6,144 £2,711 ¥369,121
CALACE, RAFFAELE	1	1	$3,618 DM6,411 £2,222 ¥441,186	$3,618 DM6,411 £2,222 ¥441,186	$3,618 DM6,411 £2,222 ¥441,186
CALCAGNI, BERNARDO	3	2	$47,481 DM66,761 £29,900 ¥4,221,073	$57,500 DM90,850 £36,800 ¥5,744,250	$52,491 DM78,805 £33,350 ¥4,982,661
CALCAGNI, BERNARDO (ascribed to)	1	1	$7,930 DM11,705 £5,175 ¥843,013	$7,930 DM11,705 £5,175 ¥843,013	$7,930 DM11,705 £5,175 ¥843,013
CALCAGNI, BERNARDO (attributed to)	1	1	$8,625 DM12,472 £5,634 ¥873,281	$8,625 DM12,472 £5,634 ¥873,281	$8,625 DM12,472 £5,634 ¥873,281

| Maker | Items | | Selling Prices | | |
	Bid	Sold	Low	High	Avg
CALLIER, FRANK	1	1	$690	$690	$690
			DM1,228	DM1,228	DM1,228
			£414	£414	£414
			¥91,756	¥91,756	¥91,756
CALOT, JOSEPH	1	0			
CALOW, WILLIAM	1	1	$1,420	$1,420	$1,420
			DM2,030	DM2,030	DM2,030
			£897	£897	£897
			¥142,610	¥142,610	¥142,610
CALVAROLA, BARTOLOMEO	1	1	$2,865	$2,865	$2,865
			DM5,076	DM5,076	DM5,076
			£1,759	£1,759	£1,759
			¥349,272	¥349,272	¥349,272
CAMILLI, CAMILLO	5	5	$40,886	$134,435	$87,078
			DM70,929	DM224,595	DM143,293
			£24,150	£80,500	£54,437
			¥5,182,832	¥16,340,695	¥10,031,895
CAMILLI, CAMILLO (attributed to)	2	1	$16,000	$16,000	$16,000
			DM27,040	DM27,040	DM27,040
			£9,600	£9,600	£9,600
			¥2,129,120	¥2,129,120	¥2,129,120
CANDI, CESARE	7	5	$12,702	$26,422	$20,074
			DM17,888	DM43,139	DM30,668
			£8,050	£17,250	£12,535
			¥1,298,723	¥2,818,133	¥2,047,685
CANDI, CESARE (attributed to)	1	0			
CANDI, ORESTE	1	0			
CANTOV, JULIUS (attributed to)	1	1	$845	$845	$845
			DM1,397	DM1,397	DM1,397
			£506	£506	£506
			¥98,822	¥98,822	¥98,822
CAPELA, ANTONIO	9	8	$549	$8,811	$5,429
			DM919	DM13,519	DM8,293
			£368	£5,750	£3,420
			¥58,390	¥990,024	¥556,546
CAPELA, D.	1	1	$5,756	$5,756	$5,756
			DM8,141	DM8,141	DM8,141
			£3,680	£3,680	£3,680
			¥584,417	¥584,417	¥584,417
CAPELA, DOMINGOS	1	0			
CAPELLI, ALDO	1	1	$2,875	$2,875	$2,875
			DM4,543	DM4,543	DM4,543
			£1,840	£1,840	£1,840
			¥287,213	¥287,213	¥287,213
CAPELLINI, VIRGILIO	2	1	$3,384	$3,384	$3,384
			DM5,074	DM5,074	DM5,074
			£2,070	£2,070	£2,070
			¥327,391	¥327,391	¥327,391
CAPICCHIONI, MARINO	2	1	$8,648	$8,648	$8,648
			DM12,966	DM12,966	DM12,966
			£5,290	£5,290	£5,290
			¥836,666	¥836,666	¥836,666
CAPICCHIONI, MARIO	2	2	$9,603	$27,336	$18,469
			DM16,043	DM46,248	DM31,145
			£5,750	£17,193	£11,471
			¥1,167,193	¥3,386,923	¥2,277,058

Maker	Items Bid	Sold	Selling Prices Low	High	Avg
CAPONNETTO, STEFANO (attributed to)	1	1	$1,930	$1,930	$1,930
			DM2,701	DM2,701	DM2,701
			£1,208	£1,208	£1,208
			¥163,270	¥163,270	¥163,270
CAPPA, GIOFFREDO	6	3	$33,350	$63,187	$48,930
			DM52,693	DM101,155	DM76,346
			£21,344	£41,100	£30,781
			¥3,331,665	¥6,396,146	¥5,111,154
CAPPA, GIOFFREDO (ascribed to)	1	0			
CAPPA, GIOFFREDO (attributed to)	1	1	$8,114	$8,114	$8,114
			DM11,297	DM11,297	DM11,297
			£5,060	£5,060	£5,060
			¥685,873	¥685,873	¥685,873
CAPPELLINI, VIRGILIO	1	1	$3,179	$3,179	$3,179
			DM5,088	DM5,088	DM5,088
			£2,070	£2,070	£2,070
			¥320,747	¥320,747	¥320,747
CARCASSI, LORENZO	2	2	$14,375	$40,176	$27,276
			DM26,105	DM56,490	DM41,297
			£8,798	£25,300	£17,049
			¥1,785,088	¥3,585,769	¥2,685,428
CARCASSI, LORENZO & TOMMASO	8	7	$28,310	$49,933	$40,838
			DM45,395	DM83,421	DM65,561
			£18,400	£31,050	£25,305
			¥2,863,500	¥6,069,401	¥4,641,088
CARCASSI, LORENZO & TOMMASO (attributed to)	1	0			
CARDI, LUIGI (ascribed to)	1	0			
CARDI, LUIGI (attributed to)	2	1	$4,481	$4,481	$4,481
			DM7,186	DM7,186	DM7,186
			£2,910	£2,910	£2,910
			¥509,803	¥509,803	¥509,803
CARDINET, D.	1	1	$1,321	$1,321	$1,321
			DM1,948	DM1,948	DM1,948
			£863	£863	£863
			¥140,907	¥140,907	¥140,907
CARESSA, ALBERT	1	0			
CARESSA & FRANCAIS	2	1	$5,463	$5,463	$5,463
			DM8,467	DM8,467	DM8,467
			£3,496	£3,496	£3,496
			¥537,018	¥537,018	¥537,018
CARLETTI, CARLO	6	2	$6,895	$10,563	$8,729
			DM9,711	DM17,647	DM13,679
			£4,370	£6,325	£5,348
			¥705,021	¥1,283,912	¥994,466
CARLETTI, CARLO (ascribed to)	1	1	$8,625	$8,625	$8,625
			DM14,908	DM14,908	DM14,908
			£5,329	£5,329	£5,329
			¥1,093,089	¥1,093,089	¥1,093,089
CARLETTI, CARLO (attributed to)	3	0			
CARLETTI, GABRIELE	1	0			
CARLETTI, GENUZIO	2	1	$4,744	$4,744	$4,744
			DM8,539	DM8,539	DM8,539
			£2,875	£2,875	£2,875
			¥684,106	¥684,106	¥684,106

Maker	Items		Selling Prices		
	Bid	Sold	Low	High	Avg
CARLETTI, GENUZIO (ascribed to)	1	1	$4,888	$4,888	$4,888
			DM8,260	DM8,260	DM8,260
			£2,933	£2,933	£2,933
			¥596,275	¥596,275	¥596,275
CARLETTI, ORFEO	2	1	$14,621	$14,621	$14,621
			DM25,295	DM25,295	DM25,295
			£8,970	£8,970	£8,970
			¥1,668,420	¥1,668,420	¥1,668,420
CARLISLE, JAMES REYNOLD	1	1	$3,450	$3,450	$3,450
			DM5,192	DM5,192	DM5,192
			£2,094	£2,094	£2,094
			¥385,641	¥385,641	¥385,641
CARLONI, ASSUNTO	1	1	$3,220	$3,220	$3,220
			DM5,509	DM5,509	DM5,509
			£1,905	£1,905	£1,905
			¥399,860	¥399,860	¥399,860
CARMICHAEL, R.	1	0			
CARROLL, JOHN	1	1	$531	$531	$531
			DM802	DM802	DM802
			£322	£322	£322
			¥60,214	¥60,214	¥60,214
CARSLAW, ROBERT	1	1	$559	$559	$559
			DM979	DM979	DM979
			£345	£345	£345
			¥67,603	¥67,603	¥67,603
CARTWRIGHT, CHARLES D.	4	2	$460	$518	$489
			DM703	DM802	DM753
			£303	£331	£317
			¥48,484	¥50,875	¥49,680
CARY, ALPHONSE	2	0			
CASELLA, MARIO	1	0			
CASINI, LAPO	2	0			
CASTAGNERI, ANDREA	5	3	$1,840	$16,100	$8,912
			DM2,814	DM24,955	DM13,366
			£1,211	£10,304	£5,678
			¥193,936	¥1,582,791	¥850,735
CASTAGNINO, GIUSEPPE	2	2	$9,220	$10,220	$9,720
			DM12,838	DM15,087	DM13,962
			£5,750	£6,670	£6,210
			¥779,401	¥1,086,550	¥932,975
CASTELLO, PAOLO	7	3	$5,750	$25,404	$13,835
			DM8,792	DM35,776	DM20,687
			£3,783	£16,100	£8,698
			¥606,050	¥2,597,445	¥1,488,732
CASTELLO, PAOLO (ascribed to)	1	1	$31,866	$31,866	$31,866
			DM55,131	DM55,131	DM55,131
			£19,550	£19,550	£19,550
			¥3,636,300	¥3,636,300	¥3,636,300
CATENAR, ENRICO	2	1	$49,450	$49,450	$49,450
			DM75,614	DM75,614	DM75,614
			£32,533	£32,533	£32,533
			¥5,212,030	¥5,212,030	¥5,212,030
CAUSSIN, F.N.	1	0			
CAUSSIN, FRANCOIS	3	2	$7,728	$9,673	$8,700
			DM13,892	DM16,365	DM15,128
			£4,600	£6,084	£5,342
			¥893,458	¥1,198,450	¥1,045,954

Maker	Items		Selling Prices		
	Bid	Sold	Low	High	Avg
CAUSSIN, FRANCOIS (attributed to)	1	1	$960	$960	$960
			DM1,587	DM1,587	DM1,587
			£575	£575	£575
			¥112,298	¥112,298	¥112,298
CAUSSIN FAMILY (MEMBER OF)	4	2	$1,075	$1,840	$1,457
			DM1,812	DM2,852	DM2,332
			£667	£1,178	£922
			¥131,975	¥180,890	¥156,433
CAVALAZZI, ANTONIO	3	1	$2,812	$2,812	$2,812
			DM4,865	DM4,865	DM4,865
			£1,725	£1,725	£1,725
			¥320,850	¥320,850	¥320,850
CAVALERI, JOSEPH	3	1	$24,705	$24,705	$24,705
			DM37,956	DM37,956	DM37,956
			£16,100	£16,100	£16,100
			¥2,704,623	¥2,704,623	¥2,704,623
CAVALLI, ARISTIDE	7	7	$1,960	$6,572	$3,672
			DM3,473	DM9,832	DM5,975
			£1,203	£3,910	£2,217
			¥238,976	¥733,047	¥421,463
CAVALLI, ARISTIDE (workshop of)	2	2	$1,255	$3,105	$2,180
			DM1,878	DM4,748	DM3,313
			£747	£2,043	£1,395
			¥140,048	¥327,267	¥233,657
CAVALLO, LUIGI	1	0			
CAVANI, GIOVANNI (ascribed to)	2	2	$2,796	$2,875	$2,835
			DM2,945	DM4,543	DM3,744
			£1,725	£1,840	£1,783
			¥213,546	¥287,213	¥250,379
CAVANI, GIOVANNI (II)	1	0			
CAVANI, VINCENZO	2	1	$5,442	$5,442	$5,442
			DM9,435	DM9,435	DM9,435
			£3,220	£3,220	£3,220
			¥679,420	¥679,420	¥679,420
CAVE, BARRY	1	1	$787	$787	$787
			DM1,331	DM1,331	DM1,331
			£528	£528	£528
			¥83,424	¥83,424	¥83,424
CAYFORD, FREDERICK	1	1	$3,187	$3,187	$3,187
			DM5,513	DM5,513	DM5,513
			£1,955	£1,955	£1,955
			¥363,630	¥363,630	¥363,630
CELESTINI, ANTONIO	1	0			
CELONIATO, GIOVANNI FRANCESCO	3	1	$30,925	$30,925	$30,925
			DM46,270	DM46,270	DM46,270
			£18,400	£18,400	£18,400
			¥3,449,632	¥3,449,632	¥3,449,632
CERMAK, JOSEF ANTONIN	1	1	$3,220	$3,220	$3,220
			DM4,846	DM4,846	DM4,846
			£1,955	£1,955	£1,955
			¥359,932	¥359,932	¥359,932
CERMAK, JOSEF ANTONIN (attributed to)	1	1	$530	$530	$530
			DM783	DM783	DM783
			£345	£345	£345
			¥56,488	¥56,488	¥56,488

Maker	Items		Selling Prices		
	Bid	Sold	Low	High	Avg
CERPI	1	1	$1,184	$1,184	$1,184
			DM1,895	DM1,895	DM1,895
			£770	£770	£770
			¥119,830	¥119,830	¥119,830
CERRUTI, RICARDO	1	0			
CERUTI, ENRICO	5	2	$30,576	$36,708	$33,642
			DM43,250	DM66,009	DM54,630
			£19,550	£21,850	£20,700
			¥3,104,716	¥4,243,926	¥3,674,321
CERUTI, ENRICO (ascribed to)	2	2	$8,625	$31,688	$20,157
			DM14,908	DM52,940	DM33,924
			£5,329	£18,975	£12,152
			¥1,093,089	¥3,851,735	¥2,472,412
CERUTI, GIOVANNI BATTISTA (attributed to)	1	1	$1,610	$1,610	$1,610
			DM2,721	DM2,721	DM2,721
			£966	£966	£966
			¥214,243	¥214,243	¥214,243
CERUTI, GIUSEPPE	1	0			
CERUTI FAMILY (MEMBER OF)	1	1	$40,572	$40,572	$40,572
			DM72,957	DM72,957	DM72,957
			£24,150	£24,150	£24,150
			¥4,690,655	¥4,690,655	¥4,690,655
CHADWICK, JOHN	1	1	$1,228	$1,228	$1,228
			DM1,735	DM1,735	DM1,735
			£782	£782	£782
			¥104,851	¥104,851	¥104,851
CHAMPION, RENE	2	1	$1,585	$1,585	$1,585
			DM2,337	DM2,337	DM2,337
			£1,035	£1,035	£1,035
			¥169,088	¥169,088	¥169,088
CHANNON, FREDERICK WILLIAM	1	1	$4,321	$4,321	$4,321
			DM7,219	DM7,219	DM7,219
			£2,588	£2,588	£2,588
			¥525,237	¥525,237	¥525,237
CHANOT	1	0			
CHANOT, FREDERICK WILLIAM	4	4	$3,489	$7,486	$5,690
			DM4,909	DM12,769	DM8,535
			£2,185	£4,830	£3,536
			¥342,053	¥827,598	¥583,985
CHANOT, G.A.	5	4	$1,671	$5,511	$3,488
			DM2,565	DM9,266	DM5,530
			£1,093	£3,450	£2,199
			¥182,379	¥676,417	¥399,313
CHANOT, GEORGE	3	1	$40,331	$40,331	$40,331
			DM67,379	DM67,379	DM67,379
			£24,150	£24,150	£24,150
			¥4,902,209	¥4,902,209	¥4,902,209
CHANOT, GEORGE ADOLPH	8	3	$3,498	$7,065	$5,725
			DM6,065	DM9,978	DM8,641
			£2,070	£4,485	£3,527
			¥436,770	¥711,469	¥594,766
CHANOT, GEORGE ADOLPH (workshop of)	1	1	$4,600	$4,600	$4,600
			DM7,774	DM7,774	DM7,774
			£2,760	£2,760	£2,760
			¥561,200	¥561,200	¥561,200

Maker	Items Bid	Sold	Selling Prices Low	High	Avg
CHANOT, GEORGES	11	10	$2,922	$32,200	$18,547
			DM4,422	DM58,475	DM30,649
			£1,840	£19,706	£11,527
			¥291,462	¥3,998,596	¥2,072,608
CHANOT, GEORGES (II)	1	1	$1,925	$1,925	$1,925
			DM3,562	DM3,562	DM3,562
			£1,150	£1,150	£1,150
			¥256,554	¥256,554	¥256,554
CHANOT, GEORGES (III)	1	0			
CHANOT, JOSEPH ANTHONY	2	1	$8,619	$8,619	$8,619
			DM13,547	DM13,547	DM13,547
			£5,520	£5,520	£5,520
			¥864,592	¥864,592	¥864,592
CHANOT FAMILY (MEMBER OF)	1	0			
CHAPPUY	5	5	$155	$1,844	$1,148
			DM270	DM2,568	DM1,731
			£92	£1,150	£713
			¥19,721	¥184,886	¥115,660
CHAPPUY (attributed to)	1	1	$679	$679	$679
			DM1,235	DM1,235	DM1,235
			£414	£414	£414
			¥85,756	¥85,756	¥85,756
CHAPPUY, A.	1	1	$1,266	$1,266	$1,266
			DM2,195	DM2,195	DM2,195
			£748	£748	£748
			¥160,421	¥160,421	¥160,421
CHAPPUY, N.	1	0			
CHAPPUY, N.A.	1	1	$1,504	$1,504	$1,504
			DM2,412	DM2,412	DM2,412
			£978	£978	£978
			¥152,123	¥152,123	¥152,123
CHAPPUY, NICOLAS AUGUSTIN	13	8	$1,033	$6,169	$2,379
			DM1,723	DM9,319	DM3,755
			£690	£4,140	£1,514
			¥106,059	¥653,333	¥263,428
CHAPPUY, NICOLAS AUGUSTIN (attributed to)	1	0			
CHAROTTE	1	1	$1,139	$1,139	$1,139
			DM1,718	DM1,718	DM1,718
			£690	£690	£690
			¥129,030	¥129,030	¥129,030
CHAROTTE, VICTOR JOSEPH	2	0			
CHAROTTE-MILLOT, JOSEPH	2	1	$1,102	$1,102	$1,102
			DM1,853	DM1,853	DM1,853
			£690	£690	£690
			¥135,283	¥135,283	¥135,283
CHAROTTE-MILLOT, JOSEPH (Workshop of)	1	1	$575	$575	$575
			DM994	DM994	DM994
			£355	£355	£355
			¥72,873	¥72,873	¥72,873
CHAROTTS	3	1	$706	$706	$706
			DM971	DM971	DM971
			£437	£437	£437
			¥58,816	¥58,816	¥58,816
CHERPITEL, L.	2	0			

Maker	Items		Selling Prices		
	Bid	Sold	Low	High	Avg
CHEVRIER (ascribed to)	1	1	$282	$282	$282
			DM502	DM502	DM502
			£173	£173	£173
			¥36,851	¥36,851	¥36,851
CHEVRIER, ANDRE	1	1	$1,660	$1,660	$1,660
			DM2,311	DM2,311	DM2,311
			£1,035	£1,035	£1,035
			¥140,292	¥140,292	¥140,292
CHEVRIER, ANDRE (ascribed to)	1	0			
CHEVRIER, CLAUDE	5	4	$633	$1,723	$1,178
			DM1,057	DM2,427	DM1,898
			£422	£1,092	£729
			¥66,292	¥176,175	¥136,209
CHIESA, CARLO	2	1	$2,823	$2,823	$2,823
			DM4,338	DM4,338	DM4,338
			£1,840	£1,840	£1,840
			¥309,100	¥309,100	¥309,100
CHIOCCHI, GAETANO	2	1	$6,085	$6,085	$6,085
			DM8,473	DM8,473	DM8,473
			£3,795	£3,795	£3,795
			¥514,405	¥514,405	¥514,405
CHIPOT, JEAN BAPTISTE	1	1	$4,032	$4,032	$4,032
			DM5,651	DM5,651	DM5,651
			£2,530	£2,530	£2,530
			¥355,427	¥355,427	¥355,427
CHIPOT, P. (attributed to)	1	1	$2,385	$2,385	$2,385
			DM3,524	DM3,524	DM3,524
			£1,553	£1,553	£1,553
			¥254,197	¥254,197	¥254,197
CHIPOT-VUILLAUME	30	26	$677	$3,680	$1,836
			DM1,146	DM5,314	DM2,947
			£414	£2,345	£1,140
			¥78,451	¥319,240	¥200,708
CHIPOT-VUILLAUME (workshop of)	3	3	$920	$1,955	$1,418
			DM1,426	DM3,304	DM2,354
			£589	£1,173	£863
			¥90,445	¥238,510	¥170,864
CIOFFI, A.	1	0			
CLARK, HOMER H.	1	1	$5,796	$5,796	$5,796
			DM10,419	DM10,419	DM10,419
			£3,450	£3,450	£3,450
			¥670,094	¥670,094	¥670,094
CLAUBOT, CHARLES	1	1	$816	$816	$816
			DM1,386	DM1,386	DM1,386
			£550	£550	£550
			¥86,783	¥86,783	¥86,783
CLAUDOT, AUGUSTIN	2	2	$3,046	$4,888	$3,967
			DM4,271	DM7,840	DM6,055
			£1,955	£3,174	£2,565
			¥307,723	¥556,148	¥431,936
CLAUDOT, CHARLES	4	2	$863	$3,416	$2,139
			DM1,491	DM5,154	DM3,323
			£533	£2,070	£1,301
			¥109,309	¥387,090	¥248,199
CLAUDOT, CHARLES II	2	2	$1,131	$2,313	$1,722
			DM2,004	DM3,913	DM2,958
			£694	£1,455	£1,075
			¥137,871	¥286,586	¥212,228

Maker	Items		Selling Prices		
	Bid	Sold	Low	High	Avg
CLEMENS, ROBERT	1	1	$1,380	$1,380	$1,380
			DM2,077	DM2,077	DM2,077
			£838	£838	£838
			¥154,256	¥154,256	¥154,256
CLEMENT, JEAN LAMBERT	1	1	$6,454	$6,454	$6,454
			DM8,987	DM8,987	DM8,987
			£4,025	£4,025	£4,025
			¥545,581	¥545,581	¥545,581
CLOTELLE, H.	2	2	$440	$1,353	$896
			DM704	DM2,166	DM1,435
			£286	£880	£583
			¥44,508	¥136,949	¥90,729
CLOUGH, GEORGE	5	2	$493	$1,272	$883
			DM744	DM1,880	DM1,312
			£303	£828	£565
			¥47,820	¥135,572	¥91,696
COCCHIONI, ERALDO (ascribed to)	1	0			
COCKER, LAWRENCE	3	1	$2,113	$2,113	$2,113
			DM3,529	DM3,529	DM3,529
			£1,265	£1,265	£1,265
			¥256,782	¥256,782	¥256,782
COFFMANN, C.R.	1	0			
COINUS, ANDRE	1	1	$3,635	$3,635	$3,635
			DM5,134	DM5,134	DM5,134
			£2,300	£2,300	£2,300
			¥324,385	¥324,385	¥324,385
COLAPIETRO, FRANCESCO	2	0			
COLE, JAMES	3	2	$1,590	$2,213	$1,902
			DM2,349	DM3,081	DM2,715
			£1,035	£1,380	£1,208
			¥169,465	¥187,056	¥178,260
COLEMAN, EDWARD E.	1	1	$1,265	$1,265	$1,265
			DM2,187	DM2,187	DM2,187
			£782	£782	£782
			¥160,320	¥160,320	¥160,320
COLIN, JEAN BAPTISTE	38	32	$863	$2,824	$1,583
			DM1,411	DM4,832	DM2,529
			£533	£1,840	£976
			¥89,135	¥313,145	¥171,823
COLIN, JEAN BAPTISTE (attributed to)	1	1	$1,078	$1,078	$1,078
			DM1,656	DM1,656	DM1,656
			£713	£713	£713
			¥114,953	¥114,953	¥114,953
COLIN, JEAN BAPTISTE (Workshop of)	1	1	$633	$633	$633
			DM1,093	DM1,093	DM1,093
			£391	£391	£391
			¥80,160	¥80,160	¥80,160
COLLENET, RAYMOND	1	1	$2,178	$2,178	$2,178
			DM3,066	DM3,066	DM3,066
			£1,380	£1,380	£1,380
			¥222,638	¥222,638	¥222,638
COLLIER & DAVIS	2	2	$1,252	$4,121	$2,686
			DM1,924	DM5,779	DM3,851
			£828	£2,645	£1,737
			¥133,494	¥416,331	¥274,913
COLLIN, J.B.	2	0			

Maker	Items		Selling Prices		
	Bid	Sold	Low	High	Avg
COLLIN, J.B. (workshop of)	1	1	$690	$690	$690
			DM1,181	DM1,181	DM1,181
			£408	£408	£408
			¥85,684	¥85,684	¥85,684
COLLIN-MEZIN (attributed to)	2	1	$2,485	$2,485	$2,485
			DM3,576	DM3,576	DM3,576
			£1,610	£1,610	£1,610
			¥252,351	¥252,351	¥252,351
COLLIN-MEZIN (workshop of)	5	4	$546	$2,523	$1,400
			DM835	DM4,269	DM2,281
			£359	£1,587	£869
			¥57,575	¥312,639	¥169,375
COLLIN-MEZIN, CH.J.B.	87	64	$734	$7,700	$3,815
			DM1,099	DM14,246	DM6,067
			£437	£4,600	£2,370
			¥81,929	¥1,026,214	¥422,083
COLLIN-MEZIN, CH.J.B. (attributed to)	7	5	$691	$3,710	$2,144
			DM1,205	DM6,212	DM3,445
			£426	£2,415	£1,334
			¥83,760	¥402,615	¥239,932
COLLIN-MEZIN, CH.J.B. (workshop of)	5	4	$978	$2,875	$1,912
			DM1,633	DM4,157	DM2,975
			£652	£1,878	£1,224
			¥102,452	¥291,094	¥201,193
COLLIN-MEZIN, CH.J.B. (FILS)	16	13	$884	$5,467	$3,404
			DM1,301	DM9,250	DM5,639
			£575	£3,439	£2,093
			¥93,817	¥677,385	¥390,119
COLLIN-MEZIN, CH.J.B. (FILS) (attributed to)	1	0			
COLLIN-MEZIN, CH.J.B. (II)	10	5	$1,586	$2,648	$2,178
			DM2,341	DM4,063	DM3,352
			£1,035	£1,725	£1,411
			¥168,603	¥289,817	¥241,151
COLLIN-MEZIN, CH.J.B. (III)	8	4	$872	$2,632	$2,109
			DM1,232	DM3,946	DM3,136
			£552	£1,610	£1,317
			¥77,852	¥279,565	¥218,581
COLOMBO, CAMILLO	2	0			
COLT, E.W.	1	0			
CONANT, WILLIAM A.	6	4	$374	$1,150	$812
			DM572	DM1,789	DM1,334
			£246	£736	£512
			¥39,393	¥131,171	¥92,767
CONE, GEORGES	1	1	$2,990	$2,990	$2,990
			DM4,724	DM4,724	DM4,724
			£1,914	£1,914	£1,914
			¥298,701	¥298,701	¥298,701
CONE, GEORGES (workshop of)	1	1	$1,610	$1,610	$1,610
			DM2,755	DM2,755	DM2,755
			£952	£952	£952
			¥199,930	¥199,930	¥199,930
CONIA, STEFANO	7	5	$1,651	$7,376	$5,108
			DM2,863	DM11,397	DM8,073
			£977	£4,600	£3,146
			¥206,147	¥820,971	¥546,022

Maker	Items		Selling Prices		
	Bid	Sold	Low	High	Avg
CONN, C.G.	1	1	$633	$633	$633
			DM980	DM980	DM980
			£405	£405	£405
			¥62,181	¥62,181	¥62,181
CONNELAN, MICHAEL	1	1	$384	$384	$384
			DM635	DM635	DM635
			£230	£230	£230
			¥44,919	¥44,919	¥44,919
CONTAVALLI	1	0			
CONTAVALLI, LUIGI	1	1	$3,392	$3,392	$3,392
			DM6,011	DM6,011	DM6,011
			£2,083	£2,083	£2,083
			¥413,612	¥413,612	¥413,612
CONTAVALLI, PRIMO	2	1	$16,822	$16,822	$16,822
			DM28,460	DM28,460	DM28,460
			£10,580	£10,580	£10,580
			¥2,084,260	¥2,084,260	¥2,084,260
CONTI, IVANO	1	1	$2,950	$2,950	$2,950
			DM4,108	DM4,108	DM4,108
			£1,840	£1,840	£1,840
			¥249,408	¥249,408	¥249,408
CONTINO, ALFREDO	7	6	$8,050	$20,284	$14,210
			DM11,640	DM34,155	DM22,948
			£5,258	£12,650	£8,850
			¥815,063	¥2,736,425	¥1,627,537
CONTINO, ALFREDO (attributed to)	1	1	$5,451	$5,451	$5,451
			DM9,457	DM9,457	DM9,457
			£3,220	£3,220	£3,220
			¥691,044	¥691,044	¥691,044
CONTRERAS, JOSE	2	2	$14,117	$25,310	$19,714
			DM21,689	DM43,908	DM32,799
			£9,200	£14,950	£12,075
			¥1,545,499	¥3,208,420	¥2,376,959
COOPER, HUGH W.	4	3	$629	$1,880	$1,104
			DM988	DM2,819	DM1,657
			£403	£1,150	£693
			¥63,043	¥181,884	¥108,811
CORATTI, IVANO	1	1	$6,561	$6,561	$6,561
			DM11,351	DM11,351	DM11,351
			£4,025	£4,025	£4,025
			¥748,650	¥748,650	¥748,650
CORDANO, GIACOMO FILIPPO	1	0			
CORDANUS, J.	2	1	$24,967	$24,967	$24,967
			DM41,711	DM41,711	DM41,711
			£14,950	£14,950	£14,950
			¥3,034,701	¥3,034,701	¥3,034,701
CORNELLISSEN, MARTEN	2	1	$6,392	$6,392	$6,392
			DM8,987	DM8,987	DM8,987
			£4,025	£4,025	£4,025
			¥568,221	¥568,221	¥568,221
CORSBY, GEORGE	4	0			
CORSINI, GIORGIO	1	0			
COSSU, FRANCESCO	2	0			
COSTA, FELIX MORI	1	1	$10,051	$10,051	$10,051
			DM15,038	DM15,038	DM15,038
			£5,980	£5,980	£5,980
			¥1,121,130	¥1,121,130	¥1,121,130

| Maker | Items | | Selling Prices | | |
---	Bid	Sold	Low	High	Avg
COUCH, C.M.	1	1	$345	$345	$345
			DM614	DM614	DM614
			£207	£207	£207
			¥45,878	¥45,878	¥45,878
COUTURIEUX	1	1	$553	$553	$553
			DM770	DM770	DM770
			£345	£345	£345
			¥46,764	¥46,764	¥46,764
COUTURIEUX (ascribed to)	2	1	$829	$829	$829
			DM1,249	DM1,249	DM1,249
			£508	£508	£508
			¥80,337	¥80,337	¥80,337
COUTURIEUX, M.	2	2	$768	$805	$787
			DM1,283	DM1,391	DM1,337
			£460	£497	£479
			¥93,375	¥102,022	¥97,699
CRAIG, JOHN	1	1	$1,546	$1,546	$1,546
			DM2,778	DM2,778	DM2,778
			£920	£920	£920
			¥178,692	¥178,692	¥178,692
CRAMOND	4	2	$402	$710	$556
			DM751	DM1,238	DM994
			£253	£437	£345
			¥47,516	¥86,023	¥66,770
CRAMOND, CHARLES	2	0			
CRASKE, GEORGE	38	25	$1,383	$7,331	$5,020
			DM1,978	DM11,397	DM8,061
			£874	£4,600	£3,116
			¥138,954	¥820,971	¥558,630
CRASKE, GEORGE (attributed to)	1	0			
CRAY, PHILLIP	1	1	$2,437	$2,437	$2,437
			DM3,445	DM3,445	DM3,445
			£1,553	£1,553	£1,553
			¥208,161	¥208,161	¥208,161
CREMONINI, VIRGILIO	1	0			
CROSS, NATHANIEL	1	1	$1,932	$1,932	$1,932
			DM3,473	DM3,473	DM3,473
			£1,150	£1,150	£1,150
			¥223,365	¥223,365	¥223,365
CROSS, NATHANIEL (attributed to)	2	1	$4,481	$4,481	$4,481
			DM7,186	DM7,186	DM7,186
			£2,910	£2,910	£2,910
			¥509,803	¥509,803	¥509,803
CROUT, THOMAS FARROW (attributed to)	1	1	$486	$486	$486
			DM744	DM744	DM744
			£311	£311	£311
			¥54,188	¥54,188	¥54,188
CUNAULT, GEORGES	4	4	$1,840	$12,617	$6,734
			DM2,769	DM21,345	DM10,549
			£1,117	£7,935	£4,189
			¥205,675	¥1,563,195	¥726,070
CUNAULT, GEORGES (workshop of)	1	0			
CURLETTO, ANSELMO	4	2	$6,351	$20,679	$13,515
			DM8,944	DM31,005	DM19,975
			£4,025	£12,650	£8,338
			¥649,361	¥2,000,724	¥1,325,043

Maker	Items		Selling Prices		
	Bid	Sold	Low	High	Avg
CURTIL, ANTOINE	1	1	$2,847	$2,847	$2,847
			DM4,787	DM4,787	DM4,787
			£1,783	£1,783	£1,783
			¥349,482	¥349,482	¥349,482
CURTIN, JOSEPH	1	1	$15,902	$15,902	$15,902
			DM23,495	DM23,495	DM23,495
			£10,350	£10,350	£10,350
			¥1,694,647	¥1,694,647	¥1,694,647
CURTIS, ROGER	1	1	$1,160	$1,160	$1,160
			DM1,735	DM1,735	DM1,735
			£690	£690	£690
			¥129,361	¥129,361	¥129,361
CUYPERS, JOHANNES	5	4	$28,756	$44,988	$38,065
			DM53,268	DM77,832	DM64,653
			£17,250	£27,600	£23,288
			¥3,585,769	¥5,133,600	¥4,420,057
CUYPERS, JOHANNES (ascribed to)	1	1	$14,128	$14,128	$14,128
			DM22,613	DM22,613	DM22,613
			£9,200	£9,200	£9,200
			¥1,425,540	¥1,425,540	¥1,425,540
CUYPERS, JOHANNES (attributed to)	1	1	$5,639	$5,639	$5,639
			DM8,324	DM8,324	DM8,324
			£3,680	£3,680	£3,680
			¥599,476	¥599,476	¥599,476
CUYPERS, JOHANNES FRANCIS	1	1	$19,205	$19,205	$19,205
			DM32,085	DM32,085	DM32,085
			£11,500	£11,500	£11,500
			¥2,334,385	¥2,334,385	¥2,334,385
CUYPERS, JOHANNES THEODORUS	3	3	$28,808	$32,712	$31,020
			DM46,204	DM53,363	DM49,232
			£17,250	£20,700	£19,263
			¥2,919,466	¥3,907,988	¥3,443,010
CUYPERS FAMILY (MEMBER OF)	1	1	$10,588	$10,588	$10,588
			DM16,267	DM16,267	DM16,267
			£6,900	£6,900	£6,900
			¥1,159,124	¥1,159,124	¥1,159,124
DAHLEN, FRANS WALDEMAR	2	2	$1,344	$2,113	$1,728
			DM2,246	DM3,529	DM2,888
			£805	£1,265	£1,035
			¥163,407	¥256,782	¥210,095
D'ALAGLIO, JOSEPH	1	1	$44,085	$44,085	$44,085
			DM74,128	DM74,128	DM74,128
			£27,600	£27,600	£27,600
			¥5,411,339	¥5,411,339	¥5,411,339
DAL CANTO, GIUSTINO	3	2	$2,313	$6,955	$4,634
			DM3,913	DM12,503	DM8,208
			£1,455	£4,140	£2,797
			¥286,586	¥804,112	¥545,349
DAL CANTO, GIUSTINO (attributed to)	1	1	$3,195	$3,195	$3,195
			DM4,598	DM4,598	DM4,598
			£2,070	£2,070	£2,070
			¥324,452	¥324,452	¥324,452
DALLA COSTA, PIETRO ANTONIO	4	3	$29,900	$56,925	$43,877
			DM47,242	DM85,905	DM68,337
			£19,136	£34,500	£27,577
			¥2,987,010	¥6,451,500	¥4,845,512

| Maker | Items | | Selling Prices | | |
---	Bid	Sold	Low	High	Avg
DALLA COSTA, PIETRO ANTONIO					
(attributed to)	2	2	$20,700	$41,124	$30,912
			DM34,983	DM62,128	DM48,555
			£12,420	£27,600	£20,010
			¥2,525,400	¥4,355,556	¥3,440,478
DALL'AGLIO, GIUSEPPE	1	0			
DALL'AGLIO, GIUSEPPE (attributed to)	2	0			
DALLINGER, SEBASTIAN	1	0			
DANIELI, SILVIO	2	1	$7,144	$7,144	$7,144
			DM10,711	DM10,711	DM10,711
			£4,370	£4,370	£4,370
			¥691,159	¥691,159	¥691,159
DARBEY, GEORGE	3	3	$2,888	$5,972	$4,243
			DM5,342	DM8,976	DM6,753
			£1,725	£3,565	£2,607
			¥384,830	¥665,090	¥490,757
DARBY	1	0			
DARCHE, HILAIRE	2	1	$11,523	$11,523	$11,523
			DM21,390	DM21,390	DM21,390
			£6,900	£6,900	£6,900
			¥1,541,736	¥1,541,736	¥1,541,736
DARCHE, NICHOLAS	1	1	$1,610	$1,610	$1,610
			DM2,924	DM2,924	DM2,924
			£985	£985	£985
			¥199,930	¥199,930	¥199,930
DARTE, AUGUSTE	2	1	$3,957	$3,957	$3,957
			DM5,597	DM5,597	DM5,597
			£2,530	£2,530	£2,530
			¥401,787	¥401,787	¥401,787
DA RUB, ANGELO (attributed to)	1	1	$12,633	$12,633	$12,633
			DM21,902	DM21,902	DM21,902
			£7,475	£7,475	£7,475
			¥1,577,225	¥1,577,225	¥1,577,225
DAY, JOHN	1	1	$6,900	$6,900	$6,900
			DM11,806	DM11,806	DM11,806
			£4,081	£4,081	£4,081
			¥856,842	¥856,842	¥856,842
DAY, SAMUEL WILLIAM	1	1	$691	$691	$691
			DM1,041	DM1,041	DM1,041
			£424	£424	£424
			¥66,948	¥66,948	¥66,948
DE ANGELIS, ERNESTO	1	1	$2,645	$2,645	$2,645
			DM4,100	DM4,100	DM4,100
			£1,693	£1,693	£1,693
			¥260,030	¥260,030	¥260,030
DEARLOVE, MARK WILLIAM	2	1	$4,485	$4,485	$4,485
			DM6,952	DM6,952	DM6,952
			£2,870	£2,870	£2,870
			¥440,920	¥440,920	¥440,920
DEAS, WILLIAM	2	1	$282	$282	$282
			DM466	DM466	DM466
			£173	£173	£173
			¥34,919	¥34,919	¥34,919
DE BARBIERI, PAOLO	5	2	$17,986	$19,960	$18,973
			DM25,441	DM28,110	DM26,776
			£11,500	£12,650	£12,075
			¥1,826,304	¥2,040,850	¥1,933,577

	Items		Selling Prices		
Maker	Bid	Sold	Low	High	Avg
DE BARBIERI, PAOLO (attributed to)	1	0			
DEBLAYE, ALBERT	7	5	$1,921	$2,824	$2,187
			DM3,066	DM4,334	DM3,511
			£1,150	£1,840	£1,360
			¥222,638	¥309,138	¥254,931
DEBLAYE, ALBERT (attributed to)	7	4	$1,034	$2,474	$1,637
			DM1,534	DM3,655	DM2,422
			£667	£1,610	£1,064
			¥111,909	¥263,612	¥173,499
DEBLAYE, ALBERT (workshop of)	2	2	$1,495	$1,840	$1,668
			DM2,558	DM3,075	DM2,816
			£884	£1,228	£1,056
			¥185,649	¥192,850	¥189,250
DE COMBLE, AMBROISE (attributed to)	1	1	$6,184	$6,184	$6,184
			DM9,137	DM9,137	DM9,137
			£4,025	£4,025	£4,025
			¥659,029	¥659,029	¥659,029
DE COMBLE, AMBROSE	1	1	$7,668	$7,668	$7,668
			DM14,205	DM14,205	DM14,205
			£4,600	£4,600	£4,600
			¥1,024,098	¥1,024,098	¥1,024,098
DECONET, MICHAEL	1	0			
DEFAT	1	0			
DEFAT, GEORGES	1	1	$9,087	$9,087	$9,087
			DM12,835	DM12,835	DM12,835
			£5,750	£5,750	£5,750
			¥810,963	¥810,963	¥810,963
DEGANI, DOMENICO (attributed to)	2	1	$7,590	$7,590	$7,590
			DM11,454	DM11,454	DM11,454
			£4,600	£4,600	£4,600
			¥860,200	¥860,200	¥860,200
DEGANI, EUGENIO	14	10	$10,162	$35,337	$24,735
			DM17,186	DM54,545	DM38,985
			£6,820	£23,000	£15,479
			¥1,077,560	¥3,968,455	¥2,775,773
DEGANI, EUGENIO (attributed to)	2	0			
DEGANI, EUGENIO (workshop of)	1	1	$10,281	$10,281	$10,281
			DM15,532	DM15,532	DM15,532
			£6,900	£6,900	£6,900
			¥1,088,889	¥1,088,889	¥1,088,889
DEGANI, GIULIO	17	12	$4,370	$30,360	$15,328
			DM6,905	DM45,816	DM25,081
			£2,797	£18,400	£9,406
			¥436,563	¥3,440,800	¥1,762,156
DEHOMMAIS & GERMAIN	1	1	$6,900	$6,900	$6,900
			DM10,902	DM10,902	DM10,902
			£4,416	£4,416	£4,416
			¥689,310	¥689,310	¥689,310
DE JONG, MATTHIJS	1	0			
DEL CANTO, GIUSTINO (attributed to)	1	0			
DELEPLANQUE, GERARD J.	2	2	$2,599	$5,654	$4,126
			DM4,808	DM8,354	DM6,581
			£1,553	£3,680	£2,616
			¥346,347	¥602,541	¥474,444
DELFOUR, DANIEL	1	0			

| Maker | Items | | Selling Prices | | |
	Bid	Sold	Low	High	Avg
DEL HIERRO, JOSE	1	1	$3,562	$3,562	$3,562
			DM6,162	DM6,162	DM6,162
			£2,185	£2,185	£2,185
			¥406,410	¥406,410	¥406,410
DELIVET, AUGUSTE	3	2	$2,070	$4,455	$3,263
			DM3,578	DM7,535	DM5,556
			£1,279	£2,990	£2,135
			¥262,341	¥472,420	¥367,381
DELLA CORTE, ALFONSO	2	1	$9,692	$9,692	$9,692
			DM14,307	DM14,307	DM14,307
			£6,325	£6,325	£6,325
			¥1,030,349	¥1,030,349	¥1,030,349
DELLA CORTE, ALFONSO (attributed to)	2	0			
DEL LUNGO, ALFREDO	2	2	$1,783	$8,832	$5,307
			DM2,875	DM14,942	DM8,908
			£1,035	£5,555	£3,295
			¥209,875	¥1,094,237	¥652,056
DE LUCCIA BROS.	1	1	$3,795	$3,795	$3,795
			DM5,882	DM5,882	DM5,882
			£2,429	£2,429	£2,429
			¥373,086	¥373,086	¥373,086
DE MEGLIO, GIOVANNI	1	0			
DE MUZIO, FRANCESCO (attributed to)	1	1	$1,885	$1,885	$1,885
			DM3,339	DM3,339	DM3,339
			£1,157	£1,157	£1,157
			¥229,784	¥229,784	¥229,784
DENNY, JAMES GORRIE	1	1	$1,250	$1,250	$1,250
			DM1,749	DM1,749	DM1,749
			£782	£782	£782
			¥105,737	¥105,737	¥105,737
DENTI, ALBERTO	1	0			
DE PLANIS, AUGUST	1	1	$38,823	$38,823	$38,823
			DM59,645	DM59,645	DM59,645
			£25,300	£25,300	£25,300
			¥4,250,122	¥4,250,122	¥4,250,122
DERAZEY, H.	4	3	$2,818	$8,694	$5,247
			DM4,155	DM15,634	DM8,673
			£1,840	£5,175	£3,258
			¥300,601	¥1,005,140	¥585,547
DERAZEY, H. (attributed to)	1	0			
DERAZEY, HONORE	22	14	$1,184	$21,416	$7,414
			DM1,785	DM37,153	DM11,926
			£726	£12,650	£4,648
			¥114,768	¥2,714,817	¥839,701
DERAZEY, HONORE (attributed to)	1	1	$8,401	$8,401	$8,401
			DM12,974	DM12,974	DM12,974
			£5,290	£5,290	£5,290
			¥837,952	¥837,952	¥837,952
DERAZEY, HONORE (Workshop of)	2	1	$1,840	$1,840	$1,840
			DM3,110	DM3,110	DM3,110
			£1,104	£1,104	£1,104
			¥224,480	¥224,480	¥224,480
DERAZEY, JUSTIN	17	11	$773	$10,708	$4,447
			DM1,292	DM18,577	DM7,216
			£518	£6,325	£2,729
			¥82,111	¥1,357,408	¥507,511
DERAZEY, JUSTIN (attributed to)	4	0			

| Maker | Items | | Selling Prices | | |
	Bid	Sold	Low	High	Avg
DERAZEY, JUSTIN (workshop of)	2	2	$1,051	$1,610	$1,331
			DM1,779	DM2,690	DM2,235
			£661	£1,074	£868
			¥130,266	¥168,744	¥149,505
DERAZEY FAMILY (MEMBER OF)	1	0			
DEROUX	1	1	$2,698	$2,698	$2,698
			DM3,816	DM3,816	DM3,816
			£1,725	£1,725	£1,725
			¥273,946	¥273,946	¥273,946
DEROUX, AUGUST S. (attributed to)	2	0			
DESIATO, GIUSEPPE (attributed to)	2	2	$3,220	$4,776	$3,998
			DM5,732	DM8,031	DM6,881
			£1,932	£2,990	£2,461
			¥428,196	¥586,228	¥507,212
DESIATO, VINCENZO (ascribed to)	1	1	$1,472	$1,472	$1,472
			DM2,490	DM2,490	DM2,490
			£926	£926	£926
			¥182,373	¥182,373	¥182,373
DESIATO, VINCENZO (attributed to)	1	0			
D'ESPINE, ALESSANDRO	5	1	$64,950	$64,950	$64,950
			DM91,739	DM91,739	DM91,739
			£41,100	£41,100	£41,100
			¥5,796,621	¥5,796,621	¥5,796,621
DE TOPPANI, ANGELO	2	2	$7,490	$12,633	$10,061
			DM12,513	DM21,902	DM17,207
			£4,485	£7,475	£5,980
			¥910,410	¥1,577,225	¥1,243,818
DEULIN, JOSEF	1	1	$403	$403	$403
			DM689	DM689	DM689
			£238	£238	£238
			¥49,982	¥49,982	¥49,982
DEVEREUX, J.	2	1	$1,006	$1,006	$1,006
			DM1,581	DM1,581	DM1,581
			£644	£644	£644
			¥100,869	¥100,869	¥100,869
DE VINCENZI, MARIO	1	1	$5,175	$5,175	$5,175
			DM8,647	DM8,647	DM8,647
			£3,453	£3,453	£3,453
			¥542,392	¥542,392	¥542,392
DE ZORZI, VALENTINO	5	3	$2,415	$29,390	$15,585
			DM3,492	DM49,419	DM26,507
			£1,577	£18,400	£9,649
			¥244,519	¥3,607,559	¥1,946,710
DE ZORZI, VALENTINO (workshop of)	1	1	$5,463	$5,463	$5,463
			DM9,346	DM9,346	DM9,346
			£3,231	£3,231	£3,231
			¥678,333	¥678,333	¥678,333
DICKENSON, EDWARD	2	1	$1,344	$1,344	$1,344
			DM2,496	DM2,496	DM2,496
			£805	£805	£805
			¥179,869	¥179,869	¥179,869
DICKIE, ROBERT	1	1	$423	$423	$423
			DM671	DM671	DM671
			£276	£276	£276
			¥42,776	¥42,776	¥42,776

Maker	Items		Selling Prices		
	Bid	Sold	Low	High	Avg
DIDELOT, DOMINIQUE	1	1	$1,150	$1,150	$1,150
			DM1,782	DM1,782	DM1,782
			£736	£736	£736
			¥113,056	¥113,056	¥113,056
DIDELOT, J.	1	0			
DIEUDONNE	3	2	$1,555	$3,123	$2,339
			DM2,696	DM5,251	DM3,973
			£920	£1,955	£1,438
			¥194,120	¥383,303	¥288,712
DIEUDONNE, AMEDEE	14	10	$1,725	$9,462	$3,419
			DM2,657	DM16,009	DM5,539
			£1,035	£5,951	£2,138
			¥159,620	¥1,172,396	¥399,597
DIEUDONNE, AMEDEE (attributed to)	5	4	$1,847	$3,518	$2,414
			DM2,835	DM5,401	DM3,674
			£1,127	£2,300	£1,532
			¥201,576	¥383,955	¥255,727
DIEUDONNE, AMEDEE (workshop of)	1	0			
DIGGNEY, CHARLES	1	1	$690	$690	$690
			DM998	DM998	DM998
			£451	£451	£451
			¥69,863	¥69,863	¥69,863
DI LELIO, ARMANDO	2	1	$5,467	$5,467	$5,467
			DM9,250	DM9,250	DM9,250
			£3,439	£3,439	£3,439
			¥677,385	¥677,385	¥677,385
DI SANTO CELLINI, MARCELLO	1	1	$2,291	$2,291	$2,291
			DM3,382	DM3,382	DM3,382
			£1,495	£1,495	£1,495
			¥243,537	¥243,537	¥243,537
DITER, JUSTIN	1	1	$6,325	$6,325	$6,325
			DM9,519	DM9,519	DM9,519
			£3,840	£3,840	£3,840
			¥707,009	¥707,009	¥707,009
DI VILONNI, ANGELO	1	1	$12,230	$12,230	$12,230
			DM17,300	DM17,300	DM17,300
			£7,820	£7,820	£7,820
			¥1,241,886	¥1,241,886	¥1,241,886
DIX, DAVID	10	6	$511	$846	$687
			DM719	DM1,343	DM1,049
			£322	£552	£447
			¥45,637	¥85,551	¥68,325
DIXON, ALFRED THOMAS	1	1	$1,160	$1,160	$1,160
			DM1,735	DM1,735	DM1,735
			£690	£690	£690
			¥129,361	¥129,361	¥129,361
DOBBS, HARRY	1	1	$1,469	$1,469	$1,469
			DM2,255	DM2,255	DM2,255
			£920	£920	£920
			¥144,022	¥144,022	¥144,022
DOBRETSOVITCH, MARCO	1	1	$17,986	$17,986	$17,986
			DM25,441	DM25,441	DM25,441
			£11,500	£11,500	£11,500
			¥1,826,304	¥1,826,304	¥1,826,304
DOBRITCHCOV, FILIP	1	1	$2,588	$2,588	$2,588
			DM4,373	DM4,373	DM4,373
			£1,553	£1,553	£1,553
			¥344,319	¥344,319	¥344,319

| Maker | Items | | Selling Prices | | |
	Bid	Sold	Low	High	Avg
DODD, THOMAS	3	1	$12,710 DM19,504 £8,280 ¥1,391,123	$12,710 DM19,504 £8,280 ¥1,391,123	$12,710 DM19,504 £8,280 ¥1,391,123
DODD, THOMAS (attributed to)	1	1	$9,664 DM14,460 £5,750 ¥1,078,010	$9,664 DM14,460 £5,750 ¥1,078,010	$9,664 DM14,460 £5,750 ¥1,078,010
DODDS, EDWARD	1	1	$1,220 DM2,101 £825 ¥126,371	$1,220 DM2,101 £825 ¥126,371	$1,220 DM2,101 £825 ¥126,371
DOERFFEL	1	1	$504 DM770 £322 ¥56,205	$504 DM770 £322 ¥56,205	$504 DM770 £322 ¥56,205
DOLLENZ, GIOVANNI (attributed to)	2	2	$1,856 DM2,971 £1,207 ¥187,838	$2,306 DM3,574 £1,380 ¥262,634	$2,081 DM3,272 £1,294 ¥225,233
DOLLENZ, GIUSEPPE	2	1	$18,328 DM25,685 £11,500 ¥1,615,578	$18,328 DM25,685 £11,500 ¥1,615,578	$18,328 DM25,685 £11,500 ¥1,615,578
DOLLENZ, GIUSEPPE (attributed to)	1	0			
DOLLING, HERMANN	1	0			
DOLLING, HERMANN (JR.)	2	2	$1,291 DM1,797 £805 ¥109,116	$1,585 DM2,337 £1,035 ¥169,088	$1,438 DM2,067 £920 ¥139,102
DOLLING, ROBERT A.	2	2	$1,495 DM2,286 £897 ¥157,573	$1,495 DM2,527 £984 ¥182,390	$1,495 DM2,406 £940 ¥169,982
DOLLING, ROBERT A. (Workshop of)	1	1	$1,093 DM1,888 £675 ¥138,458	$1,093 DM1,888 £675 ¥138,458	$1,093 DM1,888 £675 ¥138,458
DONI DE BONIS, ROCCO	1	0			
DONI DE BONIS, ROCCO (attributed to)	1	0			
DOOLEY, J.W.	1	1	$1,404 DM2,150 £897 ¥156,544	$1,404 DM2,150 £897 ¥156,544	$1,404 DM2,150 £897 ¥156,544
DORELLI, GIOVANNI (ascribed to)	1	0			
DOW, WILLIAM HENRY	1	0			
DRAKE, WINFORD E.	1	0			
DROUIN, CHARLES	1	0			
DROUIN, ETIENNE	1	1	$1,739 DM3,126 £1,035 ¥201,028	$1,739 DM3,126 £1,035 ¥201,028	$1,739 DM3,126 £1,035 ¥201,028
DROZEN, F.X.	2	1	$3,467 DM6,212 £2,070 ¥402,615	$3,467 DM6,212 £2,070 ¥402,615	$3,467 DM6,212 £2,070 ¥402,615

| Maker | Items | | Selling Prices | | |
	Bid	Sold	Low	High	Avg
DUCHENE, NICOLAS	2	2	$690 DM1,193 £426 ¥87,447	$1,234 DM1,821 £805 ¥131,135	$962 DM1,507 £616 ¥109,291
DUERER, WILHELM	2	1	$154 DM238 £92 ¥17,509	$154 DM238 £92 ¥17,509	$154 DM238 £92 ¥17,509
DUERER, WILHELM (workshop of)	1	1	$259 DM374 £165 ¥22,447	$259 DM374 £165 ¥22,447	$259 DM374 £165 ¥22,447
DUKE, RICHARD	32	22	$539 DM847 £345 ¥54,037	$11,597 DM19,543 £6,900 ¥1,407,370	$4,610 DM7,256 £2,868 ¥507,652
DUKE, RICHARD (ascribed to)	2	1	$2,823 DM4,338 £1,840 ¥309,100	$2,823 DM4,338 £1,840 ¥309,100	$2,823 DM4,338 £1,840 ¥309,100
DUKE, RICHARD (JR.)	2	2	$1,660 DM2,311 £1,035 ¥140,292	$2,582 DM3,595 £1,610 ¥218,232	$2,121 DM2,953 £1,323 ¥179,262
DUKE, RICHARD (JR.) (attributed to)	1	0			
DUKE FAMILY	2	0			
DUNCAN, ROBERT (attributed to)	1	1	$1,463 DM2,441 £978 ¥150,251	$1,463 DM2,441 £978 ¥150,251	$1,463 DM2,441 £978 ¥150,251
DUNLOP, JOHN	3	2	$357 DM605 £219 ¥41,405	$704 DM1,187 £437 ¥86,466	$531 DM896 £328 ¥63,936
DURRSCHMIDT, WILHELM	1	1	$2,415 DM4,174 £1,492 ¥306,065	$2,415 DM4,174 £1,492 ¥306,065	$2,415 DM4,174 £1,492 ¥306,065
DVORAK, CAREL BOROMAUS	2	1	$3,304 DM5,728 £1,955 ¥412,505	$3,304 DM5,728 £1,955 ¥412,505	$3,304 DM5,728 £1,955 ¥412,505
DVORAK, JAN BAPTISTA	9	8	$2,570 DM4,347 £1,725 ¥272,550	$6,110 DM9,972 £3,968 ¥729,491	$4,843 DM7,937 £3,105 ¥558,824
DVORAK, KARL	1	1	$2,300 DM3,517 £1,513 ¥242,420	$2,300 DM3,517 £1,513 ¥242,420	$2,300 DM3,517 £1,513 ¥242,420
DYKER, GEORGE	1	1	$2,390 DM3,344 £1,495 ¥202,143	$2,390 DM3,344 £1,495 ¥202,143	$2,390 DM3,344 £1,495 ¥202,143
DYKER, GEORGE (attributed to)	1	1	$2,212 DM3,546 £1,438 ¥223,711	$2,212 DM3,546 £1,438 ¥223,711	$2,212 DM3,546 £1,438 ¥223,711

Maker	Items		Selling Prices		
	Bid	Sold	Low	High	Avg
DYKES, ARTHUR WILLIAM	2	1	$1,229	$1,229	$1,229
			DM2,031	DM2,031	DM2,031
			£736	£736	£736
			¥143,741	¥143,741	¥143,741
DYKES, GEORGE	1	1	$4,609	$4,609	$4,609
			DM7,700	DM7,700	DM7,700
			£2,760	£2,760	£2,760
			¥560,252	¥560,252	¥560,252
EATON, ERIC S.	1	1	$869	$869	$869
			DM1,300	DM1,300	DM1,300
			£517	£517	£517
			¥96,927	¥96,927	¥96,927
EBERLE, EUGENE	1	1	$3,286	$3,286	$3,286
			DM4,916	DM4,916	DM4,916
			£1,955	£1,955	£1,955
			¥366,523	¥366,523	¥366,523
EBERLE, JOHANN ULRICH	6	5	$1,714	$9,240	$5,657
			DM2,898	DM17,095	DM9,148
			£1,150	£5,750	£3,527
			¥181,700	¥1,231,457	¥609,232
EBERLE, TOMASO	3	3	$28,235	$65,297	$47,533
			DM43,378	DM109,089	DM73,925
			£18,400	£39,100	£29,517
			¥3,090,998	¥7,936,909	¥5,135,702
EBERLE, TOMASO (ascribed to)	1	0			
EBERLE, TOMASO (attributed to)	1	0			
ECKLAND, DONALD	2	1	$4,025	$4,025	$4,025
			DM6,957	DM6,957	DM6,957
			£2,487	£2,487	£2,487
			¥510,108	¥510,108	¥510,108
EDLER, HANS	1	0			
EDREV, EDRIO	1	1	$2,178	$2,178	$2,178
			DM3,066	DM3,066	DM3,066
			£1,380	£1,380	£1,380
			¥222,638	¥222,638	¥222,638
EHRLICH	2	1	$4,252	$4,252	$4,252
			DM6,362	DM6,362	DM6,362
			£2,530	£2,530	£2,530
			¥474,324	¥474,324	¥474,324
EKSTRAND, GUSTAF	2	0			
ELLIOT, WILLIAM	1	1	$2,600	$2,600	$2,600
			DM4,659	DM4,659	DM4,659
			£1,553	£1,553	£1,553
			¥301,961	¥301,961	¥301,961
EMERSON, ELIJAH	1	1	$2,300	$2,300	$2,300
			DM3,935	DM3,935	DM3,935
			£1,360	£1,360	£1,360
			¥285,614	¥285,614	¥285,614
ERBA, PAOLO	1	0			
ERDESZ, OTTO ALEXANDER	3	1	$3,220	$3,220	$3,220
			DM4,924	DM4,924	DM4,924
			£2,118	£2,118	£2,118
			¥339,388	¥339,388	¥339,388
ERMINIA, MALAGUTI (attributed to)	1	1	$3,677	$3,677	$3,677
			DM5,144	DM5,144	DM5,144
			£2,300	£2,300	£2,300
			¥310,990	¥310,990	¥310,990

Maker	Items		Selling Prices		
	Bid	Sold	Low	High	Avg
ERTZ, NEIL	1	1	$1,491	$1,491	$1,491
			DM1,571	DM1,571	DM1,571
			£920	£920	£920
			¥113,891	¥113,891	¥113,891
ESPOSITO, RAFFAELE (attributed to)	1	1	$1,093	$1,093	$1,093
			DM1,945	DM1,945	DM1,945
			£666	£666	£666
			¥151,770	¥151,770	¥151,770
ESPOSTI, PIERGIUSEPPE	2	2	$1,840	$3,760	$2,800
			DM2,657	DM5,637	DM4,147
			£1,172	£2,300	£1,736
			¥159,620	¥363,768	¥261,694
EURSOLO, JOHANN GEORG	1	1	$2,898	$2,898	$2,898
			DM5,211	DM5,211	DM5,211
			£1,725	£1,725	£1,725
			¥335,047	¥335,047	¥335,047
EUSCHEN, KARL	1	1	$1,802	$1,802	$1,802
			DM2,719	DM2,719	DM2,719
			£1,092	£1,092	£1,092
			¥204,204	¥204,204	¥204,204
EVANS & CO., GEORGE	2	1	$544	$544	$544
			DM767	DM767	DM767
			£345	£345	£345
			¥55,660	¥55,660	¥55,660
EWAN, DAVID	1	0			
EWBANK, HENRY	1	1	$345	$345	$345
			DM614	DM614	DM614
			£207	£207	£207
			¥45,878	¥45,878	¥45,878
EYLES, CHARLES	1	1	$2,730	$2,730	$2,730
			DM3,904	DM3,904	DM3,904
			£1,725	£1,725	£1,725
			¥274,251	¥274,251	¥274,251
FABRICATORE, GENNARO	3	0			
FABRIS, LUIGI	2	1	$16,520	$16,520	$16,520
			DM28,641	DM28,641	DM28,641
			£9,775	£9,775	£9,775
			¥2,062,525	¥2,062,525	¥2,062,525
FABRIS, LUIGI (attributed to)	1	1	$3,006	$3,006	$3,006
			DM4,812	DM4,812	DM4,812
			£1,955	£1,955	£1,955
			¥304,245	¥304,245	¥304,245
FAGNOLA, ANNIBALE	5	3	$33,098	$54,184	$45,964
			DM57,418	DM96,010	DM80,330
			£19,550	£33,271	£27,957
			¥4,195,626	¥6,606,601	¥5,525,842
FAGNOLA, ANNIBALE (attributed to)	5	3	$12,121	$20,833	$17,681
			DM19,550	DM29,423	DM25,739
			£7,038	£13,225	£10,971
			¥1,427,150	¥2,097,921	¥1,772,652
FAGNOLA, H.	1	1	$72,979	$72,979	$72,979
			DM121,923	DM121,923	DM121,923
			£43,700	£43,700	£43,700
			¥8,870,663	¥8,870,663	¥8,870,663
FAGNOLA, H. (attributed to)	1	0			

Maker	Items		Selling Prices		
	Bid	Sold	Low	High	Avg
FALISSE, A.	9	5	$3,299	$6,325	$4,507
			DM4,623	DM9,672	DM7,073
			£2,070	£4,161	£2,872
			¥290,804	¥666,655	¥470,518
FALKNER, ARTHUR	1	1	$3,114	$3,114	$3,114
			DM5,267	DM5,267	DM5,267
			£2,090	£2,090	£2,090
			¥330,220	¥330,220	¥330,220
FANTIN, DOMENICO	2	1	$4,523	$4,523	$4,523
			DM8,014	DM8,014	DM8,014
			£2,777	£2,777	£2,777
			¥551,483	¥551,483	¥551,483
FARINA, ERMINIO	1	1	$11,064	$11,064	$11,064
			DM15,406	DM15,406	DM15,406
			£6,900	£6,900	£6,900
			¥935,281	¥935,281	¥935,281
FARLEY, CHARLES E.	2	2	$575	$1,265	$920
			DM1,024	DM1,904	DM1,464
			£345	£768	£556
			¥76,464	¥141,402	¥108,933
FAROTTI, CELESTE	4	3	$12,721	$19,435	$16,423
			DM17,968	DM33,695	DM26,421
			£8,050	£11,500	£9,829
			¥1,135,348	¥2,426,500	¥1,858,883
FAROTTO, CELESTE (attributed to)	1	1	$12,330	$12,330	$12,330
			DM18,177	DM18,177	DM18,177
			£8,050	£8,050	£8,050
			¥1,315,129	¥1,315,129	¥1,315,129
FAROTTO, CELESTINO	1	1	$31,050	$31,050	$31,050
			DM44,836	DM44,836	DM44,836
			£19,782	£19,782	£19,782
			¥2,693,588	¥2,693,588	¥2,693,588
FAWICK, THOMAS L.	1	0			
FEBBRARI, DIPENDENTE	2	0			
FELICI, ENRICO	1	1	$2,068	$2,068	$2,068
			DM3,101	DM3,101	DM3,101
			£1,265	£1,265	£1,265
			¥200,072	¥200,072	¥200,072
FENDT, BERNARD	2	0			
FENDT, BERNARD SIMON	2	1	$16,331	$16,331	$16,331
			DM22,999	DM22,999	DM22,999
			£10,350	£10,350	£10,350
			¥1,669,786	¥1,669,786	¥1,669,786
FENDT, BERNARD SIMON (attributed to)	3	1	$2,914	$2,914	$2,914
			DM4,814	DM4,814	DM4,814
			£1,783	£1,783	£1,783
			¥360,830	¥360,830	¥360,830
FENDT, FRANCOIS (attributed to)	1	0			
FENGA, GIULIANO (ascribed to)	2	1	$1,300	$1,300	$1,300
			DM1,837	DM1,837	DM1,837
			£828	£828	£828
			¥111,019	¥111,019	¥111,019
FENT, FRANCOIS	3	1	$4,235	$4,235	$4,235
			DM7,835	DM7,835	DM7,835
			£2,530	£2,530	£2,530
			¥564,418	¥564,418	¥564,418

Maker	Items		Selling Prices		
	Bid	Sold	Low	High	Avg
FENT, FRANCOIS (ascribed to)	2	1	$3,795	$3,795	$3,795
			DM5,488	DM5,488	DM5,488
			£2,479	£2,479	£2,479
			¥384,244	¥384,244	¥384,244
FERRIER, WILLIAM	1	1	$756	$756	$756
			DM1,168	DM1,168	DM1,168
			£476	£476	£476
			¥75,416	¥75,416	¥75,416
FERRONI, FERDINANDO	1	1	$4,600	$4,600	$4,600
			DM7,034	DM7,034	DM7,034
			£3,026	£3,026	£3,026
			¥484,840	¥484,840	¥484,840
FERRONI, FERNANDO	2	1	$5,175	$5,175	$5,175
			DM8,176	DM8,176	DM8,176
			£3,312	£3,312	£3,312
			¥516,982	¥516,982	¥516,982
FERRONI, FERNANDO (attributed to)	1	1	$7,246	$7,246	$7,246
			DM10,234	DM10,234	DM10,234
			£4,600	£4,600	£4,600
			¥729,712	¥729,712	¥729,712
FEYZEAU (attributed to)	2	1	$470	$470	$470
			DM776	DM776	DM776
			£288	£288	£288
			¥58,198	¥58,198	¥58,198
FICHTL, JOHANN ULRICH	4	3	$394	$3,536	$1,850
			DM602	DM5,661	DM2,913
			£253	£2,300	£1,196
			¥38,907	¥357,935	¥192,501
FICHTL, JOHANN ULRICH (attributed to)	1	1	$730	$730	$730
			DM1,027	DM1,027	DM1,027
			£460	£460	£460
			¥65,196	¥65,196	¥65,196
FICKER, AUGUST WILHELM	1	1	$282	$282	$282
			DM468	DM468	DM468
			£187	£187	£187
			¥29,316	¥29,316	¥29,316
FICKER, C.S.	1	0			
FICKER, JOHANN CHRISTIAN	8	4	$2,037	$4,626	$2,711
			DM3,267	DM7,827	DM4,550
			£1,265	£2,910	£1,694
			¥231,728	¥573,172	¥331,006
FICKER, JOHANN GOTTLOB	3	3	$920	$3,623	$2,128
			DM1,407	DM5,117	DM3,211
			£605	£2,300	£1,336
			¥96,968	¥364,856	¥228,768
FILANO, LUIGI	1	1	$6,176	$6,176	$6,176
			DM9,489	DM9,489	DM9,489
			£4,025	£4,025	£4,025
			¥676,156	¥676,156	¥676,156
FILIPPI, VITTORIO	1	1	$3,080	$3,080	$3,080
			DM5,698	DM5,698	DM5,698
			£1,840	£1,840	£1,840
			¥410,486	¥410,486	¥410,486
FILLION, G.	1	0			
FIORINI, GIUSEPPE	7	4	$3,872	$35,305	$19,721
			DM5,392	DM54,177	DM29,247
			£2,415	£23,000	£12,680
			¥327,348	¥3,864,230	¥1,953,907

Maker	Items		Selling Prices		
	Bid	Sold	Low	High	Avg
FIORINI, GIUSEPPE (ascribed to)	1	0			
FIORINI, PAOLO	4	4	$623	$2,138	$1,385
			DM1,053	DM3,706	DM2,305
			£418	£1,265	£857
			¥66,044	¥266,915	¥159,273
FIORINI, RAFFAELE	4	3	$2,444	$28,582	$13,036
			DM4,138	DM39,798	DM19,175
			£1,495	£17,825	£8,127
			¥283,297	¥2,416,143	¥1,230,506
FIORINI, RAFFAELE (attributed to)	1	1	$15,077	$15,077	$15,077
			DM26,715	DM26,715	DM26,715
			£9,258	£9,258	£9,258
			¥1,838,275	¥1,838,275	¥1,838,275
FIORIONI, CARLO	1	1	$1,705	$1,705	$1,705
			DM2,680	DM2,680	DM2,680
			£1,092	£1,092	£1,092
			¥171,039	¥171,039	¥171,039
FISCHER	1	0			
FISCHER, CARL (workshop of)	1	1	$690	$690	$690
			DM996	DM996	DM996
			£440	£440	£440
			¥59,858	¥59,858	¥59,858
FISCHER, RAY	1	0			
FISCHER, ZACHARIAS	2	2	$74	$2,523	$1,299
			DM125	DM4,269	DM2,197
			£46	£1,587	£817
			¥9,102	¥312,639	¥160,870
FIVAZ, CHARLES	1	1	$2,687	$2,687	$2,687
			DM3,769	DM3,769	DM3,769
			£1,725	£1,725	£1,725
			¥271,520	¥271,520	¥271,520
FIX, DAVID	1	1	$3,565	$3,565	$3,565
			DM5,155	DM5,155	DM5,155
			£2,329	£2,329	£2,329
			¥360,956	¥360,956	¥360,956
FLAMBEAU, PIERRE	2	1	$4,018	$4,018	$4,018
			DM5,649	DM5,649	DM5,649
			£2,530	£2,530	£2,530
			¥357,168	¥357,168	¥357,168
FORBERGER, ROBERT	1	0			
FORD, JACOB	4	2	$3,286	$6,980	$5,133
			DM4,916	DM11,737	DM8,327
			£1,955	£4,370	£3,163
			¥366,523	¥856,795	¥611,659
FORD, JOSEPH W.	2	1	$425	$425	$425
			DM742	DM742	DM742
			£253	£253	£253
			¥54,233	¥54,233	¥54,233
FORST, HANS (workshop of)	2	1	$978	$978	$978
			DM1,652	DM1,652	DM1,652
			£587	£587	£587
			¥119,255	¥119,255	¥119,255
FORSTER, WILLIAM	4	3	$4,438	$7,298	$5,748
			DM6,386	DM12,192	DM9,011
			£2,875	£4,370	£3,565
			¥450,628	¥887,066	¥625,926

Maker	Items		Selling Prices		
	Bid	Sold	Low	High	Avg
FORSTER, WILLIAM (II)	2	1	$3,226 DM4,868 £1,955 ¥365,585	$3,226 DM4,868 £1,955 ¥365,585	$3,226 DM4,868 £1,955 ¥365,585
FOSCHI, GIORGIO	2	1	$5,005 DM9,260 £2,990 ¥667,039	$5,005 DM9,260 £2,990 ¥667,039	$5,005 DM9,260 £2,990 ¥667,039
FOSTER, JOHN	2	1	$913 DM1,410 £575 ¥91,082	$913 DM1,410 £575 ¥91,082	$913 DM1,410 £575 ¥91,082
FOUCHER, HENRI J.C. (attributed to)	1	1	$1,096 DM1,541 £690 ¥97,794	$1,096 DM1,541 £690 ¥97,794	$1,096 DM1,541 £690 ¥97,794
FOUGEROLLE, CLAUDE	1	1	$2,415 DM3,487 £1,539 ¥209,501	$2,415 DM3,487 £1,539 ¥209,501	$2,415 DM3,487 £1,539 ¥209,501
FOWERS, HERBERT	1	1	$395 DM552 £247 ¥33,398	$395 DM552 £247 ¥33,398	$395 DM552 £247 ¥33,398
FRACASSI, ARTURO	2	2	$7,144 DM10,711 £4,370 ¥691,159	$10,046 DM18,066 £5,980 ¥1,161,495	$8,595 DM14,388 £5,175 ¥926,327
FRANCAIS, EMILE	1	1	$7,520 DM11,275 £4,600 ¥727,536	$7,520 DM11,275 £4,600 ¥727,536	$7,520 DM11,275 £4,600 ¥727,536
FRANKE, PAUL	1	1	$3,728 DM3,927 £2,300 ¥284,729	$3,728 DM3,927 £2,300 ¥284,729	$3,728 DM3,927 £2,300 ¥284,729
FRANKS, RAY	2	1	$798 DM1,233 £503 ¥79,605	$798 DM1,233 £503 ¥79,605	$798 DM1,233 £503 ¥79,605
FRANOT, PATRICE	1	1	$1,380 DM2,077 £838 ¥154,256	$1,380 DM2,077 £838 ¥154,256	$1,380 DM2,077 £838 ¥154,256
FREDI, CONTE FABIO	1	0			
FREDI, RODOLFO	4	3	$4,235 DM7,835 £2,530 ¥564,418	$19,550 DM29,894 £12,862 ¥2,060,570	$12,634 DM19,806 £8,197 ¥1,390,162
FREDI, RODOLFO (ascribed to)	1	0			
FREDI, RODOLFO (attributed to)	3	1	$2,138 DM3,706 £1,265 ¥266,915	$2,138 DM3,706 £1,265 ¥266,915	$2,138 DM3,706 £1,265 ¥266,915
FREYER, WILLIAM	1	1	$1,180 DM1,672 £748 ¥121,843	$1,180 DM1,672 £748 ¥121,843	$1,180 DM1,672 £748 ¥121,843

Maker	Items		Selling Prices		
	Bid	Sold	Low	High	Avg
FRIEDRICH, JOHN & BROS.	3	2	$1,265	$3,795	$2,530
			DM1,904	DM5,882	DM3,893
			£768	£2,429	£1,598
			¥141,402	¥373,086	¥257,244
FRIEDRICH, JOHN & BROS. (workshop of)	3	3	$460	$1,610	$920
			DM692	DM2,325	DM1,357
			£279	£1,026	£586
			¥51,419	¥139,668	¥87,937
FUCHS, W.K. (workshop of)	1	1	$633	$633	$633
			DM915	DM915	DM915
			£413	£413	£413
			¥64,041	¥64,041	¥64,041
FULLER, HENRY	1	1	$1,592	$1,592	$1,592
			DM2,341	DM2,341	DM2,341
			£1,035	£1,035	£1,035
			¥168,871	¥168,871	¥168,871
FURBER	3	1	$3,666	$3,666	$3,666
			DM5,880	DM5,880	DM5,880
			£2,381	£2,381	£2,381
			¥417,111	¥417,111	¥417,111
FURBER (attributed to)	1	1	$134	$134	$134
			DM201	DM201	DM201
			£80	£80	£80
			¥14,998	¥14,998	¥14,998
FURBER, JOHN	2	1	$3,385	$3,385	$3,385
			DM5,590	DM5,590	DM5,590
			£2,070	£2,070	£2,070
			¥419,028	¥419,028	¥419,028
FURBER, JOHN (attributed to)	1	1	$1,372	$1,372	$1,372
			DM1,947	DM1,947	DM1,947
			£863	£863	£863
			¥127,348	¥127,348	¥127,348
FURBER, MATTHEW	1	1	$6,184	$6,184	$6,184
			DM9,137	DM9,137	DM9,137
			£4,025	£4,025	£4,025
			¥659,029	¥659,029	¥659,029
FYDAL, M.H.	1	1	$546	$546	$546
			DM790	DM790	DM790
			£357	£357	£357
			¥55,308	¥55,308	¥55,308
GABOR, ANRISAK TIBOR	4	3	$1,270	$1,546	$1,409
			DM1,789	DM2,314	DM2,090
			£805	£920	£882
			¥129,872	¥172,482	¥152,301
GABRIELLI, GIOVANNI BATTISTA	7	5	$19,435	$50,531	$32,393
			DM33,220	DM87,607	DM52,956
			£11,500	£29,900	£19,780
			¥2,411,913	¥6,308,900	¥3,820,054
GABRIELLI, GIOVANNI BATTISTA (ascribed to)	3	1	$4,832	$4,832	$4,832
			DM7,230	DM7,230	DM7,230
			£2,875	£2,875	£2,875
			¥539,005	¥539,005	¥539,005
GADDA, GAETANO	4	2	$14,695	$19,435	$17,065
			DM24,709	DM28,716	DM26,712
			£9,200	£12,650	£10,925
			¥1,803,780	¥2,071,235	¥1,937,507

Maker	Items		Selling Prices		
	Bid	Sold	Low	High	Avg
GADDA, GAETANO (attributed to)	2	0			
GADDA, MARIO	1	1	$7,896	$7,896	$7,896
			DM11,838	DM11,838	DM11,838
			£4,830	£4,830	£4,830
			¥763,913	¥763,913	¥763,913
GADDA FAMILY (MEMBER OF) (attributed to)	1	1	$3,572	$3,572	$3,572
			DM5,355	DM5,355	DM5,355
			£2,185	£2,185	£2,185
			¥345,580	¥345,580	¥345,580
GAFFINO, JOSEPH (attributed to)	1	0			
GAGGINI (ascribed to)	1	1	$2,898	$2,898	$2,898
			DM4,830	DM4,830	DM4,830
			£1,725	£1,725	£1,725
			¥346,363	¥346,363	¥346,363
GAGGINI, PIETRO	3	1	$7,475	$7,475	$7,475
			DM10,809	DM10,809	DM10,809
			£4,883	£4,883	£4,883
			¥756,844	¥756,844	¥756,844
GAGGINI, PIETRO (attributed to)	5	0			
GAGLIANO, ALESSANDRO	4	2	$9,823	$14,751	$12,287
			DM14,680	DM24,948	DM19,814
			£5,980	£9,900	£7,940
			¥945,001	¥1,564,200	¥1,254,601
GAGLIANO, FERDINAND	11	8	$25,026	$75,266	$43,500
			DM43,638	DM105,994	DM65,931
			£14,950	£47,700	£27,056
			¥2,757,273	¥7,695,536	¥4,608,304
GAGLIANO, FERDINAND (attributed to)	1	1	$44,850	$44,850	$44,850
			DM75,797	DM75,797	DM75,797
			£26,910	£26,910	£26,910
			¥5,471,700	¥5,471,700	¥5,471,700
GAGLIANO, GENNARO	2	2	$77,300	$125,632	$101,466
			DM111,776	DM187,974	DM149,875
			£50,492	£74,750	£62,621
			¥7,826,625	¥14,014,130	¥10,920,378
GAGLIANO, GENNARO (attributed to)	2	1	$65,702	$65,702	$65,702
			DM91,924	DM91,924	DM91,924
			£41,100	£41,100	£41,100
			¥5,557,254	¥5,557,254	¥5,557,254
GAGLIANO, GIUSEPPE	5	2	$71,794	$83,481	$77,638
			DM101,106	DM133,643	DM117,374
			£45,500	£54,300	£49,900
			¥7,340,606	¥8,450,383	¥7,895,495
GAGLIANO, GIUSEPPE & ANTONIO	6	3	$27,691	$76,597	$57,361
			DM46,193	DM117,539	DM92,797
			£18,500	£49,900	£37,967
			¥2,843,616	¥8,383,699	¥6,138,772
GAGLIANO, JOHANNES (attributed to)	1	1	$6,900	$6,900	$6,900
			DM12,282	DM12,282	DM12,282
			£4,140	£4,140	£4,140
			¥917,562	¥917,562	¥917,562
GAGLIANO, JOSEPH	2	0			
GAGLIANO, JOSEPH (attributed to)	1	0			

Maker	Items		Selling Prices		
	Bid	Sold	Low	High	Avg
GAGLIANO, NICOLA	13	11	$41,358	$127,955	$89,409
			DM62,010	DM221,370	DM143,462
			£25,300	£78,500	£55,527
			¥4,001,448	¥14,601,000	¥9,900,827
GAGLIANO, NICOLA (attributed to)	2	2	$11,470	$25,026	$18,248
			DM17,622	DM46,300	DM31,961
			£7,475	£14,950	£11,213
			¥1,255,718	¥3,335,196	¥2,295,457
GAGLIANO, NICOLA (I)	1	1	$78,737	$78,737	$78,737
			DM110,883	DM110,883	DM110,883
			£49,900	£49,900	£49,900
			¥8,050,467	¥8,050,467	¥8,050,467
GAGLIANO, NICOLO (II)	2	0			
GAGLIANO, RAFFAELE & ANTONIO (II)	4	1	$23,826	$23,826	$23,826
			DM33,391	DM33,391	DM33,391
			£14,950	£14,950	£14,950
			¥2,100,251	¥2,100,251	¥2,100,251
GAGLIANO, RAFFAELE & ANTONIO (II) (attributed to)	2	2	$21,850	$30,728	$26,289
			DM36,511	DM51,336	DM43,924
			£14,581	£18,400	£16,490
			¥2,290,098	¥3,735,016	¥3,012,557
GAGLIANO FAMILY (MEMBER OF)	6	4	$19,550	$47,481	$32,275
			DM30,889	DM66,761	DM50,794
			£12,512	£29,900	£20,378
			¥1,953,045	¥4,617,963	¥3,423,946
GAGLIANO FAMILY (MEMBER OF) (attributed to)	1	1	$73,286	$73,286	$73,286
			DM108,279	DM108,279	DM108,279
			£47,700	£47,700	£47,700
			¥7,810,112	¥7,810,112	¥7,810,112
GAIANI, ROMANO	2	0			
GAIBISSO, GIOVANNI BATTISTA	6	3	$1,844	$9,488	$5,713
			DM2,568	DM14,318	DM8,354
			£1,150	£5,750	£3,527
			¥155,880	¥1,075,250	¥608,277
GAIDA, GIOVANNI	5	4	$2,399	$21,252	$13,908
			DM3,624	DM38,203	DM22,587
			£1,610	£12,650	£8,453
			¥254,074	¥2,457,010	¥1,476,100
GAILLARD, CHARLES	8	3	$1,381	$2,899	$2,204
			DM2,082	DM4,338	DM3,488
			£847	£1,725	£1,317
			¥133,895	¥323,403	¥249,493
GAILLARD, CHARLES (attributed to)	4	1	$183	$183	$183
			DM341	DM341	DM341
			£115	£115	£115
			¥21,598	¥21,598	¥21,598
GALEAZZI, ADELINO	1	1	$1,055	$1,055	$1,055
			DM1,870	DM1,870	DM1,870
			£648	£648	£648
			¥128,679	¥128,679	¥128,679
GALIMBERTI, LUIGI	3	1	$9,436	$9,436	$9,436
			DM13,288	DM13,288	DM13,288
			£5,980	£5,980	£5,980
			¥964,765	¥964,765	¥964,765

	Items		Selling Prices		
Maker	Bid	Sold	Low	High	Avg
GALLA, ANTON	4	4	$1,555	$5,479	$3,018
			DM2,696	DM7,703	DM4,853
			£920	£3,450	£1,852
			¥197,680	¥487,047	¥345,031
GALLINOTTI, PIETRO	2	0			
GAND, ADOLPHE CHARLES	2	1	$23,625	$23,625	$23,625
			DM33,370	DM33,370	DM33,370
			£14,950	£14,950	£14,950
			¥2,108,503	¥2,108,503	¥2,108,503
GAND, CHARLES	4	1	$13,609	$13,609	$13,609
			DM19,166	DM19,166	DM19,166
			£8,625	£8,625	£8,625
			¥1,391,489	¥1,391,489	¥1,391,489
GAND, CHARLES (attributed to)	1	1	$13,524	$13,524	$13,524
			DM24,311	DM24,311	DM24,311
			£8,050	£8,050	£8,050
			¥1,563,552	¥1,563,552	¥1,563,552
GAND, CHARLES FRANCOIS	6	3	$6,611	$22,559	$13,287
			DM9,881	DM33,824	DM20,746
			£4,025	£13,800	£8,050
			¥636,059	¥2,182,608	¥1,384,414
GAND BROS.	2	2	$10,626	$19,205	$14,916
			DM17,710	DM32,085	DM24,898
			£6,325	£11,500	£8,913
			¥1,269,997	¥2,334,385	¥1,802,191
GAND & BERNARDEL	15	10	$8,470	$17,659	$13,453
			DM13,013	DM28,266	DM21,750
			£5,520	£11,500	£8,374
			¥927,299	¥1,964,200	¥1,510,527
GARAVAGLIA, GARY	1	1	$2,530	$2,530	$2,530
			DM3,658	DM3,658	DM3,658
			£1,653	£1,653	£1,653
			¥256,163	¥256,163	¥256,163
GARDEN, JAMES	2	1	$874	$874	$874
			DM1,249	DM1,249	DM1,249
			£552	£552	£552
			¥87,760	¥87,760	¥87,760
GARIMBERTI, FERDINANDO	5	5	$9,436	$40,569	$26,313
			DM13,288	DM64,021	DM39,760
			£5,980	£25,300	£16,376
			¥935,281	¥4,694,910	¥2,720,382
GARIMBERTI, FERDINANDO (attributed to)	1	0			
GARTNER, EUGEN	2	1	$3,536	$3,536	$3,536
			DM5,661	DM5,661	DM5,661
			£2,300	£2,300	£2,300
			¥357,935	¥357,935	¥357,935
GASPARRI, MARIO	1	0			
GATTI, GEORGIO	7	4	$16,100	$27,600	$21,817
			DM23,281	DM43,608	DM33,153
			£10,517	£17,664	£14,070
			¥1,630,125	¥2,757,240	¥2,201,088
GAUTIE, P. & SON	1	1	$4,911	$4,911	$4,911
			DM7,340	DM7,340	DM7,340
			£2,990	£2,990	£2,990
			¥472,501	¥472,501	¥472,501

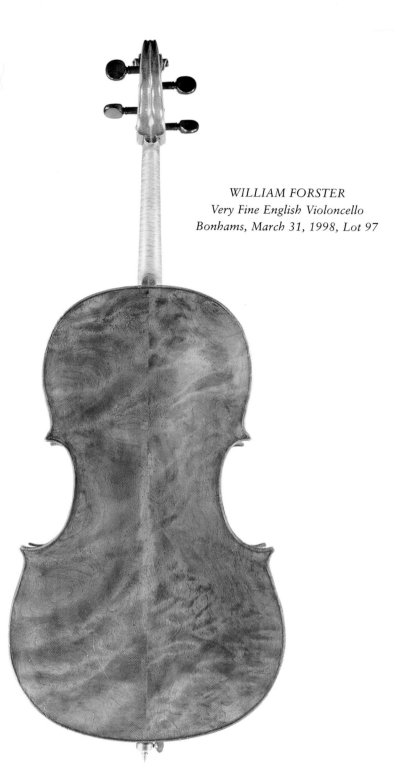

WILLIAM FORSTER
Very Fine English Violoncello
Bonhams, March 31, 1998, Lot 97

GAETANO SGARABOTTO
Good Modern Italian Violin: Parma, 1930
Skinner, November 8, 1998, Lot 82

PIETRO GIOVANNI MANTEGAZZA
Fine Italian Viola
Christie's, April 1, 1998, Lot 115

ANDREA GUARNERI
Violin: Cremona, c. 1645
Sotheby's, March 31, 1998, Lot 23

ANTONIO & GIROLAMO AMATI
Violin: Cremona, c. 1620
Sotheby's, March 31, 1998, Lot 252

CARLO GIUSEPPE TESTORE
Fine Italian Violoncello
Christie's, April 1, 1998, Lot 116

TOMASO EBERLE
Fine Neapolitan Violin: c. 1780
Bonhams, November 18, 1998, Lot 104

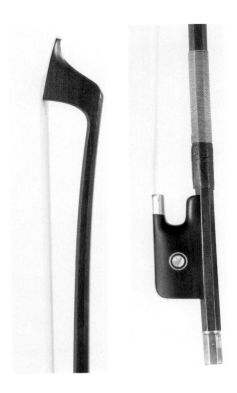

EUGENE SARTORY
Silver Violoncello Bow: Paris, c. 1920
Sotheby's, November 17, 1998, Lot 85

ETIENNE PAJEOT
Fine Nickel Violin Bow: c. 1830
Skinner, November 8, 1998, Lot 210

Maker	Items		Selling Prices		
	Bid	Sold	Low	High	Avg
GEARY, WILLIAM G.	1	1	$359	$359	$359
			DM564	DM564	DM564
			£230	£230	£230
			¥36,025	¥36,025	¥36,025
GEESMAN, EDWARD	1	0			
GEIGEN, TIM	1	1	$400	$400	$400
			DM573	DM573	DM573
			£253	£253	£253
			¥40,223	¥40,223	¥40,223
GEISSENHOF, FRANZ	15	9	$3,450	$20,165	$10,651
			DM5,192	DM34,512	DM17,763
			£2,094	£12,075	£6,577
			¥385,641	¥2,451,104	¥1,229,147
GEISSER, NICOLAUS	2	0			
GEMUNDER, AUGUST	1	1	$5,175	$5,175	$5,175
			DM8,854	DM8,854	DM8,854
			£3,061	£3,061	£3,061
			¥642,632	¥642,632	¥642,632
GEMUNDER, AUGUST & SONS	4	2	$575	$2,041	$1,308
			DM1,024	DM2,948	DM1,986
			£345	£1,300	£823
			¥76,464	¥177,078	¥126,771
GEMUNDER, AUGUST & SONS (workshop of)	2	1	$1,035	$1,035	$1,035
			DM1,558	DM1,558	DM1,558
			£628	£628	£628
			¥115,692	¥115,692	¥115,692
GEMUNDER, GEORGE (SR.)	1	0			
GENIN, LOUIS (attributed to)	1	1	$1,391	$1,391	$1,391
			DM2,137	DM2,137	DM2,137
			£920	£920	£920
			¥148,327	¥148,327	¥148,327
GENOVA, GIOVANNI BATTISTA	1	0			
GENOVESE, RICCARDO	2	2	$16,608	$23,499	$20,053
			DM23,119	DM35,233	DM29,176
			£10,350	£14,375	£12,363
			¥1,401,142	¥2,273,550	¥1,837,346
GERARD, MICHEL	1	1	$1,198	$1,198	$1,198
			DM1,668	DM1,668	DM1,668
			£747	£747	£747
			¥101,254	¥101,254	¥101,254
GERMAIN, EMILE	3	1	$6,935	$6,935	$6,935
			DM12,424	DM12,424	DM12,424
			£4,140	£4,140	£4,140
			¥805,230	¥805,230	¥805,230
GERMAIN, EMILE (attributed to)	2	1	$3,271	$3,271	$3,271
			DM4,620	DM4,620	DM4,620
			£2,070	£2,070	£2,070
			¥291,947	¥291,947	¥291,947
GIAMBERINI, SIMONE	2	1	$18,925	$18,925	$18,925
			DM32,018	DM32,018	DM32,018
			£11,903	£11,903	£11,903
			¥2,344,793	¥2,344,793	¥2,344,793
GIANNINI, FABRIZIO	1	1	$6,542	$6,542	$6,542
			DM9,241	DM9,241	DM9,241
			£4,140	£4,140	£4,140
			¥583,893	¥583,893	¥583,893

Maker	Items		Selling Prices		
	Bid	Sold	Low	High	Avg
GIANOTTI, ALFREDO	5	4	$2,786	$9,031	$5,922
			DM4,712	DM13,947	DM9,418
			£1,870	£5,687	£3,747
			¥295,460	¥900,798	¥619,912
GIBERTINI, ANTONIO	2	1	$36,347	$36,347	$36,347
			DM51,338	DM51,338	DM51,338
			£23,000	£23,000	£23,000
			¥3,243,851	¥3,243,851	¥3,243,851
GIBSON CO.	1	1	$1,360	$1,360	$1,360
			DM1,915	DM1,915	DM1,915
			£862	£862	£862
			¥139,068	¥139,068	¥139,068
GIGLI, GIULIO CESARE	1	1	$21,107	$21,107	$21,107
			DM37,400	DM37,400	DM37,400
			£12,961	£12,961	£12,961
			¥2,573,585	¥2,573,585	¥2,573,585
GILBERT, JEFFREY J.	3	2	$2,118	$3,539	$2,828
			DM3,253	DM5,674	DM4,464
			£1,380	£2,300	£1,840
			¥231,825	¥357,938	¥294,881
GILBERT, JEFFREY JAMES	5	5	$1,126	$4,057	$2,524
			DM1,595	DM5,649	DM3,545
			£713	£2,530	£1,592
			¥116,219	¥342,936	¥243,160
GILBERT, SIMON	1	1	$3,770	$3,770	$3,770
			DM6,376	DM6,376	DM6,376
			£2,530	£2,530	£2,530
			¥399,740	¥399,740	¥399,740
GILCHRIST, JAMES	1	1	$1,127	$1,127	$1,127
			DM1,954	DM1,954	DM1,954
			£667	£667	£667
			¥143,318	¥143,318	¥143,318
GILKES, WILLIAM	1	1	$2,471	$2,471	$2,471
			DM3,796	DM3,796	DM3,796
			£1,610	£1,610	£1,610
			¥270,462	¥270,462	¥270,462
GIORDANI, ENRICO	1	0			
GIORGIS, NICOLAUS	1	1	$8,642	$8,642	$8,642
			DM15,473	DM15,473	DM15,473
			£5,175	£5,175	£5,175
			¥1,189,112	¥1,189,112	¥1,189,112
GIRARDI, MARIO	3	0			
GLADSTONE, R.	1	1	$531	$531	$531
			DM780	DM780	DM780
			£345	£345	£345
			¥56,290	¥56,290	¥56,290
GLAESEL, ERNST	3	2	$751	$934	$843
			DM1,149	DM1,629	DM1,389
			£483	£575	£529
			¥74,278	¥113,189	¥93,733
GLAESEL, ERNST (workshop of)	1	1	$633	$633	$633
			DM980	DM980	DM980
			£405	£405	£405
			¥62,181	¥62,181	¥62,181
GLAESEL, LUDWIG	1	1	$2,332	$2,332	$2,332
			DM4,043	DM4,043	DM4,043
			£1,380	£1,380	£1,380
			¥291,180	¥291,180	¥291,180

Maker	Items Bid	Sold	Selling Prices Low	High	Avg
GLASS, CARL FRIEDERICH	1	0			
GLASS, FRANZ JOHANN	1	1	$2,523	$2,523	$2,523
			DM4,269	DM4,269	DM4,269
			£1,587	£1,587	£1,587
			¥312,639	¥312,639	¥312,639
GLASS, FRIEDRICH AUGUST	1	1	$403	$403	$403
			DM716	DM716	DM716
			£246	£246	£246
			¥55,915	¥55,915	¥55,915
GLASS, JOHANN	1	1	$3,335	$3,335	$3,335
			DM4,816	DM4,816	DM4,816
			£2,125	£2,125	£2,125
			¥289,311	¥289,311	¥289,311
GLASS, JOHANN (workshop of)	1	1	$2,070	$2,070	$2,070
			DM3,165	DM3,165	DM3,165
			£1,362	£1,362	£1,362
			¥218,178	¥218,178	¥218,178
GLENISTER, WILLIAM	15	8	$580	$3,030	$1,695
			DM1,042	DM4,496	DM2,727
			£345	£1,955	£1,061
			¥67,009	¥328,371	¥190,802
GLIER, OTTO R.	1	1	$355	$355	$355
			DM535	DM535	DM535
			£218	£218	£218
			¥34,430	¥34,430	¥34,430
GLIER, ROBERT	1	1	$1,495	$1,495	$1,495
			DM2,661	DM2,661	DM2,661
			£897	£897	£897
			¥198,805	¥198,805	¥198,805
GLOOR, ADOLF	3	2	$561	$635	$598
			DM977	DM1,108	DM1,043
			£345	£391	£368
			¥67,913	¥76,968	¥72,441
GLOTELLE, H.	1	0			
GOBETTI, FRANCESCO	1	1	$103,194	$103,194	$103,194
			DM145,756	DM145,756	DM145,756
			£65,300	£65,300	£65,300
			¥9,209,716	¥9,209,716	¥9,209,716
GOFFRILLER, MATTEO	4	2	$76,895	$97,297	$87,096
			DM133,315	DM164,556	DM148,936
			£45,500	£65,300	£55,400
			¥9,776,585	¥10,317,400	¥10,046,993
GOFTON, ROBERT	1	1	$537	$537	$537
			DM821	DM821	DM821
			£345	£345	£345
			¥53,055	¥53,055	¥53,055
GORDON, HUGH	1	1	$978	$978	$978
			DM1,515	DM1,515	DM1,515
			£626	£626	£626
			¥96,098	¥96,098	¥96,098
GORRIE, ANDREW	1	1	$730	$730	$730
			DM1,365	DM1,365	DM1,365
			£460	£460	£460
			¥86,393	¥86,393	¥86,393
GOSS, PHILIP	1	1	$1,557	$1,557	$1,557
			DM2,497	DM2,497	DM2,497
			£1,012	£1,012	£1,012
			¥157,493	¥157,493	¥157,493

Maker	Items		Selling Prices		
	Bid	Sold	Low	High	Avg
GOSS, PHILIP (attributed to)	3	2	$624	$799	$711
			DM926	DM1,149	DM1,038
			£403	£518	£460
			¥67,531	¥81,113	¥74,322
GOSS, WALTER S.	5	5	$690	$2,645	$1,794
			DM1,055	DM3,825	DM2,777
			£454	£1,728	£1,140
			¥72,726	¥276,916	¥198,710
GOTTI, ANSELMO	2	2	$5,532	$8,723	$7,128
			DM7,703	DM12,321	DM10,012
			£3,450	£5,520	£4,485
			¥467,641	¥778,524	¥623,082
GOTTI, ORSOLO	3	2	$5,467	$6,708	$6,088
			DM9,250	DM10,294	DM9,772
			£3,439	£4,370	£3,904
			¥677,385	¥734,204	¥705,794
GOTZ, C.A.	2	1	$207	$207	$207
			DM350	DM350	DM350
			£127	£127	£127
			¥23,971	¥23,971	¥23,971
GOTZ, CONRAD	1	0			
GOULD, JOHN ALFRED	3	0			
GOULD, JOHN ALFRED (workshop of)	1	1	$4,140	$4,140	$4,140
			DM5,978	DM5,978	DM5,978
			£2,638	£2,638	£2,638
			¥359,145	¥359,145	¥359,145
GOULDING	3	3	$394	$2,332	$1,380
			DM556	DM4,043	DM2,229
			£247	£1,380	£849
			¥34,915	¥296,521	¥160,690
GOULDING & CO.	3	2	$1,643	$2,318	$1,981
			DM2,866	DM3,864	DM3,365
			£978	£1,380	£1,179
			¥209,537	¥277,090	¥243,314
GOWAR, E. (attributed to)	5	1	$263	$263	$263
			DM469	DM469	DM469
			£161	£161	£161
			¥34,394	¥34,394	¥34,394
GRAGNANI, ANTONIO	7	4	$7,970	$64,136	$31,258
			DM14,345	DM111,194	DM52,843
			£4,830	£37,950	£19,278
			¥1,149,299	¥8,007,450	¥3,710,420
GRANCINO, GIOVANNI	8	3	$68,154	$73,196	$71,453
			DM101,633	DM112,453	DM106,223
			£44,400	£47,700	£45,867
			¥6,159,608	¥8,013,075	¥7,210,776
GRANCINO, GIOVANNI (attributed to)	1	0			
GRANDJON (attributed to)	1	1	$1,059	$1,059	$1,059
			DM1,627	DM1,627	DM1,627
			£690	£690	£690
			¥115,912	¥115,912	¥115,912
GRANDJON, J.	2	2	$2,256	$2,332	$2,294
			DM3,382	DM4,043	DM3,713
			£1,380	£1,380	£1,380
			¥218,261	¥296,521	¥257,391

| Maker | Items | | Selling Prices | | |
---	Bid	Sold	Low	High	Avg
GRANDJON, J. (workshop of)	1	1	$1,150 DM1,922 £767 ¥120,531	$1,150 DM1,922 £767 ¥120,531	$1,150 DM1,922 £767 ¥120,531
GRANDJON, JULES (FILS)	2	1	$1,198 DM2,154 £713 ¥138,486	$1,198 DM2,154 £713 ¥138,486	$1,198 DM2,154 £713 ¥138,486
GRANDJON, PROSPER GERARD	1	1	$1,495 DM2,250 £908 ¥167,111	$1,495 DM2,250 £908 ¥167,111	$1,495 DM2,250 £908 ¥167,111
GRANGEAUD, M.	1	1	$450 DM689 £288 ¥50,175	$450 DM689 £288 ¥50,175	$450 DM689 £288 ¥50,175
GRANT, DANIEL P.	1	1	$518 DM885 £306 ¥64,263	$518 DM885 £306 ¥64,263	$518 DM885 £306 ¥64,263
GRATER & SON, T.	1	1	$1,460 DM2,730 £920 ¥172,785	$1,460 DM2,730 £920 ¥172,785	$1,460 DM2,730 £920 ¥172,785
GRATER, THOMAS	1	1	$787 DM1,401 £483 ¥105,743	$787 DM1,401 £483 ¥105,743	$787 DM1,401 £483 ¥105,743
GREENWOOD, GEORGE WILLIAM	2	2	$1,414 DM2,264 £920 ¥143,174	$3,000 DM4,609 £1,955 ¥328,418	$2,207 DM3,437 £1,438 ¥235,796
GRIFFIN, WOODBURY	1	1	$1,265 DM2,164 £748 ¥157,088	$1,265 DM2,164 £748 ¥157,088	$1,265 DM2,164 £748 ¥157,088
GROBITZ	1	0			
GRULLI, PIETRO	3	2	$5,901 DM8,216 £3,680 ¥498,817	$13,840 DM19,266 £8,625 ¥1,167,618	$9,870 DM13,741 £6,153 ¥833,217
GUADAGNINI, ANTONIO (ascribed to)	1	0			
GUADAGNINI, CARLO (attributed to)	1	1	$44,158 DM74,708 £27,773 ¥5,471,183	$44,158 DM74,708 £27,773 ¥5,471,183	$44,158 DM74,708 £27,773 ¥5,471,183
GUADAGNINI, FELICE	2	1	$56,925 DM102,465 £34,500 ¥8,209,275	$56,925 DM102,465 £34,500 ¥8,209,275	$56,925 DM102,465 £34,500 ¥8,209,275
GUADAGNINI, FRANCESCO	5	2	$10,142 DM14,122 £6,325 ¥857,341	$45,230 DM80,144 £27,773 ¥5,514,825	$27,686 DM47,133 £17,049 ¥3,186,083
GUADAGNINI, GAETANO (attributed to)	2	0			

Maker	Items		Selling Prices		
	Bid	Sold	Low	High	Avg
GUADAGNINI, GIOVANNI BATTISTA	12	5	$77,751	$401,775	$220,722
			DM134,514	DM606,315	DM336,359
			£47,700	£243,500	£134,540
			¥8,872,200	¥45,534,500	¥24,729,975
GUADAGNINI, GIOVANNI BATTISTA (attributed to)	2	1	$11,474	$11,474	$11,474
			DM17,607	DM17,607	DM17,607
			£7,475	£7,475	£7,475
			¥1,255,875	¥1,255,875	¥1,255,875
GUADAGNINI, GIUSEPPE	1	0			
GUADAGNINI, GIUSEPPE (attributed to)	3	0			
GUADAGNINI, LORENZO	1	1	$123,865	$123,865	$123,865
			DM174,435	DM174,435	DM174,435
			£78,500	£78,500	£78,500
			¥12,664,562	¥12,664,562	¥12,664,562
GUADAGNINI FAMILY (MEMBER OF)	1	0			
GUADAGNINI FAMILY (MEMBER OF) (ascribed to)	1	1	$103,540	$103,540	$103,540
			DM172,980	DM172,980	DM172,980
			£62,000	£62,000	£62,000
			¥12,585,380	¥12,585,380	¥12,585,380
GUADAGNINI FAMILY (MEMBER OF) (attributed to)	3	1	$10,689	$10,689	$10,689
			DM18,532	DM18,532	DM18,532
			£6,325	£6,325	£6,325
			¥1,334,575	¥1,334,575	¥1,334,575
GUADO, LORENZO FRASSINO	2	2	$2,566	$3,795	$3,180
			DM3,596	DM6,831	DM5,213
			£1,610	£2,300	£1,955
			¥226,181	¥547,285	¥386,733
GUADO, LORENZO FRASSINO (attributed to)	1	0			
GUARNERI, ANDREA	3	2	$105,629	$149,465	$127,547
			DM195,421	DM249,705	DM222,563
			£63,100	£89,500	£76,300
			¥14,076,979	¥18,167,605	¥16,122,292
GUARNERI, GIUSEPPE (FILIUS ANDREAE)	3	2	$92,361	$278,055	$185,208
			DM138,481	DM464,535	DM301,508
			£56,500	£166,500	£111,500
			¥8,936,040	¥33,797,835	¥21,366,938
GUARNERI, JOSEPH (DEL GESU)	2	1	$932,035	$932,035	$932,035
			DM1,615,895	DM1,615,895	DM1,615,895
			£551,500	£551,500	£551,500
			¥116,366,500	¥116,366,500	¥116,366,500
GUARNERI, PIETRO (OF MANTUA)	2	1	$340,135	$340,135	$340,135
			DM544,425	DM544,425	DM544,425
			£221,500	£221,500	£221,500
			¥34,321,425	¥34,321,425	¥34,321,425
GUARNERI, PIETRO (OF MANTUA) (ascribed to)	1	0			
GUARNERI, PIETRO (OF VENICE)	1	0			
GUARNERI FAMILY (ascribed to)	1	0			
GUARNERI FAMILY (attributed to)	1	1	$27,219	$27,219	$27,219
			DM38,331	DM38,331	DM38,331
			£17,250	£17,250	£17,250
			¥2,782,977	¥2,782,977	¥2,782,977
GUASTALLA, DANTE (workshop of)	1	0			

Maker	Items Bid	Sold	Selling Prices Low	High	Avg
GUASTALLA, DANTE & ALFREDO (attributed to)	2	0			
GUERRA, EVASIO EMILE	8	5	$15,180	$33,922	$22,346
			DM27,312	DM60,108	DM37,195
			£9,200	£20,829	£14,025
			¥1,967,030	¥4,136,119	¥2,628,307
GUERSAN, LOUIS	5	5	$822	$5,444	$3,784
			DM1,433	DM8,663	DM6,045
			£506	£3,520	£2,387
			¥99,606	¥556,595	¥416,630
GUERSAN, LOUIS (attributed to)	1	0			
GUICCIARDI, GIANCARLO	1	1	$18,262	$18,262	$18,262
			DM25,677	DM25,677	DM25,677
			£11,500	£11,500	£11,500
			¥1,629,895	¥1,629,895	¥1,629,895
GUIDANTE, FLORENO	1	1	$9,220	$9,220	$9,220
			DM12,838	DM12,838	DM12,838
			£5,750	£5,750	£5,750
			¥779,401	¥779,401	¥779,401
GUIDANTE, GIOVANNI FLORENO	5	2	$9,664	$27,600	$18,632
			DM14,460	DM46,120	DM30,290
			£5,750	£18,417	£12,084
			¥1,078,010	¥2,892,756	¥1,985,383
GUIDANTE, GIOVANNI FLORENO (ascribed to)	2	0			
GUIDANTE, GIOVANNI FLORENO (attributed to)	2	1	$24,967	$24,967	$24,967
			DM46,345	DM46,345	DM46,345
			£14,950	£14,950	£14,950
			¥3,340,428	¥3,340,428	¥3,340,428
GUILLAMI	2	1	$6,556	$6,556	$6,556
			DM11,088	DM11,088	DM11,088
			£4,400	£4,400	£4,400
			¥695,200	¥695,200	¥695,200
GUILLAMI, JUAN	1	0			
GUTH, AUGUST	1	1	$2,915	$2,915	$2,915
			DM5,054	DM5,054	DM5,054
			£1,725	£1,725	£1,725
			¥363,975	¥363,975	¥363,975
GUTH, PAUL (attributed to)	1	1	$3,575	$3,575	$3,575
			DM6,048	DM6,048	DM6,048
			£2,248	£2,248	£2,248
			¥442,905	¥442,905	¥442,905
GUTTER, GEORG ADAM	1	0			
GUTTER, JOHANN GEORG	1	0			
GUTTER, JOHANN GEORG (attributed to)	2	2	$635	$1,291	$963
			DM1,108	DM2,312	DM1,710
			£391	£771	£581
			¥76,968	¥149,862	¥113,415
GYULA, CSISZAR	1	1	$1,495	$1,495	$1,495
			DM2,558	DM2,558	DM2,558
			£884	£884	£884
			¥185,649	¥185,649	¥185,649
HAAHTI, EERO	1	1	$3,262	$3,262	$3,262
			DM3,436	DM3,436	DM3,436
			£2,013	£2,013	£2,013
			¥249,137	¥249,137	¥249,137

Maker	Items Bid	Sold	Selling Prices Low	High	Avg
HADDEN, ROBERT	1	1	$690 DM1,278 £414 ¥92,169	$690 DM1,278 £414 ¥92,169	$690 DM1,278 £414 ¥92,169
HALL, GEORGE S.	1	1	$633 DM1,093 £391 ¥80,160	$633 DM1,093 £391 ¥80,160	$633 DM1,093 £391 ¥80,160
HALL, LOUIS HASTINGS	1	1	$546 DM790 £357 ¥55,308	$546 DM790 £357 ¥55,308	$546 DM790 £357 ¥55,308
HALL, R.G.	4	3	$920 DM1,407 £605 ¥96,968	$3,105 DM4,484 £1,978 ¥269,359	$2,262 DM3,292 £1,447 ¥201,919
HALL, REV. F.J. SILSEE SHIPHAM	1	0			
HALL, WILLIAM	2	1	$309 DM539 £184 ¥39,442	$309 DM539 £184 ¥39,442	$309 DM539 £184 ¥39,442
HALLIDAY, R.L.	3	3	$360 DM550 £230 ¥40,147	$588 DM873 £380 ¥63,673	$492 DM744 £318 ¥53,804
HAMM, ALBAN (workshop of)	1	1	$518 DM791 £340 ¥54,545	$518 DM791 £340 ¥54,545	$518 DM791 £340 ¥54,545
HAMM, JOHANN GOTTFRIED	3	2	$1,150 DM1,731 £698 ¥128,547	$1,977 DM2,767 £1,237 ¥167,258	$1,564 DM2,249 £968 ¥147,903
HAMM, JOHANN GOTTFRIED (workshop of)	1	1	$173 DM307 £105 ¥23,964	$173 DM307 £105 ¥23,964	$173 DM307 £105 ¥23,964
HAMMETT, THOMAS	5	3	$910 DM1,301 £575 ¥91,417	$1,549 DM2,584 £1,035 ¥159,089	$1,275 DM1,998 £823 ¥128,891
HAMMIG, LIPPOLD	1	0			
HAMMOND, JOHN	2	1	$185 DM312 £115 ¥22,754	$185 DM312 £115 ¥22,754	$185 DM312 £115 ¥22,754
HANDLEY, HENRY	1	1	$1,006 DM1,581 £644 ¥100,869	$1,006 DM1,581 £644 ¥100,869	$1,006 DM1,581 £644 ¥100,869
HANSEN, SVERRE	2	2	$1,583 DM2,430 £1,035 ¥172,780	$3,166 DM4,861 £2,070 ¥345,560	$2,375 DM3,646 £1,553 ¥259,170
HARDIE, JAMES (attributed to)	2	0			

Maker	Items		Selling Prices		
	Bid	Sold	Low	High	Avg
HARDIE, JAMES & SONS	1	1	$580	$580	$580
			DM1,042	DM1,042	DM1,042
			£345	£345	£345
			¥67,009	¥67,009	¥67,009
HARDIE, JAMES & SONS (attributed to)	3	1	$1,118	$1,118	$1,118
			DM1,178	DM1,178	DM1,178
			£690	£690	£690
			¥85,419	¥85,419	¥85,419
HARDIE, MATTHEW	6	3	$3,864	$5,677	$4,652
			DM6,440	DM9,605	DM7,704
			£2,300	£3,571	£2,915
			¥445,481	¥703,438	¥536,912
HARDIE, MATTHEW (attributed to)	4	2	$5,780	$8,554	$7,167
			DM8,686	DM13,720	DM11,203
			£3,450	£5,555	£4,502
			¥643,635	¥973,259	¥808,447
HARDIE, MATTHEW & SON (attributed to)	1	0			
HARDIE, THOMAS	2	2	$973	$5,756	$3,364
			DM1,689	DM8,141	DM4,915
			£575	£3,680	£2,128
			¥123,401	¥584,417	¥353,909
HARDWICK, JOHN E.	2	2	$530	$707	$619
			DM783	DM1,044	DM913
			£345	£460	£403
			¥56,503	¥75,337	¥65,920
HARLOW, FRANK	4	1	$672	$672	$672
			DM989	DM989	DM989
			£437	£437	£437
			¥71,301	¥71,301	¥71,301
HARPER, ANDREW	2	1	$388	$388	$388
			DM615	DM615	DM615
			£253	£253	£253
			¥39,211	¥39,211	¥39,211
HARRIS, CHARLES	2	2	$6,185	$7,728	$6,956
			DM9,254	DM12,880	DM11,067
			£3,680	£4,600	£4,140
			¥689,926	¥923,634	¥806,780
HARRIS, CHARLES (II)	1	1	$3,416	$3,416	$3,416
			DM5,154	DM5,154	DM5,154
			£2,070	£2,070	£2,070
			¥387,090	¥387,090	¥387,090
HARRIS, GEORGE E.	1	1	$368	$368	$368
			DM514	DM514	DM514
			£230	£230	£230
			¥31,099	¥31,099	¥31,099
HART, CHARLES H.	1	0			
HART, GEORGE	1	1	$4,794	$4,794	$4,794
			DM6,676	DM6,676	DM6,676
			£2,990	£2,990	£2,990
			¥405,289	¥405,289	¥405,289
HART & SON	3	3	$2,564	$3,749	$3,216
			DM3,772	DM6,486	DM5,398
			£1,668	£2,300	£1,990
			¥272,069	¥443,488	¥381,119
HART & SON (workshop of)	1	1	$1,898	$1,898	$1,898
			DM2,864	DM2,864	DM2,864
			£1,150	£1,150	£1,150
			¥215,050	¥215,050	¥215,050

Maker	Items		Selling Prices		
	Bid	Sold	Low	High	Avg
HAUSMANN, OTTOMAR	1	1	$1,840	$1,840	$1,840
			DM3,180	DM3,180	DM3,180
			£1,137	£1,137	£1,137
			¥233,192	¥233,192	¥233,192
HAVEMANN, CARL FRIEDRICH	1	1	$210	$210	$210
			DM352	DM352	DM352
			£126	£126	£126
			¥25,577	¥25,577	¥25,577
HAWKES & SON	2	2	$232	$1,022	$627
			DM385	DM1,405	DM895
			£154	£633	£393
			¥24,143	¥85,128	¥54,635
HAXTON, GEORGE	1	1	$1,557	$1,557	$1,557
			DM2,633	DM2,633	DM2,633
			£1,045	£1,045	£1,045
			¥165,110	¥165,110	¥165,110
HAYNES & CO.	1	1	$1,997	$1,997	$1,997
			DM3,378	DM3,378	DM3,378
			£1,256	£1,256	£1,256
			¥247,393	¥247,393	¥247,393
HAZELL, LEONARD W.	4	1	$186	$186	$186
			DM196	DM196	DM196
			£115	£115	£115
			¥14,236	¥14,236	¥14,236
HEATON, WALTER	1	1	$787	$787	$787
			DM1,331	DM1,331	DM1,331
			£528	£528	£528
			¥83,424	¥83,424	¥83,424
HEATON, WILLIAM	6	5	$287	$1,096	$861
			DM452	DM1,541	DM1,350
			£184	£690	£546
			¥28,820	¥110,554	¥92,600
HEBERLEIN (workshop of)	3	3	$616	$1,497	$954
			DM909	DM2,210	DM1,400
			£402	£977	£622
			¥65,486	¥159,154	¥100,108
HEBERLEIN, G.F. (JR.)	1	1	$978	$978	$978
			DM1,652	DM1,652	DM1,652
			£587	£587	£587
			¥119,255	¥119,255	¥119,255
HEBERLEIN, HEINRICH E. (JR.) (workshop of)	1	1	$518	$518	$518
			DM791	DM791	DM791
			£340	£340	£340
			¥54,545	¥54,545	¥54,545
HEBERLEIN, HEINRICH TH. (workshop of)	3	3	$978	$1,840	$1,323
			DM1,412	DM3,148	DM2,106
			£623	£1,088	£823
			¥84,798	¥228,491	¥144,833
HEBERLEIN, HEINRICH TH. (JR.)	7	6	$805	$3,179	$1,874
			DM1,360	DM5,088	DM3,026
			£483	£2,070	£1,166
			¥98,210	¥320,747	¥208,685
HEBERLEIN, HEINRICH TH. (JR.) (workshop of)	14	12	$431	$2,300	$1,313
			DM665	DM3,542	DM2,083
			£255	£1,502	£818
			¥46,575	¥257,053	¥146,936

Maker	Items Bid	Sold	Selling Prices Low	High	Avg
HEBERLEIN, L. FRITZ (attributed to)	1	1	$809 DM1,449 £483 ¥93,944	$809 DM1,449 £483 ¥93,944	$809 DM1,449 £483 ¥93,944
HEBERLEIN, LUDWIG	1	1	$1,681 DM2,695 £1,093 ¥170,020	$1,681 DM2,695 £1,093 ¥170,020	$1,681 DM2,695 £1,093 ¥170,020
HEBERLIN, FRIEDRICH	2	1	$508 DM815 £330 ¥57,831	$508 DM815 £330 ¥57,831	$508 DM815 £330 ¥57,831
HECKEL, RUDOLF	1	1	$2,185 DM3,155 £1,392 ¥189,549	$2,185 DM3,155 £1,392 ¥189,549	$2,185 DM3,155 £1,392 ¥189,549
HECKEL, RUDOLF (attributed to)	1	1	$2,206 DM3,087 £1,380 ¥186,594	$2,206 DM3,087 £1,380 ¥186,594	$2,206 DM3,087 £1,380 ¥186,594
HEESOM, EDWARD	1	0			
HEINEL, OSKAR BERNHARD	1	1	$805 DM1,360 £483 ¥98,210	$805 DM1,360 £483 ¥98,210	$805 DM1,360 £483 ¥98,210
HEINEL, OSKAR ERICH	3	1	$2,695 DM4,986 £1,610 ¥359,175	$2,695 DM4,986 £1,610 ¥359,175	$2,695 DM4,986 £1,610 ¥359,175
HEINICKE, MATHIAS	8	2	$3,887 DM6,726 £2,300 ¥421,860	$4,025 DM6,739 £2,686 ¥485,300	$3,956 DM6,732 £2,493 ¥453,580
HEL, J.	1	1	$16,324 DM27,272 £9,775 ¥1,984,227	$16,324 DM27,272 £9,775 ¥1,984,227	$16,324 DM27,272 £9,775 ¥1,984,227
HEL, JOSEPH	7	3	$7,556 DM11,292 £4,600 ¥726,924	$12,357 DM18,962 £8,050 ¥1,352,481	$10,491 DM15,875 £6,517 ¥1,122,225
HEL, JOSEPH (attributed to)	1	1	$16,295 DM30,185 £9,775 ¥2,176,208	$16,295 DM30,185 £9,775 ¥2,176,208	$16,295 DM30,185 £9,775 ¥2,176,208
HEL, JOSEPH (workshop of)	1	1	$431 DM623 £275 ¥37,411	$431 DM623 £275 ¥37,411	$431 DM623 £275 ¥37,411
HEL, PIERRE JEAN HENRI	3	1	$12,650 DM19,343 £8,322 ¥1,333,310	$12,650 DM19,343 £8,322 ¥1,333,310	$12,650 DM19,343 £8,322 ¥1,333,310
HEL, PIERRE JOSEPH	8	4	$14,404 DM20,535 £8,625 ¥1,297,540	$17,265 DM25,756 £10,925 ¥1,835,280	$15,743 DM23,685 £9,919 ¥1,606,110
HELLMER, J.G.	1	0			

Maker	Items		Selling Prices		
	Bid	Sold	Low	High	Avg
HELLMER, KARL	1	1	$489	$489	$489
			DM836	DM836	DM836
			£289	£289	£289
			¥60,693	¥60,693	¥60,693
HELMER, JOANES GEORGIUS	1	1	$2,944	$2,944	$2,944
			DM4,981	DM4,981	DM4,981
			£1,852	£1,852	£1,852
			¥364,746	¥364,746	¥364,746
HEMPEL, JULIUS	1	1	$1,093	$1,093	$1,093
			DM1,888	DM1,888	DM1,888
			£675	£675	£675
			¥138,458	¥138,458	¥138,458
HENDERSHOT, JOHN C.	1	1	$345	$345	$345
			DM590	DM590	DM590
			£204	£204	£204
			¥42,842	¥42,842	¥42,842
HENDERSON, F.V.	1	1	$518	$518	$518
			DM921	DM921	DM921
			£311	£311	£311
			¥68,817	¥68,817	¥68,817
HENDERSON, HAROLD A.	1	1	$2,415	$2,415	$2,415
			DM3,635	DM3,635	DM3,635
			£1,466	£1,466	£1,466
			¥269,949	¥269,949	¥269,949
HENNING, GUSTAV	1	1	$690	$690	$690
			DM1,166	DM1,166	DM1,166
			£414	£414	£414
			¥84,180	¥84,180	¥84,180
HENRY	1	1	$7,321	$7,321	$7,321
			DM11,002	DM11,002	DM11,002
			£4,370	£4,370	£4,370
			¥815,272	¥815,272	¥815,272
HENRY, EUGENE	3	2	$2,028	$7,941	$4,985
			DM2,824	DM12,200	DM7,512
			£1,265	£5,175	£3,220
			¥171,468	¥869,343	¥520,406
HENRY, J.B.	1	1	$3,183	$3,183	$3,183
			DM4,683	DM4,683	DM4,683
			£2,070	£2,070	£2,070
			¥337,741	¥337,741	¥337,741
HENTSCHEL, JOHANN JOSEPH	1	0			
HERBRIG, CHARLES EDWARD	1	1	$805	$805	$805
			DM1,462	DM1,462	DM1,462
			£493	£493	£493
			¥99,965	¥99,965	¥99,965
HERCLIK, FR.	1	1	$2,903	$2,903	$2,903
			DM4,089	DM4,089	DM4,089
			£1,840	£1,840	£1,840
			¥296,851	¥296,851	¥296,851
HERCLIK, LADISLAV	1	1	$1,802	$1,802	$1,802
			DM2,719	DM2,719	DM2,719
			£1,092	£1,092	£1,092
			¥204,204	¥204,204	¥204,204
HERMANN (workshop of)	1	1	$196	$196	$196
			DM348	DM348	DM348
			£119	£119	£119
			¥27,159	¥27,159	¥27,159

Maker	Items		Selling Prices		
	Bid	Sold	Low	High	Avg
HERRMANN, HEINRICH (attributed to)	1	1	$530	$530	$530
			DM783	DM783	DM783
			£345	£345	£345
			¥56,488	¥56,488	¥56,488
HERRMANN, KARL (workshop of)	4	4	$1,150	$1,495	$1,323
			DM1,758	DM2,317	DM2,044
			£757	£957	£852
			¥121,210	¥146,973	¥132,053
HERTL, ANTON	3	1	$854	$854	$854
			DM1,516	DM1,516	DM1,516
			£518	£518	£518
			¥118,451	¥118,451	¥118,451
HESKETH	1	1	$4,993	$4,993	$4,993
			DM8,342	DM8,342	DM8,342
			£2,990	£2,990	£2,990
			¥606,940	¥606,940	¥606,940
HESKETH, THOMAS EARLE	14	12	$1,733	$7,342	$4,940
			DM3,205	DM13,197	DM8,059
			£1,035	£4,600	£3,095
			¥230,898	¥887,066	¥544,212
HEVELKA, SIMON JOANNES (attributed to)	1	1	$1,463	$1,463	$1,463
			DM2,077	DM2,077	DM2,077
			£920	£920	£920
			¥135,838	¥135,838	¥135,838
HEYLIGERS, MATHIJS	2	1	$7,750	$7,750	$7,750
			DM10,789	DM10,789	DM10,789
			£4,830	£4,830	£4,830
			¥653,866	¥653,866	¥653,866
HICKS, GEORGE HERBERT	3	1	$2,566	$2,566	$2,566
			DM3,596	DM3,596	DM3,596
			£1,610	£1,610	£1,610
			¥226,181	¥226,181	¥226,181
HILAIRE, PAUL	3	1	$2,820	$2,820	$2,820
			DM4,228	DM4,228	DM4,228
			£1,725	£1,725	£1,725
			¥272,826	¥272,826	¥272,826
HILAIRE, PAUL (workshop of)	1	1	$1,725	$1,725	$1,725
			DM2,982	DM2,982	DM2,982
			£1,066	£1,066	£1,066
			¥218,618	¥218,618	¥218,618
HILL, HENRY LOCKEY	1	0			
HILL, JOSEPH	11	7	$4,240	$8,066	$6,235
			DM6,265	DM13,476	DM9,724
			£2,760	£4,830	£3,866
			¥451,906	¥980,442	¥670,675
HILL, JOSEPH (attributed to)	5	4	$748	$7,750	$3,143
			DM1,303	DM10,789	DM4,509
			£460	£4,830	£1,984
			¥90,551	¥653,866	¥292,162
HILL, LOCKEY	5	3	$1,270	$6,088	$2,968
			DM1,789	DM9,746	DM4,771
			£805	£3,960	£1,895
			¥129,872	¥616,271	¥308,278
HILL, W.E. & SONS	20	10	$5,436	$14,576	$9,206
			DM8,676	DM25,271	DM14,294
			£3,335	£8,625	£5,693
			¥524,257	¥1,819,875	¥1,002,445

Maker	Items		Selling Prices		
	Bid	Sold	Low	High	Avg
HILL, W.E. & SONS (workshop of)	1	1	$2,760	$2,760	$2,760
			DM3,985	DM3,985	DM3,985
			£1,758	£1,758	£1,758
			¥239,430	¥239,430	¥239,430
HILL FAMILY (MEMBER OF)	5	2	$2,409	$3,479	$2,944
			DM4,060	DM5,205	DM4,633
			£1,495	£2,070	£1,783
			¥295,805	¥388,084	¥341,944
HJORTH, EMIL	4	1	$6,459	$6,459	$6,459
			DM8,991	DM8,991	DM8,991
			£4,025	£4,025	£4,025
			¥544,888	¥544,888	¥544,888
HJORTH, KNUD	2	1	$5,444	$5,444	$5,444
			DM7,666	DM7,666	DM7,666
			£3,450	£3,450	£3,450
			¥556,595	¥556,595	¥556,595
HOFMANN, GEORG PHILIP	1	0			
HOFMANS, MATHIAS (attributed to)	3	1	$1,679	$1,679	$1,679
			DM2,478	DM2,478	DM2,478
			£1,092	£1,092	£1,092
			¥178,843	¥178,843	¥178,843
HOFNER, KARL	2	2	$1,060	$1,263	$1,162
			DM1,566	DM2,190	DM1,878
			£690	£748	£719
			¥112,976	¥157,723	¥135,349
HOFT	1	1	$278	$278	$278
			DM471	DM471	DM471
			£187	£187	£187
			¥29,506	¥29,506	¥29,506
HOING, CLIFFORD A.	1	0			
HOLDER, ERNEST	1	1	$1,398	$1,398	$1,398
			DM2,232	DM2,232	DM2,232
			£908	£908	£908
			¥141,229	¥141,229	¥141,229
HOLDER, T.J.	2	2	$5,780	$8,457	$7,118
			DM8,686	DM11,832	DM10,259
			£3,450	£5,290	£4,370
			¥643,635	¥715,277	¥679,456
HOLDER, T.J. (attributed to)	3	0			
HOLDER, THOMAS	1	0			
HOLDER, THOMAS (attributed to)	3	0			
HOLLISTER, W.	1	0			
HOLST, JOHANNES (attributed to)	2	1	$883	$883	$883
			DM1,460	DM1,460	DM1,460
			£529	£529	£529
			¥103,314	¥103,314	¥103,314
HOMENICK BROTHERS	1	1	$3,220	$3,220	$3,220
			DM5,566	DM5,566	DM5,566
			£1,990	£1,990	£1,990
			¥408,087	¥408,087	¥408,087
HOMOLKA, EMANUEL ADAM	1	1	$7,991	$7,991	$7,991
			DM13,519	DM13,519	DM13,519
			£5,026	£5,026	£5,026
			¥990,024	¥990,024	¥990,024
HOMOLKA, FERDINAND AUGUST	2	2	$5,264	$7,951	$6,607
			DM7,892	DM11,747	DM9,820
			£3,220	£5,175	£4,198
			¥509,275	¥847,323	¥678,299

Maker	Items		Selling Prices		
	Bid	Sold	Low	High	Avg
HOMOLKA, FERDINAND JOS.	1	1	$1,034	$1,034	$1,034
			DM1,708	DM1,708	DM1,708
			£633	£633	£633
			¥128,036	¥128,036	¥128,036
HOPF	10	5	$212	$1,008	$545
			DM312	DM1,516	DM856
			£138	£633	£336
			¥22,516	¥109,193	¥58,789
HOPF (attributed to)	1	1	$691	$691	$691
			DM1,143	DM1,143	DM1,143
			£414	£414	£414
			¥80,854	¥80,854	¥80,854
HOPF, DAVID	2	2	$1,380	$1,840	$1,610
			DM2,332	DM2,852	DM2,592
			£828	£1,178	£1,003
			¥168,360	¥180,890	¥174,625
HOPF, L.	1	0			
HOPF FAMILY (MEMBER OF)	2	2	$420	$1,536	$978
			DM649	DM2,539	DM1,594
			£265	£920	£592
			¥41,898	¥179,676	¥110,787
HOPKINS, E. (attributed to)	1	0			
HORNSTEINER	6	4	$394	$789	$584
			DM700	DM1,337	DM1,005
			£242	£483	£359
			¥52,872	¥91,527	¥71,193
HORNSTEINER (ascribed to)	1	1	$1,344	$1,344	$1,344
			DM2,246	DM2,246	DM2,246
			£805	£805	£805
			¥163,407	¥163,407	¥163,407
HORNSTEINER (attributed to)	1	0			
HORNSTEINER (workshop of)	1	1	$345	$345	$345
			DM614	DM614	DM614
			£210	£210	£210
			¥47,927	¥47,927	¥47,927
HORNSTEINER, J.	2	1	$489	$489	$489
			DM828	DM828	DM828
			£299	£299	£299
			¥56,659	¥56,659	¥56,659
HORNSTEINER, JOSEPH	2	1	$1,360	$1,360	$1,360
			DM2,359	DM2,359	DM2,359
			£805	£805	£805
			¥172,970	¥172,970	¥172,970
HORNSTEINER, JOSEPH (II)	3	3	$1,410	$3,866	$2,359
			DM2,081	DM5,784	DM3,528
			£920	£2,300	£1,437
			¥149,869	¥431,204	¥261,759
HORNSTEINER, MATHIAS	3	1	$5,175	$5,175	$5,175
			DM8,854	DM8,854	DM8,854
			£3,061	£3,061	£3,061
			¥642,632	¥642,632	¥642,632
HORNSTEINER FAMILY	4	2	$309	$466	$388
			DM556	DM816	DM686
			£184	£288	£236
			¥35,738	¥56,336	¥46,037

Maker	Items		Selling Prices		
	Bid	Sold	Low	High	Avg
HOWARD, CLARK	1	1	$1,725	$1,725	$1,725
			DM2,596	DM2,596	DM2,596
			£1,047	£1,047	£1,047
			¥192,821	¥192,821	¥192,821
HOWE, R.	1	1	$204	$204	$204
			DM344	DM344	DM344
			£127	£127	£127
			¥25,030	¥25,030	¥25,030
HOWE, ROBERT	2	0			
HOWELL, T.	1	1	$1,114	$1,114	$1,114
			DM1,727	DM1,727	DM1,727
			£667	£667	£667
			¥126,937	¥126,937	¥126,937
HOYER, ANDREAS	1	0			
HOYER, FRIEDRICH	2	2	$537	$1,380	$958
			DM994	DM2,361	DM1,678
			£322	£816	£569
			¥71,687	¥171,368	¥121,528
HOYER, JOHANN CHRISTOPH	2	0			
HUBER, JOHANN GEORG	1	0			
HUDSON, GEORGE	3	1	$1,883	$1,883	$1,883
			DM2,918	DM2,918	DM2,918
			£1,127	£1,127	£1,127
			¥214,479	¥214,479	¥214,479
HUDSON, GEORGE WULME	1	0			
HULINSKY, THOMAS	1	1	$3,887	$3,887	$3,887
			DM6,739	DM6,739	DM6,739
			£2,300	£2,300	£2,300
			¥485,300	¥485,300	¥485,300
HULL, JOHN JUSTIN	1	1	$1,725	$1,725	$1,725
			DM2,725	DM2,725	DM2,725
			£1,104	£1,104	£1,104
			¥172,327	¥172,327	¥172,327
HUME, ALEXANDER	3	2	$3,401	$5,286	$4,344
			DM4,758	DM7,804	DM6,281
			£2,128	£3,450	£2,789
			¥287,666	¥562,008	¥424,837
HUMMEL, MATHIAS	1	1	$5,264	$5,264	$5,264
			DM7,892	DM7,892	DM7,892
			£3,220	£3,220	£3,220
			¥509,275	¥509,275	¥509,275
HUMS, ALBIN	1	1	$1,035	$1,035	$1,035
			DM1,842	DM1,842	DM1,842
			£621	£621	£621
			¥137,634	¥137,634	¥137,634
HUNGER, C.F.	1	1	$3,073	$3,073	$3,073
			DM5,134	DM5,134	DM5,134
			£1,840	£1,840	£1,840
			¥373,502	¥373,502	¥373,502
HUSSON & BUTHOD	1	1	$1,089	$1,089	$1,089
			DM1,533	DM1,533	DM1,533
			£690	£690	£690
			¥111,319	¥111,319	¥111,319
HUTCHINS, CARLEEN M.	1	1	$3,450	$3,450	$3,450
			DM5,765	DM5,765	DM5,765
			£2,302	£2,302	£2,302
			¥361,594	¥361,594	¥361,594

Maker	Items		Selling Prices		
	Bid	Sold	Low	High	Avg
HYDE, ANDREW	1	0			
IGNESTI, ROBERTO	1	1	$4,180	$4,180	$4,180
			DM5,904	DM5,904	DM5,904
			£2,645	£2,645	£2,645
			¥373,043	¥373,043	¥373,043
JACOBS, H.	1	1	$28,808	$28,808	$28,808
			DM48,128	DM48,128	DM48,128
			£17,250	£17,250	£17,250
			¥3,501,578	¥3,501,578	¥3,501,578
JACOBS, HENDRIK	1	1	$16,124	$16,124	$16,124
			DM22,612	DM22,612	DM22,612
			£10,350	£10,350	£10,350
			¥1,629,121	¥1,629,121	¥1,629,121
JACQUEMIN, RENE (attributed to)	2	0			
JACQUEMIN, RENE (workshop of)	1	1	$863	$863	$863
			DM1,535	DM1,535	DM1,535
			£518	£518	£518
			¥114,695	¥114,695	¥114,695
JACQUOT, CHARLES	2	2	$6,270	$11,705	$8,987
			DM8,730	DM19,526	DM14,128
			£3,910	£7,820	£5,865
			¥529,993	¥1,202,004	¥865,999
JACQUOT, CHARLES (ascribed to)	3	1	$4,771	$4,771	$4,771
			DM7,048	DM7,048	DM7,048
			£3,105	£3,105	£3,105
			¥508,394	¥508,394	¥508,394
JACQUOT, CHARLES (attributed to)	1	1	$5,826	$5,826	$5,826
			DM8,801	DM8,801	DM8,801
			£3,910	£3,910	£3,910
			¥617,037	¥617,037	¥617,037
JACQUOT, FERNAND	1	1	$2,820	$2,820	$2,820
			DM4,658	DM4,658	DM4,658
			£1,725	£1,725	£1,725
			¥349,190	¥349,190	¥349,190
JAIS, ANDREAS	1	0			
JAIS, ANTON	2	1	$5,636	$5,636	$5,636
			DM9,772	DM9,772	DM9,772
			£3,335	£3,335	£3,335
			¥703,685	¥703,685	¥703,685
JAIS, JOHANN (attributed to)	1	0			
JAIS, JOHANNES	1	1	$10,608	$10,608	$10,608
			DM16,982	DM16,982	DM16,982
			£6,900	£6,900	£6,900
			¥1,073,806	¥1,073,806	¥1,073,806
JAMES, LESTER	1	1	$1,495	$1,495	$1,495
			DM2,159	DM2,159	DM2,159
			£952	£952	£952
			¥129,691	¥129,691	¥129,691
JAMIESON	1	0			
JAUCK, JOHANNES (ascribed to)	2	1	$2,876	$2,876	$2,876
			DM5,327	DM5,327	DM5,327
			£1,725	£1,725	£1,725
			¥384,037	¥384,037	¥384,037
JAY, HENRY (ascribed to)	1	1	$920	$920	$920
			DM1,426	DM1,426	DM1,426
			£589	£589	£589
			¥90,445	¥90,445	¥90,445

Maker	Items		Selling Prices		
	Bid	Sold	Low	High	Avg
JIROUSEK, JOSEPH	1	1	$805	$805	$805
			DM1,164	DM1,164	DM1,164
			£526	£526	£526
			¥81,506	¥81,506	¥81,506
JIROWSKY, HANS	1	0			
JOHNSON, F.M.	1	1	$1,150	$1,150	$1,150
			DM1,817	DM1,817	DM1,817
			£736	£736	£736
			¥114,885	¥114,885	¥114,885
JOHNSON, GEORGE	2	1	$863	$863	$863
			DM1,476	DM1,476	DM1,476
			£510	£510	£510
			¥107,105	¥107,105	¥107,105
JOHNSON, JOHN	11	3	$920	$4,025	$2,630
			DM1,385	DM6,058	DM4,141
			£558	£2,443	£1,618
			¥102,838	¥449,915	¥305,833
JOHNSON, W.A.	1	0			
JOLLY, LEON	4	2	$597	$1,145	$871
			DM1,044	DM1,688	DM1,366
			£368	£748	£558
			¥72,110	¥122,119	¥97,114
JOLY, LOUIS	3	2	$763	$2,028	$1,396
			DM1,081	DM2,824	DM1,952
			£483	£1,265	£874
			¥78,729	¥171,468	¥125,099
JOMBAR, P.	1	1	$8,050	$8,050	$8,050
			DM12,719	DM12,719	DM12,719
			£5,152	£5,152	£5,152
			¥804,195	¥804,195	¥804,195
JOMBAR, P. (workshop of)	1	0			
JOMBAR, PAUL	3	1	$3,882	$3,882	$3,882
			DM5,964	DM5,964	DM5,964
			£2,530	£2,530	£2,530
			¥425,012	¥425,012	¥425,012
JOMBAR, PAUL (attributed to)	2	1	$2,881	$2,881	$2,881
			DM4,761	DM4,761	DM4,761
			£1,725	£1,725	£1,725
			¥336,893	¥336,893	¥336,893
JONES, WILLIAM H.	4	1	$820	$820	$820
			DM1,217	DM1,217	DM1,217
			£529	£529	£529
			¥88,756	¥88,756	¥88,756
JORIO, VINCENZO (ascribed to)	1	0			
JUZEK, JOHN	6	6	$431	$2,070	$1,462
			DM623	DM3,243	DM2,285
			£275	£1,325	£906
			¥37,411	¥236,746	¥161,418
JUZEK, JOHN (Workshop of)	5	5	$633	$2,990	$1,645
			DM1,093	DM5,168	DM2,748
			£391	£1,848	£1,018
			¥80,160	¥378,938	¥195,129
KALTENBRUNNER, K. RICHARD	1	1	$5,750	$5,750	$5,750
			DM9,939	DM9,939	DM9,939
			£3,553	£3,553	£3,553
			¥728,726	¥728,726	¥728,726

| Maker | Items | | Selling Prices | | |
---	Bid	Sold	Low	High	Avg
KANTUSCHER, JOSEPH	1	1	$3,105 DM4,813 £1,987 ¥305,253	$3,105 DM4,813 £1,987 ¥305,253	$3,105 DM4,813 £1,987 ¥305,253
KARNER, BARTHOLOMAUS	2	1	$960 DM1,604 £575 ¥116,719	$960 DM1,604 £575 ¥116,719	$960 DM1,604 £575 ¥116,719
KARNER, BARTHOLOMAUS (II)	3	0			
KAUL, PAUL	3	1	$2,990 DM5,053 £1,794 ¥364,780	$2,990 DM5,053 £1,794 ¥364,780	$2,990 DM5,053 £1,794 ¥364,780
KEENAN, EDWARD	1	1	$3,105 DM4,813 £1,987 ¥305,253	$3,105 DM4,813 £1,987 ¥305,253	$3,105 DM4,813 £1,987 ¥305,253
KEFFER, JOANNES (attributed to)	1	1	$1,740 DM2,603 £1,035 ¥194,042	$1,740 DM2,603 £1,035 ¥194,042	$1,740 DM2,603 £1,035 ¥194,042
KEFSLER, GOTTFRIED	1	0			
KEMPTER, ANDREAS	1	1	$5,467 DM9,250 £3,439 ¥677,385	$5,467 DM9,250 £3,439 ¥677,385	$5,467 DM9,250 £3,439 ¥677,385
KEMPTER, ANDREAS (attributed to)	2	0			
KENNEDY (workshop of)	1	0			
KENNEDY, THOMAS	10	4	$1,259 DM1,781 £805 ¥127,841	$8,585 DM14,358 £5,750 ¥912,347	$5,475 DM8,422 £3,508 ¥558,211
KESSEL, M.J.H.	1	1	$2,313 DM3,913 £1,455 ¥286,586	$2,313 DM3,913 £1,455 ¥286,586	$2,313 DM3,913 £1,455 ¥286,586
KESSLER, JOHANN GEORG	1	1	$1,452 DM2,044 £920 ¥148,425	$1,452 DM2,044 £920 ¥148,425	$1,452 DM2,044 £920 ¥148,425
KESSLER, W. AUGUST (JR.)	1	1	$3,457 DM6,417 £2,070 ¥462,521	$3,457 DM6,417 £2,070 ¥462,521	$3,457 DM6,417 £2,070 ¥462,521
KEY, ALBERT E.	1	1	$690 DM1,069 £442 ¥67,834	$690 DM1,069 £442 ¥67,834	$690 DM1,069 £442 ¥67,834
KINLOCH, WILLIAM	1	1	$946 DM1,353 £598 ¥95,074	$946 DM1,353 £598 ¥95,074	$946 DM1,353 £598 ¥95,074
KINPOLTH, JOHANN CHRISTIAN (attributed to)	1	1	$1,437 DM2,258 £920 ¥144,099	$1,437 DM2,258 £920 ¥144,099	$1,437 DM2,258 £920 ¥144,099

Maker	Items		Selling Prices		
	Bid	Sold	Low	High	Avg
KLEMM, GEORGE & AUGUST	1	1	$978	$978	$978
			DM1,412	DM1,412	DM1,412
			£623	£623	£623
			¥84,798	¥84,798	¥84,798
KLINTH, ALBERT W.	1	1	$431	$431	$431
			DM768	DM768	DM768
			£259	£259	£259
			¥57,348	¥57,348	¥57,348
KLOTZ, AEGIDIUS (I)	12	7	$1,660	$6,854	$4,421
			DM2,311	DM10,355	DM7,143
			£1,035	£4,600	£2,744
			¥140,292	¥725,926	¥505,341
KLOTZ, AEGIDIUS (I) (ascribed to)	1	1	$978	$978	$978
			DM1,412	DM1,412	DM1,412
			£623	£623	£623
			¥84,798	¥84,798	¥84,798
KLOTZ, AEGIDIUS (I) (attributed to)	1	1	$1,380	$1,380	$1,380
			DM2,306	DM2,306	DM2,306
			£921	£921	£921
			¥144,638	¥144,638	¥144,638
KLOTZ, AEGIDIUS (II)	8	5	$2,645	$9,596	$5,402
			DM3,952	DM16,229	DM8,992
			£1,610	£6,440	£3,455
			¥254,423	¥1,017,520	¥603,683
KLOTZ, AEGIDIUS (II) (attributed to)	1	0			
KLOTZ, CARL FREDRICH (attributed to)	1	0			
KLOTZ, GEORG	15	9	$1,890	$7,956	$4,239
			DM2,888	DM12,737	DM6,565
			£1,208	£5,175	£2,681
			¥210,769	¥805,354	¥435,822
KLOTZ, GEORG (II)	6	3	$5,816	$8,551	$7,212
			DM8,214	DM14,826	DM11,103
			£3,680	£5,060	£4,447
			¥519,016	¥1,067,660	¥745,149
KLOTZ, JOHANN CARL	7	7	$1,113	$6,072	$3,319
			DM1,681	DM9,163	DM5,223
			£747	£3,680	£2,067
			¥117,884	¥688,160	¥364,039
KLOTZ, JOHANN CARL (ascribed to)	1	1	$2,181	$2,181	$2,181
			DM3,080	DM3,080	DM3,080
			£1,380	£1,380	£1,380
			¥194,631	¥194,631	¥194,631
KLOTZ, JOHANN CARL (attributed to)	1	1	$5,375	$5,375	$5,375
			DM7,537	DM7,537	DM7,537
			£3,450	£3,450	£3,450
			¥543,040	¥543,040	¥543,040
KLOTZ, JOSEPH	7	3	$4,237	$8,092	$6,166
			DM6,501	DM12,160	DM9,698
			£2,760	£4,830	£3,910
			¥463,708	¥901,090	¥672,972
KLOTZ, JOSEPH (attributed to)	1	1	$4,025	$4,025	$4,025
			DM6,802	DM6,802	DM6,802
			£2,415	£2,415	£2,415
			¥491,050	¥491,050	¥491,050
KLOTZ, MATHIAS (I)	4	2	$2,742	$9,664	$6,203
			DM4,637	DM14,460	DM9,548
			£1,840	£5,750	£3,795
			¥290,720	¥1,078,010	¥684,365

Maker	Items		Selling Prices		
	Bid	Sold	Low	High	Avg
KLOTZ, MATHIAS (I) (attributed to)	3	1	$5,841	$5,841	$5,841
			DM10,133	DM10,133	DM10,133
			£3,450	£3,450	£3,450
			¥740,405	¥740,405	¥740,405
KLOTZ, MATHIAS (II)	1	0			
KLOTZ, MICHAEL	5	3	$1,273	$7,345	$5,229
			DM1,873	DM11,273	DM7,863
			£828	£4,600	£3,343
			¥135,096	¥753,176	¥536,128
KLOTZ, SEBASTIAN	12	7	$2,497	$12,721	$5,570
			DM4,235	DM18,796	DM8,875
			£1,495	£8,280	£3,586
			¥272,597	¥1,355,718	¥604,793
KLOTZ, SEBASTIAN (attributed to)	3	3	$2,300	$3,802	$3,247
			DM3,326	DM5,594	DM4,708
			£1,502	£2,473	£2,092
			¥232,875	¥403,413	¥333,985
KLOTZ, SEBASTIAN (II)	4	2	$539	$3,457	$1,998
			DM847	DM5,775	DM3,311
			£345	£2,070	£1,208
			¥54,037	¥420,189	¥237,113
KLOTZ FAMILY (MEMBER OF)	26	19	$810	$8,118	$2,147
			DM1,238	DM12,146	DM3,383
			£518	£4,830	£1,316
			¥79,810	¥905,528	¥233,038
KNEDLER, VILMOS	1	1	$920	$920	$920
			DM1,385	DM1,385	DM1,385
			£558	£558	£558
			¥102,838	¥102,838	¥102,838
KNIGHT, FRANK R.	1	1	$1,724	$1,724	$1,724
			DM2,646	DM2,646	DM2,646
			£1,127	£1,127	£1,127
			¥188,138	¥188,138	¥188,138
KNILLING, JOHANN	1	1	$1,792	$1,792	$1,792
			DM2,512	DM2,512	DM2,512
			£1,150	£1,150	£1,150
			¥181,013	¥181,013	¥181,013
KNOPF, HENRY RICHARD	6	6	$1,725	$4,370	$3,115
			DM2,596	DM6,319	DM4,791
			£1,047	£2,854	£1,948
			¥192,821	¥442,463	¥349,534
KNORR, ALBERT	3	3	$2,173	$3,738	$2,775
			DM3,339	DM6,653	DM4,562
			£1,438	£2,243	£1,756
			¥231,761	¥497,013	¥327,772
KNUPFER, ALBERT	2	1	$936	$936	$936
			DM1,430	DM1,430	DM1,430
			£598	£598	£598
			¥104,381	¥104,381	¥104,381
KOBERLING, JOHANN	1	0			
KOCH, FRANZ JOSEPH	1	1	$1,150	$1,150	$1,150
			DM2,088	DM2,088	DM2,088
			£704	£704	£704
			¥142,807	¥142,807	¥142,807
KOCHLY, J. (attributed to)	1	0			

Maker	Items		Selling Prices		
	Bid	Sold	Low	High	Avg
KONIG, PAUL & HERMANN	2	1	$2,915	$2,915	$2,915
			DM5,054	DM5,054	DM5,054
			£1,725	£1,725	£1,725
			¥363,975	¥363,975	¥363,975
KRELL, ALBERT	2	2	$1,840	$2,070	$1,955
			DM2,989	DM3,110	DM3,049
			£1,104	£1,319	£1,211
			¥179,573	¥244,849	¥212,211
KREUTZINGER, ANTON (attributed to)	1	0			
KRIEGER, BOHUMIL J.	1	1	$748	$748	$748
			DM1,079	DM1,079	DM1,079
			£476	£476	£476
			¥64,846	¥64,846	¥64,846
KRIKUNOV	1	0			
KRILOV, ALESSANDRO	1	0			
KRILOV, ALESSANDRO (attributed to)	2	1	$1,081	$1,081	$1,081
			DM1,139	DM1,139	DM1,139
			£667	£667	£667
			¥82,571	¥82,571	¥82,571
KRINER, HANS B.	1	1	$2,122	$2,122	$2,122
			DM3,122	DM3,122	DM3,122
			£1,380	£1,380	£1,380
			¥225,161	¥225,161	¥225,161
KRINER, JOSEPH	3	1	$1,139	$1,139	$1,139
			DM1,718	DM1,718	DM1,718
			£690	£690	£690
			¥129,030	¥129,030	¥129,030
KRIZ, FRANTISEK	1	0			
KRUMBHOLZ, LORENZ	1	1	$7,298	$7,298	$7,298
			DM12,192	DM12,192	DM12,192
			£4,370	£4,370	£4,370
			¥887,066	¥887,066	¥887,066
KUAMME, MAGNE	2	1	$431	$431	$431
			DM668	DM668	DM668
			£276	£276	£276
			¥42,396	¥42,396	¥42,396
KUDANOWSKI, JAN	13	7	$1,328	$3,575	$2,658
			DM2,359	DM6,048	DM4,444
			£805	£2,248	£1,635
			¥184,256	¥442,905	¥324,237
KULIK, JOHAN	1	1	$8,625	$8,625	$8,625
			DM14,757	DM14,757	DM14,757
			£5,101	£5,101	£5,101
			¥1,071,053	¥1,071,053	¥1,071,053
KUN, JOSEPH	1	1	$2,645	$2,645	$2,645
			DM3,981	DM3,981	DM3,981
			£1,606	£1,606	£1,606
			¥295,658	¥295,658	¥295,658
KUNZE, WILHELM PAUL	1	1	$3,816	$3,816	$3,816
			DM5,391	DM5,391	DM5,391
			£2,415	£2,415	£2,415
			¥340,604	¥340,604	¥340,604
KURZAWA, EDWARD	1	1	$621	$621	$621
			DM1,054	DM1,054	DM1,054
			£418	£418	£418
			¥65,955	¥65,955	¥65,955

Maker	Items		Selling Prices		
	Bid	Sold	Low	High	Avg
KVAMME, MAGNE	1	1	$575	$575	$575
			DM1,024	DM1,024	DM1,024
			£345	£345	£345
			¥76,464	¥76,464	¥76,464
LABERTE, MARC	8	5	$1,145	$5,435	$3,002
			DM1,690	DM7,676	DM4,659
			£747	£3,450	£1,898
			¥121,687	¥547,284	¥337,029
LABERTE, MARC (attributed to)	1	1	$1,519	$1,519	$1,519
			DM2,634	DM2,634	DM2,634
			£897	£897	£897
			¥192,505	¥192,505	¥192,505
LABERTE, MARC (workshop of)	3	2	$863	$2,471	$1,667
			DM1,245	DM3,792	DM2,519
			£549	£1,610	£1,080
			¥74,822	¥270,496	¥172,659
LABERTE-HUMBERT BROS.	5	4	$1,128	$2,527	$1,627
			DM1,863	DM4,380	DM2,690
			£690	£1,495	£998
			¥121,660	¥315,445	¥192,582
LABERTE-MAGNIE	2	0			
LAFLEUR, J.	1	1	$937	$937	$937
			DM1,668	DM1,668	DM1,668
			£575	£575	£575
			¥125,885	¥125,885	¥125,885
LAIDLAW, JOHN W.	2	0			
LAINE, EMILE (attributed to)	1	1	$1,139	$1,139	$1,139
			DM1,747	DM1,747	DM1,747
			£713	£713	£713
			¥111,617	¥111,617	¥111,617
LAMBERT	1	1	$3,080	$3,080	$3,080
			DM5,698	DM5,698	DM5,698
			£1,840	£1,840	£1,840
			¥410,486	¥410,486	¥410,486
LAMBERT, JEAN NICOLAS	2	1	$2,766	$2,766	$2,766
			DM3,851	DM3,851	DM3,851
			£1,725	£1,725	£1,725
			¥233,820	¥233,820	¥233,820
LAMBERTON, JAMES	1	0			
LANARO, UMBERTO	3	3	$3,450	$4,874	$4,350
			DM5,347	DM8,432	DM6,818
			£2,208	£2,990	£2,729
			¥339,169	¥556,140	¥439,003
LANDOLFI, CARLO FERDINANDO	6	3	$64,541	$78,857	$71,285
			DM89,866	DM111,382	DM101,705
			£40,250	£49,900	£45,383
			¥5,455,807	¥7,515,020	¥6,669,524
LANDOLFI, PIETRO ANTONIO	2	2	$46,261	$61,380	$53,821
			DM78,266	DM86,440	DM82,353
			£29,095	£38,900	£33,998
			¥5,731,715	¥6,275,815	¥6,003,765
LANDOLFI, PIETRO ANTONIO (ascribed to)	1	1	$6,900	$6,900	$6,900
			DM10,902	DM10,902	DM10,902
			£4,416	£4,416	£4,416
			¥689,310	¥689,310	¥689,310

Maker	Items		Selling Prices		
	Bid	Sold	Low	High	Avg
LANDOLFI, PIETRO ANTONIO					
(attributed to)	2	1	$13,235	$13,235	$13,235
			DM20,333	DM20,333	DM20,333
			£8,625	£8,625	£8,625
			¥1,448,905	¥1,448,905	¥1,448,905
LANE, E.	2	1	$458	$458	$458
			DM727	DM727	DM727
			£299	£299	£299
			¥46,340	¥46,340	¥46,340
LANGE, H. FRANCIS	1	1	$748	$748	$748
			DM1,331	DM1,331	DM1,331
			£449	£449	£449
			¥99,403	¥99,403	¥99,403
LANGONET, CHARLES	1	1	$2,530	$2,530	$2,530
			DM3,921	DM3,921	DM3,921
			£1,619	£1,619	£1,619
			¥248,724	¥248,724	¥248,724
LANGONET, EUGENE	4	2	$5,089	$6,706	$5,897
			DM7,187	DM10,302	DM8,745
			£3,220	£4,370	£3,795
			¥454,139	¥734,112	¥594,126
LANGONET, EUGENE (attributed to)	1	0			
LANINI, LORIS	2	1	$2,657	$2,657	$2,657
			DM4,009	DM4,009	DM4,009
			£1,610	£1,610	£1,610
			¥301,070	¥301,070	¥301,070
LAPOLLA, ANGELO	1	0			
LAPREVOTTE, ETIENNE	2	1	$3,835	$3,835	$3,835
			DM5,392	DM5,392	DM5,392
			£2,415	£2,415	£2,415
			¥342,278	¥342,278	¥342,278
LARCHER, JEAN	2	2	$1,344	$1,921	$1,632
			DM2,246	DM3,565	DM2,905
			£805	£1,150	£978
			¥163,407	¥256,956	¥210,181
LARCHER, JEAN (attributed to)	4	1	$604	$604	$604
			DM857	DM857	DM857
			£380	£380	£380
			¥56,033	¥56,033	¥56,033
LARGOWARD, RAYBURN	1	1	$796	$796	$796
			DM1,171	DM1,171	DM1,171
			£518	£518	£518
			¥84,435	¥84,435	¥84,435
LASSI, FRANCESCO	2	1	$8,826	$8,826	$8,826
			DM13,544	DM13,544	DM13,544
			£5,750	£5,750	£5,750
			¥966,058	¥966,058	¥966,058
LATTERELL, GEORGE	1	1	$1,380	$1,380	$1,380
			DM2,506	DM2,506	DM2,506
			£845	£845	£845
			¥171,368	¥171,368	¥171,368
LAUMANN, ROBERT	1	1	$6,355	$6,355	$6,355
			DM9,752	DM9,752	DM9,752
			£4,140	£4,140	£4,140
			¥695,561	¥695,561	¥695,561

Maker	Items		Selling Prices		
	Bid	Sold	Low	High	Avg
LAURENT, EMILE	2	2	$6,900	$7,682	$7,291
			DM10,695	DM12,834	DM11,765
			£4,416	£4,600	£4,508
			¥678,339	¥933,754	¥806,047
LAURENT, EMILE (II)	1	1	$2,819	$2,819	$2,819
			DM4,162	DM4,162	DM4,162
			£1,840	£1,840	£1,840
			¥299,738	¥299,738	¥299,738
LAURENT, EMILE (II) (ascribed to)	1	0			
LAVEST, J.	1	1	$3,450	$3,450	$3,450
			DM5,903	DM5,903	DM5,903
			£2,041	£2,041	£2,041
			¥428,421	¥428,421	¥428,421
LAZZARO, GIOVANNI	1	1	$3,287	$3,287	$3,287
			DM4,622	DM4,622	DM4,622
			£2,070	£2,070	£2,070
			¥292,228	¥292,228	¥292,228
LEAVITT, F.A.	1	1	$518	$518	$518
			DM921	DM921	DM921
			£311	£311	£311
			¥68,817	¥68,817	¥68,817
LECCHI, ANTONIO	2	2	$1,055	$1,164	$1,109
			DM1,620	DM2,075	DM1,848
			£690	£713	£702
			¥115,187	¥152,318	¥133,752
LECCHI, BERNARDO GIUSEPPE	4	2	$8,473	$21,775	$15,124
			DM13,002	DM30,665	DM21,834
			£5,520	£13,800	£9,660
			¥927,415	¥2,226,382	¥1,576,898
LECCHI, GUISEPPE	5	1	$13,251	$13,251	$13,251
			DM19,579	DM19,579	DM19,579
			£8,625	£8,625	£8,625
			¥1,412,206	¥1,412,206	¥1,412,206
LECHI, ANTONIO	13	8	$654	$1,944	$1,224
			DM963	DM3,370	DM1,984
			£417	£1,150	£749
			¥69,425	¥247,101	¥141,004
LECLERC, JOSEPH NICOLAS	4	1	$3,601	$3,601	$3,601
			DM5,513	DM5,513	DM5,513
			£2,300	£2,300	£2,300
			¥401,396	¥401,396	¥401,396
LECYR, JAMES F.	1	1	$1,955	$1,955	$1,955
			DM3,345	DM3,345	DM3,345
			£1,156	£1,156	£1,156
			¥242,772	¥242,772	¥242,772
LEE, PERCY	2	2	$4,609	$5,264	$4,936
			DM7,700	DM7,892	DM7,796
			£2,760	£3,220	£2,990
			¥509,275	¥560,252	¥534,764
LEEB, JOHANN GEORG	2	2	$2,062	$9,589	$5,825
			DM3,567	DM13,352	DM8,459
			£1,265	£5,980	£3,623
			¥235,290	¥810,577	¥522,934
LEIDOLFF, JOHANN CHRISTOPH	1	0			
LEIDOLFF, JOSEPH FERDINAND	1	1	$1,651	$1,651	$1,651
			DM2,863	DM2,863	DM2,863
			£977	£977	£977
			¥206,147	¥206,147	¥206,147

Maker	Items		Selling Prices		
	Bid	Sold	Low	High	Avg
LEMARQUIS, JEAN BAPTISTE	1	0			
LEMBOCK, GABRIEL	2	2	$5,295	$9,560	$7,427
			DM8,493	DM13,375	DM10,934
			£3,439	£5,980	£4,709
			¥602,494	¥808,574	¥705,534
LE PILEUR, PIERRE	1	1	$3,652	$3,652	$3,652
			DM5,135	DM5,135	DM5,135
			£2,300	£2,300	£2,300
			¥325,979	¥325,979	¥325,979
LEWIS, WILLIAM & SON	1	0			
L'HUMBERT, E.	4	1	$6,178	$6,178	$6,178
			DM9,481	DM9,481	DM9,481
			£4,025	£4,025	£4,025
			¥676,240	¥676,240	¥676,240
LIDL, JOSEF	1	1	$2,402	$2,402	$2,402
			DM3,740	DM3,740	DM3,740
			£1,540	£1,540	£1,540
			¥237,868	¥237,868	¥237,868
LIESSEM, R.	2	2	$2,346	$4,803	$3,575
			DM4,183	DM7,445	DM5,814
			£1,438	£2,875	£2,156
			¥307,093	¥547,141	¥427,117
LINDORFER, WILLI	1	0			
LINDSAY, DAVID	1	1	$1,234	$1,234	$1,234
			DM1,821	DM1,821	DM1,821
			£805	£805	£805
			¥131,135	¥131,135	¥131,135
LINDSAY, DAVID (attributed to)	1	1	$459	$459	$459
			DM679	DM679	DM679
			£299	£299	£299
			¥48,956	¥48,956	¥48,956
LIPPOLD, CARL FREDERICK (attributed to)	1	0			
LIPPOLD, JOHANN GEORGE	2	0			
LOGAN, JOHN	1	1	$1,069	$1,069	$1,069
			DM1,587	DM1,587	DM1,587
			£690	£690	£690
			¥115,768	¥115,768	¥115,768
LONGIARU, GIOVANNI	2	2	$2,760	$3,738	$3,249
			DM3,991	DM6,245	DM5,118
			£1,803	£2,494	£2,148
			¥279,450	¥391,727	¥335,589
LONGMAN	3	1	$566	$566	$566
			DM1,029	DM1,029	DM1,029
			£345	£345	£345
			¥71,463	¥71,463	¥71,463
LONGMAN & CO.	1	1	$1,676	$1,676	$1,676
			DM2,576	DM2,576	DM2,576
			£1,093	£1,093	£1,093
			¥183,528	¥183,528	¥183,528
LONGMAN & BRODERIP	2	1	$631	$631	$631
			DM952	DM952	DM952
			£387	£387	£387
			¥61,209	¥61,209	¥61,209
LONGMAN, LUKEY & CO.	1	1	$768	$768	$768
			DM1,283	DM1,283	DM1,283
			£460	£460	£460
			¥93,375	¥93,375	¥93,375

Maker	Items		Selling Prices		
	Bid	Sold	Low	High	Avg
LONGSON (attributed to)	1	1	$643	$643	$643
			DM900	DM900	DM900
			£403	£403	£403
			¥54,423	¥54,423	¥54,423
LO SCHIAVO, ANTONIO	1	1	$4,536	$4,536	$4,536
			DM6,389	DM6,389	DM6,389
			£2,875	£2,875	£2,875
			¥463,830	¥463,830	¥463,830
LOTT, JOHN	3	2	$26,450	$31,706	$29,078
			DM40,997	DM46,741	DM43,869
			£16,928	£20,700	£18,814
			¥2,600,299	¥3,381,759	¥2,991,029
LOTT, JOHN (ascribed to)	1	0			
LOTT, JOHN (attributed to)	3	2	$15,912	$22,957	$19,435
			DM25,473	DM36,746	DM31,110
			£10,350	£14,950	£12,650
			¥1,610,708	¥2,316,503	¥1,963,605
LOTT, JOHN (SR.)	2	1	$11,141	$11,141	$11,141
			DM16,390	DM16,390	DM16,390
			£7,245	£7,245	£7,245
			¥1,182,094	¥1,182,094	¥1,182,094
LOTT, JOHN FREDERICK	1	1	$45,540	$45,540	$45,540
			DM68,724	DM68,724	DM68,724
			£27,600	£27,600	£27,600
			¥5,161,200	¥5,161,200	¥5,161,200
LOTT, JOHN FREDERICK (ascribed to)	2	0			
LOTT, JOHN FREDERICK (attributed to)	1	0			
LOUGHTON, A.J.	2	1	$251	$251	$251
			DM438	DM438	DM438
			£150	£150	£150
			¥32,047	¥32,047	¥32,047
LOWENDALL	8	7	$256	$1,450	$640
			DM363	DM2,133	DM991
			£161	£943	£407
			¥23,772	¥153,860	¥69,050
LOWENDALL, HERMANN	1	1	$546	$546	$546
			DM789	DM789	DM789
			£348	£348	£348
			¥47,387	¥47,387	¥47,387
LOWENDALL, HERMANN (workshop of)	1	1	$1,265	$1,265	$1,265
			DM2,164	DM2,164	DM2,164
			£748	£748	£748
			¥157,088	¥157,088	¥157,088
LOWENDALL, L. (workshop of)	2	2	$345	$633	$489
			DM499	DM915	DM707
			£225	£413	£319
			¥34,931	¥64,041	¥49,486
LOWENDALL, LOUIS	17	14	$282	$2,508	$888
			DM502	DM3,517	DM1,406
			£173	£1,610	£556
			¥36,851	¥253,419	¥97,140
LOWENDALL, LOUIS (workshop of)	4	4	$230	$1,495	$848
			DM394	DM2,162	DM1,280
			£136	£977	£549
			¥28,561	¥151,369	¥84,262

| Maker | Items | | Selling Prices | | |
	Bid	Sold	Low	High	Avg
LUCCA, ANTONIO	3	2	$6,185	$16,698	$11,441
			DM9,254	DM25,199	DM17,226
			£3,680	£10,120	£6,900
			¥689,926	¥1,892,440	¥1,291,183
LUCCI, GIUSEPPE	9	8	$7,512	$16,596	$11,181
			DM13,459	DM23,150	DM18,068
			£4,485	£10,350	£6,904
			¥872,333	¥1,667,598	¥1,224,154
LUCCI, GIUSEPPE (attributed to)	1	1	$5,463	$5,463	$5,463
			DM9,442	DM9,442	DM9,442
			£3,375	£3,375	£3,375
			¥692,290	¥692,290	¥692,290
LUDWIG	1	0			
LUDWIG, L. (workshop of)	1	1	$230	$230	$230
			DM352	DM352	DM352
			£151	£151	£151
			¥24,242	¥24,242	¥24,242
LUFF, WILLIAM H.	12	3	$5,997	$7,345	$6,757
			DM9,060	DM12,822	DM10,957
			£4,025	£4,370	£4,178
			¥635,185	¥923,593	¥792,688
LUNN, W.J.	3	1	$457	$457	$457
			DM649	DM649	DM649
			£288	£288	£288
			¥42,449	¥42,449	¥42,449
LUPOT, FRANCOIS	1	0			
LUPOT, NICOLAS	3	2	$103,540	$134,769	$119,155
			DM172,980	DM225,153	DM199,067
			£62,000	£80,700	£71,350
			¥12,585,380	¥16,381,293	¥14,483,337
LUTSCHG, GUSTAV	1	1	$2,123	$2,123	$2,123
			DM3,405	DM3,405	DM3,405
			£1,380	£1,380	£1,380
			¥214,763	¥214,763	¥214,763
LUTZ, IGNAZ	1	1	$4,485	$4,485	$4,485
			DM7,580	DM7,580	DM7,580
			£2,691	£2,691	£2,691
			¥547,170	¥547,170	¥547,170
LUZZATTI, GIACOMO	1	0			
LYE, HENRY	2	1	$2,297	$2,297	$2,297
			DM3,394	DM3,394	DM3,394
			£1,495	£1,495	£1,495
			¥244,782	¥244,782	¥244,782
MAAG, HENRY	7	5	$115	$460	$212
			DM205	DM819	DM380
			£70	£281	£129
			¥15,976	¥63,903	¥27,972
MACCARTHY, J.L.T.	1	0			
MACKINTOSH (attributed to)	1	1	$1,128	$1,128	$1,128
			DM1,614	DM1,614	DM1,614
			£713	£713	£713
			¥113,357	¥113,357	¥113,357
MACVEAN, ALEXANDER	1	0			
MADAY, EDWARD	1	1	$863	$863	$863
			DM1,491	DM1,491	DM1,491
			£533	£533	£533
			¥109,309	¥109,309	¥109,309

Maker	Items		Selling Prices		
	Bid	Sold	Low	High	Avg
MAGGINI, GIOVANNI PAOLO	4	3	$17,020	$168,368	$75,931
			DM23,868	DM253,029	DM113,183
			£10,925	£100,500	£46,342
			¥1,719,628	¥18,749,381	¥8,329,356
MAGIALI, CAESAR	1	1	$5,798	$5,798	$5,798
			DM8,676	DM8,676	DM8,676
			£3,450	£3,450	£3,450
			¥646,806	¥646,806	¥646,806
MAGNIERE, FOURIER	1	1	$3,778	$3,778	$3,778
			DM5,646	DM5,646	DM5,646
			£2,300	£2,300	£2,300
			¥363,462	¥363,462	¥363,462
MAGNIERE, GABRIEL	9	8	$1,344	$3,374	$2,279
			DM2,407	DM5,837	DM3,643
			£805	£2,070	£1,421
			¥184,973	¥385,020	¥257,668
MAGNIERE, GABRIEL (attributed to)	2	2	$2,308	$2,474	$2,391
			DM3,321	DM3,655	DM3,488
			£1,495	£1,610	£1,553
			¥234,326	¥263,612	¥248,969
MAGRINI, CESARE	1	1	$14,539	$14,539	$14,539
			DM20,535	DM20,535	DM20,535
			£9,200	£9,200	£9,200
			¥1,297,540	¥1,297,540	¥1,297,540
MAICH, JOHN P.	1	1	$345	$345	$345
			DM596	DM596	DM596
			£213	£213	£213
			¥43,724	¥43,724	¥43,724
MAITRE, J. CHARLES (attributed to)	1	1	$2,166	$2,166	$2,166
			DM3,062	DM3,062	DM3,062
			£1,380	£1,380	£1,380
			¥185,032	¥185,032	¥185,032
MALAGUTI, ERMINIO (attributed to)	1	0			
MALIGNAGGI, PAUL	1	1	$633	$633	$633
			DM913	DM913	DM913
			£403	£403	£403
			¥54,869	¥54,869	¥54,869
MALINE	1	1	$3,477	$3,477	$3,477
			DM5,343	DM5,343	DM5,343
			£2,300	£2,300	£2,300
			¥370,818	¥370,818	¥370,818
MALINE, JOSEPH	1	1	$2,913	$2,913	$2,913
			DM4,927	DM4,927	DM4,927
			£1,955	£1,955	£1,955
			¥308,890	¥308,890	¥308,890
MALVOLTI, PIETRO ANTONIO	1	1	$6,784	$6,784	$6,784
			DM12,022	DM12,022	DM12,022
			£4,166	£4,166	£4,166
			¥827,224	¥827,224	¥827,224
MANDELLI, CAMILLO	2	1	$23,000	$23,000	$23,000
			DM38,870	DM38,870	DM38,870
			£13,800	£13,800	£13,800
			¥3,060,610	¥3,060,610	¥3,060,610
MANGENOT, AMATI	4	2	$3,534	$3,597	$3,565
			DM5,088	DM5,221	DM5,155
			£2,300	£2,300	£2,300
			¥365,261	¥376,588	¥370,924

Maker	Items		Selling Prices		
	Bid	Sold	Low	High	Avg
MANGENOT, PAUL	3	3	$811	$1,639	$1,335
			DM1,197	DM2,772	DM2,221
			£529	£1,100	£850
			¥86,175	¥194,120	¥151,365
MANSUY	2	1	$1,835	$1,835	$1,835
			DM3,300	DM3,300	DM3,300
			£1,093	£1,093	£1,093
			¥212,196	¥212,196	¥212,196
MANTEGAZZA, PIETRO GIOVANNI	3	2	$20,125	$31,824	$25,975
			DM34,011	DM50,947	DM42,479
			£12,075	£20,700	£16,388
			¥2,678,034	¥3,221,417	¥2,949,725
MANTEGAZZA, PIETRO GIOVANNI (attributed to)	1	0			
MARAVELLI	1	1	$920	$920	$920
			DM1,353	DM1,353	DM1,353
			£598	£598	£598
			¥97,570	¥97,570	¥97,570
MARAVIGLIA, FRANCESCO	1	0			
MARAVIGLIA, GUIDO	2	1	$2,706	$2,706	$2,706
			DM4,049	DM4,049	DM4,049
			£1,610	£1,610	£1,610
			¥301,843	¥301,843	¥301,843
MARCHETTI, ENRICO	4	1	$9,184	$9,184	$9,184
			DM15,443	DM15,443	DM15,443
			£5,750	£5,750	£5,750
			¥1,127,362	¥1,127,362	¥1,127,362
MARCHETTI, ENRICO (attributed to)	2	1	$6,711	$6,711	$6,711
			DM10,741	DM10,741	DM10,741
			£4,370	£4,370	£4,370
			¥677,132	¥677,132	¥677,132
MARCHI, GIOVANNI (attributed to)	1	1	$13,605	$13,605	$13,605
			DM23,587	DM23,587	DM23,587
			£8,050	£8,050	£8,050
			¥1,729,704	¥1,729,704	¥1,729,704
MARCHI, GIOVANNI ANTONIO	3	2	$39,100	$54,418	$46,759
			DM65,336	DM94,346	DM79,841
			£26,091	£32,200	£29,146
			¥4,098,071	¥6,794,200	¥5,446,136
MARCONCINI, JOSEPH	2	1	$48,737	$48,737	$48,737
			DM84,318	DM84,318	DM84,318
			£29,900	£29,900	£29,900
			¥5,561,400	¥5,561,400	¥5,561,400
MARCONCINI, JOSEPH (attributed to)	1	0			
MARCONCINI, LUIGI ALOISIO	1	0			
MARDULA, FRANCISZEK & STANISLAW	1	0			
MARIANI (attributed to)	1	0			
MARIANI, ANTONIO (attributed to)	1	1	$5,141	$5,141	$5,141
			DM7,766	DM7,766	DM7,766
			£3,450	£3,450	£3,450
			¥544,444	¥544,444	¥544,444
MARISSAL, OLIVIER (workshop of)	1	0			
MARSHALL, JOHN (attributed to)	2	2	$3,309	$3,853	$3,581
			DM4,630	DM5,791	DM5,210
			£2,070	£2,300	£2,185
			¥279,891	¥429,090	¥354,491

Maker	Items		Selling Prices		
	Bid	Sold	Low	High	Avg
MARSIGLIESE, BIAGIO	3	1	$5,289	$5,289	$5,289
			DM7,904	DM7,904	DM7,904
			£3,220	£3,220	£3,220
			¥508,847	¥508,847	¥508,847
MARTIN	1	0			
MARTIN, E.	1	1	$403	$403	$403
			DM680	DM680	DM680
			£242	£242	£242
			¥49,105	¥49,105	¥49,105
MARTIN, E. (Workshop of)	13	12	$201	$575	$446
			DM308	DM894	DM712
			£132	£376	£276
			¥21,212	¥65,585	¥50,842
MARTINENGHI, MARCELLO G.B.	2	2	$9,176	$12,650	$10,913
			DM14,098	DM18,292	DM16,195
			£5,980	£8,263	£7,121
			¥1,004,574	¥1,280,813	¥1,142,693
MARTINI, ORESTE	2	2	$7,376	$7,984	$7,680
			DM10,270	DM11,244	DM10,757
			£4,600	£5,060	£4,830
			¥623,521	¥816,340	¥719,930
MARTINI, ORESTE (attributed to)	1	1	$3,220	$3,220	$3,220
			DM5,566	DM5,566	DM5,566
			£1,990	£1,990	£1,990
			¥408,087	¥408,087	¥408,087
MARTINO, GIUSEPPE	1	1	$2,990	$2,990	$2,990
			DM5,168	DM5,168	DM5,168
			£1,848	£1,848	£1,848
			¥378,938	¥378,938	¥378,938
MASON, GEORGE	1	1	$451	$451	$451
			DM764	DM764	DM764
			£276	£276	£276
			¥52,301	¥52,301	¥52,301
MASON, WALTER	1	1	$3,523	$3,523	$3,523
			DM5,193	DM5,193	DM5,193
			£2,300	£2,300	£2,300
			¥375,751	¥375,751	¥375,751
MAST, JEAN LAURENT	1	0			
MATSUDA, TETSUO	3	1	$8,483	$8,483	$8,483
			DM11,811	DM11,811	DM11,811
			£5,290	£5,290	£5,290
			¥717,049	¥717,049	¥717,049
MATTER, ANITA	3	1	$934	$934	$934
			DM1,629	DM1,629	DM1,629
			£575	£575	£575
			¥113,189	¥113,189	¥113,189
MATTIUZZI, BRUNO	1	0			
MAUCOTEL, CHARLES	3	2	$6,900	$18,925	$12,912
			DM10,902	DM32,018	DM21,460
			£4,416	£11,903	£8,159
			¥689,310	¥2,344,793	¥1,517,051
MAUCOTEL, ERNEST (attributed to)	1	1	$9,743	$9,743	$9,743
			DM13,632	DM13,632	DM13,632
			£6,095	£6,095	£6,095
			¥824,123	¥824,123	¥824,123
MAULE, GIOVANNI (attributed to)	1	0			

Maker	Items		Selling Prices		
	Bid	Sold	Low	High	Avg
MAURIZI, FRANCESCO	3	2	$14,980	$23,046	$19,013
			DM26,820	DM38,502	DM32,661
			£8,970	£13,800	£11,385
			¥2,061,127	¥2,801,262	¥2,431,194
MAWBEY, EDWIN	1	1	$542	$542	$542
			DM766	DM766	DM766
			£345	£345	£345
			¥46,258	¥46,258	¥46,258
MAYR, ANDREAS FERDINAND	1	1	$4,798	$4,798	$4,798
			DM8,114	DM8,114	DM8,114
			£3,220	£3,220	£3,220
			¥508,760	¥508,760	¥508,760
MAYSON, WALTER H.	29	18	$730	$3,195	$1,561
			DM1,122	DM5,411	DM2,375
			£460	£1,955	£966
			¥77,872	¥370,465	¥163,398
MEDARD, NICOLAS (III)	2	1	$7,088	$7,088	$7,088
			DM10,011	DM10,011	DM10,011
			£4,485	£4,485	£4,485
			¥632,551	¥632,551	¥632,551
MEDIO-FINO	1	1	$174	$174	$174
			DM303	DM303	DM303
			£104	£104	£104
			¥22,186	¥22,186	¥22,186
MEIER, KARL	1	1	$1,093	$1,093	$1,093
			DM1,671	DM1,671	DM1,671
			£719	£719	£719
			¥115,150	¥115,150	¥115,150
MEINEL, EUGEN	1	1	$1,495	$1,495	$1,495
			DM2,317	DM2,317	DM2,317
			£957	£957	£957
			¥146,973	¥146,973	¥146,973
MEINEL, EUGEN (workshop of)	1	1	$1,380	$1,380	$1,380
			DM1,993	DM1,993	DM1,993
			£879	£879	£879
			¥119,715	¥119,715	¥119,715
MEINEL, FRIEDRICH WILHELM	1	1	$748	$748	$748
			DM1,279	DM1,279	DM1,279
			£442	£442	£442
			¥92,825	¥92,825	¥92,825
MEINEL, OSKAR	1	1	$920	$920	$920
			DM1,638	DM1,638	DM1,638
			£552	£552	£552
			¥122,342	¥122,342	¥122,342
MEISEL, CHRISTIAN	1	1	$2,826	$2,826	$2,826
			DM4,523	DM4,523	DM4,523
			£1,840	£1,840	£1,840
			¥285,108	¥285,108	¥285,108
MEISEL, FRIEDRICH WILHELM	1	1	$558	$558	$558
			DM854	DM854	DM854
			£357	£357	£357
			¥62,216	¥62,216	¥62,216
MEISEL, JOHANN GEORG	1	1	$575	$575	$575
			DM1,024	DM1,024	DM1,024
			£345	£345	£345
			¥76,464	¥76,464	¥76,464

Maker	Items		Selling Prices		
	Bid	Sold	Low	High	Avg

Maker	Bid	Sold	Low	High	Avg
MEISEL, KARL	1	1	$259	$259	$259
			DM437	DM437	DM437
			£155	£155	£155
			¥31,568	¥31,568	¥31,568
MEISEL, KARL (workshop of)	2	2	$633	$920	$776
			DM1,126	DM1,638	DM1,382
			£380	£552	£466
			¥84,110	¥122,342	¥103,226
MEISEL, LOTHAR	1	1	$1,265	$1,265	$1,265
			DM2,164	DM2,164	DM2,164
			£748	£748	£748
			¥157,088	¥157,088	¥157,088
MEISSNER, JOHANN FRIEDERICH	1	0			
MELEGARI, MICHELE & PIETRO	2	1	$3,572	$3,572	$3,572
			DM5,355	DM5,355	DM5,355
			£2,185	£2,185	£2,185
			¥345,580	¥345,580	¥345,580
MELZL, JOHANN GEORG	2	0			
MENICHETTI, MARTINO	2	0			
MENNEGAND, CHARLES (attributed to)	1	1	$2,999	$2,999	$2,999
			DM5,189	DM5,189	DM5,189
			£1,840	£1,840	£1,840
			¥342,240	¥342,240	¥342,240
MENNESSON	1	1	$2,833	$2,833	$2,833
			DM4,235	DM4,235	DM4,235
			£1,725	£1,725	£1,725
			¥272,597	¥272,597	¥272,597
MENNESSON, EMILE	15	9	$1,929	$5,151	$3,563
			DM3,243	DM8,615	DM5,605
			£1,208	£3,450	£2,277
			¥236,746	¥547,408	¥372,572
MENZINGER, GUSTAV	1	1	$1,380	$1,380	$1,380
			DM2,456	DM2,456	DM2,456
			£828	£828	£828
			¥183,512	¥183,512	¥183,512
MERCIOLLE, JULES (workshop of)	2	1	$2,415	$2,415	$2,415
			DM4,299	DM4,299	DM4,299
			£1,449	£1,449	£1,449
			¥321,147	¥321,147	¥321,147
MERLIN, JOSEPH	1	1	$9,930	$9,930	$9,930
			DM15,433	DM15,433	DM15,433
			£6,325	£6,325	£6,325
			¥977,213	¥977,213	¥977,213
MERLING, PAULI	1	1	$7,166	$7,166	$7,166
			DM10,050	DM10,050	DM10,050
			£4,600	£4,600	£4,600
			¥724,054	¥724,054	¥724,054
MERMILLOT, MAURICE	4	2	$3,457	$5,284	$4,371
			DM6,417	DM7,790	DM7,104
			£2,070	£3,450	£2,760
			¥462,521	¥563,627	¥513,074
MERRETT, H.W.	7	3	$128	$253	$196
			DM182	DM357	DM287
			£81	£161	£127
			¥11,886	¥22,249	¥18,574

Maker	Items		Selling Prices		
	Bid	Sold	Low	High	Avg
MESSORI, PIETRO	1	1	$3,760	$3,760	$3,760
			DM5,637	DM5,637	DM5,637
			£2,300	£2,300	£2,300
			¥363,768	¥363,768	¥363,768
MEYER, KARL	3	2	$193	$1,005	$599
			DM337	DM1,807	DM1,072
			£115	£598	£357
			¥24,651	¥116,150	¥70,400
MEZZADRI, ALESSANDRO (ascribed to)	1	1	$5,796	$5,796	$5,796
			DM10,419	DM10,419	DM10,419
			£3,450	£3,450	£3,450
			¥670,094	¥670,094	¥670,094
MICHETTI, PLINIO	2	2	$7,475	$14,973	$11,224
			DM12,633	DM24,150	DM18,391
			£4,485	£8,694	£6,590
			¥911,950	¥1,762,950	¥1,337,450
MIGAZZI, LUIGI	1	1	$4,416	$4,416	$4,416
			DM7,471	DM7,471	DM7,471
			£2,777	£2,777	£2,777
			¥547,118	¥547,118	¥547,118
MILES, GEORGE	2	2	$740	$3,861	$2,300
			DM1,175	DM5,401	DM3,288
			£483	£2,415	£1,449
			¥74,857	¥326,539	¥200,698
MILES, ROLF	1	0			
MILITELLA, MARIANO	2	1	$3,565	$3,565	$3,565
			DM5,148	DM5,148	DM5,148
			£2,271	£2,271	£2,271
			¥309,264	¥309,264	¥309,264
MILLANT, MAX (workshop of)	1	1	$1,553	$1,553	$1,553
			DM2,245	DM2,245	DM2,245
			£1,014	£1,014	£1,014
			¥157,191	¥157,191	¥157,191
MILLANT, R. & M.	1	1	$8,050	$8,050	$8,050
			DM11,624	DM11,624	DM11,624
			£5,129	£5,129	£5,129
			¥698,338	¥698,338	¥698,338
MILNE, PATRICK G.	1	1	$1,933	$1,933	$1,933
			DM2,892	DM2,892	DM2,892
			£1,150	£1,150	£1,150
			¥215,602	¥215,602	¥215,602
MILTON, LOUIS	1	1	$2,459	$2,459	$2,459
			DM4,158	DM4,158	DM4,158
			£1,650	£1,650	£1,650
			¥260,700	¥260,700	¥260,700
MINNOZZI, MARCO	1	1	$2,881	$2,881	$2,881
			DM5,158	DM5,158	DM5,158
			£1,725	£1,725	£1,725
			¥396,371	¥396,371	¥396,371
MIREMONT, CLAUDE AUGUSTIN	3	3	$4,801	$12,483	$8,482
			DM8,021	DM20,855	DM14,343
			£2,875	£7,475	£5,060
			¥583,596	¥1,517,350	¥1,040,026
MISSENHASTER, CARL	1	1	$787	$787	$787
			DM1,331	DM1,331	DM1,331
			£528	£528	£528
			¥83,424	¥83,424	¥83,424

Maker	Items		Selling Prices		
	Bid	Sold	Low	High	Avg
MOCKEL, OSWALD	2	0			
MOCKEL, OTTO	3	1	$8,360	$8,360	$8,360
			DM11,808	DM11,808	DM11,808
			£5,290	£5,290	£5,290
			¥746,086	¥746,086	¥746,086
MOENNIG, WILLIAM (workshop of)	1	1	$805	$805	$805
			DM1,212	DM1,212	DM1,212
			£489	£489	£489
			¥89,983	¥89,983	¥89,983
MOINEL, CHARLES	2	0			
MOINEL, DANIEL	2	2	$1,344	$3,084	$2,214
			DM2,496	DM5,216	DM3,856
			£805	£2,070	£1,438
			¥179,869	¥327,060	¥253,465
MOINEL & CHERPITEL	2	0			
MOINIER, ALAIN	1	1	$3,672	$3,672	$3,672
			DM5,495	DM5,495	DM5,495
			£2,185	£2,185	£2,185
			¥409,644	¥409,644	¥409,644
MOITESSIER, LOUIS	5	1	$999	$999	$999
			DM1,415	DM1,415	DM1,415
			£633	£633	£633
			¥103,098	¥103,098	¥103,098
MOITESSIER, LOUIS (ascribed to)	1	0			
MOLLER, MAX	1	1	$6,325	$6,325	$6,325
			DM9,146	DM9,146	DM9,146
			£4,131	£4,131	£4,131
			¥640,406	¥640,406	¥640,406
MONK	1	1	$556	$556	$556
			DM855	DM855	DM855
			£368	£368	£368
			¥59,331	¥59,331	¥59,331
MONK, JOHN KING	5	4	$460	$812	$601
			DM781	DM1,148	DM931
			£276	£518	£382
			¥54,850	¥69,387	¥61,377
MONNIG, FRITZ	5	3	$933	$2,359	$1,832
			DM1,617	DM3,706	DM2,882
			£552	£1,495	£1,142
			¥118,608	¥270,567	¥210,122
MONTEIRO, HENRIQUE	2	1	$3,304	$3,304	$3,304
			DM5,728	DM5,728	DM5,728
			£1,955	£1,955	£1,955
			¥412,505	¥412,505	¥412,505
MONTERUMICI, ARMANDO	1	1	$6,854	$6,854	$6,854
			DM11,592	DM11,592	DM11,592
			£4,600	£4,600	£4,600
			¥726,800	¥726,800	¥726,800
MONTEVECCHI, LUIGI (attributed to)	1	1	$3,172	$3,172	$3,172
			DM4,682	DM4,682	DM4,682
			£2,070	£2,070	£2,070
			¥337,205	¥337,205	¥337,205
MONTEVERDE, CLAUDIO	7	4	$1,102	$7,064	$3,513
			DM1,853	DM11,306	DM5,557
			£690	£4,600	£2,257
			¥135,283	¥712,770	¥375,469
MONZINO, ANTONIO	2	0			

Maker	Items		Selling Prices		
	Bid	Sold	Low	High	Avg
MONZINO, ANTONIO (workshop of)	1	1	$4,830	$4,830	$4,830
			DM7,631	DM7,631	DM7,631
			£3,091	£3,091	£3,091
			¥482,517	¥482,517	¥482,517
MONZINO & FIGLI	2	1	$1,955	$1,955	$1,955
			DM3,151	DM3,151	DM3,151
			£1,150	£1,150	£1,150
			¥241,753	¥241,753	¥241,753
MOON, GEORGE	3	2	$655	$686	$671
			DM937	DM970	DM953
			£414	£437	£426
			¥58,593	¥65,820	¥62,207
MOORE, ALFRED	5	1	$1,501	$1,501	$1,501
			DM2,677	DM2,677	DM2,677
			£920	£920	£920
			¥196,540	¥196,540	¥196,540
MORARA, PAOLO	2	2	$1,312	$5,264	$3,288
			DM2,270	DM7,892	DM5,081
			£805	£3,220	£2,013
			¥149,730	¥509,275	¥329,503
MORASSI, GIOVANNI BATTISTA	4	3	$2,820	$11,945	$7,274
			DM4,228	DM17,951	DM11,008
			£1,725	£7,130	£4,485
			¥272,826	¥1,330,180	¥791,918
MORITZ, ALFRED	1	1	$730	$730	$730
			DM1,206	DM1,206	DM1,206
			£437	£437	£437
			¥85,346	¥85,346	¥85,346
MORIZOT, RENE	3	1	$3,450	$3,450	$3,450
			DM5,275	DM5,275	DM5,275
			£2,270	£2,270	£2,270
			¥363,630	¥363,630	¥363,630
MORIZOT, RENE (attributed to)	1	1	$1,674	$1,674	$1,674
			DM2,394	DM2,394	DM2,394
			£1,058	£1,058	£1,058
			¥168,207	¥168,207	¥168,207
MORLOT	1	1	$1,031	$1,031	$1,031
			DM1,834	DM1,834	DM1,834
			£633	£633	£633
			¥138,473	¥138,473	¥138,473
MORLOT, NICOLAS	1	1	$575	$575	$575
			DM994	DM994	DM994
			£355	£355	£355
			¥72,873	¥72,873	¥72,873
MORRISON, ARCHIBALD	1	1	$926	$926	$926
			DM1,562	DM1,562	DM1,562
			£575	£575	£575
			¥113,771	¥113,771	¥113,771
MORSE, JOHN	1	1	$1,380	$1,380	$1,380
			DM2,361	DM2,361	DM2,361
			£816	£816	£816
			¥171,368	¥171,368	¥171,368
MORTIMER, JOHN WILLIAM	1	1	$430	$430	$430
			DM701	DM701	DM701
			£253	£253	£253
			¥50,620	¥50,620	¥50,620

Maker	Items Bid	Sold	Selling Prices Low	High	Avg
MORTIN, LEON (attributed to)	1	1	$1,740 DM2,503 £1,127 ¥176,646	$1,740 DM2,503 £1,127 ¥176,646	$1,740 DM2,503 £1,127 ¥176,646
MOSCHELLA, SALVATORE	1	1	$1,586 DM2,341 £1,035 ¥168,603	$1,586 DM2,341 £1,035 ¥168,603	$1,586 DM2,341 £1,035 ¥168,603
MOSHER, ALEX H.	2	0			
MOSS, HENRY	1	1	$686 DM970 £437 ¥58,593	$686 DM970 £437 ¥58,593	$686 DM970 £437 ¥58,593
MOUGEL	1	0			
MOUGENOT, GEORGES	5	5	$2,125 DM3,820 £1,265 ¥245,701	$10,934 DM18,499 £6,877 ¥1,354,769	$4,723 DM8,179 £2,893 ¥592,660
MOUGENOT, GEORGES (attributed to)	1	1	$1,308 DM2,281 £805 ¥158,464	$1,308 DM2,281 £805 ¥158,464	$1,308 DM2,281 £805 ¥158,464
MOUGENOT, GEORGES (workshop of)	1	1	$920 DM1,537 £614 ¥96,425	$920 DM1,537 £614 ¥96,425	$920 DM1,537 £614 ¥96,425
MOUGENOT, LEON	16	11	$812 DM1,300 £528 ¥82,169	$4,018 DM5,649 £2,530 ¥393,406	$2,319 DM3,526 £1,461 ¥233,869
MOUGENOT, LEON (attributed to)	4	3	$2,705 DM4,508 £1,610 ¥323,272	$4,591 DM7,045 £2,875 ¥456,070	$3,942 DM5,983 £2,453 ¥409,804
MOUGENOT, LEON (workshop of)	1	1	$920 DM1,328 £586 ¥79,810	$920 DM1,328 £586 ¥79,810	$920 DM1,328 £586 ¥79,810
MOYA, HIDALGO	6	5	$1,641 DM2,951 £977 ¥189,763	$3,055 DM4,900 £1,984 ¥347,593	$2,419 DM4,041 £1,526 ¥276,776
MOYA, HIDALGO (attributed to)	1	0			
MOZZANI, LUIGI	8	6	$2,310 DM4,274 £1,380 ¥307,864	$8,481 DM13,358 £5,520 ¥928,148	$5,571 DM9,100 £3,498 ¥634,441
MOZZANI, LUIGI (attributed to)	3	1	$3,853 DM5,791 £2,300 ¥429,090	$3,853 DM5,791 £2,300 ¥429,090	$3,853 DM5,791 £2,300 ¥429,090
MOZZANI, LUIGI (workshop of)	1	0			
MUELLER, KARL	1	1	$1,225 DM2,079 £825 ¥130,175	$1,225 DM2,079 £825 ¥130,175	$1,225 DM2,079 £825 ¥130,175
MUIR, HAROLD	2	0			

Maker	Items		Selling Prices		
	Bid	Sold	Low	High	Avg
MULLER, JOSEPH	1	0			
MULLER, KARL	1	0			
MULLER, KARL (attributed to)	1	1	$1,212	$1,212	$1,212
			DM1,799	DM1,799	DM1,799
			£782	£782	£782
			¥131,204	¥131,204	¥131,204
MUMBY, ERNEST	2	1	$950	$950	$950
			DM1,467	DM1,467	DM1,467
			£598	£598	£598
			¥94,725	¥94,725	¥94,725
MUNCHER, ROMEDIO	4	4	$2,437	$6,900	$4,541
			DM4,216	DM10,385	DM7,325
			£1,495	£4,189	£2,806
			¥278,070	¥771,282	¥518,978
MUNCHER, ROMEDIO (attributed to)	1	1	$2,138	$2,138	$2,138
			DM3,706	DM3,706	DM3,706
			£1,265	£1,265	£1,265
			¥266,915	¥266,915	¥266,915
MUNCHER, ROMEDIO (workshop of)	1	0			
MUNRO, DAVID	1	0			
MURDOCH, JOHN	1	1	$1,156	$1,156	$1,156
			DM2,071	DM2,071	DM2,071
			£690	£690	£690
			¥134,205	¥134,205	¥134,205
MURDY, THOMAS (attributed to)	1	1	$462	$462	$462
			DM714	DM714	DM714
			£291	£291	£291
			¥46,087	¥46,087	¥46,087
MURRAY, THOMAS	1	1	$1,441	$1,441	$1,441
			DM2,234	DM2,234	DM2,234
			£863	£863	£863
			¥164,142	¥164,142	¥164,142
MUSCHIETTI, UMBERTO	2	1	$4,664	$4,664	$4,664
			DM8,087	DM8,087	DM8,087
			£2,760	£2,760	£2,760
			¥582,360	¥582,360	¥582,360
MUSCHKE, ANTON	1	1	$690	$690	$690
			DM971	DM971	DM971
			£437	£437	£437
			¥70,502	¥70,502	¥70,502
MUTTI, VITTORIO	2	0			
NAFISSI, CARLO (ascribed to)	1	1	$2,467	$2,467	$2,467
			DM3,642	DM3,642	DM3,642
			£1,610	£1,610	£1,610
			¥262,271	¥262,271	¥262,271
NALDI, A.	1	0			
NAMY, JEAN THEODORE	1	0			
NATIONAL DOBRO CORP.	1	1	$1,150	$1,150	$1,150
			DM1,968	DM1,968	DM1,968
			£680	£680	£680
			¥142,807	¥142,807	¥142,807
NEBEL, HANS (attributed to)	1	1	$1,598	$1,598	$1,598
			DM2,299	DM2,299	DM2,299
			£1,035	£1,035	£1,035
			¥162,226	¥162,226	¥162,226

Maker	Items		Selling Prices		
	Bid	Sold	Low	High	Avg
NEBEL, MARTIN	2	1	$2,415	$2,415	$2,415
			DM3,492	DM3,492	DM3,492
			£1,577	£1,577	£1,577
			¥244,519	¥244,519	¥244,519
NEMESSANYI, SAMUEL FELIX	2	2	$6,170	$6,325	$6,247
			DM8,688	DM9,133	DM8,911
			£3,910	£4,030	£3,970
			¥548,694	¥630,808	¥589,751
NEUBAUER, GERHARD	2	1	$1,725	$1,725	$1,725
			DM2,951	DM2,951	DM2,951
			£1,020	£1,020	£1,020
			¥214,211	¥214,211	¥214,211
NEUDORFER	1	1	$1,844	$1,844	$1,844
			DM2,568	DM2,568	DM2,568
			£1,150	£1,150	£1,150
			¥155,880	¥155,880	¥155,880
NEUDORFER, KAREL	1	1	$2,760	$2,760	$2,760
			DM4,612	DM4,612	DM4,612
			£1,842	£1,842	£1,842
			¥289,276	¥289,276	¥289,276
NEUMANN, ADOLPH (workshop of)	1	1	$345	$345	$345
			DM614	DM614	DM614
			£207	£207	£207
			¥45,878	¥45,878	¥45,878
NEUNER (workshop of)	6	6	$403	$1,380	$791
			DM606	DM2,306	DM1,238
			£244	£921	£504
			¥44,991	¥144,638	¥81,200
NEUNER, LUDWIG	2	2	$364	$3,890	$2,127
			DM676	DM6,227	DM3,451
			£218	£2,530	£1,374
			¥48,710	¥393,729	¥221,219
NEUNER, MATHIAS	8	7	$345	$5,536	$1,823
			DM583	DM7,706	DM2,853
			£207	£3,450	£1,155
			¥42,090	¥467,047	¥184,672
NEUNER & HORNSTEINER	38	25	$81	$2,359	$819
			DM124	DM3,322	DM1,324
			£52	£1,495	£518
			¥9,033	¥241,191	¥90,619
NEUNER & HORNSTEINER (workshop of)	6	5	$288	$748	$529
			DM486	DM1,331	DM887
			£173	£454	£324
			¥35,075	¥99,403	¥64,278
NICOLAS	2	1	$950	$950	$950
			DM1,467	DM1,467	DM1,467
			£598	£598	£598
			¥94,725	¥94,725	¥94,725
NICOLAS, DIDIER (L'AINE)	46	23	$489	$6,598	$1,490
			DM826	DM9,247	DM2,350
			£293	£4,140	£935
			¥59,628	¥581,608	¥159,846
NICOLAS, DIDIER (L'AINE) (attributed to)	1	1	$1,283	$1,283	$1,283
			DM1,904	DM1,904	DM1,904
			£828	£828	£828
			¥138,922	¥138,922	¥138,922

Maker	Items		Selling Prices		
	Bid	Sold	Low	High	Avg
NICOLAS, DIDIER (L'AINE) (workshop of)	1	1	$1,093 DM1,945 £656 ¥145,281	$1,093 DM1,945 £656 ¥145,281	$1,093 DM1,945 £656 ¥145,281
NICOLAS, FRANCOIS FOURRIER	1	0			
NICOLAS, JOSEPH (II)	1	1	$1,633 DM2,300 £1,035 ¥166,979	$1,633 DM2,300 £1,035 ¥166,979	$1,633 DM2,300 £1,035 ¥166,979
NIEDT, KARL (attributed to)	2	1	$758 DM1,072 £483 ¥64,761	$758 DM1,072 £483 ¥64,761	$758 DM1,072 £483 ¥64,761
NISBET, WILLIAM	1	1	$73 DM126 £50 ¥7,582	$73 DM126 £50 ¥7,582	$73 DM126 £50 ¥7,582
NOBILE, FRANCESCO (attributed to)	1	1	$4,620 DM8,548 £2,760 ¥615,728	$4,620 DM8,548 £2,760 ¥615,728	$4,620 DM8,548 £2,760 ¥615,728
NOEBE, LOUIS	2	2	$1,767 DM2,611 £1,150 ¥188,294	$3,271 DM4,620 £2,070 ¥291,947	$2,519 DM3,615 £1,610 ¥240,120
NOLLI, MARCO	1	1	$2,467 DM3,723 £1,495 ¥279,565	$2,467 DM3,723 £1,495 ¥279,565	$2,467 DM3,723 £1,495 ¥279,565
NORMAN, BARAK (ascribed to)	1	1	$963 DM1,448 £575 ¥107,273	$963 DM1,448 £575 ¥107,273	$963 DM1,448 £575 ¥107,273
NOSEK, VACLAV	2	0			
NOVELLI	1	0			
NOVELLI, NATALE	2	2	$7,633 DM10,781 £4,830 ¥681,209	$15,887 DM24,379 £10,350 ¥1,738,904	$11,760 DM17,580 £7,590 ¥1,210,056
NOVELLI, NATALE (ascribed to)	1	0			
NUNN, ERNEST S.	1	1	$1,006 DM1,428 £633 ¥93,389	$1,006 DM1,428 £633 ¥93,389	$1,006 DM1,428 £633 ¥93,389
NUPIERI, GIUSEPPE	5	4	$712 DM1,232 £437 ¥81,282	$1,495 DM2,527 £897 ¥182,390	$1,127 DM1,907 £679 ¥136,009
ODDONE, CARLO GIUSEPPE	8	5	$26,887 DM44,919 £16,100 ¥2,919,466	$45,230 DM80,144 £27,773 ¥5,514,825	$35,930 DM56,056 £22,115 ¥3,940,794
ODDONE, CARLO GIUSEPPE (ascribed to)	1	0			
ODDONE, CARLO GIUSEPPE (attributed to)	1	1	$34,339 DM57,433 £23,000 ¥3,649,387	$34,339 DM57,433 £23,000 ¥3,649,387	$34,339 DM57,433 £23,000 ¥3,649,387

| Maker | Items | | Selling Prices | | |
	Bid	Sold	Low	High	Avg
ODOARDI, GIUSEPPE	4	2	$3,276	$16,100	$9,688
			DM4,685	DM25,438	DM15,061
			£2,070	£10,304	£6,187
			¥329,101	¥1,608,390	¥968,746
ODOARDI, GIUSEPPE (ascribed to)	1	1	$6,900	$6,900	$6,900
			DM10,902	DM10,902	DM10,902
			£4,416	£4,416	£4,416
			¥689,310	¥689,310	¥689,310
ODOARDI, GIUSEPPE (attributed to)	2	2	$2,261	$3,241	$2,751
			DM4,007	DM4,962	DM4,484
			£1,389	£2,070	£1,729
			¥275,741	¥361,256	¥318,499
OETTL & HORNSTEINER	1	1	$4,140	$4,140	$4,140
			DM5,986	DM5,986	DM5,986
			£2,704	£2,704	£2,704
			¥419,175	¥419,175	¥419,175
OLDFIELD, W.	1	1	$162	$162	$162
			DM248	DM248	DM248
			£104	£104	£104
			¥18,066	¥18,066	¥18,066
OLIVER, FREEMAN ADAMS	1	1	$374	$374	$374
			DM540	DM540	DM540
			£244	£244	£244
			¥37,842	¥37,842	¥37,842
OLIVIER & BISCH	3	3	$2,305	$2,332	$2,318
			DM4,043	DM4,168	DM4,112
			£1,380	£1,380	£1,380
			¥268,037	¥317,096	¥293,885
OLRY, J. (attributed to)	4	0			
OMOND, JAMES	1	1	$1,270	$1,270	$1,270
			DM1,789	DM1,789	DM1,789
			£805	£805	£805
			¥129,872	¥129,872	¥129,872
ORLANDINI, A.	2	1	$3,887	$3,887	$3,887
			DM6,739	DM6,739	DM6,739
			£2,300	£2,300	£2,300
			¥494,201	¥494,201	¥494,201
ORNATI, GIUSEPPE	6	3	$14,752	$40,250	$23,630
			DM20,541	DM63,595	DM36,172
			£9,200	£25,760	£15,103
			¥1,247,042	¥4,020,975	¥2,335,640
ORNATI, GIUSEPPE (attributed to)	1	0			
ORNATI, GIUSEPPE (workshop of)	3	1	$10,592	$10,592	$10,592
			DM16,253	DM16,253	DM16,253
			£6,900	£6,900	£6,900
			¥1,159,269	¥1,159,269	¥1,159,269
ORSELLI, ENRICO	2	2	$3,565	$6,061	$4,813
			DM5,451	DM9,775	DM7,613
			£2,345	£3,519	£2,932
			¥375,751	¥713,575	¥544,663
ORY, F.	3	1	$601	$601	$601
			DM1,019	DM1,019	DM1,019
			£368	£368	£368
			¥69,735	¥69,735	¥69,735
OSMANEK, A.	1	1	$1,057	$1,057	$1,057
			DM1,561	DM1,561	DM1,561
			£690	£690	£690
			¥112,402	¥112,402	¥112,402

| Maker | Items | | Selling Prices | | |
	Bid	Sold	Low	High	Avg
OTTO, C.W.F.	1	1	$2,209	$2,209	$2,209
			DM3,263	DM3,263	DM3,263
			£1,438	£1,438	£1,438
			¥235,368	¥235,368	¥235,368
OTTO, WILHELM	1	1	$3,816	$3,816	$3,816
			DM5,391	DM5,391	DM5,391
			£2,415	£2,415	£2,415
			¥340,604	¥340,604	¥340,604
OTTO, WILHELM (workshop of)	1	1	$1,150	$1,150	$1,150
			DM1,661	DM1,661	DM1,661
			£733	£733	£733
			¥99,763	¥99,763	¥99,763
OWEN, JOHN W.	4	4	$1,342	$3,864	$2,473
			DM2,052	DM6,440	DM3,857
			£863	£2,300	£1,538
			¥132,639	¥461,817	¥258,102
PACHEREL, PIERRE	2	1	$26,887	$26,887	$26,887
			DM44,919	DM44,919	DM44,919
			£16,100	£16,100	£16,100
			¥3,268,139	¥3,268,139	¥3,268,139
PACHERELE, PIERRE	2	0			
PACHERELE, PIERRE (ascribed to)	2	2	$9,145	$15,902	$12,524
			DM12,980	DM23,495	DM18,237
			£5,750	£10,350	£8,050
			¥848,988	¥1,694,647	¥1,271,817
PACHERELE, PIERRE (attributed to)	3	2	$3,699	$3,761	$3,730
			DM6,211	DM6,417	DM6,314
			£2,185	£2,300	£2,243
			¥465,587	¥468,923	¥467,255
PAESOLD, RODERICH	1	1	$938	$938	$938
			DM1,673	DM1,673	DM1,673
			£575	£575	£575
			¥122,837	¥122,837	¥122,837
PAILLIOT	1	1	$1,686	$1,686	$1,686
			DM2,363	DM2,363	DM2,363
			£1,058	£1,058	£1,058
			¥148,633	¥148,633	¥148,633
PAINE, ARTHUR	1	1	$1,840	$1,840	$1,840
			DM3,275	DM3,275	DM3,275
			£1,104	£1,104	£1,104
			¥244,683	¥244,683	¥244,683
PAINE, THOMAS D.	2	1	$288	$288	$288
			DM512	DM512	DM512
			£173	£173	£173
			¥38,232	¥38,232	¥38,232
PALLAVER, GIOVANNI	1	0			
PALLOTTA, PIETRO	3	1	$55,321	$55,321	$55,321
			DM77,028	DM77,028	DM77,028
			£34,500	£34,500	£34,500
			¥4,676,406	¥4,676,406	¥4,676,406
PALMIERI, ALESSANDRO	1	1	$12,353	$12,353	$12,353
			DM18,978	DM18,978	DM18,978
			£8,050	£8,050	£8,050
			¥1,352,311	¥1,352,311	¥1,352,311
PAMPHILON, EDWARD	1	0			

Maker	Items		Selling Prices		
	Bid	Sold	Low	High	Avg
PANORMO, GEORGE	4	3	$13,771	$35,958	$23,055
			DM22,971	DM50,068	DM35,578
			£9,200	£22,425	£14,375
			¥1,414,123	¥3,039,664	¥2,293,429
PANORMO, GEORGE (attributed to)	1	1	$6,900	$6,900	$6,900
			DM11,530	DM11,530	DM11,530
			£4,604	£4,604	£4,604
			¥723,189	¥723,189	¥723,189
PANORMO, J. (attributed to)	1	1	$8,118	$8,118	$8,118
			DM12,471	DM12,471	DM12,471
			£5,290	£5,290	£5,290
			¥888,662	¥888,662	¥888,662
PANORMO, VINCENZO	9	6	$31,217	$48,364	$40,555
			DM47,909	DM81,823	DM66,429
			£19,550	£30,418	£25,032
			¥3,060,474	¥5,992,248	¥4,736,521
PANORMO, VINCENZO (ascribed to)	1	1	$18,745	$18,745	$18,745
			DM32,430	DM32,430	DM32,430
			£11,500	£11,500	£11,500
			¥2,139,000	¥2,139,000	¥2,139,000
PANORMO, VINCENZO (attributed to)	3	3	$18,975	$58,600	$32,375
			DM28,635	DM100,265	DM53,067
			£11,500	£34,660	£19,557
			¥1,921,960	¥7,276,948	¥3,783,136
PANORMO FAMILY (MEMBER OF)	1	0			
PANORMO FAMILY (MEMBER OF) (attributed to)	1	1	$16,376	$16,376	$16,376
			DM24,611	DM24,611	DM24,611
			£9,775	£9,775	£9,775
			¥1,823,634	¥1,823,634	¥1,823,634
PAOLETTI, SILVIO VEZIO	4	4	$3,618	$4,718	$4,298
			DM6,411	DM8,548	DM7,026
			£2,222	£2,990	£2,683
			¥441,186	¥615,728	¥500,751
PAOLO, ERBA (attributed to)	1	1	$8,457	$8,457	$8,457
			DM11,832	DM11,832	DM11,832
			£5,290	£5,290	£5,290
			¥715,277	¥715,277	¥715,277
PAOLUCCI, GIUSEPPE	1	1	$3,196	$3,196	$3,196
			DM4,792	DM4,792	DM4,792
			£1,955	£1,955	£1,955
			¥309,203	¥309,203	¥309,203
PAQUOTTE, JEAN BAPTIST	1	1	$7,739	$7,739	$7,739
			DM12,413	DM12,413	DM12,413
			£5,026	£5,026	£5,026
			¥880,568	¥880,568	¥880,568
PARALUPI, RODOLFO (attributed to)	1	0			
PARESCHI, GAETANO	8	3	$4,592	$15,077	$9,581
			DM7,722	DM26,715	DM15,738
			£2,875	£9,258	£5,961
			¥563,681	¥1,838,275	¥1,109,872
PARKER, DANIEL	5	1	$5,089	$5,089	$5,089
			DM7,187	DM7,187	DM7,187
			£3,220	£3,220	£3,220
			¥454,139	¥454,139	¥454,139

Maker	Items		Selling Prices		
	Bid	Sold	Low	High	Avg
PARMEGGIANI, ROMOLA	1	1	$3,015 DM5,343 £1,852 ¥367,655	$3,015 DM5,343 £1,852 ¥367,655	$3,015 DM5,343 £1,852 ¥367,655
PARMEGGIANI, ROMOLA (attributed to)	1	1	$6,611 DM10,145 £4,140 ¥648,100	$6,611 DM10,145 £4,140 ¥648,100	$6,611 DM10,145 £4,140 ¥648,100
PARRAVICINI, PIERO	2	2	$7,197 DM12,172 £4,830 ¥763,140	$14,950 DM24,981 £9,976 ¥1,566,909	$11,073 DM18,577 £7,403 ¥1,165,025
PARTL, ANDREAS NIKOLAUS II	1	1	$2,178 DM3,066 £1,380 ¥222,638	$2,178 DM3,066 £1,380 ¥222,638	$2,178 DM3,066 £1,380 ¥222,638
PASSAURO-ZUCCARO, RAYMOND	2	2	$805 DM1,360 £483 ¥98,210	$1,265 DM2,138 £759 ¥154,330	$1,035 DM1,749 £621 ¥126,270
PASTA, GAETANO	3	1	$20,407 DM35,380 £12,075 ¥2,547,825	$20,407 DM35,380 £12,075 ¥2,547,825	$20,407 DM35,380 £12,075 ¥2,547,825
PASTA FAMILY (MEMBER OF) (attributed to)	1	1	$13,708 DM20,709 £9,200 ¥1,451,852	$13,708 DM20,709 £9,200 ¥1,451,852	$13,708 DM20,709 £9,200 ¥1,451,852
PATOCKA, BENJAMIN	1	1	$1,938 DM2,861 £1,265 ¥206,070	$1,938 DM2,861 £1,265 ¥206,070	$1,938 DM2,861 £1,265 ¥206,070
PATOCKA, BENJAMIN (attributed to)	1	1	$2,120 DM3,133 £1,380 ¥225,953	$2,120 DM3,133 £1,380 ¥225,953	$2,120 DM3,133 £1,380 ¥225,953
PATZELT, FERDINAND (attributed to)	2	0			
PAUL, ADAM D.	3	1	$657 DM924 £414 ¥58,676	$657 DM924 £414 ¥58,676	$657 DM924 £414 ¥58,676
PAULI, JOSEPH	2	1	$1,265 DM1,934 £832 ¥133,331	$1,265 DM1,934 £832 ¥133,331	$1,265 DM1,934 £832 ¥133,331
PAULSEN, P.C.	2	1	$1,610 DM2,325 £1,026 ¥139,668	$1,610 DM2,325 £1,026 ¥139,668	$1,610 DM2,325 £1,026 ¥139,668
PAULUS, A.L.	1	1	$546 DM847 £350 ¥53,702	$546 DM847 £350 ¥53,702	$546 DM847 £350 ¥53,702
PAULUS, ALBIN LUDWIG	4	2	$1,059 DM1,625 £690 ¥115,927	$1,118 DM1,958 £690 ¥135,206	$1,089 DM1,792 £690 ¥125,566

Maker	Items		Selling Prices		
	Bid	Sold	Low	High	Avg

Maker	Bid	Sold	Low	High	Avg
PAULUS, KONRAD (attributed to)	2	0			
PAYNE, ALAN	1	0			
PEARCE, WILLIAM	2	1	$1,739	$1,739	$1,739
			DM3,127	DM3,127	DM3,127
			£1,035	£1,035	£1,035
			¥201,028	¥201,028	¥201,028
PEDRAZZINI, GIUSEPPE	19	12	$12,815	$57,615	$30,963
			DM21,476	DM96,255	DM50,799
			£7,869	£34,500	£19,259
			¥1,396,675	¥7,003,155	¥3,626,110
PEDRAZZINI, GIUSEPPE (ascribed to)	2	1	$13,630	$13,630	$13,630
			DM19,252	DM19,252	DM19,252
			£8,625	£8,625	£8,625
			¥1,216,444	¥1,216,444	¥1,216,444
PEDRAZZINI, GIUSEPPE (attributed to)	3	2	$1,639	$5,511	$3,575
			DM2,772	DM9,266	DM6,019
			£1,100	£3,450	£2,275
			¥173,800	¥676,417	¥425,109
PELLACANI, GIUSEPPE	2	2	$4,300	$6,325	$5,312
			DM6,030	DM9,133	DM7,582
			£2,760	£4,030	£3,395
			¥434,432	¥548,694	¥491,563
PELLACANI, GIUSEPPE (attributed to)	1	0			
PELLERANI, ANTONIO	1	1	$9,163	$9,163	$9,163
			DM13,526	DM13,526	DM13,526
			£5,980	£5,980	£5,980
			¥974,148	¥974,148	¥974,148
PELLIZON, ANTONIO (I)	2	2	$9,423	$12,721	$11,072
			DM16,697	DM17,968	DM17,332
			£5,786	£8,050	£6,918
			¥1,135,348	¥1,148,922	¥1,142,135
PERESSON, SERGIO	4	3	$18,463	$23,194	$21,144
			DM30,665	DM34,703	DM32,459
			£10,925	£13,800	£12,842
			¥2,226,382	¥2,587,224	¥2,372,927
PERR, MICHAEL	1	0			
PERRY	2	1	$251	$251	$251
			DM438	DM438	DM438
			£150	£150	£150
			¥32,047	¥32,047	¥32,047
PERRY, JAMES	4	0			
PERRY, L.A.	1	1	$668	$668	$668
			DM1,026	DM1,026	DM1,026
			£437	£437	£437
			¥72,951	¥72,951	¥72,951
PERRY, STEPHEN	1	1	$230	$230	$230
			DM384	DM384	DM384
			£153	£153	£153
			¥24,106	¥24,106	¥24,106
PERRY, THOMAS	10	6	$858	$3,770	$2,319
			DM1,336	DM6,376	DM3,703
			£550	£2,530	£1,495
			¥84,953	¥399,740	¥241,914
PERRY, THOMAS & WILKINSON, WM.	16	8	$772	$3,652	$1,767
			DM1,080	DM5,135	DM2,585
			£483	£2,300	£1,109
			¥65,308	¥325,979	¥167,401

Maker	Items Bid	Items Sold	Selling Prices Low	Selling Prices High	Selling Prices Avg
PERRY & WILKINSON	9	5	$748 DM1,303 £460 ¥90,551	$4,025 DM7,309 £2,463 ¥499,825	$1,973 DM3,533 £1,194 ¥246,279
PERRY & WILKINSON (attributed to)	1	1	$1,013 DM1,816 £605 ¥117,673	$1,013 DM1,816 £605 ¥117,673	$1,013 DM1,816 £605 ¥117,673
PETERS, WILLIAM L.	1	1	$1,610 DM2,721 £966 ¥196,420	$1,610 DM2,721 £966 ¥196,420	$1,610 DM2,721 £966 ¥196,420
PETZOLD, SIEGFRIED	2	0			
PEVERE, ERNESTO	1	1	$3,872 DM5,392 £2,415 ¥327,348	$3,872 DM5,392 £2,415 ¥327,348	$3,872 DM5,392 £2,415 ¥327,348
PFRETZSCHNER	1	0			
PFRETZSCHNER, E.R.	1	1	$92 DM164 £56 ¥12,781	$92 DM164 £56 ¥12,781	$92 DM164 £56 ¥12,781
PFRETZSCHNER, G.A. (workshop of)	1	1	$201 DM340 £121 ¥24,553	$201 DM340 £121 ¥24,553	$201 DM340 £121 ¥24,553
PFRETZSCHNER, JOHANN GOTTLOB	1	1	$900 DM1,375 £575 ¥100,366	$900 DM1,375 £575 ¥100,366	$900 DM1,375 £575 ¥100,366
PICCAGLIANI, ARMANDO	1	1	$1,960 DM3,473 £1,203 ¥238,976	$1,960 DM3,473 £1,203 ¥238,976	$1,960 DM3,473 £1,203 ¥238,976
PICKARD, H.	1	1	$3,105 DM5,367 £1,919 ¥393,512	$3,105 DM5,367 £1,919 ¥393,512	$3,105 DM5,367 £1,919 ¥393,512
PICKSTONE, HARRY	2	2	$230 DM381 £138 ¥26,951	$332 DM542 £196 ¥39,116	$281 DM461 £167 ¥33,034
PIERCE, WILLIAM	1	1	$403 DM680 £242 ¥49,105	$403 DM680 £242 ¥49,105	$403 DM680 £242 ¥49,105
PIEROTTE, JULES	1	0			
PIERRAY, CLAUDE	7	6	$2,875 DM4,602 £1,870 ¥291,017	$10,870 DM15,387 £6,900 ¥1,094,568	$7,172 DM11,051 £4,509 ¥760,030
PILAR, KAREL	2	1	$1,360 DM2,359 £805 ¥169,855	$1,360 DM2,359 £805 ¥169,855	$1,360 DM2,359 £805 ¥169,855

Maker	Items		Selling Prices		
	Bid	Sold	Low	High	Avg
PILAR, VLADIMIR	1	1	$2,467	$2,467	$2,467
			DM4,440	DM4,440	DM4,440
			£1,495	£1,495	£1,495
			¥355,735	¥355,735	¥355,735
PILAT, ERNEST PAUL	1	1	$13,159	$13,159	$13,159
			DM19,731	DM19,731	DM19,731
			£8,050	£8,050	£8,050
			¥1,273,188	¥1,273,188	¥1,273,188
PILAT, PAUL	3	1	$7,991	$7,991	$7,991
			DM13,519	DM13,519	DM13,519
			£5,026	£5,026	£5,026
			¥990,024	¥990,024	¥990,024
PILLEMENT, FRANCOIS	3	1	$2,277	$2,277	$2,277
			DM3,436	DM3,436	DM3,436
			£1,380	£1,380	£1,380
			¥258,060	¥258,060	¥258,060
PINEAU, JOSEPH	1	1	$690	$690	$690
			DM1,228	DM1,228	DM1,228
			£414	£414	£414
			¥91,756	¥91,756	¥91,756
PIQUE, FRANCOIS LOUIS	1	1	$47,179	$47,179	$47,179
			DM66,441	DM66,441	DM66,441
			£29,900	£29,900	£29,900
			¥4,823,827	¥4,823,827	¥4,823,827
PIQUE, FRANCOIS LOUIS (attributed to)	1	1	$4,600	$4,600	$4,600
			DM7,871	DM7,871	DM7,871
			£2,721	£2,721	£2,721
			¥571,228	¥571,228	¥571,228
PIRETTI, ENRICO	3	2	$1,586	$8,625	$5,105
			DM2,341	DM12,472	DM7,406
			£1,035	£5,634	£3,334
			¥168,603	¥873,281	¥520,942
PIROT, CLAUDE	2	1	$17,250	$17,250	$17,250
			DM29,153	DM29,153	DM29,153
			£10,350	£10,350	£10,350
			¥2,295,458	¥2,295,458	¥2,295,458
PIVA, GIOVANNI	1	0			
PIZZAMIGHO, CARLO	2	0			
PLACHT, FRANZ	1	1	$699	$699	$699
			DM977	DM977	DM977
			£437	£437	£437
			¥59,088	¥59,088	¥59,088
PLATNER, MICHAEL	2	0			
PLATNER, MICHAEL (attributed to)	1	0			
PLOWRIGHT, DENIS G.	2	1	$765	$765	$765
			DM1,175	DM1,175	DM1,175
			£506	£506	£506
			¥81,580	¥81,580	¥81,580
PLUMEREL, CHARLES	1	1	$345	$345	$345
			DM498	DM498	DM498
			£220	£220	£220
			¥29,929	¥29,929	¥29,929
POEHLAND & FUCHS	2	2	$863	$3,450	$2,156
			DM1,491	DM5,275	DM3,383
			£533	£2,270	£1,401
			¥109,309	¥363,630	¥236,469

Maker	Items		Selling Prices		
	Bid	Sold	Low	High	Avg
POGGI, ANSALDO	3	3	$29,956	$40,601	$34,904
			DM44,220	DM62,303	DM56,001
			£19,550	£26,450	£22,233
			¥3,184,715	¥4,925,565	¥4,184,715
POIROT, A.	1	1	$1,131	$1,131	$1,131
			DM2,004	DM2,004	DM2,004
			£694	£694	£694
			¥137,871	¥137,871	¥137,871
POIRSON, ELOPHE	1	1	$15,525	$15,525	$15,525
			DM27,635	DM27,635	DM27,635
			£9,315	£9,315	£9,315
			¥2,064,514	¥2,064,514	¥2,064,514
POLITI, ENRICO	1	1	$15,039	$15,039	$15,039
			DM22,549	DM22,549	DM22,549
			£9,200	£9,200	£9,200
			¥1,455,072	¥1,455,072	¥1,455,072
POLITI, ENRICO & RAUL	3	3	$7,520	$17,135	$13,077
			DM11,275	DM28,980	DM21,842
			£4,600	£11,500	£8,242
			¥727,536	¥1,819,875	¥1,454,804
POLITI, EUGENIO	1	0			
POLITI, EUGENIO (ascribed to)	1	0			
POLITI, RAUL	5	3	$6,641	$13,159	$10,163
			DM11,954	DM19,731	DM16,739
			£4,025	£8,050	£6,133
			¥957,749	¥1,334,575	¥1,188,504
POLLASTRI, GAETANO	10	6	$4,566	$42,757	$22,930
			DM7,310	DM74,129	DM37,244
			£2,970	£25,300	£14,017
			¥462,203	¥5,338,300	¥2,601,467
POLLASTRI, GAETANO (ascribed to)	1	1	$10,925	$10,925	$10,925
			DM19,447	DM19,447	DM19,447
			£6,555	£6,555	£6,555
			¥1,452,807	¥1,452,807	¥1,452,807
POLLASTRI, GAETANO (attributed to)	1	1	$15,040	$15,040	$15,040
			DM24,116	DM24,116	DM24,116
			£9,775	£9,775	£9,775
			¥1,521,234	¥1,521,234	¥1,521,234
POLLER, ANTON	1	1	$7,475	$7,475	$7,475
			DM10,794	DM10,794	DM10,794
			£4,762	£4,762	£4,762
			¥648,456	¥648,456	¥648,456
POLSTER, WALTER	1	0			
POSTACCHINI, ANDREA	2	2	$7,161	$40,664	$23,913
			DM12,689	DM65,099	DM38,894
			£4,397	£26,450	£15,424
			¥873,181	¥4,116,255	¥2,494,718
POSTACCHINI, ANDREA (attributed to)	3	2	$18,400	$27,600	$23,000
			DM27,692	DM41,538	DM34,615
			£11,170	£16,755	£13,962
			¥2,056,752	¥3,085,128	¥2,570,940
POSTIGLIONE, VINCENZO	10	8	$6,900	$52,703	$29,640
			DM10,695	DM80,135	DM47,208
			£4,416	£33,350	£18,270
			¥678,339	¥5,772,454	¥3,156,100

Maker	Items		Selling Prices		
	Bid	Sold	Low	High	Avg
POSTIGLIONE, VINCENZO (attributed to)	6	1	$31,719	$31,719	$31,719
			DM46,821	DM46,821	DM46,821
			£20,700	£20,700	£20,700
			¥3,372,051	¥3,372,051	¥3,372,051
POSTIGLIONE, VINCENZO (workshop of)	1	1	$15,882	$15,882	$15,882
			DM24,400	DM24,400	DM24,400
			£10,350	£10,350	£10,350
			¥1,738,686	¥1,738,686	¥1,738,686
POSTIGLIONE, VINCENZO & GIOVANNI PISTUCCI	1	0			
POUZOL, EMILE	1	1	$3,400	$3,400	$3,400
			DM5,081	DM5,081	DM5,081
			£2,070	£2,070	£2,070
			¥327,116	¥327,116	¥327,116
POWERS, CLARK	2	1	$1,093	$1,093	$1,093
			DM1,580	DM1,580	DM1,580
			£714	£714	£714
			¥110,616	¥110,616	¥110,616
POWERS, LINCOLN	1	1	$374	$374	$374
			DM572	DM572	DM572
			£246	£246	£246
			¥39,393	¥39,393	¥39,393
POWLOSKI, PATRICIA	1	0			
POWLOSKI-BANCHERO, PATRICIA	1	1	$1,840	$1,840	$1,840
			DM3,275	DM3,275	DM3,275
			£1,104	£1,104	£1,104
			¥244,683	¥244,683	¥244,683
PRAGA, EUGENIO	4	2	$8,539	$14,950	$11,744
			DM15,370	DM21,618	DM18,494
			£5,175	£9,765	£7,470
			¥1,231,391	¥1,513,688	¥1,372,539
PRAILL, RONALD WILLIAM	5	1	$1,118	$1,118	$1,118
			DM1,178	DM1,178	DM1,178
			£690	£690	£690
			¥85,419	¥85,419	¥85,419
PRESSENDA, GIOVANNI FRANCESCO	8	6	$141,120	$247,521	$179,873
			DM220,720	DM396,253	DM276,896
			£84,000	£161,000	£114,158
			¥15,969,418	¥25,055,464	¥18,752,557
PRESTON, JAMES	1	1	$1,360	$1,360	$1,360
			DM2,359	DM2,359	DM2,359
			£805	£805	£805
			¥172,970	¥172,970	¥172,970
PRICE, REGINALD (attributed to)	2	1	$704	$704	$704
			DM995	DM995	DM995
			£449	£449	£449
			¥60,135	¥60,135	¥60,135
PRIESTNALL, J.	1	1	$1,060	$1,060	$1,060
			DM1,566	DM1,566	DM1,566
			£690	£690	£690
			¥112,976	¥112,976	¥112,976
PRIESTNALL, JOHN	1	1	$538	$538	$538
			DM998	DM998	DM998
			£322	£322	£322
			¥71,948	¥71,948	¥71,948
PRIMAVERA, ALFREDO (workshop of)	1	0			

| Maker | Items | | Selling Prices | | |
	Bid	Sold	Low	High	Avg
PRINCE, W.B.	3	1	$1,316	$1,316	$1,316
			DM2,228	DM2,228	DM2,228
			£805	£805	£805
			¥152,544	¥152,544	¥152,544
PROCAK, MYRON	1	0			
PROCTER, JOSEPH (attributed to)	1	0			
PROCTOR, JOSEPH (attributed to)	3	1	$402	$402	$402
			DM571	DM571	DM571
			£253	£253	£253
			¥37,355	¥37,355	¥37,355
PROKOP, LADISLAV	2	2	$288	$374	$331
			DM497	DM646	DM571
			£178	£231	£204
			¥36,436	¥47,367	¥41,902
PROKOP, LADISLAV (II)	2	0			
PUGLISI, CONCETTO	1	0			
PUGLISI, MICHELANGELO	1	0			
PUGLISI, MICHELANGELO (attributed to)	1	1	$5,301	$5,301	$5,301
			DM7,832	DM7,832	DM7,832
			£3,450	£3,450	£3,450
			¥564,882	¥564,882	¥564,882
PUGLISI, REALE	1	1	$3,850	$3,850	$3,850
			DM7,123	DM7,123	DM7,123
			£2,300	£2,300	£2,300
			¥513,107	¥513,107	¥513,107
PULPANECK, FRITZ	1	0			
PUOZZO, EDSON	1	0			
PUPUNAT, FRANCOIS MARIE	3	1	$1,440	$1,440	$1,440
			DM2,201	DM2,201	DM2,201
			£920	£920	£920
			¥160,586	¥160,586	¥160,586
PURDAY, T.E.	1	1	$1,018	$1,018	$1,018
			DM1,633	DM1,633	DM1,633
			£661	£661	£661
			¥115,864	¥115,864	¥115,864
PUSKAS, JOSEPH	2	2	$2,875	$3,450	$3,163
			DM5,221	DM5,831	DM5,526
			£1,760	£2,070	£1,915
			¥357,018	¥459,092	¥408,055
PYNE, GEORGE	14	13	$1,999	$6,165	$4,074
			DM2,824	DM9,265	DM6,441
			£1,265	£3,910	£2,521
			¥178,412	¥686,544	¥453,104
QUENOIL, VICTOR	2	0			
RACZ, LORAND	1	1	$4,255	$4,255	$4,255
			DM6,153	DM6,153	DM6,153
			£2,779	£2,779	£2,779
			¥430,819	¥430,819	¥430,819
RADRIZZANI, ANGELO	1	1	$3,006	$3,006	$3,006
			DM4,812	DM4,812	DM4,812
			£1,955	£1,955	£1,955
			¥304,245	¥304,245	¥304,245
RAE, JOHN	7	2	$559	$777	$668
			DM979	DM1,348	DM1,163
			£345	£460	£403
			¥67,603	¥97,060	¥82,331

Maker	Items		Selling Prices		
	Bid	Sold	Low	High	Avg
RAEBURN, JOHN	1	1	$1,348	$1,348	$1,348
			DM2,416	DM2,416	DM2,416
			£805	£805	£805
			¥156,573	¥156,573	¥156,573
RAMBAUX, CLAUDE VICTOR	2	2	$3,266	$4,229	$3,748
			DM4,600	DM6,243	DM5,421
			£2,070	£2,760	£2,415
			¥333,957	¥449,607	¥391,782
RANIERI, ERACLIO	1	1	$5,076	$5,076	$5,076
			DM7,610	DM7,610	DM7,610
			£3,105	£3,105	£3,105
			¥491,087	¥491,087	¥491,087
RAPOPORT, HAIM	1	0			
RASTELLI, LODOVICO	1	0			
RATHBONE, A. (attributed to)	1	1	$848	$848	$848
			DM1,253	DM1,253	DM1,253
			£552	£552	£552
			¥90,381	¥90,381	¥90,381
RAUCH, THOMAS (attributed to)	1	1	$368	$368	$368
			DM514	DM514	DM514
			£230	£230	£230
			¥31,099	¥31,099	¥31,099
RAUCHE (attributed to)	1	1	$686	$686	$686
			DM970	DM970	DM970
			£437	£437	£437
			¥58,593	¥58,593	¥58,593
RAVIZZA, CARLO	1	0			
RAYMOND, ROBERT JOHN	2	1	$468	$468	$468
			DM717	DM717	DM717
			£299	£299	£299
			¥52,181	¥52,181	¥52,181
REED, JOSEPH	2	1	$1,273	$1,273	$1,273
			DM1,873	DM1,873	DM1,873
			£828	£828	£828
			¥135,096	¥135,096	¥135,096
REGAZZONI, DANTE PAOLO	1	1	$3,187	$3,187	$3,187
			DM5,513	DM5,513	DM5,513
			£1,955	£1,955	£1,955
			¥363,630	¥363,630	¥363,630
REICHEL	1	0			
REICHEL, E.O.	1	1	$460	$460	$460
			DM777	DM777	DM777
			£276	£276	£276
			¥56,120	¥56,120	¥56,120
REICHEL, J.G. (attributed to)	1	0			
REICHEL, JOHANN GEORG	1	1	$530	$530	$530
			DM880	DM880	DM880
			£352	£352	£352
			¥55,183	¥55,183	¥55,183
REICHEL, JOHANN GOTTFRIED	1	1	$278	$278	$278
			DM468	DM468	DM468
			£173	£173	£173
			¥34,131	¥34,131	¥34,131
REICHERT, EDUARD	4	3	$316	$575	$441
			DM534	DM1,024	DM762
			£190	£345	£265
			¥38,583	¥76,464	¥55,886

| Maker | Items | | Selling Prices | | |
	Bid	Sold	Low	High	Avg
REICHERT, EDUARD (workshop of)	2	2	$489 DM870 £293 ¥64,994	$748 DM1,081 £488 ¥75,684	$618 DM975 £391 ¥70,339
REINHARD	1	1	$820 DM1,386 £550 ¥86,900	$820 DM1,386 £550 ¥86,900	$820 DM1,386 £550 ¥86,900
REITER, JOHANN	2	1	$1,610 DM2,783 £995 ¥204,043	$1,610 DM2,783 £995 ¥204,043	$1,610 DM2,783 £995 ¥204,043
REMENYI, MIHALY	2	1	$6,308 DM10,673 £3,968 ¥781,598	$6,308 DM10,673 £3,968 ¥781,598	$6,308 DM10,673 £3,968 ¥781,598
REMY, JEAN MATHURIN	3	1	$1,452 DM2,044 £920 ¥148,425	$1,452 DM2,044 £920 ¥148,425	$1,452 DM2,044 £920 ¥148,425
RESUCHE, CHARLES	1	1	$3,524 DM5,202 £2,300 ¥374,672	$3,524 DM5,202 £2,300 ¥374,672	$3,524 DM5,202 £2,300 ¥374,672
RESUCHE, CHARLES (attributed to)	2	1	$3,834 DM7,102 £2,300 ¥512,049	$3,834 DM7,102 £2,300 ¥512,049	$3,834 DM7,102 £2,300 ¥512,049
REUTER, GUNTHER	1	1	$4,313 DM6,594 £2,837 ¥454,538	$4,313 DM6,594 £2,837 ¥454,538	$4,313 DM6,594 £2,837 ¥454,538
REYNER, JEAN	3	1	$449 DM706 £288 ¥45,031	$449 DM706 £288 ¥45,031	$449 DM706 £288 ¥45,031
RICARD, ALEXANDER	1	1	$920 DM1,385 £558 ¥102,838	$920 DM1,385 £558 ¥102,838	$920 DM1,385 £558 ¥102,838
RICE, JAMES	2	1	$1,349 DM1,908 £863 ¥136,973	$1,349 DM1,908 £863 ¥136,973	$1,349 DM1,908 £863 ¥136,973
RICHARDSON, ARTHUR	14	11	$2,213 DM3,081 £1,380 ¥187,056	$7,767 DM12,834 £5,060 ¥933,754	$5,456 DM8,580 £3,470 ¥590,158
RICHARDSON, ARTHUR (attributed to)	1	1	$2,654 DM4,256 £1,725 ¥268,453	$2,654 DM4,256 £1,725 ¥268,453	$2,654 DM4,256 £1,725 ¥268,453
RICHARDSON, E.	1	1	$1,268 DM1,791 £805 ¥127,700	$1,268 DM1,791 £805 ¥127,700	$1,268 DM1,791 £805 ¥127,700

Maker	Items		Selling Prices		
	Bid	Sold	Low	High	Avg
RICHARDSON, FRANK	1	1	$920	$920	$920
			DM1,407	DM1,407	DM1,407
			£605	£605	£605
			¥96,968	¥96,968	¥96,968
RICHTER, ECKART	1	1	$1,880	$1,880	$1,880
			DM2,819	DM2,819	DM2,819
			£1,150	£1,150	£1,150
			¥181,884	¥181,884	¥181,884
RIEGER & FIORINI (attributed to)	2	1	$999	$999	$999
			DM1,549	DM1,549	DM1,549
			£598	£598	£598
			¥113,805	¥113,805	¥113,805
RIEGER, GEORG	1	1	$2,028	$2,028	$2,028
			DM2,824	DM2,824	DM2,824
			£1,265	£1,265	£1,265
			¥171,468	¥171,468	¥171,468
RINALDI, GIOFREDO BENEDETTO	3	2	$8,483	$22,908	$15,695
			DM11,811	DM33,815	DM22,813
			£5,290	£14,950	£10,120
			¥717,049	¥2,435,370	¥1,576,209
RINALDI, MARENGO ROMANUS (ascribed to)	1	1	$23,046	$23,046	$23,046
			DM38,502	DM38,502	DM38,502
			£13,800	£13,800	£13,800
			¥2,801,262	¥2,801,262	¥2,801,262
RITCHIE, A.	1	1	$1,932	$1,932	$1,932
			DM2,984	DM2,984	DM2,984
			£1,217	£1,217	£1,217
			¥192,729	¥192,729	¥192,729
RIVA, CARLO "SEVERINO"	1	0			
RIVIERE & HAWKES	2	1	$677	$677	$677
			DM1,146	DM1,146	DM1,146
			£414	£414	£414
			¥78,451	¥78,451	¥78,451
RIVOLTA, GIACOMO	5	0			
ROBINSON	1	1	$296	$296	$296
			DM454	DM454	DM454
			£196	£196	£196
			¥31,519	¥31,519	¥31,519
ROBINSON, A.G.	2	2	$407	$608	$508
			DM598	DM935	DM767
			£265	£403	£334
			¥43,156	¥64,893	¥54,024
ROBINSON, STANLEY	1	0			
ROBINSON, WILLIAM	28	18	$533	$4,276	$2,641
			DM766	DM7,835	DM4,153
			£345	£2,645	£1,659
			¥54,075	¥564,418	¥289,875
ROBINSON, WILLIAM (attributed to)	1	1	$1,042	$1,042	$1,042
			DM1,637	DM1,637	DM1,637
			£667	£667	£667
			¥104,472	¥104,472	¥104,472
ROBINSON, WILLIAM & STANLEY	1	1	$1,069	$1,069	$1,069
			DM1,587	DM1,587	DM1,587
			£690	£690	£690
			¥115,768	¥115,768	¥115,768

Maker	Items Bid	Sold	Selling Prices Low	High	Avg
ROCCA, ENRICO	7	3	$29,900	$79,152	$47,598
			DM54,298	DM121,519	DM78,064
			£18,299	£51,750	£30,250
			¥3,712,982	¥8,638,990	¥5,400,724
ROCCA, ENRICO (attributed to)	1	0			
ROCCA, GIUSEPPE	7	4	$68,323	$165,773	$118,264
			DM96,217	DM234,147	DM170,057
			£43,300	£104,900	£74,688
			¥6,985,676	¥14,794,781	¥10,998,630
ROCCA, JOSEPH (attributed to)	1	1	$28,750	$28,750	$28,750
			DM48,588	DM48,588	DM48,588
			£17,250	£17,250	£17,250
			¥3,825,763	¥3,825,763	¥3,825,763
ROCCA, JOSEPH (workshop of)	1	0			
ROCCHI, S.	1	0			
ROCCHI, SESTO	4	3	$8,642	$14,438	$11,140
			DM14,438	DM26,712	DM19,275
			£5,175	£8,625	£6,601
			¥1,050,473	¥1,924,151	¥1,397,300
ROGERI, GIOVANNI BATTISTA	1	1	$68,427	$68,427	$68,427
			DM96,650	DM96,650	DM96,650
			£43,300	£43,300	£43,300
			¥6,106,902	¥6,106,902	¥6,106,902
ROGERI, PIETRO GIACOMO	1	1	$132,158	$132,158	$132,158
			DM229,126	DM229,126	DM229,126
			£78,200	£78,200	£78,200
			¥16,500,200	¥16,500,200	¥16,500,200
ROMBOUTS, PIETER	2	0			
ROMBOUTS, PIETER (attributed to)	1	1	$9,058	$9,058	$9,058
			DM12,793	DM12,793	DM12,793
			£5,750	£5,750	£5,750
			¥912,140	¥912,140	¥912,140
ROMER, ADOLF	2	0			
ROOT-DUERER	1	1	$316	$316	$316
			DM563	DM563	DM563
			£193	£193	£193
			¥43,933	¥43,933	¥43,933
ROPE, A.J.	2	1	$1,317	$1,317	$1,317
			DM1,869	DM1,869	DM1,869
			£828	£828	£828
			¥122,254	¥122,254	¥122,254
ROPES, WALTER S.	1	1	$1,265	$1,265	$1,265
			DM1,934	DM1,934	DM1,934
			£832	£832	£832
			¥133,331	¥133,331	¥133,331
ROSADONI, GIOVANNI	1	1	$5,005	$5,005	$5,005
			DM9,260	DM9,260	DM9,260
			£2,990	£2,990	£2,990
			¥667,039	¥667,039	¥667,039
ROSCHER, CHRISTIAN HEINRICH WILHELM	1	1	$3,220	$3,220	$3,220
			DM5,732	DM5,732	DM5,732
			£1,932	£1,932	£1,932
			¥428,196	¥428,196	¥428,196
ROSSI, DOMENICO	3	0			

Maker	Items		Selling Prices		
	Bid	Sold	Low	High	Avg
ROSSI, GIUSEPPE	4	2	$6,168	$6,182	$6,175
			DM9,104	DM11,117	DM10,111
			£3,680	£4,025	£3,853
			¥655,677	¥714,766	¥685,221
ROTH	1	0			
ROTH (attributed to)	2	1	$3,671	$3,671	$3,671
			DM6,118	DM6,118	DM6,118
			£2,185	£2,185	£2,185
			¥438,726	¥438,726	¥438,726
ROTH, ERNST HEINRICH	29	23	$546	$3,693	$2,149
			DM822	DM6,402	DM3,438
			£332	£2,358	£1,328
			¥61,060	¥469,491	¥239,562
ROTH, ERNST HEINRICH (workshop of)	13	12	$460	$2,530	$1,198
			DM819	DM3,658	DM1,814
			£276	£1,653	£763
			¥57,252	¥256,163	¥122,404
ROTH, ERNST HEINRICH (II)	2	1	$2,213	$2,213	$2,213
			DM3,081	DM3,081	DM3,081
			£1,380	£1,380	£1,380
			¥187,056	¥187,056	¥187,056
ROTH & LEDERER	1	1	$518	$518	$518
			DM875	DM875	DM875
			£311	£311	£311
			¥63,135	¥63,135	¥63,135
ROTH-PELITTI-BOTTALI	1	1	$6,854	$6,854	$6,854
			DM11,592	DM11,592	DM11,592
			£4,600	£4,600	£4,600
			¥726,800	¥726,800	¥726,800
ROUMEN, JOHANNES ARNOLDUS	1	0			
ROVATTI, LUIGI	1	0			
ROVESCALLI, A.	3	1	$4,025	$4,025	$4,025
			DM6,359	DM6,359	DM6,359
			£2,576	£2,576	£2,576
			¥402,097	¥402,097	¥402,097
ROVESCALLI, MANLIO	1	0			
ROWINSKI, STANISLAV	2	0			
RUBUS, RIGART	2	2	$115	$206	$161
			DM205	DM367	DM286
			£70	£127	£98
			¥15,976	¥27,695	¥21,835
RUBUS, RIGAT	1	1	$288	$288	$288
			DM440	DM440	DM440
			£184	£184	£184
			¥32,117	¥32,117	¥32,117
RUDDIMAN, JOSEPH	1	0			
RUFFE, CARL	1	1	$4,287	$4,287	$4,287
			DM4,516	DM4,516	DM4,516
			£2,645	£2,645	£2,645
			¥327,438	¥327,438	¥327,438
RUGGERI, FRANCESCO	3	0			
RUGGIERI, FRANCESCO	5	2	$111,356	$151,302	$131,329
			DM188,394	DM252,774	DM220,584
			£70,035	£90,600	£80,318
			¥13,796,895	¥18,390,894	¥16,093,895

Maker	Items		Selling Prices		
	Bid	Sold	Low	High	Avg
RUNNACLES, HARRY E.	1	1	$441	$441	$441
			DM699	DM699	DM699
			£288	£288	£288
			¥44,558	¥44,558	¥44,558
RUSHWORTH & DREAPER	7	6	$294	$2,038	$1,143
			DM499	DM3,436	DM1,898
			£198	£1,265	£719
			¥31,242	¥250,297	¥130,266
RUTH, BENJAMIN WARREN	1	1	$2,415	$2,415	$2,415
			DM4,132	DM4,132	DM4,132
			£1,428	£1,428	£1,428
			¥299,895	¥299,895	¥299,895
RUZIEKA, JOSEPHUS	1	1	$3,285	$3,285	$3,285
			DM6,142	DM6,142	DM6,142
			£2,070	£2,070	£2,070
			¥388,767	¥388,767	¥388,767
SACCANI, BENIGNO	4	4	$2,698	$5,651	$3,651
			DM3,816	DM9,045	DM5,613
			£1,725	£3,680	£2,329
			¥273,946	¥570,216	¥364,938
SACCANI, BENIGNO (Workshop of)	1	1	$1,840	$1,840	$1,840
			DM3,180	DM3,180	DM3,180
			£1,137	£1,137	£1,137
			¥233,192	¥233,192	¥233,192
SACCONI, SIMONE FERNANDO	2	0			
SALOMON	1	1	$1,643	$1,643	$1,643
			DM2,458	DM2,458	DM2,458
			£978	£978	£978
			¥183,262	¥183,262	¥183,262
SALOMON, J.B.	3	2	$3,478	$7,728	$5,603
			DM5,796	DM12,880	DM9,338
			£2,070	£4,600	£3,335
			¥415,635	¥923,634	¥669,635
SALOMON, JEAN BAPTISTE DESHAYES	1	0			
SALSEDO, LUIGI	1	1	$3,384	$3,384	$3,384
			DM5,074	DM5,074	DM5,074
			£2,070	£2,070	£2,070
			¥327,391	¥327,391	¥327,391
SALVADORI, GIUSEPPE	1	0			
SALVADORI, GIUSEPPE (ascribed to)	1	0			
SALZARD, FRANCOIS	1	1	$863	$863	$863
			DM1,247	DM1,247	DM1,247
			£563	£563	£563
			¥87,328	¥87,328	¥87,328
SANDER, FRIEDRICH	1	1	$1,093	$1,093	$1,093
			DM1,693	DM1,693	DM1,693
			£699	£699	£699
			¥107,404	¥107,404	¥107,404
SANINO, V.	1	0			
SANNINO, VINCENZO	7	6	$7,621	$61,900	$27,929
			DM10,733	DM104,611	DM46,799
			£4,830	£37,140	£17,153
			¥779,234	¥8,237,033	¥3,475,705
SANNINO, VINCENZO (ascribed to)	1	1	$7,498	$7,498	$7,498
			DM12,972	DM12,972	DM12,972
			£4,600	£4,600	£4,600
			¥855,600	¥855,600	¥855,600

Maker	Items		Selling Prices		
	Bid	Sold	Low	High	Avg
SANNINO, VINCENZO (attributed to)	4	1	$5,123 DM7,731 £3,105 ¥580,635	$5,123 DM7,731 £3,105 ¥580,635	$5,123 DM7,731 £3,105 ¥580,635
SANTAGIULIANA, GAETANO	2	1	$47,736 DM76,420 £31,050 ¥4,832,125	$47,736 DM76,420 £31,050 ¥4,832,125	$47,736 DM76,420 £31,050 ¥4,832,125
SANTAGIULIANA, GIACINTO	2	1	$14,517 DM20,443 £9,200 ¥1,484,254	$14,517 DM20,443 £9,200 ¥1,484,254	$14,517 DM20,443 £9,200 ¥1,484,254
SARACINI, ANTONIO (attributed to)	1	0			
SAUNDERS, S.	2	1	$544 DM943 £322 ¥69,188	$544 DM943 £322 ¥69,188	$544 DM943 £322 ¥69,188
SAUNIER	1	1	$748 DM1,279 £442 ¥92,825	$748 DM1,279 £442 ¥92,825	$748 DM1,279 £442 ¥92,825
SCARAMPELLA, GIUSEPPE (attributed to)	1	1	$8,625 DM14,412 £5,755 ¥903,986	$8,625 DM14,412 £5,755 ¥903,986	$8,625 DM14,412 £5,755 ¥903,986
SCARAMPELLA, STEFANO	6	3	$30,153 DM53,429 £18,515 ¥3,676,550	$53,903 DM99,723 £32,200 ¥7,183,498	$42,116 DM71,860 £26,105 ¥5,118,705
SCARAMPELLA, STEFANO (ascribed to)	2	2	$9,200 DM15,401 £5,520 ¥973,155	$10,904 DM16,376 £6,900 ¥1,223,416	$10,052 DM15,889 £6,210 ¥1,098,286
SCARAMPELLA, STEFANO (attributed to)	4	2	$12,783 DM17,974 £8,050 ¥1,136,443	$14,404 DM25,789 £8,625 ¥1,981,853	$13,594 DM21,881 £8,338 ¥1,559,148
SCARTABELLI, MAURO	2	2	$1,034 DM1,751 £633 ¥119,856	$1,357 DM2,404 £833 ¥165,445	$1,195 DM2,077 £733 ¥142,650
SCHAUPP, PAUL E.	3	2	$345 DM528 £227 ¥36,363	$374 DM572 £246 ¥39,393	$359 DM550 £236 ¥37,878
SCHAUPP, PAUL & CHARLES	1	0			
SCHETELIG, ERNST	2	0			
SCHEVERLE, JOANNES	1	1	$920 DM1,574 £544 ¥114,246	$920 DM1,574 £544 ¥114,246	$920 DM1,574 £544 ¥114,246
SCHILBACH, OSWALD A.	1	1	$920 DM1,574 £544 ¥114,246	$920 DM1,574 £544 ¥114,246	$920 DM1,574 £544 ¥114,246

Maker	Items		Selling Prices		
	Bid	Sold	Low	High	Avg
SCHLEGEL, KLAUS	1	1	$1,687	$1,687	$1,687
			DM2,919	DM2,919	DM2,919
			£1,035	£1,035	£1,035
			¥192,510	¥192,510	¥192,510
SCHLEMMER, JOCHEN	1	1	$540	$540	$540
			DM827	DM827	DM827
			£345	£345	£345
			¥60,209	¥60,209	¥60,209
SCHLOSSER, HERMANN	3	3	$615	$1,262	$1,019
			DM1,027	DM2,189	DM1,628
			£368	£747	£621
			¥74,700	¥157,617	¥112,557
SCHMIDT, ERNST REINHOLD	2	2	$2,070	$2,070	$2,070
			DM3,685	DM3,685	DM3,685
			£1,242	£1,242	£1,242
			¥275,269	¥275,269	¥275,269
SCHMIDT, ERNST REINHOLD (workshop of)	3	2	$518	$1,093	$805
			DM747	DM1,671	DM1,209
			£330	£719	£524
			¥44,893	¥115,150	¥80,021
SCHMIDT, E.R. & CO.	13	7	$244	$682	$413
			DM389	DM1,072	DM637
			£150	£437	£264
			¥25,470	¥68,447	¥40,575
SCHMIDT, E.R. & CO. (workshop of)	1	1	$1,380	$1,380	$1,380
			DM2,306	DM2,306	DM2,306
			£921	£921	£921
			¥144,638	¥144,638	¥144,638
SCHMIDT, OSCAR	1	1	$690	$690	$690
			DM1,069	DM1,069	DM1,069
			£442	£442	£442
			¥67,834	¥67,834	¥67,834
SCHMIDT, REINHOLD	1	1	$1,150	$1,150	$1,150
			DM2,047	DM2,047	DM2,047
			£690	£690	£690
			¥152,927	¥152,927	¥152,927
SCHMIDT, REINHOLD (workshop of)	2	1	$546	$546	$546
			DM790	DM790	DM790
			£357	£357	£357
			¥55,308	¥55,308	¥55,308
SCHMITT, LUCIEN	1	0			
SCHOLL, H. (attributed to)	1	1	$366	$366	$366
			DM656	DM656	DM656
			£219	£219	£219
			¥42,498	¥42,498	¥42,498
SCHONFELDER, ADOLF (workshop of)	1	1	$431	$431	$431
			DM623	DM623	DM623
			£275	£275	£275
			¥37,411	¥37,411	¥37,411
SCHONFELDER, HERBERT EMIL	1	1	$978	$978	$978
			DM1,495	DM1,495	DM1,495
			£643	£643	£643
			¥103,029	¥103,029	¥103,029
SCHONFELDER, JOHANN GEORG	1	1	$2,582	$2,582	$2,582
			DM4,307	DM4,307	DM4,307
			£1,725	£1,725	£1,725
			¥265,148	¥265,148	¥265,148

Maker	Items		Selling Prices		
	Bid	Sold	Low	High	Avg
SCHONFELDER, JOHANN GEORG (II)	1	1	$3,172	$3,172	$3,172
			DM4,682	DM4,682	DM4,682
			£2,070	£2,070	£2,070
			¥337,205	¥337,205	¥337,205
SCHROETTER, A.	3	2	$92	$316	$204
			DM164	DM476	DM320
			£56	£192	£124
			¥12,781	¥35,350	¥24,066
SCHUBERTH, FRANZ (workshop of)	1	1	$575	$575	$575
			DM961	DM961	DM961
			£384	£384	£384
			¥60,266	¥60,266	¥60,266
SCHULTZ, HENRY Y.	1	1	$2,185	$2,185	$2,185
			DM3,777	DM3,777	DM3,777
			£1,350	£1,350	£1,350
			¥276,916	¥276,916	¥276,916
SCHUSTER, EDOUARD	4	1	$1,926	$1,926	$1,926
			DM3,451	DM3,451	DM3,451
			£1,150	£1,150	£1,150
			¥223,675	¥223,675	¥223,675
SCHUSTER, HANS (workshop of)	1	1	$489	$489	$489
			DM706	DM706	DM706
			£311	£311	£311
			¥42,399	¥42,399	¥42,399
SCHUSTER, MAX K.	2	2	$1,380	$3,850	$2,615
			DM2,456	DM7,123	DM4,790
			£828	£2,300	£1,564
			¥183,512	¥513,107	¥348,310
SCHUSTER BROS. (workshop of)	1	1	$1,495	$1,495	$1,495
			DM2,286	DM2,286	DM2,286
			£984	£984	£984
			¥157,573	¥157,573	¥157,573
SCHUSTER & CO.	2	2	$360	$662	$511
			DM550	DM926	DM738
			£230	£414	£322
			¥40,147	¥55,978	¥48,062
SCHUSTER & CO. (workshop of)	1	1	$546	$546	$546
			DM822	DM822	DM822
			£332	£332	£332
			¥61,060	¥61,060	¥61,060
SCHWAICHER, LEOPOLD	2	1	$2,899	$2,899	$2,899
			DM4,094	DM4,094	DM4,094
			£1,840	£1,840	£1,840
			¥291,885	¥291,885	¥291,885
SCHWARTZ, ANTON	2	1	$1,265	$1,265	$1,265
			DM1,934	DM1,934	DM1,934
			£832	£832	£832
			¥133,331	¥133,331	¥133,331
SCHWARZ, HEINRICH	1	1	$783	$783	$783
			DM1,371	DM1,371	DM1,371
			£483	£483	£483
			¥94,644	¥94,644	¥94,644
SCHWEITZER, JOHANN BAPTISTE	1	1	$15,968	$15,968	$15,968
			DM22,488	DM22,488	DM22,488
			£10,120	£10,120	£10,120
			¥1,632,680	¥1,632,680	¥1,632,680

Maker	Items Bid	Sold	Selling Prices Low	High	Avg
SCIALE, GIUSEPPE	1	1	$23,046 DM38,502 £13,800 ¥2,801,262	$23,046 DM38,502 £13,800 ¥2,801,262	$23,046 DM38,502 £13,800 ¥2,801,262
SCOGGINS, MICHAEL GENE	1	1	$2,415 DM4,081 £1,449 ¥294,630	$2,415 DM4,081 £1,449 ¥294,630	$2,415 DM4,081 £1,449 ¥294,630
SCOLARI, GIORGIO	2	2	$7,305 DM10,271 £4,485 ¥649,396	$7,311 DM12,648 £4,600 ¥834,210	$7,308 DM11,459 £4,543 ¥741,803
SCOTT, JOSEPH	1	1	$460 DM738 £299 ¥46,532	$460 DM738 £299 ¥46,532	$460 DM738 £299 ¥46,532
SDERCI, IGINO	5	2	$10,350 DM14,966 £6,761 ¥1,047,938	$13,444 DM22,460 £8,050 ¥1,634,070	$11,897 DM18,713 £7,405 ¥1,341,004
SDERCI, LUCIANO	4	3	$4,798 DM8,114 £3,220 ¥508,760	$11,551 DM21,369 £6,900 ¥1,539,321	$8,980 DM15,246 £5,673 ¥1,069,117
SEAVER, GEORGE	1	1	$546 DM790 £357 ¥55,308	$546 DM790 £357 ¥55,308	$546 DM790 £357 ¥55,308
SEELMANN, PAUL	1	0			
SEIFERT	1	0			
SEIFERT, GEORGE	1	1	$1,853 DM3,123 £1,150 ¥227,543	$1,853 DM3,123 £1,150 ¥227,543	$1,853 DM3,123 £1,150 ¥227,543
SEIFERT, OTTO	5	3	$4,943 DM7,187 £3,220 ¥454,139	$6,711 DM10,741 £4,370 ¥677,132	$5,581 DM8,504 £3,603 ¥557,421
SEITZ, ANTON	2	1	$2,115 DM3,121 £1,380 ¥224,803	$2,115 DM3,121 £1,380 ¥224,803	$2,115 DM3,121 £1,380 ¥224,803
SEITZ, NICOLAS	1	1	$1,282 DM2,333 £782 ¥161,983	$1,282 DM2,333 £782 ¥161,983	$1,282 DM2,333 £782 ¥161,983
SERAPHIN, SANCTUS	4	1	$53,748 DM75,372 £34,500 ¥5,430,404	$53,748 DM75,372 £34,500 ¥5,430,404	$53,748 DM75,372 £34,500 ¥5,430,404
SERDET, PAUL	3	1	$6,900 DM11,530 £4,604 ¥723,189	$6,900 DM11,530 £4,604 ¥723,189	$6,900 DM11,530 £4,604 ¥723,189
SERDET, PAUL (attributed to)	1	1	$3,878 DM6,155 £2,530 ¥392,110	$3,878 DM6,155 £2,530 ¥392,110	$3,878 DM6,155 £2,530 ¥392,110

Maker	Items		Selling Prices		
	Bid	Sold	Low	High	Avg
SGARABOTTO, GAETANO	11	7	$26,450	$49,789	$35,462
			DM43,250	DM69,325	DM56,476
			£15,870	£31,050	£21,899
			¥3,104,716	¥4,882,164	¥3,887,024
SGARABOTTO, GAETANO (attributed to)	4	3	$5,796	$12,834	$9,085
			DM9,660	DM20,700	DM14,979
			£3,450	£7,452	£5,359
			¥692,726	¥1,511,100	¥1,085,359
SGARABOTTO, PIETRO	4	3	$11,279	$18,463	$14,527
			DM16,912	DM32,010	DM22,729
			£6,900	£10,925	£8,817
			¥1,091,304	¥2,305,175	¥1,521,366
SGARBI, ANTONIO	3	3	$2,742	$15,462	$7,333
			DM4,637	DM23,135	DM11,534
			£1,840	£9,200	£4,447
			¥290,720	¥1,724,816	¥854,274
SGARBI, ANTONIO (attributed to)	4	2	$3,177	$4,146	$3,661
			DM5,539	DM7,346	DM6,443
			£1,955	£2,546	£2,250
			¥384,842	¥505,526	¥445,184
SHAPIRO, OSCAR	1	0			
SHARLET, STACY	2	1	$920	$920	$920
			DM1,407	DM1,407	DM1,407
			£605	£605	£605
			¥96,968	¥96,968	¥96,968
SHELMERDINE, ANTHONY (attributed to)	1	1	$732	$732	$732
			DM1,311	DM1,311	DM1,311
			£437	£437	£437
			¥84,997	¥84,997	¥84,997
SHIPMAN, MARGARET	1	1	$2,300	$2,300	$2,300
			DM3,887	DM3,887	DM3,887
			£1,380	£1,380	£1,380
			¥306,061	¥306,061	¥306,061
SIEGA, IGINIO	2	1	$10,654	$10,654	$10,654
			DM17,914	DM17,914	DM17,914
			£6,670	£6,670	£6,670
			¥1,307,740	¥1,307,740	¥1,307,740
SIGNORINI, SERAFINO (attributed to)	1	0			
SILSEE, REV. F.J.	1	1	$166	$166	$166
			DM275	DM275	DM275
			£110	£110	£110
			¥17,245	¥17,245	¥17,245
SILVESTRE, HIPPOLYTE	3	3	$9,087	$15,364	$13,020
			DM12,835	DM25,668	DM19,681
			£5,750	£9,200	£8,050
			¥810,963	¥1,867,508	¥1,325,754
SILVESTRE, HIPPOLYTE CHRETIEN	12	5	$6,361	$16,304	$13,496
			DM9,398	DM28,299	DM21,003
			£4,140	£10,350	£8,349
			¥677,859	¥1,834,135	¥1,432,231
SILVESTRE, HIPPOLYTE CHRETIEN (attributed to)	1	1	$6,613	$6,613	$6,613
			DM11,770	DM11,770	DM11,770
			£3,968	£3,968	£3,968
			¥879,330	¥879,330	¥879,330

Maker	Items Bid	Sold	Selling Prices Low	High	Avg
SILVESTRE, PIERRE	9	4	$6,427 DM9,864 £4,025 ¥630,098	$26,503 DM39,158 £17,250 ¥2,824,412	$19,515 DM29,043 £12,449 ¥1,905,693
SILVESTRE, PIERRE & HIPPOLYTE	8	4	$14,751 DM24,948 £9,900 ¥1,564,200	$28,513 DM45,732 £18,515 ¥3,244,198	$22,346 DM35,780 £14,148 ¥2,333,320
SILVESTRE & MAUCOTEL	2	1	$6,613 DM11,119 £4,140 ¥811,701	$6,613 DM11,119 £4,140 ¥811,701	$6,613 DM11,119 £4,140 ¥811,701
SIMEONI, GIANNANDREA (attributed to)	1	1	$4,240 DM6,265 £2,760 ¥451,906	$4,240 DM6,265 £2,760 ¥451,906	$4,240 DM6,265 £2,760 ¥451,906
SIMONAZZI, AMADEO	4	3	$5,175 DM8,176 £3,312 ¥516,982	$18,400 DM26,606 £12,019 ¥1,863,000	$9,910 DM15,021 £6,339 ¥1,042,667
SIMONIN, CHARLES	2	1	$7,305 DM10,271 £4,600 ¥649,396	$7,305 DM10,271 £4,600 ¥649,396	$7,305 DM10,271 £4,600 ¥649,396
SIMONIN, CHARLES (attributed to)	5	1	$1,232 DM1,740 £782 ¥124,051	$1,232 DM1,740 £782 ¥124,051	$1,232 DM1,740 £782 ¥124,051
SIMOUTRE, NICHOLAS EUGENE	1	0			
SIMOUTRE, NICOLAS	2	2	$2,178 DM3,066 £1,380 ¥222,638	$3,693 DM6,402 £2,185 ¥461,035	$2,935 DM4,734 £1,783 ¥341,837
SIMPSON	1	1	$692 DM989 £437 ¥69,477	$692 DM989 £437 ¥69,477	$692 DM989 £437 ¥69,477
SIMPSON, JAMES & JOHN	2	2	$1,676 DM2,576 £1,093 ¥183,528	$2,588 DM4,373 £1,553 ¥344,319	$2,132 DM3,474 £1,323 ¥263,923
SIMPSON, THOMAS	1	1	$1,644 DM2,538 £1,035 ¥163,947	$1,644 DM2,538 £1,035 ¥163,947	$1,644 DM2,538 £1,035 ¥163,947
SIMS, BARRY	2	1	$692 DM1,072 £414 ¥78,788	$692 DM1,072 £414 ¥78,788	$692 DM1,072 £414 ¥78,788
SIRONI, AMBROGIO	2	2	$3,392 DM6,011 £2,083 ¥413,612	$12,061 DM21,372 £7,406 ¥1,470,620	$7,727 DM13,691 £4,744 ¥942,116
SIVORI	1	1	$1,014 DM1,412 £633 ¥85,734	$1,014 DM1,412 £633 ¥85,734	$1,014 DM1,412 £633 ¥85,734

Maker	Items		Selling Prices		
	Bid	Sold	Low	High	Avg
SMALLEY, G.B.	1	1	$713	$713	$713
			DM1,272	DM1,272	DM1,272
			£437	£437	£437
			¥93,356	¥93,356	¥93,356
SMILLIE, ALEXANDER	4	3	$1,247	$4,993	$3,429
			DM2,084	DM8,342	DM5,546
			£747	£2,990	£2,127
			¥151,634	¥606,940	¥400,041
SMILLIE, ANDREW Y.	2	2	$1,461	$2,889	$2,175
			DM2,054	DM4,083	DM3,069
			£920	£1,840	£1,380
			¥130,392	¥246,709	¥188,550
SMITH, ARTHUR E.	2	2	$9,633	$12,721	$11,177
			DM14,477	DM18,796	DM16,636
			£5,750	£8,280	£7,015
			¥1,072,726	¥1,355,718	¥1,214,222
SMITH, BERT	2	1	$1,598	$1,598	$1,598
			DM2,640	DM2,640	DM2,640
			£978	£978	£978
			¥197,874	¥197,874	¥197,874
SMITH, J.P.	2	1	$1,174	$1,174	$1,174
			DM1,659	DM1,659	DM1,659
			£748	£748	£748
			¥100,226	¥100,226	¥100,226
SMITH, JOHN	6	4	$1,134	$3,524	$1,961
			DM1,848	DM5,202	DM3,111
			£667	£2,300	£1,216
			¥133,453	¥374,672	¥223,288
SMITH, JOHN (attributed to)	1	1	$919	$919	$919
			DM1,357	DM1,357	DM1,357
			£598	£598	£598
			¥97,913	¥97,913	¥97,913
SMITH, THOMAS	2	2	$201	$2,119	$1,160
			DM340	DM3,796	DM2,068
			£121	£1,265	£693
			¥24,553	¥246,043	¥135,298
SMITH, WILLIAM (attributed to)	1	1	$2,889	$2,889	$2,889
			DM5,177	DM5,177	DM5,177
			£1,725	£1,725	£1,725
			¥335,513	¥335,513	¥335,513
SNEIDER, JOSEPH	1	0			
SNEIDER, JOSEPH (attributed to)	1	1	$16,100	$16,100	$16,100
			DM27,209	DM27,209	DM27,209
			£9,660	£9,660	£9,660
			¥2,142,427	¥2,142,427	¥2,142,427
SOCCOL, PIO (attributed to)	1	1	$1,010	$1,010	$1,010
			DM1,550	DM1,550	DM1,550
			£633	£633	£633
			¥99,015	¥99,015	¥99,015
SOFFRITTI, ALOYSIO LUIGI	1	0			
SOFFRITTI, ALOYSIO LUIGI (attributed to)	1	0			
SOFFRITTI, ETTORE	2	1	$18,849	$18,849	$18,849
			DM31,878	DM31,878	DM31,878
			£12,650	£12,650	£12,650
			¥1,998,700	¥1,998,700	¥1,998,700
SOFFRITTI, LUIGI	2	0			

| Maker | Items | | Selling Prices | | |
	Bid	Sold	Low	High	Avg
SOFFRITTI, LUIGI (ascribed to)	1	1	$5,796 DM10,419 £3,450 ¥670,094	$5,796 DM10,419 £3,450 ¥670,094	$5,796 DM10,419 £3,450 ¥670,094
SOLFERINO, REMO	1	0			
SOLIANI, ANGELO	3	1	$38,851 DM62,185 £25,300 ¥3,920,235	$38,851 DM62,185 £25,300 ¥3,920,235	$38,851 DM62,185 £25,300 ¥3,920,235
SOLIANI, ANGELO (attributed to)	2	0			
SOLLNER, FRANZ JOSEF	3	1	$932 DM982 £575 ¥71,182	$932 DM982 £575 ¥71,182	$932 DM982 £575 ¥71,182
SORIOT & DIDION	1	1	$4,637 DM8,338 £2,760 ¥536,075	$4,637 DM8,338 £2,760 ¥536,075	$4,637 DM8,338 £2,760 ¥536,075
SORIOT, D.	1	1	$820 DM1,386 £550 ¥86,900	$820 DM1,386 £550 ¥86,900	$820 DM1,386 £550 ¥86,900
SORSANO, SPIRITO	2	2	$35,650 DM55,257 £22,816 ¥3,504,751	$53,774 DM96,278 £32,200 ¥7,398,916	$44,712 DM75,768 £27,508 ¥5,451,834
SORSANO, SPIRITO (attributed to)	1	1	$3,092 DM4,627 £1,840 ¥344,963	$3,092 DM4,627 £1,840 ¥344,963	$3,092 DM4,627 £1,840 ¥344,963
SPATAFFI, GUERRIERO	1	0			
SPIDLEN, FRANTISEK F.	3	1	$10,573 DM15,607 £6,900 ¥1,124,017	$10,573 DM15,607 £6,900 ¥1,124,017	$10,573 DM15,607 £6,900 ¥1,124,017
SPIDLEN, OTAKAR FRANTISEK	4	2	$3,850 DM6,763 £2,300 ¥487,074	$4,582 DM7,123 £2,990 ¥513,107	$4,216 DM6,943 £2,645 ¥500,090
SPIDLEN, OTAKAR FRANTISEK (attributed to)	2	1	$8,333 DM11,769 £5,290 ¥839,169	$8,333 DM11,769 £5,290 ¥839,169	$8,333 DM11,769 £5,290 ¥839,169
SPIDLEN, PREMYSL OTAKAR	3	2	$5,479 DM7,703 £3,450 ¥488,968	$8,247 DM11,558 £5,175 ¥727,010	$6,863 DM9,631 £4,313 ¥607,989
SQUIER, JEROME BONAPARTE	4	4	$1,150 DM1,663 £751 ¥116,438	$3,795 DM5,803 £2,497 ¥399,993	$2,128 DM3,258 £1,394 ¥214,731
SQUIER, VICTOR CARROLL	2	1	$978 DM1,690 £604 ¥123,883	$978 DM1,690 £604 ¥123,883	$978 DM1,690 £604 ¥123,883

Maker	Items		Selling Prices		
	Bid	Sold	Low	High	Avg
SQUIRE, V.C.	1	1	$374	$374	$374
			DM665	DM665	DM665
			£224	£224	£224
			¥49,701	¥49,701	¥49,701
STADLMANN, JOHANN JOSEPH	3	3	$1,093	$11,279	$6,275
			DM1,580	DM16,912	DM9,159
			£714	£6,900	£3,880
			¥110,616	¥1,091,304	¥582,500
STADLMANN, JOHANN JOSEPH (attributed to)	1	0			
STAINER, JACOB	5	1	$57,615	$57,615	$57,615
			DM96,255	DM96,255	DM96,255
			£34,500	£34,500	£34,500
			¥7,003,155	¥7,003,155	¥7,003,155
STAINER, JACOB (attributed to)	2	2	$2,698	$7,194	$4,946
			DM3,816	DM10,177	DM6,996
			£1,725	£4,600	£3,163
			¥273,946	¥730,521	¥502,233
STANLEY, C.F.	2	2	$1,265	$1,840	$1,553
			DM1,829	DM3,275	DM2,552
			£826	£1,104	£965
			¥128,081	¥244,683	¥186,382
STANLEY, FREELAN OSCAR	2	2	$1,495	$1,610	$1,553
			DM2,317	DM2,328	DM2,323
			£957	£1,052	£1,004
			¥146,973	¥163,013	¥154,993
STEFANINI, GIUSEPPE	4	4	$4,255	$10,106	$7,433
			DM7,355	DM17,521	DM12,733
			£2,629	£5,980	£4,464
			¥539,257	¥1,261,780	¥925,289
STIRRAT, DAVID	4	2	$2,833	$8,710	$5,772
			DM4,235	DM12,266	DM8,250
			£1,725	£5,520	£3,623
			¥272,597	¥890,553	¥581,575
STONEMAN, HENRY (attributed to)	1	1	$989	$989	$989
			DM1,462	DM1,462	DM1,462
			£644	£644	£644
			¥105,445	¥105,445	¥105,445
STORCH	1	0			
STORIONI, CARLO	12	8	$668	$2,332	$1,608
			DM1,026	DM4,043	DM2,485
			£437	£1,380	£990
			¥72,951	¥291,180	¥178,296
STORIONI, LORENZO	4	2	$50,757	$229,460	$140,109
			DM76,104	DM388,080	DM232,092
			£31,050	£154,000	£92,525
			¥4,910,868	¥24,332,000	¥14,621,434
STOSS, IGNAZ GEORG	1	1	$1,348	$1,348	$1,348
			DM2,493	DM2,493	DM2,493
			£805	£805	£805
			¥179,587	¥179,587	¥179,587
STOTT, GEORGE T. (attributed to)	1	1	$684	$684	$684
			DM1,047	DM1,047	DM1,047
			£437	£437	£437
			¥76,265	¥76,265	¥76,265
STOUGHTENBERG, HARRY	1	1	$748	$748	$748
			DM1,249	DM1,249	DM1,249
			£499	£499	£499
			¥78,345	¥78,345	¥78,345

Maker	Items		Selling Prices		
	Bid	Sold	Low	High	Avg
STRAATEMEIER, BARTOLOME	1	1	$867	$867	$867
			DM1,225	DM1,225	DM1,225
			£552	£552	£552
			¥74,013	¥74,013	¥74,013
STRADIVARI, ANTONIO	10	7	$219,328	$1,582,325	$661,635
			DM308,872	DM2,937,250	DM1,078,097
			£139,000	£947,500	£404,957
			¥22,425,148	¥211,709,400	¥74,538,533
STRADIVARI, FRANCESCO	1	0			
STRADIVARI, OMOBONO	1	0			
STRAINER, J.	1	1	$348	$348	$348
			DM534	DM534	DM534
			£230	£230	£230
			¥37,082	¥37,082	¥37,082
STRAUB, JOSEPH	1	1	$5,377	$5,377	$5,377
			DM8,984	DM8,984	DM8,984
			£3,220	£3,220	£3,220
			¥653,628	¥653,628	¥653,628
STRELLINI	1	1	$3,354	$3,354	$3,354
			DM5,147	DM5,147	DM5,147
			£2,185	£2,185	£2,185
			¥367,102	¥367,102	¥367,102
STRIEBIG, JEAN	1	1	$4,592	$4,592	$4,592
			DM7,722	DM7,722	DM7,722
			£2,875	£2,875	£2,875
			¥563,681	¥563,681	¥563,681
STRINKOVSKY, LEV	2	0			
STRNAD, CASPAR	1	1	$11,523	$11,523	$11,523
			DM19,251	DM19,251	DM19,251
			£6,900	£6,900	£6,900
			¥1,400,631	¥1,400,631	¥1,400,631
STROH	1	1	$516	$516	$516
			DM861	DM861	DM861
			£345	£345	£345
			¥53,030	¥53,030	¥53,030
STUMPEL, H.C.	1	1	$403	$403	$403
			DM716	DM716	DM716
			£242	£242	£242
			¥53,524	¥53,524	¥53,524
SUCHY, FRANZ	1	1	$1,043	$1,043	$1,043
			DM1,876	DM1,876	DM1,876
			£621	£621	£621
			¥120,617	¥120,617	¥120,617
SUZUKI	1	1	$104	$104	$104
			DM189	DM189	DM189
			£63	£63	£63
			¥13,102	¥13,102	¥13,102
SWAIN, JOSEPH	1	1	$317	$317	$317
			DM504	DM504	DM504
			£207	£207	£207
			¥32,082	¥32,082	¥32,082
SWET, JOAL B.	1	1	$1,785	$1,785	$1,785
			DM2,676	DM2,676	DM2,676
			£1,092	£1,092	£1,092
			¥172,711	¥172,711	¥172,711

Maker	Items		Selling Prices		
	Bid	Sold	Low	High	Avg
SZEPESSY, BELA	12	7	$3,110	$9,724	$6,074
			DM5,391	DM15,567	DM9,422
			£1,840	£6,325	£3,844
			¥388,240	¥984,322	¥634,160
TARANTINO, GIUSEPPE	1	1	$6,417	$6,417	$6,417
			DM10,350	DM10,350	DM10,350
			£3,726	£3,726	£3,726
			¥755,550	¥755,550	¥755,550
TARASCONI, G.	2	1	$19,435	$19,435	$19,435
			DM33,695	DM33,695	DM33,695
			£11,500	£11,500	£11,500
			¥2,426,500	¥2,426,500	¥2,426,500
TARR, THOMAS	2	1	$1,176	$1,176	$1,176
			DM2,089	DM2,089	DM2,089
			£713	£713	£713
			¥163,199	¥163,199	¥163,199
TARR, WILLIAM	3	1	$2,415	$2,415	$2,415
			DM3,635	DM3,635	DM3,635
			£1,466	£1,466	£1,466
			¥269,949	¥269,949	¥269,949
TARTAGLIA, FRANCESCO	1	0			
TASSINI, MARCO	4	3	$2,181	$4,276	$3,440
			DM3,080	DM7,413	DM5,813
			£1,380	£2,530	£2,070
			¥194,631	¥533,830	¥391,730
TATEM	1	1	$817	$817	$817
			DM1,158	DM1,158	DM1,158
			£518	£518	£518
			¥84,353	¥84,353	¥84,353
TATUM, D.J.	2	2	$695	$1,403	$1,049
			DM986	DM1,991	DM1,489
			£437	£900	£669
			¥64,523	¥142,699	¥103,611
TAUSCHER, EDUARD	3	2	$500	$720	$610
			DM774	DM1,103	DM938
			£299	£460	£380
			¥56,903	¥80,279	¥68,591
TAYLOR, GULIELMUS (attributed to)	2	2	$267	$2,827	$1,547
			DM397	DM4,177	DM2,287
			£173	£1,840	£1,006
			¥28,942	¥301,271	¥165,106
TAYLOR, JOSEPH	1	1	$1,004	$1,004	$1,004
			DM1,412	DM1,412	DM1,412
			£633	£633	£633
			¥89,644	¥89,644	¥89,644
TAYLOR, N.S.	1	1	$1,380	$1,380	$1,380
			DM1,993	DM1,993	DM1,993
			£879	£879	£879
			¥119,715	¥119,715	¥119,715
TECCHLER, DAVID	6	3	$23,005	$30,309	$27,506
			DM42,614	DM50,963	DM48,080
			£13,800	£18,975	£16,675
			¥3,072,294	¥3,720,295	¥3,498,204
TECCHLER, DAVID (attributed to)	1	1	$76,626	$76,626	$76,626
			DM122,649	DM122,649	DM122,649
			£49,900	£49,900	£49,900
			¥7,732,005	¥7,732,005	¥7,732,005

Maker	Items		Selling Prices		
	Bid	Sold	Low	High	Avg
TELLER, ROMAN (workshop of)	1	1	$863	$863	$863
			DM1,319	DM1,319	DM1,319
			£567	£567	£567
			¥90,908	¥90,908	¥90,908
TERRY, JOHN	1	1	$2,645	$2,645	$2,645
			DM4,572	DM4,572	DM4,572
			£1,634	£1,634	£1,634
			¥335,214	¥335,214	¥335,214
TESTORE, CARLO ANTONIO	10	6	$30,728	$66,548	$46,460
			DM46,508	DM94,133	DM68,656
			£18,400	£42,550	£29,038
			¥3,001,086	¥6,757,323	¥4,928,542
TESTORE, CARLO ANTONIO (attributed to)	3	2	$14,950	$16,324	$15,637
			DM25,841	DM27,272	DM26,557
			£9,238	£9,775	£9,506
			¥1,894,688	¥1,984,227	¥1,939,458
TESTORE, CARLO GIUSEPPE	1	1	$48,300	$48,300	$48,300
			DM76,314	DM76,314	DM76,314
			£30,912	£30,912	£30,912
			¥4,825,170	¥4,825,170	¥4,825,170
TESTORE, CARLO GIUSEPPE (ascribed to)	1	0			
TESTORE, PAOLO ANTONIO	5	2	$6,784	$15,771	$11,278
			DM12,022	DM26,681	DM19,351
			£4,166	£9,919	£7,042
			¥827,224	¥1,953,994	¥1,390,609
TESTORE, PAOLO ANTONIO (attributed to)	1	0			
TESTORE FAMILY (MEMBER OF)	5	3	$11,523	$32,258	$22,656
			DM21,390	DM48,680	DM34,662
			£6,900	£19,550	£13,992
			¥1,541,736	¥3,655,850	¥2,547,089
THEODORE, JACOB	1	0			
THIBOUT, JACQUES PIERRE	5	3	$4,722	$23,421	$13,592
			DM7,058	DM37,566	DM22,175
			£2,875	£15,209	£8,520
			¥454,328	¥2,664,877	¥1,565,477
THIBOUVILLE-LAMY, J.	148	115	$90	$8,834	$862
			DM141	DM13,053	DM1,344
			£58	£5,750	£540
			¥9,006	¥941,471	¥93,537
THIBOUVILLE-LAMY, J. (workshop of)	12	11	$288	$2,185	$829
			DM492	DM3,155	DM1,313
			£170	£1,392	£517
			¥35,702	¥189,549	¥89,412
THIER (attributed to)	1	1	$1,445	$1,445	$1,445
			DM2,588	DM2,588	DM2,588
			£863	£863	£863
			¥167,756	¥167,756	¥167,756
THIER, JOSEPH	3	3	$1,745	$2,467	$1,997
			DM2,934	DM3,723	DM3,245
			£1,092	£1,495	£1,227
			¥203,112	¥279,565	¥232,292
THIR, ANTON	2	0			
THIR, JOHANN GEORG	2	1	$1,555	$1,555	$1,555
			DM2,696	DM2,696	DM2,696
			£920	£920	£920
			¥194,120	¥194,120	¥194,120

Maker	Items		Selling Prices		
	Bid	Sold	Low	High	Avg
THIR, MATHIAS	7	5	$1,150	$6,768	$3,921
			DM1,663	DM10,147	DM6,360
			£751	£4,140	£2,404
			¥116,438	¥711,471	¥460,587
THOMASSIN	1	1	$8,349	$8,349	$8,349
			DM15,028	DM15,028	DM15,028
			£5,060	£5,060	£5,060
			¥1,204,027	¥1,204,027	¥1,204,027
THOMPSON, CHARLES & SAMUEL	34	20	$205	$3,450	$1,383
			DM236	DM5,275	DM2,130
			£127	£2,270	£874
			¥17,084	¥363,630	¥146,901
THOMPSON, E.A.	1	1	$288	$288	$288
			DM512	DM512	DM512
			£175	£175	£175
			¥39,940	¥39,940	¥39,940
THOMPSON & SON	1	1	$1,955	$1,955	$1,955
			DM3,379	DM3,379	DM3,379
			£1,208	£1,208	£1,208
			¥247,767	¥247,767	¥247,767
THOUVENEL	1	0			
THOUVENEL, HENRY	1	1	$863	$863	$863
			DM1,319	DM1,319	DM1,319
			£567	£567	£567
			¥90,908	¥90,908	¥90,908
THUMHARD, JOHANN STEPHAN	1	1	$1,391	$1,391	$1,391
			DM2,137	DM2,137	DM2,137
			£920	£920	£920
			¥148,327	¥148,327	¥148,327
THUMHARD, JOHANN STEPHAN (attributed to)	1	1	$4,777	$4,777	$4,777
			DM7,660	DM7,660	DM7,660
			£3,105	£3,105	£3,105
			¥483,216	¥483,216	¥483,216
TIEDEMANN, JAKOB	3	1	$1,682	$1,682	$1,682
			DM2,932	DM2,932	DM2,932
			£1,035	£1,035	£1,035
			¥203,740	¥203,740	¥203,740
TILLER, G.W.	1	1	$375	$375	$375
			DM669	DM669	DM669
			£230	£230	£230
			¥49,135	¥49,135	¥49,135
TILLER, WILFRED	2	2	$318	$656	$487
			DM511	DM1,167	DM839
			£207	£403	£305
			¥32,214	¥88,119	¥60,167
TINSLEY, CHARLES	1	1	$250	$250	$250
			DM450	DM450	DM450
			£149	£149	£149
			¥28,940	¥28,940	¥28,940
TIPPER, J.W.	1	1	$1,191	$1,191	$1,191
			DM1,968	DM1,968	DM1,968
			£713	£713	£713
			¥139,249	¥139,249	¥139,249
TIVOLI, ARRIGO	2	2	$6,179	$7,072	$6,626
			DM8,728	DM11,322	DM10,025
			£3,910	£4,600	£4,255
			¥551,455	¥715,870	¥633,663

Maker	Items		Selling Prices		
	Bid	Sold	Low	High	Avg
TOBIN, RICHARD (ascribed to)	1	0			
TONONI, CARLO	3	0			
TONONI, GIOVANNI	4	1	$43,550	$43,550	$43,550
			DM61,330	DM61,330	DM61,330
			£27,600	£27,600	£27,600
			¥4,452,763	¥4,452,763	¥4,452,763
TONONI, GIOVANNI (attributed to)	1	0			
TONONI FAMILY (MEMBER OF)	1	1	$94,190	$94,190	$94,190
			DM131,118	DM131,118	DM131,118
			£58,700	£58,700	£58,700
			¥7,946,571	¥7,946,571	¥7,946,571
TOOMEY, T.	2	2	$559	$1,796	$1,177
			DM589	DM2,822	DM1,706
			£345	£1,150	£748
			¥42,709	¥180,123	¥111,416
TOSELLO, BENITO	1	0			
TOSELLO, BENITO (ascribed to)	2	0			
TOTH, JOANNES	1	1	$2,990	$2,990	$2,990
			DM4,500	DM4,500	DM4,500
			£1,815	£1,815	£1,815
			¥334,222	¥334,222	¥334,222
TOTH, THERESIA	1	0			
TRAPANI, RAFFAELE (ascribed to)	1	1	$7,882	$7,882	$7,882
			DM13,331	DM13,331	DM13,331
			£5,290	£5,290	£5,290
			¥835,820	¥835,820	¥835,820
TRIFFAUX, PIERRE	1	1	$1,381	$1,381	$1,381
			DM2,082	DM2,082	DM2,082
			£847	£847	£847
			¥133,895	¥133,895	¥133,895
TROIANI, CARLO	2	1	$3,651	$3,651	$3,651
			DM5,610	DM5,610	DM5,610
			£2,415	£2,415	£2,415
			¥389,358	¥389,358	¥389,358
TUA, SILVIO	1	1	$4,888	$4,888	$4,888
			DM7,328	DM7,328	DM7,328
			£2,990	£2,990	£2,990
			¥472,898	¥472,898	¥472,898
TURCSAK, TIBOR GABOR	1	1	$1,730	$1,730	$1,730
			DM2,775	DM2,775	DM2,775
			£1,124	£1,124	£1,124
			¥196,868	¥196,868	¥196,868
TURNER, WILLIAM	1	1	$3,237	$3,237	$3,237
			DM4,579	DM4,579	DM4,579
			£2,070	£2,070	£2,070
			¥328,735	¥328,735	¥328,735
TURRINI, GAETANO	1	0			
TURRINI, GAETANO (ascribed to)	1	0			
TWEEDALE, CHARLES L.	6	3	$805	$949	$896
			DM1,212	DM1,685	DM1,508
			£489	£575	£546
			¥89,983	¥131,612	¥111,594
TYSON, HERBERT W.	2	1	$1,378	$1,378	$1,378
			DM2,036	DM2,036	DM2,036
			£897	£897	£897
			¥146,869	¥146,869	¥146,869
UDALRICUS, JOHANNES (attributed to)	1	0			

Maker	Items		Selling Prices		
	Bid	Sold	Low	High	Avg
ULCIGRAI, NICOLO	1	0			
ULLMANN, GIORGIO	1	1	$13,122	$13,122	$13,122
			DM22,701	DM22,701	DM22,701
			£8,050	£8,050	£8,050
			¥1,497,300	¥1,497,300	¥1,497,300
URBINO, RICHARD ALEXANDER	1	0			
URFF, WILLIAM	1	1	$431	$431	$431
			DM729	DM729	DM729
			£259	£259	£259
			¥52,613	¥52,613	¥52,613
UTILI, NICOLO	1	0			
VACCARI, ALBERTO	3	1	$3,046	$3,046	$3,046
			DM4,271	DM4,271	DM4,271
			£1,955	£1,955	£1,955
			¥307,723	¥307,723	¥307,723
VACCARI, GIUSEPPE	2	2	$2,126	$2,513	$2,320
			DM3,709	DM4,383	DM4,046
			£1,265	£1,495	£1,380
			¥271,165	¥320,468	¥295,817
VACCARI, RAFFAELLO	8	4	$9,226	$11,272	$10,619
			DM12,844	DM19,543	DM15,800
			£5,750	£6,900	£6,555
			¥778,412	¥1,407,370	¥1,023,258
VALENTIN, GEORG	1	0			
VAN DER GEEST, JACOB JAN	4	1	$3,091	$3,091	$3,091
			DM5,152	DM5,152	DM5,152
			£1,840	£1,840	£1,840
			¥369,454	¥369,454	¥369,454
VAN HOOF, ALPHONS	1	1	$6,930	$6,930	$6,930
			DM12,822	DM12,822	DM12,822
			£4,140	£4,140	£4,140
			¥923,593	¥923,593	¥923,593
VAUTELINT, N. PIERRE	1	0			
VAUTRIN, JOSEPH	3	2	$1,035	$2,397	$1,716
			DM1,789	DM3,338	DM2,563
			£640	£1,495	£1,067
			¥131,171	¥202,644	¥166,907
VAVRA, KAREL (I)	4	2	$2,185	$4,536	$3,361
			DM3,341	DM6,389	DM4,865
			£1,437	£2,875	£2,156
			¥230,299	¥463,830	¥347,064
VENTAPANE, LORENZO	4	3	$49,114	$50,467	$49,937
			DM73,399	DM90,298	DM83,026
			£29,900	£31,740	£30,513
			¥4,725,007	¥6,252,780	¥5,595,088
VENTAPANE, LORENZO (ascribed to)	1	0			
VENTAPANE, LORENZO (attributed to)	3	2	$8,118	$16,584	$12,351
			DM12,146	DM29,386	DM20,766
			£4,830	£10,183	£7,507
			¥905,528	¥2,022,103	¥1,463,815
VENTAPANE, PASQUALE	3	1	$4,033	$4,033	$4,033
			DM6,738	DM6,738	DM6,738
			£2,415	£2,415	£2,415
			¥490,221	¥490,221	¥490,221
VENTAPANE, PASQUALE (attributed to)	2	1	$3,536	$3,536	$3,536
			DM5,661	DM5,661	DM5,661
			£2,300	£2,300	£2,300
			¥357,935	¥357,935	¥357,935

Maker	Items		Selling Prices		
	Bid	Sold	Low	High	Avg
VENTAPANE, VINCENZO	1	0			
VENTAPANE, VINCENZO (attributed to)	1	1	$18,400	$18,400	$18,400
			DM28,135	DM28,135	DM28,135
			£12,105	£12,105	£12,105
			¥1,939,360	¥1,939,360	¥1,939,360
VENTURINI, LUCIANO	1	0			
VERINI, ANDREA	1	0			
VETTORI, CARLO	7	6	$3,457	$8,218	$5,628
			DM5,775	DM12,022	DM8,705
			£2,070	£5,175	£3,568
			¥420,189	¥827,224	¥600,569
VETTORI, DARIO	1	0			
VETTORI, PAULO	4	4	$3,565	$5,047	$4,237
			DM5,451	DM8,538	DM6,955
			£2,345	£3,174	£2,689
			¥375,751	¥625,278	¥499,685
VICKERS	2	0			
VICKERS, E.	2	1	$320	$320	$320
			DM541	DM541	DM541
			£196	£196	£196
			¥37,046	¥37,046	¥37,046
VICKERS, J.E.	2	0			
VIDOUDEZ, ALFRED	1	0			
VIERTEL, HOLM	1	1	$2,571	$2,571	$2,571
			DM3,945	DM3,945	DM3,945
			£1,610	£1,610	£1,610
			¥252,039	¥252,039	¥252,039
VILLA, LUIGI	4	3	$1,824	$3,073	$2,616
			DM3,047	DM5,134	DM4,096
			£1,092	£1,840	£1,591
			¥221,665	¥373,502	¥281,525
VILLAUME, G. (attributed to)	1	1	$2,899	$2,899	$2,899
			DM4,094	DM4,094	DM4,094
			£1,840	£1,840	£1,840
			¥291,885	¥291,885	¥291,885
VILLAUME, GUSTAVE EUGENE	4	2	$1,687	$3,110	$2,398
			DM2,919	DM5,391	DM4,155
			£1,035	£1,840	£1,438
			¥192,510	¥388,240	¥290,375
VINACCIA, GAETANO	1	0			
VINACCIA, GENNARO	2	1	$11,551	$11,551	$11,551
			DM21,369	DM21,369	DM21,369
			£6,900	£6,900	£6,900
			¥1,539,321	¥1,539,321	¥1,539,321
VINACCIA FAMILY (MEMBER OF)	1	1	$29,130	$29,130	$29,130
			DM49,266	DM49,266	DM49,266
			£19,550	£19,550	£19,550
			¥3,088,900	¥3,088,900	¥3,088,900
VINCENT, ALFRED	16	10	$1,096	$5,509	$3,500
			DM1,613	DM8,455	DM5,305
			£713	£3,450	£2,266
			¥116,333	¥579,562	¥356,362
VINCENT, ARTHUR	1	1	$6,936	$6,936	$6,936
			DM10,423	DM10,423	DM10,423
			£4,140	£4,140	£4,140
			¥772,363	¥772,363	¥772,363

Maker	Items		Selling Prices		
	Bid	Sold	Low	High	Avg
VISTOLI, LUIGI	3	1	$9,718	$9,718	$9,718
			DM16,848	DM16,848	DM16,848
			£5,750	£5,750	£5,750
			¥1,213,250	¥1,213,250	¥1,213,250
VITERBO, AUGUSTO DA RUB	3	0			
VIVENET	3	1	$1,315	$1,315	$1,315
			DM1,849	DM1,849	DM1,849
			£828	£828	£828
			¥117,352	¥117,352	¥117,352
VLUMMENS, DOMINIC	1	1	$5,883	$5,883	$5,883
			DM8,231	DM8,231	DM8,231
			£3,680	£3,680	£3,680
			¥497,584	¥497,584	¥497,584
VLUMMENS, DOMINIC (attributed to)	1	1	$3,461	$3,461	$3,461
			DM4,981	DM4,981	DM4,981
			£2,243	£2,243	£2,243
			¥351,489	¥351,489	¥351,489
VOGLER, JOHANN GEORG	1	1	$1,380	$1,380	$1,380
			DM1,995	DM1,995	DM1,995
			£901	£901	£901
			¥139,725	¥139,725	¥139,725
VOIGT, ARNOLD	3	3	$541	$1,610	$1,147
			DM944	DM2,423	DM1,721
			£322	£977	£701
			¥69,024	¥179,966	¥119,369
VOIGT, JOHANN GEORG	2	1	$768	$768	$768
			DM1,426	DM1,426	DM1,426
			£460	£460	£460
			¥102,782	¥102,782	¥102,782
VOIGT, PAUL	2	2	$900	$1,475	$1,187
			DM1,601	DM2,054	DM1,827
			£552	£920	£736
			¥120,849	¥124,704	¥122,777
VOIGT, WERNER	3	1	$1,926	$1,926	$1,926
			DM3,451	DM3,451	DM3,451
			£1,150	£1,150	£1,150
			¥223,675	¥223,675	¥223,675
VOLLER BROTHERS	3	1	$9,938	$9,938	$9,938
			DM15,014	DM15,014	DM15,014
			£6,670	£6,670	£6,670
			¥1,052,593	¥1,052,593	¥1,052,593
VUILLAUME (workshop of)	1	1	$5,216	$5,216	$5,216
			DM9,024	DM9,024	DM9,024
			£3,200	£3,200	£3,200
			¥595,200	¥595,200	¥595,200
VUILLAUME, GUSTAVE	1	0			
VUILLAUME, JEAN BAPTISTE	40	28	$3,749	$99,203	$44,455
			DM6,486	DM171,991	DM70,946
			£2,300	£58,700	£27,556
			¥427,800	¥12,385,700	¥4,928,934
VUILLAUME, JEAN BAPTISTE (attributed to)	3	2	$13,629	$21,419	$17,524
			DM23,643	DM36,225	DM29,934
			£8,050	£14,375	£11,213
			¥1,727,611	¥2,271,250	¥1,999,430
VUILLAUME, JEAN BAPTISTE (workshop of)	4	2	$8,910	$25,126	$17,018
			DM15,070	DM37,595	DM26,332
			£5,980	£14,950	£10,465
			¥944,840	¥2,802,826	¥1,873,833

Maker	Items Bid	Sold	Selling Prices Low	High	Avg
VUILLAUME, NICOLAS	11	3	$2,504 DM4,486 £1,495 ¥290,778	$4,200 DM5,906 £2,645 ¥374,876	$3,270 DM5,068 £2,042 ¥323,635
VUILLAUME, NICOLAS (attributed to)	1	1	$1,653 DM2,536 £1,035 ¥162,025	$1,653 DM2,536 £1,035 ¥162,025	$1,653 DM2,536 £1,035 ¥162,025
VUILLAUME, NICOLAS (workshop of)	2	2	$4,455 DM6,730 £2,990 ¥471,852	$5,025 DM7,519 £2,990 ¥560,565	$4,740 DM7,125 £2,990 ¥516,209
VUILLAUME, NICOLAS FRANCOIS	10	6	$3,727 DM5,953 £2,420 ¥376,610	$21,107 DM32,405 £13,800 ¥2,303,731	$12,676 DM19,689 £7,974 ¥1,383,744
VUILLAUME, SEBASTIAN	5	1	$8,551 DM14,826 £5,060 ¥1,067,660	$8,551 DM14,826 £5,060 ¥1,067,660	$8,551 DM14,826 £5,060 ¥1,067,660
WADE, H.F.	1	1	$690 DM1,228 £414 ¥91,756	$690 DM1,228 £414 ¥91,756	$690 DM1,228 £414 ¥91,756
WAGNER, JOSEPH	1	0			
WALKER, JOHN	2	2	$2,250 DM3,446 £1,438 ¥250,873	$3,303 DM5,076 £2,185 ¥352,277	$2,777 DM4,261 £1,811 ¥301,575
WALKER, WILLIAM	1	1	$2,652 DM4,246 £1,725 ¥268,451	$2,652 DM4,246 £1,725 ¥268,451	$2,652 DM4,246 £1,725 ¥268,451
WALMSLEY, PETER	4	1	$1,220 DM2,175 £748 ¥159,688	$1,220 DM2,175 £748 ¥159,688	$1,220 DM2,175 £748 ¥159,688
WALTERS, PHILIP	3	1	$552 DM772 £345 ¥46,648	$552 DM772 £345 ¥46,648	$552 DM772 £345 ¥46,648
WALTON, WILLIAM	2	2	$1,454 DM2,054 £920 ¥129,754	$1,766 DM2,827 £1,150 ¥178,193	$1,610 DM2,440 £1,035 ¥153,973
WAMSLEY, PETER	7	4	$895 DM1,541 £605 ¥92,672	$6,900 DM10,902 £4,416 ¥689,310	$2,938 DM4,612 £1,859 ¥301,101
WARD, GEORGE	1	1	$2,705 DM4,864 £1,610 ¥312,710	$2,705 DM4,864 £1,610 ¥312,710	$2,705 DM4,864 £1,610 ¥312,710
WARD, GEORGE (ascribed to)	1	1	$1,159 DM1,766 £747 ¥128,559	$1,159 DM1,766 £747 ¥128,559	$1,159 DM1,766 £747 ¥128,559

Maker	Items		Selling Prices		
	Bid	Sold	Low	High	Avg

Maker	Bid	Sold	Low	High	Avg
WARD, GEORGE (attributed to)	2	0			
WARRICK, A.	1	1	$2,758	$2,758	$2,758
			DM3,858	DM3,858	DM3,858
			£1,725	£1,725	£1,725
			¥233,242	¥233,242	¥233,242
WARWICK, A.	2	1	$1,191	$1,191	$1,191
			DM1,968	DM1,968	DM1,968
			£713	£713	£713
			¥139,249	¥139,249	¥139,249
WASSERMANN, JOSEPH	2	0			
WATSON, FRANK	2	2	$1,225	$2,305	$1,765
			DM2,079	DM3,850	DM2,965
			£825	£1,380	£1,103
			¥130,175	¥280,126	¥205,151
WATT, WALTER	3	2	$746	$1,440	$1,093
			DM1,067	DM2,405	DM1,736
			£472	£862	£667
			¥74,962	¥174,977	¥124,970
WEBB, R.J.	1	1	$6,569	$6,569	$6,569
			DM10,948	DM10,948	DM10,948
			£3,910	£3,910	£3,910
			¥785,089	¥785,089	¥785,089
WEBER, ROBERT E.	1	1	$920	$920	$920
			DM1,328	DM1,328	DM1,328
			£586	£586	£586
			¥79,810	¥79,810	¥79,810
WEBSTER, GEORGE	1	1	$1,212	$1,212	$1,212
			DM1,975	DM1,975	DM1,975
			£713	£713	£713
			¥142,657	¥142,657	¥142,657
WEICHOLD, RICHARD	1	0			
WEISS, EUGENIO	1	1	$2,412	$2,412	$2,412
			DM4,274	DM4,274	DM4,274
			£1,481	£1,481	£1,481
			¥294,124	¥294,124	¥294,124
WELLER, FREDERICK	7	2	$973	$1,632	$1,302
			DM1,560	DM3,029	DM2,295
			£633	£977	£805
			¥98,433	¥218,301	¥158,367
WELLER, FREDERICK (attributed to)	4	1	$307	$307	$307
			DM476	DM476	DM476
			£184	£184	£184
			¥35,017	¥35,017	¥35,017
WELLER, MICHAEL	1	1	$2,300	$2,300	$2,300
			DM3,935	DM3,935	DM3,935
			£1,360	£1,360	£1,360
			¥285,614	¥285,614	¥285,614
WENGER, GREGORI FERDINAND	1	1	$5,816	$5,816	$5,816
			DM8,214	DM8,214	DM8,214
			£3,680	£3,680	£3,680
			¥519,016	¥519,016	¥519,016
WERLE, J. PAUL (attributed to)	1	1	$1,153	$1,153	$1,153
			DM1,787	DM1,787	DM1,787
			£690	£690	£690
			¥131,314	¥131,314	¥131,314
WERRO, JEAN	1	0			

Maker	Items		Selling Prices		
	Bid	Sold	Low	High	Avg
WERRO, JEAN & HENRI	2	1	$2,485	$2,485	$2,485
			DM3,576	DM3,576	DM3,576
			£1,610	£1,610	£1,610
			¥252,351	¥252,351	¥252,351
WESTON, A.T.	1	1	$863	$863	$863
			DM1,566	DM1,566	DM1,566
			£528	£528	£528
			¥107,105	¥107,105	¥107,105
WHITE, ASA WARREN	4	4	$489	$1,955	$1,358
			DM747	DM3,345	DM2,256
			£322	£1,156	£826
			¥51,514	¥242,772	¥158,958
WHITE, IRA	1	1	$1,725	$1,725	$1,725
			DM2,951	DM2,951	DM2,951
			£1,020	£1,020	£1,020
			¥214,211	¥214,211	¥214,211
WHITE, NEHEMIAH	1	1	$805	$805	$805
			DM1,212	DM1,212	DM1,212
			£489	£489	£489
			¥89,983	¥89,983	¥89,983
WHITE, WILFRED	1	1	$1,715	$1,715	$1,715
			DM2,424	DM2,424	DM2,424
			£1,093	£1,093	£1,093
			¥146,483	¥146,483	¥146,483
WHITMARSH, E.	3	3	$1,800	$1,932	$1,865
			DM2,751	DM3,474	DM3,163
			£1,150	£1,150	£1,150
			¥200,733	¥225,343	¥216,480
WHITMARSH, EDWIN (attributed to)	1	1	$1,759	$1,759	$1,759
			DM2,700	DM2,700	DM2,700
			£1,150	£1,150	£1,150
			¥191,978	¥191,978	¥191,978
WHITMARSH, EMANUEL	19	13	$874	$6,016	$2,187
			DM1,515	DM9,020	DM3,376
			£517	£3,680	£1,360
			¥111,088	¥582,029	¥231,972
WHITMARSH, EMANUEL (attributed to)	2	2	$2,226	$2,912	$2,569
			DM3,289	DM4,164	DM3,727
			£1,449	£1,840	£1,645
			¥237,251	¥292,534	¥264,892
WHITMARSH, EMANUEL (SR.)	2	2	$1,201	$2,060	$1,631
			DM1,870	DM3,446	DM2,658
			£770	£1,380	£1,075
			¥118,934	¥218,963	¥168,949
WHITMARSH, EMANUEL (SR.) (attributed to)	1	1	$1,893	$1,893	$1,893
			DM3,159	DM3,159	DM3,159
			£1,265	£1,265	£1,265
			¥194,442	¥194,442	¥194,442
WICKENS, KENNETH	1	1	$241	$241	$241
			DM402	DM402	DM402
			£161	£161	£161
			¥24,747	¥24,747	¥24,747
WIDHALM, LEOPOLD	9	6	$5,750	$11,072	$8,171
			DM9,838	DM15,413	DM12,383
			£3,401	£6,900	£5,033
			¥714,035	¥934,094	¥850,814

Maker	Items Bid	Sold	Low	Selling Prices High	Avg
WIDHALM, LEOPOLD (attributed to)	2	1	$1,820 DM2,603 £1,150 ¥182,834	$1,820 DM2,603 £1,150 ¥182,834	$1,820 DM2,603 £1,150 ¥182,834
WIDHALM, MARTIN LEOPOLD	2	2	$9,220 DM12,838 £5,750 ¥779,401	$9,603 DM16,043 £5,750 ¥1,167,193	$9,411 DM14,440 £5,750 ¥973,297
WIEGANET, A.G.	2	1	$1,035 DM1,583 £681 ¥109,089	$1,035 DM1,583 £681 ¥109,089	$1,035 DM1,583 £681 ¥109,089
WILD, ANDREA (ascribed to)	1	0			
WILD, FRANK	1	1	$144 DM204 £92 ¥12,335	$144 DM204 £92 ¥12,335	$144 DM204 £92 ¥12,335
WILKANOWSKI, W.	9	9	$460 DM692 £279 ¥44,893	$1,093 DM1,580 £714 ¥110,616	$712 DM1,099 £449 ¥75,461
WILKINSON, JOHN	6	2	$3,570 DM5,514 £2,248 ¥356,130	$4,175 DM6,300 £2,530 ¥473,110	$3,872 DM5,907 £2,389 ¥414,620
WILKINSON, JOHN (attributed to)	3	1	$1,789 DM3,344 £1,127 ¥211,662	$1,789 DM3,344 £1,127 ¥211,662	$1,789 DM3,344 £1,127 ¥211,662
WILLARD, ELI A.	1	1	$489 DM826 £293 ¥59,628	$489 DM826 £293 ¥59,628	$489 DM826 £293 ¥59,628
WILLER, JOANNES MICHAEL	1	1	$2,645 DM4,420 £1,765 ¥277,222	$2,645 DM4,420 £1,765 ¥277,222	$2,645 DM4,420 £1,765 ¥277,222
WILLIAMS, F.C.	1	1	$920 DM1,555 £552 ¥122,424	$920 DM1,555 £552 ¥122,424	$920 DM1,555 £552 ¥122,424
WILMET, F.J.	1	1	$2,444 DM4,138 £1,495 ¥283,297	$2,444 DM4,138 £1,495 ¥283,297	$2,444 DM4,138 £1,495 ¥283,297
WILSON, H.	1	0			
WILSON, R.	2	1	$147 DM227 £93 ¥14,664	$147 DM227 £93 ¥14,664	$147 DM227 £93 ¥14,664
WINFIELD	1	1	$548 DM770 £345 ¥48,897	$548 DM770 £345 ¥48,897	$548 DM770 £345 ¥48,897
WINTER & SON (attributed to)	2	1	$927 DM1,375 £598 ¥100,332	$927 DM1,375 £598 ¥100,332	$927 DM1,375 £598 ¥100,332

Maker	Items		Selling Prices		
	Bid	Sold	Low	High	Avg
WINTERLING, GEORG	2	2	$6,765	$8,085	$7,425
			DM10,122	DM14,959	DM12,540
			£4,025	£4,830	£4,428
			¥754,607	¥1,077,525	¥916,066
WITHERS, EDWARD	2	2	$1,701	$2,722	$2,212
			DM2,386	DM3,833	DM3,109
			£1,092	£1,725	£1,409
			¥171,884	¥278,298	¥225,091
WITHERS, EDWARD (workshop of)	1	1	$2,178	$2,178	$2,178
			DM3,066	DM3,066	DM3,066
			£1,380	£1,380	£1,380
			¥222,638	¥222,638	¥222,638
WITHERS, GEORGE	4	2	$2,319	$5,294	$3,807
			DM3,470	DM8,133	DM5,802
			£1,380	£3,450	£2,415
			¥258,722	¥579,562	¥419,142
WITHERS, GEORGE (attributed to)	1	1	$1,739	$1,739	$1,739
			DM2,456	DM2,456	DM2,456
			£1,104	£1,104	£1,104
			¥175,131	¥175,131	¥175,131
WITHERS, GEORGE & SONS	3	2	$1,329	$3,467	$2,398
			DM2,166	DM6,212	DM4,189
			£782	£2,070	£1,426
			¥156,463	¥402,615	¥279,539
WITHERS, JOSEPH	2	1	$2,068	$2,068	$2,068
			DM3,416	DM3,416	DM3,416
			£1,265	£1,265	£1,265
			¥256,073	¥256,073	¥256,073
WITTMANN, ANTON	1	1	$4,934	$4,934	$4,934
			DM7,283	DM7,283	DM7,283
			£3,220	£3,220	£3,220
			¥524,541	¥524,541	¥524,541
WOLFF BROS.	24	19	$138	$1,460	$757
			DM230	DM2,730	DM1,169
			£92	£920	£475
			¥14,141	¥172,785	¥78,943
WOLFF BROS. (workshop of)	1	1	$345	$345	$345
			DM576	DM576	DM576
			£230	£230	£230
			¥36,159	¥36,159	¥36,159
WOOD, OTIS W.	1	1	$431	$431	$431
			DM768	DM768	DM768
			£259	£259	£259
			¥57,348	¥57,348	¥57,348
WOODWARD, CECIL F.	7	5	$235	$413	$301
			DM332	DM649	DM466
			£150	£265	£193
			¥20,045	¥41,428	¥29,530
WRONA, ANTHONY	2	1	$460	$460	$460
			DM713	DM713	DM713
			£294	£294	£294
			¥45,223	¥45,223	¥45,223
WULME-HUDSON, GEORGE	15	11	$3,866	$9,410	$6,577
			DM5,784	DM15,722	DM10,469
			£2,300	£5,635	£4,031
			¥431,204	¥1,143,849	¥758,328

| Maker | Items | | Selling Prices | | |
	Bid	Sold	Low	High	Avg
WULME-HUDSON, GEORGE (attributed to)	1	1	$3,467	$3,467	$3,467
			DM6,212	DM6,212	DM6,212
			£2,070	£2,070	£2,070
			¥402,615	¥402,615	¥402,615
WURLITZER CO., RUDOLPH	1	1	$403	$403	$403
			DM716	DM716	DM716
			£242	£242	£242
			¥53,524	¥53,524	¥53,524
YOUNG, JOHN	1	1	$695	$695	$695
			DM1,069	DM1,069	DM1,069
			£460	£460	£460
			¥74,164	¥74,164	¥74,164
ZACH & CO., CARL	1	1	$7,788	$7,788	$7,788
			DM13,510	DM13,510	DM13,510
			£4,600	£4,600	£4,600
			¥987,206	¥987,206	¥987,206
ZAHN, UTE	2	1	$935	$935	$935
			DM1,621	DM1,621	DM1,621
			£552	£552	£552
			¥118,465	¥118,465	¥118,465
ZANI, ALDO	2	2	$4,121	$7,211	$5,666
			DM6,892	DM10,881	DM8,887
			£2,760	£4,370	£3,565
			¥437,926	¥817,190	¥627,558
ZANIER, FERRUCCIO	2	1	$5,640	$5,640	$5,640
			DM8,456	DM8,456	DM8,456
			£3,450	£3,450	£3,450
			¥545,652	¥545,652	¥545,652
ZANISI, FILIPPO	1	0			
ZANOLI, FRANCESCO	1	1	$2,734	$2,734	$2,734
			DM4,625	DM4,625	DM4,625
			£1,719	£1,719	£1,719
			¥338,692	¥338,692	¥338,692
ZANOLI, GIACOMO (attributed to)	2	0			
ZARI BROTHERS	1	1	$3,738	$3,738	$3,738
			DM5,397	DM5,397	DM5,397
			£2,381	£2,381	£2,381
			¥324,228	¥324,228	¥324,228
ZETTWITZ, WILLIAM	1	1	$980	$980	$980
			DM1,664	DM1,664	DM1,664
			£660	£660	£660
			¥104,140	¥104,140	¥104,140
ZIMMERMANN, JULIUS HEINRICH	1	1	$358	$358	$358
			DM616	DM616	DM616
			£242	£242	£242
			¥37,069	¥37,069	¥37,069
ZIMMERMANN, JULIUS HEINRICH (attributed to)	1	1	$1,061	$1,061	$1,061
			DM1,561	DM1,561	DM1,561
			£690	£690	£690
			¥112,580	¥112,580	¥112,580
ZURLINI, NICOLO	2	0			
ZUST, J. EMILE	1	1	$3,286	$3,286	$3,286
			DM4,916	DM4,916	DM4,916
			£1,955	£1,955	£1,955
			¥366,523	¥366,523	¥366,523

Maker	Items		Selling Prices		
	Bid	Sold	Low	High	Avg
ZWERGER, ANTON	2	1	$2,624	$2,624	$2,624
			DM4,549	DM4,549	DM4,549
			£1,553	£1,553	£1,553
			¥327,578	¥327,578	¥327,578

VIOLIN BOW

Maker	Items		Selling Prices		
ADAM	1	0			
ADAM (attributed to)	2	1	$6,338	$6,338	$6,338
			DM11,765	DM11,765	DM11,765
			£3,795	£3,795	£3,795
			¥847,955	¥847,955	¥847,955
ADAM, JEAN (attributed to)	2	1	$1,380	$1,380	$1,380
			DM2,077	DM2,077	DM2,077
			£838	£838	£838
			¥154,256	¥154,256	¥154,256
ALLEN, SAMUEL	1	0			
ALLEN, SAMUEL (attributed to)	3	2	$5,654	$7,246	$6,450
			DM8,354	DM10,234	DM9,294
			£3,680	£4,600	£4,140
			¥602,541	¥729,712	¥666,126
ALVEY, BRIAN	1	0			
ASCHAR, J.N.	1	1	$474	$474	$474
			DM758	DM758	DM758
			£308	£308	£308
			¥47,932	¥47,932	¥47,932
ASHMEAD, RALPH	1	0			
AUBRY, JOSEPH	3	3	$525	$3,177	$1,554
			DM908	DM4,876	DM2,463
			£322	£2,070	£989
			¥59,892	¥347,781	¥174,797
AUDINOT, JACQUES	1	1	$1,155	$1,155	$1,155
			DM2,137	DM2,137	DM2,137
			£690	£690	£690
			¥153,932	¥153,932	¥153,932
AUDINOT, NESTOR	1	0			
BAILEY, G.E.	1	1	$971	$971	$971
			DM1,491	DM1,491	DM1,491
			£633	£633	£633
			¥106,253	¥106,253	¥106,253
BAILLY, CHARLES	1	1	$1,433	$1,433	$1,433
			DM2,010	DM2,010	DM2,010
			£920	£920	£920
			¥144,811	¥144,811	¥144,811
BALMFORTH, LEONARD PERCY	1	1	$2,028	$2,028	$2,028
			DM2,824	DM2,824	DM2,824
			£1,265	£1,265	£1,265
			¥171,468	¥171,468	¥171,468
BARBE, AUGUSTE	4	3	$3,427	$4,774	$4,151
			DM5,796	DM7,327	DM6,495
			£2,300	£2,990	£2,607
			¥363,400	¥474,324	¥435,266
BASTIEN, E.	2	1	$1,348	$1,348	$1,348
			DM2,493	DM2,493	DM2,493
			£805	£805	£805
			¥179,587	¥179,587	¥179,587

Maker	Items		Selling Prices		
	Bid	Sold	Low	High	Avg
BAUSCH	9	6	$122	$734	$277
			DM187	DM1,099	DM416
			£81	£437	£169
			¥12,382	¥81,929	¥29,012
BAUSCH (workshop of)	1	1	$575	$575	$575
			DM831	DM831	DM831
			£376	£376	£376
			¥58,219	¥58,219	¥58,219
BAUSCH, L. (workshop of)	1	1	$518	$518	$518
			DM791	DM791	DM791
			£340	£340	£340
			¥54,545	¥54,545	¥54,545
BAUSCH, LUDWIG	1	1	$690	$690	$690
			DM1,228	DM1,228	DM1,228
			£414	£414	£414
			¥91,756	¥91,756	¥91,756
BAUSCH, LUDWIG & SOHN	5	3	$673	$949	$766
			DM1,167	DM1,708	DM1,373
			£402	£575	£464
			¥77,004	¥136,821	¥101,169
BAUSCH, LUDWIG (II)	1	1	$1,234	$1,234	$1,234
			DM1,821	DM1,821	DM1,821
			£805	£805	£805
			¥131,135	¥131,135	¥131,135
BAUSCH, LUDWIG CHRISTIAN AUGUST	1	1	$863	$863	$863
			DM1,491	DM1,491	DM1,491
			£533	£533	£533
			¥109,309	¥109,309	¥109,309
BAUSCH, LUDWIG CHRISTIAN AUGUST (workshop of)	1	1	$374	$374	$374
			DM562	DM562	DM562
			£227	£227	£227
			¥41,778	¥41,778	¥41,778
BAUSCH, OTTO	1	1	$805	$805	$805
			DM1,433	DM1,433	DM1,433
			£491	£491	£491
			¥111,831	¥111,831	¥111,831
BAUSCH, OTTO (workshop of)	1	1	$805	$805	$805
			DM1,377	DM1,377	DM1,377
			£476	£476	£476
			¥99,965	¥99,965	¥99,965
BAZIN	19	9	$232	$2,899	$978
			DM405	DM4,338	DM1,620
			£138	£1,725	£591
			¥29,582	¥323,403	¥116,379
BAZIN (workshop of)	2	1	$2,113	$2,113	$2,113
			DM3,529	DM3,529	DM3,529
			£1,265	£1,265	£1,265
			¥256,782	¥256,782	¥256,782
BAZIN, C.	3	3	$2,332	$5,756	$3,802
			DM4,043	DM8,141	DM5,602
			£1,380	£3,680	£2,377
			¥280,584	¥584,417	¥385,394
BAZIN, CHARLES	22	18	$1,093	$5,412	$2,460
			DM1,694	DM8,097	DM3,705
			£656	£3,335	£1,552
			¥109,039	¥603,686	¥253,001

| Maker | Items | | Selling Prices | | |
	Bid	Sold	Low	High	Avg
BAZIN, CHARLES NICHOLAS	25	16	$1,089	$4,941	$2,135
			DM1,533	DM7,591	DM3,353
			£690	£3,220	£1,329
			¥111,319	¥540,925	¥241,684
BAZIN, LOUIS	20	17	$518	$4,416	$2,081
			DM894	DM7,471	DM3,322
			£320	£2,777	£1,292
			¥65,585	¥547,118	¥228,750
BAZIN, LOUIS (II)	3	1	$347	$347	$347
			DM641	DM641	DM641
			£207	£207	£207
			¥46,180	¥46,180	¥46,180
BAZIN FAMILY (MEMBER OF)	3	1	$1,612	$1,612	$1,612
			DM2,902	DM2,902	DM2,902
			£977	£977	£977
			¥232,477	¥232,477	¥232,477
BAZIN FAMILY (MEMBER OF) (attributed to)	1	0			
BEARE, JOHN & ARTHUR	7	5	$1,588	$5,442	$3,156
			DM2,440	DM9,435	DM5,064
			£1,035	£3,220	£1,897
			¥173,869	¥691,881	¥372,792
BERNARD, J.P.	1	1	$1,009	$1,009	$1,009
			DM1,708	DM1,708	DM1,708
			£635	£635	£635
			¥125,056	¥125,056	¥125,056
BERNARDEL, GUSTAVE	1	1	$3,427	$3,427	$3,427
			DM5,796	DM5,796	DM5,796
			£2,300	£2,300	£2,300
			¥363,400	¥363,400	¥363,400
BERNARDEL, GUSTAVE (workshop of)	1	1	$3,680	$3,680	$3,680
			DM5,538	DM5,538	DM5,538
			£2,234	£2,234	£2,234
			¥411,350	¥411,350	¥411,350
BERNARDEL, GUSTAVE ADOLPHE	1	1	$1,518	$1,518	$1,518
			DM2,291	DM2,291	DM2,291
			£920	£920	£920
			¥172,040	¥172,040	¥172,040
BERNARDEL, LEON	13	8	$412	$2,829	$1,256
			DM713	DM4,529	DM2,062
			£253	£1,840	£788
			¥47,058	¥286,348	¥136,384
BERNARDEL, LEON (workshop of)	2	2	$2,530	$4,025	$3,278
			DM3,808	DM6,058	DM4,933
			£1,536	£2,443	£1,990
			¥282,803	¥449,915	¥366,359
BERNARDEL, RENE	1	0			
BETTS	1	1	$2,497	$2,497	$2,497
			DM4,635	DM4,635	DM4,635
			£1,495	£1,495	£1,495
			¥334,043	¥334,043	¥334,043
BETTS, JOHN	2	2	$1,786	$2,721	$2,254
			DM3,022	DM4,717	DM3,870
			£1,124	£1,610	£1,367
			¥221,339	¥339,710	¥280,525

Maker	Items		Selling Prices		
	Bid	Sold	Low	High	Avg
BEYER, HERMANN	1	1	$633	$633	$633
			DM915	DM915	DM915
			£413	£413	£413
			¥64,041	¥64,041	¥64,041
BLONDELET, EMILE	1	1	$1,437	$1,437	$1,437
			DM2,258	DM2,258	DM2,258
			£920	£920	£920
			¥144,099	¥144,099	¥144,099
BLONDELET, H. EMILE	2	2	$1,942	$2,207	$2,074
			DM2,980	DM3,734	DM3,357
			£1,265	£1,388	£1,327
			¥212,533	¥273,446	¥242,989
BOLLINGER, JOSEPH	1	1	$920	$920	$920
			DM1,555	DM1,555	DM1,555
			£552	£552	£552
			¥122,424	¥122,424	¥122,424
BOUVIN, JEAN	2	1	$805	$805	$805
			DM1,162	DM1,162	DM1,162
			£513	£513	£513
			¥69,834	¥69,834	¥69,834
BRAMBACH, P. OTTO	1	0			
BRISTOW, S.E.	4	2	$883	$1,065	$974
			DM1,305	DM1,533	DM1,419
			£575	£690	£633
			¥94,147	¥108,151	¥101,149
BRISTOW, STEPHEN	3	3	$777	$1,845	$1,438
			DM1,348	DM3,200	DM2,361
			£460	£1,092	£862
			¥98,840	¥234,638	¥165,725
BRYANT	2	0			
BRYANT, PERCIVAL WILFRED	11	10	$714	$2,444	$1,438
			DM1,071	DM3,664	DM2,166
			£437	£1,495	£889
			¥69,116	¥236,449	¥145,181
BULTITUDE, ARTHUR RICHARD	26	22	$453	$5,390	$2,313
			DM824	DM9,972	DM3,699
			£276	£3,335	£1,444
			¥57,171	¥718,350	¥262,989
BUTHOD	3	2	$155	$169	$162
			DM270	DM286	DM278
			£92	£104	£98
			¥19,613	¥19,721	¥19,667
BUTHOD, CHARLES LOUIS	6	3	$1,125	$2,204	$1,638
			DM2,001	DM3,706	DM2,683
			£690	£1,380	£1,035
			¥151,062	¥270,567	¥196,744
BYROM, H.	1	1	$691	$691	$691
			DM1,238	DM1,238	DM1,238
			£414	£414	£414
			¥95,129	¥95,129	¥95,129
BYRON, J.	2	1	$468	$468	$468
			DM715	DM715	DM715
			£299	£299	£299
			¥52,190	¥52,190	¥52,190
CALLIER, FRANK	3	3	$345	$863	$613
			DM583	DM1,319	DM956
			£207	£567	£397
			¥42,090	¥90,908	¥66,554

| Maker | Items | | Selling Prices | | |
	Bid	Sold	Low	High	Avg
CALLIER, PAUL J.	1	1	$1,495	$1,495	$1,495
			DM2,286	DM2,286	DM2,286
			£984	£984	£984
			¥157,573	¥157,573	¥157,573
CAPELA, ANTONIO	1	0			
CARESSA, ALBERT	5	3	$1,255	$3,304	$2,226
			DM2,256	DM5,728	DM3,706
			£747	£1,955	£1,361
			¥145,090	¥412,505	¥261,183
CARESSA & FRANCAIS	3	2	$1,749	$3,354	$2,552
			DM3,033	DM5,147	DM4,090
			£1,035	£2,185	£1,610
			¥218,385	¥367,102	¥292,743
CARESSA & FRANCAIS (workshop of)	1	1	$2,300	$2,300	$2,300
			DM3,321	DM3,321	DM3,321
			£1,465	£1,465	£1,465
			¥199,525	¥199,525	¥199,525
CHALUPETZKY, F.	1	1	$1,057	$1,057	$1,057
			DM1,561	DM1,561	DM1,561
			£690	£690	£690
			¥112,402	¥112,402	¥112,402
CHANOT	1	1	$675	$675	$675
			DM1,167	DM1,167	DM1,167
			£414	£414	£414
			¥77,004	¥77,004	¥77,004
CHANOT (attributed to)	1	1	$12,523	$12,523	$12,523
			DM18,820	DM18,820	DM18,820
			£7,475	£7,475	£7,475
			¥1,394,543	¥1,394,543	¥1,394,543
CHANOT, G.A.	1	1	$2,298	$2,298	$2,298
			DM3,215	DM3,215	DM3,215
			£1,438	£1,438	£1,438
			¥194,369	¥194,369	¥194,369
CHANOT, GEORGE ADOLPH	1	1	$3,995	$3,995	$3,995
			DM6,759	DM6,759	DM6,759
			£2,513	£2,513	£2,513
			¥495,012	¥495,012	¥495,012
CHANOT & CHARDON	1	0			
CHARDON, ANDRE	1	1	$1,579	$1,579	$1,579
			DM2,920	DM2,920	DM2,920
			£943	£943	£943
			¥210,374	¥210,374	¥210,374
CHARDON, CHANOT	1	0			
CHARDON, JOSEPH MARIE	2	0			
CHIPOT, JEAN BAPTISTE	1	1	$1,198	$1,198	$1,198
			DM1,668	DM1,668	DM1,668
			£747	£747	£747
			¥101,254	¥101,254	¥101,254
CLARK, JULIAN B.	1	1	$972	$972	$972
			DM1,685	DM1,685	DM1,685
			£575	£575	£575
			¥121,325	¥121,325	¥121,325
CLASQUIN, G.	6	3	$1,508	$2,453	$2,048
			DM2,671	DM3,889	DM3,342
			£926	£1,552	£1,263
			¥183,828	¥290,561	¥231,093
CLAUDOT, ALBERT	1	0			

Maker	Items		Selling Prices		
	Bid	Sold	Low	High	Avg
CLUTTERBUCK, JOHN	2	2	$564	$1,058	$811
			DM846	DM1,957	DM1,401
			£345	£632	£489
			¥54,565	¥140,993	¥97,779
COCKER, L.	2	1	$174	$174	$174
			DM303	DM303	DM303
			£104	£104	£104
			¥22,186	¥22,186	¥22,186
COCKER, LAWRENCE	2	0			
COLAS, PROSPER	6	4	$693	$2,820	$1,529
			DM1,282	DM4,228	DM2,392
			£414	£1,725	£952
			¥92,359	¥272,826	¥162,171
COLAS, PROSPER (attributed to)	2	0			
COLLIN-MEZIN	3	1	$2,113	$2,113	$2,113
			DM3,529	DM3,529	DM3,529
			£1,265	£1,265	£1,265
			¥256,782	¥256,782	¥256,782
COLLIN-MEZIN, CH.J.B.	6	6	$960	$2,915	$2,042
			DM1,604	DM5,054	DM3,177
			£575	£1,725	£1,269
			¥116,719	¥370,651	¥223,333
COLLIN-MEZIN, CH.J.B. (FILS)	1	0			
COLLIN-MEZIN, CH.J.B. (II)	1	0			
CONE, GEORGES & FILS	1	0			
COROLLA	1	0			
CORSBY, GEORGE	1	1	$3,416	$3,416	$3,416
			DM5,154	DM5,154	DM5,154
			£2,070	£2,070	£2,070
			¥387,090	¥387,090	¥387,090
CUNIOT-HURY	8	6	$1,235	$2,113	$1,562
			DM1,883	DM3,922	DM2,643
			£805	£1,265	£956
			¥135,231	¥282,652	¥193,514
CUNIOT-HURY, EUGENE	26	21	$578	$1,885	$1,089
			DM998	DM3,188	DM1,711
			£357	£1,265	£676
			¥73,189	¥199,870	¥115,421
DARBEY, GEORGE	5	3	$879	$1,291	$1,045
			DM1,350	DM1,797	DM1,628
			£575	£805	£652
			¥95,989	¥111,682	¥105,596
DARCHE, HILAIRE	5	5	$214	$1,733	$1,173
			DM345	DM3,205	DM2,146
			£124	£1,035	£703
			¥25,185	¥232,477	¥159,382
DARCHE, NICHOLAS	1	1	$968	$968	$968
			DM1,430	DM1,430	DM1,430
			£632	£632	£632
			¥102,953	¥102,953	¥102,953
DELIVET, AUGUSTE	1	1	$2,467	$2,467	$2,467
			DM3,723	DM3,723	DM3,723
			£1,495	£1,495	£1,495
			¥279,565	¥279,565	¥279,565
DEROUX, AUGUST S. (workshop of)	1	1	$1,610	$1,610	$1,610
			DM2,690	DM2,690	DM2,690
			£1,074	£1,074	£1,074
			¥168,744	¥168,744	¥168,744

Maker	Items		Selling Prices		
	Bid	Sold	Low	High	Avg
DIDIER, PAUL	2	0			
DITER, PAUL FRANCOIS	1	0			
DITER BROTHERS	1	0			
DODD	18	11	$850	$5,289	$1,694
			DM1,270	DM7,904	DM2,628
			£518	£3,220	£1,045
			¥77,940	¥508,847	¥178,348
DODD (ascribed to)	1	1	$1,013	$1,013	$1,013
			DM1,411	DM1,411	DM1,411
			£632	£632	£632
			¥85,666	¥85,666	¥85,666
DODD (attributed to)	4	3	$700	$1,413	$1,117
			DM1,213	DM2,088	DM1,710
			£414	£920	£713
			¥87,354	¥150,635	¥123,265
DODD, J.	6	2	$556	$960	$758
			DM937	DM1,604	DM1,271
			£345	£575	£460
			¥68,263	¥116,719	¥92,491
DODD, JAMES	4	2	$1,150	$1,452	$1,301
			DM1,988	DM2,044	DM2,016
			£711	£920	£815
			¥145,745	¥148,425	¥147,085
DODD, JOHN	23	18	$1,265	$6,000	$2,792
			DM1,789	DM9,218	DM4,493
			£759	£3,910	£1,749
			¥119,715	¥688,637	¥317,723
DODD, JOHN (attributed to)	2	2	$989	$1,260	$1,125
			DM1,462	DM1,946	DM1,704
			£644	£794	£719
			¥105,445	¥125,693	¥115,569
DODD FAMILY	1	0			
DODD FAMILY (MEMBER OF)	2	1	$3,084	$3,084	$3,084
			DM4,660	DM4,660	DM4,660
			£2,070	£2,070	£2,070
			¥326,667	¥326,667	¥326,667
DOLLING, BERND	1	1	$740	$740	$740
			DM1,092	DM1,092	DM1,092
			£483	£483	£483
			¥78,681	¥78,681	¥78,681
DOLLING, HEINZ	8	6	$169	$1,845	$1,023
			DM300	DM2,569	DM1,575
			£104	£1,150	£639
			¥22,659	¥182,373	¥107,833
DOLMETSCH, ARNOLD	1	1	$441	$441	$441
			DM699	DM699	DM699
			£288	£288	£288
			¥44,558	¥44,558	¥44,558
DORFLER, EGIDIUS	1	1	$1,150	$1,150	$1,150
			DM1,944	DM1,944	DM1,944
			£690	£690	£690
			¥153,031	¥153,031	¥153,031
DOTSCHKAIL, R.	1	0			
DUBOIS, VICTOR	1	1	$39	$39	$39
			DM67	DM67	DM67
			£23	£23	£23
			¥4,930	¥4,930	¥4,930

Maker	Items		Selling Prices		
	Bid	*Sold*	*Low*	*High*	*Avg*
DUCHAINE	1	0			
DUCHENE, NICOLAS (II)	1	0			
DUGAD, ANDRE	4	3	$637	$1,996	$1,103
			DM1,083	DM2,811	DM1,666
			£391	£1,265	£699
			¥68,475	¥204,085	¥115,095
DUGAD, C.	1	1	$738	$738	$738
			DM1,027	DM1,027	DM1,027
			£460	£460	£460
			¥62,352	¥62,352	¥62,352
DUPUY	5	3	$1,049	$1,771	$1,526
			DM1,679	DM2,836	DM2,127
			£682	£1,093	£937
			¥106,136	¥217,578	¥152,986
DUPUY, GEORGE	2	1	$2,261	$2,261	$2,261
			DM4,007	DM4,007	DM4,007
			£1,389	£1,389	£1,389
			¥275,741	¥275,741	¥275,741
DUPUY, GEORGE (workshop of)	1	1	$1,725	$1,725	$1,725
			DM2,596	DM2,596	DM2,596
			£1,047	£1,047	£1,047
			¥192,821	¥192,821	¥192,821
DUPUY, PHILIPPE	2	0			
DURRSCHMIDT, OTTO	5	3	$201	$530	$410
			DM310	DM783	DM623
			£127	£345	£257
			¥20,038	¥56,903	¥44,476
DURRSCHMIDT, OTTO (workshop of)	1	1	$345	$345	$345
			DM576	DM576	DM576
			£230	£230	£230
			¥36,159	¥36,159	¥36,159
DURRSCHMIDT, WOLFGANG	2	0			
ENEL, CHARLES	4	4	$570	$1,567	$1,261
			DM920	DM2,625	DM2,056
			£331	£978	£773
			¥67,160	¥191,652	¥142,795
ENEL, PIERRE	1	1	$1,265	$1,265	$1,265
			DM1,829	DM1,829	DM1,829
			£826	£826	£826
			¥128,081	¥128,081	¥128,081
EURY (attributed to)	1	1	$9,183	$9,183	$9,183
			DM14,698	DM14,698	DM14,698
			£5,980	£5,980	£5,980
			¥926,601	¥926,601	¥926,601
EURY, FRANCOIS	2	1	$2,829	$2,829	$2,829
			DM4,529	DM4,529	DM4,529
			£1,840	£1,840	£1,840
			¥286,348	¥286,348	¥286,348
EURY, FRANCOIS (ascribed to)	1	1	$1,412	$1,412	$1,412
			DM2,167	DM2,167	DM2,167
			£920	£920	£920
			¥154,569	¥154,569	¥154,569
EURY, NICOLAS	7	4	$3,534	$10,541	$7,980
			DM5,221	DM15,503	DM12,375
			£2,300	£6,670	£4,945
			¥376,588	¥1,000,559	¥829,556

Maker	Items		Selling Prices		
	Bid	Sold	Low	High	Avg
EURY, NICOLAS (ascribed to)	1	1	$3,693	$3,693	$3,693
			DM6,402	DM6,402	DM6,402
			£2,185	£2,185	£2,185
			¥461,035	¥461,035	¥461,035
EURY, NICOLAS (attributed to)	1	1	$2,119	$2,119	$2,119
			DM3,392	DM3,392	DM3,392
			£1,380	£1,380	£1,380
			¥213,831	¥213,831	¥213,831
FAROTTO, CELESTINO	1	0			
FARY, WILLIAM	1	1	$440	$440	$440
			DM704	DM704	DM704
			£286	£286	£286
			¥44,508	¥44,508	¥44,508
FERRON & KROEPLIN	1	0			
FETIQUE, CHARLES	3	2	$863	$4,081	$2,472
			DM1,442	DM7,076	DM4,259
			£517	£2,415	£1,466
			¥104,946	¥509,565	¥307,255
FETIQUE, JULES	5	4	$3,688	$7,348	$5,787
			DM5,135	DM12,355	DM9,048
			£2,300	£4,600	£3,594
			¥311,760	¥901,890	¥620,706
FETIQUE, MARCEL	10	9	$3,154	$5,905	$4,151
			DM4,924	DM8,220	DM6,418
			£1,984	£3,680	£2,606
			¥339,388	¥527,464	¥446,622
FETIQUE, VICTOR	49	36	$910	$15,614	$4,707
			DM1,301	DM26,254	DM7,372
			£575	£9,775	£2,949
			¥91,417	¥1,916,516	¥505,890
FETIQUE, VICTOR (attributed to)	1	0			
FETIQUE, VICTOR (workshop of)	1	1	$978	$978	$978
			DM1,740	DM1,740	DM1,740
			£587	£587	£587
			¥129,988	¥129,988	¥129,988
FINKEL	3	1	$304	$304	$304
			DM539	DM539	DM539
			£184	£184	£184
			¥42,116	¥42,116	¥42,116
FINKEL, JOHANN S.	5	4	$883	$1,187	$1,062
			DM1,413	DM1,669	DM1,542
			£575	£748	£676
			¥89,096	¥109,578	¥101,624
FINKEL, JOHANN S. (workshop of)	2	2	$316	$345	$331
			DM541	DM590	DM566
			£187	£204	£196
			¥39,272	¥42,842	¥41,057
FINKEL, JOHANNES S.	3	1	$2,695	$2,695	$2,695
			DM4,986	DM4,986	DM4,986
			£1,610	£1,610	£1,610
			¥359,175	¥359,175	¥359,175
FINKEL, SIEGFRIED	3	2	$1,898	$1,955	$1,926
			DM2,864	DM3,030	DM2,947
			£1,150	£1,251	£1,201
			¥192,196	¥215,050	¥203,623

Maker	Items		Selling Prices		
	Bid	Sold	Low	High	Avg
FLEURY, H.	3	2	$169	$407	$288
			DM300	DM653	DM477
			£104	£265	£184
			¥22,659	¥46,346	¥34,502
FONCLAUSE, JOSEPH	3	1	$4,626	$4,626	$4,626
			DM7,825	DM7,825	DM7,825
			£3,105	£3,105	£3,105
			¥490,590	¥490,590	¥490,590
FORSTER, WILLIAM (II)	1	1	$2,846	$2,846	$2,846
			DM4,295	DM4,295	DM4,295
			£1,725	£1,725	£1,725
			¥322,575	¥322,575	¥322,575
FOURNIER, GEORGE	1	1	$1,844	$1,844	$1,844
			DM2,568	DM2,568	DM2,568
			£1,150	£1,150	£1,150
			¥155,880	¥155,880	¥155,880
FRANCAIS, EMILE	2	2	$600	$2,467	$1,533
			DM1,038	DM3,642	DM2,340
			£368	£1,610	£989
			¥68,448	¥262,271	¥165,359
FRANCAIS, LUCIEN	3	1	$1,921	$1,921	$1,921
			DM3,209	DM3,209	DM3,209
			£1,150	£1,150	£1,150
			¥233,439	¥233,439	¥233,439
GAND BROS.	2	2	$525	$1,944	$1,234
			DM908	DM3,370	DM2,139
			£322	£1,150	£736
			¥59,892	¥242,650	¥151,271
GAND & BERNARDEL	18	12	$1,312	$5,301	$2,510
			DM1,973	DM7,832	DM3,998
			£805	£3,450	£1,572
			¥127,319	¥564,882	¥266,627
GAULARD	2	2	$2,228	$5,053	$3,640
			DM3,365	DM8,761	DM6,063
			£1,495	£2,990	£2,243
			¥235,926	¥630,890	¥433,408
GAUTIE, P. & SON	1	1	$581	$581	$581
			DM818	DM818	DM818
			£368	£368	£368
			¥59,370	¥59,370	¥59,370
GERMAIN, EMILE	2	1	$1,500	$1,500	$1,500
			DM2,401	DM2,401	DM2,401
			£977	£977	£977
			¥151,386	¥151,386	¥151,386
GEROME, ROGER	4	3	$960	$1,380	$1,164
			DM1,783	DM2,139	DM1,999
			£575	£838	£701
			¥128,478	¥154,256	¥145,636
GILLET	2	0			
GILLET, LOUIS	1	1	$1,452	$1,452	$1,452
			DM2,044	DM2,044	DM2,044
			£920	£920	£920
			¥148,425	¥148,425	¥148,425
GOHDE, GREGORY	1	1	$540	$540	$540
			DM825	DM825	DM825
			£345	£345	£345
			¥60,220	¥60,220	¥60,220

Maker	Items		Selling Prices		
	Bid	Sold	Low	High	Avg
GOTZ, CONRAD	2	1	$428	$428	$428
			DM741	DM741	DM741
			£253	£253	£253
			¥53,383	¥53,383	¥53,383
GOTZ, CONRAD (workshop of)	3	3	$201	$1,093	$661
			DM291	DM1,644	DM1,029
			£128	£663	£417
			¥17,458	¥122,120	¥70,632
GOULD, JOHN ALFRED	1	1	$920	$920	$920
			DM1,328	DM1,328	DM1,328
			£586	£586	£586
			¥79,810	¥79,810	¥79,810
GRAND ADAM	2	0			
GREEN, HOWARD	3	3	$691	$963	$795
			DM1,155	DM1,781	DM1,385
			£414	£575	£475
			¥84,038	¥128,277	¥100,340
GRIMM	2	2	$789	$1,880	$1,335
			DM1,337	DM3,183	DM2,260
			£483	£1,150	£817
			¥91,527	¥217,920	¥154,723
GRINKE, R.	1	1	$812	$812	$812
			DM1,300	DM1,300	DM1,300
			£528	£528	£528
			¥82,169	¥82,169	¥82,169
GRUNKE, RICHARD	3	3	$920	$1,765	$1,393
			DM1,555	DM2,709	DM2,171
			£552	£1,150	£870
			¥112,240	¥193,212	¥157,521
HART & SON	6	5	$460	$3,008	$1,632
			DM713	DM4,510	DM2,601
			£294	£1,840	£1,025
			¥45,223	¥291,014	¥172,494
HART & SON (workshop of)	3	2	$1,610	$1,840	$1,725
			DM2,423	DM2,657	DM2,540
			£977	£1,172	£1,075
			¥159,620	¥179,966	¥169,793
HAWKES & SON	1	1	$266	$266	$266
			DM472	DM472	DM472
			£161	£161	£161
			¥36,851	¥36,851	¥36,851
HAWKES & SON (workshop of)	1	0			
HEBERLEIN (workshop of)	1	1	$575	$575	$575
			DM830	DM830	DM830
			£366	£366	£366
			¥49,881	¥49,881	¥49,881
HEBERLEIN, HEINRICH TH.	1	1	$1,049	$1,049	$1,049
			DM1,820	DM1,820	DM1,820
			£621	£621	£621
			¥131,031	¥131,031	¥131,031
HEL, PIERRE JOSEPH	1	0			
HENRI (attributed to)	1	1	$13,587	$13,587	$13,587
			DM19,189	DM19,189	DM19,189
			£8,625	£8,625	£8,625
			¥1,368,210	¥1,368,210	¥1,368,210

Maker	Items		Selling Prices		
	Bid	Sold	Low	High	Avg
HENRY	1	1	$20,226	$20,226	$20,226
			DM36,237	DM36,237	DM36,237
			£12,075	£12,075	£12,075
			¥2,348,588	¥2,348,588	¥2,348,588
HENRY, E.	1	0			
HENRY, EUGENE	1	0			
HENRY, J.V.	2	0			
HENRY, JACQUES	1	1	$4,798	$4,798	$4,798
			DM8,114	DM8,114	DM8,114
			£3,220	£3,220	£3,220
			¥508,760	¥508,760	¥508,760
HENRY, JOSEPH	5	4	$2,819	$18,400	$9,905
			DM4,162	DM26,570	DM14,951
			£1,840	£11,723	£6,335
			¥299,738	¥1,596,200	¥933,524
HENRY, JOSEPH (attributed to)	3	1	$6,714	$6,714	$6,714
			DM9,920	DM9,920	DM9,920
			£4,370	£4,370	£4,370
			¥715,518	¥715,518	¥715,518
HERMANN, ADOLF	1	1	$334	$334	$334
			DM562	DM562	DM562
			£207	£207	£207
			¥40,958	¥40,958	¥40,958
HERMANN, EMIL	1	1	$1,265	$1,265	$1,265
			DM2,252	DM2,252	DM2,252
			£772	£772	£772
			¥175,734	¥175,734	¥175,734
HERNOULT, HENRI (attributed to)	1	1	$1,921	$1,921	$1,921
			DM3,209	DM3,209	DM3,209
			£1,150	£1,150	£1,150
			¥233,439	¥233,439	¥233,439
HERRMANN, A.	7	4	$293	$1,199	$625
			DM473	DM2,029	DM1,015
			£173	£805	£405
			¥36,263	¥127,190	¥68,715
HERRMANN, AUGUST FRIEDRICH	1	1	$1,147	$1,147	$1,147
			DM1,760	DM1,760	DM1,760
			£747	£747	£747
			¥125,503	¥125,503	¥125,503
HERRMANN, E.	2	2	$389	$773	$581
			DM572	DM1,390	DM981
			£253	£460	£357
			¥41,279	¥89,346	¥65,313
HERRMANN, EDWARD	1	1	$403	$403	$403
			DM624	DM624	DM624
			£258	£258	£258
			¥39,570	¥39,570	¥39,570
HERRMANN, EMIL	2	1	$690	$690	$690
			DM1,055	DM1,055	DM1,055
			£454	£454	£454
			¥72,726	¥72,726	¥72,726
HERRMANN, EMIL (workshop of)	1	1	$1,380	$1,380	$1,380
			DM2,110	DM2,110	DM2,110
			£908	£908	£908
			¥145,452	¥145,452	¥145,452

Maker	Items Bid	Sold	Selling Prices Low	High	Avg
HILL	4	3	$684	$2,078	$1,442
			DM1,045	DM3,105	DM2,121
			£437	£1,265	£901
			¥76,278	¥199,904	¥145,024
HILL, WILLIAM EBSWORTH	1	1	$1,380	$1,380	$1,380
			DM2,332	DM2,332	DM2,332
			£828	£828	£828
			¥168,360	¥168,360	¥168,360
HILL, W.E. & SONS	336	299	$318	$7,996	$2,398
			DM511	DM14,246	DM3,801
			£196	£5,060	£1,500
			¥32,214	¥1,026,214	¥262,841
HOUFFLACK, G.	1	1	$1,829	$1,829	$1,829
			DM3,383	DM3,383	DM3,383
			£1,093	£1,093	£1,093
			¥243,726	¥243,726	¥243,726
HOYER (attributed to)	1	1	$1,148	$1,148	$1,148
			DM1,697	DM1,697	DM1,697
			£748	£748	£748
			¥122,391	¥122,391	¥122,391
HOYER, ADOLF	1	1	$849	$849	$849
			DM1,249	DM1,249	DM1,249
			£552	£552	£552
			¥90,064	¥90,064	¥90,064
HOYER, C.A.	5	3	$58	$1,051	$606
			DM101	DM1,779	DM1,004
			£35	£661	£385
			¥7,395	¥130,266	¥69,750
HOYER, HERMANN ALBERT	2	2	$385	$472	$429
			DM546	DM669	DM608
			£247	£299	£273
			¥39,163	¥48,737	¥43,950
HOYER, OTTO	5	4	$493	$1,265	$1,015
			DM876	DM2,252	DM1,709
			£299	£759	£623
			¥68,438	¥168,220	¥124,045
HOYER, OTTO (workshop of)	1	1	$920	$920	$920
			DM1,574	DM1,574	DM1,574
			£544	£544	£544
			¥114,246	¥114,246	¥114,246
HOYER, OTTO A.	25	16	$387	$3,635	$1,089
			DM674	DM5,134	DM1,737
			£230	£2,300	£674
			¥48,213	¥324,385	¥121,460
HUMS, ALBIN	3	2	$792	$794	$793
			DM1,169	DM1,218	DM1,194
			£517	£517	£517
			¥84,220	¥86,861	¥85,540
HURY, CUNIOT	2	2	$406	$1,360	$883
			DM565	DM2,359	DM1,462
			£253	£805	£529
			¥34,294	¥172,970	¥103,632
HUSSON, AUGUST	3	2	$856	$3,073	$1,964
			DM1,380	DM5,134	DM3,257
			£497	£1,840	£1,168
			¥100,740	¥373,502	¥237,121

Maker	Items		Selling Prices		
	Bid	Sold	Low	High	Avg
HUSSON, CHARLES CLAUDE	8	4	$713	$1,955	$1,359
			DM1,150	DM2,942	DM2,123
			£414	£1,187	£831
			¥83,950	¥218,530	¥154,831
HUSSON, CHARLES CLAUDE (attributed to)	2	1	$1,324	$1,324	$1,324
			DM1,957	DM1,957	DM1,957
			£862	£862	£862
			¥141,139	¥141,139	¥141,139
HUSSON, CHARLES CLAUDE (II)	2	0			
JOMBAR, PAUL	9	6	$1,164	$4,798	$2,101
			DM1,632	DM8,114	DM3,273
			£747	£3,220	£1,366
			¥117,580	¥508,760	¥210,264
KAUL, PAUL	1	0			
KEY, ALBERT E.	1	1	$374	$374	$374
			DM639	DM639	DM639
			£221	£221	£221
			¥46,412	¥46,412	¥46,412
KITTEL, NICOLAUS (attributed to)	1	1	$2,588	$2,588	$2,588
			DM4,699	DM4,699	DM4,699
			£1,584	£1,584	£1,584
			¥321,316	¥321,316	¥321,316
KNOPF	1	0			
KNOPF (workshop of)	1	1	$748	$748	$748
			DM1,331	DM1,331	DM1,331
			£449	£449	£449
			¥99,403	¥99,403	¥99,403
KNOPF, HEINRICH	6	5	$616	$2,812	$1,395
			DM1,140	DM4,865	DM2,452
			£368	£1,725	£856
			¥82,097	¥320,850	¥167,218
KNOPF, HENRY RICHARD	1	0			
KOUCKY, WILLIAM H.	1	1	$633	$633	$633
			DM1,093	DM1,093	DM1,093
			£391	£391	£391
			¥80,160	¥80,160	¥80,160
KOVANDA, FRANK	6	5	$480	$1,113	$805
			DM811	DM1,882	DM1,362
			£322	£747	£540
			¥50,876	¥118,026	¥85,383
KREUSLER, ERNST	1	1	$360	$360	$360
			DM550	DM550	DM550
			£230	£230	£230
			¥40,147	¥40,147	¥40,147
KUEHNL, EMIL	3	2	$115	$1,495	$805
			DM193	DM2,558	DM1,375
			£69	£884	£477
			¥14,006	¥185,649	¥99,828
KUHNLA, STEFFEN	1	1	$315	$315	$315
			DM532	DM532	DM532
			£198	£198	£198
			¥38,967	¥38,967	¥38,967
KUN, JOSEPH	1	1	$1,495	$1,495	$1,495
			DM2,558	DM2,558	DM2,558
			£884	£884	£884
			¥185,649	¥185,649	¥185,649
LABERTE	2	0			

Maker	Items		Selling Prices		
	Bid	Sold	Low	High	Avg
LABERTE, MARC	8	6	$187	$1,762	$981
			DM334	DM2,601	DM1,447
			£115	£1,150	£621
			¥25,177	¥187,336	¥97,599
LABERTE, MARC (workshop of)	3	1	$115	$115	$115
			DM173	DM173	DM173
			£70	£70	£70
			¥12,855	¥12,855	¥12,855
LAFLEUR	1	0			
LAFLEUR, JOSEPH RENE	6	5	$1,997	$3,841	$3,190
			DM3,378	DM6,417	DM4,885
			£1,256	£2,404	£2,020
			¥247,393	¥466,877	¥344,210
LAFLEUR, JOSEPH RENE (ascribed to)	1	1	$1,597	$1,597	$1,597
			DM2,395	DM2,395	DM2,395
			£977	£977	£977
			¥154,522	¥154,522	¥154,522
LAFLEUR, JOSEPH RENE (attributed to)	1	1	$631	$631	$631
			DM1,067	DM1,067	DM1,067
			£397	£397	£397
			¥78,160	¥78,160	¥78,160
LAMBERT, N.	2	2	$1,437	$1,518	$1,477
			DM2,258	DM2,732	DM2,495
			£920	£920	£920
			¥144,099	¥218,914	¥181,506
LAMY, A.	12	8	$3,319	$12,483	$8,219
			DM4,622	DM20,855	DM13,418
			£2,070	£7,475	£4,988
			¥280,584	¥1,517,350	¥948,562
LAMY, A. (attributed to)	3	1	$749	$749	$749
			DM1,111	DM1,111	DM1,111
			£483	£483	£483
			¥81,038	¥81,038	¥81,038
LAMY, ALFRED	29	23	$1,403	$13,697	$5,264
			DM1,991	DM19,761	DM8,096
			£900	£8,625	£3,264
			¥142,699	¥1,272,117	¥551,978
LAMY, ALFRED (attributed to)	1	1	$1,265	$1,265	$1,265
			DM2,297	DM2,297	DM2,297
			£774	£774	£774
			¥157,088	¥157,088	¥157,088
LAMY, ALFRED JOSEPH	32	27	$1,087	$17,992	$5,748
			DM1,691	DM30,429	DM9,235
			£667	£12,075	£3,571
			¥109,130	¥1,907,850	¥644,043
LAMY, HIPPOLYTE CAMILLE	1	0			
LAMY, JULES	2	0			
LAMY, LOUIS	3	2	$1,765	$3,872	$2,819
			DM2,709	DM5,392	DM4,050
			£1,150	£2,415	£1,783
			¥193,212	¥327,348	¥260,280
LAMY, LOUIS (attributed to)	1	1	$835	$835	$835
			DM1,260	DM1,260	DM1,260
			£506	£506	£506
			¥94,622	¥94,622	¥94,622
LANGONET, EUGENE	1	0			

| Maker | Items | | Selling Prices | | |
	Bid	Sold	Low	High	Avg
LANGONET, EUGENE (workshop of)	1	1	$1,955	$1,955	$1,955
			DM2,942	DM2,942	DM2,942
			£1,187	£1,187	£1,187
			¥218,530	¥218,530	¥218,530
LAPIERRE, MARCEL	7	7	$1,093	$3,172	$1,666
			DM1,693	DM4,682	DM2,590
			£699	£2,070	£1,041
			¥107,404	¥337,205	¥180,443
LATOUR, ARMAND	1	1	$905	$905	$905
			DM1,603	DM1,603	DM1,603
			£555	£555	£555
			¥110,297	¥110,297	¥110,297
LAURENT, EMILE	1	1	$1,889	$1,889	$1,889
			DM2,823	DM2,823	DM2,823
			£1,150	£1,150	£1,150
			¥181,731	¥181,731	¥181,731
LAURY, N.	2	1	$1,697	$1,697	$1,697
			DM3,088	DM3,088	DM3,088
			£1,035	£1,035	£1,035
			¥214,390	¥214,390	¥214,390
LAUXERROIS, JEAN-PAUL	2	2	$1,145	$2,185	$1,665
			DM1,690	DM3,651	DM2,670
			£747	£1,458	£1,103
			¥121,687	¥229,010	¥175,348
LAVEST, J.	1	1	$817	$817	$817
			DM1,154	DM1,154	DM1,154
			£517	£517	£517
			¥72,916	¥72,916	¥72,916
LAVEST, MICHEL	1	1	$551	$551	$551
			DM927	DM927	DM927
			£345	£345	£345
			¥67,642	¥67,642	¥67,642
LE JEUNE	1	1	$1,924	$1,924	$1,924
			DM2,697	DM2,697	DM2,697
			£1,208	£1,208	£1,208
			¥169,636	¥169,636	¥169,636
LECCHI, BERNARDO GIUSEPPE	1	0			
LECLERC FAMILY (MEMBER OF)	1	0			
LEE, JOHN NORWOOD	4	2	$1,380	$1,380	$1,380
			DM2,110	DM2,361	DM2,236
			£816	£908	£862
			¥145,452	¥171,368	¥158,410
LEICHT, MAX	2	2	$673	$715	$694
			DM1,210	DM1,245	DM1,227
			£402	£450	£426
			¥88,581	¥89,682	¥89,132
LENOBLE, AUGUSTE	2	0			
LENOBLE, AUGUSTE (attributed to)	3	3	$343	$1,028	$685
			DM518	DM1,553	DM1,035
			£230	£690	£460
			¥36,296	¥108,889	¥72,593
LIU, LLOYD	1	0			
LORANGE, PAUL	1	0			
LOTTE, FRANCOIS	15	11	$1,089	$2,305	$1,502
			DM1,533	DM3,850	DM2,494
			£690	£1,380	£915
			¥111,319	¥280,126	¥179,226

Maker	Items		Selling Prices		
	Bid	Sold	Low	High	Avg
LOTTE, ROGER	4	2	$2,523	$7,731	$5,127
			DM4,269	DM11,568	DM7,918
			£1,587	£4,600	£3,094
			¥312,639	¥862,408	¥587,524
LOTTE, ROGER-FRANCOIS	5	4	$1,752	$3,055	$2,222
			DM2,962	DM4,900	DM3,795
			£1,035	£1,984	£1,364
			¥212,436	¥347,593	¥272,624
LOUIS, A.N.	2	2	$5,658	$5,750	$5,704
			DM8,315	DM9,057	DM8,686
			£3,680	£3,756	£3,718
			¥572,696	¥582,188	¥577,442
LUCCHI, GIOVANNI	1	0			
LUPOT	4	3	$845	$7,398	$3,514
			DM1,506	DM10,906	DM5,433
			£518	£4,830	£2,243
			¥110,554	¥789,077	¥401,897
LUPOT, FRANCOIS (attributed to)	1	0			
LUPOT, FRANCOIS (II)	8	5	$2,648	$8,648	$5,329
			DM4,063	DM12,966	DM8,097
			£1,725	£5,290	£3,289
			¥289,817	¥836,666	¥536,285
LUPOT, FRANCOIS (II) (ascribed to)	1	1	$1,679	$1,679	$1,679
			DM2,688	DM2,688	DM2,688
			£1,092	£1,092	£1,092
			¥169,941	¥169,941	¥169,941
LUPOT, NICOLAS	1	0			
MAGNIERE, GABRIEL	1	0			
MAIRE, N. (workshop of)	2	2	$676	$5,762	$3,219
			DM1,216	DM9,626	DM5,421
			£403	£3,450	£1,926
			¥78,178	¥700,316	¥389,247
MAIRE, NICOLAS	9	4	$4,725	$25,300	$16,880
			DM6,674	DM43,288	DM28,971
			£2,990	£14,964	£10,095
			¥421,701	¥3,141,754	¥2,083,774
MAIRE, NICOLAS (attributed to)	3	1	$11,645	$11,645	$11,645
			DM16,331	DM16,331	DM16,331
			£7,475	£7,475	£7,475
			¥1,176,587	¥1,176,587	¥1,176,587
MAIRE, NICOLAS (workshop of)	1	1	$3,877	$3,877	$3,877
			DM5,723	DM5,723	DM5,723
			£2,530	£2,530	£2,530
			¥412,140	¥412,140	¥412,140
MAIRE, NICOLAS (II)	1	1	$6,729	$6,729	$6,729
			DM11,384	DM11,384	DM11,384
			£4,232	£4,232	£4,232
			¥833,704	¥833,704	¥833,704
MALINE, GUILLAUME	11	8	$2,122	$25,126	$9,269
			DM3,396	DM37,595	DM15,049
			£1,380	£14,950	£5,697
			¥214,761	¥2,802,826	¥1,065,452
MALINE, GUILLAUME (attributed to)	1	0			
MALINE, GUILLAUME (workshop of)	1	0			
MARCHAND, EUGENE	1	1	$2,399	$2,399	$2,399
			DM4,057	DM4,057	DM4,057
			£1,610	£1,610	£1,610
			¥254,380	¥254,380	¥254,380

Maker	Items Bid	Sold	Selling Prices Low	High	Avg
MARISSAL, OLIVIER	1	1	$2,742	$2,742	$2,742
			DM4,637	DM4,637	DM4,637
			£1,840	£1,840	£1,840
			¥290,720	¥290,720	¥290,720
MARTIN, JEAN JOSEPH	10	7	$2,300	$4,417	$3,565
			DM4,261	DM7,380	DM5,644
			£1,380	£2,780	£2,259
			¥290,720	¥536,909	¥393,219
MAUCOTEL & DESCHAMPS	5	3	$347	$1,236	$895
			DM641	DM1,896	DM1,463
			£207	£805	£567
			¥46,180	¥135,283	¥105,570
MCGILL, A.	1	0			
MEINEL, F.	1	0			
MENNESSON, EMILE	2	0			
METTAL, WALTER	2	1	$690	$690	$690
			DM1,253	DM1,253	DM1,253
			£422	£422	£422
			¥85,684	¥85,684	¥85,684
MILLANT, B.	3	2	$2,899	$3,816	$3,358
			DM4,338	DM5,391	DM4,864
			£1,725	£2,415	£2,070
			¥323,403	¥340,604	¥332,004
MILLANT, JEAN-JACQUES	2	2	$2,329	$3,887	$3,108
			DM3,266	DM6,739	DM5,003
			£1,495	£2,300	£1,898
			¥235,317	¥485,300	¥360,309
MILLANT, M.	2	1	$1,360	$1,360	$1,360
			DM2,359	DM2,359	DM2,359
			£805	£805	£805
			¥169,855	¥169,855	¥169,855
MILLANT, MAX	1	1	$2,570	$2,570	$2,570
			DM4,347	DM4,347	DM4,347
			£1,725	£1,725	£1,725
			¥272,550	¥272,550	¥272,550
MILLANT, R. & M.	1	1	$2,657	$2,657	$2,657
			DM4,009	DM4,009	DM4,009
			£1,610	£1,610	£1,610
			¥301,070	¥301,070	¥301,070
MILLANT, R. & M. (workshop of)	1	1	$2,300	$2,300	$2,300
			DM3,843	DM3,843	DM3,843
			£1,535	£1,535	£1,535
			¥241,063	¥241,063	¥241,063
MIQUEL FAMILY (MEMBER OF)	1	0			
MIQUEL, E.	2	1	$1,160	$1,160	$1,160
			DM1,735	DM1,735	DM1,735
			£690	£690	£690
			¥129,361	¥129,361	¥129,361
MOHR, RODNEY D.	2	2	$546	$690	$618
			DM789	DM1,228	DM1,008
			£348	£414	£381
			¥47,387	¥91,756	¥69,572
MOINEL, DANIEL	1	1	$1,633	$1,633	$1,633
			DM2,300	DM2,300	DM2,300
			£1,035	£1,035	£1,035
			¥166,979	¥166,979	¥166,979

| Maker | Items | | Selling Prices | | |
	Bid	Sold	Low	High	Avg
MOLLER, M.	1	1	$1,642	$1,642	$1,642
			DM2,457	DM2,457	DM2,457
			£977	£977	£977
			¥183,168	¥183,168	¥183,168
MOLLER & ZOON	2	1	$1,635	$1,635	$1,635
			DM3,026	DM3,026	DM3,026
			£977	£977	£977
			¥217,959	¥217,959	¥217,959
MONNIG, A. HERMANN	2	1	$450	$450	$450
			DM778	DM778	DM778
			£276	£276	£276
			¥51,336	¥51,336	¥51,336
MORIZOT	2	2	$922	$2,397	$1,660
			DM1,284	DM3,338	DM2,311
			£575	£1,495	£1,035
			¥77,940	¥202,644	¥140,292
MORIZOT (attributed to)	1	0			
MORIZOT, LOUIS	39	30	$615	$3,635	$1,883
			DM884	DM5,134	DM2,935
			£368	£2,300	£1,194
			¥64,064	¥347,781	¥198,340
MORIZOT, LOUIS (II)	10	7	$1,218	$4,206	$2,526
			DM2,107	DM7,346	DM4,148
			£747	£2,645	£1,563
			¥138,942	¥521,065	¥297,873
MORIZOT (FRERES), LOUIS	2	2	$1,150	$1,344	$1,247
			DM2,047	DM2,246	DM2,146
			£690	£805	£748
			¥152,927	¥163,407	¥158,167
MORIZOT FAMILY	4	3	$978	$2,530	$1,591
			DM1,652	DM4,503	DM2,764
			£587	£1,518	£955
			¥119,255	¥336,439	¥203,341
MOUGENOT, LEON	3	1	$794	$794	$794
			DM1,218	DM1,218	DM1,218
			£517	£517	£517
			¥86,861	¥86,861	¥86,861
NAPIER, FRANK D.	1	1	$4,313	$4,313	$4,313
			DM7,206	DM7,206	DM7,206
			£2,878	£2,878	£2,878
			¥451,993	¥451,993	¥451,993
NEHR, J.P.	1	0			
NEUDORFER	3	3	$233	$718	$451
			DM356	DM1,129	DM683
			£150	£460	£288
			¥22,991	¥72,049	¥43,633
NEUVILLE	1	1	$396	$396	$396
			DM605	DM605	DM605
			£253	£253	£253
			¥44,161	¥44,161	¥44,161
NOLDER, T.J.	1	1	$701	$701	$701
			DM976	DM976	DM976
			£437	£437	£437
			¥59,234	¥59,234	¥59,234
NORRIS	1	1	$1,128	$1,128	$1,128
			DM1,691	DM1,691	DM1,691
			£690	£690	£690
			¥109,130	¥109,130	¥109,130

Maker	Items Bid	Sold	Selling Prices Low	High	Avg
NURNBERGER	3	1	$719	$719	$719
			DM1,018	DM1,018	DM1,018
			£460	£460	£460
			¥73,052	¥73,052	¥73,052
NURNBERGER (workshop of)	1	1	$1,265	$1,265	$1,265
			DM2,252	DM2,252	DM2,252
			£759	£759	£759
			¥168,220	¥168,220	¥168,220
NURNBERGER, ALBERT	70	63	$288	$4,748	$1,489
			DM433	DM6,676	DM2,318
			£175	£2,990	£940
			¥32,137	¥422,107	¥160,174
NURNBERGER, ALBERT (attributed to)	3	1	$1,121	$1,121	$1,121
			DM1,955	DM1,955	DM1,955
			£690	£690	£690
			¥135,827	¥135,827	¥135,827
NURNBERGER, ALBERT (workshop of)	2	1	$805	$805	$805
			DM1,391	DM1,391	DM1,391
			£497	£497	£497
			¥102,022	¥102,022	¥102,022
NURNBERGER, AUGUST	1	1	$978	$978	$978
			DM1,412	DM1,412	DM1,412
			£623	£623	£623
			¥84,798	¥84,798	¥84,798
NURNBERGER, CH.	1	1	$575	$575	$575
			DM879	DM879	DM879
			£378	£378	£378
			¥60,605	¥60,605	¥60,605
NURNBERGER, CHRISTIAN ALBERT	5	3	$1,536	$2,523	$1,879
			DM2,567	DM4,269	DM3,167
			£920	£1,587	£1,166
			¥186,751	¥312,639	¥231,559
NURNBERGER, FRANZ ALBERT	1	1	$3,811	$3,811	$3,811
			DM5,366	DM5,366	DM5,366
			£2,415	£2,415	£2,415
			¥389,617	¥389,617	¥389,617
NURNBERGER, FRANZ ALBERT (II)	1	1	$2,570	$2,570	$2,570
			DM4,347	DM4,347	DM4,347
			£1,725	£1,725	£1,725
			¥272,550	¥272,550	¥272,550
NURNBERGER, KARL ALBERT	29	23	$865	$3,457	$1,729
			DM1,278	DM5,775	DM2,836
			£517	£2,070	£1,058
			¥92,766	¥420,189	¥204,735
NURNBERGER, KARL ALBERT (II)	1	1	$2,295	$2,295	$2,295
			DM3,521	DM3,521	DM3,521
			£1,495	£1,495	£1,495
			¥251,175	¥251,175	¥251,175
NURNBERGER-SUESS, AUGUST	1	1	$1,162	$1,162	$1,162
			DM2,011	DM2,011	DM2,011
			£713	£713	£713
			¥132,618	¥132,618	¥132,618
OUCHARD, B.	2	2	$3,785	$5,693	$4,739
			DM6,404	DM8,591	DM7,497
			£2,381	£3,450	£2,915
			¥468,959	¥645,150	¥557,054
OUCHARD, BERNARD	1	0			

Maker	Items		Selling Prices		
	Bid	Sold	Low	High	Avg
OUCHARD, E.	1	1	$4,592	$4,592	$4,592
			DM7,722	DM7,722	DM7,722
			£2,875	£2,875	£2,875
			¥563,681	¥563,681	¥563,681
OUCHARD, EMILE	21	15	$1,068	$6,325	$3,689
			DM1,835	DM10,203	DM5,984
			£632	£4,048	£2,256
			¥118,125	¥736,575	¥418,366
OUCHARD, EMILE A.	9	7	$519	$6,765	$4,718
			DM960	DM10,122	DM7,316
			£310	£4,025	£2,893
			¥69,158	¥754,607	¥518,474
OUCHARD, EMILE FRANCOIS	11	10	$909	$23,590	$4,656
			DM1,283	DM33,220	DM6,934
			£575	£14,950	£2,938
			¥81,096	¥2,411,913	¥485,021
OUCHARD, J.CL. (ascribed to)	1	0			
OUCHARD, J.CL. (attributed to)	2	0			
OUDINOT	1	0			
PAJEOT	6	4	$5,901	$11,765	$9,462
			DM8,216	DM21,176	DM15,062
			£3,680	£7,130	£5,865
			¥498,817	¥1,696,584	¥1,073,027
PAJEOT (FILS)	2	1	$8,840	$8,840	$8,840
			DM14,152	DM14,152	DM14,152
			£5,750	£5,750	£5,750
			¥894,838	¥894,838	¥894,838
PAJEOT, ETIENNE	14	6	$2,291	$13,800	$7,442
			DM3,382	DM23,322	DM12,431
			£1,495	£8,280	£4,505
			¥243,537	¥1,683,600	¥898,958
PAJEOT, LOUIS SIMON	6	2	$1,682	$2,363	$2,022
			DM2,846	DM3,337	DM3,092
			£1,058	£1,495	£1,277
			¥208,426	¥210,850	¥209,638
PAJEOT, LOUIS SIMON (attributed to)	1	0			
PANORMO, LOUIS	1	1	$960	$960	$960
			DM1,604	DM1,604	DM1,604
			£575	£575	£575
			¥116,719	¥116,719	¥116,719
PAQUOTTE, ALBERT	1	1	$5,452	$5,452	$5,452
			DM7,701	DM7,701	DM7,701
			£3,450	£3,450	£3,450
			¥486,578	¥486,578	¥486,578
PARISOT, A.	1	1	$1,272	$1,272	$1,272
			DM1,797	DM1,797	DM1,797
			£805	£805	£805
			¥113,535	¥113,535	¥113,535
PASSA, FRANK	1	1	$690	$690	$690
			DM1,055	DM1,055	DM1,055
			£454	£454	£454
			¥72,726	¥72,726	¥72,726
PATIGNY, PIERRE	2	1	$3,009	$3,009	$3,009
			DM4,969	DM4,969	DM4,969
			£1,840	£1,840	£1,840
			¥372,470	¥372,470	¥372,470

Maker	Items		Selling Prices		
	Bid	Sold	Low	High	Avg
PAULUS, GUNTER A.	2	1	$1,344	$1,344	$1,344
			DM2,496	DM2,496	DM2,496
			£805	£805	£805
			¥179,869	¥179,869	¥179,869
PAULUS, JOHANNES O.	3	2	$726	$792	$759
			DM1,022	DM1,169	DM1,096
			£460	£517	£489
			¥74,213	¥84,220	¥79,216
PAULUS, OTTO	1	1	$792	$792	$792
			DM1,169	DM1,169	DM1,169
			£517	£517	£517
			¥84,220	¥84,220	¥84,220
PECATTE, C.	1	0			
PECCATTE, CHARLES	7	6	$1,999	$14,097	$6,005
			DM2,824	DM20,809	DM9,276
			£1,265	£9,200	£3,910
			¥178,412	¥1,498,689	¥639,311
PECCATTE, CHARLES (ascribed to)	1	1	$1,291	$1,291	$1,291
			DM1,797	DM1,797	DM1,797
			£805	£805	£805
			¥109,116	¥109,116	¥109,116
PECCATTE, CHARLES (attributed to)	1	0			
PECCATTE, DOMINIQUE	14	8	$5,286	$29,900	$18,946
			DM7,804	DM50,543	DM30,173
			£3,450	£19,136	£12,023
			¥562,008	¥3,639,750	¥2,011,872
PECCATTE, DOMINIQUE (ascribed to)	2	1	$27,209	$27,209	$27,209
			DM47,173	DM47,173	DM47,173
			£16,100	£16,100	£16,100
			¥3,397,100	¥3,397,100	¥3,397,100
PECCATTE, DOMINIQUE (attributed to)	2	2	$3,738	$12,650	$8,194
			DM5,793	DM19,987	DM12,890
			£2,392	£8,096	£5,244
			¥367,434	¥1,263,735	¥815,584
PECCATTE, FRANCOIS	2	1	$7,258	$7,258	$7,258
			DM10,222	DM10,222	DM10,222
			£4,600	£4,600	£4,600
			¥742,127	¥742,127	¥742,127
PECCATTE, FRANCOIS (attributed to)	1	1	$10,925	$10,925	$10,925
			DM17,262	DM17,262	DM17,262
			£6,992	£6,992	£6,992
			¥1,091,408	¥1,091,408	¥1,091,408
PECCATTE FAMILY (MEMBER OF)	2	2	$4,874	$8,050	$6,462
			DM8,432	DM13,452	DM10,942
			£2,990	£5,372	£4,181
			¥556,140	¥843,720	¥699,930
PECCATTE, D. & HENRY, J.	1	1	$7,682	$7,682	$7,682
			DM13,754	DM13,754	DM13,754
			£4,600	£4,600	£4,600
			¥1,056,988	¥1,056,988	¥1,056,988
PENZEL	1	1	$367	$367	$367
			DM641	DM641	DM641
			£219	£219	£219
			¥46,838	¥46,838	¥46,838
PENZEL, E.M.	2	2	$863	$978	$920
			DM1,298	DM1,515	DM1,407
			£524	£626	£575
			¥96,098	¥96,410	¥96,254

Maker	Items		Selling Prices		
	Bid	Sold	Low	High	Avg
PENZEL, GUSTAV	1	0			
PENZEL, K. GERHARD	2	1	$2,118	$2,118	$2,118
			DM3,251	DM3,251	DM3,251
			£1,380	£1,380	£1,380
			¥231,854	¥231,854	¥231,854
PERSOIS	6	4	$6,542	$20,165	$10,746
			DM9,241	DM37,433	DM18,551
			£4,140	£12,075	£6,785
			¥583,893	¥2,698,038	¥1,252,020
PEYROT, ALFRED	1	0			
PFRETZSCHNER	2	2	$469	$2,029	$1,249
			DM834	DM3,249	DM2,041
			£288	£1,320	£804
			¥62,942	¥205,424	¥134,183
PFRETZSCHNER (attributed to)	1	1	$940	$940	$940
			DM1,553	DM1,553	DM1,553
			£575	£575	£575
			¥116,397	¥116,397	¥116,397
PFRETZSCHNER, C.F.	1	0			
PFRETZSCHNER, F.C.	2	2	$509	$1,061	$785
			DM719	DM1,698	DM1,208
			£322	£690	£506
			¥45,414	¥107,381	¥76,397
PFRETZSCHNER, G.A.	5	5	$546	$1,380	$799
			DM915	DM2,332	DM1,328
			£323	£828	£488
			¥64,041	¥183,637	¥100,413
PFRETZSCHNER, G.A. (workshop of)	1	1	$748	$748	$748
			DM1,249	DM1,249	DM1,249
			£499	£499	£499
			¥78,345	¥78,345	¥78,345
PFRETZSCHNER, H.R.	35	28	$375	$3,785	$1,290
			DM649	DM6,404	DM2,122
			£230	£2,381	£803
			¥42,780	¥468,959	¥154,065
PFRETZSCHNER, H.R. (workshop of)	1	1	$489	$489	$489
			DM826	DM826	DM826
			£293	£293	£293
			¥59,628	¥59,628	¥59,628
PFRETZSCHNER, L.	4	2	$575	$1,552	$1,064
			DM961	DM2,183	DM1,572
			£384	£978	£681
			¥60,266	¥137,997	¥99,131
PFRETZSCHNER, L. (attributed to)	1	1	$1,007	$1,007	$1,007
			DM1,488	DM1,488	DM1,488
			£656	£656	£656
			¥107,328	¥107,328	¥107,328
PFRETZSCHNER, W.A.	4	4	$690	$1,380	$969
			DM1,181	DM2,139	DM1,560
			£408	£883	£607
			¥85,684	¥135,668	¥107,192
PILLOT	2	2	$1,728	$2,178	$1,953
			DM3,066	DM3,209	DM3,137
			£1,035	£1,380	£1,208
			¥222,638	¥231,260	¥226,949
POIRSON	1	0			

Maker	Items		Selling Prices		
	Bid	Sold	Low	High	Avg
POIRSON, JUSTIN	10	4	$294	$3,941	$1,978
			DM498	DM6,665	DM3,118
			£185	£2,645	£1,283
			¥36,475	¥417,910	¥198,138
PRAGA, EUGENIO	1	0			
PRAGER, AUGUST EDWIN	17	15	$576	$2,310	$1,354
			DM898	DM4,274	DM2,288
			£345	£1,495	£831
			¥54,490	¥307,864	¥165,561
PRAGER, GUSTAV	8	5	$352	$2,742	$1,059
			DM593	DM4,637	DM1,738
			£219	£1,840	£691
			¥43,233	¥290,720	¥115,852
PRAGER, GUSTAV OSKAR	2	2	$922	$1,093	$1,008
			DM1,540	DM1,850	DM1,695
			£552	£688	£620
			¥112,050	¥135,477	¥123,764
PRELL, HERMAN WILHELM	6	4	$403	$1,114	$769
			DM673	DM1,642	DM1,234
			£269	£725	£480
			¥42,186	¥118,209	¥87,391
RAHM, WILHELM	1	1	$1,412	$1,412	$1,412
			DM2,167	DM2,167	DM2,167
			£920	£920	£920
			¥154,569	¥154,569	¥154,569
RAPOPORT, HAIM (attributed to)	6	2	$338	$338	$338
			DM602	DM602	DM602
			£207	£207	£207
			¥44,221	¥44,221	¥44,221
RAU, AUGUST	2	2	$963	$1,304	$1,133
			DM1,781	DM2,206	DM1,993
			£575	£820	£697
			¥128,277	¥161,530	¥144,903
REIDEL, E.	2	2	$316	$460	$388
			DM457	DM787	DM622
			£207	£272	£239
			¥32,020	¥57,123	¥44,572
RETFORD, WILLIAM C.	1	0			
RICHAUME, ANDRE	4	4	$2,056	$5,798	$4,214
			DM3,478	DM8,676	DM6,362
			£1,380	£3,680	£2,674
			¥218,040	¥646,806	¥455,831
RIEDL, RUDOLF	1	0			
ROBICHAUD	1	1	$1,536	$1,536	$1,536
			DM2,567	DM2,567	DM2,567
			£920	£920	£920
			¥186,751	¥186,751	¥186,751
ROCKWELL, DAVID BAILEY	1	1	$403	$403	$403
			DM689	DM689	DM689
			£238	£238	£238
			¥49,982	¥49,982	¥49,982
ROLLAND	1	1	$5,762	$5,762	$5,762
			DM9,626	DM9,626	DM9,626
			£3,450	£3,450	£3,450
			¥700,316	¥700,316	¥700,316

Maker	Items		Selling Prices		
	Bid	Sold	Low	High	Avg
ROLLAND, BENOIT	2	1	$1,380	$1,380	$1,380
			DM2,385	DM2,385	DM2,385
			£853	£853	£853
			¥174,894	¥174,894	¥174,894
ROTH, ERNST HEINRICH (workshop of)	1	1	$805	$805	$805
			DM1,212	DM1,212	DM1,212
			£489	£489	£489
			¥89,983	¥89,983	¥89,983
ROTH, EUGEN	1	1	$173	$173	$173
			DM244	DM244	DM244
			£109	£109	£109
			¥17,808	¥17,808	¥17,808
SARTORY, EUGENE	109	95	$734	$30,576	$8,547
			DM1,320	DM43,250	DM13,497
			£437	£19,550	£5,321
			¥84,879	¥3,104,716	¥946,479
SARTORY, EUGENE (ascribed to)	1	1	$4,798	$4,798	$4,798
			DM8,114	DM8,114	DM8,114
			£3,220	£3,220	£3,220
			¥508,760	¥508,760	¥508,760
SARTORY, EUGENE (attributed to)	2	2	$2,689	$3,498	$3,094
			DM4,492	DM6,065	DM5,279
			£1,610	£2,070	£1,840
			¥326,814	¥436,770	¥381,792
SARTORY, EUGENE (workshop of)	2	2	$3,226	$3,658	$3,442
			DM4,868	DM6,767	DM5,817
			£1,955	£2,185	£2,070
			¥365,585	¥487,452	¥426,518
SCHAFFNER, M.	1	1	$1,283	$1,283	$1,283
			DM1,798	DM1,798	DM1,798
			£805	£805	£805
			¥113,090	¥113,090	¥113,090
SCHICKER, HORST	2	0			
SCHMIDT, C. HANS CARL	1	1	$991	$991	$991
			DM1,589	DM1,589	DM1,589
			£644	£644	£644
			¥100,223	¥100,223	¥100,223
SCHMIDT, E.R. & CO.	1	1	$374	$374	$374
			DM579	DM579	DM579
			£239	£239	£239
			¥36,743	¥36,743	¥36,743
SCHMIDT, HANS KARL	1	0			
SCHMITT, LUCIEN	1	1	$1,518	$1,518	$1,518
			DM2,732	DM2,732	DM2,732
			£920	£920	£920
			¥218,914	¥218,914	¥218,914
SCHUBERT, PAUL	3	2	$240	$863	$552
			DM334	DM1,221	DM777
			£150	£552	£351
			¥20,264	¥87,663	¥53,963
SCHULLER	1	1	$601	$601	$601
			DM885	DM885	DM885
			£391	£391	£391
			¥63,796	¥63,796	¥63,796
SCHULTZ, T.	1	1	$348	$348	$348
			DM534	DM534	DM534
			£230	£230	£230
			¥37,082	¥37,082	¥37,082

Maker	Items		Selling Prices		
	Bid	Sold	Low	High	Avg
SCHUSTER, ADOLF	5	3	$633	$1,150	$901
			DM1,057	DM1,988	DM1,458
			£422	£711	£578
			¥66,292	¥145,745	¥101,729
SCHUSTER, ADOLPH CURT	4	4	$546	$1,265	$926
			DM847	DM1,829	DM1,375
			£350	£826	£592
			¥53,702	¥128,081	¥97,116
SCHUSTER, GOTHARD	2	2	$186	$966	$576
			DM326	DM1,737	DM1,031
			£115	£575	£345
			¥22,534	¥111,682	¥67,108
SCHUSTER, MAX K.	1	1	$1,035	$1,035	$1,035
			DM1,842	DM1,842	DM1,842
			£621	£621	£621
			¥137,634	¥137,634	¥137,634
SCHUSTER, WILHELM R.	1	1	$805	$805	$805
			DM1,212	DM1,212	DM1,212
			£489	£489	£489
			¥89,983	¥89,983	¥89,983
SCHWARZ	1	1	$258	$258	$258
			DM359	DM359	DM359
			£161	£161	£161
			¥21,823	¥21,823	¥21,823
SCHWARZ BROS.	1	1	$3,084	$3,084	$3,084
			DM5,216	DM5,216	DM5,216
			£2,070	£2,070	£2,070
			¥327,060	¥327,060	¥327,060
SEIFERT, LOTHAR	16	9	$288	$2,138	$846
			DM440	DM3,706	DM1,454
			£173	£1,265	£515
			¥30,303	¥266,915	¥103,558
SEIFERT, W.	1	1	$487	$487	$487
			DM748	DM748	DM748
			£322	£322	£322
			¥51,914	¥51,914	¥51,914
SERDET, PAUL	3	1	$2,122	$2,122	$2,122
			DM3,396	DM3,396	DM3,396
			£1,380	£1,380	£1,380
			¥214,761	¥214,761	¥214,761
SILVESTRE, HIPPOLYTE CHRETIEN	1	1	$4,057	$4,057	$4,057
			DM5,649	DM5,649	DM5,649
			£2,530	£2,530	£2,530
			¥342,936	¥342,936	¥342,936
SILVESTRE & MAUCOTEL	5	2	$1,880	$2,819	$2,350
			DM2,819	DM4,162	DM3,490
			£1,150	£1,840	£1,495
			¥181,884	¥299,738	¥240,811
SILVESTRE & MAUCOTEL (workshop of)	2	1	$1,725	$1,725	$1,725
			DM2,596	DM2,596	DM2,596
			£1,047	£1,047	£1,047
			¥192,821	¥192,821	¥192,821
SIMON	1	1	$13,191	$13,191	$13,191
			DM21,117	DM21,117	DM21,117
			£8,580	£8,580	£8,580
			¥1,335,254	¥1,335,254	¥1,335,254

Maker	Items		Selling Prices		
	Bid	Sold	Low	High	Avg
SIMON, F.R.	1	0			
SIMON, PAUL	6	5	$2,118	$6,325	$3,566
			DM3,253	DM11,259	DM6,038
			£1,380	£3,795	£2,208
			¥231,825	¥841,098	¥436,758
SIMON, PAUL (ascribed to)	1	1	$4,664	$4,664	$4,664
			DM8,087	DM8,087	DM8,087
			£2,760	£2,760	£2,760
			¥582,360	¥582,360	¥582,360
SIMON, PAUL (attributed to)	1	1	$4,140	$4,140	$4,140
			DM7,369	DM7,369	DM7,369
			£2,484	£2,484	£2,484
			¥550,537	¥550,537	¥550,537
SIMON BROS.	3	2	$1,033	$1,874	$1,454
			DM1,549	DM3,243	DM2,396
			£632	£1,150	£891
			¥99,957	¥213,900	¥156,929
SIRDEVAN, JOHN	3	3	$575	$920	$709
			DM831	DM1,328	DM1,025
			£376	£586	£458
			¥58,219	¥79,810	¥67,356
STUBER, JOHANN	1	1	$1,234	$1,234	$1,234
			DM1,821	DM1,821	DM1,821
			£805	£805	£805
			¥131,135	¥131,135	¥131,135
SUARD, ARNAUD	1	1	$1,495	$1,495	$1,495
			DM2,498	DM2,498	DM2,498
			£998	£998	£998
			¥156,691	¥156,691	¥156,691
SUESS, AUGUST NURNBERGER	1	1	$410	$410	$410
			DM718	DM718	DM718
			£253	£253	£253
			¥49,575	¥49,575	¥49,575
SUSS	1	1	$1,100	$1,100	$1,100
			DM1,541	DM1,541	DM1,541
			£690	£690	£690
			¥96,935	¥96,935	¥96,935
SZEPESSY, BELA	2	2	$752	$1,061	$906
			DM1,127	DM1,698	DM1,413
			£460	£690	£575
			¥72,754	¥107,381	¥90,067
TAYLOR, MALCOLM	9	5	$478	$1,996	$1,173
			DM766	DM2,811	DM1,765
			£311	£1,265	£735
			¥48,322	¥204,085	¥125,202
TAYLOR, MICHAEL J.	3	3	$626	$2,295	$1,571
			DM878	DM3,521	DM2,304
			£402	£1,495	£1,016
			¥63,276	¥251,175	¥165,155
TECHLER	1	1	$149	$149	$149
			DM204	DM204	DM204
			£92	£92	£92
			¥12,382	¥12,382	¥12,382
THIBOUT, JACQUES PIERRE	1	1	$3,001	$3,001	$3,001
			DM4,605	DM4,605	DM4,605
			£1,955	£1,955	£1,955
			¥328,460	¥328,460	¥328,460

Maker	Items		Selling Prices		
	Bid	Sold	Low	High	Avg
THIBOUVILLE-LAMY, J.	16	12	$416	$1,646	$866
			DM621	DM2,784	DM1,474
			£253	£1,035	£542
			¥39,981	¥203,895	¥102,216
THIBOUVILLE-LAMY, J. (workshop of)	1	1	$1,610	$1,610	$1,610
			DM2,328	DM2,328	DM2,328
			£1,052	£1,052	£1,052
			¥163,013	¥163,013	¥163,013
THOMA, ADOLF	1	1	$1,018	$1,018	$1,018
			DM1,633	DM1,633	DM1,633
			£661	£661	£661
			¥115,864	¥115,864	¥115,864
THOMASSIN	1	1	$1,068	$1,068	$1,068
			DM1,852	DM1,852	DM1,852
			£632	£632	£632
			¥133,352	¥133,352	¥133,352
THOMASSIN, C.	6	4	$1,059	$6,762	$3,031
			DM1,959	DM12,160	DM5,173
			£633	£4,025	£1,840
			¥141,104	¥781,776	¥352,546
THOMASSIN, CLAUDE	37	29	$673	$5,750	$2,511
			DM1,138	DM9,616	DM4,015
			£414	£3,680	£1,575
			¥77,004	¥692,694	¥279,395
THOMASSIN, CLAUDE (attributed to)	2	1	$4,238	$4,238	$4,238
			DM6,784	DM6,784	DM6,784
			£2,760	£2,760	£2,760
			¥427,662	¥427,662	¥427,662
THOMASSIN, LOUIS	1	0			
TILLOTSON, J.	1	1	$730	$730	$730
			DM1,365	DM1,365	DM1,365
			£460	£460	£460
			¥86,393	¥86,393	¥86,393
TOURNIER, JOSEPH ALEXIS	2	1	$3,416	$3,416	$3,416
			DM5,154	DM5,154	DM5,154
			£2,070	£2,070	£2,070
			¥387,090	¥387,090	¥387,090
TOURNIER, JOSEPH ALEXIS (workshop of)	1	1	$2,530	$2,530	$2,530
			DM3,808	DM3,808	DM3,808
			£1,536	£1,536	£1,536
			¥282,803	¥282,803	¥282,803
TOURTE, FRANCOIS	2	1	$76,684	$76,684	$76,684
			DM122,994	DM122,994	DM122,994
			£49,795	£49,795	£49,795
			¥8,725,080	¥8,725,080	¥8,725,080
TOURTE, FRANCOIS (ascribed to)	1	0			
TOURTE, FRANCOIS (attributed to)	1	1	$9,775	$9,775	$9,775
			DM14,711	DM14,711	DM14,711
			£5,934	£5,934	£5,934
			¥1,092,650	¥1,092,650	¥1,092,650
TOURTE, FRANCOIS XAVIER	8	3	$4,180	$38,164	$17,749
			DM5,904	DM53,905	DM25,070
			£2,645	£24,150	£11,232
			¥373,043	¥3,406,044	¥1,584,081
TOURTE, LOUIS (PERE) (workshop of)	1	0			

Maker	Items		Selling Prices		
	Bid	Sold	Low	High	Avg
TOURTE, XAVIER (ascribed to)	1	1	$5,303	$5,303	$5,303
			DM8,971	DM8,971	DM8,971
			£3,335	£3,335	£3,335
			¥656,995	¥656,995	¥656,995
TOURTE, XAVIER (L'AINE) (ascribed to)	1	0			
TOURTE FAMILY	2	0			
TUA, SILVIO	3	0			
TUBBS	2	2	$664	$1,312	$988
			DM1,179	DM2,335	DM1,757
			£403	£805	£604
			¥92,128	¥176,239	¥134,183
TUBBS (attributed to)	1	0			
TUBBS (workshop of)	1	1	$1,955	$1,955	$1,955
			DM3,267	DM3,267	DM3,267
			£1,305	£1,305	£1,305
			¥204,904	¥204,904	¥204,904
TUBBS, ALFRED	1	0			
TUBBS, C.E.	3	1	$2,950	$2,950	$2,950
			DM4,108	DM4,108	DM4,108
			£1,840	£1,840	£1,840
			¥249,408	¥249,408	¥249,408
TUBBS, JAMES	120	91	$884	$43,616	$4,787
			DM1,415	DM61,606	DM7,543
			£575	£27,600	£2,983
			¥89,484	¥3,892,621	¥518,431
TUBBS, JAMES (attributed to)	5	4	$720	$3,470	$1,662
			DM1,103	DM4,879	DM2,541
			£460	£2,185	£1,029
			¥80,279	¥309,680	¥174,645
TUBBS, T. (attributed to)	3	1	$103	$103	$103
			DM171	DM171	DM171
			£63	£63	£63
			¥12,804	¥12,804	¥12,804
TUBBS, THOMAS	2	1	$3,348	$3,348	$3,348
			DM4,942	DM4,942	DM4,942
			£2,185	£2,185	£2,185
			¥355,939	¥355,939	¥355,939
TUBBS, WILLIAM	3	0			
TUBBS, WILLIAM (ascribed to)	1	1	$1,221	$1,221	$1,221
			DM1,831	DM1,831	DM1,831
			£747	£747	£747
			¥118,146	¥118,146	¥118,146
TUBBS, WILLIAM (attributed to)	3	2	$2,109	$2,120	$2,114
			DM3,133	DM3,906	DM3,519
			£1,265	£1,380	£1,323
			¥225,953	¥281,627	¥253,790
UEBEL, K. WERNER	2	0			
ULLMANN, GIORGIO	3	1	$856	$856	$856
			DM1,380	DM1,380	DM1,380
			£497	£497	£497
			¥100,740	¥100,740	¥100,740
VAN DER MEER, KAREL	3	1	$940	$940	$940
			DM1,409	DM1,409	DM1,409
			£575	£575	£575
			¥90,942	¥90,942	¥90,942

Maker	Items		Selling Prices		
	Bid	Sold	Low	High	Avg
VAUTRIN, JOSEPH	1	1	$1,371	$1,371	$1,371
			DM2,318	DM2,318	DM2,318
			£920	£920	£920
			¥145,360	¥145,360	¥145,360
VICKERS, J.E.	3	1	$226	$226	$226
			DM382	DM382	DM382
			£138	£138	£138
			¥26,150	¥26,150	¥26,150
VICTOR, T.	1	1	$1,864	$1,864	$1,864
			DM3,264	DM3,264	DM3,264
			£1,150	£1,150	£1,150
			¥225,343	¥225,343	¥225,343
VIDOUDEZ, PIERRE	8	5	$480	$3,816	$2,149
			DM889	DM5,391	DM3,256
			£287	£2,415	£1,355
			¥64,027	¥344,319	¥229,614
VIGNERON, A.	9	6	$2,650	$5,878	$4,496
			DM3,916	DM9,884	DM6,846
			£1,725	£3,680	£2,856
			¥282,441	¥721,512	¥483,744
VIGNERON, A. (attributed to)	2	0			
VIGNERON, ANDRE	18	15	$841	$7,269	$4,011
			DM1,423	DM11,230	DM6,314
			£529	£4,600	£2,491
			¥104,213	¥817,035	¥438,177
VIGNERON, ARTHUR	2	2	$3,543	$8,694	$6,119
			DM5,004	DM15,629	DM10,316
			£2,242	£5,175	£3,709
			¥316,205	¥1,005,140	¥660,673
VIGNERON, JOSEPH ARTHUR	33	27	$589	$10,925	$3,941
			DM996	DM16,442	DM6,238
			£370	£6,632	£2,426
			¥72,949	¥1,221,197	¥448,491
VOIGT	2	1	$151	$151	$151
			DM226	DM226	DM226
			£92	£92	£92
			¥14,538	¥14,538	¥14,538
VOIGT, ARNOLD	10	7	$630	$1,320	$803
			DM890	DM2,402	DM1,345
			£402	£805	£492
			¥63,921	¥166,748	¥94,514
VOIGT, ARNOLD (workshop of)	1	1	$690	$690	$690
			DM996	DM996	DM996
			£440	£440	£440
			¥59,858	¥59,858	¥59,858
VOIGT, WERNER	1	1	$451	$451	$451
			DM764	DM764	DM764
			£276	£276	£276
			¥52,301	¥52,301	¥52,301
VOIRIN, FRANCOIS NICOLAS	72	50	$1,009	$18,463	$6,108
			DM1,708	DM32,054	DM9,733
			£635	£10,925	£3,809
			¥125,056	¥2,347,455	¥681,212
VOIRIN, FRANCOIS NICOLAS (ascribed to)	2	0			

Maker	Items		Selling Prices		
	Bid	Sold	Low	High	Avg
VOIRIN, FRANCOIS NICOLAS					
(attributed to)	1	1	$2,867	$2,867	$2,867
			DM4,020	DM4,020	DM4,020
			£1,840	£1,840	£1,840
			¥289,622	¥289,622	¥289,622
VOIRIN, J.	4	1	$1,031	$1,031	$1,031
			DM1,834	DM1,834	DM1,834
			£633	£633	£633
			¥138,473	¥138,473	¥138,473
VOIRIN, JOSEPH	6	2	$2,650	$4,590	$3,620
			DM3,916	DM7,043	DM5,479
			£1,725	£2,990	£2,358
			¥282,441	¥502,350	¥392,396
VUILLAUME (workshop of)	2	1	$4,081	$4,081	$4,081
			DM7,076	DM7,076	DM7,076
			£2,415	£2,415	£2,415
			¥509,565	¥509,565	¥509,565
VUILLAUME, JEAN BAPTISTE	32	24	$1,059	$12,633	$5,712
			DM1,625	DM21,902	DM9,626
			£690	£7,935	£3,537
			¥115,927	¥1,606,153	¥668,682
VUILLAUME, JEAN BAPTISTE (ascribed to)	1	1	$2,068	$2,068	$2,068
			DM3,101	DM3,101	DM3,101
			£1,265	£1,265	£1,265
			¥200,072	¥200,072	¥200,072
VUILLAUME, JEAN BAPTISTE (workshop of)	6	5	$2,829	$6,900	$5,330
			DM4,529	DM11,530	DM8,146
			£1,840	£4,604	£3,442
			¥286,348	¥723,189	¥507,809
WATSON, WILLIAM	4	3	$1,344	$2,387	$1,857
			DM2,496	DM3,664	DM3,145
			£805	£1,495	£1,135
			¥179,869	¥244,683	¥219,530
WEICHOLD	8	6	$283	$863	$546
			DM515	DM1,442	DM925
			£173	£517	£332
			¥35,732	¥104,946	¥68,024
WEICHOLD, RICHARD	28	23	$288	$3,008	$1,074
			DM446	DM4,510	DM1,721
			£184	£1,840	£666
			¥28,264	¥291,014	¥120,918
WEIDEMANN, R.	1	1	$696	$696	$696
			DM1,251	DM1,251	DM1,251
			£414	£414	£414
			¥80,411	¥80,411	¥80,411
WEIDHAAS, PAUL	5	2	$1,415	$1,682	$1,548
			DM2,081	DM2,846	DM2,464
			£920	£1,058	£989
			¥150,107	¥208,426	¥179,267
WEISCHOLD, R.	2	1	$495	$495	$495
			DM731	DM731	DM731
			£322	£322	£322
			¥52,722	¥52,722	¥52,722
WERNER, EMIL	1	0			
WERRO, JEAN	1	1	$1,198	$1,198	$1,198
			DM1,668	DM1,668	DM1,668
			£747	£747	£747
			¥101,254	¥101,254	¥101,254

Maker	Items		Selling Prices		
	Bid	Sold	Low	High	Avg
WERRO, JEAN (workshop of)	1	0			
WILSON, GARNER	15	13	$524	$1,967	$1,264
			DM887	DM3,326	DM1,954
			£352	£1,320	£806
			¥55,616	¥208,560	¥127,104
WILSON, J.J.	1	1	$761	$761	$761
			DM1,218	DM1,218	DM1,218
			£495	£495	£495
			¥77,034	¥77,034	¥77,034
WINKLER, F.	2	2	$205	$575	$390
			DM359	DM879	DM619
			£127	£378	£252
			¥24,788	¥60,605	¥42,696
WITHERS, EDWARD	2	2	$576	$726	$651
			DM882	DM1,022	DM952
			£368	£460	£414
			¥64,223	¥74,213	¥69,218
WITHERS, EDWARD & SONS	1	0			
WITHERS, GEORGE	3	2	$705	$811	$758
			DM1,040	DM1,197	DM1,119
			£460	£529	£495
			¥74,934	¥86,175	¥80,555
WITHERS, GEORGE & SONS	3	2	$773	$1,541	$1,157
			DM1,157	DM2,761	DM1,959
			£460	£920	£690
			¥86,241	¥178,940	¥132,590
WITHERS, GEORGE & SONS (workshop of)	1	1	$1,380	$1,380	$1,380
			DM1,993	DM1,993	DM1,993
			£879	£879	£879
			¥119,715	¥119,715	¥119,715
WUNDERLICH, F.R.	1	1	$451	$451	$451
			DM764	DM764	DM764
			£276	£276	£276
			¥52,301	¥52,301	¥52,301
WUNDERLICH, FRIEDRICH	6	6	$690	$2,228	$1,298
			DM1,181	DM3,365	DM2,003
			£408	£1,495	£829
			¥85,684	¥235,926	¥144,245
WUNDERLICH, GUSTAV	1	1	$748	$748	$748
			DM1,249	DM1,249	DM1,249
			£499	£499	£499
			¥78,345	¥78,345	¥78,345
WUNDERLICH, MAX (workshop of)	1	0			
YOUNG, DAVID RUSSELL	1	0			
ZABINSKI, ROGER ALFONS	2	2	$518	$546	$532
			DM921	DM972	DM947
			£311	£328	£319
			¥68,817	¥72,640	¥70,729
ZIMMERMANN, JULIUS HEINRICH	1	0			

VIOLINO D'AMORE

Maker	Items		Selling Prices		
BISIACH, LEANDRO	1	0			

VIOLONCELLO

Maker	Items		Selling Prices		
ALBANI, MICHAEL	1	0			
ALBERTI, FERDINANDO (attributed to)	1	0			

Maker	Items		Selling Prices		
	Bid	Sold	Low	High	Avg
ALDRIC, NICOLAS (ascribed to)	1	1	$2,726	$2,726	$2,726
			DM3,850	DM3,850	DM3,850
			£1,725	£1,725	£1,725
			¥243,289	¥243,289	¥243,289
ALLETSEE, PAULUS	1	1	$15,882	$15,882	$15,882
			DM24,400	DM24,400	DM24,400
			£10,350	£10,350	£10,350
			¥1,738,686	¥1,738,686	¥1,738,686
ANTONIAZZI, RICCARDO (attributed to)	1	0			
APPARUT, GEORGES (workshop of)	2	0			
ARCANGELI, ULDERICO	1	0			
ARDOLI, MASSIMO	1	0			
BACZYNSKI, LADISLAUS	1	0			
BAILEY, G.E.	1	0			
BAILLY, CHARLES	1	1	$6,914	$6,914	$6,914
			DM11,551	DM11,551	DM11,551
			£4,140	£4,140	£4,140
			¥840,379	¥840,379	¥840,379
BAILLY, PAUL	2	1	$31,370	$31,370	$31,370
			DM43,669	DM43,669	DM43,669
			£19,550	£19,550	£19,550
			¥2,646,601	¥2,646,601	¥2,646,601
BANDINI, MARIO	1	1	$6,738	$6,738	$6,738
			DM12,465	DM12,465	DM12,465
			£4,025	£4,025	£4,025
			¥897,937	¥897,937	¥897,937
BANKS, BENJAMIN	1	1	$35,650	$35,650	$35,650
			DM55,257	DM55,257	DM55,257
			£22,816	£22,816	£22,816
			¥3,504,751	¥3,504,751	¥3,504,751
BANKS, STEPHENSON (attributed to)	2	1	$1,738	$1,738	$1,738
			DM2,672	DM2,672	DM2,672
			£1,150	£1,150	£1,150
			¥185,409	¥185,409	¥185,409
BANKS, JAMES & HENRY	2	1	$7,305	$7,305	$7,305
			DM10,271	DM10,271	DM10,271
			£4,600	£4,600	£4,600
			¥651,958	¥651,958	¥651,958
BARKER	1	1	$1,217	$1,217	$1,217
			DM1,870	DM1,870	DM1,870
			£805	£805	£805
			¥129,786	¥129,786	¥129,786
BERNARDEL, AUGUST SEBASTIEN PHILIPPE	1	1	$61,289	$61,289	$61,289
			DM102,393	DM102,393	DM102,393
			£36,700	£36,700	£36,700
			¥7,449,733	¥7,449,733	¥7,449,733
BERNARDEL, GUSTAVE	5	1	$24,714	$24,714	$24,714
			DM37,924	DM37,924	DM37,924
			£16,100	£16,100	£16,100
			¥2,704,961	¥2,704,961	¥2,704,961
BERNARDEL, GUSTAVE ADOLPHE	1	0			
BERNARDEL, LEON	3	2	$15,576	$22,770	$19,173
			DM27,020	DM40,986	DM34,003
			£9,200	£13,800	£11,500
			¥1,974,412	¥3,283,710	¥2,629,061

Maker	Items		Selling Prices		
	Bid	Sold	Low	High	Avg
BERNARDEL, LEON (workshop of)	1	1	$10,350	$10,350	$10,350
			DM14,966	DM14,966	DM14,966
			£6,761	£6,761	£6,761
			¥1,047,938	¥1,047,938	¥1,047,938
BETTS	1	1	$34,983	$34,983	$34,983
			DM60,651	DM60,651	DM60,651
			£20,700	£20,700	£20,700
			¥4,367,700	¥4,367,700	¥4,367,700
BETTS, JOHN	2	0			
BETTS, ARTHUR & JOHN	1	1	$44,148	$44,148	$44,148
			DM70,665	DM70,665	DM70,665
			£28,750	£28,750	£28,750
			¥4,454,813	¥4,454,813	¥4,454,813
BINA, J.	2	1	$6,165	$6,165	$6,165
			DM9,088	DM9,088	DM9,088
			£4,025	£4,025	£4,025
			¥657,564	¥657,564	¥657,564
BISIACH (workshop of)	1	1	$37,950	$37,950	$37,950
			DM68,310	DM68,310	DM68,310
			£23,000	£23,000	£23,000
			¥5,472,850	¥5,472,850	¥5,472,850
BISIACH, GIACOMO & LEANDRO	2	1	$34,983	$34,983	$34,983
			DM60,651	DM60,651	DM60,651
			£20,700	£20,700	£20,700
			¥4,447,809	¥4,447,809	¥4,447,809
BLANCHI, ALBERTO	2	2	$18,890	$28,117	$23,504
			DM28,230	DM48,645	DM38,438
			£11,500	£17,250	£14,375
			¥1,817,310	¥3,208,500	¥2,512,905
BLONDELET, EMILE	1	1	$1,475	$1,475	$1,475
			DM2,495	DM2,495	DM2,495
			£990	£990	£990
			¥156,420	¥156,420	¥156,420
BOLINK, JAAP	1	1	$4,947	$4,947	$4,947
			DM7,309	DM7,309	DM7,309
			£3,220	£3,220	£3,220
			¥527,223	¥527,223	¥527,223
BONNETT, CHRIS	1	0			
BONORA, GIUSEPPE (ascribed to)	1	1	$10,925	$10,925	$10,925
			DM18,693	DM18,693	DM18,693
			£6,462	£6,462	£6,462
			¥1,356,667	¥1,356,667	¥1,356,667
BOULANGEOT, EMILE	1	0			
BOULLANGIER, CHARLES	1	0			
BRIGGS, JAMES WILLIAM	3	3	$15,674	$23,194	$18,432
			DM21,825	DM34,703	DM27,036
			£9,775	£13,800	£11,117
			¥1,324,982	¥2,587,224	¥1,914,941
BRIGGS, JAMES WILLIAM (attributed to)	1	0			
BRYANT, PAUL	1	1	$1,604	$1,604	$1,604
			DM2,380	DM2,380	DM2,380
			£1,035	£1,035	£1,035
			¥173,652	¥173,652	¥173,652
BUCHESTETTER, GABRIEL DAVID	1	1	$13,782	$13,782	$13,782
			DM20,362	DM20,362	DM20,362
			£8,970	£8,970	£8,970
			¥1,468,694	¥1,468,694	¥1,468,694

| Maker | Items | | Selling Prices | | |
	Bid	Sold	Low	High	Avg
BUTHOD, CHARLES LOUIS	5	5	$3,889	$21,202	$11,896
			DM5,742	DM31,326	DM17,401
			£2,530	£13,800	£7,590
			¥414,353	¥2,259,529	¥1,262,963
CALCAGNI, BERNARDO	1	1	$156,500	$156,500	$156,500
			DM284,204	DM284,204	DM284,204
			£95,778	£95,778	£95,778
			¥19,434,170	¥19,434,170	¥19,434,170
CARCASSI, TOMMASO	1	0			
CARCASSI, LORENZO & TOMMASO	1	1	$73,220	$73,220	$73,220
			DM112,357	DM112,357	DM112,357
			£47,700	£47,700	£47,700
			¥8,014,077	¥8,014,077	¥8,014,077
CARLETTI, NATALE	2	0			
CASTAGNERI, ANDREA	1	1	$9,724	$9,724	$9,724
			DM15,567	DM15,567	DM15,567
			£6,325	£6,325	£6,325
			¥984,322	¥984,322	¥984,322
CAUSSIN, FRANCOIS	1	1	$6,176	$6,176	$6,176
			DM9,489	DM9,489	DM9,489
			£4,025	£4,025	£4,025
			¥676,156	¥676,156	¥676,156
CERUTI, GIUSEPPE (ascribed to)	3	1	$16,203	$16,203	$16,203
			DM24,808	DM24,808	DM24,808
			£10,350	£10,350	£10,350
			¥1,806,282	¥1,806,282	¥1,806,282
CHANOT, GEORGES (II)	2	1	$56,775	$56,775	$56,775
			DM96,053	DM96,053	DM96,053
			£35,708	£35,708	£35,708
			¥7,034,378	¥7,034,378	¥7,034,378
CHANOT, JOSEPH ANTHONY	1	1	$17,874	$17,874	$17,874
			DM30,239	DM30,239	DM30,239
			£11,241	£11,241	£11,241
			¥2,214,526	¥2,214,526	¥2,214,526
CHAROTTE, VICTOR JOSEPH	1	1	$3,457	$3,457	$3,457
			DM5,775	DM5,775	DM5,775
			£2,070	£2,070	£2,070
			¥420,189	¥420,189	¥420,189
CHAROTTE-MILLOT, JOSEPH	1	1	$6,854	$6,854	$6,854
			DM10,355	DM10,355	DM10,355
			£4,600	£4,600	£4,600
			¥725,926	¥725,926	¥725,926
CHRISTA, JOSEPH PAULUS	1	0			
COCKER, LAWRENCE	1	1	$5,659	$5,659	$5,659
			DM8,325	DM8,325	DM8,325
			£3,680	£3,680	£3,680
			¥600,429	¥600,429	¥600,429
COLAS, PROSPER	1	1	$12,563	$12,563	$12,563
			DM18,797	DM18,797	DM18,797
			£7,475	£7,475	£7,475
			¥1,401,413	¥1,401,413	¥1,401,413
COLIN, JEAN BAPTISTE	1	1	$7,072	$7,072	$7,072
			DM11,322	DM11,322	DM11,322
			£4,600	£4,600	£4,600
			¥715,870	¥715,870	¥715,870

Maker	Items		Selling Prices		
	Bid	Sold	Low	High	Avg
COLLIN-MEZIN, CH.J.B.	10	8	$6,325	$30,905	$18,080
			DM9,993	DM51,690	DM28,240
			£4,048	£20,700	£11,704
			¥631,868	¥3,284,448	¥1,902,615
COLLIN-MEZIN, CH.J.B. (workshop of)	1	1	$4,888	$4,888	$4,888
			DM8,363	DM8,363	DM8,363
			£2,891	£2,891	£2,891
			¥606,930	¥606,930	¥606,930
COLLIN-MEZIN, CH.J.B. (FILS) (attributed to)	1	1	$7,316	$7,316	$7,316
			DM10,384	DM10,384	DM10,384
			£4,600	£4,600	£4,600
			¥679,190	¥679,190	¥679,190
COLLIN-MEZIN, CH.J.B. (III)	2	1	$2,305	$2,305	$2,305
			DM3,850	DM3,850	DM3,850
			£1,380	£1,380	£1,380
			¥280,126	¥280,126	¥280,126
COLLINS, DAVID	1	1	$2,300	$2,300	$2,300
			DM3,843	DM3,843	DM3,843
			£1,535	£1,535	£1,535
			¥241,063	¥241,063	¥241,063
CONIA, STEFANO	1	1	$16,740	$16,740	$16,740
			DM24,711	DM24,711	DM24,711
			£10,925	£10,925	£10,925
			¥1,779,693	¥1,779,693	¥1,779,693
CONTAL, F.	1	1	$2,742	$2,742	$2,742
			DM4,142	DM4,142	DM4,142
			£1,840	£1,840	£1,840
			¥290,370	¥290,370	¥290,370
CRASKE, GEORGE	7	4	$6,895	$17,087	$13,026
			DM9,711	DM26,056	DM19,797
			£4,370	£10,925	£8,136
			¥705,021	¥1,734,988	¥1,332,922
CUISSET, A.	3	0			
CULLIER, MARTIN	1	0			
CUNAULT, GEORGES	1	1	$21,216	$21,216	$21,216
			DM33,965	DM33,965	DM33,965
			£13,800	£13,800	£13,800
			¥2,147,611	¥2,147,611	¥2,147,611
CURLETTO, ANSELMO	2	1	$11,385	$11,385	$11,385
			DM17,181	DM17,181	DM17,181
			£6,900	£6,900	£6,900
			¥1,290,300	¥1,290,300	¥1,290,300
DARCHE, HILAIRE	3	1	$13,605	$13,605	$13,605
			DM23,587	DM23,587	DM23,587
			£8,050	£8,050	£8,050
			¥1,729,704	¥1,729,704	¥1,729,704
DEARLOVE, MARK WILLIAM	1	1	$9,853	$9,853	$9,853
			DM17,718	DM17,718	DM17,718
			£5,865	£5,865	£5,865
			¥1,139,159	¥1,139,159	¥1,139,159
DE COMBLE, AMBROISE	3	1	$3,532	$3,532	$3,532
			DM4,855	DM4,855	DM4,855
			£2,185	£2,185	£2,185
			¥294,079	¥294,079	¥294,079
DECONET, MICHAEL	1	0			
DECONET, MICHAEL (ascribed to)	1	0			

Maker	Items		Selling Prices		
	Bid	Sold	Low	High	Avg
DEGANI, EUGENIO	3	2	$32,200	$59,700	$45,950
			DM55,658	DM89,849	DM72,753
			£19,896	£36,241	£28,069
			¥4,080,867	¥6,673,266	¥5,377,067
DERAZEY, HONORE	1	1	$36,992	$36,992	$36,992
			DM64,173	DM64,173	DM64,173
			£21,850	£21,850	£21,850
			¥4,689,229	¥4,689,229	¥4,689,229
DERAZEY, HONORE (workshop of)	1	1	$4,025	$4,025	$4,025
			DM6,239	DM6,239	DM6,239
			£2,576	£2,576	£2,576
			¥395,698	¥395,698	¥395,698
DERAZEY, JUSTIN	1	0			
DIEUDONNE, AMEDEE	1	0			
DODD, THOMAS	8	3	$17,001	$34,776	$26,076
			DM25,407	DM62,535	DM43,244
			£10,350	£20,700	£15,993
			¥1,635,579	¥4,020,561	¥2,766,165
DOLLENZ, GIOVANNI	2	0			
DOLLENZ, GIUSEPPE	1	0			
DOLLING, HERMANN (JR.)	1	1	$2,846	$2,846	$2,846
			DM5,123	DM5,123	DM5,123
			£1,725	£1,725	£1,725
			¥410,464	¥410,464	¥410,464
DUKE, RICHARD (attributed to)	1	1	$16,376	$16,376	$16,376
			DM24,611	DM24,611	DM24,611
			£9,775	£9,775	£9,775
			¥1,823,634	¥1,823,634	¥1,823,634
EDLER, HANS	1	1	$8,910	$8,910	$8,910
			DM13,461	DM13,461	DM13,461
			£5,980	£5,980	£5,980
			¥943,704	¥943,704	¥943,704
EMDE, J.F.C.	1	1	$1,945	$1,945	$1,945
			DM2,862	DM2,862	DM2,862
			£1,265	£1,265	£1,265
			¥206,397	¥206,397	¥206,397
EMERY, JEAN	1	1	$6,574	$6,574	$6,574
			DM9,244	DM9,244	DM9,244
			£4,140	£4,140	£4,140
			¥586,762	¥586,762	¥586,762
EMERY, JULIAN	1	1	$5,796	$5,796	$5,796
			DM9,660	DM9,660	DM9,660
			£3,450	£3,450	£3,450
			¥692,726	¥692,726	¥692,726
ENZENSPERGER, BERNARD (II)	1	1	$7,315	$7,315	$7,315
			DM13,534	DM13,534	DM13,534
			£4,370	£4,370	£4,370
			¥974,903	¥974,903	¥974,903
EVANS & SON	1	1	$1,025	$1,025	$1,025
			DM1,637	DM1,637	DM1,637
			£666	£666	£666
			¥103,568	¥103,568	¥103,568
FANTIN, DOMENICO	1	0			
FARINA, ERMINIO	2	2	$18,564	$32,649	$25,606
			DM29,719	DM54,545	DM42,132
			£12,075	£19,550	£15,813
			¥1,879,160	¥3,968,455	¥2,923,807

| Maker | Items | | Selling Prices | | |
	Bid	Sold	Low	High	Avg
FAROTTI, CELESTE	1	1	$68,500	$68,500	$68,500
			DM121,930	DM121,930	DM121,930
			£41,100	£41,100	£41,100
			¥9,109,130	¥9,109,130	¥9,109,130
FAROTTO, CELESTE	1	1	$12,590	$12,590	$12,590
			DM17,809	DM17,809	DM17,809
			£8,050	£8,050	£8,050
			¥1,278,412	¥1,278,412	¥1,278,412
FENDT, BERNARD SIMON	1	1	$31,706	$31,706	$31,706
			DM46,741	DM46,741	DM46,741
			£20,700	£20,700	£20,700
			¥3,381,759	¥3,381,759	¥3,381,759
FORSTER, SIMON ANDREW	1	1	$38,410	$38,410	$38,410
			DM64,170	DM64,170	DM64,170
			£23,000	£23,000	£23,000
			¥4,668,770	¥4,668,770	¥4,668,770
FORSTER, WILLIAM	10	7	$18,029	$46,202	$33,671
			DM30,492	DM85,477	DM55,156
			£12,100	£29,440	£21,090
			¥1,911,800	¥6,157,284	¥3,836,556
FORSTER, WILLIAM (II)	2	2	$17,395	$30,728	$24,062
			DM26,027	DM51,336	DM38,682
			£10,350	£18,400	£14,375
			¥1,940,418	¥3,735,016	¥2,837,717
FRANCAIS, LUCIEN (attributed to)	1	1	$4,816	$4,816	$4,816
			DM8,628	DM8,628	DM8,628
			£2,875	£2,875	£2,875
			¥559,188	¥559,188	¥559,188
FRANKS, RAY	1	1	$4,194	$4,194	$4,194
			DM4,418	DM4,418	DM4,418
			£2,588	£2,588	£2,588
			¥320,320	¥320,320	¥320,320
FUCHS, WENZEL	1	1	$2,990	$2,990	$2,990
			DM5,322	DM5,322	DM5,322
			£1,794	£1,794	£1,794
			¥397,610	¥397,610	¥397,610
FURBER (FAMILY OF)	1	0			
GABOR, ANRISAK TIBOR	1	1	$3,448	$3,448	$3,448
			DM4,855	DM4,855	DM4,855
			£2,185	£2,185	£2,185
			¥352,510	¥352,510	¥352,510
GABRIELLI, GIOVANNI BATTISTA	2	1	$115,187	$115,187	$115,187
			DM162,213	DM162,213	DM162,213
			£73,000	£73,000	£73,000
			¥11,777,236	¥11,777,236	¥11,777,236
GAGLIANO, ALESSANDRO	1	1	$125,723	$125,723	$125,723
			DM176,305	DM176,305	DM176,305
			£80,700	£80,700	£80,700
			¥12,702,422	¥12,702,422	¥12,702,422
GAGLIANO, JOSEPH	1	0			
GAGLIANO, RAFFAELE & ANTONIO (II)	2	2	$74,924	$115,968	$95,446
			DM132,759	DM173,514	DM153,137
			£46,006	£69,000	£57,503
			¥9,135,428	¥12,936,120	¥11,035,774
GAGLIANO FAMILY (MEMBER OF)	1	0			

Maker	Items		Selling Prices		
	Bid	Sold	Low	High	Avg
GAND, CHARLES	1	1	$56,397	$56,397	$56,397
			DM84,559	DM84,559	DM84,559
			£34,500	£34,500	£34,500
			¥5,456,520	¥5,456,520	¥5,456,520
GAND BROS.	3	0			
GARINI	2	2	$1,025	$1,259	$1,142
			DM1,781	DM1,795	DM1,788
			£633	£805	£719
			¥123,938	¥127,841	¥125,890
GATTI, ERNESTO	1	1	$13,609	$13,609	$13,609
			DM19,166	DM19,166	DM19,166
			£8,625	£8,625	£8,625
			¥1,391,489	¥1,391,489	¥1,391,489
GIANOTTI, ALFREDO (attributed to)	1	1	$3,082	$3,082	$3,082
			DM5,522	DM5,522	DM5,522
			£1,840	£1,840	£1,840
			¥357,880	¥357,880	¥357,880
GILBERT, JEFFREY J.	3	2	$4,228	$7,342	$5,785
			DM6,768	DM13,202	DM9,985
			£2,750	£4,370	£3,560
			¥427,966	¥848,785	¥638,376
GILBERT, JEFFREY JAMES	1	0			
GLOOR, ADOLF	4	2	$1,028	$2,504	$1,766
			DM1,792	DM4,486	DM3,139
			£633	£1,495	£1,064
			¥124,508	¥290,778	¥207,643
GOATER, MICHAEL	1	0			
GODDARD, CHARLES (attributed to)	1	1	$784	$784	$784
			DM1,164	DM1,164	DM1,164
			£506	£506	£506
			¥84,897	¥84,897	¥84,897
GOTZ, C.A.	1	1	$1,230	$1,230	$1,230
			DM1,296	DM1,296	DM1,296
			£759	£759	£759
			¥93,960	¥93,960	¥93,960
GOTZ, CONRAD	1	0			
GOULDING & CO.	2	2	$4,830	$14,801	$9,815
			DM8,685	DM26,641	DM17,663
			£2,875	£8,970	£5,923
			¥558,411	¥2,134,412	¥1,346,411
GRANCINO, FRANCESCO & GIOVANNI (ascribed to)	1	1	$4,025	$4,025	$4,025
			DM6,887	DM6,887	DM6,887
			£2,381	£2,381	£2,381
			¥499,825	¥499,825	¥499,825
GRANCINO, GIOVANNI	6	2	$60,881	$307,280	$184,081
			DM97,464	DM513,360	DM305,412
			£39,600	£184,000	£111,800
			¥6,162,710	¥37,350,160	¥21,756,435
GRANDJON, J. (attributed to)	1	1	$10,601	$10,601	$10,601
			DM15,663	DM15,663	DM15,663
			£6,900	£6,900	£6,900
			¥1,129,765	¥1,129,765	¥1,129,765
GRULLI, PIETRO	1	1	$27,553	$27,553	$27,553
			DM46,330	DM46,330	DM46,330
			£17,250	£17,250	£17,250
			¥3,382,087	¥3,382,087	¥3,382,087

| Maker | Items | | Selling Prices | | |
	Bid	Sold	Low	High	Avg
GUADAGNINI, FRANCESCO	1	0			
GUADAGNINI, GIOVANNI BATTISTA	1	1	$259,390	$259,390	$259,390
			DM363,753	DM363,753	DM363,753
			£166,500	£166,500	£166,500
			¥26,207,600	¥26,207,600	¥26,207,600
GUERRA, ALBERTO	2	1	$16,100	$16,100	$16,100
			DM23,248	DM23,248	DM23,248
			£10,257	£10,257	£10,257
			¥1,396,675	¥1,396,675	¥1,396,675
GUERSAN, LOUIS	3	2	$2,277	$12,851	$7,564
			DM3,436	DM19,415	DM11,426
			£1,380	£8,625	£5,003
			¥258,060	¥1,361,111	¥809,586
GUINOT, CHARLES	1	1	$5,640	$5,640	$5,640
			DM8,456	DM8,456	DM8,456
			£3,450	£3,450	£3,450
			¥545,652	¥545,652	¥545,652
HAIDE, JAY	1	0			
HAMMIG, JOHANN CHRISTIAN	1	1	$2,147	$2,147	$2,147
			DM3,283	DM3,283	DM3,283
			£1,380	£1,380	£1,380
			¥212,222	¥212,222	¥212,222
HAMMIG, W.H.	1	0			
HARDIE, MATTHEW	3	3	$3,278	$18,354	$12,439
			DM5,544	DM30,590	DM19,323
			£2,200	£10,925	£7,633
			¥347,600	¥2,193,631	¥1,288,177
HARRIS, CHARLES	3	3	$4,228	$13,216	$8,391
			DM5,916	DM19,509	DM13,106
			£2,645	£8,625	£5,290
			¥357,638	¥1,405,021	¥885,373
HAUSMANN, OTTOMAR	1	1	$3,910	$3,910	$3,910
			DM6,758	DM6,758	DM6,758
			£2,416	£2,416	£2,416
			¥495,534	¥495,534	¥495,534
HEBERLEIN, HEINRICH TH. (JR.) (workshop of)	1	1	$2,185	$2,185	$2,185
			DM3,651	DM3,651	DM3,651
			£1,458	£1,458	£1,458
			¥229,010	¥229,010	¥229,010
HEBERLEIN, LUDWIG	1	1	$4,759	$4,759	$4,759
			DM7,554	DM7,554	DM7,554
			£3,105	£3,105	£3,105
			¥481,225	¥481,225	¥481,225
HEELEY, JOHN LINACRE (attributed to)	1	1	$2,927	$2,927	$2,927
			DM4,154	DM4,154	DM4,154
			£1,840	£1,840	£1,840
			¥271,676	¥271,676	¥271,676
HEL, JOSEPH	1	1	$67,012	$67,012	$67,012
			DM100,708	DM100,708	DM100,708
			£40,000	£40,000	£40,000
			¥7,462,440	¥7,462,440	¥7,462,440
HEL, PIERRE JOSEPH	1	1	$11,474	$11,474	$11,474
			DM17,607	DM17,607	DM17,607
			£7,475	£7,475	£7,475
			¥1,255,875	¥1,255,875	¥1,255,875

Maker	Items		Selling Prices		
	Bid	Sold	Low	High	Avg
HELMER, JOANES GEORGIUS (ascribed to)	1	1	$2,497 DM4,171 £1,495 ¥303,470	$2,497 DM4,171 £1,495 ¥303,470	$2,497 DM4,171 £1,495 ¥303,470
HERRMANN, KARL (workshop of)	1	1	$1,610 DM2,423 £977 ¥179,966	$1,610 DM2,423 £977 ¥179,966	$1,610 DM2,423 £977 ¥179,966
HILL, HENRY LOCKEY	2	1	$19,668 DM33,264 £13,200 ¥2,085,600	$19,668 DM33,264 £13,200 ¥2,085,600	$19,668 DM33,264 £13,200 ¥2,085,600
HILL, JOSEPH	9	7	$10,350 DM16,042 £6,624 ¥1,017,508	$45,336 DM67,752 £27,600 ¥4,361,545	$26,686 DM42,346 £16,521 ¥2,803,669
HILL, JOSEPH (ascribed to)	1	1	$6,641 DM11,954 £4,025 ¥957,749	$6,641 DM11,954 £4,025 ¥957,749	$6,641 DM11,954 £4,025 ¥957,749
HILL, LOCKEY	6	4	$6,002 DM9,210 £3,910 ¥656,919	$25,266 DM43,804 £14,950 ¥3,154,450	$11,710 DM20,014 £7,135 ¥1,414,797
HILL FAMILY (MEMBER OF)	1	1	$2,823 DM4,338 £1,840 ¥309,100	$2,823 DM4,338 £1,840 ¥309,100	$2,823 DM4,338 £1,840 ¥309,100
HOFNER, KARL	1	0			
HORNSTEINER	1	1	$3,961 DM7,206 £2,415 ¥500,243	$3,961 DM7,206 £2,415 ¥500,243	$3,961 DM7,206 £2,415 ¥500,243
HORNSTEINER, JOSEPH (attributed to)	1	1	$13,449 DM20,846 £8,050 ¥1,531,996	$13,449 DM20,846 £8,050 ¥1,531,996	$13,449 DM20,846 £8,050 ¥1,531,996
HUSSON & BUTHOD	1	1	$1,270 DM1,789 £805 ¥129,872	$1,270 DM1,789 £805 ¥129,872	$1,270 DM1,789 £805 ¥129,872
JONES, EDWARD B. (attributed to)	1	1	$2,721 DM4,717 £1,610 ¥339,710	$2,721 DM4,717 £1,610 ¥339,710	$2,721 DM4,717 £1,610 ¥339,710
KENNEDY, THOMAS	15	10	$13,490 DM19,081 £8,625 ¥1,362,983	$46,092 DM77,004 £27,600 ¥5,602,524	$25,504 DM39,745 £16,055 ¥2,753,371
KENNEDY, THOMAS (ascribed to)	1	0			
KENNEDY, THOMAS (attributed to)	2	2	$2,742 DM4,637 £1,840 ¥290,720	$5,630 DM10,040 £3,450 ¥737,024	$4,186 DM7,338 £2,645 ¥513,872
KLIER, OTTO JOSEPH	1	1	$1,518 DM2,291 £920 ¥172,040	$1,518 DM2,291 £920 ¥172,040	$1,518 DM2,291 £920 ¥172,040

Maker	Items		Selling Prices		
	Bid	Sold	Low	High	Avg
KLOTZ, AEGIDIUS (I)	1	1	$3,465	$3,465	$3,465
			DM6,411	DM6,411	DM6,411
			£2,070	£2,070	£2,070
			¥461,796	¥461,796	¥461,796
KLOTZ, SEBASTIAN (II) (attributed to)	1	0			
KLOTZ FAMILY (MEMBER OF)	1	0			
KOBERLING, JOHANN	1	0			
LABERTE, MARC (attributed to)	2	1	$6,167	$6,167	$6,167
			DM10,751	DM10,751	DM10,751
			£3,795	£3,795	£3,795
			¥747,046	¥747,046	¥747,046
LABERTE-HUMBERT BROS.	2	1	$9,673	$9,673	$9,673
			DM16,365	DM16,365	DM16,365
			£6,084	£6,084	£6,084
			¥1,198,450	¥1,198,450	¥1,198,450
LAMBERT, JEAN NICOLAS	1	1	$18,330	$18,330	$18,330
			DM29,399	DM29,399	DM29,399
			£11,903	£11,903	£11,903
			¥2,085,556	¥2,085,556	¥2,085,556
LANG, BENEDIKT	3	2	$1,826	$2,138	$1,982
			DM2,568	DM3,706	DM3,137
			£1,150	£1,265	£1,208
			¥162,349	¥266,915	¥214,632
LANG, RUDOLF	1	1	$2,827	$2,827	$2,827
			DM4,177	DM4,177	DM4,177
			£1,840	£1,840	£1,840
			¥301,271	¥301,271	¥301,271
LECAVELLE, FRANCOIS	1	1	$5,377	$5,377	$5,377
			DM8,984	DM8,984	DM8,984
			£3,220	£3,220	£3,220
			¥653,628	¥653,628	¥653,628
LEE, PERCY	1	1	$6,580	$6,580	$6,580
			DM9,865	DM9,865	DM9,865
			£4,025	£4,025	£4,025
			¥636,594	¥636,594	¥636,594
LE LIEVRE, PIERRE	2	1	$9,718	$9,718	$9,718
			DM14,358	DM14,358	DM14,358
			£6,325	£6,325	£6,325
			¥1,035,618	¥1,035,618	¥1,035,618
LONGMAN & BRODERIP	4	3	$752	$6,219	$4,348
			DM1,242	DM10,930	DM7,651
			£460	£3,680	£2,607
			¥93,117	¥875,656	¥581,751
LONGMAN, LUKEY & CO.	2	0			
LOTT, JOHN FREDERICK (attributed to)	1	0			
LOWENDALL	1	1	$5,475	$5,475	$5,475
			DM10,236	DM10,236	DM10,236
			£3,450	£3,450	£3,450
			¥647,945	¥647,945	¥647,945
LOWENDALL, L.	1	1	$4,637	$4,637	$4,637
			DM8,338	DM8,338	DM8,338
			£2,760	£2,760	£2,760
			¥536,075	¥536,075	¥536,075
LOWENDALL, LOUIS	1	1	$1,540	$1,540	$1,540
			DM2,849	DM2,849	DM2,849
			£920	£920	£920
			¥205,243	¥205,243	¥205,243

Maker	Items		Selling Prices		
	Bid	Sold	Low	High	Avg
MANGENOT WORKSHOP	1	0			
MARCHETTI, ENRICO (attributed to)	1	0			
MARTIN, E. (Workshop of)	1	1	$1,955	$1,955	$1,955
			DM3,379	DM3,379	DM3,379
			£1,208	£1,208	£1,208
			¥247,767	¥247,767	¥247,767
MAYNARD, BRIAN	1	0			
MAYSON, WALTER H.	1	1	$8,692	$8,692	$8,692
			DM13,358	DM13,358	DM13,358
			£5,750	£5,750	£5,750
			¥927,044	¥927,044	¥927,044
MEINEL, OSKAR	1	1	$2,875	$2,875	$2,875
			DM5,118	DM5,118	DM5,118
			£1,725	£1,725	£1,725
			¥382,317	¥382,317	¥382,317
MEINEL, PAUL	1	1	$15,523	$15,523	$15,523
			DM21,826	DM21,826	DM21,826
			£9,775	£9,775	£9,775
			¥1,379,966	¥1,379,966	¥1,379,966
MEISEL, JOHANN GEORG	1	1	$3,587	$3,587	$3,587
			DM5,066	DM5,066	DM5,066
			£2,277	£2,277	£2,277
			¥361,207	¥361,207	¥361,207
MELEGARI, ENRICO CLODOVEO	1	1	$47,945	$47,945	$47,945
			DM66,758	DM66,758	DM66,758
			£29,900	£29,900	£29,900
			¥4,052,885	¥4,052,885	¥4,052,885
MERIOTTE, CHARLES (attributed to)	1	1	$1,607	$1,607	$1,607
			DM2,260	DM2,260	DM2,260
			£1,012	£1,012	£1,012
			¥143,431	¥143,431	¥143,431
MERLING, PAULI	1	1	$10,310	$10,310	$10,310
			DM17,837	DM17,837	DM17,837
			£6,325	£6,325	£6,325
			¥1,176,450	¥1,176,450	¥1,176,450
MESSORI, PIETRO	3	1	$3,018	$3,018	$3,018
			DM5,491	DM5,491	DM5,491
			£1,840	£1,840	£1,840
			¥381,138	¥381,138	¥381,138
METHFESSEL, GUSTAV	1	1	$11,500	$11,500	$11,500
			DM16,606	DM16,606	DM16,606
			£7,327	£7,327	£7,327
			¥997,625	¥997,625	¥997,625
METHFESSEL, GUSTAV (attributed to)	1	0			
MILNES, JOHN	2	2	$2,616	$3,018	$2,817
			DM4,283	DM4,561	DM4,422
			£1,610	£1,898	£1,754
			¥280,166	¥316,929	¥298,547
MORASSI, GIOVANNI BATTISTA	3	3	$16,436	$23,005	$20,156
			DM23,109	DM42,614	DM33,766
			£10,350	£13,800	£12,458
			¥1,466,906	¥3,072,294	¥2,381,508
MORASSI, GIOVANNI BATTISTA (attributed to)	1	0			
MORRISON, JOHN	1	0			

Maker	Items		Selling Prices		
	Bid	Sold	Low	High	Avg
MOUGENOT, LEON	4	3	$7,414	$11,202	$9,847
			DM11,377	DM17,966	DM15,047
			£4,830	£7,274	£6,413
			¥811,488	¥1,274,506	¥1,064,050
MUELLER, KARL (workshop of)	1	1	$748	$748	$748
			DM1,081	DM1,081	DM1,081
			£488	£488	£488
			¥75,684	¥75,684	¥75,684
MULLER, KARL	1	1	$3,941	$3,941	$3,941
			DM5,527	DM5,527	DM5,527
			£2,530	£2,530	£2,530
			¥398,230	¥398,230	¥398,230
NEUNER & HORNSTEINER	7	5	$759	$9,179	$3,945
			DM1,348	DM14,086	DM6,415
			£460	£5,980	£2,484
			¥105,289	¥1,004,700	¥462,308
NILSSON, GOTTFRIED	1	1	$6,940	$6,940	$6,940
			DM9,757	DM9,757	DM9,757
			£4,370	£4,370	£4,370
			¥619,360	¥619,360	¥619,360
NORMAN, BARAK	8	3	$3,018	$24,398	$10,681
			DM5,491	DM43,505	DM18,941
			£1,840	£14,950	£6,567
			¥381,138	¥3,193,769	¥1,382,693
NURNBERGER, ALBERT	1	1	$1,265	$1,265	$1,265
			DM2,164	DM2,164	DM2,164
			£748	£748	£748
			¥157,088	¥157,088	¥157,088
ODDY, DAVID	1	1	$2,997	$2,997	$2,997
			DM4,756	DM4,756	DM4,756
			£1,955	£1,955	£1,955
			¥302,994	¥302,994	¥302,994
OTTO, C.W.F. (attributed to)	1	1	$3,310	$3,310	$3,310
			DM5,742	DM5,742	DM5,742
			£1,955	£1,955	£1,955
			¥419,563	¥419,563	¥419,563
OWEN, JOHN W.	3	1	$9,364	$9,364	$9,364
			DM13,836	DM13,836	DM13,836
			£6,095	£6,095	£6,095
			¥997,959	¥997,959	¥997,959
PACHERELE, PIERRE	1	0			
PADDAY, A.L.	1	0			
PADEWET, JOHANN II	2	1	$4,276	$4,276	$4,276
			DM7,413	DM7,413	DM7,413
			£2,530	£2,530	£2,530
			¥533,830	¥533,830	¥533,830
PANORMO, VINCENZO	2	0			
PANORMO, VINCENZO (attributed to)	1	1	$7,668	$7,668	$7,668
			DM14,205	DM14,205	DM14,205
			£4,600	£4,600	£4,600
			¥1,024,098	¥1,024,098	¥1,024,098
PARESCHI, GAETANO	1	1	$16,871	$16,871	$16,871
			DM29,187	DM29,187	DM29,187
			£10,350	£10,350	£10,350
			¥1,925,100	¥1,925,100	¥1,925,100

Maker	Items		Selling Prices		
	Bid	Sold	Low	High	Avg
PARMEGGIANI, ROMOLA	1	1	$26,432	$26,432	$26,432
			DM39,018	DM39,018	DM39,018
			£17,250	£17,250	£17,250
			¥2,810,042	¥2,810,042	¥2,810,042
PAROCHE, LEON	1	1	$1,502	$1,502	$1,502
			DM2,405	DM2,405	DM2,405
			£977	£977	£977
			¥152,045	¥152,045	¥152,045
PARRAMON, RAMON	1	0			
PEDRAZZINI, GIUSEPPE	3	3	$37,598	$62,978	$54,011
			DM56,373	DM102,672	DM84,003
			£23,000	£41,100	£33,633
			¥3,637,680	¥7,470,032	¥5,934,314
PEDRAZZINI, GIUSEPPE (attributed to)	2	0			
PELLIZON FAMILY (MEMBER OF)	2	0			
PETERNELLA, JAGO	1	0			
PFRETZSCHNER (workshop of)	2	2	$575	$1,380	$978
			DM972	DM2,332	DM1,652
			£345	£828	£587
			¥70,150	¥168,360	¥119,255
PFRETZSCHNER, C.G.	1	1	$2,645	$2,645	$2,645
			DM3,825	DM3,825	DM3,825
			£1,728	£1,728	£1,728
			¥267,806	¥267,806	¥267,806
PIATTELLINI, A.	1	1	$57,615	$57,615	$57,615
			DM96,255	DM96,255	DM96,255
			£34,500	£34,500	£34,500
			¥7,003,155	¥7,003,155	¥7,003,155
PICCAGLIANI (workshop of)	1	0			
PICCAGLIANI, ARMANDO	1	1	$15,447	$15,447	$15,447
			DM21,819	DM21,819	DM21,819
			£9,775	£9,775	£9,775
			¥1,378,637	¥1,378,637	¥1,378,637
PICKARD, H.	1	1	$4,325	$4,325	$4,325
			DM7,143	DM7,143	DM7,143
			£2,645	£2,645	£2,645
			¥535,425	¥535,425	¥535,425
PIERRAY, CLAUDE (attributed to)	1	0			
POGGI, ANSALDO	1	1	$79,850	$79,850	$79,850
			DM147,727	DM147,727	DM147,727
			£47,700	£47,700	£47,700
			¥10,641,393	¥10,641,393	¥10,641,393
POGGI, ANSALDO (attributed to)	1	1	$17,336	$17,336	$17,336
			DM31,060	DM31,060	DM31,060
			£10,350	£10,350	£10,350
			¥2,013,075	¥2,013,075	¥2,013,075
POLITI, ENRICO	1	1	$22,984	$22,984	$22,984
			DM36,795	DM36,795	DM36,795
			£14,950	£14,950	£14,950
			¥2,326,579	¥2,326,579	¥2,326,579
POLLASTRI, CESARE FEDERICO	1	0			
POSCH, ANTON	2	0			
POSTIGLIONE, VINCENZO	2	0			
POT, JOHANNES	1	1	$5,304	$5,304	$5,304
			DM8,491	DM8,491	DM8,491
			£3,450	£3,450	£3,450
			¥536,903	¥536,903	¥536,903

Maker	Items		Selling Prices		
	Bid	Sold	Low	High	Avg
PRESSENDA, GIOVANNI FRANCESCO	1	1	$343,170	$343,170	$343,170
			DM634,885	DM634,885	DM634,885
			£205,000	£205,000	£205,000
			¥45,733,450	¥45,733,450	¥45,733,450
PRESTON	2	2	$3,044	$4,917	$3,981
			DM4,873	DM8,316	DM6,595
			£1,980	£3,300	£2,640
			¥308,136	¥521,400	¥414,768
PRESTON, JAMES	1	0			
PRESTON, JOHN	1	0			
PRINCE, W.B.	1	1	$5,775	$5,775	$5,775
			DM10,685	DM10,685	DM10,685
			£3,450	£3,450	£3,450
			¥769,661	¥769,661	¥769,661
PROKOP, LADISLAV	1	1	$4,313	$4,313	$4,313
			DM6,236	DM6,236	DM6,236
			£2,817	£2,817	£2,817
			¥436,641	¥436,641	¥436,641
REGAZZONI, DANTE PAOLO	1	1	$3,850	$3,850	$3,850
			DM7,123	DM7,123	DM7,123
			£2,300	£2,300	£2,300
			¥513,107	¥513,107	¥513,107
RENAUDIN, LEOPOLD	3	2	$12,357	$14,517	$13,437
			DM18,962	DM20,443	DM19,703
			£8,050	£9,200	£8,625
			¥1,352,481	¥1,484,254	¥1,418,367
RICHARDSON, ARTHUR	1	0			
RIECHERS, AUGUST (attributed to)	2	1	$3,259	$3,259	$3,259
			DM6,037	DM6,037	DM6,037
			£1,955	£1,955	£1,955
			¥435,242	¥435,242	¥435,242
RIVOLTA, GIACOMO (attributed to)	1	1	$49,933	$49,933	$49,933
			DM83,421	DM83,421	DM83,421
			£29,900	£29,900	£29,900
			¥6,069,401	¥6,069,401	¥6,069,401
ROADWATER, HORROBIN	1	1	$1,638	$1,638	$1,638
			DM2,342	DM2,342	DM2,342
			£1,035	£1,035	£1,035
			¥164,551	¥164,551	¥164,551
ROBINSON, WILLIAM	1	0			
ROCCA, ENRICO	1	1	$160,564	$160,564	$160,564
			DM239,957	DM239,957	DM239,957
			£97,750	£97,750	£97,750
			¥15,447,139	¥15,447,139	¥15,447,139
ROCCA, GIUSEPPE	1	1	$344,104	$344,104	$344,104
			DM515,935	DM515,935	DM515,935
			£210,500	£210,500	£210,500
			¥33,292,680	¥33,292,680	¥33,292,680
ROSSI, GIOVANNI	1	1	$33,922	$33,922	$33,922
			DM60,108	DM60,108	DM60,108
			£20,829	£20,829	£20,829
			¥4,136,119	¥4,136,119	¥4,136,119
ROTH, ERNST HEINRICH	1	1	$6,146	$6,146	$6,146
			DM10,267	DM10,267	DM10,267
			£3,680	£3,680	£3,680
			¥747,003	¥747,003	¥747,003
ROUGIER, MAURICE	2	0			

Maker	Items		Selling Prices		
	Bid	Sold	Low	High	Avg
RUBIO, DAVID	1	0			
RUGGERI, FRANCESCO	3	2	$83,481	$193,281	$138,381
			DM133,643	DM289,191	DM211,417
			£54,300	£115,000	£84,650
			¥8,450,383	¥21,560,200	¥15,005,292
RUNNACLES, HARRY E.	4	3	$1,890	$2,130	$2,047
			DM2,919	DM3,133	DM3,039
			£1,190	£1,380	£1,317
			¥188,539	¥225,953	¥210,264
RUSHWORTH & DREAPER	1	1	$3,572	$3,572	$3,572
			DM5,355	DM5,355	DM5,355
			£2,185	£2,185	£2,185
			¥345,580	¥345,580	¥345,580
SACQUIN, CLAUDE	1	1	$21,202	$21,202	$21,202
			DM31,326	DM31,326	DM31,326
			£13,800	£13,800	£13,800
			¥2,259,529	¥2,259,529	¥2,259,529
SALSEDO, LUIGI	1	1	$7,590	$7,590	$7,590
			DM11,454	DM11,454	DM11,454
			£4,600	£4,600	£4,600
			¥860,200	¥860,200	¥860,200
SANDNER, ANTON	1	1	$4,588	$4,588	$4,588
			DM7,049	DM7,049	DM7,049
			£2,990	£2,990	£2,990
			¥502,287	¥502,287	¥502,287
SANNINO, VINCENZO	1	1	$31,227	$31,227	$31,227
			DM52,507	DM52,507	DM52,507
			£19,550	£19,550	£19,550
			¥3,833,032	¥3,833,032	¥3,833,032
SANTAGIULIANA, GAETANO	1	0			
SCARAMPELLA, STEFANO	1	0			
SCARAMPELLA, STEFANO (ascribed to)	1	0			
SCHUSTER, JOSEF	2	1	$1,739	$1,739	$1,739
			DM3,126	DM3,126	DM3,126
			£1,035	£1,035	£1,035
			¥201,028	¥201,028	¥201,028
SCHWARZ BROS.	1	1	$10,514	$10,514	$10,514
			DM18,239	DM18,239	DM18,239
			£6,210	£6,210	£6,210
			¥1,332,728	¥1,332,728	¥1,332,728
SCIORILLI, LUIGI	1	1	$2,113	$2,113	$2,113
			DM3,529	DM3,529	DM3,529
			£1,265	£1,265	£1,265
			¥256,782	¥256,782	¥256,782
SILVESTRE, HIPPOLYTE CHRETIEN	2	1	$36,800	$36,800	$36,800
			DM65,504	DM65,504	DM65,504
			£22,080	£22,080	£22,080
			¥4,893,664	¥4,893,664	¥4,893,664
SMILLIE, ALEXANDER	2	1	$3,093	$3,093	$3,093
			DM5,395	DM5,395	DM5,395
			£1,840	£1,840	£1,840
			¥394,422	¥394,422	¥394,422
SMITH, ARTHUR E.	1	1	$18,529	$18,529	$18,529
			DM28,467	DM28,467	DM28,467
			£12,075	£12,075	£12,075
			¥2,028,467	¥2,028,467	¥2,028,467

| Maker | Items | | Selling Prices | | |
---	Bid	Sold	Low	High	Avg
SMITH, THOMAS	10	6	$2,555 DM4,777 £1,610 ¥302,374	$16,764 DM25,756 £10,925 ¥1,835,280	$8,394 DM12,946 £5,371 ¥860,524
SMITH, THOMAS (attributed to)	2	1	$2,632 DM4,348 £1,610 ¥325,911	$2,632 DM4,348 £1,610 ¥325,911	$2,632 DM4,348 £1,610 ¥325,911
SMITH, WILLIAM	1	1	$1,874 DM3,243 £1,150 ¥213,900	$1,874 DM3,243 £1,150 ¥213,900	$1,874 DM3,243 £1,150 ¥213,900
SMITH, WILLIAM EDWARD	1	1	$2,277 DM3,436 £1,380 ¥258,060	$2,277 DM3,436 £1,380 ¥258,060	$2,277 DM3,436 £1,380 ¥258,060
SPIEGEL, JANOS	1	1	$10,080 DM14,127 £6,325 ¥888,568	$10,080 DM14,127 £6,325 ¥888,568	$10,080 DM14,127 £6,325 ¥888,568
STEWART, C.G.	1	0			
STOSS, JOHANN MARTIN	2	1	$9,664 DM14,460 £5,750 ¥1,078,010	$9,664 DM14,460 £5,750 ¥1,078,010	$9,664 DM14,460 £5,750 ¥1,078,010
TARASCONI, CAROL	1	0			
TECCHLER, DAVID	1	0			
TECCHLER, DAVID (attributed to)	1	0			
TESTORE, CARLO ANTONIO	1	0			
TESTORE, CARLO ANTONIO (attributed to)	1	1	$66,993 DM115,902 £41,100 ¥7,644,600	$66,993 DM115,902 £41,100 ¥7,644,600	$66,993 DM115,902 £41,100 ¥7,644,600
TESTORE, CARLO GIUSEPPE	1	1	$158,650 DM294,500 £95,000 ¥21,226,800	$158,650 DM294,500 £95,000 ¥21,226,800	$158,650 DM294,500 £95,000 ¥21,226,800
THIBOUT, JACQUES PIERRE	1	1	$19,384 DM28,613 £12,650 ¥2,060,698	$19,384 DM28,613 £12,650 ¥2,060,698	$19,384 DM28,613 £12,650 ¥2,060,698
THIBOUVILLE-LAMY, J.	32	26	$585 DM831 £368 ¥54,335	$6,402 DM10,808 £4,025 ¥789,765	$2,479 DM3,892 £1,553 ¥264,972
THIBOUVILLE-LAMY, J. (attributed to)	1	1	$4,907 DM6,931 £3,105 ¥437,920	$4,907 DM6,931 £3,105 ¥437,920	$4,907 DM6,931 £3,105 ¥437,920
THIBOUVILLE-LAMY, J. (workshop of)	1	1	$575 DM1,024 £345 ¥76,464	$575 DM1,024 £345 ¥76,464	$575 DM1,024 £345 ¥76,464
THIERRY (attributed to)	1	0			

Maker	Items Bid	Sold	Selling Prices Low	High	Avg
THIR, MATHIAS (attributed to)	1	1	$1,939 DM3,077 £1,265 ¥196,055	$1,939 DM3,077 £1,265 ¥196,055	$1,939 DM3,077 £1,265 ¥196,055
THOMA, MATHIAS (workshop of)	1	1	$575 DM984 £340 ¥71,404	$575 DM984 £340 ¥71,404	$575 DM984 £340 ¥71,404
THOMPSON, ALFRED	1	0			
THOMPSON, ROBERT (attributed to)	1	1	$2,971 DM5,504 £1,783 ¥396,838	$2,971 DM5,504 £1,783 ¥396,838	$2,971 DM5,504 £1,783 ¥396,838
TOMAS, OTIS A.	1	1	$1,610 DM2,783 £995 ¥204,043	$1,610 DM2,783 £995 ¥204,043	$1,610 DM2,783 £995 ¥204,043
TRAPP, HERMANN	2	1	$2,610 DM4,569 £1,610 ¥315,480	$2,610 DM4,569 £1,610 ¥315,480	$2,610 DM4,569 £1,610 ¥315,480
UCHIYAMA, MASAYUKI	2	0			
UEBEL, ERHARD	1	1	$8,050 DM11,640 £5,258 ¥815,063	$8,050 DM11,640 £5,258 ¥815,063	$8,050 DM11,640 £5,258 ¥815,063
VALENCE (attributed to)	1	1	$10,530 DM17,391 £6,440 ¥1,303,643	$10,530 DM17,391 £6,440 ¥1,303,643	$10,530 DM17,391 £6,440 ¥1,303,643
VAN DER MEER, KAREL	1	1	$8,500 DM12,704 £5,175 ¥817,790	$8,500 DM12,704 £5,175 ¥817,790	$8,500 DM12,704 £5,175 ¥817,790
VAN HOOF, ALPHONS	1	1	$11,454 DM16,908 £7,475 ¥1,217,685	$11,454 DM16,908 £7,475 ¥1,217,685	$11,454 DM16,908 £7,475 ¥1,217,685
VENTAPANE, LORENZO	2	2	$85,514 DM148,258 £50,600 ¥10,676,600	$87,458 DM151,628 £51,750 ¥10,919,250	$86,486 DM149,943 £51,175 ¥10,797,925
VENTAPANE, LORENZO (attributed to)	1	0			
VERHASSELT, F.	1	1	$8,746 DM15,163 £5,175 ¥1,091,925	$8,746 DM15,163 £5,175 ¥1,091,925	$8,746 DM15,163 £5,175 ¥1,091,925
VERINI, ANDREA	1	1	$5,467 DM9,250 £3,439 ¥677,385	$5,467 DM9,250 £3,439 ¥677,385	$5,467 DM9,250 £3,439 ¥677,385
VETTORI, CARLO	1	0			
VICKERS, J.E.	1	0			
VILLA, LUIGI	1	0			
VOIGT, E.R. & SON	1	1	$3,947 DM6,684 £2,415 ¥457,633	$3,947 DM6,684 £2,415 ¥457,633	$3,947 DM6,684 £2,415 ¥457,633

Maker	Items		Selling Prices		
	Bid	Sold	Low	High	Avg
VUILLAUME, JEAN BAPTISTE	7	6	$68,634	$131,120	$106,511
			DM126,977	DM221,760	DM168,082
			£41,000	£88,000	£66,756
			¥9,146,690	¥13,904,000	¥11,582,967
VUILLAUME, JEAN BAPTISTE (workshop of)	1	1	$39,982	$39,982	$39,982
			DM56,472	DM56,472	DM56,472
			£25,300	£25,300	£25,300
			¥3,568,236	¥3,568,236	¥3,568,236
VUILLAUME, NICOLAS FRANCOIS	1	1	$65,388	$65,388	$65,388
			DM98,040	DM98,040	DM98,040
			£40,000	£40,000	£40,000
			¥6,326,400	¥6,326,400	¥6,326,400
WAMSLEY, PETER	6	3	$2,118	$9,373	$5,469
			DM3,251	DM16,215	DM9,261
			£1,380	£5,750	£3,477
			¥231,854	¥1,069,500	¥607,585
WEIGERT, JOHANN BLASIUS	2	0			
WERNER, ERICH	6	1	$2,687	$2,687	$2,687
			DM3,769	DM3,769	DM3,769
			£1,725	£1,725	£1,725
			¥271,520	¥271,520	¥271,520
WERNER, FRANZ EMANUEL	1	1	$7,064	$7,064	$7,064
			DM11,306	DM11,306	DM11,306
			£4,600	£4,600	£4,600
			¥712,770	¥712,770	¥712,770
WHITAKER, MAURICE	1	1	$11,560	$11,560	$11,560
			DM17,372	DM17,372	DM17,372
			£6,900	£6,900	£6,900
			¥1,287,271	¥1,287,271	¥1,287,271
WHITMARSH, EDWIN (attributed to)	1	1	$3,673	$3,673	$3,673
			DM5,636	DM5,636	DM5,636
			£2,300	£2,300	£2,300
			¥360,056	¥360,056	¥360,056
WHITMARSH, EMANUEL	2	1	$3,286	$3,286	$3,286
			DM4,916	DM4,916	DM4,916
			£1,955	£1,955	£1,955
			¥366,523	¥366,523	¥366,523
WITHERS, EDWARD	1	1	$11,645	$11,645	$11,645
			DM16,331	DM16,331	DM16,331
			£7,475	£7,475	£7,475
			¥1,176,587	¥1,176,587	¥1,176,587
WITHERS, GEORGE & SONS	1	1	$2,444	$2,444	$2,444
			DM3,664	DM3,664	DM3,664
			£1,495	£1,495	£1,495
			¥236,449	¥236,449	¥236,449
WOLFF BROS.	4	3	$2,571	$5,025	$3,782
			DM3,945	DM7,519	DM5,983
			£1,610	£2,990	£2,300
			¥252,039	¥560,565	¥413,468
WOODWARD, CECIL F.	1	1	$1,365	$1,365	$1,365
			DM2,108	DM2,108	DM2,108
			£860	£860	£860
			¥136,167	¥136,167	¥136,167
ZAHARIC, MARK	1	1	$1,995	$1,995	$1,995
			DM3,081	DM3,081	DM3,081
			£1,256	£1,256	£1,256
			¥199,014	¥199,014	¥199,014

| Maker | Items | | Selling Prices | | |
	Bid	Sold	Low	High	Avg
ZANOLI, GIACOMO	1	1	$67,815	$67,815	$67,815
			DM102,339	DM102,339	DM102,339
			£41,100	£41,100	£41,100
			¥7,685,700	¥7,685,700	¥7,685,700
ZANOLI, JOANNES BAPTISTA (ascribed to)	1	1	$26,979	$26,979	$26,979
			DM38,162	DM38,162	DM38,162
			£17,250	£17,250	£17,250
			¥2,739,455	¥2,739,455	¥2,739,455
ZAPOLSKI, ALEX	1	1	$1,093	$1,093	$1,093
			DM1,693	DM1,693	DM1,693
			£699	£699	£699
			¥107,404	¥107,404	¥107,404
ZIMMERMANN, JULIUS HEINRICH	1	1	$972	$972	$972
			DM1,685	DM1,685	DM1,685
			£575	£575	£575
			¥121,325	¥121,325	¥121,325

VIOLONCELLO BOW

| Maker | Items | | Selling Prices | | |
	Bid	Sold	Low	High	Avg
ACOULON, ALFRED	1	0			
ADAM, JEAN DOMINIQUE	1	1	$2,950	$2,950	$2,950
			DM4,108	DM4,108	DM4,108
			£1,840	£1,840	£1,840
			¥249,408	¥249,408	¥249,408
ADAM, JEAN DOMINIQUE (attributed to)	1	0			
ADAM FAMILY (MEMBER OF)	1	0			
ALVEY, BRIAN	3	1	$274	$274	$274
			DM441	DM441	DM441
			£161	£161	£161
			¥33,845	¥33,845	¥33,845
BAILEY, G.E.	3	2	$743	$773	$758
			DM1,197	DM1,349	DM1,273
			£437	£460	£449
			¥91,866	¥98,606	¥95,236
BARBE, AUGUSTE	2	1	$5,826	$5,826	$5,826
			DM9,853	DM9,853	DM9,853
			£3,910	£3,910	£3,910
			¥617,780	¥617,780	¥617,780
BAUSCH	5	3	$56	$460	$272
			DM94	DM676	DM404
			£35	£299	£176
			¥6,826	¥48,785	¥29,170
BAUSCH, L.	1	1	$1,380	$1,380	$1,380
			DM2,361	DM2,361	DM2,361
			£816	£816	£816
			¥171,368	¥171,368	¥171,368
BAZIN	3	3	$1,610	$3,936	$3,004
			DM2,755	DM6,810	DM5,325
			£952	£2,415	£1,812
			¥199,930	¥461,796	¥370,305
BAZIN (attributed to)	1	0			
BAZIN (workshop of)	1	1	$1,765	$1,765	$1,765
			DM2,711	DM2,711	DM2,711
			£1,150	£1,150	£1,150
			¥193,187	¥193,187	¥193,187

Maker	Items Bid	Sold	Selling Prices Low	High	Avg
BAZIN, CHARLES	4	3	$2,544	$3,401	$2,896
			DM3,594	DM5,897	DM4,709
			£1,610	£2,013	£1,821
			¥227,070	¥424,638	¥314,142
BAZIN, CHARLES NICHOLAS	11	8	$570	$4,404	$2,405
			DM920	DM7,059	DM3,758
			£331	£2,875	£1,487
			¥67,160	¥513,565	¥274,168
BAZIN, LOUIS	4	2	$1,062	$3,364	$2,213
			DM1,909	DM5,692	DM3,800
			£632	£2,116	£1,374
			¥122,753	¥416,852	¥269,803
BAZIN, LOUIS (workshop of)	2	1	$768	$768	$768
			DM1,270	DM1,270	DM1,270
			£460	£460	£460
			¥89,838	¥89,838	¥89,838
BEARE, JOHN & ARTHUR	4	3	$849	$3,055	$1,791
			DM1,544	DM4,900	DM2,900
			£518	£1,984	£1,140
			¥107,195	¥347,593	¥199,603
BEARE & SON	1	1	$1,155	$1,155	$1,155
			DM2,137	DM2,137	DM2,137
			£690	£690	£690
			¥153,932	¥153,932	¥153,932
BECHINI, RENZO	1	0			
BEILKE, MARTIN O.	1	1	$1,398	$1,398	$1,398
			DM1,473	DM1,473	DM1,473
			£863	£863	£863
			¥106,773	¥106,773	¥106,773
BERNARDEL, GUSTAVE	2	2	$1,462	$2,875	$2,169
			DM2,601	DM5,221	DM3,911
			£897	£1,760	£1,328
			¥196,380	¥357,018	¥276,699
BERNARDEL, GUSTAVE ADOLPHE	2	1	$637	$637	$637
			DM1,103	DM1,103	DM1,103
			£391	£391	£391
			¥72,726	¥72,726	¥72,726
BERNARDEL, LEON	4	2	$428	$1,733	$1,080
			DM690	DM3,205	DM1,948
			£248	£1,035	£642
			¥50,370	¥230,898	¥140,634
BETTS	1	1	$1,028	$1,028	$1,028
			DM1,553	DM1,553	DM1,553
			£690	£690	£690
			¥108,889	¥108,889	¥108,889
BOURGUIGNON, MAURICE	1	1	$2,118	$2,118	$2,118
			DM3,918	DM3,918	DM3,918
			£1,265	£1,265	£1,265
			¥282,209	¥282,209	¥282,209
BOUVIN, JEAN	2	2	$1,035	$2,415	$1,725
			DM1,495	DM3,743	DM2,619
			£659	£1,546	£1,102
			¥89,786	¥237,419	¥163,602
BRISTOW, S.E.	1	1	$411	$411	$411
			DM717	DM717	DM717
			£253	£253	£253
			¥49,803	¥49,803	¥49,803

Maker	Items		Selling Prices		
	Bid	Sold	Low	High	Avg
BRYANT, PERCIVAL WILFRED	3	3	$1,540	$1,792	$1,675
			DM2,512	DM2,849	DM2,633
			£920	£1,150	£1,035
			¥163,696	¥205,243	¥183,317
BULTITUDE, ARTHUR RICHARD	15	11	$705	$4,832	$2,477
			DM1,039	DM7,230	DM3,932
			£460	£2,875	£1,579
			¥75,150	¥539,005	¥261,235
BUTHOD	2	1	$87	$87	$87
			DM134	DM134	DM134
			£58	£58	£58
			¥9,270	¥9,270	¥9,270
BUTHOD, CHARLES LOUIS	2	2	$1,633	$1,892	$1,763
			DM2,300	DM3,202	DM2,751
			£1,035	£1,190	£1,113
			¥166,979	¥234,479	¥200,729
BUTHOD, CHARLES LOUIS (workshop of)	1	1	$1,380	$1,380	$1,380
			DM2,110	DM2,110	DM2,110
			£908	£908	£908
			¥145,452	¥145,452	¥145,452
BYROM, GEORGE	1	1	$970	$970	$970
			DM1,489	DM1,489	DM1,489
			£632	£632	£632
			¥106,182	¥106,182	¥106,182
BYROM, H.	1	0			
CARESSA, ALBERT	1	1	$1,152	$1,152	$1,152
			DM1,925	DM1,925	DM1,925
			£690	£690	£690
			¥140,063	¥140,063	¥140,063
CHANOT & CHARDON	1	0			
CHERPITEL, MOINEL	1	0			
CLUTTERBUCK, JOHN	1	1	$1,106	$1,106	$1,106
			DM1,541	DM1,541	DM1,541
			£690	£690	£690
			¥93,528	¥93,528	¥93,528
COCKER, L.	2	2	$348	$463	$406
			DM534	DM688	DM611
			£230	£299	£265
			¥37,082	¥50,166	¥43,624
COCKER, LAWRENCE	2	2	$494	$1,149	$821
			DM783	DM1,691	DM1,237
			£322	£748	£535
			¥49,905	¥121,962	¥85,933
COLAS, PROSPER	6	3	$1,402	$2,319	$1,836
			DM2,432	DM3,470	DM2,975
			£828	£1,380	£1,111
			¥177,697	¥258,722	¥219,253
COLLIN-MEZIN (Workshop of)	1	1	$3,450	$3,450	$3,450
			DM5,963	DM5,963	DM5,963
			£2,132	£2,132	£2,132
			¥437,236	¥437,236	¥437,236
COLLIN-MEZIN, CH.J.B.	1	0			
COLLINS, ROY	2	2	$442	$529	$485
			DM653	DM839	DM746
			£288	£345	£316
			¥47,074	¥53,469	¥50,272

Maker	Items		Selling Prices		
	Bid	Sold	Low	High	Avg
CUNIOT-HURY	5	2	$1,271	$3,105	$2,188
			DM2,278	DM4,365	DM3,321
			£759	£1,955	£1,357
			¥147,626	¥275,993	¥211,809
CUNIOT-HURY, EUGENE	1	0			
DABERT, J.F.	1	1	$1,953	$1,953	$1,953
			DM2,810	DM2,810	DM2,810
			£1,265	£1,265	£1,265
			¥198,276	¥198,276	¥198,276
DARCHE, HILAIRE	1	1	$1,938	$1,938	$1,938
			DM2,861	DM2,861	DM2,861
			£1,265	£1,265	£1,265
			¥206,070	¥206,070	¥206,070
DARTE, AUGUSTE (workshop of)	1	1	$2,990	$2,990	$2,990
			DM4,500	DM4,500	DM4,500
			£1,815	£1,815	£1,815
			¥334,222	¥334,222	¥334,222
DAVIS	1	1	$2,497	$2,497	$2,497
			DM4,635	DM4,635	DM4,635
			£1,495	£1,495	£1,495
			¥334,043	¥334,043	¥334,043
DODD	11	9	$1,031	$7,700	$4,539
			DM1,526	DM14,246	DM7,654
			£633	£4,600	£2,766
			¥109,578	¥1,026,214	¥545,175
DODD FAMILY	1	1	$777	$777	$777
			DM1,348	DM1,348	DM1,348
			£460	£460	£460
			¥97,060	¥97,060	¥97,060
DODD FAMILY (MEMBER OF)	2	2	$857	$2,913	$1,885
			DM1,294	DM4,401	DM2,848
			£575	£1,955	£1,265
			¥90,741	¥308,519	¥199,630
DODD, EDWARD	1	0			
DODD, J.	1	1	$2,823	$2,823	$2,823
			DM4,338	DM4,338	DM4,338
			£1,840	£1,840	£1,840
			¥309,100	¥309,100	¥309,100
DODD, JAMES	2	1	$4,355	$4,355	$4,355
			DM6,133	DM6,133	DM6,133
			£2,760	£2,760	£2,760
			¥445,276	¥445,276	¥445,276
DODD, JOHN	9	9	$1,590	$7,064	$3,369
			DM2,349	DM11,306	DM5,433
			£977	£4,600	£2,123
			¥169,465	¥793,563	¥382,063
DODD, JOHN (attributed to)	3	1	$2,424	$2,424	$2,424
			DM3,810	DM3,810	DM3,810
			£1,553	£1,553	£1,553
			¥243,167	¥243,167	¥243,167
DOLLING, HEINZ	2	2	$1,055	$1,221	$1,138
			DM1,620	DM1,831	DM1,726
			£690	£747	£719
			¥115,187	¥118,146	¥116,666
DUPREE, EMILE	1	1	$1,495	$1,495	$1,495
			DM2,159	DM2,159	DM2,159
			£952	£952	£952
			¥129,691	¥129,691	¥129,691

Violoncello Bow

| Maker | Items | | Selling Prices | | |
	Bid	Sold	Low	High	Avg
DUPUY, GEORGE	1	1	$1,612 DM2,902 £977 ¥232,477	$1,612 DM2,902 £977 ¥232,477	$1,612 DM2,902 £977 ¥232,477
DURRSCHMIDT, OTTO	1	1	$251 DM395 £161 ¥25,217	$251 DM395 £161 ¥25,217	$251 DM395 £161 ¥25,217
DURRSCHMIDT, OTTO (workshop of)	1	1	$633 DM952 £384 ¥70,701	$633 DM952 £384 ¥70,701	$633 DM952 £384 ¥70,701
EURY, NICOLAS	1	0			
FETIQUE, VICTOR	12	10	$1,555 DM2,696 £920 ¥194,120	$8,066 DM13,476 £4,830 ¥980,442	$4,296 DM6,726 £2,651 ¥484,455
FINKEL, JOHANN S.	3	2	$1,352 DM2,431 £805 ¥156,355	$1,944 DM2,872 £1,265 ¥207,124	$1,648 DM2,651 £1,035 ¥181,739
FINKEL, JOHANNES S.	2	0			
FINKEL, SIEGFRIED	2	2	$972 DM1,685 £575 ¥121,325	$1,433 DM2,010 £920 ¥144,811	$1,203 DM1,847 £748 ¥133,068
FORSTER	1	1	$3,887 DM5,743 £2,530 ¥414,247	$3,887 DM5,743 £2,530 ¥414,247	$3,887 DM5,743 £2,530 ¥414,247
FORSTER, WILLIAM	1	1	$2,399 DM3,624 £1,610 ¥254,074	$2,399 DM3,624 £1,610 ¥254,074	$2,399 DM3,624 £1,610 ¥254,074
FORSTER, WILLIAM (III)	1	0			
FRANCAIS, EMILE	2	2	$1,502 DM2,778 £897 ¥200,112	$4,146 DM7,346 £2,546 ¥505,526	$2,824 DM5,062 £1,721 ¥352,819
FRITSCH, JEAN	1	1	$1,840 DM3,148 £1,088 ¥228,491	$1,840 DM3,148 £1,088 ¥228,491	$1,840 DM3,148 £1,088 ¥228,491
GAND BROS.	1	1	$2,496 DM4,025 £1,449 ¥293,825	$2,496 DM4,025 £1,449 ¥293,825	$2,496 DM4,025 £1,449 ¥293,825
GAND & BERNARDEL	4	3	$1,676 DM2,572 £1,092 ¥171,468	$3,529 DM5,422 £2,300 ¥386,375	$2,411 DM3,606 £1,552 ¥247,103
GEROME, ROGER	2	2	$1,561 DM2,625 £978 ¥191,652	$1,725 DM2,915 £1,035 ¥210,450	$1,643 DM2,770 £1,006 ¥201,051

Maker	Items		Selling Prices		
	Bid	Sold	Low	High	Avg
GILLET, LOUIS	4	3	$862	$5,762	$2,821
			DM1,492	DM9,626	DM4,731
			£529	£3,450	£1,736
			¥98,394	¥700,316	¥330,520
GOTZ	1	0			
GOTZ, CONRAD	1	1	$424	$424	$424
			DM624	DM624	DM624
			£276	£276	£276
			¥45,032	¥45,032	¥45,032
GRAND ADAM (attributed to)	1	0			
GRANDCHAMP, ERIC	1	1	$1,540	$1,540	$1,540
			DM2,849	DM2,849	DM2,849
			£920	£920	£920
			¥205,243	¥205,243	¥205,243
GRANIER, ANDRE	1	1	$3,220	$3,220	$3,220
			DM4,656	DM4,656	DM4,656
			£2,103	£2,103	£2,103
			¥326,025	¥326,025	¥326,025
GRANIER, DENIS	1	1	$1,238	$1,238	$1,238
			DM1,981	DM1,981	DM1,981
			£805	£805	£805
			¥125,277	¥125,277	¥125,277
GRUNKE	1	0			
GRUNKE, RICHARD	1	1	$1,591	$1,591	$1,591
			DM2,547	DM2,547	DM2,547
			£1,035	£1,035	£1,035
			¥161,071	¥161,071	¥161,071
HAMMIG, W.H.	1	1	$869	$869	$869
			DM1,300	DM1,300	DM1,300
			£517	£517	£517
			¥96,927	¥96,927	¥96,927
HART	1	1	$2,041	$2,041	$2,041
			DM3,538	DM3,538	DM3,538
			£1,208	£1,208	£1,208
			¥254,783	¥254,783	¥254,783
HART & SON	2	2	$526	$1,149	$837
			DM937	DM1,806	DM1,372
			£322	£736	£529
			¥68,789	¥115,279	¥92,034
HAWKES & SON	1	1	$1,068	$1,068	$1,068
			DM1,852	DM1,852	DM1,852
			£632	£632	£632
			¥135,798	¥135,798	¥135,798
HEBERLIN, FRIEDRICH	1	1	$1,412	$1,412	$1,412
			DM2,169	DM2,169	DM2,169
			£920	£920	£920
			¥154,550	¥154,550	¥154,550
HEL, PIERRE JOSEPH (workshop of)	1	1	$1,093	$1,093	$1,093
			DM1,644	DM1,644	DM1,644
			£663	£663	£663
			¥122,120	¥122,120	¥122,120
HENRY (attributed to)	2	1	$7,064	$7,064	$7,064
			DM11,306	DM11,306	DM11,306
			£4,600	£4,600	£4,600
			¥712,770	¥712,770	¥712,770

Maker	Items		Selling Prices		
	Bid	Sold	Low	High	Avg
HENRY, JOSEPH	2	2	$3,713	$9,436	$6,574
			DM5,944	DM13,288	DM9,616
			£2,415	£5,980	£4,198
			¥375,832	¥964,765	¥670,299
HERRMANN, EDWIN OTTO	2	2	$883	$1,938	$1,410
			DM1,354	DM2,861	DM2,108
			£575	£1,265	£920
			¥96,606	¥206,070	¥151,338
HERRMANN, EMIL	1	1	$1,725	$1,725	$1,725
			DM2,494	DM2,494	DM2,494
			£1,127	£1,127	£1,127
			¥174,656	¥174,656	¥174,656
HERRMANN, PAUL	1	1	$773	$773	$773
			DM1,390	DM1,390	DM1,390
			£460	£460	£460
			¥89,346	¥89,346	¥89,346
HILAIRE, PAUL	1	0			
HILL	4	2	$336	$1,191	$764
			DM494	DM1,670	DM1,082
			£219	£748	£483
			¥35,650	¥105,013	¥70,331
HILL, W.E. & SONS	96	81	$168	$5,479	$2,226
			DM293	DM9,260	DM3,498
			£104	£3,450	£1,395
			¥20,374	¥667,039	¥241,714
HURY, CUNIOT	1	0			
HUSSON, CHARLES CLAUDE	3	2	$3,534	$7,475	$5,504
			DM5,221	DM11,810	DM8,516
			£2,300	£4,784	£3,542
			¥376,588	¥746,752	¥561,670
JOMBAR, PAUL	1	1	$192	$192	$192
			DM321	DM321	DM321
			£115	£115	£115
			¥23,344	¥23,344	¥23,344
KITTEL, NICOLAUS (ascribed to)	1	1	$1,714	$1,714	$1,714
			DM2,898	DM2,898	DM2,898
			£1,150	£1,150	£1,150
			¥181,700	¥181,700	¥181,700
KNOPF, HEINRICH	1	1	$1,597	$1,597	$1,597
			DM2,395	DM2,395	DM2,395
			£977	£977	£977
			¥154,522	¥154,522	¥154,522
KOLSTEIN, SAMUEL	1	1	$1,380	$1,380	$1,380
			DM2,110	DM2,110	DM2,110
			£908	£908	£908
			¥145,452	¥145,452	¥145,452
LABERTE, MARC	1	1	$1,234	$1,234	$1,234
			DM1,821	DM1,821	DM1,821
			£805	£805	£805
			¥131,135	¥131,135	¥131,135
LAFLEUR, JACQUES RENE	1	1	$22,770	$22,770	$22,770
			DM34,362	DM34,362	DM34,362
			£13,800	£13,800	£13,800
			¥2,580,600	¥2,580,600	¥2,580,600
LAMY, A.	7	3	$3,044	$4,776	$3,836
			DM4,873	DM8,031	DM6,013
			£1,980	£2,990	£2,423
			¥308,136	¥586,228	¥402,041

Maker	Items		Selling Prices		
	Bid	Sold	Low	High	Avg
LAMY, ALFRED	17	13	$1,725	$10,925	$4,932
			DM2,674	DM17,262	DM7,757
			£1,104	£6,992	£3,163
			¥169,585	¥1,091,408	¥519,176
LAMY, ALFRED JOSEPH	9	7	$2,497	$9,603	$5,937
			DM4,171	DM16,043	DM10,025
			£1,495	£5,750	£3,598
			¥303,470	¥1,167,193	¥717,822
LAMY, JULES	2	0			
LAPIERRE, MARCEL	1	0			
LAPIERRE, MARCEL (attributed to)	1	1	$2,889	$2,889	$2,889
			DM5,177	DM5,177	DM5,177
			£1,725	£1,725	£1,725
			¥335,513	¥335,513	¥335,513
LEE, JOHN NORWOOD	4	2	$1,265	$3,427	$2,346
			DM2,187	DM5,796	DM3,991
			£782	£2,300	£1,541
			¥160,320	¥363,400	¥261,860
LEWIS, WILLIAM & SON	2	2	$611	$1,096	$853
			DM980	DM1,541	DM1,260
			£397	£690	£543
			¥69,519	¥97,409	¥83,464
LOTTE, FRANCOIS	4	3	$428	$809	$587
			DM690	DM1,496	DM1,031
			£248	£483	£351
			¥50,370	¥107,752	¥72,671
LOTTE, ROGER-FRANCOIS	3	2	$2,689	$2,695	$2,692
			DM4,986	DM4,991	DM4,989
			£1,610	£1,610	£1,610
			¥359,175	¥359,738	¥359,457
MAIRE, NICOLAS	4	2	$2,899	$4,776	$3,837
			DM4,094	DM8,031	DM6,062
			£1,840	£2,990	£2,415
			¥291,885	¥586,228	¥439,057
MAIRE, NICOLAS (ascribed to)	1	1	$6,900	$6,900	$6,900
			DM9,977	DM9,977	DM9,977
			£4,507	£4,507	£4,507
			¥698,625	¥698,625	¥698,625
MALINE, GUILLAUME	1	0			
MARTIN, J.	1	0			
MARTIN, JEAN JOSEPH	2	1	$673	$673	$673
			DM1,245	DM1,245	DM1,245
			£402	£402	£402
			¥89,682	¥89,682	¥89,682
METTAL, WALTER	3	2	$96	$1,005	$550
			DM172	DM1,504	DM838
			£57	£598	£328
			¥11,071	¥112,113	¥61,592
MILLANT, MAX	1	0			
MILLANT, R. & M.	1	1	$3,084	$3,084	$3,084
			DM5,216	DM5,216	DM5,216
			£2,070	£2,070	£2,070
			¥327,060	¥327,060	¥327,060
MOINEL & CHERPITEL	4	2	$712	$1,540	$1,126
			DM1,232	DM2,849	DM2,041
			£437	£920	£679
			¥81,282	¥205,243	¥143,262

Maker	Items		Selling Prices		
	Bid	Sold	Low	High	Avg
MORIZOT, LOUIS	3	2	$576 DM1,070 £345 ¥77,087	$1,344 DM2,496 £805 ¥179,869	$960 DM1,783 £575 ¥128,478
MORIZOT, LOUIS (II)	2	2	$1,328 DM2,004 £805 ¥150,535	$2,648 DM4,063 £1,725 ¥289,817	$1,988 DM3,034 £1,265 ¥220,176
MORIZOT (FRERES), LOUIS	1	0			
MORIZOT FAMILY	1	1	$1,380 DM2,332 £828 ¥168,360	$1,380 DM2,332 £828 ¥168,360	$1,380 DM2,332 £828 ¥168,360
NEUDORFER, RUDOLPH	2	1	$342 DM607 £207 ¥47,380	$342 DM607 £207 ¥47,380	$342 DM607 £207 ¥47,380
NEUVEVILLE, R.C.	1	1	$1,316 DM1,973 £805 ¥127,319	$1,316 DM1,973 £805 ¥127,319	$1,316 DM1,973 £805 ¥127,319
NEUVILLE	1	0			
NICOLAS, FRANCOIS	1	0			
NORRIS, JOHN	1	0			
NURNBERGER, ALBERT	11	6	$604 DM903 £368 ¥58,154	$2,881 DM4,813 £1,725 ¥350,158	$1,685 DM2,621 £1,027 ¥183,260
NURNBERGER, CHRISTIAN ALBERT	1	1	$1,218 DM2,107 £747 ¥138,942	$1,218 DM2,107 £747 ¥138,942	$1,218 DM2,107 £747 ¥138,942
NURNBERGER, KARL ALBERT	5	4	$1,360 DM1,915 £862 ¥137,793	$2,068 DM3,101 £1,265 ¥200,072	$1,650 DM2,487 £1,049 ¥162,367
OUCHARD, E.	1	1	$3,523 DM5,193 £2,300 ¥375,751	$3,523 DM5,193 £2,300 ¥375,751	$3,523 DM5,193 £2,300 ¥375,751
OUCHARD, EMILE	4	4	$2,300 DM3,935 £1,360 ¥285,614	$5,750 DM8,854 £3,491 ¥642,735	$4,241 DM6,960 £2,531 ¥508,776
OUCHARD, EMILE (FILS)	1	1	$3,220 DM5,381 £2,149 ¥337,488	$3,220 DM5,381 £2,149 ¥337,488	$3,220 DM5,381 £2,149 ¥337,488
OUCHARD, EMILE (FILS) (attributed to)	2	1	$6,569 DM10,948 £3,910 ¥785,089	$6,569 DM10,948 £3,910 ¥785,089	$6,569 DM10,948 £3,910 ¥785,089
OUCHARD, EMILE A.	4	4	$1,542 DM2,171 £977 ¥157,621	$10,925 DM16,442 £6,632 ¥1,221,197	$5,951 DM8,973 £3,714 ¥657,695

Maker	Items		Selling Prices		
	Bid	Sold	Low	High	Avg
OUCHARD, EMILE FRANCOIS	4	3	$2,359	$4,066	$3,170
			DM3,322	DM6,510	DM4,725
			£1,495	£2,645	£2,032
			¥241,191	¥411,625	¥322,740
OUCHARD, EMILE F. & EMILE A.	1	1	$5,270	$5,270	$5,270
			DM7,444	DM7,444	DM7,444
			£3,335	£3,335	£3,335
			¥470,358	¥470,358	¥470,358
PAESOLD, RODERICH	1	1	$514	$514	$514
			DM869	DM869	DM869
			£345	£345	£345
			¥54,510	¥54,510	¥54,510
PAJEOT	1	1	$8,797	$8,797	$8,797
			DM12,329	DM12,329	DM12,329
			£5,520	£5,520	£5,520
			¥775,477	¥775,477	¥775,477
PAJEOT (FILS)	2	0			
PAJEOT, ETIENNE	1	1	$12,334	$12,334	$12,334
			DM22,201	DM22,201	DM22,201
			£7,475	£7,475	£7,475
			¥1,778,676	¥1,778,676	¥1,778,676
PAJEOT, LOUIS SIMON	1	0			
PANORMO, LOUIS	5	2	$1,371	$3,524	$2,448
			DM2,071	DM5,202	DM3,637
			£920	£2,300	£1,610
			¥145,185	¥374,672	¥259,929
PAQUOTTE, PLACIDE	1	1	$2,497	$2,497	$2,497
			DM4,171	DM4,171	DM4,171
			£1,495	£1,495	£1,495
			¥303,470	¥303,470	¥303,470
PAULUS, GUNTER A.	3	2	$654	$978	$816
			DM926	DM1,413	DM1,170
			£414	£639	£526
			¥67,482	¥98,972	¥83,227
PAULUS, JOHANNES O.	2	1	$960	$960	$960
			DM1,783	DM1,783	DM1,783
			£575	£575	£575
			¥128,478	¥128,478	¥128,478
PECATTE, CHARLES	2	1	$10,563	$10,563	$10,563
			DM18,912	DM18,912	DM18,912
			£6,325	£6,325	£6,325
			¥1,453,359	¥1,453,359	¥1,453,359
PECCATTE, CHARLES	5	3	$7,682	$16,331	$11,431
			DM12,834	DM22,999	DM17,122
			£4,600	£10,350	£7,283
			¥933,754	¥1,669,786	¥1,230,810
PECCATTE, DOMINIQUE	2	2	$10,689	$30,843	$20,766
			DM18,532	DM52,164	DM35,348
			£6,325	£20,700	£13,513
			¥1,334,575	¥3,270,600	¥2,302,588
PECCATTE, FRANCOIS	2	2	$7,896	$15,005	$11,450
			DM11,838	DM23,025	DM17,432
			£4,830	£9,775	£7,303
			¥763,913	¥1,642,298	¥1,203,105
PECCATTE, FRANCOIS (workshop of)	1	1	$3,073	$3,073	$3,073
			DM5,134	DM5,134	DM5,134
			£1,840	£1,840	£1,840
			¥373,502	¥373,502	¥373,502

Maker	Items		Selling Prices		
	Bid	Sold	Low	High	Avg
PECCATTE, FRANCOIS & DOMINIQUE	1	1	$13,476	$13,476	$13,476
			DM24,931	DM24,931	DM24,931
			£8,050	£8,050	£8,050
			¥1,795,875	¥1,795,875	¥1,795,875
PECCATTE FAMILY (MEMBER OF)	1	1	$3,067	$3,067	$3,067
			DM5,682	DM5,682	DM5,682
			£1,840	£1,840	£1,840
			¥409,639	¥409,639	¥409,639
PENZEL, E.M.	1	1	$1,035	$1,035	$1,035
			DM1,558	DM1,558	DM1,558
			£628	£628	£628
			¥115,692	¥115,692	¥115,692
PFRETZSCHNER, CARL FRIEDRICH	1	1	$997	$997	$997
			DM1,404	DM1,404	DM1,404
			£632	£632	£632
			¥101,962	¥101,962	¥101,962
PFRETZSCHNER, CARL FRIEDRICH (III)	1	0			
PFRETZSCHNER, G.A.	1	1	$920	$920	$920
			DM1,574	DM1,574	DM1,574
			£544	£544	£544
			¥114,246	¥114,246	¥114,246
PFRETZSCHNER, H.R.	13	12	$489	$3,110	$1,813
			DM736	DM5,391	DM3,052
			£297	£1,840	£1,095
			¥54,632	¥388,240	¥223,938
PIERNOT, MARIE LOUIS	2	2	$1,725	$3,635	$2,680
			DM2,596	DM5,134	DM3,865
			£1,047	£2,300	£1,674
			¥192,821	¥324,385	¥258,603
POIRSON, JUSTIN	4	2	$570	$2,865	$1,717
			DM920	DM5,076	DM2,998
			£331	£1,759	£1,045
			¥67,160	¥349,272	¥208,216
PRAGER, AUGUST EDWIN	4	2	$637	$1,117	$877
			DM953	DM2,066	DM1,509
			£379	£667	£523
			¥71,055	¥148,801	¥109,928
PRAGER, GUSTAV	1	1	$705	$705	$705
			DM1,040	DM1,040	DM1,040
			£460	£460	£460
			¥74,934	¥74,934	¥74,934
PRELL, HERMAN WILHELM	1	1	$748	$748	$748
			DM1,249	DM1,249	DM1,249
			£499	£499	£499
			¥78,345	¥78,345	¥78,345
RAU, AUGUST	1	0			
REICHEL, AUGUST ANTON	1	1	$1,353	$1,353	$1,353
			DM2,024	DM2,024	DM2,024
			£805	£805	£805
			¥150,921	¥150,921	¥150,921
RETFORD, WILLIAM C.	1	1	$4,813	$4,813	$4,813
			DM8,904	DM8,904	DM8,904
			£2,875	£2,875	£2,875
			¥641,384	¥641,384	¥641,384
ROLLAND, BENOIT	2	2	$2,852	$3,562	$3,207
			DM4,600	DM6,162	DM5,381
			£1,656	£2,185	£1,921
			¥335,800	¥406,410	¥371,105

Maker	Items		Selling Prices		
	Bid	Sold	Low	High	Avg
ROTH, ERNST HEINRICH (workshop of)	1	1	$1,150 DM1,731 £698 ¥128,547	$1,150 DM1,731 £698 ¥128,547	$1,150 DM1,731 £698 ¥128,547
SARTORY, EUGENE	28	21	$3,287 DM4,622 £2,070 ¥292,228	$23,046 DM39,177 £13,800 ¥2,822,089	$9,844 DM16,102 £6,051 ¥1,122,883
SCHULLER, OTTO	1	1	$188 DM318 £115 ¥21,792	$188 DM318 £115 ¥21,792	$188 DM318 £115 ¥21,792
SCHUSTER, ADOLF	3	3	$944 DM1,338 £598 ¥97,474	$1,035 DM1,690 £681 ¥123,883	$986 DM1,537 £628 ¥110,149
SCHUSTER, GOTHARD	2	1	$805 DM1,360 £483 ¥98,210	$805 DM1,360 £483 ¥98,210	$805 DM1,360 £483 ¥98,210
SEIFERT, LOTHAR	1	0			
SEIFERT, W.	1	1	$155 DM270 £92 ¥19,721	$155 DM270 £92 ¥19,721	$155 DM270 £92 ¥19,721
SILVESTRE & MAUCOTEL	5	3	$315 DM487 £198 ¥31,423	$5,654 DM8,354 £3,680 ¥602,541	$2,605 DM4,013 £1,657 ¥289,534
SIMON (attributed to)	1	0			
SIMON, F.R.	2	0			
SIMON, F.R. (attributed to)	1	0			
SIMON, PAUL	3	1	$2,103 DM3,558 £1,323 ¥260,533	$2,103 DM3,558 £1,323 ¥260,533	$2,103 DM3,558 £1,323 ¥260,533
SIMON, PIERRE	3	1	$7,941 DM12,200 £5,175 ¥869,343	$7,941 DM12,200 £5,175 ¥869,343	$7,941 DM12,200 £5,175 ¥869,343
SIMON BROS.	2	0			
SOMNY, JOSEPH MAURICE	1	0			
STENGEL, V.	1	1	$159 DM283 £98 ¥21,400	$159 DM283 £98 ¥21,400	$159 DM283 £98 ¥21,400
TAYLOR, MALCOLM	1	1	$1,768 DM2,830 £1,150 ¥178,968	$1,768 DM2,830 £1,150 ¥178,968	$1,768 DM2,830 £1,150 ¥178,968
TAYLOR, ROBERT	1	0			
THIBOUVILLE-LAMY, J.	5	3	$1,383 DM1,926 £828 ¥116,910	$1,695 DM2,548 £1,012 ¥188,800	$1,493 DM2,302 £901 ¥161,136
THOMA, ARTHUR	1	0			

Maker	Items		Selling Prices		
	Bid	Sold	Low	High	Avg
THOMASSIN, CLAUDE	1	1	$3,196	$3,196	$3,196
			DM4,792	DM4,792	DM4,792
			£1,955	£1,955	£1,955
			¥309,203	¥309,203	¥309,203
TORRES, FRANK	1	0			
TOURNIER, JOSEPH ALEXIS	1	1	$989	$989	$989
			DM1,517	DM1,517	DM1,517
			£644	£644	£644
			¥108,198	¥108,198	¥108,198
TOURNIER, JOSEPH ALEXIS (workshop of)	1	1	$1,955	$1,955	$1,955
			DM2,942	DM2,942	DM2,942
			£1,187	£1,187	£1,187
			¥218,530	¥218,530	¥218,530
TOURTE	1	1	$11,334	$11,334	$11,334
			DM16,938	DM16,938	DM16,938
			£6,900	£6,900	£6,900
			¥1,090,386	¥1,090,386	¥1,090,386
TOURTE, FRANCOIS XAVIER	1	0			
TOURTE, LOUIS (PERE)	1	0			
TUBBS, JAMES	10	8	$3,760	$9,218	$5,843
			DM5,637	DM15,401	DM9,160
			£2,300	£5,520	£3,680
			¥363,768	¥1,120,505	¥617,286
TUBBS, THOMAS	1	1	$10,018	$10,018	$10,018
			DM15,056	DM15,056	DM15,056
			£5,980	£5,980	£5,980
			¥1,115,635	¥1,115,635	¥1,115,635
TUBBS, THOMAS (attributed to)	2	1	$2,120	$2,120	$2,120
			DM3,133	DM3,133	DM3,133
			£1,380	£1,380	£1,380
			¥225,953	¥225,953	¥225,953
TUBBS, WILLIAM	1	0			
VAN DER MEER, KAREL	4	4	$1,006	$3,182	$1,915
			DM1,060	DM5,095	DM2,869
			£621	£2,070	£1,233
			¥76,877	¥322,142	¥181,809
VAN HEMERT, KEES	1	1	$805	$805	$805
			DM1,377	DM1,377	DM1,377
			£476	£476	£476
			¥99,965	¥99,965	¥99,965
VICKERS, J.E.	2	1	$201	$201	$201
			DM282	DM282	DM282
			£127	£127	£127
			¥17,929	¥17,929	¥17,929
VIDOUDEZ, PIERRE	1	1	$3,353	$3,353	$3,353
			DM5,151	DM5,151	DM5,151
			£2,185	£2,185	£2,185
			¥367,056	¥367,056	¥367,056
VIGNERON, A.	1	0			
VIGNERON, ANDRE	3	2	$3,105	$4,950	$4,028
			DM5,188	DM7,925	DM6,557
			£2,072	£3,220	£2,646
			¥325,435	¥501,109	¥413,272
VIGNERON, JOSEPH ARTHUR	8	5	$1,035	$9,200	$5,444
			DM1,583	DM14,536	DM8,288
			£681	£5,888	£3,476
			¥109,089	¥919,080	¥557,492

Maker	Items		Selling Prices		
	Bid	*Sold*	*Low*	*High*	*Avg*
VOIGT, ARNOLD	1	1	$1,089	$1,089	$1,089
			DM1,533	DM1,533	DM1,533
			£690	£690	£690
			¥111,319	¥111,319	¥111,319
VOIGT, CARL HERMANN	1	0			
VOIRIN, FRANCOIS NICOLAS	21	13	$1,536	$12,075	$4,968
			DM2,513	DM17,436	DM7,440
			£920	£7,693	£3,127
			¥183,300	¥1,047,506	¥501,704
VUILLAUME, JEAN BAPTISTE	8	4	$768	$11,523	$5,522
			DM1,283	DM19,251	DM8,827
			£460	£6,900	£3,414
			¥93,375	¥1,400,631	¥639,200
WATSON, WILLIAM	2	1	$1,128	$1,128	$1,128
			DM1,791	DM1,791	DM1,791
			£736	£736	£736
			¥114,068	¥114,068	¥114,068
WEICHOLD	1	0			
WEICHOLD, RICHARD	7	6	$321	$1,768	$781
			DM514	DM2,830	DM1,242
			£209	£1,150	£495
			¥32,525	¥178,968	¥82,952
WERNER, ERNST	1	1	$1,380	$1,380	$1,380
			DM2,077	DM2,077	DM2,077
			£838	£838	£838
			¥154,256	¥154,256	¥154,256
WERNER, FRANZ EMANUEL					
(workshop of)	1	0			
WERRO, JEAN	1	1	$248	$248	$248
			DM364	DM364	DM364
			£161	£161	£161
			¥26,269	¥26,269	¥26,269
WILLBANKS, HOYT L.	1	1	$403	$403	$403
			DM673	DM673	DM673
			£269	£269	£269
			¥42,186	¥42,186	¥42,186
WILSON, GARNER	9	8	$951	$2,062	$1,393
			DM1,350	DM3,567	DM2,199
			£598	£1,265	£874
			¥88,295	¥235,290	¥146,936
WINKLER, FRANZ	1	1	$1,093	$1,093	$1,093
			DM1,580	DM1,580	DM1,580
			£714	£714	£714
			¥110,616	¥110,616	¥110,616
WITHERS, EDWARD	1	0			
WITHERS, GEORGE & SONS	3	0			

VIOLONCELLO PICCOLO

Maker	Items		Selling Prices		
EBNER, GOTTHARD	1	0			

XYLOPHONE

Maker	Items		Selling Prices		
COSLEV	1	1	$556	$556	$556
			DM855	DM855	DM855
			£368	£368	£368
			¥59,331	¥59,331	¥59,331

Maker	Items		Selling Prices		
	Bid	Sold	Low	High	Avg
PREMIER	2	2	$193	$789	$491
			DM289	DM1,120	DM704
			£115	£506	£311
			¥21,560	¥80,228	¥50,894
WARNE, REUBEN	3	1	$39	$39	$39
			DM67	DM67	DM67
			£23	£23	£23
			¥4,930	¥4,930	¥4,930

ZITHER

Maker	Items		Selling Prices		
KIENDL, A.	2	2	$194	$495	$345
			DM287	DM731	DM509
			£127	£322	£224
			¥20,712	¥52,722	¥36,717
KIENDL, KARL	1	1	$354	$354	$354
			DM520	DM520	DM520
			£230	£230	£230
			¥37,527	¥37,527	¥37,527
PUGH, JOHANNES	1	1	$476	$476	$476
			DM792	DM792	DM792
			£287	£287	£287
			¥55,489	¥55,489	¥55,489
SCHUSTER, CARL GOTTLOB (JR.)	1	1	$575	$575	$575
			DM1,065	DM1,065	DM1,065
			£345	£345	£345
			¥76,807	¥76,807	¥76,807
TIEFENBRUNNER, GEORG	2	2	$112	$271	$191
			DM195	DM383	DM289
			£69	£173	£121
			¥13,583	¥23,129	¥18,356

ZITHER-BANJO

Maker	Items		Selling Prices		
CAMMEYER, ALFRED D.	1	1	$339	$339	$339
			DM618	DM618	DM618
			£207	£207	£207
			¥42,878	¥42,878	¥42,878
DALLAS	1	1	$63	$63	$63
			DM96	DM96	DM96
			£40	£40	£40
			¥7,026	¥7,026	¥7,026
GORDON, GERALD	1	1	$97	$97	$97
			DM169	DM169	DM169
			£58	£58	£58
			¥12,326	¥12,326	¥12,326
WINDSOR	2	2	$50	$116	$83
			DM77	DM178	DM127
			£32	£75	£53
			¥4,952	¥11,495	¥8,224
WINDSOR, A.O.	1	1	$115	$115	$115
			DM166	DM166	DM166
			£75	£75	£75
			¥11,644	¥11,644	¥11,644